Daniel Davis

THOMAS CARLYLE'S WORKS.

"The Ashburton Edition"

IN SEVENTEEN VOLUMES.

VOLUME II.

THE FRENCH REVOLUTION.

Volume II.—THE GUILLOTINE. Books I—vii.

PAST AND PRESENT.

THE FRENCH REVOLUTION

𝔄 𝔥𝔦𝔰𝔱𝔬𝔯𝔶

BY

THOMAS CARLYLE

Μέγα ὁ ἀγὼν ἔστι, θεῖον γὰρ ἔργον· ὑπὲρ βασιλείας, ὑπὲρ ἐλευθερίας, ὑπὲρ εὐροίας, ὑπὲρ ἀταραξίας. ARRIANUS.
Δόγμα γὰρ αὐτῶν τίς μεταβάλλει; χωρὶς δὲ δογμάτων μεταβολῆς, τί ἄλλο ἢ δουλεία στενόντων καὶ πείθεσθαι προσποιουμένων; ANTONINUS.

VOLUME II.

THE GUILLOTINE. Books I—VII.

LONDON: CHAPMAN AND HALL
LIMITED
1885

Diesem Ambos vergleich' ich das Land, den Hammer dem Herrscher;
Und dem Volke das Blech, das in der Mitte sich krümmt.
Wehe dem armen Blech, wenn nur willkürliche Schläge
Ungewiß treffen, und nie fertig der Kessel erscheint!

Goethe.

R. CLAY AND SONS, LONDON AND BUNGAY.

CONTENTS OF VOLUME II.

THE FRENCH REVOLUTION.

THE GUILLOTINE.

BOOK I.—*Continued.*

BOOK II.

BOOK III.

THE GIRONDINS.

BOOK IV.

TERROR.

BOOK V.

TERROR THE ORDER OF THE DAY.

THE GUILLOTINE.

THE CULPRIT

BOOK FIRST.

(continued.)

SEPTEMBER.

THE FRENCH REVOLUTION.

CHAPTER V.

A TRILOGY.

As all Delineation, in these ages, were it never so Epic,. 'speaking itself and not singing itself,' must either found on Belief and provable Fact, or have no foundation at all (nor, except as floating cobweb, any existence at all),—the Reader will perhaps prefer to take a glance with the very eyes of eye-witnesses; and see, in that way, for himself, how it was. Brave Jourgniac, innocent Abbé Sicard, judicious Advocate Maton, these, greatly compressing themselves, shall speak, each an instant. Jourgniac's *Agony of Thirty-eight Hours* went through 'above a hundred editions,' though intrinsically a poor work. Some portion of it may here go through above the hundred-and-first, for want of a better.

'*Towards seven o'clock*' (Sunday night at the Abbaye; for Jourgniac goes by dates): 'We saw two men enter, their hands 'bloody and armed with sabres; a turnkey, with a torch, lighted 'them; he pointed to the bed of the unfortunate Swiss, Reding. 'Reding spoke with a dying voice. One of them paused; but the 'other cried, *Allons donc;* lifted the unfortunate man; carried him 'out on his back to the street. He was massacred there.

'We all looked at one another in silence, we clasped each other's 'hands. Motionless, with fixed eyes, we gazed on the pavement 'of our prison; on which lay the moonlight, chequered with the 'triple stancheons of our windows.'

'*Three in the morning:* They were breaking-in one of the 'prison-doors. We at first thought they were coming to kill us 'in our room; but heard, by voices on the staircase, that it was a 'room where some Prisoners had barricaded themselves. They 'were all butchered there, as we shortly gathered.'

'*Ten o'clock:* The Abbé Lenfant and the Abbé de Chapt- 'Rastignac appeared in the pulpit of the Chapel, which was our 'prison; they had entered by a door from the stairs. They said 'to us that our end was at hand; that we must compose ourselves, 'and receive their last blessing. An electric movement, not to be 'defined, threw us all on our knees, and we received it. These 'two white-haired old men, blessing us from their place above; 'death hovering over our heads, on all hands environing us; the 'moment is never to be forgotten. Half an hour after, they were 'both massacred, and we heard their cries.'[1]—Thus Jourgniac in his *Agony* in the Abbaye: how it ended with Jourgniac, we shall see anon.

But now let the good Maton speak, what he, over in La Force, in the same hours, is suffering and witnessing. This *Résurrection* by him is greatly the best, the least theatrical of these Pamphlets; and stands testing by documents:

'Towards seven o'clock,' on Sunday night, 'prisoners were called 'frequently, and they did not reappear. Each of us reasoned, in 'his own way, on this singularity: but our ideas became calm, as 'we persuaded ourselves that the Memorial I had drawn up for 'the National Assembly was producing effect.'

'At one in the morning, the grate which led to our quarter 'opened anew. Four men in uniform, each with a drawn sabre 'and blazing torch, came up to our corridor, preceded by a turn- 'key; and entered an apartment close to ours, to investigate a box 'there, which we heard them break up. This done, they stept 'into the gallery, and questioned the man Cuissa, to know where 'Lamotte' (Necklace's Widower) 'was. Lamotte, they said, had 'some months ago, under pretext of a treasure he knew of, swindled 'a sum of three-hundred livres from one of them, inviting him to 'dinner for that purpose. The wretched Cuissa, now in their 'hands, who indeed lost his life this night, answered trembling, 'That he remembered the fact well, but could not tell what was 'become of Lamotte. Determined to find Lamotte and confront

[1] Jourgniac Saint-Méard, *Mon Agonie de trente-huit heures* (reprinted in *Hist. Parl.* xviii. 103-135).

'him with Cuissa, they rummaged, along with this latter, through
'various other apartments; but without effect, for we heard them
'say : "Come search among the corpses, then; for, *nom de Dieu!*
'we must find where he is."

'At this same time, I heard Louis Bardy, the Abbé Bardy's
'name called : he was brought out; and directly massacred, as I
'learnt. He had been accused, along with his concubine, five or
'six years before, of having murdered and cut in pieces his own
'Brother, Auditor of the *Chambre des Comptes* of Montpelier; but
'had by his subtlety, his dexterity, nay his eloquence, outwitted
'the judges, and escaped.

'One may fancy what terror these words, "Come search among
'the corpses, then," had thrown me into. I saw nothing for it
'now but resigning myself to die. I wrote my last-will; conclud-
'ing it by a petition and adjuration, that the paper should be sent
'to its address. Scarcely had I quitted the pen, when there came
'two other men in uniform; one of them, whose arm and sleeve
'up to the very shoulder, as well as his sabre, were covered with
'blood, said, He was as weary as a hodman that had been beating
'plaster.'

'Baudin de la Chenaye was called ; sixty years of virtues could
'not save him. They said, *À l'Abbaye :* he passed the fatal outer-
'gate ; gave a cry of terror, at sight of the heaped corpses; covered
'his eyes with his hands, and died of innumerable wounds. At
'every new opening of the grate, I thought I should hear my own
'name called, and see Rossignol enter.'

'I flung off my nightgown and cap; I put on a coarse unwashed
'shirt, a worn frock without waistcoat, an old round hat ; these
'things I had sent for, some days ago, in the fear of what might
'happen.

'The rooms of this corridor had been all emptied but ours. We
'were four together ; whom they seemed to have forgotten : we
'addressed our prayers in common to the Eternal to be delivered
'from this peril.'

'Baptiste the turnkey came up by himself, to see us. I took
'him by the hands; I conjured him to save us ; promised him a
'hundred louis, if he would conduct me home. A noise coming
'from the grates made him hastily withdraw.

'It was the noise of some dozen or fifteen men, armed to the
'teeth ; as we, lying flat to escape being seen, could see from our
'windows. "Up stairs !" said they : "Let not one remain." I

'took out my penknife; I considered where I should strike my-
'self,'—but reflected 'that the blade was too short,' and also 'on
religion.'

Finally, however, between seven and eight o'clock in the morning,
enter four men with bludgeons and sabres!—'To one of whom
'Gérard my comrade whispered, earnestly, apart. During their
'colloquy I searched everywhere for shoes, that I might lay off the
Advocate pumps (*pantoufles de Palais*) I had on,' but could find
none.—'Constant, called le Sauvage, Gérard, and a third whose
'name escapes me, they let clear off: as for me, four sabres were
'crossed over my breast, and they led me down. I was brought
'to their bar; to the Personage with the scarf, who sat as judge
'there. He was a lame man, of tall lank stature. He recognised
'me on the streets and spoke to me, seven months after. I have
'been assured that he was son of a retired attorney, and named
'Chepy. Crossing the Court called *Des Nourrices*, I saw Manuel
'haranguing in tricolor scarf.' The trial, as we see, ends in
acquittal and *resurrection*.[2]

Poor Sicard, from the *violon* of the Abbaye, shall say but a few
words; true-looking, though tremulous. Towards three in the
morning, the killers bethink them of this little *violon;* and knock
from the court. 'I tapped gently, trembling lest the murderers
'might hear, on the opposite door, where the Section Committee
'was sitting: they answered gruffly, that they had no key. There
'were three of us in this *violon;* my companions thought they
'perceived a kind of loft overhead. But it was very high; only
'one of us could reach it by mounting on the shoulders of both the
'others. One of them said to me, that my life was usefuller than
'theirs: I resisted, they insisted: no denial! I fling myself on
'the neck of these two deliverers; never was scene more touching.
'I mount on the shoulders of the first, then on those of the second,
'finally on the loft; and address to my two comrades the expres-
'sion of a soul overwhelmed with natural emotions.'[3]

The two generous companions, we rejoice to find, did not perish.
But it is time that Jourgniac de Saint-Méard should speak his last
words, and end this singular trilogy. The night had become day;
and the day has again become night. Jourgniac, worn down with
uttermost agitation, was fallen asleep, and had a cheering dream:

[2] Maton de la Varenne, *Ma Résurrection* (in *Hist. Parl.* xviii. 135-156).

[3] Abbé Sicard, *Relation adressée à un de ses amis* (in *Hist. Parl.* xviii. 98-
103).

he has also contrived to make acquaintance with one of the
volunteer bailiffs, and spoken in native Provençal with him.   On
Tuesday, about one in the morning, his *Agony* is reaching its crisis.

'By the glare of two torches, I now descried the terrible tribunal,
'where lay my life or my death.   The President, in gray coat, with
'a sabre at his side, stood leaning with his hands against a table,
'on which were papers, an inkstand, tobacco-pipes and bottles.
'Some ten persons were around, seated or standing; two of whom
'had jackets and aprons: others were sleeping stretched on benches.
'Two men, in bloody shirts, guarded the door of the place; an old
'turnkey had his hand on the lock.   In front of the President
'three men held a Prisoner, who might be about sixty' (or seventy:
he was old Marshal Maillé, of the Tuileries and August Tenth).
'They stationed me in a corner; my guards crossed their sabres
'on my breast.   I looked on all sides for my Provençal: two
'National Guards, one of them drunk, presented some appeal from
'the Section of Croix Rouge in favour of the Prisoner; the Man
'in Gray answered: "They are useless, these appeals for traitors."
'Then the Prisoner exclaimed: "It is frightful; your judgment is
'a murder."   The President answered: "My hands are washed of
'it; take M. Maillé away."   They drove him into the street;
'where, through the opening of the door, I saw him massacred.

'The President sat down to write; registering, I suppose, the
'name of this one whom they had finished; then I heard him
'say: "Another, *À un autre !*"

'Behold me then haled before this swift and bloody judgment-
'bar, where the best protection was to have no protection, and
'all resources of ingenuity became null if they were not founded
'on truth.   Two of my guards held me each by a hand, the
'third by the collar of my coat.   "Your name, your profession?"
'said the President.   "The smallest lie ruins you," added one
'of the Judges.—"My name is Jourgniac Saint-Méard; I have
'served, as an officer, twenty years: and I appear at your tribunal
'with the assurance of an innocent man, who therefore will not
'lie."—"We shall see that," said the President: "Do you know
'why you are arrested?"—"Yes, Monsieur le Président; I am
'accused of editing the Journal *De la Cour et de la Ville*.   But
'I hope to prove the falsity"'—But no; Jourgniac's proof of the
falsity, and defence generally, though of excellent result as a
defence, is not interesting to read.   It is longwinded; there is a
loose theatricality in the reporting of it, which does not amount

to unveracity, yet which tends that way. We shall suppose him successful, beyond hope, in proving and disproving; and skip largely,—to the catastrophe, almost at two steps.

'"But after all," said one of the Judges, "there is no smoke 'without kindling; tell us why they accuse you of that."—"I 'was about to do so"'—Jourgniac does so; with more and more success.

'"Nay," continued I, "they accuse me even of recruiting for 'the Emigrants!" At these words there arose a general murmur. '"O Messieurs, Messieurs," I exclaimed, raising my voice, "it is 'my turn to speak; I beg M. le Président to have the kindness 'to maintain it for me; I never needed it more."—"True enough, 'true enough," said almost all the Judges with a laugh: "Silence!"'

'While they were examining the testimonials I had produced, 'a new Prisoner was brought in, and placed before the President. '"It was one Priest more," they said, "whom they had ferreted 'out of the Chapelle." After very few questions: "*À la Force!*" 'He flung his breviary on the table; was hurled forth, and 'massacred. I reappeared before the tribunal.

'"You tell us always," cried one of the Judges, with a tone 'of impatience, "that you are not this, that you are not that; 'what are you, then?"—"I was an open Royalist."—There arose 'a general murmur; which was miraculously appeased by another 'of the men, who had seemed to take an interest in me: "We are 'not here to judge opinions," said he, "but to judge the results of 'them." Could Rousseau and Voltaire both in one, pleading for 'me, have said better?—"Yes, Messieurs," cried I, "always till 'the Tenth of August I was an open Royalist. Ever since the 'Tenth of August that cause has been finished. I am a Frenchman, 'true to my country. I was always a man of honour."'

'"My soldiers never distrusted me. Nay, two days before that 'business of Nanci, when their suspicion of their officers was at 'its height, they chose me for commander, to lead them to Luné-'ville, to get back the prisoners of the Regiment Mestre-de-Camp, 'and seize General Malseigne."' Which fact there is, most luckily, an individual present who by a certain token can confirm.

'The President, this cross-questioning being over, took off his 'hat and said: "I see nothing to suspect in this man: I am for 'granting him his liberty. Is that your vote?" To which all 'the Judges answered: "*Oui, Oui;* it is just!"'

And there arose vivats within doors and without; 'escort of

three,' amid shoutings and embracings : thus Jourgniac escaped
from jury-trial and the jaws of death.[4] Maton and Sicard did,
either by trial and no bill found, lank President Chepy finding
'absolutely nothing;' or else by evasion, and new favour of Moton
the brave watchmaker, likewise escape ; and were embraced and
wept over ; weeping in return, as they well might.

Thus they three, in wondrous trilogy, or triple soliloquy :
uttering simultaneously, through the dread night-watches, their
Night-thoughts,—grown audible to us ! They Three are become
audible : but the other 'Thousand and Eighty-nine, of whom
Two-hundred and two were Priests,' who also had Night-thoughts,
remain inaudible ; choked forever in black Death. Heard only
of President Chepy and the Man in Gray !—

CHAPTER VI.

THE CIRCULAR.

BUT the Constituted Authorities, all this while ? The Legislative Assembly ; the Six Ministers ; the Townhall ; Santerre
with the National Guard ?—It is very curious to think what a
City is. Theatres, to the number of some twenty-three, were
open every night during these prodigies ; while right-arms here
grew weary with slaying, right-arms there were twiddledeeing on
melodious catgut : at the very instant when Abbé Sicard was
clambering up his second pair of shoulders three-men high, five
hundred thousand human individuals were lying horizontal, as
if nothing were amiss.

As for the poor Legislative, the sceptre had departed from it.
The Legislative did send Deputation to the Prisons, to these
Street-Courts ; and poor M. Dusaulx did harangue there ; but
produced no conviction whatsoever : nay at last, as he continued
haranguing, the Street-Court interposed, not without threats ; and
he had to cease, and withdraw. This is the same poor worthy
old M. Dusaulx who told, or indeed almost sang (though with

[4] *Mon Agonie* (ut suprà, *Hist. Parl.* xviii. 128).

cracked voice), the *Taking of the Bastille*, to our satisfaction, long since. He was wont to announce himself, on such and on all occasions, as *the Translator of Juvenal*. "Good Citizens, you see before you a man who loves his country, who is the Translator of Juvenal," said he once.—"Juvenal?" interrupts Sansculottism: "Who the devil is Juvenal? One of your *sacrés Aristocrates?* To the *Lanterne!*" From an orator of this kind, conviction was not to be expected. The Legislative had much ado to save one of its own Members, or ex-Members, Deputy Jounneau, who chanced to be lying in arrest for mere Parliamentary delinquencies, in these Prisons. As for poor old Dusaulx and Company, they returned to the Salle de Manége, saying, "It was dark; and they could not see well what was going on."[1]

Roland writes indignant messages, in the name of Order, Humanity and the Law; but there is no Force at his disposal. Santerre's National Force seems lazy to rise: though he made requisitions, he says,—which always dispersed again. Nay did not we, with Advocate Maton's eyes, see 'men in uniform' too, with their 'sleeves bloody to the shoulder'? Pétion goes in tricolor scarf; speaks 'the austere language of the law:' the killers give up, while he is there; when his back is turned, recommence. Manuel too in scarf we, with Maton's eyes, transiently saw haranguing, in the Court called of Nurses, *Cour des Nourrices*. On the other hand, cruel Billaud, likewise in scarf, 'with that small puce coat and black wig we are used to on him,'[2] audibly delivers, 'standing among corpses,' at the Abbaye, a short but ever-memorable harangue, reported in various phraseology, but always to this purpose: "Brave Citizens, you are extirpating the Enemies of Liberty: you are at your duty. A grateful Commune and Country would wish to recompense you adequately; but cannot, for you know its want of funds. Whoever shall have worked (*travaillé*) in a Prison shall receive a draft of one louis, payable by our cashier. Continue your work."[3] The Constituted Authorities are of yesterday: all pulling different ways: there is properly no Constituted Authority, but every man is his own King; and all are kinglets, belligerent, allied, or armed-neutral, without king over them.

'O everlasting infamy,' exclaims Montgaillard, 'that Paris

[1] *Moniteur*, Debate of 2d September 1792.
[2] Méhée Fils (ut suprà, in *Hist. Parl.* xviii. p. 189).
[3] Montgaillard, iii. 191.

'stood looking on in stupor for four days, and did not interfere!'
Very desirable indeed that Paris had interfered; yet not unnatural
that it stood even so, looking on in stupor. Paris is in death-
panic, the enemy and gibbets at its door: whosoever in Paris
has the heart to front death, finds it more pressing to do it
fighting the Prussians, than fighting the killers of Aristocrats.
Indignant abhorrence, as in Roland, may be here; gloomy sanction, premeditation or not, as in Marat and Committee of Salvation,
may be there; dull disapproval, dull approval, and acquiescence
in Necessity and Destiny, is the general temper. The Sons of
Darkness, 'two-hundred or so,' risen from their lurking-places,
have scope to do their work. Urged on by fever-frenzy of
Patriotism, and the madness of Terror;—urged on by lucre, and
the gold louis of wages? Nay, not lucre; for the gold watches,
rings, money of the Massacred, are punctually brought to the
Townhall, by Killers sans-indispensables, who higgle afterwards
for their twenty shillings of wages; and Sergent sticking an
uncommonly fine agate on his finger (fully 'meaning to account
for it') becomes *Agate*-Sergent. But the temper, as we say, is
dull acquiescence. Not till the Patriotic or Frenetic part of the
work is finished for want of material; and Sons of Darkness,
bent clearly on lucre alone, begin wrenching watches and purses,
brooches from ladies' necks, "to equip volunteers," in daylight,
on the streets,—does the temper from dull grow vehement; does
the Constable raise his truncheon, and striking heartily (like a
cattle-driver in earnest) beat the 'course of things' back into its
old regulated drove-roads. The *Garde-Meuble* itself was surreptitiously plundered, on the 17th of the month, to Roland's new
horror; who anew bestirs himself, and is, as Sieyes says, 'the veto
of scoundrels,' Roland *veto des coquins*.[4]—

This is the September Massacre, otherwise called 'Severe
Justice of the People.' These are the Septemberers (*Septembri-
seurs*); a name of some note and lucency,—but lucency of the
Nether-fire sort; very different from that of our Bastille Heroes,
who shone, disputable by no Friend of Freedom, as in Heavenly
light-radiance: to such phasis of the business have we advanced
since then! The numbers massacred are in the Historical *fantasy*,
'between two and three thousand;' or indeed they are 'upwards
of six thousand,' for Peltier (in vision) saw them massacring the
very patients of the Bicêtre Madhouse 'with grape-shot;' nay

4 Helen Maria Williams, iii. 27.

finally they are 'twelve-thousand' and odd hundreds,—not more than that.[5] In Arithmetical ciphers, and Lists drawn up by accurate Advocate Maton, the number, including two-hundred and two priests, three 'persons unknown,' and 'one thief killed at the Bernardins,' is, as above hinted, a Thousand and Eighty-nine,—not less than that.

A Thousand and eighty-nine lie dead, 'two-hundred and sixty heaped carcasses on the Pont au Change' itself;—among which, Robespierre pleading afterwards will 'nearly weep' to reflect that there was said to be one slain innocent.[6] One; not two, O thou seagreen Incorruptible? If so, Themis Sansculotte must be lucky; for she was brief!—In the dim Registers of the Townhall, which are preserved to this day, men read, with a certain sickness of heart, items and entries not usual in Town Books: 'To workers 'employed in preserving the salubrity of the air in the Prisons, 'and persons who presided over these dangerous operations,' so much,—in various items, nearly seven hundred pounds sterling. To carters employed to 'the Burying-grounds of Clamart, Mont-rouge and Vaugirard,' at so much a journey, per cart; this also is an entry. Then so many francs and odd sous 'for the necessary quantity of quick-lime'![7] Carts go along the streets; full of stript human corpses, thrown pell-mell; limbs sticking up :—seest thou that cold Hand sticking up, through the heaped embrace of brother corpses, in its yellow paleness, in its cold rigour; the palm opened towards Heaven, as if in dumb prayer, in expostulation *de profundis*, Take pity on the Sons of Men!—Mercier saw it, as he walked down 'the Rue Saint-Jacques from Montrouge, on the 'morrow of the Massacres;' but not a Hand; it was a Foot,—which he reckons still more significant, one understands not well why. Or was it as the Foot of one *spurning* Heaven? Rushing, like a wild diver, in disgust and despair, towards the depths of Annihilation? Even there shall His hand find thee, and His right-hand hold thee,—surely for right not for wrong, for good not evil! 'I saw that Foot,' says Mercier; 'I shall know it again 'at the great Day of Judgment, when the Eternal, throned on His 'thunders, shall judge both Kings and Septemberers.'[8]

That a shriek of inarticulate horror rose over this thing, not

[5] See *Hist. Parl.* xvii. 421, 422.
[6] *Moniteur* of 6th November (Debate of 5th November 1793).
[7] *Etat des sommes payées par la Commune de Paris* (*Hist. Parl.* xviii. 231).
[8] Mercier, *Nouveau Paris*, vi. 21.

only from French Aristocrats and Moderates, but from all Europe, and has prolonged itself to the present day, was most natural and right. The thing lay done, irrevocable; a thing to be counted beside some other things, which lie very black in our Earth's Annals, yet which will not erase therefrom. For man, as was remarked, has transcendentalisms in him; standing, as he does, poor creature, every way 'in the confluence of Infinitudes;' a mystery to himself and others: in the centre of two Eternities, of three Immensities,—in the intersection of primeval Light with the everlasting Dark!—Thus have there been, especially by vehement tempers reduced to a state of desperation, very miserable things done. Sicilian Vespers, and 'eight thousand slaughtered in two hours,' are a known thing. Kings themselves, not in desperation, but only in difficulty, have sat hatching, for year and day (nay De Thou says for seven years), their Bartholomew Business; and then, at the right moment, also on an Autumn Sunday, this very Bell (they say it is the identical metal) of Saint-Germain l'Auxerrois was set a-pealing—with effect.[9] Nay the same black boulder-stones of these Paris Prisons have seen Prison-massacres before now; men massacring countrymen, Burgundies massacring Armagnacs, whom they had suddenly imprisoned, till, as now, there were piled heaps of carcasses, and the streets ran red;—the Mayor Pétion of the time speaking the austere language of the law, and answered by the Killers, in old French (it is some four hundred years old): "*Maugré bieu, Sire*,—Sir, God's malison on your 'justice,' your 'pity,' your 'right reason.' Cursed be of God whoso shall have pity on these false traitorous Armagnacs, English; dogs they are; they have destroyed us, wasted this realm of France, and sold it to the English." [10] And so they slay, and fling aside the slain, to the extent of 'fifteen hundred and eighteen, 'among whom are found four Bishops of false and damnable 'counsel, and two Presidents of Parlement.' For though it is not Satan's world this that we live in, Satan always has his place in it (underground properly); and from time to time bursts up. Well may mankind shriek, inarticulately anathematising as they can. There are actions of such emphasis that no shrieking can be too emphatic for them. Shriek ye; acted have they.

Shriek who might in this France, in this Paris Legislative or Paris Townhall, there are Ten Men who do not shriek. A

[9] 9th to 13th September 1572 (Dulaure, *Hist. de Paris*, iv. 289).
[10] Dulaure, iii. 494.

Circular goes out from the Committee of *Salut Public*, dated 3d of September 1792; directed to all Townhalls: a State-paper too remarkable to be overlooked. 'A part of the ferocious conspirators 'detained in the Prisons,' it says, 'have been put to death by the 'People; and we cannot doubt but the whole Nation, driven to the 'edge of ruin by such endless series of treasons, will make haste 'to adopt *this* means of public salvation: and all Frenchmen will 'cry as the men of Paris: We go to fight the enemy; but we will 'not leave robbers behind us, to butcher our wives and children.' To which are legibly appended these signatures: Panis; Sergent; Marat, Friend of the People; [11] with Seven others;—carried down thereby, in a strange way, to the late remembrance of Antiquarians. We remark, however, that their Circular rather recoiled on themselves. The Townhalls made no use of it; even the distracted Sansculottes made little; they only howled and bellowed, but did not bite. At Rheims 'about eight persons' were killed; and two afterwards were hanged for doing it. At Lyons, and a few other places, some attempt was made; but with hardly any effect, being quickly put down.

Less fortunate were the Prisoners of Orléans; was the good Duke de la Rochefoucault. He journeying, by quick stages, with his Mother and Wife, towards the Waters of Forges, or some quieter country, was arrested at Gisors; conducted along the streets, amid effervescing multitudes, and killed dead 'by the stroke of a paving-stone hurled through the coach-window.' Killed as a once Liberal now Aristocrat; Protector of Priests, Suspender of virtuous Pétions, and most unfortunate Hot-grown-cold, detestable to Patriotism. He dies lamented of Europe; his blood spattering the cheeks of his old Mother, ninety-three years old.

As for the Orléans Prisoners, they are State Criminals: Royalist Ministers, Delessarts, Montmorins; who have been accumulating on the High Court of Orléans, ever since that Tribunal was set up. Whom now it seems good that we should get transferred to our new Paris Court of the Seventeenth; which proceeds far quicker. Accordingly hot Fournier from Martinique, Fournier *l'Américain*, is off, missioned by Constituted Authority; with stanch National Guards, with Lazouski the Pole; sparingly provided with road-money. These, through bad quarters, through difficulties, perils, for Authorities cross each other in this time,— do triumphantly bring off the Fifty or Fifty-three Orléans Prisoners,

[11] *Hist. Parl.* xvii. 433.

towards Paris; where a swifter Court of the Seventeenth will do justice on them.[12] But lo, at Paris, in the interim, a still swifter and swiftest Court of the *Second*, and of *September*, has instituted itself: enter not Paris, or that will judge you!—What shall hot Fournier do? It was his duty, as volunteer Constable, had he been a perfect character, to guard those men's lives never so Aristocratic, at the expense of his own valuable life never so Sansculottic, till some Constituted Court had disposed of them. But he was an imperfect character and Constable; perhaps one of the more imperfect.

Hot Fournier, ordered to turn hither by one Authority, to turn thither by another Authority, is in a perplexing multiplicity of orders; but finally he strikes off for Versailles. His Prisoners fare in tumbrils, or open carts, himself and Guards riding and marching around: and at the last village, the worthy Mayor of Versailles comes to meet him, anxious that the arrival and locking-up were well over. It is Sunday, the ninth day of the month. Lo, on entering the Avenue of Versailles, what multitudes, stirring, swarming in the September sun, under the dull-green September foliage; the Four-rowed Avenue all humming and swarming, as if the Town had emptied itself! Our tumbrils roll heavily through the living sea; the Guards and Fournier making way with ever more difficulty; the Mayor speaking and gesturing his persuasivest; amid the inarticulate growling hum, which growls ever the deeper even by hearing itself growl, not without sharp yelpings here and there:—Would to God we were out of this strait place, and wind and separation had cooled the heat, which seems about igniting here!

And yet if the wide Avenue is too strait, what will the Street *de Surintendance* be, at leaving of the same? At the corner of Surintendance Street, the compressed yelpings become a continuous yell: savage figures spring on the tumbril-shafts; first spray of an endless coming tide! The Mayor pleads, pushes, half-desperate; is pushed, carried off in men's arms: the savage tide has entrance, has mastery. Amid horrid noise, and tumult as of fierce wolves, the Prisoners sink massacred,—all but some eleven, who escaped into houses, and found mercy. The Prisons, and what other Prisoners they held, were with difficulty saved. The stript clothes are burnt in bonfire; the corpses lie heaped in the ditch on

[12] *Hist. Parl.* xvii. 434.

the morrow morning.[13] All France, except it be the Ten Men of the Circular and their people, moans and rages, inarticulately shrieking; all Europe rings.

But neither did Danton shriek; though, as Minister of Justice, it was more his part to do so. Brawny Danton is in the breach, as of stormed Cities and Nations; amid the sweep of Tenth-of-August cannon, the rustle of Prussian gallows-ropes, the smiting of September sabres; destruction all around him, and the rushing-down of worlds: Minister of Justice is his name; but Titan of the Forlorn Hope, and *Enfant Perdu* of the Revolution, is his quality, —and the man acts according to that. "We must put our enemies in fear!" Deep fear, is it not, as of its own accord, falling on our enemies? The Titan of the Forlorn Hope, he is not the man that would swiftest of all prevent its so falling. Forward, thou lost Titan of an *Enfant Perdu;* thou must dare, and again dare, and without end dare; there is nothing left for thee but that! *"Que mon nom soit flétri,* Let my name be blighted:" what am I? The Cause alone is great; and shall live, and not perish.—So, on the whole, here too is a Swallower of Formulas; of still wider gulp than Mirabeau: this Danton, Mirabeau of the Sansculottes. In the September days, this Minister was not heard of as coöperating with strict Roland; his business might lie elsewhere,—with Brunswick and the Hôtel-de-Ville. When applied to by an official person, about the Orléans Prisoners, and the risks they ran, he answered gloomily, twice over, "Are not these men guilty?"—When pressed, he 'answered in a terrible voice,' and turned his back.[14] A thousand slain in the Prisons; horrible if you will; but Brunswick is within a day's journey of us; and there are Five-and-twenty Millions yet, to slay or to save. Some men have tasks,—frightfuller than ours! It seems strange, but is not strange, that this Minister of Moloch-Justice, when any suppliant for a friend's life got access to him, was found to have human compassion; and yielded and granted 'always;' 'neither did one personal enemy of Danton perish in these days.'[15]

To shriek, we say, when certain things are acted, is proper and unavoidable. Nevertheless, articulate speech, not shrieking, is the faculty of man: when speech is not yet possible, let there be, with the shortest delay, at least—silence. Silence, accordingly, in this

---

[13] *Pièces officielles relatives au massacre des Prisonniers à Versailles* (in *Hist. Parl.* xviii. 236-249).

[14] *Biographie des Ministres,* p. 97.   [15] Ibid. p. 103.

forty-fourth year of the business, and eighteen hundred and thirty-sixth of an 'Era called Christian as *lucus à non*,' is the thing we recommend and practise. Nay, instead of shrieking more, it were perhaps edifying to remark, on the other side, what a singular thing Customs (in Latin, *Mores*) are ; and how fitly the Virtue, *Vir-tus*, Manhood or Worth, that is in a man, is called his *Morality* or *Customariness*. Fell Slaughter, one of the most authentic products of the Pit you would say, once give it Customs, becomes War, with Laws of War ; and is Customary and Moral enough ; and red individuals carry the tools of it girt round their haunches, not without an air of pride,—which do thou nowise blame. While, see ! so long as it is but dressed in hodden or russet ; and Revolution, less frequent than War, has not yet got its Laws of Revolution, but the hodden or russet individuals are Uncustomary—O shrieking beloved brother blockheads of Mankind, let us close those wide mouths of ours ; let us cease shrieking, and begin considering !

CHAPTER VII.

SEPTEMBER IN ARGONNE.

PLAIN, at any rate, is one thing : that the *fear*, whatever of fear those Aristocrat enemies might need, has been brought about. The matter is getting serious, then ! Sansculottism too has become a Fact, and seems minded to assert itself as such ? This huge moon-calf of Sansculottism, staggering about, as young calves do, is not mockable only, and soft like another calf ; but terrible too, if you prick it ; and, through its hideous nostrils, blows fire !—Aristocrats, with pale panic in their hearts, fly towards covert ; and a light rises to them over several things ; or rather a confused transition towards light, whereby for the moment darkness is only darker than ever. But what will become of this France ? Here is a question ! France is dancing its desert-waltz, as Sahara does when the winds waken ; in whirl-blasts twenty-five millions in number ; waltzing towards Townhalls, Aristocrat Prisons and Election Committee-rooms ; towards Brunswick and the frontiers ; towards a New Chapter of

Universal History; if indeed it be not the *Finis*, and winding-up
of that !

In Election Committee-rooms there is now no dubiety; but the
work goes bravely along. The Convention is getting chosen,—
really in a decisive spirit; in the Townhall we already date *First
year of the Republic.* Some Two-hundred of our best Legislators
may be reëlected, the Mountain bodily: Robespierre, with Mayor
Pétion, Buzot, Curate Grégoire, Rabaut, some threescore Old-
Constituents; though we once had only 'thirty voices.' All these;
and along with them, friends long known to Revolutionary fame:
Camille Desmoulins, though he stutters in speech: Manuel, Tallien
and Company; Journalists Gorsas, Carra, Mercier, Louvet of
Faublas; Clootz Speaker of Mankind; Collot d'Herbois, tearing
a passion to rags; Fabre d'Eglantine, speculative Pamphleteer;
Legendre, the solid Butcher; nay Marat, though rural France can
hardly believe it, or even believe that there *is* a Marat, except in
print. Of Minister Danton, who will lay down his Ministry for a
Membership, we need not speak. Paris is fervent; nor is the
Country wanting to itself. Barbaroux, Rebecqui, and fervid
Patriots are coming from Marseilles. Seven-hundred and forty-
five men (or indeed forty-nine, for Avignon now sends Four) are
gathering: so many are to meet; not so many are to part !
Attorney Carrier from Aurillac, Ex-Priest Lebon from Arras,
these shall both gain a *name.* Mountainous Auvergne re-elects
her Romme; hardy tiller of the soil, once Mathematical Professor;
who, unconscious, carries in petto a remarkable *New Calendar*, with
Messidors, Pluvioses, and such-like;—and having given it well
forth, shall depart with the death they call Roman. Sieyes Old-
Constituent comes; to make new Constitutions as many as wanted :
for the rest, peering out of his clear cautious eyes, he will cower
low in many an emergency, and find silence safest. Young Saint-
Just is coming, deputed by Aisne in the North; more like a
Student than a Senator; not four-and-twenty yet; who has written
Books; a youth of slight stature, with mild mellow voice, enthusiast
olive-complexion and long black hair. Féraud, from the far valley
D'Aure in the folds of the Pyrenees, is coming; an ardent Re-
publican; doomed to fame, at least in death.
All manner of Patriot men are coming: Teachers, Husbandmen,
Priests and Ex-Priests, Traders, Doctors; above all, Talkers, or
the Attorney species. Man-midwives, as Levasseur of the Sarthe,

are not wanting. Nor Artists: gross David, with the swoln cheek, has long painted, with genius in a state of convulsion; and will now legislate. The swoln cheek, choking his words in the birth, totally disqualifies him as an orator; but his pencil, his head, his gross hot heart, with genius in a state of convulsion, will be there. A man bodily and mentally swoln-cheeked, disproportionate; flabby-large, instead of great; weak withal as in a state of convulsion, not strong in a state of composure: so let him play his part. Nor are naturalised Benefactors of the Species forgotten: Priestley, elected by the Orne Department, but declining; Paine the rebellious Needleman, by the Pas de Calais, who accepts.

Few Nobles come, and yet not none. Paul-François Barras, 'noble as the Barrases, old as the rocks of Provence;' he is one. The reckless, shipwrecked man: flung ashore on the coast of the Maldives long ago, while sailing and soldiering as Indian Fighter; flung ashore since then, as hungry Parisian pleasure-hunter and half-pay, on many a Circe Island, with temporary enchantment, temporary conversion into beasthood and hoghood; —the remote Var Department has now sent him hither. A man of heat and haste; defective in utterance; defective indeed in anything to utter; yet not without a certain rapidity of glance, a certain swift transient courage; who in these times, Fortune favouring, may go far. He is tall, handsome to the eye, 'only the complexion a little yellow;' but 'with a robe of purple, with a scarlet cloak and plume of tricolor, on occasions of solemnity,' the man will look well.[1] Lepelletier Saint-Fargeau, Old-Constituent, is a kind of noble, and of enormous wealth; he too has come hither:—to have the Pain of Death *abolished?* Hapless Ex-Parlementeer! Nay among our Sixty Old-Constituents, see Philippe d'Orléans, a Prince of the Blood! Not now *D'Orléans:* for, Feudalism being swept from the world, he demands of his worthy friends the Electors of Paris, to have a new name of their choosing; whereupon Procureur Manuel, like an antithetic literary man, recommends *Equality*, Egalité. A Philippe Egalité therefore will sit; seen of the Earth and Heaven.

Such a Convention is gathering itself together. Mere angry poultry in moulting season; whom Brunswick's grenadiers and cannoneers will give short account of. Would the weather, as Bertrand is always praying, only mend a little![2]

[1] *Dictionnaire des Hommes Marquans*, § Barras.
[2] Bertrand-Moleville, *Mémoires*, ii. 225.

In vain, O Bertrand! The weather will not mend a whit: nay even if it did? Dumouriez Polymetis, though Bertrand knows it not, started from brief slumber at Sedan, on that morning of the 29th of August; with stealthiness, with promptitude, audacity. Some three mornings after that, Brunswick, opening wide eyes, perceives the Passes of the Argonne all seized; blocked with felled trees, fortified with camps; and that it is a most shifty swift Dumouriez this, who has outwitted him!

The manœuvre may cost Brunswick 'a loss of three weeks,' very fatal in these circumstances. A Mountain-wall of forty miles lying between him and Paris: which he should have pre-occupied; —which how now to get possession of? Also the rain it raineth every day; and we are in a hungry Champagne Pouilleuse, a land flowing only with ditch-water. How to cross this Mountain-wall of the Argonne; or what in the world to do with it?—There are marchings and wet splashings by steep paths, with *sackerments* and guttural interjections; forcings of Argonne Passes,—which unhappily will not force. Through the woods, volleying War reverberates, like huge gong-music, or Moloch's kettledrum, borne by the echoes; swoln torrents boil angrily round the foot of rocks, floating pale carcasses of men. In vain! Islettes Village, with its church-steeple, rises intact in the Mountain-pass, between the embosoming heights; your forced marchings and climbings have become forced slidings and tumblings back. From the hill-tops thou seest nothing but dumb crags, and endless wet moaning woods; the Clermont *Vache* (huge Cow that she is) disclosing herself[3] at intervals; flinging-off her cloud-blanket, and soon taking it on again, drowned in the pouring Heaven. The Argonne Passes will not force: you must *skirt* the Argonne: go round by the end of it.

But fancy whether the Emigrant Seigneurs have not got their brilliancy dulled a little; whether that 'Foot Regiment in red-facings with nankeen trousers' could be in field-day order! In place of gasconading, a sort of desperation, and hydrophobia from *excess* of water, is threatening to supervene. Young Prince de Ligne, son of that brave literary De Ligne the Thundergod of Dandies, fell backwards; shot dead in Grand-Pré, the Northmost of the Passes: Brunswick is skirting and rounding, laboriously, by the extremity of the South. Four days; days of a rain as of Noah, —without fire, without food! For fire you cut down green trees,

[3] See Helen Maria Williams, *Letters*, iii. 79-81.

and produce smoke; for food you eat green grapes, and produce
colic, pestilential dysentery, ὀλέκοντο δὲ λαοί. And the Peasants
assassinate us, they do not join us; shrill women cry shame on us,
threaten to draw their very scissors on us! O ye hapless dulled-
bright Seigneurs, and hydrophobic splashed Nankeens;—but O,
ten times more, ye poor *sackerment*ing ghastly-visaged Hessians
and Hulans, fallen on your backs; who had no call to die there,
except compulsion and three-halfpence a-day! Nor has Mrs. Le
Blanc of the Golden Arm a good time of it, in her bower of
dripping rushes. Assassinating Peasants are hanged; Old-Constituent Honourable Members, though of venerable age, ride in
carts with their hands tied: these are the woes of war.

Thus they; sprawling and wriggling, far and wide, on the slopes
and passes of the Argonne;—a loss to Brunswick of five-and-
twenty disastrous days. There is wriggling and struggling; facing,
backing and right-about facing; as the positions shift, and the
Argonne gets partly rounded, partly forced:—but still Dumouriez,
force him, round him as you will, sticks like a rooted fixture on
the ground; fixture with many *hinges;* wheeling now this way,
now that; showing always new front, in the most unexpected
manner: nowise consenting to take himself away. Recruits stream
up on him: full of heart; yet rather difficult to deal with. Behind
Grand-Pré, for example, Grand-Pré which is on the wrong side of
the Argonne, for we are now forced and rounded,—the full heart,
in one of those wheelings and showings of new front, did as it
were overset itself, as full hearts are liable to do; and there rose
a shriek of *sauve qui peut,* and a death-panic which had nigh
ruined all! So that the General had to come galloping; and, with
thunder-words, with gesture, stroke of drawn sword even, check
and rally, and bring back the sense of shame;[4]—nay to seize the
first shriekers and ringleaders; 'shave their heads and eyebrows,'
and pack them forth into the world as a sign. Thus too (for
really the rations are short, and wet camping with hungry stomach
brings bad humour) there is like to be mutiny. Whereupon again
Dumouriez 'arrives at the head of their line, with his staff, and an
'escort of a hundred hussars. He had placed some squadrons behind
'them, the artillery in front; he said to them: "As for you, for I
'will neither call you citizens, nor soldiers, nor my men (*ni mes
'enfans*), you see before you this artillery, behind you this cavalry.
'You have dishonoured yourselves by crimes. If you amend, and

---

[4] Dumouriez, *Mémoires,* iii. 29.

'grow to behave like this brave Army which you have the honour
'of belonging to, you will find in me a good father. But
'plunderers and assassins I do not suffer here. At the smallest
'mutiny I will have you shivered in pieces (*hacher en pièces*). Seek
'out the Scoundrels that are among you, and dismiss them your-
'selves; I hold you responsible for them." ' [5]

Patience, O Dumouriez! This uncertain heap of shriekers,
mutineers, were they once drilled and inured, will become a
phalanxed mass of Fighters; and wheel and whirl, to order,
swiftly like the wind or the whirlwind: tanned mustachio-figures;
often bare-foot, even bare-backed; with sinews of iron; who
require only bread and gunpowder: very Sons of Fire, the
adroitest, hastiest, hottest ever seen perhaps since Attila's time.
They may conquer and overrun amazingly, much as that same
Attila did;—whose Attila's-Camp and Battlefield thou now seest,
on this very ground; [6] who, after sweeping bare the world, was,
with difficulty, and days of tough fighting, checked *here* by Roman
Ætius and Fortune; and his dust-cloud made to vanish in the
East again!—

Strangely enough, in this shrieking Confusion of a Soldiery,
which we saw long since fallen all suicidally out of square, in
suicidal collision,—at Nanci, or on the streets of Metz, where
brave Bouillé stood with drawn sword; and which has collided
and ground itself to pieces worse and worse ever since, down now
to such a state: in this shrieking Confusion, and not elsewhere,
lies the first germ of returning Order for France! Round which,
we say, poor France nearly all ground down suicidally likewise
into rubbish and Chaos, will be glad to rally; to begin growing,
and new-shaping her inorganic dust; very slowly, through centuries, through Napoleons, Louis-Philippes, and other the like
media and phases,—into a new, infinitely preferable France, we
can hope!—

These wheelings and movements in the region of the Argonne,
which are all faithfully described by Dumouriez himself, and more
interesting to us than Hoyle's or Philidor's best Game of Chess,
let us nevertheless, O Reader, entirely omit;—and hasten to remark two things: the first a minute private, the second a large
public thing. Our minute private thing is: the presence, in the
Prussian host, in that war-game of the Argonne, of a certain

[5] Dumouriez, *Mémoires*, iii. 55.   [6] Helen Maria Williams, iii. 32.

Man, belonging to the sort called Immortal; who, in days since then, is becoming visible more and more in that character, as the Transitory more and more vanishes: for from of old it was remarked that when the Gods appear among men, it is seldom in recognisable shape; thus Admetus's neatherds give Apollo a draught of their goatskin whey-bottle (well if they do not give him strokes with their oxrungs), not dreaming that he is the Sun-god! This man's name is *Johann Wolfgang von Goethe*. He is Herzog Weimar's Minister, come with the small contingent of Weimar; to do insignificant unmilitary duty here; very irrecognisable to nearly all! He stands at present, with drawn bridle, on the height near Sainte-Menehould, making an experiment on the 'cannon-fever;' having ridden thither against persuasion, into the dance and firing of the cannon-balls, with a scientific desire to understand what that same cannon-fever may be: 'The sound 'of them,' says he, 'is curious enough; as if it were compounded 'of the humming of tops, the gurgling of water and the whistle of 'birds. By degrees you get a very uncommon sensation; which 'can only be described by similitude. It seems as if you were in 'some place extremely hot, and at the same time were completely 'penetrated by the heat of it; so that you feel as if you and this 'element you are in were perfectly on a par. The eyesight loses 'nothing of its strength or distinctness; and yet it is as if all 'things had got a kind of brown-red colour, which makes the 'situation and the objects still more impressive on you.' [7]

This is the cannon-fever, as a World-Poet feels it.—A man entirely irrecognisable! In whose irrecognisable head, meanwhile, there verily is the spiritual counterpart (and call it complement) of this same huge Death-Birth of the World; which now effectuates itself, outwardly in the Argonne, in such cannon-thunder; inwardly, in the irrecognisable head, quite otherwise than by thunder! Mark that man, O Reader, as the memorablest of all the memorable in this Argonne Campaign. What we say of him is not dream, nor flourish of rhetoric, but scientific historic fact; as many men, now at this distance, see or begin to see.

But the large public thing we had to remark is this: That the Twentieth of September 1792 was a raw morning covered with mist; that from three in the morning, Sainte-Menehould, and those Villages and homesteads we know of old, were stirred by the rumble of artillery-wagons, by the clatter of hoofs and many-footed

[7] Goethe, *Campagne in Frankreich* (*Werke*, xxx. 73).

tramp of men: all manner of military, Patriot and Prussian, taking up positions, on the Heights of La Lune and other Heights; shifting and shoving,—seemingly in some dread chess-game; which may the Heavens turn to good! The Miller of Valmy has fled dusty under ground; his Mill, were it never so windy, will have rest today. At seven in the morning the mist clears off: see Kellermann, Dumouriez' second in command, with 'eighteen pieces of cannon,' and deep-serried ranks, drawn up round that same silent Windmill, on his knoll of strength; Brunswick, also with serried ranks and cannon, glooming over to him from the Height of La Lune: only the little brook and its little dell now parting them.

So that the much-longed-for has come at last! Instead of hunger and dysentery, we shall have sharp shot; and then!— Dumouriez, with force and firm front, looks on from a neighbouring height; can help only with his wishes, in silence. Lo, the eighteen pieces do bluster and bark, responsive to the bluster of La Lune; and thunder-clouds mount into the air; and echoes roar through all dells, far into the depths of Argonne Wood (deserted now); and limbs and lives of men fly dissipated, this way and that. Can Brunswick make an impression on them? The dulled-bright Seigneurs stand biting their thumbs; these Sansculottes seem *not* to fly like poultry! Towards noontide a cannon-shot blows Kellermann's horse from under him; there bursts a powder-cart high into the air, which knell heard over all: some swagging and swaying observable;—Brunswick will try! "*Camarades*," cries Kellermann, "*Vive la Patrie! Allons vaincre pour elle*, Come let us conquer for her." "Live the Fatherland!" rings responsive to the welkin, like rolling-fire from side to side: our ranks are as firm as rocks; and Brunswick may *re*cross the dell, ineffectual; regain his old position on La Lune; not unbattered by the way. And so, for the length of a September day,—with bluster and bark; with bellow far-echoing! The cannonade lasts till sunset; and no impression made. Till an hour after sunset, the few remaining Clocks of the District striking Seven; at this late time of day Brunswick tries again. With not a whit better fortune! He is met by rock-ranks, by shout of *Vive la Patrie;* and driven back, not unbattered. Whereupon he ceases; retires 'to the Tavern of La Lune;' and sets to raising a redoute lest *he* be attacked!

Verily so, ye dulled-bright Seigneurs, make of it what ye may.

Ah, and France does not rise round us in mass; and the Peasants do not join us, but assassinate us: neither hanging nor any persuasion will induce them! They have lost their old distinguishing love of King and King's-cloak,—I fear, altogether; and will even fight to be rid of it: that seems now their humour. Nor does Austria prosper, nor the siege of Thionville. The Thionvillers, carrying their insolence to the epigrammatic pitch, have put a Wooden Horse on their walls, with a bundle of Hay hung from him, and this Inscription: "When I finish my hay, you will take Thionville." [8] To such height has the frenzy of mankind risen.

The trenches of Thionville may shut; and what though those of Lille open? The Earth smiles not on us, nor the Heaven; but weeps and blears itself, in sour rain, and worse. Our very friends insult us; we are wounded in the house of our friends: 'His 'Majesty of Prussia had a greatcoat, when the rain came; and '(contrary to all known laws) he put it on, though our two French 'Princes, the hope of their country, had none!' To which indeed, as Goethe admits, what answer could be made? [9]—Cold and Hunger and Affront, Colic and Dysentery and Death; and we here, cowering *redouted*, most unredoubtable, amid the 'tattered corn-shocks and deformed stubble,' on the splashy Height of La Lune, round the mean Tavern de la Lune!—

This is the Cannonade of Valmy; wherein the World-Poet experimented on the cannon-fever; wherein the French Sans-culottes did not fly like poultry. Precious to France! Every soldier did his duty, and Alsatian Kellermann (how preferable to old Lückner the dismissed!) began to become greater; and *Égalité Fils*, Equality Junior, a light gallant Field-Officer, distinguished himself by intrepidity:—it is the same intrepid individual who now, as Louis-Philippe, without the Equality, struggles, under sad circumstances, to be called King of the French for a season.

[8] *Hist. Parl.* xix. 177.   [9] Goethe, xxx. 49.

CHAPTER VIII.

EXEUNT.

BUT this Twentieth of September is otherwise a great day. For, observe, while Kellermann's horse was flying blown from under him at the Mill of Valmy, our new National Deputies, that shall be a NATIONAL CONVENTION, are hovering and gathering about the Hall of the Hundred Swiss: with intent to constitute themselves!

On the morrow, about noontide, Camus the Archivist is busy 'verifying their powers;' several hundreds of them already here. Whereupon the Old Legislative comes solemnly over, to merge its old ashes phœnix-like in the body of the new ;—and so forthwith, returning all solemnly back to the Salle de Manége, there sits a National Convention, Seven-hundred and Forty-nine complete, or complete enough; presided by Pétion ;—which proceeds directly to do business. Read that reported afternoon's-debate, O Reader; there are few debates like it: dull reporting *Moniteur* itself becomes more dramatic than a 'very Shakspeare. For epigrammatic Manuel rises, speaks strange things; how the President shall have a guard of honour, and lodge in the Tuileries :—*rejected*. And Danton rises and speaks; and Collot d'Herbois rises, and Curate Grégoire, and lame Couthon of the Mountain rises; and in rapid Melibœan stanzas, only a few lines each, they propose motions not a few: That the corner-stone of our new Constitution is, Sovereignty of the People; that our Constitution shall be accepted by the People or be null; further that the People ought to be avenged, and have right Judges; that the Imposts must continue till new order; that Landed and other Property be sacred forever; finally that 'Royalty from this day is abolished in France:' —*Decreed* all, before four o'clock strike, with acclamation of the world![1] The tree was all so ripe; only shake it, and there fall such yellow cartloads.

[1] *Hist Parl.* xix. 19.

And so over in the Valmy Region, as soon as the news come, what stir is this, audible, visible from our muddy Heights of La Lune ?[2] Universal shouting of the French on their opposite hill-side ; caps raised on bayonets : and a sound as of *République : Vive la République* borne dubious on the winds !—On the morrow morning, so to speak, Brunswick slings his knapsacks before day, lights any fires he has ; and marches without tap of drum. Dumouriez finds ghastly symptoms in that camp ; '*latrines* full of blood' ![3] The chivalrous King of Prussia,—for he, as we saw, is here in person,—may long rue the day ; may look colder than ever on these dulled-bright Seigneurs, and French Princes their Country's hope ;—and, on the whole, put on his greatcoat without ceremony, happy that he has one. They retire, all retire with convenient despatch, through a Champagne trodden into a quagmire, the wild weather pouring on them : Dumouriez, through his Kellermanns and Dillons, pricking them a little in the hinder parts. A little, not much ; now pricking, now negotiating : for Brunswick has his eyes opened ; and the Majesty of Prussia is a repentant Majesty.

Nor has Austria prospered ; nor the Wooden Horse of Thionville bitten his hay ; nor Lille City surrendered itself. The Lille trenches opened on the 29th of the month ; with balls and shells, and redhot balls ; as if not trenches but Vesuvius and the Pit had opened. It was frightful, say all eye-witnesses ; but it is ineffectual. The Lillers have risen to such temper ; especially after these news from Argonne and the East. Not a Sans-indispensables in Lille that would surrender for a King's ransom. Redhot balls rain, day and night ; 'six-thousand,' or so, and bombs 'filled internally with oil of turpentine which splashes up in flame ;'—mainly on the dwellings of the Sansculottes and Poor ; the streets of the Rich being spared. But the Sansculottes get water-pails ; form quenching-regulations : "The ball is in Peter's house !" "The ball is in John's !" They divide their lodging and substance with each other ; shout *Vive la République ;* and faint not in heart. A ball thunders through the main chamber of the Hôtel-de-Ville while the Commune is there assembled : "We are in permanence," says one coldly, proceeding with his business ; and the ball remains permanent too, sticking in the wall, probably to this day.[4]

The Austrian Archduchess (Queen's Sister) will herself see red

---

[2] Williams, iii. 71. [3] 1st October 1792 : Dumouriez, iii. 73.
[4] *Bombardement de Lille* (in *Hist. Parl.* xx. 63-71).

artillery fired: in their over-haste to satisfy an Archduchess, 'two mortars explode and kill thirty persons.' It is in vain; Lille, often burning, is always quenched again; Lille will not yield. The very boys deftly wrench the matches out of fallen bombs: 'a man clutches a rolling ball with his hat, which takes fire; when cool, they crown it with a *bonnet rouge.*' Memorable also be that nimble Barber, who when the bomb burst beside him, snatched up a sherd of it, introduced soap and lather into it, crying, " *Voilà mon plat à barbe,* My new shaving-dish!" and shaved 'fourteen people' on the spot. Bravo, thou nimble Shaver; worthy to shave old spectral Redcloak, and find treasures!—On the eighth day of this desperate siege, the sixth day of October, Austria, finding it fruitless, draws off, with no pleasurable consciousness; rapidly, Dumouriez tending thitherward; and Lille too, black with ashes and smoulder, but jubilant skyhigh, flings its gates open. The *Plat à barbe* became fashionable; 'no Patriot of an elegant turn,' says Mercier several years afterwards, 'but shaves himself out of the splinter of a Lille bomb.'

Quid multa, Why many words? The Invaders are in flight; Brunswick's Host, the third part of it gone to death, staggers disastrous along the deep highways of Champagne; spreading out also into 'the fields of a tough spongy red-coloured clay:'—'like Pharaoh through a Red Sea of mud,' says Goethe; 'for here also 'lay broken chariots, and riders and foot seemed sinking around.' [5] On the eleventh morning of October, the World-Poet, struggling Northwards out of Verdun, which he had entered Southwards, some five weeks ago, in quite other order, discerned the following Phenomenon and formed part of it:

'Towards three in the morning, without having had any sleep, 'we were about mounting our carriage, drawn up at the door; 'when an insuperable obstacle disclosed itself: for there rolled on 'already, between the pavement-stones which were crushed up 'into a ridge on each side, an uninterrupted column of sick- 'wagons through the Town, and all was trodden as into a morass. 'While we stood waiting what could be made of it, our Landlord 'the Knight of Saint-Louis pressed past us, without salutation.' He had been a Calonne's Notable in 1787, an Emigrant since; had returned to his home, jubilant, with the Prussians; but must

[5] *Campagne in Frankreich,* p. 103.

now forth again into the wide world, 'followed by a servant
carrying a little bundle on his stick.'

'The activity of our alert Lisieux shone eminent, and on this
'occasion too brought us on: for he struck into a small gap of
'the wagon-row; and held the advancing team back till we,
'with our six and our four horses, got intercalated; after which,
'in my light little coachlet, I could breathe freer. We were now
'under way; at a funeral pace, but still under way. The day
'broke; we found ourselves at the outlet of the Town, in a tumult
'and turmoil without measure. All sorts of vehicles, few horsemen,
'innumerable foot-people, were crossing each other on the great
'esplanade before the Gate. We turned to the right, with our
'Column, towards Estain, on a limited highway, with ditches at
'each side. Self-preservation, in so monstrous a press, knew now
'no pity, no respect of aught. Not far before us there fell down a
'horse of an ammunition-wagon; they cut the traces, and let it
'lie. And now as the three others could not bring their load
'along, they cut them also loose, tumbled the heavy-packed
'vehicle into the ditch; and with the smallest retardation, we
'had to drive on right over the horse, which was just about to
'rise; and I saw too clearly how its legs, under the wheels, went
'crashing and quivering.

'Horse and foot endeavoured to escape from the narrow laborious
'highway into the meadows: but these too were rained to ruin;
'overflowed by full ditches, the connexion of the footpaths every-
'where interrupted. Four gentleman-like, handsome, well-dressed
'French soldiers waded for a time beside our carriage; wonderfully
'clean and neat: and had such art of picking their steps, that
'their foot-gear testified no higher than the ankle to the muddy
'pilgrimage these good people found themselves engaged in.

'That under such circumstances one saw, in ditches, in meadows,
'in fields and crofts, dead horses enough, was natural to the case:
'by and by, however, you found them also flayed, the fleshy parts
'even cut away; sad token of the universal distress.

'Thus we fared on; every moment in danger, at the smallest
'stoppage on our own part, of being ourselves tumbled overboard;
'under which circumstances, truly, the careful dexterity of our
'Lisieux could not be sufficiently praised. The same talent
'showed itself at Estain; where we arrived towards noon; and
'descried, over the beautiful well-built little Town, through streets
'and on squares, around and beside us, one sense-confusing

'tumult: the mass rolled this way and that; and, all struggling
'forward, each hindered the other. Unexpectedly our carriage
'drew up before a stately house in the marketplace; master and
'mistress of the mansion saluted us in reverent distance.' Dexterous
Lisieux, though we knew it not, had said we were the King of
Prussia's Brother!

'But now, from the ground-floor windows, looking over the
'whole marketplace, we had the endless tumult lying, as it were,
'palpable. All sorts of walkers, soldiers in uniform, marauders,
'stout but sorrowing citizens and peasants, women and children,
'crushed and jostled each other, amid vehicles of all forms:
'ammunition-wagons, baggage-wagons; carriages, single, double
'and multiplex; such hundredfold miscellany of teams, requisitioned
'or lawfully owned, making way, hitting together, hindering each
'other, rolled here to right and to left. Horned-cattle too were
'struggling on; probably herds that had been put in requisition.
'Riders you saw few; but the elegant carriages of the Emigrants,
'many-coloured, lackered, gilt and silvered, evidently by the best
'builders, caught your eye.[6]

'The crisis of the strait, however, arose farther on a little;
'where the crowded marketplace had to introduce itself into a
'street,—straight indeed and good, but proportionably far too
'narrow. I have, in my life, seen nothing like it: the aspect of
'it might perhaps be compared to that of a swoln river which has
'been raging over meadows and fields, and is now again obliged
'to press itself through a narrow bridge, and flow on in its
'bounded channel. Down the long street, all visible from our
'windows, there swelled continually the strangest tide: a high
'double-seated travelling coach towered visible over the flood of
'things. We thought of the fair Frenchwomen we had seen in the
'morning. It was not they, however; it was Count Haugwitz;
'him you could look at, with a kind of sardonic malice, rocking
'onwards, step by step, there.'[7]

In such untriumphant Procession has the Brunswick Manifesto
issued! Nay in worse, 'in Negotiation with these miscreants,'—
the first news of which produced such a revulsion in the Emigrant
nature, as put our scientific World-Poet 'in fear for the wits of
several.'[8] There is no help: they must fare on, these poor

[6] See *Hermann und Dorothea* (also by Goethe), Buch *Kalliope*.
[7] *Campagne in Frankreich*, Goethe's *Werke* (Stuttgart, 1829), xxx. 133.
[8] *Campagne in Frankreich*, Goethe's *Werke*, xxx. 152.

Emigrants, angry with all persons and things, and making all persons angry in the hapless course they struck into. Landlord and landlady testify to you, at *tables-d'hôte*, how insupportable these Frenchmen are : how, in spite of such humiliation, of poverty and probable beggary, there is ever the same struggle for precedence, the same forwardness and want of discretion. High in honour, at the head of the table, you with your own eyes observe not a Seigneur, but the automaton of a Seigneur fallen into dotage; still worshipped, reverently waited on and fed. In miscellaneous seats is a miscellany of soldiers, commissaries, adventurers; consuming silently their barbarian victuals. 'On 'all brows is to be read a hard destiny; all are silent, for each 'has his own sufferings to bear, and looks forth into misery without 'bounds.' One hasty wanderer, coming in, and eating without ungraciousness what is set before him, the landlord lets off almost scot-free. "He is," whispered the landlord to me, "the first of these cursed people I have seen condescend to taste our German black bread." [9]

And Dumouriez is in Paris ; lauded and feasted ; paraded in glittering saloons, floods of beautifulest blonde-dresses and broad-cloth-coats flowing past him, endless, in admiring joy. One night, nevertheless, in the splendour of one such scene, he sees himself suddenly apostrophised by a squalid unjoyful Figure, who has come in *un*invited, nay despite of all lackeys ; an unjoyful Figure ! The Figure is come "in express mission from the Jacobins," to inquire sharply, better then than later, touching certain things : "Shaven eyebrows of Volunteer Patriots, for instance ? " Also, "your threats of shivering in pieces ? " Also, " why you have not chased Brunswick hotly enough ? " Thus, with sharp croak, inquires the Figure.—" *Ah, c'est vous qu'on appelle Marat*, You are he they call Marat ! " answers the General, and turns coldly on his heel.[10]— " Marat ! " The blonde-gowns quiver like aspens; the dress-coats gather round ; Actor Talma (for it is his house), Actor Talma, and almost the very chandelier-lights, are blue : till this obscene Spectrum, swart unearthly Visual-Appearance, vanish, back into its native Night.

[9] *Campagne in Frankreich*, Goethe's *Werke*, xxx. 210-12.

[10] Dumouriez, iii. 115.—Marat's account, in the *Débats des Jacobins* and *Journal de la République* (*Hist. Parl.* xix. 317-21), agrees to the turning on the heel, but strives to interpret it differently.

General Dumouriez, in few brief days, is gone again, towards the Netherlands; will attack the Netherlands, winter though it be. And General Montesquiou, on the Southeast, has driven in the Sardinian Majesty; nay, almost without a shot fired, has taken Savoy from him, which longs to become a piece of the Republic. And General Custine, on the Northeast, has dashed forth on Spires and its Arsenal; and then on Electoral Mentz, not uninvited, wherein are German Democrats and no shadow of an Elector now : so that in the last days of October, Frau Forster, a daughter of Heyne's, somewhat democratic, walking out of the Gate of Mentz with her Husband, finds French Soldiers playing at bowls with cannon-balls there. Forster trips cheerfully over one iron bomb, with " Live the Republic ! " A black-bearded National Guard answers : " *Elle vivra bien 'sans vous*, It will probably live independently of you." [11]

[11] Johann Georg Forster's *Briefwechsel* (Leipzig, 1829), i. 83.

BOOK SECOND.

REGICIDE.

CHAPTER I.

THE DELIBERATIVE.

FRANCE therefore has done two things very completely: she has hurled back her Cimmerian Invaders far over the marches; and likewise she has shattered her own internal Social Constitution, even to the minutest fibre of it, into wreck and dissolution. Utterly it is all altered: from King down to Parish Constable, all Authorities, Magistrates, Judges, persons that bore rule, have had, on the sudden, to alter themselves, so far as needful; or else, on the sudden, and not without violence, to be altered; a Patriot 'Executive Council of Ministers,' with a Patriot Danton in it, and then a whole Nation and National Convention, have taken care of that. Not a Parish Constable, in the farthest hamlet, who has said *De par le Roi,* and shown loyalty, but must retire, making way for a new improved Parish Constable who can say *De par la République.*

It is a change such as History must beg her readers to imagine, *un*described. An instantaneous change of the whole body-politic, the soul-politic being all changed; such a change as few bodies, politic or other, can experience in this world. Say, perhaps, such as poor Nymph Semele's body did experience, when she would needs, with woman's humour, see her Olympian Jove as very Jove; —and so stood, poor Nymph, this moment Semele, next moment not Semele, but Flame and a Statue of red-hot Ashes! France has looked upon Democracy; seen it face to face.—The Cimmerian Invaders will rally, in humbler temper, with better or worse luck: the wreck and dissolution must *re*shape itself into a social

Arrangement as it can and may. But as for this National Convention, which is to settle everything, if it do, as Deputy Paine and France generally expects, get all finished 'in a few months,' we shall call it a most deft Convention.

In truth, it is very singular to see how this mercurial French People plunges suddenly from *Vive le Roi* to *Vive la République;* and goes simmering and dancing, shaking off daily (so to speak), and trampling into the dust, its old social garnitures, ways of thinking, rules of existing; and cheerfully dances towards the Ruleless, Unknown, with such hope in its heart, and nothing but *Freedom, Equality and Brotherhood* in its mouth. Is it two centuries, or is it only two years, since all France roared simultaneously to the welkin, bursting forth into sound and smoke at its *Feast of Pikes*, "Live the Restorer of French Liberty"? Three short years ago there was still Versailles and an Œil-de-Bœuf: now there is that watched Circuit of the Temple, girt with dragon-eyed Municipals, where, as in its final limbo, Royalty lies extinct. In the year 1789, Constituent Deputy Barrère 'wept,' in his *Break-of-Day* Newspaper, at sight of a reconciled King Louis; and now in 1792, Convention Deputy Barrère, perfectly tearless, may be considering, whether the reconciled King Louis shall be guillotined or not!

Old garnitures and social vestures drop off (we say) so fast, being indeed quite decayed, and are trodden under the National dance. And the new vestures, where are they; the new modes and rules? Liberty, Equality, Fraternity: not vestures, but the wish for vestures! The Nation is for the present, figuratively speaking, *naked;* it has no rule or vesture; but is naked,—a Sansculottic Nation.

So far therefore, and in such manner, have our Patriot Brissots, Guadets triumphed. Vergniaud's Ezekiel-visions of the fall of thrones and crowns, which he spake hypothetically and prophetically in the Spring of the year, have suddenly come to fulfilment in the Autumn. Our eloquent Patriots of the Legislative, like strong Conjurors, by the word of their mouth, have swept Royalism with its old moods and formulas to the winds; and shall now govern a France free of formulas. Free of formulas! And yet man lives not except with formulas; with customs, *ways* of doing and living: no text truer than this; which will hold true from the Tea-table and Tailor's shopboard up to the High Senate-houses, Solemn Temples; nay through all provinces of Mind and Imagination, onwards to the outmost confines of articulate Being,—*Ubi homines sunt modi sunt.* There are modes wherever there are men. It is the deepest law of man's nature; whereby man is a craftsman and 'tool-using animal;' not the slave of Impulse, Chance and brute Nature, but in some measure their lord. Twenty-five millions of men, suddenly stript bare of their *modi,* and dancing them down in that manner, are a terrible thing to govern!

Eloquent Patriots of the Legislative, meanwhile, have precisely this problem to solve. Under the name and nickname of 'statesmen, *hommes d'état,'* of 'moderate men, *modérantins,'* of Brissotins, Rolandins, finally of *Girondins,* they shall become world-famous in solving it. For the Twenty-five millions are Gallic effervescent too;—filled both with hope of the unutterable, of universal Fraternity and Golden Age; and with terror of the unutterable, Cimmerian Europe all rallying on us. It is a problem like few. Truly, if man, as the Philosophers brag, did to any extent look before and after, what, one may ask, in many cases would become of him? What, in this case, would become of these Seven-hundred and Forty-nine men? The Convention, seeing clearly before and after, were a paralysed Convention. Seeing clearly to the length of its own nose, it is not paralysed.

To the Convention itself neither the work nor the method of doing it is doubtful! To make the Constitution; to defend the Republic till that be made. Speedily enough, accordingly, there has been a 'Committee of the Constitution' got together. Sieyes, Old-Constituent, Constitution-builder by trade; Condorcet, fit for better things; Deputy Paine, foreign Benefactor of the Species, with that 'red carbuncled face and the black beaming eyes;' Hérault de Séchelles, Ex-Parlementeer, one of the handsomest men in France; these, with inferior guild-brethren, are girt cheerfully to the work; will once more 'make the Constitution;' let us hope, more effectually than last time. For that the Constitution can be made, who doubts,—unless the Gospel of Jean Jacques came into the world in vain? True, our last Constitution did tumble within the year, so lamentably. But what then; except sort the rubbish and boulders, and build them up again better? 'Widen your basis,' for one thing,—to Universal Suffrage, if need be; exclude rotten materials, Royalism and suchlike, for another thing. And in brief, *build,* O unspeakable Sieyes and Company, unwearied! Frequent perilous downrushing of scaffolding and rubblework, be that an irritation, no discouragement. Start ye always again, clearing aside the wreck; if with broken limbs, yet

with whole hearts; and build, we say, in the name of Heaven,—
till either the work do stand ; or else mankind abandon it, and the
Constitution-builders be paid off, with laughter and tears ! One
good time, in the course of Eternity, it was appointed that this of
Social Contract too should try itself out. And so the Committee
of Constitution shall toil : with hope and faith ;—with no disturbance from any reader of these pages.

To make the Constitution, then, and return home joyfully in a
few months; this is the prophecy our National Convention gives
of itself; by this scientific program shall its operations and events
go on. But from the best scientifio program, in such a case, to
the actual fulfilment, what a difference ! Every reunion of men,
is it not, as we often say, a reunion of incalculable Influences ;
every unit of it a microcosm of Influences ;—of which how shall
Science calculate or prophesy ? Science, which cannot, with all its
calculuses, differential, integral and of variations, calculate the
Problem of Three gravitating Bodies, ought to hold her peace here,
and say only : In this National Convention there are Seven-
hundred and Forty-nine very singular Bodies, that gravitate and
do much else ;—who, probably in an amazing manner, will work
the appointment of Heaven.

Of National Assemblages, Parliaments, Congresses, which have
long sat; which are of saturnine temperament; above all, which
are not 'dreadfully in earnest,' something may be computed or
conjectured : yet even these are a kind of Mystery in progress,—
whereby accordingly we see the Journalist Reporter find liveli-
hood : even these jolt madly out of the ruts, from time to time.
How much more a poor National Convention, of French vehemence ; urged on at such velocity ; without routine, without rut,
track or landmark ; and dreadfully in earnest every man of. them !
It is a Parliament literally such as there was never elsewhere in
the world. Themselves are new, unarranged ; they are the Heart
and presiding centre of a France fallen wholly into maddest dis-
arrangement. From all cities, hamlets, from the utmost ends of
this France with its Twenty-five million vehement souls, thick-
streaming influences storm-in on that same Heart, in the Salle de
Manége, and storm-out again : such fiery venous-arterial circulation
is the function of that Heart. Seven-hundred and Forty-nine
human individuals, we say, never sat together on our Earth under
more original circumstances. Common individuals most of them,
or not far from common : yet in virtue of the position they occupied,

so notable. How, in this wild piping of the whirlwind of human passions, with death, victory, terror, valour, and all height and all depth pealing and piping, these men, left to their own guidance, will speak and act?

Readers know well that this French National Convention (quite contrary to its own Program) became the astonishment and horror of mankind; a kind of Apocalyptic Convention, or black *Dream become real;* concerning which History seldom speaks except in the way of interjection : how it covered France with wo, delusion and delirium ; and from its bosom there went forth Death on the pale Horse. To hate this poor National Convention is easy; to praise and love it has not been found impossible. It is, as we say, a Parliament in the most original circumstances. To us, in these pages, be it as a fuliginous fiery mystery, where Upper has met Nether, and in such alternate glare and blackness of darkness poor bedazzled mortals know not which is Upper, which is Nether; but rage and plunge distractedly, as mortals in that case will do. A Convention which has to consume itself, suicidally; and become dead ashes—with its World! Behoves us, not to enter exploratively its dim embroiled deeps; yet to stand with unwavering eyes, looking how it welters; what notable phases and occurrences it will successively throw up.

One general superficial circumstance we remark with praise : the force of Politeness. To such depth has the sense of civilisation penetrated man's life; no Drouet, no Legendre, in the maddest tug of war, can altogether shake it off. Debates of Senates dreadfully in earnest are seldom given frankly to the world; else perhaps they would surprise it. Did not the Grand Monarque himself once chase his Louvois with a pair of brandished tongs? But reading long volumes of these Convention Debates, all in a foam with furious earnestness, earnest many times to the extent of life and death, one is struck rather with the degree of continence they manifest in speech ; and how in such wild ebullition, there is still a kind of polite rule struggling for mastery, and the forms of social life never altogether disappear. These men, though they menace with clenched right-hands, do not clutch one another by the collar; they draw no daggers, except for oratorical purposes, and this not often : profane swearing is almost unknown, though the Reports are frank enough ; we find only one or two oaths, oaths by Marat, reported in all.

For the rest, that there is ' effervescence ' who doubts ? Effervescence enough ; Decrees passed by acclamation today, repealed by vociferation tomorrow ; temper fitful, most rotatory-changeful, always headlong ! The 'voice of the orator is covered with rumours ;' a hundred ' honourable Members rush with menaces towards the Left side of the Hall ; ' President has ' broken three ' bells in succession,'—claps on his hat, as signal that the country is near ruined. A fiercely effervescent Old-Gallic Assemblage !— Ah, how the loud sick sounds of Debate, and of Life, which is a *debate,* sink silent one after another : so loud now, and in a little while so low ! Brennus, and those antique Gael Captains, in their way to Rome, to Galatia and such places, whither they were in the habit of marching in the most fiery manner, had Debates as effervescent, doubt it not ; though no *Moniteur* has reported them. They scolded in Celtic Welsh, those Brennuses ; neither were they Sansculotte ; nay rather breeches (*braccæ,* say of felt or rough-leather) were the only thing they had ; being, as Livy testifies, naked down *to* the haunches :—and, see, it is the same sort of work and of men still, now when they have got coats, and speak nasally a kind of broken Latin ! But, on the whole, does not TIME envelope this present National Convention ; as it did those Brennuses, and ancient august Senates in felt breeches ? Time surely : and also Eternity. Dim dusk of Time,—or noon which will be dusk ; and then there is night, and silence ; and Time with all its sick noises is swallowed in the still sea. Pity thy brother, O son of Adam ! The angriest frothy jargon that he utters, is it not properly the whimpering of an infant which cannot *speak* what ails it, but is in distress clearly, in the inwards of it ; and so must squall and whimper continually, till its Mother take it, and it get—to sleep !

This Convention is not four days old, and the melodious Melibœan stanzas that shook down Royalty are still fresh in our ear, when there bursts out a new diapason,—unhappily, of Discord, this time. For speech has been made of a thing difficult to speak of well : the September Massacres. How deal with these September Massacres ; with the Paris Commune that presided over them ? A Paris Commune hateful-terrible ; before which the poor effete Legislative had to quail, and sit quiet. And now if a young omnipotent Convention will not so quail and sit, what steps shall it take ? Have a Departmental Guard in its pay, answer the Girondins and Friends of Order ! A Guard of National Volunteers, missioned from all the Eighty-three or Eighty-five Departments, for that express end; these will keep Septemberers, tumultuous Communes in a due state of submissiveness, the Convention in a due state of sovereignty. So have the Friends of Order answered, sitting in Committee, and reporting; and even a Decree has been passed of the required tenour. Nay certain Departments, as the Var or Marseilles, in mere expectation and assurance of a Decree, have their contingent of Volunteers already on march; brave Marseillese, foremost on the Tenth of August, will not be hindmost here: 'fathers gave their sons a musket and twenty-five louis,' says Barbaroux, 'and bade them march.'

Can anything be properer? A Republic that will found itself on justice must needs investigate September Massacres; a Convention calling itself National, ought it not to be guarded by a National force?—Alas, Reader, it seems so to the eye: and yet there is much to be said and argued. Thou beholdest here the small beginning of a Controversy, which mere logic will not settle. Two small well-springs, September, Departmental Guard, or rather at bottom they are but one and the same small well-spring; which will swell and widen into waters of bitterness; all manner of subsidiary streams and brooks of bitterness flowing in, from this side and that; till it become a wide river of bitterness, of rage and separation,—which can subside only into the Catacombs. This Departmental Guard, decreed by overwhelming majorities, and then repealed for peace's sake, and not to insult Paris, is again decreed more than once; nay it is partially executed, and the very men that are to be of it are seen visibly parading the Paris streets, —shouting once, being overtaken with liquor: "*À bas Marat*, Down with Marat!" [1] Nevertheless, decreed never so often, it is repealed just as often; and continues, for some seven months an angry noisy Hypothesis only: a fair Possibility struggling to become a Reality, but which shall never be one; which, after endless struggling, shall, in February next, sink into sad rest,— dragging much along with it. So singular are the ways of men and honourable Members.

But on this fourth day of the Convention's existence, as we said, which is the 25th of September 1792, there comes Committee Report on that Decree of the Departmental Guard, and speech of repealing it; there come denunciations of Anarchy, of a Dictatorship,—which let the incorruptible Robespierre consider: there

<hr>

[1] *Hist. Parl.* xx. 184.

come denunciations of a certain *Journal de la République,* once
called *Ami du Peuple;* and so thereupon there comes, visibly
stepping up, visibly standing aloft on the Tribune, ready to speak,
—the Bodily Spectrum of People's-Friend Marat! Shriek, ye
Seven-hundred and Forty-nine; it is verily Marat, he and not
another. Marat is no phantasm of the brain, or mere lying im-
press of Printer's Types; but a thing material, of joint and sinew,
and a certain small stature; ye behold him there, in his blackness,
in his dingy squalor, a living fraction of Chaos and Old Night;
visibly incarnate, desirous to speak. "It appears," says Marat to
the shrieking Assembly, "that a great many persons here are
enemies of mine."—"All! all!" shriek hundreds of voices: enough
to drown any People's-Friend. But Marat will not drown: he
speaks and croaks explanation; croaks with such reasonableness,
air of sincerity, that repentant pity smothers anger, and the
shrieks subside, or even become applauses. For this Convention
is unfortunately the crankest of machines: it shall be pointing
eastward with stiff violence this moment; and then do but touch
some spring dexterously, the whole machine, clattering and jerking
seven-hundredfold, will whirl with huge crash, and, next moment,
is pointing westward! Thus Marat, absolved and applauded, victorious in his turn of fence, is, as the Debate goes on, prickt at
again by some dexterous Girondin; and then the shrieks rise anew,
and Decree of Accusation is on the point of passing; till the
dingy People's-Friend bobs aloft once more; croaks once more persuasive stillness, and the Decree of Accusation sinks. Whereupon
he draws forth—a Pistol; and setting it to his Head, the seat of
such thought and prophecy, says: 'If they had passed their Ac-
'cusation Decree, he, the People's-Friend, would have blown his
'brains out.' A People's-Friend has that faculty in him. For the
rest, as to this of the two-hundred and sixty-thousand Aristocrat
Heads, Marat candidly says, "*C'est là mon avis,* Such is my
opinion." Also is it not indisputable: "No power on Earth can
prevent me from seeing into traitors, and unmasking them,"—by
my superior originality of mind?[2] An honourable member like
this Friend of the People few terrestrial Parliaments have had.

We observe, however, that this first onslaught by the Friends of
Order, as sharp and prompt as it was, has failed. For neither can

---

[2] *Moniteur* Newspaper, Nos. 271, 280, 294, Année première; Moore's
Journal, ii. 21, 157, &c. (which, however, may perhaps, as in similar cases, be
only a copy of the Newspaper).

Robespierre, summoned out by talk of Dictatorship, and greeted with the like rumour on showing himself, be thrown into Prison, into Accusation; not though Barbaroux openly bear testimony against him, and sign it on paper. With such sanctified meekness does the Incorruptible lift his seagreen cheek to the smiter; lift his thin voice, and with jesuitic dexterity plead, and prosper; asking at last, in a prosperous manner: "But what witnesses has the Citoyen Barbaroux to support his testimony?" "*Moi!*" cries hot Rebecqui, standing up, striking his breast with both hands, and answering "Me!"[3] Nevertheless the Seagreen pleads again, and makes it good: the long hurly-burly, 'personal merely,' while so much public matter lies fallow, has ended in the order of the day. O Friends of the Gironde, why will you occupy our august sessions with mere paltry Personalities, while the grand Nationality lies in such a state?—The Gironde has touched, this day, on the foul black-spot of its fair Convention Domain; has trodden on it, and yet *not* trodden it down. Alas, it is a *well-spring*, as we said, this black-spot; and will not tread down!

CHAPTER II.

THE EXECUTIVE.

MAY we not conjecture therefore that round this grand enterprise of Making the Constitution, there will, as heretofore, very strange embroilments gather, and questions and interests complicate themselves; so that after a few or even several months, the Convention will not have settled everything? Alas, a whole tide of questions comes rolling, boiling; growing ever wider, without end! Among which, apart from this question of September and Anarchy, let us notice three, which emerge oftener than the others, and promise to become Leading Questions: Of the Armies; of the Subsistences; thirdly, of the Dethroned King.

As to the Armies, Public Defence must evidently be put on a proper footing; for Europe seems coalising itself again; one is apprehensive even England will join it. Happily Dumouriez

[3] *Moniteur*, ut suprà: Séance du 25 Septembre.

prospers in the North;—nay, what if he should prove *too* prosperous, and become *Liberticide*, Murderer of Freedom!—Dumouriez prospers, through this winter season; yet not without
lamentable complaints.   Sleek Pache, the Swiss Schoolmaster, he
that sat frugal in his Alley, the wonder of neighbours, has got
lately—whither thinks the Reader?   To be Minister of War!
Madame Roland, struck with his sleek ways, recommended him
to her husband as Clerk; the sleek Clerk had no need of salary,
being of true Patriotic temper; he would come with a bit of
bread in his pocket, to save dinner and time; and munching
incidentally, do three men's work in a day; punctual, silent, frugal,
—the sleek Tartuffe that he was.   Wherefore Roland, in the late
Overturn, recommended him to be War-Minister.   And now, it
would seem, he is secretly undermining Roland; playing into the
hands of your hotter Jacobins and September Commune; and
cannot, like strict Roland, be the *Veto des Coquins!*[1]

How the sleek Pache might mine and undermine, one knows
not well; this however one does know: that his War-Office has
become a den of thieves and confusion, such as all men shudder to
behold.   That the Citizen Hassenfratz, as Head-Clerk, sits there
in *bonnet rouge*, in rapine, in violence, and some Mathematical
calculation; a most insolent, red-nightcapped man.   That Pache
munches his pocket-loaf, amid head-clerks and sub-clerks, and has
spent all the War-Estimates.   That Furnishers scour in gigs, over
all districts of France, and drive bargains.   And lastly that the
Army gets next to no furniture: no shoes, though it is winter; no
clothes; some have not even arms; 'in the Army of the South,'
complains an honourable Member, 'there are thirty-thousand pairs
of breeches wanting,'—a most scandalous want.

Roland's strict soul is sick to see the course things take: but
what can he do?   Keep his own Department strict; rebuke, and
repress wheresoever possible; at lowest, complain.   He can complain in Letter after Letter, to a National Convention, to France,
to Posterity, the Universe; grow ever more querulous-indignant;—
till at last, may he not grow wearisome?   For is not this continual
text of his, at bottom, a rather barren one: How astonishing that
in a time of Revolt and abrogation of all Law but Cannon Law,
there should be such Unlawfulness?   Intrepid Veto-of-Scoundrels,
narrow-faithful, respectable, methodic man, work thou in that
manner, since happily it is thy manner, and wear thyself away;

[1] Madame Roland, *Mémoires*, ii. 237, &c.

though ineffectual, not profitless in it—then nor *now!*—The brave Dame Roland, bravest of all French women, begins to have misgivings: The figure of Danton has too much of the 'Sardanapalus character,' at a Republican Rolandin Dinner-table: Clootz, Speaker of Mankind, proses sad stuff about a Universal Republic, or union of all Peoples and Kindreds in one and the same Fraternal Bond; of which Bond, how it is to be *tied*, one unhappily sees not.

It is also an indisputable, unaccountable or accountable fact, that Grains are becoming scarcer and scarcer. Riots for grain, tumultuous Assemblages demanding to have the price of grain fixed, abound far and near. The Mayor of Paris and other poor Mayors are like to have their difficulties. Pétion was reëlected Mayor of Paris; but has declined; being now a Convention Legislator. Wise surely to decline: for, besides this of Grains and all the rest, there is in these times an Improvised Insurrectionary Commune passing into an Elected legal one; getting their accounts settled,—not without irritancy! Pétion has declined: nevertheless many do covet and canvass. After months of scrutinising, balloting, arguing and jargoning, one Doctor Chambon gets the post of honour: who will not long keep it; but be, as we shall see, literally *crushed* out of it.[2]

Think also if the private Sansculotte has not his difficulties, in a time of dearth! Bread, according to the People's-Friend, may be some 'six sous per pound, a day's wages some fifteen;' and grim winter here. How the Poor Man continues living, and so seldom starves; by miracle! Happily, in these days, he can enlist, and have himself shot by the Austrians, in an unusually satisfactory manner: for the Rights of Man.—But Commandant Santerre, in this so straitened condition of the flour-market, and state of Equality and Liberty, proposes, through the Newspapers, two remedies, or at least palliatives: *First*, that all classes of men should live two days of the week on potatoes; then, *second*, that every man should hang his dog. Hereby, as the Commandant thinks, the saving, which indeed he computes to so many sacks, would be very considerable. Cheerfuler form of inventive-stupidity than Commandant Santerre's dwells in no human soul. Inventive-stupidity, imbedded in health, courage and good-nature: much to be commended. "My whole strength," he tells the Convention once, "is, day and night, at the service of my fellow-citizens: if

[2] *Dictionnaire des Hommes Marquans*, § Chambon.

they find me worthless, they will dismiss me; I will return, and
brew beer." [3]

Or figure what correspondences a poor Roland, Minister of the
Interior, must have, on this of Grains alone! Free-trade in Grain,
impossibility to fix the Prices of Grain; on the other hand, clamour
and necessity to fix them: Political Economy lecturing from the
Home Office, with demonstration clear as Scripture;—ineffectual
for the empty National Stomach. The Mayor of Chartres, like to
be eaten himself, cries to the Convention; the Convention sends
honourable Members in Deputation; who endeavour to feed the
multitude by miraculous spiritual methods; but cannot. The
multitude, in spite of all Eloquence, come bellowing round; will
have the Grain-Prices fixed, and at a moderate elevation; or else—
the honourable Deputies hanged on the spot! The honourable
Deputies, reporting this business, admit that, on the edge of horrid
death, they did fix, or affect to fix the Price of Grain: for which,
be it also noted, the Convention, a Convention that will not be
trifled with, sees good to reprimand them. [4]

But as to the origin of these Grain-Riots, is it not most probably
your secret Royalists again? Glimpses of Priests were discernible
in this of Chartres,—to the eye of Patriotism. Or indeed may
not 'the root of it all lie in the Temple Prison, in the heart of a
perjured King,' well as we guard him? [5] Unhappy perjured King!
—And so there shall be Bakers' Queues by and by, more sharp-
tempered than ever: on every Baker's door-rabbet an iron ring,
and coil of rope; whereon, with firm grip, on this side and that,
we form our Queue: but mischievous deceitful persons cut the
rope, and our Queue becomes a ravelment; wherefore the coil
must be made of iron chain. [6] Also there shall be Prices of Grain
well fixed; but then no grain purchasable by them: bread not to
be had except by Ticket from the Mayor, few ounces per mouth
daily; after long swaying, with firm grip, on the chain of the
Queue. And Hunger shall stalk direful; and Wrath and Suspicion, whetted to the Preternatural pitch, shall stalk; as those
other preternatural 'shapes of Gods in their wrathfulness' were
discerned stalking, 'in glare and gloom of that fire-ocean,' when
Troy Town fell!—

[3] *Moniteur* (in *Hist. Parl.* xx. 412).   [4] *Hist. Parl.* xx. 431-440.
[5] *Hist. Parl.* xx. 409.   [6] Mercier, *Nouveau Paris.*

CHAPTER III.

DISCROWNED.

But the question more pressing than all on the Legislator, as yet, is this third : What shall be done with King Louis ?

King Louis, now King and Majesty to his own family alone, in their own Prison Apartment alone, has, for months past, been mere Louis Capet and the Traitor Veto with the rest of France. Shut in his Circuit of the Temple, he has heard and seen the loud whirl of things; yells of September Massacres, Brunswick war-thunders dying off in disaster and discomfiture; he passive, a spectator merely; waiting whither it would please to whirl with him. From the neighbouring windows, the curious, not without pity, might see him walk daily, at a certain hour, in the Temple Garden, with his Queen, Sister and two Children, all that now belongs to him in this Earth.[1] Quietly he walks and waits; for he is not of lively feelings, and is of a devout heart. The wearied Irresolute has, at least, no need of resolving now. His daily meals, lessons to his Son, daily walk in the Garden, daily game at ombre or draughts, fill up the day : the morrow will provide for itself.

The morrow indeed; and yet How ? Louis asks, How ? France, with perhaps still more solicitude, asks, How ? A King dethroned by insurrection is verily not easy to dispose of. Keep him prisoner, he is a secret centre for the Disaffected, for endless plots, attempts and hopes of theirs. Banish him, he is an open centre for them; his royal war-standard, with what of divinity it has, unrolls itself, summoning the world. Put him to death ? A cruel questionable extremity that too : and yet the likeliest in these extreme circumstances, of insurrectionary men, whose own life and death lies staked : accordingly it is said, from the last step of the throne to the first of the scaffold there is short distance.

But, on the whole, we will remark here that this business of Louis looks altogether different now, as seen over Seas and at the

[1] Moore, i. 123 ; ii. 224. &c.

distance of forty-four years, from what it looked then, in France, and struggling confused all round one. For indeed it is a most lying thing that same Past Tense always: so beautiful, sad, almost Elysian-sacred, 'in the moonlight of Memory,' it seems; and *seems* only. For observe, always one most important element is surreptitiously (we not noticing it) withdrawn from the Past Time: the haggard element of Fear! Not *there* does Fear dwell, nor Uncertainty, nor Anxiety; but it dwells *here;* haunting us, tracking us; running like an accursed ground-discord through all the music-tones of our Existence;—making the Tense a mere Present one! Just so is it with this of Louis. Why smite the fallen? asks Magnanimity, out of danger now. He is fallen so low this once-high man; no criminal nor traitor, how far from it; but the unhappiest of Human Solecisms: whom if abstract Justice had to pronounce upon, she might well become concrete Pity, and pronounce only sobs and dismissal!

So argues retrospective Magnanimity: but Pusillanimity, present, prospective? Reader, thou hast never lived, for months, under the rustle of Prussian gallows-ropes; never wert thou portion of a National Sahara-waltz, Twenty-five millions running distracted to fight Brunswick! Knights Errant themselves, when they conquered Giants, usually slew the Giants: quarter was only for other Knights Errant, who knew courtesy and the laws of battle. The French Nation, in simultaneous, desperate dead-pull, and as if by miracle of madness, has pulled down the most dread Goliath, huge with the growth of ten centuries; and cannot believe, though his giant bulk, covering acres, lies prostrate, bound with peg and packthread, that he will not rise again, man-devouring; that the victory is not partly a dream. Terror has its scepticism; miraculous victory its rage of vengeance. Then as to criminality, is the prostrated Giant, who will devour us if he rise, an innocent Giant? Curate Grégoire, who indeed is now Constitutional Bishop Grégoire, asserts, in the heat of eloquence, that Kingship by the very nature of it is a crime capital; that Kings' Houses are as wild-beasts' dens.[2] Lastly consider this: that there is on record a Trial of Charles First! This printed *Trial of Charles First* is sold and read everywhere at present:[3]—*Quel spectacle!* Thus did the English People judge their Tyrant, and become the first of Free Peoples: which feat, by the grace of Destiny, may

[2] *Moniteur*, Séance du 21 Septembre, An 1ᵉʳ (1792).
[3] Moore's *Journal*, ii. 165.

not France now rival? Scepticism of terror, rage of miraculous victory, sublime spectacle to the universe,—all things point one fatal way.

Such leading questions, and their endless incidental ones,— of September Anarchists and Departmental Guard; of Grain-Riots, plaintive Interior Ministers; of Armies, Hassenfratz dilapidations; and what is to be done with Louis,—beleaguer and embroil this Convention; which would so gladly make the Constitution rather. All which questions, too, as we often urge of such things, are in *growth;* they grow in every French head; and can be *seen* growing also, very curiously, in this mighty welter of Parliamentary Debate, of Public Business which the Convention has to do. A question emerges, so small at first; is put off, submerged; but always reëmerges bigger than before. It is a curious, indeed an indescribable sort of growth which such things have.

We perceive, however, both by its frequent reëmergence and by its rapid enlargement of bulk, that this Question of King Louis will take the lead of all the rest. And truly, in that case, it will take the *lead* in a much deeper sense. For as Aaron's Rod swallowed all the other serpents; so will the Foremost Question, whichever may get foremost, absorb all other questions and interests; and from it and the decision of it will they all, so to speak, be *born,* or new-born, and have shape, physiognomy and destiny corresponding. It was appointed of Fate that, in this wide-weltering, strangely growing, monstrous stupendous imbroglio of Convention Business, the grand First-Parent of all the questions, controversies, measures and enterprises which were to be evolved there to the world's astonishment, should be this Question of King Louis.

CHAPTER IV.

THE LOSER PAYS.

THE Sixth of November 1792 was a great day for the Republic: outwardly, over the Frontiers; inwardly, in the *Salle de Manége.*

Outwardly: for Dumouriez, overrunning the Netherlands, did, on that day, come in contact with Saxe-Teschen and the Austrians; Dumouriez wide-winged, they wide-winged; at and around the village of Jemappes, near Mons. And fire-hail is whistling far and wide there, the great guns playing, and the small; so many green Heights getting fringed and maned with red Fire. And Dumouriez is swept back on this wing, and swept back on that, and is like to be swept back utterly; when he rushes up in person, the prompt Polymetis; speaks a prompt word or two; and then, with clear tenor-pipe, 'uplifts the Hymn of the Marseillese, *entonna la Marseillaise,*'[1] ten-thousand tenor or bass pipes joining; or say, some Forty-thousand in all; for every heart leaps at the sound; and so with rhythmic march-melody, waxing ever quicker, to double and to treble quick, they rally, they advance, they rush, death-defying, man-devouring; carry batteries, redoutes, whatsoever is to be carried; and, like the fire-whirlwind, sweep all manner of Austrians from the scene of action. Thus, through the hands of Dumouriez, may Rouget de Lille, in figurative speech, be said to have gained, miraculously, like another Orpheus, by his Marseillese fiddle-strings (*fidibus canoris*), a Victory of Jemappes; and conquered the Low Countries.

Young General Egalité, it would seem, shone brave among the bravest on this occasion. Doubtless a brave Egalité:—whom however does not Dumouriez rather talk of oftener than need were? The Mother Society has her own thoughts. As for the Elder Egalité, he flies low at this time; appears in the Convention for some half-hour daily, with rubicund, preoccupied or impassive quasi-contemptuous countenance; and then takes himself away.[2]

[1] Dumouriez, *Mémoires*, iii. 174.   [2] Moore, ii. 143.

The Netherlands are conquered, at least overrun. Jacobin missionaries, your Prolys, Pereiras, follow in the train of the Armies; also Convention Commissioners, melting church-plate, revolutionising and remodeling,—among whom Danton, in brief space, does immensities of business; not neglecting his own wages and trade-profits, it is thought. Hassenfratz dilapidates at home; Dumouriez grumbles and they dilapidate abroad: within the walls there is sinning, and without the walls there is sinning.

But in the Hall of the Convention, at the same hour with this victory of Jemappes, there went another thing forward: Report, of great length, from the proper appointed Committee, on the Crimes of Louis. The Galleries listen breathless; take comfort, ye Galleries: Deputy Valazé, Reporter on this occasion, thinks Louis very criminal; and that, if convenient, he should be tried;—poor Girondin Valazé, who may be tried himself, one day! Comfortable so far. Nay here comes a second Committee-reporter, Deputy Mailhe, with a Legal Argument, very prosy to read now, very refreshing to hear then, That, by the Law of the Country, Louis Capet was only called Inviolable by a figure of rhetoric; but at bottom was perfectly violable, triable; that he can, and even should be tried. This Question of Louis, emerging so often as an angry confused possibility, and submerging again, has emerged now in an articulate shape.

Patriotism growls indignant joy. The so-called reign of Equality is not to be a mere name, then, but a thing! Try Louis Capet? scornfully ejaculates Patriotism. Mean criminals go to the gallows for a purse cut; and this chief criminal, guilty of a France cut; of a France slashed asunder with Clotho-scissors and Civil war; with his victims 'twelve-hundred on the Tenth of August alone' lying low in the Catacombs, fattening the passes of Argonne Wood, of Valmy and far Fields; he, such chief criminal, shall not even come to the bar?—For, alas, O Patriotism! add we, it was from of old said, *The loser pays!* It is he who has to pay *all* scores, run up by whomsoever; on him must all breakages and charges fall; and the twelve-hundred on the Tenth of August are not rebel traitors, but victims and martyrs: such is the law of quarrel.

Patriotism, nothing doubting, watches over this Question of the trial, now happily emerged in an articulate shape; and will see it to maturity, if the gods permit. With a keen solicitude Patriotism watches; getting ever keener, at every new difficulty, as Girondins and false brothers interpose delays; till it get a keenness as of fixed-idea, and will have this Trial and no earthly thing instead of it,—if Equality be not a name. Love of Equality; then scepticism of terror, rage of victory, sublime spectacle to the universe : all these things are strong.

But indeed this Question of the Trial, is it not to all persons a most grave one; filling with dubiety many a Legislative head! Regicide? asks the Gironde Respectability. To kill a king, and become the horror of respectable nations and persons? But then also, to save a king; to lose one's footing with the decided Patriot; the undecided Patriot, though never so respectable, being mere hypothetic froth and no footing?—The dilemma presses sore; and between the horns of it you wriggle round and round. Decision is nowhere, save in the Mother Society and her Sons. These have decided, and go forward : the others wriggle round uneasily within their dilemma-horns, and make way nowhither.

CHAPTER V.

STRETCHING OF FORMULAS.

But how this Question of the Trial grew laboriously, through the weeks of gestation, now that it has been articulated or conceived, were superfluous to trace here. It emerged and submerged among the infinite of questions and embroilments. The Veto of Scoundrels writes plaintive Letters as to Anarchy; 'concealed Royalists,' aided by Hunger, produce Riots about Grain. Alas, it is but a week ago, these Girondins made a new fierce onslaught on the September Massacres!

For, one day, among the last of October, Robespierre, being summoned to the tribune by some new hint of that old calumny of the Dictatorship, was speaking and pleading there, with more and more comfort to himself; till rising high in heart, he cried out valiantly : Is there any man here that dare specifically accuse me? "*Moi!*" exclaimed one. Pause of deep silence : a lean angry little Figure, with broad bald brow, strode swiftly towards the tribune, taking papers from its pocket: "I accuse thee, Robespierre,"—I, Jean Baptiste Louvet! The Seagreen became tallowgreen; shrinking to a corner of the tribune: Danton cried, "Speak, Robespierre; there are many good citizens that listen;" but the tongue refused its office. And so Louvet, with a shrill tone, read and recited crime after crime: dictatorial temper, exclusive popularity, bullying at elections, mob-retinue, September Massacres;—till all the Convention shrieked again, and had almost indicted the Incorruptible there on the spot. Never did the Incorruptible run such a risk. Louvet, to his dying day, will regret that the Gironde did not take a bolder attitude, and extinguish him there and then.

Not so, however: the Incorruptible, about to be indicted in this sudden manner, could not be refused a week of delay. That week he is not idle; nor is the Mother Society idle,—fierce-tremulous for her chosen son. He is ready at the day with his written Speech; smooth as a Jesuit Doctor's; and convinces some. And now? Why now lazy Vergniaud does *not* rise with Demosthenic thunder; poor Louvet, unprepared, can do little or nothing: Barrère proposes that these comparatively despicable 'personalities' be dismissed by order of the day! Order of the day it accordingly is. Barbaroux cannot even get a hearing; not though he rush down to the Bar, and demand to be heard there as a petitioner.[1] The Convention, eager for public business (with that first articulate emergence of the Trial just coming on), dismisses these comparative *misères* and despicabilities: splenetic Louvet must digest his spleen, regretfully forever: Robespierre, dear to Patriotism, is dearer for the dangers he has run.

This is the second grand attempt by our Girondin Friends of Order to extinguish that black-spot in their domain; and we see they have made it far blacker and wider than before! Anarchy, September Massacre: it is a thing that lies hideous in the general imagination; very detestable to the undecided Patriot, of Respectability: a thing to be harped on as often as need is. Harp on it, denounce it, trample it, ye Girondin Patriots:—and yet behold, the black-spot will not trample down; it will only, as we say, trample blacker and wider: fools, it is no black-spot of the surface, but a well-spring of the deep! Consider rightly, it is the Apex of the everlasting Abyss, this black-spot, looking up as water

---

[1] Louvet, *Mémoires* (Paris, 1823), p. 52; *Moniteur* (Séances du 29 Octobre, 5 Novembre, 1792); Moore, ii. 178, &c.

through thin ice;—say, as the region of Nether Darkness through
your thin film of Gironde Regulation and Respectability : trample
it *not*, lest the film break, and then— !

The truth is, if our Gironde Friends had an understanding of
it, where were French Patriotism, with all its eloquence, at this
moment, had *not* that same great Nether Deep, of Bedlam,
Fanaticism and Popular wrath and madness, risen unfathomable
on the Tenth of August ?   French Patriotism were an eloquent
Reminiscence; swinging on Prussian gibbets.   Nay, where, in few
months, were it still, should the same great Nether Deep subside ?
—Nay, as readers of Newspapers pretend to recollect, this hate-
fulness of the September Massacre is itself partly an after-thought:
readers of Newspapers can quote Gorsas and various Brissotins
approving of the September Massacre, at the time it happened;
and calling it a salutary vengeance.[2]   So that the real grief, after
all, were not so much righteous horror, as grief that one's own
power was departing ?   Unhappy Girondins !

In the Jacobin Society, therefore, the decided Patriot complains
that here are men who with their private ambitions and animosities
will ruin Liberty, Equality and Brotherhood, all three : they check
the spirit of Patriotism; throw stumbling-blocks in its way; and
instead of pushing on, all shoulders at the wheel, will stand idle
there, spitefully clamouring what foul ruts there are, what rude
jolts we give !   To which the Jacobin Society answers with angry
roar;—with angry shriek, for there are Citoyennes too, thick
crowded in the galleries here.   Citoyennes who bring their seam
with them, or their knitting-needles; and shriek or knit as the
case needs; famed *Tricoteuses*, Patriot Knitters; *Mère Duchesse*, or
the like Deborah and Mother of the Faubourgs, giving the key-
note.   It is a changed Jacobin Society; and a still changing.
Where Mother Duchess now sits, authentic Duchesses have sat.
High-rouged dames went once in jewels and spangles; now, instead
of jewels, you may take the knitting-needles and leave the rouge :
the rouge will gradually give place to natural brown, clean washed
or even unwashed : and Demoiselle Théroigne herself get scandal-
ously fustigated.   Strange enough; it is the same tribune raised
in mid-air, where a high Mirabeau, a high Barnave and Aristocrat
Lameths once thundered; whom gradually your Brissots, Guadets,
Vergniauds, a hotter style of Patriots in *bonnet rouge*, did displace;

[2] See *Hist. Parl.* xvii. 401 ; Newspapers by Gorsas and others (cited *ibid.*
428).

red heat, as one may say, superseding light. And now your Brissots in turn, and Brissotins, Rolandins, Girondins, are becoming supernumerary; must desert the sittings, or be expelled: the light of the Mighty Mother is burning not red but blue!—Provincial Daughter Societies loudly disapprove these things; loudly demand the swift reinstatement of such eloquent Girondins, the swift 'erasure of Marat, *radiation de Marat.*' The Mother Society, so far as natural reason can predict, seems ruining herself. Nevertheless she has at all crises seemed so; she has a *preter*natural life in her, and will not ruin.

But, in a fortnight more, this great Question of the Trial, while the fit Committee is assiduously but silently working on it, receives an unexpected stimulus. Our readers remember poor Louis's turn for smith-work: how, in old happier days, a certain Sieur Gamain of Versailles was wont to come over and instruct him in lockmaking;—often scolding him, they say, for his numbness. By whom, nevertheless, the royal Apprentice had learned something of that craft. Hapless Apprentice; perfidious Master-Smith! For now, on this 20th of November 1792, dingy Smith Gamain comes over to the Paris Municipality, over to Minister Roland, with hints that he, Smith Gamain, knows a thing; that, in May last, when traitorous Correspondence was so brisk, he and the royal Apprentice fabricated an 'Iron Press, *Armoire de Fer,*' cunningly inserting the same in a wall of the royal chamber in the Tuileries; invisible under the wainscot; where doubtless it still sticks! Perfidious Gamain, attended by the proper Authorities, finds the wainscot panel which none else can find; wrenches it up; discloses the Iron Press,—full of Letters and Papers! Roland clutches them out; conveys them over in towels to the fit assiduous Committee, which sits hard by. In towels, we say, and without notarial inventory; an oversight on the part of Roland.

Here, however, are Letters enough: which disclose to a demonstration the Correspondence of a traitorous self-preserving Court; and this not with Traitors only, but even with Patriots so-called! Barnave's treason, of Correspondence with the Queen, and friendly advice to her, ever since that Varennes Business, is hereby manifest: how happy that we have him, this Barnave, lying safe in the Prison of Grenoble, since September last, for he had long been suspect! Talleyrand's treason, many a man's treason if not manifest hereby, is next to it. Mirabeau's treason: wherefore his Bust in the Hall of the Convention 'is veiled with gauze,' till we ascertain. Alas, it is too ascertainable! His Bust in the Hall of the Jacobins, denounced by Robespierre from the tribune in mid-air, is not veiled, it is instantly broken to sherds; a Patriot mounting swiftly with a ladder, and shivering it down on the floor;—it and others: amid shouts.[3] Such is *their* recompense and amount of wages, at this date: on the principle of supply and demand. Smith Gamain, inadequately recompensed for the present, comes, some fifteen months after, with a humble Petition; setting forth that no sooner was that important Iron Press finished off by him, than (as he now bethinks himself) Louis gave him a large glass of wine. Which large glass of wine did produce in the stomach of Sieur Gamain the terriblest effects, evidently tending towards death, and was then brought up by an emetic; but has, notwithstanding, entirely ruined the constitution of Sieur Gamain; so that he cannot work for his family (as he now bethinks himself). The recompense of *which* is 'Pension of Twelve-hundred Francs,' and 'honourable mention.' So different is the ratio of demand and supply at different times.

Thus, amid obstructions and stimulating furtherances, has the Question of the Trial to grow; emerging and submerging; fostered by solicitous Patriotism. Of the Orations that were spoken on it, of the painfully devised Forms of Process for managing it, the Law Arguments to prove it lawful, and all the infinite floods of Juridical and other ingenuity and oratory, be no syllable reported in this History. Lawyer ingenuity is good: but what can it profit here? If the truth must be spoken, O august Senators, the only Law in this case is: *Væ victis*, The loser pays! Seldom did Robespierre say a wiser word than the hint he gave to that effect, in his oration, That it was needless to speak of Law; that here, if never elsewhere, our Right was Might. An oration admired almost to ecstasy by the Jacobin Patriot: who shall say that Robespierre is not a thorough-going man; bold in Logic at least? To the like effect, or still more plainly, spake young Saint-Just, the black-haired, mild-toned youth. Danton is on mission, in the Netherlands, during this preliminary work. The rest, far as one reads, welter amid Law of Nations, Social Contract, Juristics, Syllogistics; to us barren as the East wind. In fact,

[3] *Journal des Débats des Jacobins* (in *Hist. Parl.* xxii. 296).

what can be more unprofitable than the sight of Seven-hundred
and Forty-nine ingenious men struggling with their whole force
and industry, for a long course of weeks, to do at bottom this:
To stretch out the old Formula and Law Phraseology, so that it
may cover the new, contradictory, entirely *un*coverable Thing?
Whereby the poor Formula does but *crack*, and one's honesty
along with it! The thing that is palpably *hot*, burning, wilt thou
prove it, by syllogism, to be a freezing-mixture? This of stretching out Formulas till they crack, is, especially in times of swift
change, one of the sorrowfulest tasks poor Humanity has.

CHAPTER VI.

AT THE BAR.

MEANWHILE, in a space of some five weeks, we have got to
another emerging of the Trial, and a more practical one than ever.

On Tuesday eleventh of December, the King's Trial has *emerged*,
very decidedly: into the streets of Paris; in the shape of that
green Carriage of Mayor Chambon, within which sits the King
himself, with attendants, on his way to the Convention Hall!
Attended, in that green carriage, by Mayors Chambon, Procureurs
Chaumette; and outside of it by Commandants Santerre, with
cannon, cavalry and double row of infantry; all Sections under
arms, strong Patrols scouring all streets; so fares he, slowly
through the dull drizzling weather: and about two o'clock we
behold him, 'in walnut-coloured greatcoat, *redingote noisette*,' descending through the Place Vendôme, towards that Salle de
Manége; to be indicted, and judicially interrogated. The mysterious Temple Circuit has given up its secret; which now, in
this walnut-coloured coat, men behold with eyes. The same
bodily Louis who was once Louis the Desired, fares there: hapless
King, he is getting now towards port; his deplorable farings and
voyagings draw to a close. What duty remains to him henceforth,
that of placidly enduring, he is fit to do.

The singular Procession fares on; in silence, says Prudhomme,
or amid growlings of the Marseillese Hymn; in silence, ushers

itself into the Hall of the Convention, Santerre holding Louis's arm with his hand. Louis looks round him, with composed air, to see what kind of Convention and Parliament it is. Much changed indeed : — since February gone two years, when our Constituent, then busy, spread fleur-de-lys velvet for us; and we came over to say a kind word here, and they all started up swearing Fidelity; and all France started up swearing, and made it a Feast of Pikes; which has ended in this! Barrère, who once 'wept' looking up from his Editor's-Desk, looks down now from his President's-Chair, with a list of Fifty-seven Questions; and says, dry-eyed : "Louis, you may sit down." Louis sits down : it is the very seat, they say, same timber and stuffing, from which he accepted the Constitution, amid dancing and illumination, autumn gone a year. So much woodwork remains identical; so much else is not identical. Louis sits and listens, with a composed look and mind.

Of the Fifty-seven Questions we shall not give so much as one. They are questions captiously embracing all the main Documents seized on the Tenth of August, or found lately in the Iron Press; embracing all the main incidents of the Revolution History; and they ask, in substance, this : Louis, who wert King, art thou not guilty to a certain extent, by act and written document, of trying to continue King? Neither in the Answers is there much notable. Mere quiet negations, for most part; an accused man standing on the simple basis of *No:* I do not recognise that document; I did not do that act; or did it according to the law that then was. Where-upon the Fifty-seven Questions, and Documents to the number of a Hundred and Sixty-two, being exhausted in this manner, Barrère finishes, after some three hours, with his : " Louis, I invite you to withdraw."

Louis withdraws, under Municipal escort, into a neighbouring Committee-room; having first, in leaving the bar, demanded to have Legal Counsel. He declines refreshment, in this Committee-room; then, seeing Chaumette busy with a small loaf which a grenadier had divided with him, says, he will take a bit of bread. It is five o'clock; and he had breakfasted but slightly, in a morning of such drumming and alarm. Chaumette breaks his half-loaf: the King eats of the crust; mounts the green Carriage, eating; asks now, What he shall do with the crumb? Chaumette's clerk takes it from him; flings it out into the street. Louis says, It is pity to fling out bread, in a time of dearth. " My grandmother," remarks Chaumette, "used to say to me, Little boy, never waste a crumb of bread; you cannot make one." "Monsieur Chaumette," answers Louis, "your grandmother seems to have been a sensible woman."[1] Poor innocent mortal; so quietly he waits the drawing of the lot;—fit to do this at least well; Passivity alone, without Activity, sufficing for it! He talks once of travelling over France by and by, to have a geographical and topographical view of it; being from of old fond of geography.—The Temple Circuit again receives him, closes on him; gazing Paris may retire to its hearths and coffee-houses, to its clubs and theatres: the damp Darkness has sunk, and with it the drumming and patrolling of this strange Day.

Louis is now separated from his Queen and Family; given up to his simple reflections and resources. Dull lie these stone walls round him; of his loved ones none with him. 'In this state of uncertainty,' providing for the worst, he writes his Will: a Paper which can still be read; full of placidity, simplicity, pious sweetness. The Convention, after debate, has granted him Legal Counsel, of his own choosing. Advocate Target feels himself 'too old,' being turned of fifty-four; and declines. He had gained great honour once, defending Rohan the Necklace-Cardinal; but will gain none here. Advocate Tronchet, some ten years older, does not decline. Nay behold, good old Malesherbes steps forward voluntarily; to the last of his fields, the good old hero! He is gray with seventy years: he says, "I was twice called to the Council of "him who was my Master, when all the world coveted that "honour; and I owe him the same service now, when it has "become one which many reckon dangerous." These two, with a younger Desèze, whom they will select for pleading, are busy over that Fifty-and-sevenfold Indictment, over the Hundred and Sixty-two Documents; Louis aiding them as he can.

A great Thing is now therefore in open progress; all men, in all lands, watching it. By what Forms and Methods shall the Convention acquit itself, in such manner that there rest not on it even the suspicion of blame? Difficult that will be! The Convention, really much at a loss, discusses and deliberates. All day from morning to night, day after day, the Tribune drones with oratory on this matter; one must stretch the old Formula to cover the new Thing. The Patriots of the Mountain, whetted ever keener, clamour for despatch above all; the only good Form will

---

[1] Prudhomme's Newspaper (in *Hist. Parl.* xxi. 314).

be a swift one. Nevertheless the Convention deliberates; the Tribune drones,—drowned indeed in tenor, and even in treble, from time to time; the whole Hall shrilling up round it into pretty frequent wrath and provocation. It has droned and shrilled well-nigh a fortnight, before we can decide, this shrillness getting ever shriller, That on Wednesday 26th of December, Louis shall appear and plead. His Advocates complain that it is fatally soon; which they well might as Advocates: but without remedy; to Patriotism it seems endlessly late.

On Wednesday therefore, at the cold dark hour of eight in the morning, all Senators are at their post. Indeed they warm the cold hour, as we find, by a violent effervescence, such as is too common now; some Louvet or Buzot attacking some Tallien, Chabot; and so the whole Mountain effervescing against the whole Gironde. Scarcely is this done, at nine, when Louis and his three Advocates, escorted by the clang of arms and Santerre's National force, enter the Hall.

Desèze unfolds his papers; honourably fulfilling his perilous office, pleads for the space of three hours. An honourable Pleading, 'composed almost overnight;' courageous yet discreet; not without ingenuity, and soft pathetic eloquence: Louis fell on his neck, when they had withdrawn, and said with tears, "*Mon pauvre Desèze!*" Louis himself, before withdrawing, had added a few words, "perhaps the last he would utter to them:" how it pained his heart, above all things, to be held guilty of that bloodshed on the Tenth of August; or of ever shedding or wishing to shed French blood. So saying, he withdrew from that Hall;—having indeed finished his work there. Many are the strange errands he has had thither; but this strange one is the last.

And now, why will the Convention loiter? Here is the Indictment and Evidence; here is the Pleading: does not the rest follow of itself? The Mountain, and Patriotism in general, clamours still louder for despatch; for Permanent-session, till the task be done. Nevertheless a doubting, apprehensive Convention decides that it will still deliberate first; that all Members, who desire it, shall have leave to speak.—To your desks, therefore, ye eloquent Members! Down with your thoughts, your echoes and hearsays of thoughts; now is the time to show oneself; France and the Universe listens! Members are not wanting: Oration, spoken Pamphlet follows spoken Pamphlet, with what eloquence it can:

President's List swells ever higher with names claiming to speak; from day to day, all days and all hours, the constant Tribune drones;—shrill Galleries supplying, very variably, the tenor and treble. It were a dull tone otherwise.

The Patriots, in Mountain and Galleries, or taking counsel nightly in Section-house, in Mother Society, amid their shrill *Tricoteuses*, have to watch lynx-eyed; to give voice when needful; occasionally very loud. Deputy Thuriot, he who was Advocate Thuriot, who was Elector Thuriot, and from the top of the Bastille saw Saint-Antoine rising like the ocean; this Thuriot can stretch a Formula as heartily as most men. Cruel Billaud is not silent, if you incite him. Nor is cruel Jean-Bon silent; a kind of Jesuit he too;—write him not, as the Dictionaries too often do, *Jambon*, which signifies mere *Ham!*

But, on the whole, let no man conceive it possible that Louis is not guilty. The only question for a reasonable man is or was: Can the Convention judge Louis? Or must it be the whole People; in Primary Assembly, and with delay? Always delay, ye Girondins, false *hommes d'état!* so bellows Patriotism, its patience almost failing.—But indeed, if we consider it, what shall these poor Girondins do? Speak their conviction that Louis is a Prisoner of War; and cannot be put to death without injustice, solecism, peril? Speak such conviction; and lose utterly your footing with the decided Patriot! Nay properly it is not even a conviction, but a conjecture and dim puzzle. How many poor Girondins are sure of but one thing: That a man and Girondin ought to *have* footing somewhere, and to stand firmly on it; keeping well with the Respectable Classes! *This* is what conviction and assurance of faith they have. They must wriggle painfully between their dilemma-horns.[2]

Nor is France idle, nor Europe. It is a Heart this Convention, as we said, which sends out influences, and receives them. A King's Execution, call it Martyrdom, call it Punishment, were an influence!—Two notable influences this Convention has already sent forth over all Nations; much to its own detriment. On the 19th of November, it emitted a Decree, and has since confirmed and unfolded the details of it, That any Nation which might see good to shake off the fetters of Despotism was thereby, so to speak, the Sister of France, and should have help and countenance. A

[2] See Extracts from their Newspapers, in *Hist. Parl.* xxi. 1-38, &c.

Decree much noised of by Diplomatists, Editors, International
Lawyers; such a Decree as no living Fetter of Despotism, nor
Person in Authority anywhere, can approve of! It was Deputy
Chambon the Girondin who propounded this Decree;—at bottom
perhaps as a flourish of rhetoric.

The second influence we speak of had a still poorer origin:
in the restless loud-rattling slightly-furnished head of one Jacob
Dupont from the Loire country. The Convention is speculating
on a plan of National Education: Deputy Dupont in his speech
says, "I am free to avow, M. le Président, that I for my part am
an Atheist," [3]—thinking the world might like to know that. The
French world received it without commentary; or with no audible
commentary, so *loud* was France otherwise. The Foreign world
received it with confutation, with horror and astonishment; [4] a
most miserable influence this! And now if to these two were
added a third influence and sent pulsing abroad over all the Earth:
that of Regicide?

Foreign Courts interfere in this Trial of Louis; Spain, England:
not to be listened to; though they come, as it were, at least Spain
comes, with the olive-branch in one hand, and the sword without
scabbard in the other. But at home too, from out of this circumambient Paris and France, what influences come thick-pulsing!
Petitions flow in; pleading for equal justice, in a reign of so-called
Equality. The living Patriot pleads;—O ye National Deputies, do
not the dead Patriots plead? The Twelve-hundred that lie in cold
obstruction, do not they plead; and petition, in Death's dumb-
show, from their narrow house there, more eloquently than speech?
Crippled Patriots hop on crutches round the Salle de Manége,
demanding justice. The Wounded of the Tenth of August, the
Widows and Orphans of the Killed petition in a body; and hop
and defile, eloquently mute, through the Hall: one wounded
Patriot, unable to hop, is borne on his bed thither, and passes
shoulder-high, in the horizontal posture.[5] The Convention Tribune,
which has paused at such sight, commences again,—droning mere
Juristic Oratory. But out of doors Paris is piping ever higher.
Bull-voiced St.-Huruge is heard; and the hysteric eloquence of
Mother Duchess; 'Varlet, Apostle of Liberty,' with pike and red
cap, flies hastily, carrying his oratorical folding-stool. Justice on

---

[3] *Moniteur*, Séance du 14 Décembre 1792.
[4] Mrs. Hannah More, *Letter to Jacob Dupont* (London, 1793); &c. &c.
[5] *Hist. Parl.* xxii. 131; Moore, &c.

the Traitor! cries all the Patriot world. Consider also this other cry, heard loud on the streets: " Give us Bread, or else kill us!" Bread and Equality; Justice on the Traitor, that we may have Bread!

The Limited or undecided Patriot is set against the Decided. Mayor Chambon heard of dreadful rioting at the *Théâtre de la Nation:* it had come to rioting, and even to fist-work, between the Decided and the Undecided, touching a new Drama called *Ami des Lois* (Friend of the Laws). One of the poorest Dramas ever written; but which had didactic applications in it; wherefore powdered wigs of Friends of Order and black hair of Jacobin heads are flying there; and Mayor Chambon hastens with Santerre, in hopes to quell it. Far from quelling it, our poor Mayor gets so ' squeezed,' says the Report, and likewise so blamed and bullied, say we,—that he, with regret, quits the brief Mayoralty altogether, ' his lungs being affected.' This miserable *Ami des Lois* is debated of in the Convention itself; so violent, mutually-enraged, are the Limited Patriots and the Unlimited.[6]

Between which two classes, are not Aristocrats enough, and Crypto-Aristocrats, busy? Spies running over from London with important Packets; spies pretending to run! One of these latter, Viard was the name of him, pretended to accuse Roland, and even the Wife of Roland: to the joy of Chabot and the Mountain. But the Wife of Roland came, being summoned, on the instant, to the Convention Hall; came, in her high clearness; and, with few clear words, dissipated this Viard into despicability and air; all Friends of Order applauding.[7] So, with Theatre-riots, and ' Bread, or else kill us;' with Rage, Hunger, preternatural Suspicion, does this wild Paris pipe. Roland grows ever more querulous, in his Messages and Letters; rising almost to the hysterical pitch. Marat, whom no power on Earth can prevent seeing into traitors and Rolands, takes to bed for three days; almost dead, the invaluable People's-Friend, with heart-break, with fever and headache: ' *O Peuple babillard, si tu savais agir,* People of Babblers, if thou ' couldst but *act!* '

To crown all, victorious Dumouriez, in these New-year's days, is arrived in Paris;—one fears for no good. He pretends to be complaining of Minister Pache, and Hassenfratz dilapidations; to be

[6] *Hist. Parl.* xxiii. 31, 48, &c.
[7] *Moniteur,* Séance du 7 Décembre 1792.

concerting measures for the spring Campaign : one finds him much
in the company of the Girondins. Plotting with them against
Jacobinism, against Equality, and the Punishment of Louis ?   We
have Letters of his to the Convention itself.   Will he act the old
Lafayette part, this new victorious General ?   Let him withdraw
again; not undenounced.[8]

And still in the Convention Tribune, it drones continually, mere
Juristic Eloquence, and Hypothesis without Action; and there are
still fifties on the President's List.   Nay these Gironde Presidents
give their own party preference : we suspect they play foul with
the List; men of the Mountain cannot be heard.   And still it
drones, all through December into January and a New year; and
there is no end!   Paris pipes round it; multitudinous; ever
higher, to the note of the whirlwind.   Paris will 'bring cannon
from Saint-Denis;' there is talk of 'shutting the Barriers,'—to
Roland's horror.

Whereupon, behold, the Convention Tribune suddenly ceases
droning : we cut short, be on the List who likes; and *make* end.
On Tuesday next, the Fifteenth of January 1793, it shall go to the
Vote, name by name; and one way or other, this great game play
itself out!

CHAPTER VII.

THE THREE VOTINGS.

Is Louis Capet guilty of conspiring against Liberty ?   Shall our
Sentence be itself final, or need ratifying by Appeal to the People ?
If guilty, what Punishment ?   This is the form agreed to, after
uproar and 'several hours of tumultuous indecision :' these are
the Three successive Questions, whereon the Convention shall
now pronounce.   Paris floods round their Hall; multitudinous,
many-sounding.   Europe and all Nations listen for their answer.
Deputy after Deputy shall answer to his name : Guilty or Not
guilty ?

As to the Guilt, there is, as above hinted, no doubt in the mind

[8] Dumouriez, *Mémoires*, iii. c. 4.

of Patriot men. Overwhelming majority pronounces Guilt; the
unanimous Convention votes for Guilt, only some feeble twenty-
eight voting not Innocence, but refusing to vote at all. Neither
does the Second Question prove doubtful, whatever the Girondins
might calculate. Would not Appeal to the People be another
name for civil war? Majority of two to one answers that there
shall be no Appeal: this also is settled. Loud Patriotism, now at
ten o'clock, may hush itself for the night; and retire to its bed
not without hope. Tuesday has gone well. On the morrow comes.
What Punishment? On the morrow is the tug of war.

Consider therefore if, on this Wednesday morning, there is an
affluence of Patriotism; if Paris stands a-tiptoe, and all Deputies
are at their post! Seven-hundred and Forty-nine honourable
Deputies; only some twenty absent on mission, Duchâtel and
some seven others absent by sickness. Meanwhile expectant
Patriotism and Paris standing a-tiptoe have need of patience. For
this Wednesday again passes in debate and effervescence; Girondins
proposing that a 'majority of three-fourths' shall be required;
Patriots fiercely resisting them. Danton, who has just got back
from mission in the Netherlands, does obtain 'order of the day' on
this Girondin proposal; nay he obtains farther that we decide *sans
désemparer*, in Permanent-session, till we have done.

And so, finally, at eight in the evening this Third stupendous
Voting, by roll-call or *appel nominal*, does begin. What Punish-
ment? Girondins undecided, Patriots decided, men afraid of
Royalty, men afraid of Anarchy, must answer here and now.
Infinite Patriotism, dusky in the lamp-light, floods all corridors,
crowds all galleries; sternly waiting to hear. Shrill-sounding
Ushers summon you by Name and Department; you must rise to
the Tribune, and say.

Eye-witnesses have represented this scene of the Third Voting,
and of the votings that grew out of it,—a scene protracted, like to
be endless, lasting, with few brief intervals, from Wednesday till
Sunday morning,—as one of the strangest seen in the Revolution.
Long night wears itself into day, morning's paleness is spread over
all faces; and again the wintry shadows sink, and the dim lamps
are lit: but through day and night and the vicissitudes of hours,
Member after Member is mounting continually those Tribune-
steps; pausing aloft there, in the clearer upper light, to speak his
Fate-word; then diving down into the dusk and throng again.

Like Phantoms in the hour of midnight; most spectral, pandemonial! Never did President Vergniaud, or any terrestrial
President, superintend the like. A King's Life, and so much else
that depends thereon, hangs trembling in the balance. Man after
man mounts; the buzz hushes itself till he have spoken: Death;
Banishment; Imprisonment till the Peace. Many say, Death;
with what cautious well-studied phrases and paragraphs they could
devise, of explanation, of enforcement, of faint recommendation to
mercy. Many too say, Banishment; something short of Death.
The balance trembles, none can yet guess whitherward. Whereat
anxious Patriotism bellows; irrepressible by Ushers.

The poor Girondins, many of them, under such fierce bellowing
of Patriotism, say Death; justifying, *motivant*, that most miserable
word of theirs by some brief casuistry and jesuitry. Vergniaud
himself says, Death; justifying by jesuitry. Rich Lepelletier
Saint-Fargeau had been of the Noblesse, and then of the Patriot
Left Side, in the Constituent; and had argued and reported, there
and elsewhere, not a little, *against* Capital Punishment: nevertheless he now says, Death; a word which may cost him dear. Manuel
did surely rank with the Decided in August last; but he has been
sinking and backsliding ever since September and the scenes of
September. In this Convention, above all, no word he could speak
would find favour; he says now, Banishment; and in mute wrath
quits the place forever,—much hustled in the corridors. Philippe
Egalité votes, in his soul and conscience, Death: at the sound of
which and of whom, even Patriotism shakes its head; and there
runs a groan and shudder through this Hall of Doom. Robespierre's
vote cannot be doubtful; his speech is long. Men see the figure
of shrill Sieyes ascend; hardly pausing, passing merely, this figure
says, "*La Mort sans phrase,* Death without phrases;" and fares
onward and downward. Most spectral, pandemonial!

And yet if the Reader fancy it of a funereal, sorrowful or even
grave character, he is far mistaken: 'the Ushers in the Mountain
'quarter,' says Mercier, 'had become as Box-keepers at the Opera;'
opening and shutting of Galleries for privileged persons, for
'D'Orléans Egalité's mistresses,' or other high-dizened women of
condition, rustling with laces and tricolor. Gallant Deputies pass
and repass thitherward, treating them with ices, refreshments and
small-talk; the high-dizened heads beck responsive; some have
their card and pin, pricking down the Ayes and Noes, as at a game
of *Rouge-et-Noir.* Farther aloft reigns Mère Duchesse with her

unrouged Amazons; she cannot be prevented making long *Hahas*,
when the vote is not *La Mort*. In these Galleries there is refection,
drinking of wine and brandy 'as in open tavern, *en pleine tabagie.*'
Betting goes on in all coffeehouses of the neighbourhood. But
within doors, fatigue, impatience, uttermost weariness sits now on
all visages; lighted up only from time to time by turns of the
game. Members have fallen asleep; Ushers come and awaken
them to vote: other Members calculate whether they shall not
have time to run and dine. Figures rise, like phantoms, pale in
the dusky lamp-light; utter from this Tribune, only one word:
Death. '*Tout est optique,*' says Mercier, 'The world is all an
optical shadow.'[1] Deep in the Thursday night, when the Voting
is done, and Secretaries are summing it up, sick Duchâtel, more
spectral than another, comes borne on a chair, wrapped in blankets,
in 'nightgown and nightcap,' to vote for Mercy: one vote it is
thought may turn the scale.

Ah no! In profoundest silence, President Vergniaud, with a
voice full of sorrow, has to say: "I declare, in the name of the
Convention, that the punishment it pronounces on Louis Capet
is that of Death." Death by a small majority of Fifty-three.
Nay, if we deduct from the one side, and add to the other, a
certain Twenty-six, who said Death but coupled some faintest
ineffectual surmise of mercy with it, the majority will be but *One*.

Death is the sentence: but its execution? It is not executed
yet! Scarcely is the vote declared when Louis's Three Advocates
enter: with Protest in his name, with demand for Delay, for
Appeal to the People. For this do Desèze and Tronchet plead,
with brief eloquence: brave old Malesherbes pleads for it with
eloquent want of eloquence, in broken sentences, in embarrassment
and sobs; that brave time-honoured face, with its gray strength,
its broad sagacity and honesty, is mastered with emotion, melts
into dumb tears.[2]—They reject the Appeal to the People; that
having been already settled. But as to the Delay, what they
call *Sursis*, it *shall* be considered; shall be voted for tomorrow:
at present we adjourn. Whereupon Patriotism 'hisses' from
the Mountain: but a 'tyrannical majority' has so decided, and
adjourns.

[1] Mercier, *Nouveau Paris*, vi. 156-59; Montgaillard, iii. 348-87; Moore, &c.
[2] *Moniteur* (in *Hist. Parl.* xxiii. 210). See Boissy d'Anglas, *Vie de
Malesherbes*, ii. 139.

There is still this *fourth* Vote, then, growls indignant Patriotism : —this vote, and who knows what other votes, and adjournments of voting; and the whole matter still hovering hypothetical! And at every new vote those Jesuit Girondins, even they who voted for Death, would so fain find a loophole! Patriotism must watch and rage. Tyrannical adjournments there have been; one, and now another at midnight on plea of fatigue,—all Friday wasted in hesitation and higgling; in *re*-counting of the votes, which are found correct as they stood! Patriotism bays fiercer than ever; Patriotism, by long watching, has become red-eyed, almost rabid.

"Delay: yes or no?" men do vote it finally, all Saturday, all day and night. Men's nerves are worn out, men's hearts are desperate; now it shall end. Vergniaud, spite of the baying, ventures to say Yes, Delay; though he had voted Death. Philippe Egalité says, in his soul and conscience, No. The next Member mounting: "Since Philippe says No, I for my part say Yes, *moi je dis Oui.*" The balance still trembles. Till finally, at three o'clock on Sunday morning, we have: *No Delay*, by a majority of Seventy; *Death within four-and-twenty hours!*

Garat, Minister of Justice, has to go to the Temple with this stern message: he ejaculates repeatedly, "*Quelle commission affreuse*, What a frightful function!"[3] Louis begs for a Confessor; for yet three days of life, to prepare himself to die. The Confessor is granted; the three days and all respite are refused.

There is no deliverance, then? Thick stone walls answer, None. Has King Louis no friends? Men of action, of courage grown desperate, in this his extreme need? King Louis's friends are feeble and far. Not even a voice in the coffeehouses rises for him. At Méot the Restaurateur's no Captain Dampmartin now dines; or sees death-doing whiskerandoes on furlough exhibit daggers of improved structure. Méot's gallant Royalists on furlough are far across the marches; they are wandering distracted over the world: or their bones lie whitening Argonne Wood. Only some weak Priests 'leave Pamphlets on all the bourne-stones,' this night, calling for a rescue: calling for the pious women to rise; or are taken distributing Pamphlets, and sent to prison.[4]

Nay there is one death-doer, of the ancient Méot sort, who, with

[3] *Biographie des Ministres*, p. 157.

[4] See Prudhomme's Newspaper; *Révolutions de Paris* (in *Hist. Parl.* xxiii. 318).

effort, has done even less and worse: slain a Deputy, and set all the Patriotism of Paris on edge! It was five on Saturday evening when Lepelletier Saint-Fargeau, having given his vote, *No Delay*, ran over to Février's in the Palais Royal to snatch a morsel of dinner. He had dined, and was paying. A thickset man 'with black hair and blue beard,' in a loose kind of frock, stept up to him; it was, as Février and the bystanders bethought them, one Pâris of the old King's-Guard. "Are you Lepelletier?" asks he. —"Yes."—"You voted in the King's Business--?"—"I voted Death."—" *Scélérat*, take that!" cries Pâris, flashing out a sabre from under his frock, and plunging it deep in Lepelletier's side. Février clutches him: but he breaks off; is gone.

The voter Lepelletier lies dead; he has expired in great pain, at one in the morning;—two hours before that Vote of *No Delay* was fully summed up. Guardsman Pâris is flying over France; cannot be taken; will be found some months after, self-shot in a remote inn.[5]—Robespierre sees reason to think that Prince d'Artois himself is privately in Town; that the Convention will be butchered in the lump. Patriotism sounds mere wail and vengeance: Santerre doubles and trebles all his patrols. Pity is lost in rage and fear; the Convention has refused the three days of life and all respite.

[5] *Hist. Parl.* xxiii. 275, 318 ; Félix Lepelletier, *Vie de Michel Lepelletier son Frère*, p. 61, &c. Félix, with due love of the miraculous, will have it that the Suicide in the inn was not Pâris, but some *double-ganger* of his.

CHAPTER VIII.

PLACE DE LA RÉVOLUTION.

To this conclusion, then, hast thou come, O hapless Louis! The Son of Sixty Kings is to die on the Scaffold by form of Law. Under Sixty Kings this same form of Law, form of Society, has been fashioning itself together these thousand years; and has become, one way and another, a most strange Machine. Surely, if needful, it is also frightful, this Machine; dead, blind; not what it should be; which, with swift stroke, or by cold slow torture, has wasted the lives and souls of innumerable men. And behold now a King himself, or say rather Kinghood in his person, is to expire here in cruel tortures;—like a Phalaris shut in the belly of his own red-heated Brazen Bull! It is ever so; and thou shouldst know it, O haughty tyrannous man: injustice breeds injustice; curses and falsehoods do verily return 'always *home*,' wide as they may wander. Innocent Louis bears the sins of many generations: he too experiences that man's tribunal is not in this Earth; that if he had no Higher one, it were not well with him.

A King dying by such violence appeals impressively to the imagination; as the like must do, and ought to do. And yet at bottom it is not the King dying, but the man! Kingship is a coat: the grand loss is of the skin. The man from whom you take his Life, to him can the whole combined world do *more?* Lally went on his hurdle; his mouth filled with a gag. Miserablest mortals, doomed for picking pockets, have a whole five-act Tragedy in them, in that dumb pain, as they go to the gallows, unregarded; they consume the cup of trembling down to the lees. For Kings and for Beggars, for the justly doomed and the unjustly, it is a hard thing to die. Pity them all: thy utmost pity, with all aids and appliances and throne-and-scaffold contrasts, how far short is it of the thing pitied!

A Confessor has come; Abbé Edgeworth, of Irish extraction, whom the King knew by good report, has come promptly on this

solemn mission. Leave the Earth alone, then, thou hapless King;
it with its malice will go its way, thou also canst go thine. A hard
scene yet remains: the parting with our loved ones. Kind hearts,
environed in the same grim peril with us; to be left *here!* Let the
Reader look with the eyes of Valet Cléry through these glass-doors,
where also the Municipality watches; and see the cruelest of scenes:

'At half-past eight, the door of the ante-room opened: the
'Queen appeared first, leading her Son by the hand; then Madame
'Royale and Madame Elizabeth: they all flung themselves into
'the arms of the King. Silence reigned for some minutes; inter-
'rupted only by sobs. The Queen made a movement to lead his
'Majesty towards the inner room, where M. Edgeworth was waiting
'unknown to them: "No," said the King, "let us go into the
'dining-room; it is there only that I can see you." They entered
'there; I shut the door of it, which was of glass. The King sat
'down, the Queen on his left hand, Madame Elizabeth on his
'right, Madame Royale almost in front; the young Prince re-
'mained standing between his father's legs. They all leaned
'towards him, and often held him embraced. This scene of wo
'lasted an hour and three quarters; during which we could hear
'nothing; we could see only that always when the King spoke,
'the sobbings of the Princesses redoubled, continued for some
'minutes; and that then the King began again to speak.'[1]—And
so our meetings and our partings do now end! The sorrows we
gave each other; the poor joys we faithfully shared, and all our
lovings and our sufferings, and confused toilings under the earthly
Sun, are over. Thou good soul, I shall never, never through all
ages of Time, see thee any more!—NEVER! O Reader, knowest
thou that hard word?

For nearly two hours this agony lasts; then they tear themselves
asunder. "Promise that you will see us on the morrow." He
promises:—Ah yes, yes; yet once; and go now, ye loved ones;
cry to God for yourselves and me!—It was a hard scene, but it is
over. He will not see them on the morrow. The Queen, in passing
through the ante-room, glanced at the Cerberus Municipals; and,
with woman's vehemence, said through her tears, "*Vous êtes tous
des scélérats.*"

King Louis slept sound, till five in the morning, when Cléry, as
he had been ordered, awoke him. Cléry dressed his hair: while
this went forward, Louis took a ring from his watch, and kept

[1] Cléry's *Narrative* (London, 1798), cited in Weber, iii. 312.

trying it on his finger; it was his wedding-ring, which he is now
to return to the Queen as a mute farewell. At half-past six, he
took the Sacrament; and continued in devotion, and conference
with Abbé Edgeworth. He will not see his Family: it were too
hard to bear.

At eight, the Municipals enter: the King gives them his Will,
and messages and effects; which they, at first, brutally refuse to
take charge of: he gives them a roll of gold pieces, a hundred and
twenty-five louis; these are to be returned to Malesherbes, who
had lent them. At nine, Santerre says the hour is come. The
King begs yet to retire for three minutes. At the end of three
minutes, Santerre again says the hour is come. 'Stamping on the
ground with his right-foot, Louis answers: "*Partons*, Let us go."'
—How the rolling of those drums comes in, through the Temple
bastions and bulwarks, on the heart of a queenly wife; soon to be
a widow! He is gone, then, and has not seen us? A Queen
weeps bitterly; a King's Sister and Children. Over all these
Four does Death also hover: all shall perish miserably save one;
she, as Duchesse d'Angoulême, will live,—not happily.

At the Temple Gate were some faint cries, perhaps from voices
of pitiful women: "*Grâce! Grâce!*" Through the rest of the
streets there is silence as of the grave. No man not armed
is allowed to be there: the armed, did any even pity, dare not
express it, each man overawed by all his neighbours. All windows
are down, none seen looking through them. All shops are shut.
No wheel-carriage rolls, this morning, in these streets but one
only. Eighty-thousand armed men stand ranked, like armed
statues of men; cannons bristle, cannoneers with match burning,
but no word or movement: it is as a city enchanted into silence
and stone: one carriage with its escort, slowly rumbling, is the
only sound. Louis reads, in his Book of Devotion, the Prayers of
the Dying: clatter of this death-march falls sharp on the ear, in
the great silence; but the thought would fain struggle heavenward,
and forget the Earth.

As the clocks strike ten, behold the Place de la Révolution,
once Place de Louis Quinze: the Guillotine, mounted near the old
Pedestal where once stood the Statue of that Louis! Far round,
all bristles with cannons and armed men: spectators crowding in
the rear; D'Orléans Egalité there in cabriolet. Swift messengers,
hoquetons, speed to the Townhall, every three minutes: near by is
the Convention sitting,—vengeful for Lepelletier. Heedless of all,

Louis reads his Prayers of the Dying; not till five minutes yet has he finished; then the Carriage opens. What temper he is in? Ten different witnesses will give ten different accounts of it. He is in the collision of all tempers; arrived now at the black Mahlstrom and descent of Death: in sorrow, in indignation, in resignation struggling to be resigned. "Take care of M. Edgeworth," he straitly charges the Lieutenant who is sitting with them: then they two descend.

The drums are beating: "*Taisez-vous*, Silence!" he cries 'in a terrible voice, *d'une voix terrible.*' He mounts the scaffold, not without delay; he is in puce coat, breeches of gray, white stockings. He strips off the coat; stands disclosed in a sleeve-waistcoat of white flannel. The Executioners approach to bind him: he spurns, resists; Abbé Edgeworth has to remind him how the Saviour, in whom men trust, submitted to be bound. His hands are tied, his head bare; the fatal moment is come. He advances to the edge of the Scaffold, 'his face very red,' and says: "Frenchmen, I die innocent: it is from the Scaffold and near appearing before God that I tell you so. I pardon my enemies; I desire that France——" A General on horseback, Santerre or another, prances out, with uplifted hand: "*Tambours!*" The drums drown the voice. "Executioners, do your duty!" The Executioners, desperate lest themselves be murdered (for Santerre and his Armed Ranks will strike, if they do not), seize the hapless Louis: six of them desperate, him singly desperate, struggling there; and bind him to their plank. Abbé Edgeworth, stooping, bespeaks him: "Son of Saint Louis, ascend to Heaven." The Axe clanks down; a King's Life is shorn away. It is Monday the 21st of January 1793. He was aged Thirty-eight years four months and twenty-eight days.[2]

Executioner Samson shows the Head: fierce shout of *Vive la République* rises, and swells; caps raised on bayonets, hats waving: students of the College of Four Nations take it up, on the far Quais; fling it over Paris. D'Orléans drives off in his cabriolet: the Townhall Councillors rub their hands, saying, "It is done, It is done." There is dipping of handkerchiefs, of pike-points in the blood. Headsman Samson, though he afterwards denied it,[3] sells locks of the hair: fractions of the puce coat are long after worn

[2] Newspapers, Municipal Records, &c. &c. (in *Hist. Parl.* xxiii. 298-349); *Deux Amis*, ix. 369-373; Mercier, *Nouveau Paris*, iii. 3-8.

[3] His Letter in the Newspapers (*Hist. Parl.* ubi suprà).

in rings.[4]—And so, in some half-hour it is done; and the multitude has all departed. Pastry-cooks, coffee-sellers, milkmen sing out their trivial quotidian cries: the world wags on, as if this were a common day. In the coffeehouses that evening, says Prudhomme, Patriot shook hands with Patriot in a more cordial manner than usual. Not till some days after, according to Mercier, did public men see what a grave thing it was.

A grave thing it indisputably is; and will have consequences. On the morrow morning, Roland, so long steeped to the lips in disgust and chagrin, sends in his demission. His accounts lie all ready, correct in black-on-white to the uttermost farthing: these he wants but to have audited, that he might retire to remote obscurity, to the country and his books. They will never be audited, those accounts; he will never get retired thither.

It was on Tuesday that Roland demitted. On Thursday comes Lepelletier St.-Fargeau's Funeral, and passage to the Pantheon of Great Men. Notable as the wild pageant of a winter day. The Body is borne aloft, half-bare; the winding-sheet disclosing the death-wound: sabre and bloody clothes parade themselves; a 'lugubrious music' wailing harsh *nœniæ*. Oak-crowns shower down from windows; President Vergniaud walks there, with Convention, with Jacobin Society, and all Patriots of every colour, all mourning brotherlike.

Notable also for another thing this Burial of Lepelletier: it was the last act these men ever did with concert! All Parties and figures of Opinion, that agitate this distracted France and its Convention, now stand, as it were, face to face, and dagger to dagger; the King's Life, round which they all struck and battled, being hurled down. Dumouriez, conquering Holland, growls ominous discontent, at the head of Armies. Men say Dumouriez will have a King; that young D'Orléans Egalité shall be his King. Deputy Fauchet, in the *Journal des Amis*, curses his day, more bitterly than Job did; invokes the poniards of Regicides, of 'Arras Vipers' or Robespierres, of Pluto Dantons, of horrid Butchers Legendre and Simulacra d'Herbois, to send him swiftly to another world than *theirs*.[5] This is *Te-Deum* Fauchet, of the Bastille Victory, of the *Cercle Social*. Sharp was the death-hail rattling round one's Flag-of-truce, on that Bastille day: but it was soft to such wreckage of

---

[4] Forster's *Briefwechsel*, i. 473.   [5] *Hist. Parl.* ubi suprà.

high Hope as this; one's New Golden Era going down in leaden
dross, and sulphurous black of the Everlasting Darkness!

At home this Killing of a King has divided all friends; and
abroad it has united all enemies. Fraternity of Peoples, Revolutionary Propagandism; Atheism, Regicide; total destruction of
social order in this world! All Kings, and lovers of Kings, and
haters of Anarchy, rank in coalition; as in a war for life. England
signifies to Citizen Chauvelin, the Ambassador or rather Ambassador's-Cloak, that he must quit the country in eight days. Ambassador's-Cloak and Ambassador, Chauvelin and Talleyrand, depart
accordingly.[6] Talleyrand, implicated in that Iron Press of the
Tuileries, thinks it safest to make for America.

England has cast out the Embassy: England declares war,—
being shocked principally, it would seem, at the condition of the
River Scheldt. Spain declares war; being shocked principally at
some other thing; which doubtless the Manifesto indicates.[7] Nay
we find it was not England that declared war first, or Spain first;
but that France herself declared war first on both of them;[8]—
a point of immense Parliamentary and Journalistic interest in
those days, but which has become of no interest whatever in these.
They all declare war. The sword is drawn, the scabbard thrown
away. It is even as Danton said, in one of his all-too gigantic
figures: "The coalised Kings threaten us; we hurl at their feet,
as gage of battle, the Head of a King."

[6] *Annual Register* of 1793, pp. 114-28.
[7] 23d March (*Annual Register*, p. 161).
[8] 1st February; 7th March (*Moniteur* of these dates).

BOOK THIRD.

THE GIRONDINS.

CHAPTER I.

CAUSE AND EFFECT.

THIS huge Insurrectionary Movement, which we liken to a breaking-out of Tophet and the Abyss, has swept away Royalty, Aristocracy, and a King's life. The question is, What will it next do; how will it henceforth shape itself? Settle down into a reign of Law and Liberty; according as the habits, persuasions and endeavours of the educated, moneyed, respectable class prescribe? That is to say: the volcanic lava-flood, bursting up in the manner described, will explode and flow according to Girondin Formula and preëstablished rule of Philosophy? If so, for our Girondin friends it will be well.

Meanwhile were not the prophecy rather, that as no external force, Royal or other, now remains which could control this Movement, the Movement will follow a course of its own; probably a very original one? Farther, that whatsoever man or men can best interpret the inward tendencies it has, and give them voice and activity, will obtain the lead of it? For the rest, that as a thing *without* order, a thing proceeding from beyond and beneath the region of order, it must work and welter, not as a Regularity but as a Chaos; destructive and self-destructive; always till something that *has* order arise, strong enough to bind it into subjection again? Which something, we may farther conjecture, will not be a Formula, with philosophical propositions and forensic eloquence; but a Reality, probably with a sword in its hand!

As for the Girondin Formula, of a respectable Republic for the

Middle Classes, all manner of Aristocracies being now sufficiently demolished, there seems little reason to expect that the business will stop there. *Liberty, Equality, Fraternity,* these are the words; enunciative and prophetic. Republic for the respectable washed Middle Classes, how can that be the fulfilment thereof? Hunger and nakedness, and nightmare oppression lying heavy on Twenty-five million hearts; this, not the wounded vanities or contradicted philosophies of philosophical Advocates, rich Shopkeepers, rural Noblesse, was the prime mover in the French Revolution; as the like will be in all such Revolutions, in all countries. Feudal Fleur-de-lys had become an insupportably bad marching-banner, and needed to be torn and trampled: but Moneybag of Mammon (for that, in these times, is what the respectable Republic for the Middle Classes will signify) is a still worse, while it lasts. Properly, indeed, it is the worst and basest of all banners and symbols of dominion among men; and indeed is possible only in a time of general Atheism, and Unbelief in anything save in brute Force and Sensualism; pride of birth, pride of office, any known kind of pride being a degree better than purse-pride. Freedom, Equality, Brotherhood: not in the Moneybag, but far elsewhere, will Sansculottism seek these things.

We say therefore that an Insurrectionary France, loose of control from without, destitute of supreme order from within, will form one of the most tumultuous Activities ever seen on this Earth; such as no Girondin Formula can regulate. An immeasurable force, made up of forces manifold, heterogeneous, compatible and incompatible. In plainer words, this France must needs split into Parties; each of which seeking to make itself good, contradiction, exasperation will arise; and Parties on Parties find that they cannot work together, cannot exist together.

As for the number of Parties, there will, strictly counting, be as many Parties as there are opinions. According to which rule, in this National Convention itself, to say nothing of France generally, the number of Parties ought to be Seven-hundred and Forty-nine; for every unit entertains his opinion. But now, as every unit has at once an individual nature or necessity to follow his own road, and a gregarious nature or necessity to see himself travelling by the side of others,—what can there be but dissolutions, precipitations, endless turbulence of attracting and repelling; till once the master-element get evolved, and this wild alchemy arrange itself again?

To the length of Seven-hundred and Forty-nine Parties, however, no Nation was ever yet seen to go. Nor indeed much beyond the length of Two Parties; two at a time;—so invincible is man's tendency to unite, with all the invincible divisiveness he has! Two Parties, we say, are the usual number at one time : let these two fight it out, all minor shades of party rallying under the shade likest them; when the one has fought down the other, then it, in its turn, may divide, self-destructive; and so the process continue, as far as needful. This is the way of Revolutions, which spring up as the French one has done; when the so-called Bonds of Society snap asunder; and all Laws that are not Laws of Nature become naught and Formulas merely.

But, quitting these somewhat abstract considerations, let History note this concrete reality which the streets of Paris exhibit, on Monday the 25th of February 1793. Long before daylight that morning, these streets are noisy and angry. Petitioning enough there has been; a Convention often solicited. It was but yesterday there came a Deputation of Washerwomen with Petition; complaining that not so much as soap could be had; to say nothing of bread, and condiments of bread. The cry of women, round the Salle de Manége, was heard plaintive: "*Du pain et du savon,* Bread and soap." [1]

And now from six o'clock, this Monday morning, one perceives the Bakers' Queues unusually expanded, angrily agitating themselves. Not the Baker alone, but two Section Commissioners to help him, manage with difficulty the daily distribution of loaves. Soft-spoken assiduous, in the early candle-light, are Baker and Commissioners: and yet the pale chill February sunrise discloses an unpromising scene. Indignant Female Patriots, partly supplied with bread, rush now to the shops, declaring that they will have groceries. Groceries enough : sugar-barrels rolled forth into the street, Patriot Citoyennes weighing it out at a just rate of elevenpence a pound; likewise coffee-chests, soap-chests, nay cinnamon and cloves-chests, with *aquavitæ* and other forms of alcohol,—at a just rate, which some do not pay; the pale-faced Grocer silently wringing his hands! What help? The distributive Citoyennes are of violent speech and gesture, their long Eumenides-hair hanging out of curl; nay in their girdles pistols are seen sticking : some, it is even said, have *beards,*—male Patriots in petticoats and

---

[1] *Moniteur,* &c. (*Hist. Parl.* xxiv. 332-348).

mob-cap. Thus, in the street of Lombards, in the street of Five-Diamonds, street of Pulleys, in most streets of Paris does it effervesce, the livelong day; no Municipality, no Mayor Pache, though he was War-Minister lately, sends military against it, or aught against it but persuasive-eloquence, till seven at night, or later.

On Monday gone five weeks, which was the twenty-first of January, we saw Paris, beheading its King, stand silent, like a petrified City of Enchantment: and now on this Monday it is so noisy, selling sugar! Cities, especially Cities in Revolution, are subject to these alternations; the secret courses of civic business and existence effervescing and efflorescing, in this manner, as a concrete Phenomenon to the eye. Of which Phenomenon, when secret existence becoming public effloresces on the street, the philosophical cause and effect is not so easy to find. What, for example, may be the accurate philosophical meaning, and meanings, of this sale of sugar? These things that have become visible in the street of Pulleys and over Paris, whence are they, we say; and whither?—

That Pitt has a hand in it, the gold of Pitt: so much, to all reasonable Patriot men, may seem clear. But then, through what agents of Pitt? Varlet, Apostle of Liberty, was discerned again of late with his pike and red nightcap. Deputy Marat published in his Journal, this very day, complaining of the bitter scarcity, and sufferings of the people, till he seemed to get wroth: 'If your Rights of Man were anything but a piece of written 'paper, the plunder of a few shops, and a forestaller or two hung 'up at the door-lintels, would put an end to such things.' [2] Are not these, say the Girondins, pregnant indications? Pitt has bribed the Anarchists; Marat is the agent of Pitt: hence this sale of sugar. To the Mother Society, again, it is clear that the scarcity is factitious; is the work of Girondins, and suchlike; a set of men sold partly to Pitt; sold wholly to their own ambitions and hard-hearted pedantries; who will not fix the grain-prices, but prate pedantically of free-trade; wishing to starve Paris into violence, and embroil it with the Departments: *hence* this sale of sugar.

And, alas, if to these two notabilities, of a Phenomenon and such Theories of a Phenomenon, we add this third notability,

[2] *Hist. Parl.* xxiv. 353-356.

That the French Nation has believed, for several years now, in the possibility, nay certainty and near advent, of a universal Millennium, or reign of Freedom, Equality, Fraternity, wherein man should be the brother of man, and sorrow and sin flee away? Not bread to eat, nor soap to wash with; and the reign of Perfect Felicity ready to arrive, due always since the Bastille fell! How did our hearts burn within us, at that Feast of Pikes, when brother flung himself on brother's bosom; and in sunny jubilee, Twenty-five millions burst forth into sound and cannon-smoke! Bright was our Hope then, as sunlight; red-angry is our Hope grown now, as consuming fire. But, O Heavens, what enchantment is it, or devilish legerdemain, of such effect, that Perfect Felicity, always within arm's length, could never be laid hold of, but only in her stead Controversy and Scarcity? This set of traitors after that set! Tremble, ye traitors; dread a People which calls itself patient, long-suffering; but which cannot always submit to have its pocket picked, in this way,—of a Millennium!

Yes, Reader, here is the miracle. Out of that putrescent rubbish of Scepticism, Sensualism, Sentimentalism, hollow Macchiavelism, such a Faith has verily risen; flaming in the heart of a People. A whole People, awakening as it were to consciousness in deep misery, believes that it is within reach of a Fraternal Heaven-on-Earth. With longing arms, it struggles to embrace the Unspeakable; cannot embrace it, owing to certain causes.—Seldom do we find that a whole People can be said to have any Faith at all; except in things which it can eat and handle. Whensoever it gets any Faith, its history becomes spirit-stirring, noteworthy. But since the time when steel Europe shook itself simultaneously at the word of Hermit Peter, and rushed towards the Sepulchre where God had lain, there was no universal impulse of Faith that one could note. Since Protestantism went silent, no Luther's voice, no Zisca's drum any longer proclaiming that God's Truth was *not* the Devil's Lie; and the Last of the Cameronians (Renwick was the name of him; honour to the name of the brave!) sank, shot, on the Castle-hill of Edinburgh, there was no partial impulse of Faith among Nations. Till now, behold, once more, this French Nation believes! Herein, we say, in that astonishing Faith of theirs, lies the miracle. It is a Faith undoubtedly of the more prodigious sort, even among Faiths; and will embody itself in prodigies. It is the soul of that world-prodigy named French Revolution; whereat the world still gazes and shudders.

But, for the rest, let no man ask History to explain by cause and effect how the business proceeded henceforth. This battle of Mountain and Gironde, and what follows, is the battle of Fanaticisms and Miracles; unsuitable for cause and effect. The sound of it, to the mind, is as a hubbub of voices in distraction; little of articulate is to be gathered by long listening and studying; only battle-tumult, shouts of triumph, shrieks of despair. The Mountain has left no Memoirs; the Girondins have left Memoirs, which are too often little other than long-drawn Interjections, of *Woe is me*, and *Cursed be ye*. So soon as History can philosophically delineate the conflagration of a kindled Fireship, she may try this other task. Here lay the bitumen-stratum, there the brimstone one; so ran the vein of gunpowder, of nitre, terebinth and foul grease: this, were she inquisitive enough, History might partly know. But how they acted and reacted below decks, one firestratum playing into the other, by its nature and the art of man, now when all hands ran raging, and the flames lashed high over shrouds and topmast: this let not History attempt.

The Fireship is old France, the old French Form of Life; her crew a Generation of men. Wild are their cries and their ragings there, like spirits tormented in that flame. But, on the whole, are they not *gone*, O Reader? Their Fireship and they, frightening the world, have sailed away; its flames and its thunders quite away, into the Deep of Time. One thing therefore History will do: pity them all; for it went hard with them all. Not even the seagreen Incorruptible but shall have some pity, some human love, though it takes an effort. And now, so much once thoroughly attained, the rest will become easier. To the eye of equal brotherly pity, innumerable perversions dissipate themselves; exaggerations and execrations fall off, of their own accord. Standing wistfully on the safe shore, we will look, and see, what is of interest to us, what is adapted to us.

CHAPTER II.

CULOTTIC AND SANSCULOTTIC.

GIRONDE and Mountain are now in full quarrel; their mutual rage, says Toulongeon, is growing a 'pale' rage. Curious, lamentable: all these men have the word Republic on their lips; in the heart of every one of them is a passionate wish for something which he calls Republic: yet see their death-quarrel! So, however, are men made. Creatures who live in confusion; who, once thrown together, can readily fall into that confusion of confusions which quarrel is, simply because their confusions differ from one another; still more because they seem to differ! Men's words are a poor exponent of their thought; nay their thought itself is a poor exponent of the inward unnamed Mystery, wherefrom both thought and action have their birth. No man can explain himself, can get himself explained; men see not one another, but distorted phantasms which they call one another; which they hate and go to battle with: for all battle is well said to be *misunderstanding*.

But indeed that similitude of the Fireship; of our poor French brethren, so fiery themselves, working also in an *element* of fire, was not insignificant. Consider it well, there is a shade of the truth in it. For a man, once committed headlong to republican or any other Transcendentalism, and fighting and fanaticising amid a Nation of his like, becomes as it were enveloped in an ambient atmosphere of Transcendentalism and Delirium: his individual self is lost in something that is not himself, but foreign though inseparable from him. Strange to think of, the man's cloak still seems to hold the same man: and yet the man is not there, his volition is not there; nor the source of what he will do and devise; instead of the man and his volition there is a piece of Fanaticism and Fatalism incarnated in the shape of him. He, the hapless incarnated Fanaticism, goes his road; no man can help him, he himself least of all. It is a wonderful, tragical predicament;—such as human language, unused to deal with these things, being contrived for the uses of common life, struggles to shadow out in figures. The ambient element of material fire is not wilder than this of Fanaticism; nor, though visible to the eye, is it more real. Volition bursts forth involuntary-voluntary; rapt along; the movement of free human minds becomes a raging tornado of fatalism, blind as the winds; and Mountain and Gironde, when they recover themselves, are alike astounded to see *where* it has flung and dropt them. To such height of miracle can men work on men; the Conscious and the Unconscious blended inscrutably in this our inscrutable Life; endless Necessity environing Freewill!

The weapons of the Girondins are Political Philosophy, Respectability and Eloquence. Eloquence, or call it rhetoric, really of a superior order; Vergniaud, for instance, turns a period as sweetly as any man of that generation. The weapons of the Mountain are those of mere Nature: Audacity and Impetuosity which may become Ferocity, as of men complete in their determination, in their conviction; nay of men, in some cases, who as Septemberers must either prevail or perish. The ground to be fought for is Popularity: farther you may either seek Popularity with the friends of Freedom and Order, or with the friends of Freedom Simple; to seek it with both has unhappily become impossible. With the former sort, and generally with the Authorities of the Departments, and such as read Parliamentary Debates, and are of Respectability, and of a peace-loving moneyed nature, the Girondins carry it. With the extreme Patriot again, with the indigent Millions, especially with the Population of Paris who do not read so much as hear and see, the Girondins altogether lose it, and the Mountain carries it.

Egoism, nor meanness of mind, is not wanting on either side. Surely not on the Girondin side; where in fact the instinct of self-preservation, too prominently unfolded by circumstances, cuts almost a sorry figure; where also a certain finesse, to the length even of shuffling and shamming, now and then shows itself. They are men skilful in Advocate-fence. They have been called the Jesuits of the Revolution;[1] but that is too hard a name. It must be owned likewise that this rude blustering Mountain has a sense in it of what the Revolution means; which these eloquent Girondins are totally void of. Was the Revolution made, and fought for, against the world, these four weary years, that a Formula might

[1] Dumouriez, *Mémoires*, iii. 314.

be substantiated; that Society might become *methodic*, demonstrable by logic; and the old Noblesse with their pretensions vanish? Or ought it not withal to bring some glimmering of light and alleviation to the Twenty-five Millions, who sat in darkness, heavy-laden, till they rose with pikes in their hands? At least and lowest, one would think, it should bring them a proportion of bread to live on? There is in the Mountain here and there; in Marat People's-friend; in the incorruptible Seagreen himself, though otherwise so lean and formulary, a heartfelt knowledge of this latter fact;—without which knowledge all other knowledge here is naught, and the choicest forensic eloquence is as sounding brass and a tinkling cymbal. Most cold, on the other hand, most patronising, unsubstantial is the tone of the Girondins towards ' our poorer brethren;'—those brethren whom one often hears of under the collective name of 'the masses,' as if they were not persons at all, but mounds of combustible explosive material, for blowing down Bastilles with! In very truth, a Revolutionist of this kind, is he not a Solecism? Disowned by Nature and Art; deserving only to be erased, and disappear! Surely, to our poorer brethren of Paris, all this Girondin patronage sounds deadening and killing: if fine-spoken and incontrovertible in logic, then all the falser, all the hatefuler in fact.

Nay doubtless, pleading for Popularity, here among our poorer brethren of Paris, the Girondin has a hard game to play. If he gain the ear of the Respectable at a distance, it is by insisting on September and suchlike; it is at the expense of this Paris where he dwells and perorates. Hard to perorate in such an auditory! Wherefore the question arises: Could not we get ourselves out of this Paris? Twice or oftener such an attempt is made. If not we ourselves, thinks Guadet, then at least our *Suppléans* might do it. For every Deputy has his *Suppléant*, or Substitute, who will take his place if need be: might not these assemble, say at Bourges, which is a quiet episcopal Town, in quiet Berri, forty good leagues off? In that case, what profit were it for the Paris Sansculottery to insult us; our *Suppléans* sitting quiet in Bourges, to whom we could run? Nay, even the Primary electoral Assemblies, thinks Guadet, might be reconvoked, and a New Convention got, with new orders from the Sovereign People; and right glad were Lyons, were Bourdeaux, Rouen, Marseilles, as yet Provincial Towns, to welcome us in their turn, and become a sort of Capital Towns; and teach these Parisians reason.

Fond schemes; which all misgo! If decreed, in heat of eloquent logic, today, they are repealed, by clamour and passionate wider considerations, on the morrow.[2] Will you, O Girondins, parcel us into separate Republics, then; like the Swiss, like your Americans; so that there be no Metropolis or indivisible French Nation any more? Your Departmental Guard seemed to point that way! Federal Republic? Federalist? Men and Knitting-women repeat *Fédéraliste*, with or without much Dictionary-meaning; but go on repeating it, as is usual in such cases, till the meaning of it becomes almost magical, fit to designate all mystery of Iniquity; and *Fédéraliste* has grown a word of Exorcism and *Apage-Satanas*. But furthermore, consider what 'poisoning of public opinion' in the Departments, by these Brissot, Gorsas, Caritat-Condorcet Newspapers! And then also what counter-poisoning, still feller in quality, by a *Père Duchesne* of Hébert, brutalest Newspaper yet published on Earth; by a *Rougiff* of Guffroy; by the 'incendiary leaves of Marat'! More than once, on complaint given and effervescence rising, it is decreed that a man cannot both be Legislator and Editor; that he shall choose between the one function and the other.[3] But this too, which indeed could help little, is revoked or eluded; remains a pious wish mainly.

Meanwhile, as the sad fruit of such strife, behold, O ye National Representatives, how, between the friends of Law and the friends of Freedom everywhere, mere heats and jealousies have arisen; fevering the whole Republic! Department, Provincial Town is set against Metropolis, Rich against Poor, Culottic against Sansculottic, man against man. From the Southern Cities come Addresses of an almost inculpatory character; for Paris has long suffered Newspaper calumny. Bourdeaux demands a reign of Law and Respectability, meaning Girondism, with emphasis. With emphasis Marseilles demands the like. Nay, from Marseilles there come *two* Addresses : one Girondin; one Jacobin Sansculottic. Hot Rebecqui, sick of this Convention-work, has given place to his Substitute, and gone home; where also, with such jarrings, there is work to be sick of.

Lyons, a place of Capitalists and Aristocrats, is in still worse state; almost in revolt. Chalier the Jacobin Town-Councillor has got, too literally, to daggers-drawn with Nièvre-Chol the *Modératin*

[2] *Moniteur*, 1793, No. 140, &c.
[3] *Hist. Parl.* xxv. 25, &c.

Mayor; one of your Moderate, perhaps Aristocrat, Royalist or Federalist Mayors ! Chalier, who pilgrimed to Paris ' to behold Marat and the Mountain,' has verily kindled himself at their sacred urn : for on the 6th of February last, History or Rumour has seen him haranguing his Lyons Jacobins in a quite transcendental manner, with a drawn dagger in his hand; recommending (they say) sheer September methods, patience being worn out; and that the Jacobin Brethren should, impromptu, work the Guillotine themselves ! One sees him still, in Engravings: mounted on a table; foot advanced, body contorted; a bald, rude, slope-browed, infuriated visage of the canine species, the eyes starting from their sockets; in his puissant right-hand the brandished dagger, or horse-pistol, as some give it; other dog-visages kindling under him :—a man not likely to end well ! However, the Guillotine was *not* got together impromptu, that day, ' on the Pont Saint-Clair,' or elsewhere; but indeed continued lying rusty in its loft :[4] Nièvre-Chol with military went about, rumbling cannon, in the most confused manner; and the ' nine-hundred prisoners' received no hurt. So distracted is Lyons grown, with its cannons rumbling. Convention Commissioners must be sent thither forthwith : if even they can appease it, and keep the Guillotine in its loft ?

Consider finally if, on all these mad jarrings of the Southern Cities, and of France generally, a traitorous Crypto-Royalist class is not looking and watching; ready to strike in, at the right season ! Neither is there bread; neither is there soap: see the Patriot women selling out sugar, at a just rate of twenty-two sous per pound ! Citizen Representatives, it were verily well that your quarrels finished, and the reign of Perfect Felicity began.

[4] *Hist. Parl.* xxiv. 385-93 ; xxvi. 229, &c.

CHAPTER III.

GROWING SHRILL.

On the whole, one cannot say that the Girondins are wanting to themselves, so far as good-will might go. They prick assiduously into the sore-places of the Mountain; from principle, and also from Jesuitism.

Besides September, of which there is now little to be made except effervescence, we discern two sore-places where the Mountain often suffers: Marat, and Orléans Egalité. Squalid Marat, for his own sake and for the Mountain's, is assaulted ever and anon; held up to France, as a squalid bloodthirsty Portent, inciting to the pillage of shops; of whom let the Mountain have the credit! The Mountain murmurs, ill at ease: this ' Maximum of Patriotism,' how shall they either own him or disown him? As for Marat personally, he, with his fixed-idea, remains invulnerable to such things; nay the People's-friend is very evidently rising in importance, as his befriended People rises. No shrieks now, when he goes to speak; occasional applauses rather, furtherance which breeds confidence. The day when the Girondins proposed to 'decree him accused' (*décréter d'accusation*, as they phrase it) for that February Paragraph, of 'hanging up a Forestaller or two at the door-lintels,' Marat proposes to have *them* 'decreed insane;' and, descending the Tribune-steps, is heard to articulate these most unsenatorial ejaculations: " *Les cochons, les imbécilles*, Pigs, idiots!" Oftentimes he croaks harsh sarcasm, having really a rough rasping tongue, and a very deep fund of contempt for fine outsides; and once or twice, he even laughs, nay 'explodes into laughter, *rit aux éclats*,' at the gentilities and superfine airs of these Girondin " men of statesmanship," with their pedantries, plausibilities, pusillanimities: " these two years," says he, " you have been whining about attacks, and plots, and danger from Paris; and you have not a scratch to show for yourselves." [1]—Danton gruffly rebukes him, from time to time: a Maximum of Patriotism whom one can neither own nor disown!

[1] *Moniteur*, Séance du 20 Mai 1793.

But the second sore-place of the Mountain is this anomalous
Monseigneur Equality Prince d'Orléans. Behold these men, says
the Gironde; with a whilom Bourbon Prince among them: they
are creatures of the D'Orléans Faction; they will have Philippe
made King; one King no sooner guillotined than another made
in his stead! Girondins have moved, Buzot moved long ago,
from principle and also from jesuitism, that the whole race of
Bourbons should be marched forth from the soil of France; this
Prince Egalité to bring up the rear. Motions which might
produce some effect on the public;—which the Mountain, ill at
ease, knows not what to do with.

And poor Orléans Egalité himself, for one begins to pity even
him, what does he do with them? The disowned of all parties,
the rejected and foolishly bedrifted hither and thither, to what
corner of Nature can he now drift with advantage? Feasible
hope remains not for him: unfeasible hope, in pallid doubtful
glimmers, there may still come, bewildering, not cheering or
illuminating,—from the Dumouriez quarter; and how if not
the time-wasted Orléans Egalité, then perhaps the young unworn
Chartres Egalité might rise to be a kind of King? Sheltered,
if shelter it be, in the clefts of the Mountain, poor Egalité will
wait: one refuge in Jacobinism, one in Dumouriez and Counter-
Revolution, are there not two chances? However, the look of
him, Dame Genlis says, is grown gloomy; sad to see. Sillery
also, the Genlis's Husband, who hovers about the Mountain,
not on it, is in a bad way. Dame Genlis is come to Raincy,
out of England and Bury St. Edmunds, in these days; being
summoned by Egalité, with her young charge, Mademoiselle
Egalité,—that so Mademoiselle might not be counted among
Emigrants and hardly dealt with. But it proves a ravelled
business: Genlis and charge find that they must retire to the
Netherlands; must wait on the Frontiers, for a week or two;
till Monseigneur, by Jacobin help, get it wound up. 'Next
'morning,' says Dame Genlis, 'Monseigneur, gloomier than ever,
'gave me his arm, to lead me to the carriage. I was greatly
'troubled; Mademoiselle burst into tears; her Father was pale
'and trembling. After I had got seated, he stood immovable
'at the carriage-door, with his eyes fixed on me; his mournful
'and painful look seemed to implore pity;—"Adieu, Madame!"
'said he. The altered sound of his voice completely over-
'came me; unable to utter a word, I held out my hand;

'he grasped it close; then turning, and advancing sharply
'towards the postillions, he gave them a sign, and we rolled
'away.'[2]

Nor are Peace-makers wanting; of whom likewise we mention
two; one fast on the crown of the Mountain, the other not yet
alighted anywhere: Danton and Barrère. Ingenious Barrère,
Old-Constituent and Editor, from the slopes of the Pyrenees, is
one of the usefulest men of this Convention, in his way. Truth
may lie on both sides, on either side, or on neither side; my
friends, ye must give and take: for the rest, success to the winning
side! This is the motto of Barrère. Ingenious, almost genial;
quick-sighted, supple, graceful; a man that will prosper. Scarcely
Belial in the assembled Pandemonium was plausibler to ear and
eye. An indispensable man: in the great *Art of Varnish* he
may be said to seek his fellow. Has there an explosion arisen,
as many do arise, a confusion, unsightliness, which no tongue
can speak of, nor eye look on; give it to Barrère; Barrère shall
be Committee-Reporter of it; you shall see it transmute itself
into a regularity, into the very beauty and improvement that
was needed. Without one such man, we say, how were this
Convention bested? Call him not, as exaggerative Mercier does,
'the greatest liar in France:' nay it may be argued there is
not truth enough in him to make a real lie of. Call him, with
Burke, Anacreon of the Guillotine, and a man serviceable to this
Convention.

The other Peace-maker whom we name is Danton. Peace,
O peace with one another! cries Danton often enough: Are we
not alone against the world; a little band of brothers? Broad
Danton is loved by all the Mountain; but they think him too
easy-tempered, deficient in suspicion: he has stood between
Dumouriez and much censure, anxious not to exasperate our
only General: in the shrill tumult Danton's strong voice reverberates, for union and pacification. Meetings there are; dinings
with the Girondins: it is so pressingly essential that there be
union. But the Girondins are haughty and respectable: this
Titan Danton is not a man of Formulas, and there rests on
him a shadow of September. "Your Girondins have no confidence in me:" this is the answer a conciliatory Meillan gets
from him; to all the arguments and pleadings this conciliatory

[2] Genlis, *Mémoires*, (London, 1825), iv. 118.

Meillan can bring, the repeated answer is, "*Ils n'ont point de confiance.*" [3]—The tumult will get ever shriller; rage is growing pale.

In fact, what a pang is it to the heart of a Girondin, this first withering probability that the despicable unphilosophic anarchic Mountain, after all, may triumph! Brutal Septemberers, a fifth-floor Tallien, 'a Robespierre without an idea in his head,' as Condorcet says, 'or a feeling in his heart:' and yet we, the flower of France, cannot stand against them; behold the sceptre departs from us; from us and goes to them! Eloquence, Philosophism, Respectability avail not: 'against Stupidity the very gods fight to no purpose,

'*Mit der Dummheit kämpfen Götter selbst vergebens!*'

Shrill are the plaints of Louvet; his thin existence all acidified into rage and preternatural insight of suspicion. Wroth is young Barbaroux; wroth and scornful. Silent, like a Queen with the aspic on her bosom, sits the wife of Roland; Roland's Accounts never yet got audited, his name become a byword. Such is the fortune of war, especially of revolution. The great gulf of Tophet and Tenth of August opened itself at the magic of your eloquent voice; and lo now, it will not close at your voice! It is a dangerous thing such magic. The Magician's Famulus got hold of the forbidden Book, and summoned a goblin: *Plait-il*, What is your will? said the goblin. The Famulus, somewhat struck, bade him fetch water: the swift goblin fetched it, pail in each hand; but lo, would not cease fetching it! Desperate, the Famulus shrieks at him, smites at him, cuts him in two; lo, *two* goblin water-carriers ply; and the house will be swum away in Deucalion Deluges.

[3] *Mémoires de Meillan, Représentant du Peuple* (Paris, 1823), p. 51.

CHAPTER IV.

FATHERLAND IN DANGER.

OR rather we will say, this Senatorial war might have lasted long; and Party tugging and throttling with Party might have suppressed and smothered one another, in the ordinary bloodless Parliamentary way; on one condition : that France had been at least able to exist, all the while. But this Sovereign People has a digestive faculty, and cannot do without bread. Also we are at war, and must have victory; at war with Europe, with Fate and Famine : and behold, in the spring of the year, all victory deserts us.

Dumouriez had his outposts stretched as far as Aix-la-Chapelle, and the beautifulest plan for pouncing on Holland, by stratagem, flat-bottomed boats and rapid intrepidity; wherein too he had prospered so far; but unhappily could prosper no farther. Aix-la-Chapelle is lost; Maestricht will not surrender to mere smoke and noise : the flat-bottomed boats have to launch themselves again, and return the way they came. Steady now, ye rapidly intrepid men; retreat with firmness, Parthian-like ! Alas, were it General Miranda's fault; were it the War-minister's fault; or were it Dumouriez's own fault and that of Fortune : enough, there is nothing for it but retreat,—well if it be not even flight; for already terror-stricken cohorts and stragglers pour off, not waiting for order; flow disastrous, as many as ten thousand of them, without halt till they see France again.[1] Nay worse : Dumouriez himself is perhaps secretly turning traitor? Very sharp is the tone in which he writes to our Committees. Commissioners and Jacobin Pillagers have done such incalculable mischief; Hassenfratz sends neither cartridges nor clothing; shoes we have, deceptively ' soled with wood and pasteboard.' Nothing in short is right. Danton and Lacroix, when it was they that were Commissioners, would needs join Belgium to France ;—of which Dumouriez might have made the prettiest little Duchy for his own secret

[1] Dumouriez, iv. 16-73.

behoof! With all these things the General is wroth; and writes to us in a sharp tone. Who knows what this hot little General is meditating? Dumouriez Duke of Belgium or Brabant; and say, Egalité the Younger King of France: there were an end for our Revolution!—Committee of Defence gazes, and shakes its head: who except Danton, defective in suspicion, could still struggle to be of hope?

And General Custine is rolling back from the Rhine Country; conquered Mentz will be reconquered, the Prussians gathering round to bombard it with shot and shell. Mentz may resist, Commissioner Merlin, the Thionviller, 'making sallies, at the head of the besieged;'—resist to the death; but not longer than that. How sad a reverse for Mentz! Brave Forster, brave Lux planted Liberty-trees, amid ça-ira-ing music, in the snow-slush of last winter, there; and made Jacobin Societies; and got the Territory incorporated with France; they came hither to Paris, as Deputies or Delegates, and have their eighteen francs a-day: but see, before once the Liberty-tree is got rightly in leaf, Mentz is changing into an explosive crater; vomiting fire, bevomited with fire!

Neither of these men shall again see Mentz; they have come hither only to die. Forster has been round the Globe; he saw Cook perish under Owyhee clubs; but like this Paris he has yet seen or suffered nothing. Poverty escorts him: from home there can nothing come, except Job's-news; the eighteen daily francs, which we here as Deputy or Delegate with difficulty 'touch,' are in paper *assignats*, and sink fast in value. Poverty, disappointment, inaction, obloquy; the brave heart slowly breaking! Such is Forster's lot. For the rest, Demoiselle Théroigne smiles on you in the Soirées; '.a beautiful brownlocked face,' of an exalted temper; and contrives to keep her carriage. Prussian Trenck, the poor subterranean Baron, jargons and jangles in an unmelodious manner. Thomas Paine's face is red-pustuled, 'but the eyes uncommonly bright.' Convention Deputies ask you to dinner: very courteous; and 'we all play at *plumpsack*.'[2] 'It is the Explosion and New-'creation of a World,' says Forster; 'and the actors in it, such small 'mean objects, buzzing round one like a handful of flies.'—

Likewise there is war with Spain. Spain will advance through the gorges of the Pyrenees; rustling with Bourbon banners, jingling with artillery and menace. And England has donned the red coat; and marches, with Royal Highness of York,—whom some once

---

[2] Forster's *Briefwechsel*, ii. 514, 460, 631.

spake of inviting to be our King. Changed that humour now: and ever more changing; till no hatefuler thing walk this Earth than a denizen of that tyrannous Island; and Pitt be declared and decreed, with effervescence, '*L'ennemi du genre humain,* The enemy of mankind;' and, very singular to say, you make order that no Soldier of Liberty give quarter to an Englishman. Which order, however, the Soldier of Liberty does but partially obey. We will take no Prisoners then, say the Soldiers of Liberty; they shall all be 'Deserters' that we take.[3] It is a frantic order; and attended with inconvenience. For surely, if you give no quarter, the plain issue is that you will get none; and so the business become as broad as it was long.—Our 'recruitment of Three-hundred Thousand men,' which was the decreed force for this year, is like to have work enough laid to its hand.

So many enemies come wending on; penetrating through throats of mountains, steering over the salt sea; towards all points of our territory; rattling chains at us. Nay, worst of all: there is an enemy within our own territory itself. In the early days of March, the Nantes Postbags do not arrive; there arrive only instead of them Conjecture, Apprehension, bodeful wind of Rumour. The bodefulest proves true. Those fanatic Peoples of La Vendée will no longer keep under: their fire of insurrection, heretofore dissipated with difficulty, blazes out anew, after the King's Death, as a wide conflagration; not riot, but civil war. Your Cathelineaus, your Stofflets, Charettes, are other men than was thought: behold how their Peasants, in mere russet and hodden, with their rude arms, rude array, with their fanatic Gaelic frenzy and wild-yelling battle-cry of *God and the King,* dash at us like a dark whirlwind; and blow the best-disciplined Nationals we can get into panic and *sauve-qui-peut!* Field after field is theirs; one sees not where it will end. Commandant Santerre may be sent there; but with non-effect; he might as well have returned and brewed beer.

It has become peremptorily necessary that a National Convention cease arguing, and begin acting. Yield one party of you to the other, and do it swiftly. No theoretic outlook is here, but the close certainty of ruin; the very day that is passing over us must be provided for.

It was Friday the Eighth of March when this Job's-post from Dumouriez, thickly preceded and escorted by so many other Job's-

---

[3] See Dampmartin, *E énemens,* ii. 213-30.

posts, reached the National Convention. Blank enough are most
faces. Little will it avail whether our Septemberers be punished
or go unpunished; if Pitt and Cobourg are coming in, with one
punishment for us all; nothing now between Paris itself and the
Tyrants but a doubtful Dumouriez, and hosts in loose-flowing loud
retreat !—Danton the Titan rises in this hour as always in the hour
of need. Great is his voice, reverberating from the domes :—
Citizen-Representatives, shall we not, in such crisis of Fate, lay
aside discords ? Reputation: O what is the reputation of this man
or of that ? *" Que mon nom soit flétri ; que la France soit libre:*
Let my name be blighted; let France be free !" It is necessary
now again that France rise, in swift vengeance, with her million
right-hands, with her heart as of one man. Instantaneous recruitment in Paris ; let every Section of Paris furnish its thousands;
every Section of France ! Ninety-six Commissioners of us, two for
each Section of the Forty-eight, they must go forthwith, and tell
Paris what the Country needs of her. Let Eighty more of us be
sent, post-haste, over France ; to spread the fire-cross, to call forth
the might of men. Let the Eighty also be on the road, before this
sitting rise. Let them go, and think what their errand is. Speedy
Camp of Fifty-thousand between Paris and the North Frontier;
for Paris will pour forth her volunteers ! Shoulder to shoulder ;
one strong universal death-defiant rising and rushing; we shall
hurl back these Sons of Night yet again ; and France, in spite of
the world, be free ! [4]—So sounds the Titan's voice : into all Section-
houses ; into all French hearts. Sections sit in Permanence, for
recruitment, enrolment, that very night. Convention Commissioners, on swift wheels, are carrying the fire-cross from Town to
Town, till all France blaze.

And so there is Flag of *Fatherland in Danger* waving from the
Townhall, Black Flag from the top of Notre-Dame Cathedral ;
there is Proclamation, hot eloquence ; Paris rushing out once again
to strike its enemies down. That, in such circumstances, Paris was
in no mild humour can be conjectured. Agitated streets ; still
more agitated round the Salle de Manége ! Feuillans-Terrace
crowds itself with angry Citizens, angrier Citizenesses ; Varlet
perambulates with portable chair : ejaculations of no measured
kind, as to perfidious fine-spoken *Hommes d'état*, friends of
Dumouriez, secret-friends of Pitt and Cobourg, burst from the
hearts and lips of men. To fight the enemy ? Yes, and even to

[4] *Moniteur* (in *Hist. Parl.* xxv. 6).

'freeze him with terror, *glacer d'effroi:*' but first to have domestic
Traitors punished! Who are they that, carping and quarrelling,
in their jesuitic most *moderate* way, seek to shackle the Patriotic
movement? That divide France against Paris, and poison public
opinion in the Departments? That when we ask for bread, and a
Maximum fixed-price, treat us with lectures on Free-trade in
grains? Can the human stomach satisfy itself with lectures on
Free-trade; and are we to fight the Austrians in a moderate
manner, or in an immoderate? This Convention must be *purged.*

"Set up a swift Tribunal for Traitors, a Maximum for Grains:"
thus speak with energy the Patriot Volunteers, as they defile
through the Convention Hall, just on the wing to the Frontiers;—
perorating in that heroical Cambyses' vein of theirs: beshouted by
the Galleries and Mountain; bemurmured by the Right-side and
Plain. Nor are prodigies wanting: lo, while a Captain of the
Section Poissonnière perorates with vehemence about Dumouriez,
Maximum and Crypto-Royalist Traitors, and his troop beat chorus
with him, waving their Banner overhead, the eye of a Deputy
discerns, in this same Banner, that the *cravates* or streamers of it
have Royal fleurs-de-lys! The Section-Captain shrieks; his troop
shriek, horror-struck, and 'trample the Banner under foot:'
seemingly the work of some Crypto-Royalist Plotter? Most
probable:[5]—or perhaps at bottom, only the *old* Banner of the
Section, manufactured prior to the Tenth of August, when such
streamers were according to rule![6]

History, looking over the Girondin Memoirs, anxious to dis-
entangle the truth of them from the hysterics, finds these days of
March, especially this Sunday the Tenth of March, play a great
part. Plots, plots; a plot for murdering the Girondin Deputies;
Anarchists and Secret-Royalists plotting, in hellish concert, for that
end! The far greater part of which is hysterics. What we do
find indisputable is, that Louvet and certain Girondins were
apprehensive they might be murdered on Saturday, and did not
go to the evening sitting; but held council with one another, each
inciting his fellow to do something resolute, and end these
Anarchists: to which, however, Pétion, opening the window, and
finding the night very wet, answered only, " *Ils ne feront rien,*" and
'composedly resumed his violin,' says Louvet;[7] thereby, with soft
Lydian tweedledeeing, to wrap himself against eating cares. Also

---

[5] *Choix des Rapports,* xi. 277.   [6] *Hist. Parl.* xxv. 78.
[7] Louvet, *Mémoires,* p. 72.

that Louvet felt especially liable to being killed; that several
Girondins went abroad to seek beds: liable to being killed; but
were not. Farther that, in very truth, Journalist Deputy Gorsas,
poisoner of the Departments, he and his Printer had their houses
broken into (by a tumult of Patriots, among whom redcapped
Varlet, American Fournier loom forth, in the darkness of the rain
and riot); had their wives put in fear; their presses, types and
circumjacent equipments beaten to ruin; no Mayor interfering in
time; Gorsas himself escaping, pistol in hand, 'along the coping
of the back wall.' Farther that Sunday, the morrow, was not a
workday; and the streets were more agitated than ever: Is it a
new September, then, that these Anarchists intend? Finally, that
no September came;—and also that hysterics, not unnaturally,
had reached almost their acme.[8]

Vergniaud denounces and deplores; in sweetly-turned periods.
Section Bonconseil, *Good-counsel* so-named, not Mauconseil or *Ill-
counsel* as it once was,—does a far notabler thing: demands that
Vergniaud, Brissot, Guadet, and other denunciatory, fine-spoken
Girondins, to the number of Twenty-two, be put under arrest!
Section Good-counsel, so named ever since the Tenth of August, is
sharply rebuked, like a Section of Ill-counsel:[9] but its word is
spoken, and will not fall to the ground.

In fact, one thing strikes us in these poor Girondins: their fatal
shortness of vision; nay fatal poorness of character, for that is the
root of it. They are as strangers to the People they would govern;
to the thing they have come to work in. Formulas, Philosophies,
Respectabilities, what has been written in Books, and admitted by
the Cultivated Classes: *this* inadequate *Scheme* of Nature's working
is all that Nature, let her work as she will, can reveal to these
men. So they perorate and speculate; and call on the Friends of
Law, when the question is not Law or No-Law, but Life or No-
Life. Pedants of the Revolution, if not Jesuits of it! Their
Formalism is great; great also is their Egoism. France rising to
fight Austria has been raised only by plot of the Tenth of March,
to kill Twenty-two of *them!* This Revolution Prodigy, unfolding
itself into terrific stature and articulation, by its own laws and
Nature's, not by the laws of Formula, has become unintelligible,
incredible as an impossibility, the 'waste chaos of a Dream.' A
Republic founded on what they call the Virtues; on what we call

---

[8] Meillan, pp. 23, 24; Louvet, pp. 71-80.
[9] *Moniteur* (Séance du 12 Mars), 15 Mars.

the Decencies and Respectabilities: this they will have, and nothing but this. Whatsoever other Republic Nature and Reality send, shall be considered as not sent; as a kind of Nightmare Vision, and thing non-extant; disowned by the Laws of Nature and of Formula. Alas, dim for the best eyes is this Reality; and as for these men, they will not look at it with eyes at all, but only through 'facetted spectacles' of Pedantry, wounded Vanity; which yield the most portentous fallacious spectrum. Carping and complaining forever of Plots and Anarchy, they will do one thing; prove, to demonstration, that the Reality will not translate into their Formula; that they and their Formula are incompatible with the Reality: and, in its dark wrath, the Reality will extinguish it and them! What a man *kens* he *cans*. But the beginning of a man's doom is, that vision be withdrawn from him; that he see not the reality, but a false spectrum of the reality; and following that, step darkly, with more or less velocity, downwards to the utter Dark; to Ruin, which is the great Sea of Darkness, whither all falsehoods, winding or direct, continually flow!

This Tenth of March we may mark as an epoch in the Girondin destinies; the rage so exasperated itself, the misconception so darkened itself. Many desert the sittings; many come to them armed.[10] An honourable Deputy, setting out after breakfast, must now, besides taking his Notes, see whether his Priming is in order.

Meanwhile with Dumouriez in Belgium it fares ever worse. Were it again General Miranda's fault, or some other's fault, there is no doubt whatever but the 'Battle of Nerwinden,' on the 18th of March, is lost; and our rapid retreat has become a far too rapid one. Victorious Cobourg, with his Austrian prickers, hangs like a dark cloud on the rear of us: Dumouriez never off horseback night or day; engagement every three hours; our whole discomfited Host rolling rapidly inwards, full of rage, suspicion and *sauve-qui-peut!* And then Dumouriez himself, what his intents may be? Wicked seemingly and not charitable! His despatches to Committee openly denounce a factious Convention, for the woes it has brought on France and him. And his speeches—for the General has no reticence! The execution of the Tyrant this Dumouriez calls the Murder of the King. Danton and Lacroix, flying thither as Commissioners once more, return very doubtful; even Danton now doubts.

[10] Meillan, *Mémoires*, pp. 85, 24.

Three Jacobin Missionaries, Proly, Dubuisson, Pereyra, have flown forth; sped by a wakeful Mother Society: they are struck dumb to hear the General speak. The Convention, according to this General, consists of three-hundred scoundrels and four-hundred imbeciles: France cannot do without a King. "But we have executed our King." "And what is it to me," hastily cries Dumouriez, a General of no reticence, "whether the King's name be *Ludovicus* or *Jacobus?*" "Or *Philippus!*" rejoins Proly;— and hastens to report progress. Over the Frontiers such hope is there.

CHAPTER V.

SANSCULOTTISM ACCOUTRED.

LET us look, however, at the grand internal Sansculottism and Revolution Prodigy, whether it stirs and waxes: there and not elsewhere may hope still be for France. The Revolution Prodigy, as Decree after Decree issues from the Mountain, like creative *fiats*, accordant with the nature of the Thing,—is shaping itself rapidly, in these days, into terrific stature and articulation, limb after limb. Last March 1792, we saw all France flowing in blind terror; shutting town-barriers, boiling pitch for Brigands: happier, this March, that it is a seeing terror; that a creative Mountain exists, which can say *fiat!* Recruitment proceeds with fierce celerity: nevertheless our Volunteers hesitate to set out, till Treason be punished at home; they do not fly to the frontiers; but only fly hither and thither, demanding and denouncing, The Mountain must speak new *fiat* and new *fiats*.

And does it not speak such? Take, as first example, those *Comités Révolutionnaires* for the arrestment of Persons Suspect. Revolutionary Committee, of Twelve chosen Patriots, sits in every Township of France; examining the Suspect, seeking arms, making domiciliary visits and arrestments;—caring, generally, that the Republic suffer no detriment. Chosen by universal suffrage, each in its Section, they are a kind of elixir of Jacobinism; some Forty-four Thousand of them awake and alive over France! In Paris and all Towns, every house-door must have the names of the

inmates legibly printed on it, 'at a height not exceeding five feet
from the ground;' every Citizen must produce his certificatory
Carte de Civisme, signed by Section-President; every man be ready
to give account of the faith that is in him. Persons Suspect had
as well depart this soil of Liberty! And yet departure too is bad:
all Emigrants are declared Traitors, their property become National;
they are 'dead in Law,'—save, indeed, that for *our* behoof they
shall 'live yet fifty years in Law,' and what heritages may fall to
them in that time become National too! A mad vitality of
Jacobinism, with Forty-four Thousand centres of activity, circulates
through all fibres of France.

Very notable also is the *Tribunal Extraordinaire:*[1] decreed by
the Mountain; some Girondins dissenting, for surely such a Court
contradicts every formula;—other Girondins assenting, nay co-
operating, for do not we all hate Traitors, O ye people of Paris?—
Tribunal of the Seventeenth, in Autumn last, was swift; but this
shall be swifter. Five Judges; a standing Jury, which is named
from Paris and the Neighbourhood, that there be not delay in
naming it: they are subject to no Appeal; to hardly any Law-
forms, but must 'get themselves convinced' in all readiest ways;
and for security are bound 'to vote audibly;' audibly, in the hearing of a Paris Public. This is the *Tribunal Extraordinaire;* which,
in few months, getting into most lively action, shall be entitled
Tribunal Révolutionnaire; as indeed it from the very first has
entitled itself: with a Herman or a Dumas for Judge-President,
with a Fouquier-Tinville for Attorney-General, and a Jury of such
as Citizen Leroi, who has surnamed himself *Aix-Août*, 'Leroi
August-Tenth,' it will become the wonder of the world. Herein
has Sansculottism fashioned for itself a Sword of Sharpness: a
weapon magical; tempered in the Stygian hell-waters; to the edge
of it all armour, and defence of strength or of cunning shall be soft;
it shall mow down Lives and Brazen-gates; and the waving of it
shed terror through the souls of men.

But speaking of an amorphous Sansculottism taking form, ought
we not, above all things, to specify how the Amorphous gets itself
a Head? Without metaphor, this Revolution Government continues hitherto in a very anarchic state. Executive Council of
Ministers, Six in number, there is: but they, especially since
Roland's retreat, have hardly known whether they were Ministers
or not. Convention Committees sit supreme over them; but then

---

[1] *Moniteur*, No. 70 (du 11 Mars), No. 76, &c.

each Committee as supreme as the others: Committee of Twenty-one, of Defence, of General Surety; simultaneous or successive, for specific purposes. The Convention alone is all-powerful,—especially if the Commune go with it; but is too numerous for an administrative body. Wherefore, in this perilous quick-whirling condition of the Republic, before the end of March we obtain our small *Comité de Salut Public;* [2] as it were, for miscellaneous accidental purposes requiring despatch;—as it proves, for a sort of universal supervision, and universal subjection. They are to report weekly, these new Committee-men; but to deliberate in secret. Their number is Nine, firm Patriots all, Danton one of them; renewable every month;—yet why not reëlect them if they turn out well? The flower of the matter is, that they are but nine; that they sit in secret. An insignificant-looking thing at first, this Committee; but with a principle of growth in it! Forwarded by fortune, by internal Jacobin energy, it will reduce all Committees and the Convention itself to mute obedience, the Six Ministers to Six assiduous Clerks; and work its will on the Earth and under Heaven, for a season. A 'Committee of Public Salvation' whereat the world still shrieks and shudders.

If we call that Revolutionary Tribunal a Sword, which Sansculottism has provided for itself, then let us call the 'Law of the Maximum' a Provender-scrip, or Haversack, wherein, better or worse, some ration of bread may be found. It is true, Political Economy, Girondin free-trade, and all law of supply and demand, are hereby hurled topsyturvy: but what help? Patriotism must live; the 'cupidity of farmers' seems to have no bowels. Wherefore this Law of the Maximum, fixing the highest price of grains, is, with infinite effort, got passed; [3] and shall gradually extend itself into a Maximum for all manner of *comestibles* and commodities: with such scrambling and topsyturvying as may be fancied! For now if, for example, the farmer will not sell? The farmer shall be forced to sell. An accurate Account of what grain he has shall be delivered in to the Constituted Authorities: let him see that he say not too much; for in that case, his rents, taxes and contributions will rise proportionally: let him see that he say not too little; for, on or before a set day, we shall suppose in April, *less* than one-third of this declared quantity must remain in his

[2] *Moniteur*, No. 83 (du 24 Mars 1793), Nos. 86, 98, 99, 100.
[3] *Moniteur* (du 20 Avril, &c. to 20 Mai, 1793).

barns, more than two-thirds of it must have been thrashed and sold. One can denounce him, and raise penalties.

By such inextricable overturning of all Commercial relations will Sansculottism keep life in; since not otherwise. On the whole, as Camille Desmoulins says once, "while the Sansculottes fight, the Monsieurs must pay." So there come *Impôts Progressifs*, Ascending Taxes; which consume, with fast-increasing voracity, the 'superfluous-revenue' of men: beyond fifty-pounds a-year, you are not exempt; rising into the hundreds, you bleed freely; into the thousands and tens of thousands, you bleed gushing. Also there come Requisitions; there comes 'Forced-Loan of a Milliard,' some Fifty-Millions Sterling; which of course they that *have* must lend. Unexampled enough; it has grown to be no country for the Rich, this; but a country for the Poor! And then if one fly, what steads it? Dead in Law; nay kept alive fifty years yet, for *their* accursed behoof! In this manner therefore it goes; topsyturvying, *ça-ira*-ing;—and withal there is endless sale of Emigrant National-Property, there is Cambon with endless cornucopia of Assignats. The Trade and Finance of Sansculottism; and how, with Maximum and Bakers' queues, with Cupidity, Hunger, Denunciation and Paper-money, it led its galvanic-life, and began and ended,— remains the most interesting of all Chapters in Political Economy: still to be written.

All which things, are they not clean against Formula? O Girondin Friends, it is not a Republic of the Virtues we are getting; but only a Republic of the Strengths, virtuous and other!

CHAPTER VI.

THE TRAITOR.

But Dumouriez, with his fugitive Host, with his King *Ludovicus* or King *Philippus?* There lies the crisis; there hangs the question: Revolution Prodigy, or Counter-Revolution? — One wide shriek covers that North-east region. Soldiers, full of rage, suspicion and terror, flock hither and thither; Dumouriez, the many-counselled, never off horseback, knows now no counsel that were not worse than none: the counsel, namely, of joining himself with Cobourg; marching to Paris, extinguishing Jacobinism, and, with some new King Ludovicus or King Philippus, restoring the Constitution of 1791![1]

Is wisdom quitting Dumouriez; the herald of Fortune quitting him? Principle, faith political or other, beyond a certain faith of mess-rooms, and honour of an officer, had him not to quit. At any rate his quarters in the Burgh of Saint-Amand; his head-quarters in the Village of Saint-Amand des Boues, a short way off,—have become a Bedlam. National Representatives, Jacobin Missionaries are riding and running; of the 'three Towns,' Lille, Valenciennes or even Condé, which Dumouriez wanted to snatch for himself, not one can be snatched; your Captain is admitted, but the Town-gate is closed on him, and then alas the Prison-gate, and 'his men wander about the ramparts.' Couriers gallop breathless; men wait, or seem waiting, to assassinate, to be assassinated; Battalions nigh frantic with such suspicion and uncertainty, with *Vive-la-République* and *Sauve-qui-peut*, rush this way and that;—Ruin and Desperation in the shape of Cobourg lying entrenched close by.

Dame Genlis and her fair Princess d'Orléans find this Burgh of Saint-Amand no fit place for them; Dumouriez's protection is grown worse than none. Tough Genlis, one of the toughest women; a woman, as it were, with nine lives in her; whom nothing will beat: she packs her bandboxes; clear for flight in a private manner. Her beloved Princess she will—leave here, with the

---

[1] Dumouriez, *Mémoires,* iv. c. 7-10.

Prince Chartres Egalité her Brother. In the cold gray of the April morning, we find her accordingly established in her hired vehicle, on the street of Saint-Amand; postillions just cracking their whips to go,—when behold the young Princely Brother, struggling hitherward, hastily calling; bearing the Princess in his arms! Hastily he has clutched the poor young lady up, in her very night-gown, nothing saved of her goods except the watch from the pillow: with brotherly despair he flings her in, among the band-boxes, into Genlis's chaise, into Genlis's arms: Leave her not, in the name of Mercy and Heaven! A shrill scene, but a brief one: —the postillions crack and go. Ah, whither? Through by-roads and broken hill-passes; seeking their way with lanterns after nightfall; through perils, and Cobourg Austrians and suspicious French Nationals: finally, into Switzerland; safe though nigh moneyless.[2] The brave young Egalité has a most wild Morrow to look for; but now only himself to carry through it.

For indeed over at that Village named *of the Mudbaths*, Saint-Amand des Boues, matters are still worse. About four o'clock on Tuesday afternoon, the 2d of April 1793, two Couriers come galloping as if for life; *Mon Général!* Four National Represent-atives, War-Minister at their head, are posting hitherward from Valenciennes; are close at hand,—with what intents one may guess! While the Couriers are yet speaking, War-Minister and National Representatives, old Camus the Archivist for chief speaker of them, arrive. Hardly has *Mon Général* had time to order out the Hussar Regiment de Berchigny; that it take rank and wait near by, in case of accident. And so, enter War-Minister Beurnonville, with an embrace of friendship, for he is an old friend; enter Archivist Camus and the other three following him.

They produce Papers, invite the General to the bar of the Con-vention: merely to give an explanation or two. The General finds it unsuitable, not to say impossible, and that "the service will suffer." Then comes reasoning; the voice of the old Archivist getting loud. Vain to reason loud with this Dumouriez; he answers mere angry irreverences. And so, amid plumed staff-officers, very gloomy-looking; in jeopardy and uncertainty, these poor National messengers debate and consult, retire and reënter, for the space of some two hours: without effect. Whereupon Archivist Camus, getting quite loud, proclaims, in the name of the

[2] Genlis, iv. 139.

H 2

National Convention, for he has the power to do it, That General
Dumouriez is *arrested:* "Will you obey the National mandate,
General!"—"*Pas dans ce moment-ci,* Not at this particular moment,"
answers the General also aloud; then glancing the other way,
utters certain unknown vocables, in a mandatory manner; seemingly a German word-of-command.[3] Hussars clutch the Four
National Representatives, and Beurnonville the War-Minister;
pack them out of the apartment; out of the Village, over the lines
to Cobourg, in two chaises that very night,—as hostages, prisoners;
to lie long in Maestricht and Austrian strongholds![4] *Jacta est alea.*

This night Dumouriez prints his 'Proclamation;' this night
and the morrow the Dumouriez Army, in such darkness visible,
and rage of semi-desperation as there is, shall meditate what
the General is doing, what they themselves will do in it. Judge
whether this Wednesday was of halcyon nature, for any one!
But on the Thursday morning, we discern Dumouriez with
small escort, with Chartres Egalité and a few staff-officers, ambling
along the Condé Highway: perhaps they are for Condé, and trying
to persuade the Garrison there; at all events, they are for an
interview with Cobourg, who waits in the woods by appointment,
in that quarter. Nigh the Village of Doumet, three National
Battalions, a set of men always full of Jacobinism, sweep past us;
marching rather swiftly,—seemingly in mistake, by a way we had
not ordered. The General dismounts, steps into a cottage, a little
from the wayside; will give them right order in writing. Hark!
what strange growling is heard; what barkings are heard, loud
yells of "*Traitors,*" of "*Arrest:*" the National Battalions have
wheeled round, are emitting shot! Mount, Dumouriez, and spring
for life! Dumouriez and Staff strike the spurs in, deep; vault
over ditches, into the fields, which prove to be morasses; sprawl
and plunge for life; bewhistled with curses and lead. Sunk to
the middle, with or without horses, several servants killed, they
escape out of shot-range, to General Mack the Austrian's quarters.
Nay they return on the morrow, to Saint-Amand and faithful
foreign Berchigny; but what boots it? The Artillery has all
revolted, is jingling off to Valenciennes; all have revolted, are
revolting; except only foreign Berchigny, to the extent of some
poor fifteen hundred, none will follow Dumouriez against France
and Indivisible Repulic: Dumouriez's occupation's gone.[5]

[3] Dumouriez, iv. 159, &c.

[4] Their Narrative, written by Camus (in Toulongeon, iii. app. 60-87).

[5] *Mémoires,* iv. 162-80.

Such an instinct of Frenchhood and Sansculottism dwells in these men: they will follow no Dumouriez nor Lafayette, nor any mortal on such errand. Shriek may be of *Sauve-qui-peut,* but will also be of *Vive-la-République.* New National Representatives arrive; new General Dampierre, soon killed in battle; new General Custine: the agitated Hosts draw back to some Camp of Famars; make head against Cobourg as they can.

And so Dumouriez is in the Austrian quarters; his drama ended, in this rather sorry manner. A most shifty, wiry man; one of Heaven's Swiss; that wanted only work. Fifty years of unnoticed toil and valour; one year of toil and valour, not unnoticed, but seen of all countries and centuries; then thirty other years again unnoticed, of Memoir-writing, English Pension, scheming and projecting to no purpose: Adieu, thou Swiss of Heaven, worthy to have been something else!

His Staff go different ways. Brave young Egalité reaches Switzerland and the Genlis Cottage; with a strong crabstick in his hand, a strong heart in his body: his Princedom is now reduced to that. Egalité the Father sat playing whist, in his Palais Egalité, at Paris, on the 6th day of this same month of April, when a catchpole entered: Citoyen Egalité is wanted at the Convention Committee![6] Examination, requiring Arrestment; finally requiring Imprisonment, transference to Marseilles and the Castle of If! Orléansdom has sunk in the black waters; Palais Egalité, which was Palais Royal, is like to become Palais National.

[6] See Montgaillard, iv. 144.

CHAPTER VII.

IN FIGHT.

OUR Republic, by paper Decree, may be 'One and Indivisible;'
but what profits it while these things are? Federalists in the
Senate, renegadoes in the Army, traitors everywhere! France, all
in desperate recruitment since the Tenth of March, does not fly to
the frontier, but only flies hither and thither. This defection of
contemptuous diplomatic Dumouriez falls heavy on the fine-spoken
high-sniffing *Hommes d'état* whom he consorted with; forms a
second epoch in their destinies.

Or perhaps more strictly we might say, the second Girondin
epoch, though little noticed then, began on the day when, in reference to this defection, the Girondins broke with Danton. It was
the first day of April; Dumouriez had not yet plunged across the
morasses to Cobourg, but was evidently meaning to do it, and our
Commissioners were off to arrest him; when what does the
Girondin Lasource see good to do, but rise, and jesuitically
question and insinuate at great length, whether a main accomplice
of Dumouriez had not probably been—Danton! Gironde grins
sardonic assent; Mountain holds its breath. The figure of Danton,
Levasseur says, while this speech went on, was noteworthy. He
sat erect with a kind of internal convulsion struggling to keep
itself motionless; his eye from time to time flashing wilder, his
lip curling in Titanic scorn.[1] Lasource, in a fine-spoken attorney
manner, proceeds : there is this probability to his mind, and there
is that; probabilities which press painfully on him, which cast the
Patriotism of Danton under a painful shade;—which painful shade,
he, Lasource, will hope that Danton may find it not impossible to
dispel.

"*Les Scélérats!*" cries Danton, starting up, with clenched right-
hand, Lasource having done; and descends from the Mountain,
like a lava-flood : his answer not unready. Lasource's probabilities
fly like idle dust; but leave a result behind them. "Ye were right,

[1] *Mémoires de Réné Levasseur* (Bruxelles, 1830), i. 164.

"friends of the Mountain," begins Danton, "and I was wrong: "there is no peace possible with these men. Let it be war, then! "They will not save the Republic with us: it shall be saved "without them; saved in spite of them." Really a burst of rude Parliamentary eloquence this; which is still worth reading in the old *Moniteur.* With fire-words the exasperated rude Titan rives and smites these Girondins; at every hit the glad Mountain utters chorus; Marat, like a musical *bis,* repeating the last phrase.[2] Lasource's probabilities are gone; but Danton's pledge of battle remains lying.

A third epoch, or scene in the Girondin Drama, or rather it is but the completion of this second epoch, we reckon from the day when the patience of virtuous Pétion finally boiled over; and the Girondins, to speak, took up this battle-pledge of Danton's, and decreed Marat accused. It was the eleventh of the same month of April, on some effervescence rising, such as often rose; and President had covered himself, mere Bedlam now ruling; and Mountain and Gironde were rushing on one another with clenched right-hands, and even with pistols in them; when, behold, the Girondin Duperret drew a sword! Shriek of horror rose, instantly quenching all other effervescence, at sight of the clear murderous steel; whereupon Duperret returned it to the leather again;—confessing that he did indeed draw it, being instigated by a kind of sacred madness, "*sainte fureur,*" and pistols held at him; but that if he parricidally had chanced to scratch the outmost skin of National Representation with it, he too carried pistols, and would have blown his brains out on the spot.[3]

But now in such posture of affairs, virtuous Pétion rose, next morning, to lament these effervescences, this endless Anarchy invading the Legislative Sanctuary itself; and here, being growled at and howled at by the Mountain, his patience, long tried, did, as we say, boil over; and he spake vehemently, in high key, with foam on his lips; "whence," says Marat, "I concluded he had got *la rage*," the rabidity, or dog-madness. Rabidity smites others rabid: so there rises new foam-lipped demand to have Anarchists extinguished; and specially to have Marat put under Accusation. Send a representative to the Revolutionary Tribunal? Violate the inviolability of a Representative? Have a care, O Friends!

[2] Séance du 1 Avril 1793 (in *Hist. Parl.* xxv. 24-35).
[3] *Hist. Parl.* xv. 397.

This poor Marat has faults enough ; but against Liberty or Equality, what fault ? That he has loved and fought for it, not wisely but too well. In dungeons and cellars, in pinching poverty, under anathema of men; even so, in such fight, has he grown so dingy, bleared; even so has his head become a Stylites one ! Him you will fling to your Sword of Sharpness ; while Cobourg and Pitt advance on us, fire-spitting ?

The Mountain is loud, the Gironde is loud and deaf; all lips are foamy. With ' Permanent-Session of twenty-four hours,' with vote by roll-call, and a deadlift effort, the Gironde carries it : Marat is ordered to the Revolutionary Tribunal, to answer for that February Paragraph of Forestallers at the door-lintel, with other offences; and, after a little hesitation, he obeys.[4]

Thus is Danton's battle-pledge taken up ; there is, as he said there would be, ' war without truce or treaty, *ni trêve ni composition.*' Wherefore, close now with one another, Formula and Reality, in death-grips, and wrestle it out; both of you cannot live, but only one !

CHAPTER VIII.

IN DEATH-GRIPS.

IT proves what strength, were it only of inertia, there is in established Formulas, what weakness in nascent Realities, and illustrates several things, that this death-wrestle should still have lasted some six weeks or more. National business, discussion of the Constitutional Act, for our Constitution should decidedly be got ready, proceeds along with it. We even change our Locality ; we shift, on the Tenth of May, from the old Salle de Manége into our new Hall, in the Palace, once a King's but now the Republic's, of the Tuileries. Hope and ruth, flickering against despair and rage, still struggle in the minds of men.

It is a most dark confused death-wrestle, this of the six weeks. Formalist frenzy against Realist frenzy ; Patriotism, Egoism, Pride, Anger, Vanity, Hope and Despair, all raised to the frenetic pitch :

[4] *Moniteur* (du 16 Avril 1793, et seqq.).

Frenzy meets Frenzy, like dark clashing whirlwinds; neither understands the other; the weaker, one day, will understand that *it* is verily swept down! Girondism is strong as established Formula and Respectability: do not as many as Seventy-two of the Departments, or say respectable Heads of Departments, declare for us? Calvados, which loves its Buzot, will even rise in revolt, so hint the Addresses; Marseilles, cradle of Patriotism, will rise; Bordeaux will rise, and the Gironde Department, as one man; in a word, who will *not* rise, were our *Représentation Nationale* to be insulted, or one hair of a Deputy's head harmed! The Mountain, again, is strong as Reality and Audacity. To the Reality of the Mountain are not all furthersome things possible? A new Tenth of August, if needful; nay a new Second of September!—

But, on Wednesday afternoon, Twenty-fourth day of April, year 1793, what tumult as of fierce jubilee is this? It is Marat returning from the Revolutionary Tribunal! A week or more of death-peril: and now there is triumphant acquittal; Revolutionary Tribunal can find no accusation against this man. And so the eye of History beholds Patriotism, which had gloomed unutterable things all week, break into loud jubilee, embrace its Marat; lift him into a chair of triumph, bear him shoulder-high through the streets. Shoulder-high is the injured People's-friend, crowned with an oak-garland; amid the wavy sea of red night-caps, carmagnole jackets, grenadier bonnets and female mob-caps; far-sounding like a sea! The injured People's-friend has here reached his culminating point; he too strikes the stars with his sublime head.

But the Reader can judge with what face President Lasource, he of the 'painful probabilities,' who presides in this Convention Hall, might welcome such jubilee-tide, when it got thither, and the Decreed of Accusation floating on the top of it! A National Sapper, spokesman on the occasion, says, the People know their Friend, and love his life as their own; "whosoever wants Marat's head must get the Sapper's first."[1] Lasource answered with some vague painful mumblement,—which, says Levasseur, one could not help tittering at.[2] Patriot Sections, Volunteers not yet gone to the Frontiers, come demanding the "purgation of traitors from your own bosom;" the expulsion, or even the trial and sentence, of a factious Twenty-two.

[1] Séance du 26 Avril, An 1ᵉʳ (in *Moniteur*, No. 116).
[2] Levasseur, *Mémoires*, i. c. 6.

Nevertheless the Gironde has got its Commission of Twelve;
a Commission specially appointed for investigating these troubles
of the Legislative Sanctuary: let Sansculottism say what it will,
Law shall triumph. Old-Constituent Rabaut Saint-Etienne presides over this Commission: 'it is the last plank whereon a
wrecked Republic may perhaps still save herself.' Rabaut and they
therefore sit, intent; examining witnesses; launching arrestments;
looking out into a waste dim sea of troubles,—the womb of
Formula, or perhaps her grave! Enter not that sea, O Reader!
There are dim desolation and confusion; raging women and raging
men. Sections come demanding Twenty-two; for the *number* first
given by Section Bonconseil still holds, though the names should
even vary. Other Sections, of the wealthier kind, come denouncing
such demand; nay the same Section will demand today, and denounce the demand tomorrow, according as the wealthier sit, or the
poorer. Wherefore, indeed, the Girondins decree that all Sections
shall close ' at ten in the evening;' before the working people come:
which Decree remains without effect. And nightly the Mother of
Patriotism wails doleful; doleful, but her eye kindling! And
Fournier l'Américain is busy, and the two banker Freys, and Varlet
Apostle of Liberty; the bull-voice of Marquis St.-Huruge is heard.
And shrill women vociferate from all Galleries, the Convention ones
and downwards. Nay a 'Central Committee' of all the Forty-
eight Sections looms forth huge and dubious; sitting dim in the
Archevêché, sending Resolutions, receiving them: a Centre of the
Sections; in dread deliberation as to a New Tenth of August!

One thing we will specify, to throw light on many: the aspect
under which, seen through the eyes of these Girondin Twelve, or
even seen through one's own eyes, the Patriotism of the softer sex
presents itself. There are Female Patriots, whom the Girondins
call Megæras, and count to the extent of eight thousand; with
serpent-hair, all out of curl; who have changed the distaff for
the dagger. They are of ' the Society called Brotherly,' *Fraternelle*,
say *Sisterly*, which meets under the roof of the Jacobins. 'Two
thousand daggers,' or *so*, have been ordered,—doubtless for them.
They rush to Versailles, to raise more women; but the Versailles
women will not rise.[3]

Nay behold, in National Garden of Tuileries,—Demoiselle
Théroigne herself is become as a brown-locked Diana (were that

[3] Buzot, *Mémoires*, pp. 69, 84; Meillan, *Mémoires*, pp. 192, 195, 196. See
Commission des Douze (in *Choix des Rapports*, xii. 69-131).

possible) attacked by her own dogs, or she-dogs! The Demoiselle,
keeping her carriage, is for Liberty indeed, as she has full well
shown; but then for Liberty with Respectability: whereupon
these serpent-haired Extreme She Patriots do now fasten on her,
tatter her, shamefully fustigate her, in their shameful way; almost
fling her into the Garden-ponds, had not help intervened. Help,
alas, to small purpose. The poor Demoiselle's head and nervous-
system, none of the soundest, is so tattered and fluttered that it
will never recover; but flutter worse and worse, till it crack; and
within year and day we hear of her in madhouse and strait-waist-
coat, which proves permanent!—Such brown-locked Figure did
flutter, and inarticulately jabber and gesticulate, little able to
speak the obscure meaning it had, through some segment of the
Eighteenth Century of Time. She disappears here from the
Revolution and Public History forevermore.[4]

Another thing we will not again specify, yet again beseech the
Reader to imagine: the reign of Fraternity and Perfection.
Imagine, we say, O Reader, that the Millennium were struggling
on the threshold, and yet not so much as groceries could be had,—
owing to traitors. With what impetus would a man strike traitors,
in that case! Ah, thou canst not imagine it; thou hast thy
groceries safe in the shops, and little or no hope of a Millennium
ever coming!—But indeed, as to the temper there was in men
and women, does not this one fact say enough: the height
SUSPICION had risen to? Preternatural we often called it; seemingly in the language of exaggeration: but listen to the cold
deposition of witnesses. Not a musical Patriot can blow himself
a snatch of melody from the French Horn, sitting mildly pensive
on the housetop, but Mercier will recognise it to be a signal which
one Plotting Committee is making to another. Distraction has
possessed Harmony herself; lurks in the sound of *Marseillaise* and
Ça-ira.[5] Louvet, who can see as deep into a millstone as the
most, discerns that we shall be invited back to our old Hall of
the Manége, by a Deputation; and then the Anarchists will
massacre Twenty-two of us, as we walk over. It is Pitt and
Cobourg; the gold of Pitt.—Poor Pitt! They little know what
work he has with his own Friends of the People; getting them

---

[4] *Deux Amis*, vii. 77-80; Forster, i. 514; Moore, i. 70. She did not die
till 1817; in the Salpêtrière, in the most abject state of insanity: see Esquirol,
Des Maladies Mentales (Paris, 1838), i. 445-50.

[5] Mercier, *Nouveau Paris*, vi. 63.

bespied, beheaded, their habeas-corpuses suspended, and his own Social Order and strong-boxes kept tight,—to fancy him raising mobs among his neighbours!

But the strangest fact connected with French or indeed with human Suspicion, is perhaps this of Camille Desmoulins. Camille's head, one of the clearest in France, has got itself so saturated through every fibre with Preternaturalism of Suspicion, that looking back on that Twelfth of July 1789, when the thousands rose round him, yelling responsive at his word in the Palais-Royal Garden, and took cockades, he finds it explicable only on this hypothesis, That they were all hired to do it, and set on by the Foreign and other Plotters. "It was not for nothing," says Camille with insight, "that this multitude burst up round me when I spoke!" No, not for nothing. Behind, around, before, it is one huge Preternatural Puppet-play of Plots; Pitt pulling the wires.[6] Almost I conjecture that I, Camille myself, am a Plot, and wooden with wires.—The force of insight could no farther go.

Be this as it will, History remarks that the Commission of Twelve, now clear enough as to the Plots; and luckily having ' got the threads of them all by the end,' as they say,—are launching Mandates of Arrest rapidly in these May days; and carrying matters with a high hand; resolute that the sea of troubles shall be restrained. What chief Patriot, Section-President even, is safe? They can arrest him; tear him from his warm bed, because he has made irregular Section Arrestments! They arrest Varlet Apostle of Liberty. They arrest Procureur-Substitute Hébert, *Père Duchesne;* a Magistrate of the People, sitting in Townhall; who, with high solemnity of martyrdom, takes leave of his colleagues; prompt he, to obey the Law; and solemnly acquiescent, disappears into prison.

The swifter fly the Sections, energetically demanding him back; demanding not arrestment of Popular Magistrates, but of a traitorous Twenty-two. Section comes flying after Section;— defiling energetic, with their Cambyses-vein of oratory: nay the Commune itself comes, with Mayor Pache at its head; and with question not of Hébert and the Twenty-two alone, but with this ominous old question made new, "Can you save the Republic, or

[6] See *Histoire des Brissotins,* par Camille Desmoulins (a Pamphlet of Camille's, Paris, 1793).

must we do it?" To whom President Max Isnard makes fiery answer: If by fatal chance, in any of those tumults which since the Tenth of March are ever returning, Paris were to lift a sacrilegious finger against the National Representation, France would rise as one man, in never-imagined vengeance, and shortly 'the traveller would ask, on which side of the Seine Paris had stood!'[7] Whereat the Mountain bellows only louder, and every Gallery; Patriot Paris boiling round.

And Girondin Valazé has nightly conclaves at his house; sends billets, 'Come punctually, and well armed, for there is to be business.' And Megæra women perambulate the streets, with flags, with lamentable *alleleu*.[8] And the Convention-doors are obstructed by roaring multitudes: fine-spoken *Hommes d'état* are hustled, maltreated, as they pass; Marat will apostrophise you, in such death-peril, and say, Thou too art of them. If Roland ask leave to quit Paris, there is order of the day. What help? Substitute Hébert, Apostle Varlet, must be given back; to be crowned with oak-garlands. The Commission of Twelve, in a Convention overwhelmed with roaring Sections, is broken; then on the morrow, in a Convention of rallied Girondins, is reinstated. Dim Chaos, or the sea of troubles, is struggling through all its elements; writhing and chafing towards some Creation.

[7] *Moniteur*, Séance du 25 Mai 1793.
[8] Meillan, *Mémoires*, p. 195 ; Buzot, pp. 69, 84.

CHAPTER IX.

EXTINCT.

ACCORDINGLY, on Friday the Thirty-first of May 1793, there comes forth into the summer sunlight one of the strangest scenes. Mayor Pache with Municipality arrives at the Tuileries Hall of Convention; sent for, Paris being in visible ferment; and gives the strangest news.

How, in the gray of this morning, while we sat Permanent in Townhall, watchful for the commonweal, there entered, precisely as on a Tenth of August, some Ninety-six extraneous persons; who declared themselves to be in a state of Insurrection; to be plenipotentiary Commissioners from the Forty-eight Sections, sections or members of the Sovereign People, all in a state of Insurrection; and farther that we, in the name of said Sovereign in Insurrection, were dismissed from office. How we thereupon laid off our sashes, and withdrew into the adjacent Saloon of Liberty. How, in a moment or two, we were called back; and reinstated; the Sovereign pleasing to think us still worthy of confidence. Whereby, having taken new oath of office, we on a sudden find ourselves Insurrectionary Magistrates, with extraneous Committee of Ninety-six sitting by us; and a Citoyen Henriot, one whom some accuse of Septemberism, is made Generalissimo of the National Guard; and, since six o'clock, the tocsins ring, and the drums beat:—Under which peculiar circumstances, what would an august National Convention please to direct us to do ? [1]

Yes, there is the question! "Break the Insurrectionary Authorities," answer some with vehemence. Vergniaud at least will have "the National Representatives all die at their post;" this is sworn to, with ready loud acclaim. But as to breaking the Insurrectionary Authorities,—alas, while we yet debate, what sound is that? Sound of the Alarm-Cannon on the Pont Neuf; which it is death by the Law to fire without order from us!

---

[1] *Débats de la Convention* (Paris, 1828), iv. 187-223 ; *Moniteur*, Nos. 152, 3, 4, An 1ᵉʳ.

It does boom off there nevertheless; sending a stound through all hearts. And the tocsins discourse stern music; and Henriot with his Armed Force has enveloped us! And Section succeeds Section, the livelong day; demanding with Cambyses-oratory, with the rattle of muskets, That traitors, Twenty-two or more, be punished; that the Commission of Twelve be irrecoverably broken. The heart of the Gironde dies within it; distant are the Seventy-two respectable Departments, this fiery Municipality is near! Barrère is for a middle course; granting something. The Commission of Twelve declares that, not waiting to be broken, it hereby breaks itself, and is no more. Fain would Reporter Rabaut speak his and its last words; but he is bellowed off. Too happy that the Twenty-two are still left unviolated!—Vergniaud, carrying the laws of refinement to a great length, moves, to the amazement of some, that 'the Sections of Paris have deserved well of their country.' Whereupon, at a late hour of the evening, the deserving Sections retire to their respective places of abode. Barrère shall report on it. With busy quill and brain he sits, secluded; for him no sleep tonight. Friday the last of May has ended in this manner.

The Sections have deserved well: but ought they not to deserve better? Faction and Girondism is struck down for the moment, and consents to be a nullity; but will it not, at another favourabler moment, rise, still feller; and the Republic have to be saved in spite of it? So reasons Patriotism, still Permanent; so reasons the Figure of Marat, visible in the dim Section-world, on the morrow. To the conviction of men!—And so at eventide of Saturday, when Barrère had just got the thing all varnished by the labour of a night and day, and his Report was setting off in the evening mail-bags, tocsin peals out *again*. *Générale* is beating; armed men taking station in the Place Vendôme and elsewhere, for the night; supplied with provisions and liquor. There, under the summer stars, will they wait, this night, what is to be seen and to be done, Henriot and Townhall giving due signal.

The Convention, at the sound of *générale*, hastens back to its Hall; but to the number only of a Hundred; and does little business. puts off business till the morrow. The Girondins do not stir out thither, the Girondins are abroad seeking beds.—Poor Rabaut, on the morrow morning, returning to his post, with Louvet and some others, through streets all in ferment, wrings his hands, ejaculating, '*Illa suprema dies!*' [2] It has become Sunday the 2d day of June,

2 Louvet, *Mémoires*, p. 89.

year 1793, by the old style; by the new style, year One of Liberty,
Equality, Fraternity. We have got to the last scene of all, that
ends this history of the Girondin Senatorship.

It seems doubtful whether any terrestrial Convention had ever
met in such circumstances as this National one now does. Tocsin
is pealing; Barriers shut; all Paris is on the gaze, or under arms.
As many as a Hundred Thousand under arms they count: National
Force; and the Armed Volunteers, who should have flown to the
Frontiers and La Vendée; but would not, treason being unpunished; and only flew hither and thither! So many, steady
under arms, environ the National Tuileries and Garden. There
are horse, foot, artillery, sappers with beards: the artillery one can
see with their camp-furnaces in this National Garden, heating
bullets red, and their match is lighted. Henriot in plumes rides,
amid a plumed Staff: all posts and issues are safe; reserves lie
out, as far as the Wood of Boulogne; the choicest Patriots nearest
the scene. One other circumstance we will note: that a careful
Municipality, liberal of camp-furnaces, has not forgotten provision-
carts. No member of the Sovereign need now go home to dinner;
but can keep rank—plentiful victual circulating unsought. Does
not this People understand Insurrection? Ye, *not* uninventive,
Gualches!—

Therefore let a National Representation, 'mandatories of the
Sovereign,' take thought of it. Expulsion of your Twenty-two,
and your Commission of Twelve: we stand here till it be done!
Deputation after Deputation, in ever stronger language, comes
with that message. Barrère proposes a middle course:—Will not
perhaps the inculpated Deputies consent to withdraw voluntarily;
to make a generous demission and self-sacrifice for the sake of one's
country? Isnard, repentant of that search on which river-bank
Paris stood, declares himself ready to demit. Ready also is *Te-
Deum* Fauchet; old Dusaulx of the Bastille, '*vieux radoteur*, old
dotard,' as Marat calls him, is still readier. On the contrary,
Lanjuinais the Breton declares that there is one man who never
will demit voluntarily; but will protest to the uttermost, while
a voice is left him. And he accordingly goes on protesting; amid
rage and clangour; Legendre crying at last: "Lanjuinais, come
down from the Tribune, or I will fling thee down, *ou je te jette en
bas!*" For matters are come to extremity. Nay they do clutch
hold of Lanjuinais, certain zealous Mountain-men; but cannot

fling him down, for he 'cramps himself on the railing;' and 'his clothes get torn.' Brave Senator, worthy of pity! Neither will Barbaroux demit; he "has sworn to die at his post, and will keep that oath." Whereupon the Galleries all rise with explosion; brandishing weapons, some of them; and rush out, saying: "*Allons*, then; we must save our country!" Such a Session is this of Sunday the second of June.

Churches fill, over Christian Europe, and then empty themselves; but this Convention empties not, the while: a day of shrieking contention, of agony, humiliation and tearing of coatskirts; *illa suprema dies!* Round stand Henriot and his Hundred Thousand, copiously refreshed from tray and basket: nay he is 'distributing five francs a-piece,' we Girondins saw it with our eyes; five francs to keep them in heart! And distraction of armed riot encumbers our borders, jangles at our Bar; we are prisoners in our own Hall: Bishop Grégoire could not get out for a *besoin actuel* without four gendarmes to wait on him! What is the character of a National Representative become? And now the sunlight falls yellower on western windows, and the chimney-tops are flinging longer shadows; the refreshed Hundred Thousand, nor their shadows, stir not! What to resolve on? Motion rises, superfluous one would think, That the Convention go forth in a body; ascertain with its own eyes whether it is free or not. Lo, therefore, from the Eastern Gate of the Tuileries, a distressed Convention issuing; handsome Hérault Séchelles at their head; he with hat on, in sign of public calamity, the rest bareheaded,— towards the Gate of the Carrousel; wondrous to see: towards Henriot and his plumed Staff. "In the name of the National Convention, make way!" Not an inch of way does Henriot make: "I receive no orders, till the Sovereign, yours and mine, have been obeyed." The Convention presses on; Henriot prances back, with his Staff, some fifteen paces, "To arms! Cannoneers, to your guns!"—flashes out his puissant sword, as the Staff all do, and the Hussars all do. Cannoneers brandish the lit match; Infantry present arms,—alas, in the level way, as if for firing! Hatted Hérault leads his distressed flock, through their pinfold of a Tuileries again; across the Garden, to the Gate on the opposite side. Here is Feuillans-Terrace, alas, there is our old Salle de Manége; but neither at this Gate of the Pont Tournant is there egress. Try the other; and the other: no egress! We wander disconsolate through armed ranks; who indeed salute with *Live the Republic,* but also with *Die the Gironde.* Other such sight, in the Year One of Liberty, the westering sun never saw.

And now behold Marat meets us; for he lagged in this Suppliant Procession of ours: he has got some hundred elect Patriots at his heels; he orders us, in the Sovereign's name, to return to our place, and do as we are bidden and bound. The Convention returns. "Does not the Convention," says Couthon with a singular power of face, "see that it is free,"—none but friends round it? The Convention, overflowing with friends and armed Sectioners, proceeds to vote as bidden. Many will not vote, but remain silent; some one or two protest, in words, the Mountain has a clear unanimity. Commission of Twelve, and the denounced Twenty-two, to whom we add Ex-Ministers Clavière and Lebrun: these, with some slight extempore alterations (this or that orator proposing, but Marat disposing), are voted to be under 'Arrestment in their own houses.' Brissot, Buzot, Vergniaud, Guadet, Louvet, Gensonné, Barbaroux, Lasource, Lanjuinais, Rabaut,— Thirty-two, by the tale; all that we have known as Girondins, and more than we have known. They, 'under the safeguard of the French People;' by and by, under the safeguard of two Gendarmes each, shall dwell peaceably in their own houses; as Non-Senators; till farther order. Herewith ends *Séance* of Sunday the second of June 1793.

At ten o'clock, under mild stars, the Hundred Thousand, their work well finished, turn homewards. Already yesterday, Central Insurrection Committee had arrested Madame Roland; imprisoned her in the Abbaye. Roland has fled, no man knows whither.

Thus fell the Girondins, by Insurrection; and became extinct as a Party: not without a sigh from most Historians. The men were men of parts, of Philosophic culture, decent behaviour; not condemnable in that they were but Pedants, and had not better parts; not condemnable, but most unfortunate. They wanted a Republic of the Virtues, wherein themselves should be head; and they could only get a Republic of the Strengths, wherein others than they were head.

For the rest, Barrère shall make Report of it. The night concludes with a 'civic promenade by torchlight:'[3] surely the true reign of Fraternity is now not far?

[3] Buzot, *Mémoires,* p. 310. See *Pièces Justificatives,* of Narratives, Commentaries, &c. in Buzot, Louvet, Meillan; *Documens Complémentaires,* in *Hist. Parl.* xxviii. 1-78.

BOOK FOURTH.

TERROR.

CHAPTER I.

CHARLOTTE CORDAY.

In the leafy months of June and July, several French Department-ments germinate a set of rebellious *paper*-leaves, named Pro-clamations, Resolutions, Journals, or Diurnals, 'of the Union for Resistance to Oppression.' In particular, the Town of Caen, in Calvados, sees its paper-leaf of *Bulletin de Caen* suddenly bud, suddenly establish itself as Newspaper there; under the Editorship of Girondin National Representatives!

For among the proscribed Girondins are certain of a more desperate humour. Some, as Vergniaud, Valazé, Gensonné, 'arrested in their own houses,' will await with stoical resignation what the issue may be. Some, as Brissot, Rabaut, will take to flight, to concealment; which, as the Paris Barriers are opened again in a day or two, is not yet difficult. But others there are who will rush, with Buzot, to Calvados; or far over France, to Lyons, Toulon, Nantes and elsewhither, and then rendezvous at Caen: to awaken as with war-trumpet the respectable Departments; and strike down an anarchic Mountain Faction; at least not yield without a stroke at it. Of this latter temper we count some score or more, of the Arrested, and of the Not-yet-arrested: a Buzot, a Barbaroux, Louvet, Guadet, Pétion, who have escaped from Arrestment in their own homes; a Salles, a Pythagorean Valady, a Duchâtel, the Duchâtel that came in blanket and nightcap to vote for the life of Louis, who have escaped from danger and likelihood of Arrestment. These, to the number at one time of

I 2

Twenty-seven, do accordingly lodge here, at the '*Intendance,* or
Departmental Mansion,' of the town of Caen in Calvados; welcomed by Persons in Authority; welcomed and defrayed, having
no money of their own.   And the *Bulletin de Caen* comes forth,
with the most animating paragraphs: How the Bourdeaux
Department, the Lyons Deparment, this Department after the
other is declaring itself; sixty, or say sixty-nine, or seventy-two;
respectable Departments either declaring, or ready to declare.
Nay Marseilles, it seems, will march on Paris by itself, if need be.
So has Marseilles Town said, That she will march.   But on the
other hand, that Montélimart Town has said, No thoroughfare;
and means even to 'bury herself' under her own stone and mortar
first,—of this be no mention in *Bulletin de Caen.*

Such animating paragraphs we read in this new Newspaper;
and fervours and eloquent sarcasm : tirades against the Mountain,
from the pen of Deputy Salles; which resemble, say friends,
Pascal's *Provincials.* What is more to the purpose, these Girondins have got a General in chief, one Wimpfen, formerly under
Dumouriez; also a secondary questionable General Puisaye, and
others; and are doing their best to raise a force for war.   National
Volunteers, whosoever is of right heart: gather in, ye National
Volunteers, friends of Liberty; from our Calvados Townships, from
the Eure, from Brittany, from far and near : forward to Paris, and
extinguish Anarchy!   Thus at Caen, in the early July days,
there is a drumming and parading, a perorating and consulting:
Staff and Army; Council; Club of *Carabots,* Anti-jacobin friends
cf Freedom, to denounce atrocious Marat.   With all which, and
the editing of *Bulletins,* a National Representative has his hands
full.

At Caen it is most animated; and, as one hopes, more or less
animated in the 'Seventy-two Departments that adhere to us.'
And in a France begirt with Cimmerian invading Coalitions, and
torn with an internal La Vendée, *this* is the conclusion we have
arrived at: To put down Anarchy by Civil War! *Durum et
durum,* the Proverb says, *non faciunt murum.* La Vendée burns:
Santerre can do nothing there; he may return home and brew
beer.   Cimmerian bombshells fly all along the North.   That Siege
of Mentz is become famed ;—lovers of the Picturesque (as Goethe
will testify), washed country-people of both sexes, stroll thither
on Sundays, to see the artillery work and counterwork; 'you

[1] Meillan, pp. 72, 73 ; Louvet, p. 129.

only duck a little while the shot whizzes past.' [2] Condé is
capitulating to the Austrians; Royal Highness of York, these
several weeks, fiercely batters Valenciennes. For, alas, our fortified
Camp of Famars was stormed; General Dampierre was killed;
General Custine was blamed,—and indeed is now come to Paris to
give ' explanations.'

Against all which the Mountain and atrocious Marat must even
make head as they can. They, anarchic Convention as they are,
publish Decrees, expostulatory, explanatory, yet not without severity;
they ray-forth Commissioners, singly or in pairs, the olive-branch in
one hand, yet the sword in the other. Commissioners come even
to Caen; but without effect. Mathematical Romme, and Prieur
named of the Côte d'Or, venturing thither, with their olive and
sword, are packed into prison : there may Romme lie, under lock
and key, 'for fifty days;' and meditate his New Calendar, if
he please. Cimmeria, La Vendée, and Civil War ! Never was
Republic One and Indivisible at a lower ebb.—

Amid which dim ferment of Caen and the World, History specially notices one thing : in the lobby of the Mansion *de l'Intendance*,
where busy Deputies are coming and going, a young Lady with an
aged valet, taking grave graceful leave of Deputy Barbaroux.[3]
She is of stately Norman figure ; in her twenty-fifth year; of
beautiful still countenance : her name is Charlotte Corday, heretofore styled D'Armans, while Nobility still was. Barbaroux has
given her a Note to Deputy Duperret,—him who once drew his
sword in the effervescence. Apparently she will to Paris on some
errand ? 'She was a Republican before the Revolution, and never
wanted energy.' A completeness, a decision is in this fair female
Figure : 'by energy she means the spirit that will prompt one to
' sacrifice himself for his country.' What if she, this fair young
Charlotte, had emerged from her secluded stillness, suddenly like
a Star ; cruel-lovely, with half-angelic, half-dæmonic splendour; to
gleam for a moment, and in a moment be extinguished : to be held
in memory, so bright complete was she, through long centuries !—
Quitting Cimmerian Coalitions without, and the dim-simmering
Twenty-five millions within, History will look fixedly at this one
fair Apparition of a Charlotte Corday; will note whither Charlotte
moves, how the little Life burns forth so radiant, then vanishes
swallowed of the Night.

[2] *Belagerung von Mainz* (Goethe's *Werke*, xxx. 278-334).
[3] Meillan, p. 75 ; Louvet, p. 114.

With Barbaroux's Note of Introduction, and slight stock of luggage, we see Charlotte on Tuesday the 9th of July seated in the Caen Diligence, with a place for Paris. None takes farewell of her, wishes her Good-journey: her Father will find a line left, signifying that she is gone to England, that he must pardon her, and forget her. The drowsy Diligence lumbers along; amid drowsy talk of Politics, and praise of the Mountain; in which she mingles not: all night, all day, and again all night. On Thursday, not long before noon, we are at the bridge of Neuilly; here is Paris with her thousand black domes, the goal and purpose of thy journey! Arrived at the Inn de la Providence in the Rue des Vieux Augustins, Charlotte demands a room; hastens to bed; sleeps all afternoon and night, till the morrow morning.

On the morrow morning, she delivers her Note to Duperret. It relates to certain Family Papers which are in the Minister of the Interior's hands; which a Nun at Caen, an old Convent-friend of Charlotte's, has need of; which Duperret shall assist her in getting: this then was Charlotte's errand to Paris? She has finished this, in the course of Friday;—yet says nothing of return-ing. She has seen and silently investigated several things. The Convention, in bodily reality, she has seen; what the Mountain is like. The living physiognomy of Marat she could not see; he is sick at present, and confined to home.

About eight on the Saturday morning, she purchases a large sheath-knife in the Palais Royal; then straightway, in the Place des Victoires, take a hackney-coach: "To the Rue de l'Ecole de Médecine, No. 44." It is the residence of the Citoyen Marat! —The Citoyen Marat is ill, and cannot be seen; which seems to disappoint her much. Her business is with Marat, then? Hapless beautiful Charlotte; hapless squalid Marat! From Caen in the utmost West, from Neuchâtel in the utmost East, they two are drawing nigh each other; they two have, very strangely, business together.—Charlotte, returning to her Inn, despatches a short Note to Marat; signifying that she is from Caen, the seat of rebellion; that she desires earnestly to see him, and 'will put it in his power to do France a great service.' No answer. Charlotte writes another Note, still more pressing; sets out with it by coach, about seven in the evening, herself. Tired day-labourers have again finished their Week; huge Paris is circling and simmering, manifold, according to its vague wont: this one fair Figure has decision in it; drives straight,—towards a purpose.

It is yellow July evening, we say, the thirteenth of the month; eve of the Bastille day,—when 'M. Marat,' four years ago, in the crowd of the Pont Neuf, shrewdly required of that Besenval Hussar-party, which had such friendly dispositions, "to dismount, and give up their arms, then;" and became notable among Patriot men. Four years: what a road he has travelled;—and sits now, about half-past seven of the clock, stewing in slipper-bath; sore afflicted; ill of Revolution Fever,—of what other malady this History had rather not name. Excessively sick and worn, poor man: with precisely elevenpence-halfpenny of ready-money, in paper; with slipper-bath; strong three-footed stool for writing on, the while: and a squalid—Washerwoman, one may call her: that is his civic establishment in Medical-School Street; thither and not elsewhither has his road led him. Not to the reign of Brotherhood and Perfect Felicity; yet surely on the way towards that?—Hark, a rap again! A musical woman's voice, refusing to be rejected: it is the Citoyenne who would do France a service. Marat, recognising from within, cries, Admit her. Charlotte Corday is admitted.

Citoyen Marat, I am from Caen the seat of rebellion, and wished to speak with you.—Be seated, *mon enfant.* Now what are the traitors doing at Caen? What Deputies are at Caen? —Charlotte names some Deputies. "Their heads shall fall within a fortnight," croaks the eager People's-friend, clutching his tablets to write: *Barbaroux, Pétion,* writes he with bare shrunk arm, turning aside in the bath: *Pétion,* and *Louvet,* and—Charlotte has drawn her knife from the sheath; plunges it, with one sure stroke, into the writer's heart. "*A moi, chère amie,* Help, dear!" no more could the Death-choked say or shriek. The helpful Washerwoman running in, there is no Friend of the People, or Friend of the Washerwoman left; but his life with a groan gushes out, indignant, to the shades below.[4]

And so Marat People's-friend is ended; the lone Stylites has got hurled down suddenly from his Pillar,—*whitherward* He that made him knows. Patriot Paris may sound triple and tenfold, in dole and wail; reëchoed by Patriot France; and the Convention, 'Chabot pale with terror, declaring that they are to be all assassinated,' may decree him Pantheon Honours, Public Funeral, Mirabeau's dust making way for him; and Jacobin

4 *Moniteur,* Nos. 197, 198, 199; *Hist. Parl.* xxviii. 301-5; *Deux Amis,* x. 368-374.

Societies, in lamentable oratory, summing up his character, parallel him to One, whom they think it honour to call 'the good Sansculotte,'—whom we name not here;[5] also a Chapel may be made, for the urn that holds his Heart, in the Place du Carrousel; and new-born children be named Marat; and Lago-di-Como Hawkers bake mountains of stucco into unbeautiful Busts; and David paint his Picture, or Death-Scene; and such other Apotheosis take place as the human genius, in these circumstances, can devise: but Marat returns no more to the light of this Sun. One sole circumstance we have read with clear sympathy, in the old *Moniteur* Newspaper: how Marat's Brother comes from Neuchâtel to ask of the Convention, 'that the deceased Jean-Paul Marat's musket be given him.'[6] For Marat too had a brother and natural affections; and was wrapped once in swaddling-clothes, and slept safe in a cradle like the rest of us. Ye children of men!—A sister of his, they say, lives still to this day in Paris.

As for Charlotte Corday, her work is accomplished; the recompense of it is near and sure. The *chère amie*, and neighbours of the house, flying at her, she 'overturns some movables,' entrenches herself till the gendarmes arrive; then quietly surrenders; goes quietly to the Abbaye Prison: she alone quiet, all Paris sounding, in wonder, in rage or admiration, round her. Duperret is put in arrest, on account of her; his Papers sealed,—which may lead to consequences. Fauchet, in like manner; though Fauchet had not so much as heard of her. Charlotte, confronted with these two Deputies, praises the great firmness of Duperret, censures the dejection of Fauchet.

On Wednesday morning, the thronged Palais de Justice and Revolutionary Tribunal can see her face; beautiful and calm: she dates it 'fourth day of the Preparation of Peace.' A strange murmur ran through the Hall, at sight of her; you could not say of what character.[7] Tinville has his indictments and tape-papers: the cutler of the Palais Royal will testify that he sold her the sheath-knife; "All these details are needless," interrupted Charlotte; "it is I that killed Marat." By whose instigation?— "By no one's." What tempted you, then? His crimes. "I killed one man," added she, raising her voice extremely (*extrêmement*),

[5] See *Eloge funèbre de Jean-Paul Marat*, prononcé à Strasbourg (in Barbaroux, pp. 125-131); Mercier, &c.

[6] Séance du 16 Septembre 1793.

[7] *Procès de Charlotte Corday*, &c. (*Hist. Parl.* xxviii. 311-338).

as they went on with their questions, "I killed one man to save a hundred thousand; a villain to save innocents; a savage wild-beast to give repose to my country. I was a Republican before the Revolution; I never wanted energy." There is therefore nothing to be said. The public gazes astonished: the hasty limners sketch her features, Charlotte not disapproving: the men of law proceed with their formalities. The doom is Death as a murderess. To her Advocate she gives thanks; in gentle phrase, in high-flown classical spirit. To the Priest they send her she gives thanks; but needs not any shriving, any ghostly or other aid from him.

On this same evening therefore, about half-past seven o'clock, from the gate of the Conciergerie, to a City all on tiptoe, the fatal Cart issues; seated on it a fair young creature, sheeted in red smock of Murderess; so beautiful, serene, so full of life; journeying towards death,—alone amid the World. Many take off their hats, saluting reverently; for what heart but must be touched? [8] Others growl and howl. Adam Lux, of Mentz, declares that she is greater than Brutus; that it were beautiful to die with her: the head of this young man seems turned. At the Place de la Révolution, the countenance of Charlotte wears the same still smile. The executioners proceed to bind her feet; she resists, thinking it meant as an insult; on a word of explanation, she submits with cheerful apology. As the last act, all being now, ready, they take the neckerchief from her neck; a blush of maidenly shame overspreads that fair face and neck; the cheeks were still tinged with it when the executioner lifted the severed head, to show it to the people. 'It is most true,' says Forster, 'that he struck 'the cheek insultingly; for I saw it with my eyes: the Police 'imprisoned him for it.' [9]

In this manner have the Beautifulest and the Squalidest come in collision, and extinguished one another. Jean-Paul Marat and Marie-Anne Charlotte Corday both, suddenly, are no more. 'Day of the Preparation of Peace'? Alas, how were peace possible or preparable, while, for example, the hearts of lovely Maidens, in their convent-stillness, are dreaming not of Love-paradises and the light of Life, but of Codrus'-sacrifices and Death well-earned? That Twenty-five million hearts have got to such temper, this *is* the Anarchy; the soul of it lies in this: whereof not peace can be the embodiment! The death of Marat, whetting old animosities tenfold, will be worse than any life. O ye hapless Two, mutually

[8] *Deux Amis*, x. 374-384.   [9] *Briefwechsel*, i. 508.

extinctive, the Beautiful and the Squalid, sleep ye well,—in the
Mother's bosom that bore you both!

This is the History of Charlotte Corday; most definite, most
complete; angelic-dæmonic: like a Star! Adam Lux goes home,
half-delirious; to pour forth his Apotheosis of her, in paper and
print; to propose that she have a statue with this inscription,
Greater than Brutus. Friends represent his danger; Lux is reckless;
thinks it were beautiful to die with her.

CHAPTER II.

IN CIVIL WAR.

But during these same hours, another guillotine is at work, on
another: Charlotte, for the Girondins, dies at Paris today; Chalier,
by the Girondins, dies at Lyons tomorrow.

From rumbling of cannon along the streets of that City, it has
come to firing of them, to rabid fighting: Nièvre Chol and the
Girondins triumph;—behind whom there is, as everywhere, a
Royalist Faction waiting to strike in. Trouble enough at Lyons;
and the dominant party carrying it with a high hand! For,
indeed, the whole South is astir; incarcerating Jacobins; arming
for Girondins: wherefore we have got a 'Congress of Lyons;' also
a 'Revolutionary Tribunal of Lyons,' and Anarchists shall tremble.
So Chalier was soon found guilty, of Jacobinism, of murderous
Plot, 'address with drawn dagger on the sixth of February last;'
and, on the morrow, he also travels his final road, along the streets
of Lyons, 'by the side of an ecclesiastic, with whom he seems to
speak earnestly,'—the axe now glittering nigh. He could weep, in
old years, this man, and 'fall on his knees on the pavement,'
blessing Heaven at sight of Federation Programs or the like; then
he pilgrimed to Paris, to worship Marat and the Mountain: now
Marat and he are both gone;—we said he could not end well.
Jacobinism groans inwardly, at Lyons; but dare not outwardly.
Chalier, when the Tribunal sentenced him, made answer: "My
death will cost this City dear."

Montélimart Town is not buried under its ruins; yet Marseilles

is actually marching, under order of a 'Lyons Congress;' is incarcerating Patriots; the very Royalists now showing face. Against
which a General Cartaux fights, though in small force; and with
him an Artillery Major, of the name of—Napoleon Buonaparte.
This Napoleon, to prove that the Marseillese have no chance
ultimately, not only fights but writes; publishes his *Supper of
Beaucaire*, a Dialogue which has become curious.[1] Unfortunate
Cities, with their actions and their reactions! Violence to be paid
with violence in geometrical ratio; Royalism and Anarchism both
striking in;—the final net-amount of which geometrical series,
what man shall sum?

The Bar of Iron has never yet floated in Marseilles Harbour;
but the body of Rebecqui was found floating, self-drowned there.
Hot Rebecqui, seeing how confusion deepened, and Respectability
grew poisoned with Royalism, felt that there was no refuge for
a Republican but death. Rebecqui disappeared: no one knew
whither; till, one morning, they found the empty case or body of
him risen to the top, tumbling on the salt waves;[2] and perceived
that Rebecqui had withdrawn forever.—Toulon likewise is incarcerating Patriots; sending delegates to Congress; intriguing, in
case of necessity, with the Royalists and English. Montpellier,
Bourdeaux, Nantes: all France, that is not under the swoop of
Austria and Cimmeria, seems rushing into madness and suicidal
ruin. The Mountain labours; like a volcano in a burning volcanic
Land. Convention Committees, of Surety, of Salvation, are busy
night and day: Convention Commissioners whirl on all highways;
bearing olive-branch and sword, or now perhaps sword only.
Chaumette and Municipals come daily to the Tuileries demanding
a Constitution: it is some weeks now since he resolved, in Townhall, that a Deputation 'should go every day,' and demand a
Constitution, till one were got;[3] whereby suicidal France might
rally and pacify itself; a thing inexpressibly desirable.

This then is the fruit your Antianarchic Girondins have got from
that Levying of War in Calvados? This fruit, we may say; and
no other whatsoever. For indeed, before either Charlotte's or
Chalier's head had fallen, the Calvados War itself had, as it were,
vanished, dreamlike, in a shriek! With 'seventy-two Departments'
on our side, one might have hoped better things. But it turns
out that Respectabilities, though they will vote, will not fight.
Possession always is nine points in Law; but in Lawsuits of *this*

---

[1] See Hazlitt, ii. 529-41.　　　[2] Barbaroux, p. 29.　　　[3] *Deux Amis*, x. 345.

kind, one may say, it is ninety-and-nine points. Men do what they were wont to do; and have immense irresolution and inertia: they obey him who has the symbols that claim obedience. Consider what, in modern society, this one fact means: the Metropolis is with our enemies! Metropolis, *Mother-city ;* rightly so named: all the rest are but as her children, her nurselings. Why, there is not a leathern Diligence, with its post-bags and luggage-boots, that lumbers out from her, but is as a huge life-pulse; she is the heart of all. Cut short that one leathern Diligence, how much is cut short!—General Wimpfen, looking practically into the matter, can see nothing for it but that one should fall back on Royalism; get into communication with Pitt! Dark innuendos he flings out, to that effect: whereat we Girondins start, horrorstruck. He produces as his Second in command a certain '*Ci-devant*,' one Comte Puisaye; entirely unknown to Louvet; greatly suspected by him.

Few wars, accordingly, were ever levied of a more insufficient character than this of Calvados. He that is curious in such things may read the details of it in the Memoirs of that same *Ci-devant* Puisaye, the much-enduring man and Royalist: How our Girondin National forces, marching off with plenty of wind-music, were drawn out about the old Château of Brécourt, in the wood-country near Vernon, to meet the Mountain National forces advancing from Paris. How on the fifteenth afternoon of July, they did meet;— and, as it were, shrieked mutually, and took mutually to flight, without loss. How Puisaye thereafter,—for the Mountain Nationals fled first, and we thought ourselves the victors,—was roused from his warm bed in the Castle of Brécourt; and had to gallop without boots; our Nationals, in the night-watches, having fallen unexpectedly into *sauve-qui-peut :*—and in brief the Calvados War had burnt priming; and the only question now was, Whitherward to vanish, in what hole to hide oneself![4]

The National Volunteers rush homewards, faster than they came. The Seventy-two Respectable Departments, says Meillan, 'all turned round and forsook us, in the space of four-and-twenty hours.' Unhappy those who, as at Lyons for instance, have gone too far for turning! 'One morning,' we find placarded on our Intendance Mansion, the Decree of Convention which casts us *Hors la loi,* into Outlawry; placarded by our Caen Magistrates;—clear hint that we also are to vanish. Vanish indeed: but whitherward? Gorsas has friends in Rennes; he will hide there,—unhappily will

[4] *Mémoires de Puisaye* (London, 1803), ii. 142-67.

not lie hid. Gaudet, Lanjuinais are on cross roads; making for Bourdeaux. To Bourdeaux! cries the general voice, of Valour alike and of Despair. Some flag of Respectability still floats there, or is thought to float.

Thitherward therefore; each as he can! Eleven of these ill-fated Deputies, among whom we may count as twelfth, Friend Riouffe the Man of Letters, do an original thing: Take the uniform of National Volunteers, and retreat southward with the Breton Battalion, as private soldiers of that corps. These brave Bretons had stood truer by us than any other. Nevertheless, at the end of a day or two, they also do now get dubious, self-divided; we must part from them; and, with some half-dozen as convoy or guide, retreat by ourselves,—a solitary marching detachment, through waste regions of the West.[5]

CHAPTER III.

RETREAT OF THE ELEVEN.

It is one of the notablest Retreats, this of the Eleven, that History presents: The handful of forlorn Legislators retreating there, continually, with shouldered firelock and well-filled cartridge-box, in the yellow autumn; long hundreds of miles between them and Bourdeaux; the country all getting hostile, suspicious of the truth; simmering and buzzing on all sides, more and more. Louvet has preserved the Itinerary of it; a piece worth all the rest he ever wrote.

O virtuous Pétion, with thy early-white head, O brave young Barbaroux, has it come to this? Weary ways, worn shoes, light purse;—encompassed with perils as with a sea! Revolutionary Committees are in every Township; of Jacobin temper; our friends all cowed, our cause the losing one. In the Borough of Moncontour, by ill chance, it is market-day: to the gaping public such transit of a solitary Marching Detachment is suspicious; we have need of energy, of promptitude and luck, to be allowed to march through. Hasten, ye weary pilgrims! The country is getting up; noise of you is bruited day after day, a solitary Twelve retreating in

⁵ Louvet, pp. 101-37; Meillan, pp. 81, 241-70.

this mysterious manner: with every new day, a wider wave of inquisitive pursuing tumult is stirred up, till the whole West will be in motion. 'Cussy is tormented with gout, Buzot is too fat for marching.' Riouffe, blistered, bleeding, marches only on tiptoe; Barbaroux limps with sprained ankle, yet ever cheery, full of hope and valour. Light Louvet glances hare-eyed, not hare-hearted: only virtuous Pétion's serenity 'was but once seen ruffled.'[1] They lie in straw-lofts, in woody brakes; rudest paillasse on the floor of a secret friend is luxury. They are seized in the dead of night by Jacobin mayors and tap of drum; get off by firm countenance, rattle of muskets and ready wit.

Of Bourdeaux, through fiery La Vendée and the long geographical spaces that remain, it were madness to think: well if you can get to Quimper on the sea-coast, and take shipping there. Faster, ever faster! Before the end of the march, so hot has the country grown, it is found advisable to march all night. They do it; under the still night-canopy they plod along;—and yet behold, Rumour has outplodded them. In the paltry Village of Carhaix (be its thatched huts and bottomless peat-bogs long notable to the Traveller), one is astonished to find light still glimmering: citizens are awake, with rushlights burning, in that nook of the terrestrial Planet; as we traverse swiftly the one poor street, a voice is heard saying, "There they are, *Les voilà qui passent !* "[2] Swifter, ye doomed lame Twelve: speed ere they can arm; gain the Woods of Quimper before day, and lie squatted there!

The doomed Twelve do it; though with difficulty, with loss of road, with peril and the mistakes of a night. In Quimper are Girondin friends, who perhaps will harbour the homeless, till a Bourdeaux ship weigh. Wayworn, heartworn, in agony of suspense, till Quimper friendship get warning, they lie there, squatted under the thick wet boscage; suspicious of the face of man. Some pity to the brave; to the unhappy! Unhappiest of all Legislators, O when ye packed your luggage, some score or two-score months ago, and mounted this or the other leathern vehicle, to be Conscript Fathers of a regenerated France, and reap deathless laurels,—did you think your journey was to lead *hither?* The Quimper Samaritans find them squatted; lift them up to help and comfort; will hide them in sure places. Thence let them dissipate gradually; or there they can lie quiet, and write *Memoirs*, till a Bourdeaux ship sail.

<hr>

[1] Meillan, pp. 119-137.   [2] Louvet, pp. 138-164.

And thus, in Calvados all is dissipated; Romme is out of prison, meditating his Calendar; ringleaders are locked in his room. At Caen the Corday family mourns in silence: Buzot's House is a heap of dust and demolition; and amid the rubbish sticks a Gallows, with this inscription, *Here dwelt the Traitor Buzot, who conspired against the Republic.* Buzot and the other vanished Deputies are *hors la loi,* as we saw; their lives free to take where they can be found. The worse fares it with the poor Arrested visible Deputies at Paris. 'Arrestment at home' threatens to become 'Confinement in the Luxembourg;' to end: *where?* For example, what pale-visaged thin man is this, journeying towards Switzerland as a Merchant of Neuchâtel, whom they arrest in the town of Moulins? To Revolutionary Committee he is suspect. To Revolutionary Committee, on probing the matter, he is evidently: Deputy Brissot! Back to thy Arrestment, poor Brissot; or indeed to strait confinement,—whither others are fated to follow. Rabaut has built himself a false-partition, in a friend's house; lives, in invisible darkness, between two walls. It will end, this same Arrestment business, in Prison, and the Revolutionary Tribunal.

Nor must we forget Duperret, and the seal put on his papers by reason of Charlotte. One Paper is there, fit to breed woe enough : A secret solemn Protest against that *suprema dies* of the Second of June! This Secret Protest our poor Duperret had drawn up, the same week, in all plainness of speech; waiting the time for publishing it: to which Secret Protest his signature, and that of other honourable Deputies not a few, stands legibly appended. And now, if the seals were once broken, the Mountain still victorious? Such Protesters, your Merciers, Bailleuls, Seventy-three by the tale, what yet remains of Respectable Girondism in the Convention, may tremble to think!—These are the fruits of levying civil war.

Also we find, that in these last days of July, the famed Siege of Mentz is *finished:* the Garrison to march out with honours of war; not to serve against the Coalition for a year. Lovers of the Picturesque, and Goethe standing on the Chaussée of Mentz, saw, with due interest, the Procession issuing forth, in all solemnity :

'Escorted by Prussian horse came first the French Garrison. 'Nothing could look stranger than this latter; a column of Mar- 'seillese, slight, swarthy, parti-coloured, in patched clothes, came 'tripping on;—as if King Edwin had opened the Dwarf Hill, and 'sent out his nimble Host of Dwarfs. Next followed regular 'troops; serious, sullen; not as if downcast or ashamed. But the

'remarkablest appearance, which struck every one, was that of the
'Chasers (*Chasseurs*) coming out mounted: they had advanced
'quite silent to where we stood, when their Band struck up the
'*Marseillaise.* This revolutionary *Te-Deum* has in itself something
mournful and bodeful, however briskly played; but at present
'they gave it in altogether slow time, proportionate to the creeping
'step they rode at. It was piercing and fearful, and a most serious-
'looking thing, as these cavaliers, long, lean men, of a certain age,
'with mien suitable to the music, came pacing on: singly you
'might have likened them to Don Quixote; in mass, they were
'highly dignified.

   'But now a single troop became notable: that of the Commis-
'sioners or *Représentans.* Merlin of Thionville, in hussar uniform,
'distinguishing himself by wild beard and look, had another person
'in similar costume on his left; the crowd shouted out, with rage,
'at sight of this latter, the name of a Jacobin Townsman and
'Clubbist; and shook itself to seize him. Merlin drew bridle;
'referred to his dignity as French Representative, to the vengeance
'that should follow any injury done; he would advise every one to
'compose himself, for this was not the *last time* they would see
'him here.'[3] Thus rode Merlin; threatening in defeat. But
what now shall stem that tide of Prussians setting-in through
the opened Northeast? Lucky if fortified Lines of Weissembourg, and impassabilities of Vosges Mountains confine it to
French Alsace, keep it from submerging the very heart of the
country!

   Furthermore, precisely in the same days, Valenciennes Siege is
finished, in the Northwest:—fallen, under the red hail of York!
Condé fell some fortnight since. Cimmerian Coalition presses on.
What seems very notable too, on all these captured French Towns
there flies not the Royalist fleur-de-lys, in the name of a new Louis
the Pretender; but the Austrian flag flies; as if Austria meant to
keep them for herself! Perhaps General Custine, still in Paris,
can give some explanation of the fall of these strong-places?
Mother Society, from tribune and gallery, growls loud that he
ought to do it;—remarks, however, in a splenetic manner that
'the *Monsieurs* of the Palais Royal' are calling Long-life to this
General.

   The Mother Society, purged now, by successive 'scrutinies or
épurations,' from all taint of Girondism, has become a great

   [3] *Belagerung von Mainz* (Goethe's *Works*, xxx. 315).

Authority: what we can call shield-bearer or bottle-holder, nay call it fugleman, to the purged National Convention itself. The Jacobins Debates are reported in the *Moniteur*, like Parliamentary ones.

CHAPTER IV.

O NATURE.

BUT looking more specially into Paris City, what is this that History, on the 10th of August, Year One of Liberty, 'by old-style, year 1793,' discerns there? Praised be the Heavens, a new Feast of Pikes!

For Chaumette's 'Deputation every day' has worked out its result: a Constitution. It was one of the rapidest Constitutions ever put together; made, some say in eight days, by Hérault Séchelles and others; probably a workmanlike, roadworthy Constitution enough;—on which point, however, we are, for some reasons, little called to form a judgment. Workmanlike or not, the Forty-four Thousand Communes of France, by overwhelming majorities, did hasten to accept it; glad of any Constitution whatsoever. Nay Departmental Deputies have come, the venerablest Republicans of each Department, with solemn message of Acceptance; and now what remains but that our new Final Constitution be proclaimed, and sworn to, in Feast of Pikes? The Departmental Deputies, we say, are come some time ago; Chaumette very anxious about them, lest Girondin *Monsieurs*, Agio-jobbers, or were it even *Filles de joie* of a Girondin temper, corrupt their morals.[1] Tenth of August, immortal Anniversary, greater almost than Bastille July, is the Day.

Painter David has not been idle. Thanks to David and the French genius, there steps forth into the sunlight, this day, a Scenic Phantasmagory unexampled:—whereof History, so occupied with Real Phantasmagories, will say but little.

For one thing, History can notice with satisfaction, on the ruins of the Bastille, a *Statue of Nature*; gigantic, spouting water from

[1] *Deux Amis*, xi. 73.

her two *mammelles*. Not a Dream this; but a fact, palpable visible. There she spouts, great Nature; dim, before daybreak. But as the coming Sun ruddies the East, come countless Multitudes, regulated and unregulated; come Departmental Deputies, come Mother Society and Daughters; comes National Convention, led on by handsome Hérault; soft wind-music breathing note of expectation. Lo, as great Sol scatters his first fire-handful, tipping the hills and chimney-heads with gold, Hérault is at great Nature's feet (she is plaster-of-paris merely); Hérault lifts, in an iron saucer, water spouted from the sacred breasts; drinks of it, with an eloquent Pagan Prayer, beginning, "O Nature!" and all the Departmental Deputies drink, each with what best suitable ejaculation or prophetic-utterance is in him;—amid breathings, which become blasts, of wind-music; and the roar of artillery and human throats : finishing well the first act of this solemnity.

Next are processionings along the Boulevards: Deputies or Officials bound together by long indivisible tricolor riband; general 'members of the Sovereign' walking pell-mell, with pikes, with hammers, with the tools and emblems of their crafts; among which we notice a Plough, and ancient Baucis and Philemon seated on it, drawn by their children. Many-voiced harmony and dissonance filling the air. Through Triumphal Arches enough: at the basis of the first of which, we descry — whom thinkest thou ? — the Heroines of the Insurrection of Women. Strong Dames of the Market, they sit there (Théroigne too ill to attend, one fears), with oak-branches, tricolor bedizenment; firm seated on their Cannons. To whom handsome Hérault, making pause of admiration, addresses soothing eloquence; whereupon they rise and fall into the march.

And now mark, in the Place de la Révolution, what other august Statue may this be; veiled in canvas,—which swiftly we shear off, by pulley and cord? The *Statue of Liberty !* She too is of plaster, hoping to become of metal; stands where a Tyrant Louis Quinze once stood. 'Three thousand birds' are let loose, into the whole world, with labels round their neck, *We are free; imitate us.* Holocaust of Royalist and *ci-devant* trumpery, such as one could still gather, is burnt; pontifical eloquence must be uttered, by handsome Hérault, and Pagan orisons offered up.

And then forward across the River; where is new enormous Statuary; enormous plaster Mountain; Hercules-*Peuple*, with uplifted all-conquering club; 'many-headed Dragon of Girondin Federalism rising from fetid marsh :'—needing new eloquence from

O NATURE.   131

Hérault.   To say nothing of Champ-de-Mars, and Fatherland's
Altar there; with urn of slain Defenders, Carpenter's-level of the
Law; and such exploding, gesticulating and perorating, that
Hérault's lips must be growing white, and his tongue cleaving to
the roof of his mouth.[2]

Towards six o'clock let the wearied President, let Paris Patriotism
generally sit down to what repast, and social repasts, can be had;
and with flowing tankard or light-mantling glass, usher in this
New and Newest Era. In fact, is not Romme's New Calendar
getting ready ? On all house-tops flicker little tricolor Flags, their
flagstaff a Pike and Liberty-Cap. On all house-walls,—for no
Patriot not suspect will be behind another,—there stand printed
these words: *Republic one and indivisible; Liberty, Equality,
Fraternity, or Death.*

As to the New Calendar, we may say here rather than elsewhere
that speculative men have long been struck with the inequalities
and incongruities of the Old Calendar; that a New one has long
been as good as determined on. Maréchal the Atheist, almost ten
years ago, proposed a New Calendar, free at least from superstition: this the Paris Municipality would now adopt, in defect of a
better; at all events, let us have either this of Maréchal's or a
better,—the New Era being come. Petitions, more than once,
have been sent to that effect; and indeed, for a year past, all
Public Bodies, Journalists, and Patriots in general, have dated
First Year of the Republic. It is a subject not without difficulties.
But the Convention has taken it up; and Romme, as we say, has
been meditating it; not Maréchal's New Calendar, but a better
New one of Romme's and our own. Romme, aided by a Monge,
a Lagrange and others, furnishes mathematics; Fabre d'Eglantine
furnishes poetic nomenclature: and so, on the 5th of October 1793,
after trouble enough, they bring forth this New Republican
Calendar of theirs, in a complete state; and by Law get it put in
action.

Four equal Seasons, Twelve equal Months of Thirty days each;
this makes three hundred and sixty days; and five odd days
remain to be disposed of. The five odd days we will make
Festivals, and name the five *Sansculottides,* or Days without
Breeches. Festival of Genius; Festival of Labour; of Actions;
of Rewards; of Opinion : these are the five Sansculottides.

_____

[2] *Choix des Rapports,* xii. 432-42.

K 2

Whereby the great Circle, or Year, is made complete: solely every fourth year, whilom called Leap-year, we introduce a sixth Sansculottide; and name it Festival of the Revolution. Now as to the day of commencement, which offers difficulties, is it not one of the luckiest coincidences that the Republic herself commenced on the 21st of September; close on the Autumnal Equinox? Autumnal Equinox, at midnight for the meridian of Paris, in the year whilom Christian 1792, from that moment shall the New Era reckon itself to begin. *Vendémiaire, Brumaire, Frimaire;* or as one might say, in mixed English, *Vintagearious, Fogarious, Frostarious:* these are our three Autumn months. *Nivose, Pluviose, Ventose,* or say, *Snowous, Rainous, Windous,* make our Winter season. *Germinal, Floréal, Prairial,* or *Buddal, Floweral, Meadowal,* are our Spring season. *Messidor, Thermidor, Fructidor,* that is to say (*dor* being Greek for *gift*), *Reapidor, Heatidor, Fruitidor,* are Republican Summer. These Twelve, in a singular manner, divide the Republican Year. Then as to minuter subdivisions, let us venture at once on a bold stroke: adopt your decimal subdivision; and instead of the world-old Week, or *Se'ennight,* make it a *Tennight,* or *Décade;*—not without results. There are three Decades, then, in each of the months, which is very regular; and the *Décadi,* or Tenth-day, shall always be the 'Day of Rest.' And the Christian Sabbath, in that case? Shall shift for itself!

This, in brief, is the New Calendar of Romme and the Convention; calculated for the meridian of Paris, and Gospel of Jean Jacques: not one of the least afflicting occurrences for the actual British reader of French History;—confusing the soul with *Messidors, Meadowals;* till at last, in self-defence, one is forced to construct some ground-scheme, or rule of Commutation from Newstyle to Old-style, and have it lying by him. Such ground-scheme, almost worn out in our service, but still legible and printable, we shall now in a Note, present to the reader. For the Romme Calendar, in so many Newspapers, Memoirs, Public Acts, has stamped itself deep into that section of Time: a New Era that lasts some Twelve years and odd is not to be despised.[3] Let the Reader, therefore, with such ground-scheme, help himself, where needful, out of New-style into Old-style, called also 'slave-style, *stile-esclave;*'—whereof we, in these pages, shall as much as possible use the latter only.

Thus with new Feast of Pikes, and New Era or New Calendar,

[3] For footnote see opposite page.

did France accept her New Constitution: the most Democratic Constitution ever committed to paper. How it will work in practice? Patriot Deputations, from time to time, solicit fruition of it; that it be set a-going. Always, however, this seems questionable; for the moment, unsuitable. Till, in some weeks, *Salut Public,* through the organ of Saint-Just, makes report, that, in the present alarming circumstances, the state of France is Revolutionary; that her 'Government must be Revolutionary till the Peace.' Solely as Paper, then, and as a Hope, must this poor new Constitution exist;—in which shape we may conceive it lying, even now, with an infinity of other things, in that Limbo near the Moon. Farther than paper it never got, nor ever will get.

[3] September 22d of 1792 is Vendémiaire 1st of Year One, and the new months are all of 30 days each; therefore:

		ADD			DAYS
	Vendémiaire . .	21		September . .	30
	Brumaire . . .	21		October . . .	31
To the number of the day in	Frimaire . . .	20	We have the number of the day in	November. . .	30
	Nivose . . .	20		December . . .	31
	Pluviose . . .	19		January . . .	31
	Ventose . . .	18		February . . .	28
	Germinal . . .	20		March . . .	31
	Floréal . . .	19		April. . . .	30
	Prairial . . .	19		May . . .	31
	Messidor . . .	18		June. . . .	30
	Thermidor . .	18		July	31
	Fructidor . . .	17		August . . .	31

There are 5 Sansculottides, and in leap-year a sixth, to be added at the end of Fructidor. Romme's first Leap-year is "*An* 4" (1795, not 1796), which is another troublesome circumstance, every fourth year, from 'September 23d' round to 'February 29' again.

The New Calendar ceased on the 1st of January 1806. See *Choix des Rapports,* xiii. 83-99; xix. 199.

CHAPTER V.

SWORD OF SHARPNESS.

In fact, it is something quite other than paper theorems, it is iron and audacity that France now needs.

Is not La Vendée still blazing; — alas too literally; rogue Rossignol burning the very corn-mills? General Santerre could do nothing there; General Rossignol, in blind fury, often in liquor, can do less than nothing. Rebellion spreads, grows ever madder. Happily those lean Quixote-figures, whom we saw retreating out of Mentz, 'bound not to serve against the Coalition for a year,' have got to Paris. National Convention packs them into post-vehicles and conveyances; sends them swiftly, by post, into La Vendée. There valiantly struggling, in obscure battle and skirmish, under rogue Rossignol, let them, unlaureled, save the Republic, and 'be cut down gradually to the last man.' [1]

Does not the Coalition, like a fire-tide, pour in; Prussia through the opened Northeast; Austria, England through the Northwest? General Houchard prospers no better there than General Custine did: let him look to it! Through the Eastern and the Western Pyrenees Spain has deployed itself; spreads, rustling with Bourbon banners, over the face of the South. Ashes and embers of confused Girondin civil war covered that region already. Marseilles is damped down, not quenched; to be quenched in blood. Toulon, terror-struck, too far gone for turning, has flung itself, ye righteous Powers, into the hands of the English! On Toulon Arsenal there flies a flag, — nay not even the Fleur-de-lys of a Louis Pretender; there flies that accursed St. George's Cross of the English and Admiral Hood! What remnant of sea-craft, arsenals, roperies, war-navy France had, has given itself to these enemies of human nature, '*ennemis du genre humain*.' Beleaguer it, bombard it, ye Commissioners Barras, Fréron, Robespierre Junior; thou General Cartaux, General Dugommier; above all, thou remarkable Artillery-

---

[1] *Deux Amis*, xi. 147; xiii. 160-92, &c.

Major, Napoleon Buonaparte! Hood is fortifying himself, victualling himself; means, apparently, to make a new Gibraltar of it.

But lo, in the Antumn night, late night, among the last of August, what sudden red sunblaze is this that has risen over Lyons City; with a noise to deafen the world? It is the Powder-tower of Lyons, nay the Arsenal with four Powder-towers, which has caught fire in the Bombardment; and sprung into the air, carrying 'a hundred and seventeen houses' after it. With a light, one fancies, as of the noon sun; with a roar second only to the Last Trumpet! All living sleepers far and wide it has awakened. What a sight was that, which the eye of History saw, in the sudden nocturnal sunblaze! The roofs of hapless Lyons, and all its domes and steeples made momentarily clear; Rhone and Soane streams flashing suddenly visible; and height and hollow, hamlet and smooth stubblefield, and all the region round;—heights, alas, all scarped and counter-scarped, into trenches, curtains, redoubts; blue Artillerymen, little Powder-devilkins, plying their hell-trade there through the *not* ambrosial night! Let the darkness cover it again; for it pains the eye. Of a truth, Chalier's death is costing the City dear. Convention Commissioners, Lyons Congresses have come and gone; and action there was and reaction; bad ever growing worse; till it has come to this; Commissioner Dubois-Crancé, 'with seventy-thousand men, and all the Artillery of several Provinces,' bombarding Lyons day and night.

Worse things still are in store. Famine is in Lyons, and ruin and fire. Desperate are the sallies of the besieged; brave Précy, their National Colonel and Commandant, doing what is in man: desperate but ineffectual. Provisions cut off; nothing entering our city but shot and shells! The Arsenal has roared aloft; the very Hospital will be battered down, and the sick buried alive. A black Flag hung on this latter noble Edifice, appealing to the pity of the besiegers; for though maddened, were they not still our brethren? In their blind wrath, they took it for a flag of defiance, and aimed thitherward the more. Bad is growing ever worse here: and how will the worse stop, till it have grown worst of all? Commissioner Dubois will listen to no pleading, to no speech, save this only, We surrender at discretion. Lyons contains in it subdued Jacobins; dominant Girondins; secret Royalists. And now, mere deaf madness and cannon-shot enveloping them, will not the desperate Municipality fly, at last, into the arms of Royalism itself?

Majesty of Sardinia was to bring help, but it failed. Emigrant
d'Autichamp, in name of the Two Pretender Royal Highnesses,
is coming through Switzerland with help; coming, not yet come:
Précy hoists the Fleur-de-lys!

At sight of which all true Girondins sorrowfully fling down their
arms :—Let our Tricolor brethren storm us, then, and slay us in
their wrath; with *you* we conquer not. The famishing women
and children are sent forth : deaf Dubois sends them back ;—rains
in mere fire and madness. Our 'redoubts of cotton-bags' are
taken, retaken; Précy under his Fleur-de-lys is valiant as Despair.
What will become of Lyons? It is a siege of seventy days.[2]

Or see, in these same weeks, far in the Western waters: breast-
ing through the Bay of Biscay, a greasy dingy little Merchant-ship,
with Scotch skipper ; under hatches whereof sit, disconsolate,—
the last forlorn nucleus of Girondism, the Deputies from Quimper!
Several have dissipated themselves, whithersoever they could.
Poor Riouffe fell into the talons of Revolutionary Committee and
Paris Prison. The rest sit here under hatches; reverend Pétion
with his gray hair, angry Buzot, suspicious Louvet, brave young
Barbaroux, and others. They have escaped from Quimper, in this
sad craft; are now tacking and struggling; in danger from the
waves, in danger from the English, in still worse danger from the
French ;—banished by Heaven and Earth to the greasy belly of
this Scotch skipper's Merchant-vessel, unfruitful Atlantic raving
round. They are for Bourdeaux, if peradventure hope yet linger
there. Enter not Bourdeaux, O Friends! Bloody Convention
Representatives, Tallien and suchlike, with their Edicts, with their
Guillotine, have arrived there ; Respectability is driven under
ground: Jacobinism lords it on high. From that Réole landing-
place, or *Beak of Ambès*, as it were, pale Death, waving his Revolutionary Sword of Sharpness, waves you elsewhither!

On one side or the other of that Bec d'Ambès, the Scotch
Skipper with difficulty moors, a dexterous greasy man; with
difficulty lands his Girondins ;—who, after reconnoitering, must
rapidly burrow in the Earth ; and so, in subterranean ways, in
friends' back-closets, in cellars, barn-lofts, in caves of Saint-
Emilion and Libourne, stave-off cruel Death.[3] Unhappiest of all
Senators!

[2] *Deux Amis*, xi. 80-143.   [3] Louvet, pp. 180-199.

CHAPTER VI.

RISEN AGAINST TYRANTS.

AGAINST all which incalculable impediments, horrors and dis-asters, what can a Jacobin Convention oppose ? The uncalculating Spirit of Jacobinism, and Sansculottic sansformulistic Frenzy ! Our Enemies press-in on us, says Danton, but they shall not conquer us, " we will burn France to ashes rather, *nous brûlerons la France.*"

Committees, of *Sureté*, of *Salut*, have raised themselves ' *à la hauteur*, to the height of circumstances.' Let all mortals raise themselves *à la hauteur*. Let the Forty-four thousand Sections and their Revolutionary Committees stir every fibre of the Re-public; and every Frenchman feel that he is to do or die. They are the life-circulation of Jacobinism, these Sections and Com-mittees : Danton, through the organ of Barrère and *Salut Public*, gets decreed, That there be in Paris, by law, two meetings of Section weekly ; also that the Poorer Citizen be *paid* for attending, and have his day's-wages of Forty Sous.[1] This is the celebrated ' Law of the Forty Sous ; ' fiercely stimulant to Sansculottism, to the life-circulation of Jacobinism.

On the twenty-third of August, Committee of Public Salvation, as usual through Barrère, had promulgated, in words not unworthy of remembering, their Report, which is soon made into a Law, of *Levy in Mass*. ' All France, and whatsoever it contains of men or resources, is put under requisition,' says Barrère ; really in Tyrtæan words, the best we know of his. 'The Republic is one vast be-sieged city.' Two-hundred and fifty Forges shall, in these days, be set up in the Luxembourg Garden, and round the outer wall of the Tuileries ; to make gun-barrels; in sight of Earth and Heaven ! From all hamlets, towards their Departmental Town ; from all Departmental Towns, towards the appointed Camp and seat of war, the Sons of Freedom shall march ; their banner is to bear : ' *Le Peuple Français debout contre les Tyrans*, The French People

[1] *Moniteur*, Séance du 5 Septembre 1793.

'risen against Tyrants. The young men shall go to the battle; it
'is their task to conquer: the married men shall forge arms, trans-
'port baggage and artillery; provide subsistence: the women shall
'work at soldiers' clothes, make tents; serve in the hospitals: the
'children shall scrape old-linen into surgeon's-lint: the aged men
'shall have themselves carried into public places; and there, by
'their words, excite the courage of the young; preach hatred to
'Kings and unity to the Republic.'[2] Tyrtæan words; which tingle
through all French hearts.

In this humour, then, since no other serves, will France rush
against its enemies. Headlong, reckoning no cost or consequence;
heeding no law or rule but that supreme law, Salvation of the
People! The weapons are, all the iron that is in France; the
strength is, that of all the men, women and children that are in
France. There, in their two-hundred and fifty shed-smithies, in
Garden of Luxembourg or Tuileries, let them forge gun-barrels, in
sight of Heaven and Earth.

Nor with heroic daring against the Foreign foe, can black
vengeance against the Domestic be wanting. Life-circulation of
the Revolutionary Committees being quickened by that *Law of
the Forty Sous*, Deputy Merlin,—not the Thionviller, whom we saw
ride out of Mentz, but Merlin of Douai, named subsequently
Merlin *Suspect*,—comes, about a week after, with his world-famous
Law of the Suspect: ordering all Sections, by their Committees,
instantly to arrest all Persons Suspect; and explaining withal who
the Arrestable and Suspect specially are. 'Are suspect,' says he,
'all who by their actions, by their connexions, speakings, writings
'have'—in short become Suspect.[3] Nay Chaumette, illuminating
the matter still farther, in his Municipal Placards and Proclamations, will bring it about that you may almost recognise a Suspect
on the streets, and clutch him there,—off to Committee and Prison.
Watch well your words, watch well your looks: if Suspect of
nothing else, you may grow, as came to be a saying, 'Suspect of
being Suspect'! For are we not in a state of Revolution?

No frightfuler Law ever ruled in a Nation of men. All Prisons
and Houses of Arrest in French land are getting crowded to the
ridge-tile: Forty-four thousand Committees, like as many companies of reapers or gleaners, gleaning France, are gathering their

[2] *Débats*, Séance du 23 Août 1793.
[3] *Moniteur*, Séance du 17 Septembre 1793.

harvest, and storing it in these Houses. Harvest of Aristocrat tares ! Nay, lest the Forty-four thousand, each on its own harvest-field, prove insufficient, we are to have an ambulant ' Revolutionary Army :' six-thousand strong, under right captains, this shall per-ambulate the country at large, and strike-in wherever it finds such harvest-work slack. So have Municipality and Mother Society petitioned ; so has Convention decreed.[4] Let Aristocrats, Feder-alists, Monsieurs vanish, and all men tremble : ' the Soil of Liberty shall be purged,'—with a vengeance !

Neither hitherto has the Revolutionary Tribunal been keeping holiday. Blanchelande, for losing Saint-Domingo ; ' Conspirators of Orléans,' for 'assassinating,' for assaulting the sacred Deputy Léonard-Bourdon : these with many Nameless, to whom life was sweet, have died. Daily the great Guillotine has its due. Like a black Spectre, daily at eventide glides the Death-tumbril through the variegated throng of things. The variegated street shudders at it, for the moment ; next moment forgets it : The Aristocrats ! They were guilty against the Republic ; their death, were it only that their goods are confiscated, will be useful to the Republic ; *Vive la République !*

In the last days of August fell a notabler head : General Custine's. Custine was accused of harshness, of unskilfulness, perfidiousness ; accused of many things : found guilty, we may say, of one thing, unsuccessfulness. Hearing his unexpected Sentence, ' Custine fell down before the Crucifix,' silent for the space of two hours : he fared, with moist eyes and a look of prayer, towards the Place de la Révolution ; glanced upwards at the clear suspended axe ; then mounted swiftly aloft,[5] swiftly was struck away from the lists of the Living. He had fought in America ; he was a proud, brave man ; and his fortune led him *hither.*

On the 2d of this same month, at three in the morning, a vehicle rolled off, with closed blinds, from the Temple to the Con-ciergerie. Within it were two Municipals ; and Marie-Antoinette, once Queen of France ! There in that Conciergerie, in ignominious dreary cell, she, secluded from children, kindred, friend and hope, sits long weeks ; expecting when the end will be.[6]

The Guillotine, we find, gets always a quicker motion, as other

[4] *Moniteur*, Séances du 5, 9, 11 Septembre.
[5] *Deux Amis*, xi. 148-188.
[6] See *Mémoires particuliers de la Captivité à la Tour du Temple* (by the Duchesse d'Angoulême, Paris, 21 Janvier 1817).

things are quickening. The Guillotine, by its speed of going, will give index of the general velocity of the Republic. The clanking of its huge axe, rising and falling there, in horrid systole-diastole, is portion of the whole enormous life-movement and pulsation of the Sansculottic System!—'Orléans Conspirators' and Assaulters had to die, in spite of much weeping and entreating; so sacred is the person of a Deputy. Yet the sacred can become desecrated: your very Deputy is not greater than the Guillotine. Poor Deputy Journalist Gorsas: we saw him hide at Rennes, when the Calvados War burnt priming. He stole, afterwards, in August, to Paris; lurked several weeks about the Palais ci-devant Royal; was seen there, one day; was clutched, identified, and without ceremony, being already 'out of the Law,' was sent to the Place de la Révolution. He died, recommending his wife and children to the pity of the Republic. It is the ninth day of October 1793. Gorsas is the first Deputy that dies on the scaffold; he will not be the last.

Ex-Mayor Bailly is in Prison; Ex-Procureur Manuel. Brissot and our poor Arrested Girondins have become Incarcerated In-dicted Girondins; universal Jacobinism clamouring for their punishment. Duperret's Seals are *broken!* Those Seventy-three Secret Protesters, suddenly one day, are reported upon, are decreed accused; the Convention-doors being 'previously shut,' that none implicated might escape. They were marched, in a very rough manner, to Prison that evening. Happy those of them who chanced to be absent! Condorcet has vanished into darkness; perhaps, like Rabaut, sits between two walls, in the house of a friend.

CHAPTER VII.

MARIE-ANTOINETTE.

ON Monday the Fourteenth of October 1793, a Cause is pending
in the Palais de Justice, in the new Revolutionary Court, such as
those old stone-walls never witnessed: the Trial of Marie-
Antoinette. The once brightest of Queens, now tarnished, defaced,
forsaken, stands here at Fouquier-Tinville's Judgment-bar; answering for her life. The Indictment was delivered her last
night.[1] To such changes of human fortune what words are
adequate? Silence alone is adequate.

There are few Printed things one meets with of such tragic,
almost ghastly, significance as those bald Pages of the *Bulletin du
Tribunal Révolutionnaire*, which bear title, *Trial of the Widow
Capet*. Dim, dim, as if in disastrous eclipse; like the pale
kingdoms of Dis! Plutonic Judges, Plutonic Tinville; encircled,
nine times, with Styx and Lethe, with Fire-Phlegethon and
Cocytus named of Lamentation! The very witnesses summoned
are like Ghosts: exculpatory, inculpatory, they themselves are all
hovering over death and doom; they are known, in our imagination, as the prey of the Guillotine. Tall *ci-devant* Count d'Estaing,
anxious to show himself Patriot, cannot escape; nor Bailly, who,
when asked If he knows the Accused, answers with a reverent
inclination towards her, "Ah, yes, I know Madame." Ex-Patriots
are here, sharply dealt with, as Procureur Manuel; Ex-Ministers,
shorn of their splendour. We have cold Aristocratic impassivity
faithful to itself even in Tartarus; rabid stupidity, of Patriot
Corporals, Patriot Washerwomen, who have much to say of Plots,
Treasons, August Tenth, old Insurrection of Women. For all now
has become a crime in her who has *lost*.

Marie-Antoinette, in this her utter abandonment, and hour
of extreme need, is not wanting to herself, the imperial woman.
Her look, they say, as that hideous Indictment was reading,
continued calm; 'she was sometimes observed moving her fingers,

[1] *Procès de la Reine (Deux Amis*, xi. 251-381).

as when one plays on the piano.' You discern, not without
interest, across that dim Revolutionary Bulletin itself, how she
bears herself queenlike. Her answers are prompt, clear, often of
Laconic brevity; resolution, which has grown contemptuous without ceasing to be dignified, veils itself in calm words. "You
persist, then, in denial?"—"My plan is not denial: it is the
truth I have said, and I persist in that." Scandalous Hébert has
borne his testimony as to many things: as to one thing, concerning
Marie-Antoinette and her little Son,—wherewith Human Speech
had better not farther be soiled. She has answered Hébert; a
Juryman begs to observe that she has not answered as to *this*.
"I have not answered," she exclaims with noble emotion, "because
Nature refuses to answer such a charge brought against a Mother.
I appeal to all the Mothers that are here." Robespierre, when
he heard of it, broke out into something almost like swearing at
the brutish blockheadism of this Hebért;[2] on whose foul head
his foul lie has recoiled. At four o'clock on Wednesday morning,
after two days and two nights of interrogating, jury-charging, and
other darkening of counsel, the result comes out: sentence of
Death. "Have you anything to say?" The Accused shook her
head, without speech. Night's candles are burning out; and
with her too Time is finishing, and it will be Eternity and Day.
This Hall of Tinville's is dark, ill-lighted except where she stands.
Silently she withdraws from it, to die.

Two Processions, or Royal Progresses, three-and-twenty years
apart, have often struck us with a strange feeling of contrast.
The first is of a beautiful Archduchess and Dauphiness, quitting
her Mother's City, at the age of Fifteen; towards hopes such as
no other Daughter of Eve then had: 'On the morrow,' says Weber,
an eye-witness, 'the Dauphiness left Vienna. The whole city
'crowded out; at first with a sorrow which was silent. She
'appeared: you saw her sunk back into her carriage; her face
'bathed in tears; hiding her eyes now with her handkerchief,
'now with her hands; several times putting out her head to see
'yet again this Palace of her Fathers, whither she was to return
'no more. She motioned her regret, her gratitude to the good
'Nation, which was crowding here to bid her farewell. Then
'arose not only tears; but piercing cries, on all sides. Men and
'women alike abandoned themselves to such expression of their

---

[2] Villate, *Causes secrètes de la Révolution de Thermidor* (Paris, 1825),
p. 179.

'sorrow. It was an audible sound of wail, in the streets and
'avenues of Vienna. The last Courier that followed her dis-
'appeared, and the crowd melted away.'[3]

The young imperial Maiden of Fifteen has now become a worn
discrowned Widow of Thirty-eight; gray before her time : this is
the last Procession : 'Few minutes after the Trial ended, the
'drums were beating to arms in all Sections; at sunrise the armed
'force was on foot, cannons getting placed at the extremities of
'the Bridges, in the Squares, Crossways, all along from the Palais
'de Justice to the Place de la Révolution. By ten o'clock,
'numerous patrols were circulating in the Streets; thirty thousand
'foot and horse drawn up under arms. At eleven, Marie-Antoinette
'was brought out. She had on an undress of *piqué blanc* : she was
'led to the place of execution, in the same manner as an ordinary
'criminal; bound, on a Cart; accompanied by a Constitutional
'Priest in Lay dress; escorted by numerous detachments of
'infantry and cavalry. These, and the double row of troops all
'along her road, she appeared to regard with indifference. On
'her countenance there was visible neither abashment nor pride.
'To the cries of *Vive la Republique* and *Down with Tyranny*,
'which attended her all the way, she seemed to pay no heed.
'She spoke little to her Confessor. The tricolor Streamers on the
'housetops occupied her attention, in the Streets du Roule and
'Saint-Honoré; she also noticed the Inscriptions on the house-
'fronts. On reaching the Place de la Révolution, her looks turned
'towards the *Jardin National*, whilom Tuileries; her face at that
'moment gave signs of lively emotion. She mounted the Scaffold
'with courage enough; at a quarter past Twelve, her head fell;
'the Executioner showed it to the people, amid universal long-
'continued cries of *Vive la Republique.*'

[3] Weber, i. 6.   [4] *Deux Amis*, xi. 301.

CHAPTER VIII.

THE TWENTY-TWO.

WHOM next, O Tinville! The next are of a different colour: our poor Arrested Girondin Deputies. What of them could still be laid hold of; our Vergniaud, Brissot, Fauchet, Valazé, Gensonné; the once flower of French Patriotism, Twenty-two by the tale: *hither*, at Tinville's Bar, onward from 'safeguard of the French People,' from confinement in the Luxembourg, imprisonment in the Conciergerie, have they now, by the course of things, arrived. Fouquier-Tinville must give what account of them he can.

Undoubtedly this Trial of the Girondins is the greatest that Fouquier has yet had to do. Twenty-two, all chief Republicans, ranged in a line there; the most eloquent in France; Lawyers too; not without friends in the auditory. How will Tinville prove these men guilty of Royalism, Federalism, Conspiracy against the Republic? Vergniaud's eloquence awakes once more; 'draws tears,' they say. And Journalists report, and the Trial lengthens itself out day after day; 'threatens to become eternal,' murmur many. Jacobinism and Municipality rise to the aid of Fouquier. On the 28th of the month, Hébert and others come in deputation to inform a Patriot Convention that the Revolutionary Tribunal is quite 'shackled by Forms of Law;' that a Patriot Jury ought to have 'the power of cutting short, of *terminer les débats*, when they feel themselves convinced.' Which pregnant suggestion, of cutting short, passes itself, with all despatch, into a Decree.

Accordingly, at ten o'clock on the night of the 30th of October, the Twenty-two, summoned back once more, receive this information, That the Jury feeling themselves convinced have cut short, have brought in their verdict; that the Accused are found guilty, and the Sentence on one and all of them is, Death with confiscation of goods.

Loud natural clamour rises among the poor Girondins; tumult; which can only be repressed by the gendarmes. Valazé stabs himself; falls down dead on the spot. The rest, amid loud clamour and confusion, are driven back to their Conciergerie; Lasource exclaiming, "I die on the day when the People have lost their reason; ye will die when they recover it." [1] No help! Yielding

---

[1] Δημοσθένους εἰπόντος, 'Αποκτενοῦσί σε 'Αθηναῖοι, Φωκίων· "Αν μανῶσιν, εἶπε σὲ δ', ἐὰν σωφρονῶσι.—Plut. *Opp.* t. iv. p. 310, ed. Reiske, 1776.

to violence, the Doomed uplift the Hymn of the Marseillese; return singing to their dungeon.

Riouffe, who was their Prison-mate in these last days, has lovingly recorded what death they made. To our notions, it is not an edifying death. Gay satirical *Pot-pourri* by Ducos; rhymed Scenes of Tragedy, wherein Barrère and Robespierre discourse with Satan; death's eve spent in 'singing' and 'sallies of gaiety,' with 'discourses on the happiness of peoples:' these things, and the like of these, we have to accept for what they are worth. It is the manner in which the Girondins make *their* Last Supper. Valazé, with bloody breast, sleeps cold in death; hears not the singing. Vergniaud has his dose of poison; but it is not enough for his friends, it is enough only for himself; wherefore he flings it from him; presides at this Last Supper of the Girondins, with wild coruscations of eloquence, with song and mirth. Poor human Will struggles to assert itself; if not in this way, then in that.[2]

But on the morrow morning all Paris is out; such a crowd as no man had seen. The Death-carts, Valazé's cold corpse stretched among the yet living Twenty-one, roll along. Bareheaded, hands bound; in their shirt-sleeves, coat flung loosely round the neck: so fare the eloquent of France; bemurmured, beshouted. To the shouts of *Vive la République*, some of them keep answering with counter-shouts of *Vive la République*. Others, as Brissot, sit sunk in silence. At the foot of the scaffold they again strike up, with appropriate variations, the Hymn of the Marseillese. Such an act of music; conceive it well! The yet Living chant there; the chorus so rapidly wearing weak! Samson's axe is rapid; one head per minute, or little less. The chorus is wearing weak; the chorus is worn *out;*—farewell forevermore, ye Girondins. Te-Deum Fauchet has become silent; Valazé's dead head is lopped: the sickle of the Guillotine has reaped the Girondins all away. 'The eloquent, the young, the beautiful and brave!' exclaims Riouffe. O Death, what feast is toward in thy ghastly Halls!

Nor, alas, in the far Bourdeaux region will Girondism fare better. In caves of Saint-Emilion, in loft and cellar, the weariest months roll on; apparel worn, purse empty; wintry November come; under Tallien and his Guillotine, all hope now gone. Danger drawing ever nigher, difficulty pressing ever straiter, they determine to separate. Not unpathetic the farewell; tall Barbaroux, cheeriest of brave men, stoops to clasp his Louvet:

[2] *Mémoires de Riouffe* (in *Mémoires sur les Prisons*, Paris, 1823), pp. 48-55.

" In what place soever thou findest my Mother," cries he, " try
" to be instead of a son to her: no resource of mine but I will
" share with thy Wife, should chance ever lead me where she is." [3]

Louvet went with Guadet, with Salles and Valadi; Barbaroux
with Buzot and Pétion. Valadi soon went southward, on a way
of his own. The two friends and Louvet had a miserable day and
night; the 14th of the November month, 1793. Sunk in wet,
weariness and hunger, they knock, on the morrow, for help, at a
friend's country-house; the fainthearted friend refuses to admit
them. They stood therefore under trees, in the pouring rain.
Flying desperate, Louvet thereupon will to Paris. He sets forth,
there and then, splashing the mud on each side of him, with a
fresh strength gathered from fury or frenzy. He passes villages,
finding ' the sentry asleep in his box in the thick rain ;' he is gone,
before the man can call after him. He bilks Revolutionary Committees; rides in carriers' carts, covered carts and open; lies hidden
in one, under knapsacks and cloaks of soldiers' wives on the Street
of Orléans, while men search for him; has hairbreadth escapes that
would fill three romances: finally he gets to Paris to his fair
Helpmate; gets to Switzerland, and waits better days.

Poor Guadet and Salles were both taken, ere long; they died
by the Guillotine in Bourdeaux; drums beating to drown their
voice. Valadi also is caught, and guillotined. Barbaroux and his
two comrades weathered it longer, into the summer of 1794; but
not long enough. One July morning, changing their hiding-place,
as they have often to do, ' about a league from Saint-Emilion, they
' observe a great crowd of country-people:' doubtless Jacobins
come to take them? Barbaroux draws a pistol, shoots himself
dead. Alas, and it was not Jacobins; it was harmless villagers
going to a village wake. Two days afterwards, Buzot and Pétion
were found in a Cornfield, their bodies half-eaten by dogs.[4]

Such was the end of Girondism. They arose to regenerate
France, these men; and have accomplished *this*. Alas, whatever
quarrel we had with them, has not their cruel fate abolished it?
Pity only survives. So many excellent souls of heroes sent down
to Hades; they themselves given as a prey of dogs and all manner
of birds! But, here too, the will of the Supreme Power was
accomplished. As Vergniaud said : ' the Revolution, like Saturn,
is devouring its own children.'

[3] Louvet, p. 213.
[4] *Recherches Historiques sur les Girondins* (in *Mémoires de Buzot*), p. 107.

BOOK FIFTH.

TERROR THE ORDER OF THE DAY.

CHAPTER I.

RUSHING DOWN.

WE are now, therefore, got to that black precipitous Abyss; whither all things have long been tending; where, having now arrived on the giddy verge, they hurl down, in confused ruin; headlong, pellmell, down, down;—till Sansculottism have consummated itself; and in this wondrous French Revolution, as in a Doomsday, a World have been rapidly, if not born again, yet destroyed and engulfed. Terror has long been terrible: but to the actors themselves it has now become manifest that their appointed course is one of Terror; and they say, Be it so. "*Que la Terreur soit à l'ordre du jour.*"

So many centuries, say only from Hugh Capet downwards, had been adding together, century transmitting it with increase to century, the sum of Wickedness, of Falsehood, Oppression of man by man. Kings were sinners, and Priests were, and People. Open Scoundrels rode triumphant, bediademed, becoronetted, bemitred; or the still fataler species of Secret-Scoundrels, in their fair-sounding formulas, speciosities, respectabilities, hollow within: the race of Quacks was grown many as the sands of the sea. Till at length such a sum of Quackery had accumulated itself as, in brief, the Earth and the Heavens were weary of. Slow seemed the Day of Settlement; coming on, all imperceptible, across the bluster and fanfaronade of Courtierisms, Conquering-Heroisms, Most Christian *Grand Monarque*-isms, Well-beloved Pompadourisms: yet behold it was always coming; behold it has come, suddenly, unlooked for by any man! The harvest of long centuries was

ripening and whitening so rapidly of late; and now it is grown
white, and is reaped rapidly, as it were, in one day.   Reaped, in
this Reign of Terror; and carried home, to Hades and the Pit!—
Unhappy Sons of Adam: it is ever so; and never do they know
it, nor will they know it.   With cheerfully smoothed countenances,
day after day, and generation after generation, they, calling cheerfully to one another, Well-speed-ye, are at work, *sowing the wind*.
And yet, as God lives, they *shall reap the whirlwind :* no other
thing, we say, is possible,—since God is a Truth, and His World is
a Truth.

History, however, in dealing with this Reign of Terror, has had
her own difficulties.   While the Phenomenon continued in its
primary state, as mere 'Horrors of the French Revolution,' there
was abundance to be said and shrieked.   With and also without
profit.   Heaven knows, there were terrors and horrors enough :
yet that was not all the Phenomenon; nay, more properly, that
was not the Phenomenon at all, but rather was the *shadow* of it,
the negative part of it.   And now, in a new stage of the business,
when History, ceasing to shriek, would try rather to include under
her old Forms of speech or speculation this new amazing Thing ;
that so some accredited scientific Law of Nature might suffice for
the unexpected Product of Nature, and History might get to
speak of it articulately, and draw inferences and profit from it;   in
this new stage, History, we must say, babbles and flounders perhaps
in a still painfuler manner.   Take, for example, the latest Form of
speech we have seen propounded on the subject as adequate to it,
almost in these months, by our worthy M. Roux, in his *Histoire
Parlementaire*.   The latest and the strangest : that the French
Revolution was a dead-lift effort, after eighteen hundred years of
preparation, to realise—the Christian Religion ! [1]   *Unity, Indivisi-
bility, Brotherhood or Death*, did indeed stand printed on all Houses
of the Living ; also on Cemeteries, or Houses of the Dead, stood
printed, by order of Procureur Chaumette, *Here is Eternal Sleep :* [2]
but a Christian Religion realised by the Guillotine and Death-
Eternal 'is suspect to me,' as Robespierre was wont to say, '*m'est
suspecte.*'
      Alas, no, M. Roux!   A Gospel of Brotherhood, not according to
any of the Four old Evangelists, and calling on men to repent, and
amend *each his own* wicked existence, that they might be saved;

---

[1] *Hist. Parl.* (Introd.), i. 1 et seqq.   [2] *Deux Amis*, xii. 78.

but a Gospel rather, as we often hint, according to a new Fifth
Evangelist Jean-Jacques, calling on men to amend *each the whole
world's* wicked existence, and be saved by making the Constitution.
A thing different and distant *toto cœlo*, as they say: the whole
breadth of the sky, and farther if possible!—It is thus, however,
that History, and indeed all human Speech and Reason does yet,
what Father Adam began life by doing: strive to *name* the new
Things it sees of Nature's producing,—often helplessly enough.

But what if History were to admit, for once, that all the Names
and Theorems yet known to her fall short? That this grand
Product of Nature was even grand, and new, in that it came not
to range itself under old recorded Laws of Nature at all, but to
disclose new ones? In that case, History, renouncing the pretension to *name* it at present, will *look* honestly at it, and name what
she can of it! Any approximation to the right Name has value:
were the right Name itself once here, the thing is known henceforth; the Thing is then ours, and can be dealt with.

Now surely not realisation, of Christianity or of aught earthly,
do we discern in this Reign of Terror, in this French Revolution
of which it is the consummating. Destruction rather we discern,
—of all that was destructible. It is as if Twenty-five millions,
risen at length into the Pythian mood, had stood up simultaneously
to say, with a sound which goes through far lands and times, that
this Untruth of an Existence had become insupportable. O ye
Hypocrisies and Speciosities, Royal mantles, Cardinal plush-cloaks,
ye Credos, Formulas, Respectabilities, fair-painted Sepulchres full of
dead men's bones,—behold, ye appear to us to be altogether a Lie.
Yet our Life is not a Lie; yet our Hunger and Misery is not a Lie!
Behold we lift up, one and all, our Twenty-five million right-
hands; and take the Heavens, and the Earth and also the Pit of
Tophet to witness, that either ye shall be abolished, or else we
shall be abolished!

No inconsiderable Oath, truly; forming, as has been often said,
the most remarkable transaction in these last thousand years.
Wherefrom likewise there follow, and will follow, results. The
fulfilment of this Oath; that is to say, the black desperate battle
of Men against their whole Condition and Environment,—a battle,
alas, withal, against the Sin and Darkness that was in themselves
as in others: this is the Reign of Terror. Transcendental despair
was the purport of it, though not consciously so. False hopes,
of Fraternity, Political Millennium, and what not, we have always

seen: but the unseen heart of the whole, the transcendental despair, was not false; neither has it been of no effect. Despair, pushed far enough, completes the circle, so to speak; and becomes a kind of genuine productive hope again.

Doctrine of Fraternity, out of old Catholicism, does, it is true, very strangely in the vehicle of a Jean-Jacques Evangel, suddenly plump down out of its cloud-firmament; and from a theorem determine to make itself a practice. But just so do all creeds, intentions, customs, knowledges, thoughts and things, which the French have, suddenly plump down; Catholicism, Classicism, Sentimentalism, Cannibalism: all *isms* that make up Man in France are rushing and roaring in that gulf; and the theorem has become a practice, and whatsoever cannot swim sinks. Not Evangelist Jean-Jacques alone; there is not a Village School-master but has contributed his quota: do we not *thou* one another, according to the Free Peoples of Antiquity? The French Patriot, in red Phrygian nightcap of Liberty, christens his poor little red infant Cato,—Censor, or else of Utica. Gracchus has become Babœuf, and edites Newspapers; Mutius Scævola, Cordwainer of that ilk, presides in the Section Mutius-Scævola: and in brief, there is a world wholly jumbling itself, to try what will swim.

Wherefore we will, at all events, call this Reign of Terror a very strange one. Dominant Sansculottism makes, as it were, free arena; one of the strangest temporary states Humanity was ever seen in. A nation of men full of wants and void of habits! The old habits are gone to wreck because they were old: men, driven forward by Necessity and fierce Pythian Madness, have, on the spur of the instant, to devise for the want the *way* of satisfying it. The Wonted tumbles down; by imitation, by invention, the Unwonted hastily builds itself up. What the French National head has in it comes out: if not a great result, surely one of the strangest.

Neither shall the Reader fancy that it was all black, this Reign of Terror: far from it. How many hammermen and squaremen, bakers and brewers, washers and wringers, over this France, must ply their old daily work, let the Government be one of Terror or one of Joy! In this Paris there are Twenty-three Theatres nightly; some count as many as Sixty Places of Dancing.[3] The Playwright manufactures,—pieces of a strictly Republican character. Ever fresh Novel-garbage, as of old, fodders the Circulating Libraries.[4] The 'Cesspool of *Agio*,' now in a time of Paper

<hr>

[3] Mercier, ii. 124.　　　　[4] *Moniteur* of these months, passim.

Money, works with a vivacity unexampled, unimagined; exhales from itself 'sudden fortunes,' like Aladdin-Palaces: really a kind of miraculous Fata-Morganas, since you *can* live in them, for a time.   Terror is as a sable ground, on which the most variegated of scenes paints itself.   In startling transitions, in colours all intensated, the sublime, the ludicrous, the horrible succeed one another; or rather, in crowding tumult, accompany one another.

Here, accordingly, if anywhere, the 'hundred tongues,' which the old Poets often clamour for, were of supreme service! In defect of any such organ on our part, let the Reader stir up his own imaginative organ: let us snatch for him this or the other significant glimpse of things, in the fittest sequence we can.

CHAPTER II.

DEATH.

In the early days of November there is one transient glimpse of things that is to be noted: the last transit to his long home of Philippe d'Orléans Egalité.   Philippe was 'decreed accused,' along with the Girondins, much to his and their surprise; but not tried along with them.   They are doomed and dead, some three days, when Philippe, after his long half-year of durance at Marseilles, arrives in Paris.   It is, as we calculate, the third of November 1793.

On which same day, two notable Female Prisoners are also put in ward there: Dame Dubarry and Josephine Beauharnais. Dame whilom Countess Dubarry, Unfortunate-female, had returned from London; they snatched her, not only as Ex-harlot of a whilom Majesty, and therefore suspect; but as having 'furnished the Emigrants with money.'   Contemporaneously with whom there comes the wife Beauharnais, soon to be the widow: she that is Josephine Tascher Beauharnais; that shall be Josephine Empress Buonaparte,—for a black Divineress of the Tropics prophesied long since that she should be a Queen and more. Likewise, in the same hours, poor Adam Lux, nigh turned in the head, who, according to Forster, 'has taken no food these three weeks,' marches to the Guillotine for his Pamphlet on Charlotte Corday:

he 'sprang to the scaffold;' said 'he died for her with great joy.'
Amid such fellow-travellers does Philippe arrive. For, be the
month named Brumaire year 2 of Liberty, or November year
1793 of Slavery, the Guillotine goes always, *Guillotine va toujours.*

Enough, Philippe's indictment is soon drawn, his jury soon convinced. He finds himself made guilty of Royalism, Conspiracy
and much else; nay, it is a guilt in him that he voted Louis's
Death, though he answers, "I voted in my soul and conscience."
The doom he finds is death forthwith; this present 6th dim day
of November is the last day that Philippe is to see. Philippe,
says Montgaillard, thereupon called for breakfast: sufficiency of
'oysters, two cutlets, best part of an excellant bottle of claret;'
and consumed the same with apparent relish. A Revolutionary
Judge, or some official Convention Emissary, then arrived, to
signify that he might still do the State some service by revealing
the truth about a plot or two. Philippe answered that, on him,
in the pass things had come to, the State had, he thought, small
claim; that nevertheless, in the interest of Liberty, he, having
still some leisure on his hands, was willing, were a reasonable
question asked him, to give a reasonable answer. And so, says
Montgaillard, he leant his elbow on the mantel-piece, and conversed
in an undertone with great seeming composure; till the leisure
was done, or the Emissary went his ways.

At the door of the Conciergerie, Philippe's attitude was erect
and easy, almost commanding. It is five years, all but a few days,
since Philippe, within these same stone walls, stood up with an air
of graciosity, and asked King Louis, "Whether it was a Royal
Session, then, or a Bed of Justice?" O Heaven!—Three poor
blackguards were to ride and die with him: some say, they
objected to such company, and had to be flung in, neck and
heels;[1] but it seems not true. Objecting or not objecting, the
gallows-vehicle gets under way. Philippe's dress is remarked for
its elegance; green frock, waistcoat of white *piqué*, yellow buckskins, boots clear as Warren: his air, as before, entirely composed,
impassive, not to say easy and Brummellean-polite. Through street
after street; slowly, amid execrations;—past the Palais Egalité,
whilom Palais Royal! The cruel Populace stopped him there, some
minutes: Dame de Buffon, it is said, looked out on him, in Jezebel
headtire; along the ashlar Wall there ran these words in huge
tricolor print, REPUBLIC ONE AND INDIVISIBLE; LIBERTY, EQUALITY,

---

[1] Forster, ii. 628 ; Montgaillard, iv. 141-57.

FRATERNITY OR DEATH: *National Property.* Philippe's eyes flashed hellfire, one instant; but the next instant it was gone, and he sat impassive, Brummellean-polite. On the scaffold, Samson was for drawing off his boots: "Tush," said Philippe, "they will come better off *after;* let us have done, *dépêchons-nous!*"

So Philippe was not without virtue, then? God forbid that there should be any living man without it! He had the virtue to keep living for five-and-forty years;—other virtues perhaps more than we know of. But probably no mortal ever had such things recorded of him: such facts, and also such lies. For he was a *Jacobin Prince of the Blood;* consider what a combination! Also, unlike any Nero, any Borgia, he lived in the Age of Pamphlets. Enough for us: Chaos *has* reabsorbed him; may it late or never bear his like again!—Brave young Orléans Egalité, deprived of all, only not deprived of himself, is gone to Coire in the Grisons, under the name of Corby, to teach Mathematics. The Egalité Family is at the darkest depths of the Nadir.

A far nobler Victim follows; one who will claim remembrance from several centuries: Jeanne-Marie Phlipon, the Wife of Roland. Queenly, sublime in her uncomplaining sorrow, seemed she to Riouffe in her Prison. 'Something more than is usually found in 'the looks of women painted itself,' says Riouffe,[2] 'in those large 'black eyes of hers, full of expression and sweetness. She spoke to 'me often, at the Grate: we were all attentive round her, in a sort 'of admiration and astonishment; she expressed herself with a 'purity, with a harmony and prosody that made her language like 'music, of which the ear could never have enough. Her conversa-'tion was serious, not cold; coming from the mouth of a beautiful 'woman, it was frank and courageous as that of a great man.' 'And yet her maid said: "Before you, she collects her strength; 'but in her own room, she will sit three hours sometimes leaning 'on the window, and weeping."' She has been in Prison, liberated once, but recaptured the same hour, ever since the first of June: in agitation and uncertainty; which has gradually settled down into the last stern certainty, that of death. In the Abbaye Prison, she occupied Charlotte Corday's apartment. Here in the Conciergerie, she speaks with Riouffe, with Ex-Minister Clavière; calls the beheaded Twenty-two "*Nos amis,* our Friends,"—whom we are soon to follow. During these five months, those *Memoirs* of hers were written, which all the world still reads.

[2] *Mémoires (Sur les Prisons,* i.), pp. 55-7.

But now, on the 8th of November, 'clad in white,' says Riouffe, 'with her long black hair hanging down to her girdle,' she is gone to the Judgment-bar. She returned with a quick step; lifted her finger, to signify to us that she was doomed: her eyes seemed to have been wet. Fouquier-Tinville's questions had been 'brutal;' offended female honour flung them back on him, with scorn, not without tears. And now, short preparation soon done, she too shall go her last road. There went with her a certain Lamarche, 'Director of Assignat-printing;' whose dejection she endeavoured to cheer. Arrived at the foot of the scaffold, she asked for pen and paper, "to write the strange thoughts that were rising in her:" [3] a remarkable request; which was refused. Looking at the Statue of Liberty which stands there, she says bitterly: "O Liberty, what things are done in thy name!" For Lamarche's sake, she will die first; show him how easy it is to die: "Contrary to the order," said Samson.—"Pshaw, you cannot refuse the last request of a Lady;" and Samson yielded.

Noble white Vision, with its high queenly face, its soft proud eyes, long black hair flowing down to the girdle; and as brave a heart as ever beat in woman's bosom! Like a white Grecian Statue, serenely complete, she shines in that black wreck of things;—long memorable. Honour to great Nature who, in Paris City, in the Era of Noble-Sentiment and Pompadourism, can make a Jeanne Phlipon, and nourish her to clear perennial Womanhood, though but on Logics, *Encyclopédies*, and the Gospel according to Jean-Jacques! Biography will long remember that trait of asking for a pen "to write the strange thoughts that were rising in her." It is as a little light-beam, shedding softness, and a kind of sacredness, over all that preceded: so in her too there was an Unnameable; she too was a Daughter of the Infinite; there were mysteries which Philosophism had not dreamt of!—She left long written counsels to her little Girl; she said her Husband would not survive her.

Still crueler was the fate of poor Bailly, First National President, First Mayor of Paris: doomed now for Royalism, Fayettism; for that Red-Flag Business of the Champ-de-Mars;—one may say in general, for leaving his Astronomy to meddle with Revolution. It is the 10th of November 1793, a cold bitter drizzling rain, as poor Bailly is led through the streets; howling Populace covering him with curses, with mud; waving over his face a burning or smoking mockery of a Red Flag. Silent, unpitied, sits the innocent old

[3] *Mémoires de Madame Roland* (Introd.), i. 68.

man. Slow faring through the sleety drizzle, they have got to the Champ-de-Mars: Not there! vociferates the cursing Populace; such Blood ought not to stain an Altar of the Fatherland: not there; but on that dung-heap by the River-side! So vociferates the cursing Populace; Officiality gives ear to them. The Guillotine is taken down, though with hands numbed by the sleety drizzle; is carried to the River-side; is there set up again, with slow numbness; pulse after pulse still counting itself out in the old man's weary heart. For hours long; amid curses and bitter frost-rain! "Bailly, thou tremblest," said one. "*Mon ami*, it is for cold," said Bailly, "*c'est de froid.*" Crueler end had no mortal.[4]

Some days afterwards, Roland, hearing the news of what happened on the 8th, embraces his kind Friends at Rouen, leaves their kind house which had given him refuge; goes forth, with farewell too sad for tears. On the morrow morning, 16th of the month, 'some four leagues from Rouen, Paris-ward, near Bourg-Baudoin, in M. Normand's Avenue,' there is seen sitting leant against a tree the figure of a rigorous wrinkled man; stiff now in the rigour of death; a cane-sword run through his heart; and at his feet this writing: ' Whoever thou art that findest me lying, 'respect my remains: they are those of a man who consecrated all 'his life to being useful; and who has died as he lived, virtuous 'and honest.' ' Not fear, but indignation, made me quit my 'retreat, on learning that my Wife had been murdered. I wished 'not to remain longer on an Earth polluted with crimes.'[5]

Barnave's appearance at the Revolutionary Tribunal was of the bravest; but it could not stead him. They have sent for him from Grenoble; to pay the common smart. Vain is eloquence, forensic or other, against the dumb Clotho-shears of Tinville. He is still but two-and-thirty, this Barnave, and has known such changes. Short while ago, we saw him at the top of Fortune's wheel, his word a law to all Patriots: and now surely he is at the *bottom* of the wheel; in stormful altercation with a Tinville Tribunal, which is dooming him to die![6] And Pétion, once also of the Extreme Left, and named *Pétion Virtue,* where is he? Civilly dead; in the Caves of Saint-Emilion; to be devoured of dogs. And Robespierre, who rode along with him on the shoulders of the people, is in Committee of *Salut;* civilly alive: not to live always. So giddy-swift whirls and spins this immeasurable *tor-*

---

[4] *Vie de Bailly* (in *Mémoires,* i.), p. 29.
[5] *Mémoires de Madame Roland* (Introd.), i. 88.   [6] Forster, ii. 629.

mentum of a Revolution; wild-booming; not to be followed by the eye. Barnave, on the Scaffold, stamped with his foot; and looking upwards was heard to ejaculate, "This, then, is my reward!"

Deputy Ex-Procureur Manuel is already gone; and Deputy Osselin, famed also in August and September, is about to go: and Rabaut, discovered treacherously between his two walls, and the Brother of Rabaut. National Deputies not a few! And Generals: the memory of General Custine cannot be defended by his Son; his Son is already guillotined. Custine the Ex-Noble was replaced by Houchard the Plebeian: he too could not prosper in the North; for him too there was no mercy; he has perished in the Place de la Révolution, after attempting suicide in Prison. And Generals Biron, Beauharnais, Brunet, whatsoever General prospers not; tough old Lückner, with his eyes grown rheumy; Alsatian Westermann, valiant and diligent in La Vendée: *none of them can*, as the Psalmist sings, *his soul from death deliver.*

How busy are the Revolutionary Committees; Sections with their Forty Halfpence a-day! Arrestment on arrestment falls quick, continual; followed by death. Ex-Minister Clavière has killed himself in Prison. Ex-Minister Lebrun, seized in a hayloft, under the disguise of a working man, is instantly conducted to death.[7] Nay, withal, is it not what Barrère calls 'coining money on the Place de la Révolution'? For always the 'property of the guilty, if property he have,' is confiscated. To avoid accidents, we even make a Law that suicide shall not defraud us; that a criminal who kills himself does not the less incur forfeiture of goods. Let the guilty tremble, therefore, and the suspect, and the rich, and in a word all manner of Culottic men! Luxembourg Palace, once Monsieur's, has become a huge loathsome Prison; Chantilly Palace too, once Condé's:—And their landlords are at Blankenberg, on the wrong side of the Rhine. In Paris are now some Twelve Prisons; in France some Forty-four Thousand: thitherward, thick as brown leaves in Autumn, rustle and travel the suspect; shaken down by Revolutionary Committees, they are swept thitherward, as into their storehouse,—to be consumed by Samson and Tinville. 'The Guillotine goes not ill, *La Guillotine ne va pas mal.*'

[7] *Moniteur*, 11, 30 Décembre 1793; Louvet, p. 287.

CHAPTER III.

DESTRUCTION.

THE suspect may well tremble; but how much more the open rebels;—the Girondin Cities of the South! Revolutionary Army is gone forth, under Ronsin the Playwright; six thousand strong; 'in red nightcap, in tricolor waistcoat, in black-shag trousers, 'black-shag spencer, with enormous mustachioes, enormous sabre,— 'in *carmagnole complète;* '[1] and has portable guillotines. Representative Carrier has got to Nantes, by the edge of blazing La Vendée, which Rossignol has literally set on fire: Carrier will try what captives you make; what accomplices thay have, Royalist or Girondin: his guillotine goes always, *va toujours;* and his wool-capped 'Company of Marat.' Little children are guillotined, and aged men. Swift as the machine is, it will not serve; the Headsman and all his valets sink, worn down with work; declare that the human muscles can no more.[2] Whereupon you must try fusillading; to which perhaps still frightfuler methods may succeed.

In Brest, to like purpose, rules Jean-Bon Saint-André; with an Army of Red Nightcaps. In Bourdeaux rules Tallien, with his Isabeau and henchmen; Guadets, Cussys, Salleses, many fall; the bloody Pike and Nightcap bearing supreme sway; the Guillotine coining money. Bristly fox-haired Tallien, once Able Editor, still young in years, is now become most gloomy, potent; a Pluto on Earth, and has the keys of Tartarus. One remarks, however, that a certain Senhorina Cabarus, or call her rather *Senhora* and wedded not yet widowed *Dame de Fontenai*, brown beautiful woman, daughter of Cabarus the Spanish Merchant,—has softened the red bristly countenance; pleading for herself and friends; and prevailing. The keys of Tartarus, or any kind of power, are something to a woman; gloomy Pluto himself is not insensible to love. Like a new Proserpine, she, by this red gloomy Dis, is gathered; and, they say, softens his stone heart a little.

[1] See Louvet, p. 301.   [2] *Deux Amis*, xii. 249-51.

Maignet, at Orange in the South; Lebon, at Arras in the North, become world's wonders. Jacobin Popular Tribunal, with its National Representative, perhaps where Girondin Popular Tribunal had lately been, rises here and rises there; wheresoever needed. Fouchés, Maignets, Barrases, Frérons scour the Southern Departments; like reapers, with their guillotine-sickle. Many are the labourers, great is the harvest. By the hundred and the thousand, men's lives are cropt; cast like brands into the burning.

Marseilles is taken, and put under martial law : lo, at Marseilles, what one besmutted red-bearded corn-ear is this which they cut;— one gross Man, we mean, with copper-studded face; plenteous beard, or beard-stubble, of a tile-colour ? By Nemesis and the Fatal Sisters, it is Jourdan Coupe-tête ! Him they have clutched, in these martial-law districts; him too, with their 'national razor,' their *rasoir national*, they sternly shave away. Low now is Jourdan the Headsman's own head;—low as Deshuttes's and Varigny's, which he sent on pikes, in the Insurrection of Women ! No more shall he, as a copper Portent, be seen gyrating through the Cities of the South; no more sit judging, with pipes and brandy, in the Ice-tower of Avignon. The all-hiding Earth has received him, the bloated Tilebeard: may we never look upon his like again !— Jourdan one names; the other Hundreds are not named. Alas, they, like confused faggots, lie massed together for us; counted by the cart-load : and yet not an individual faggot-twig of them but had a Life and History; and was cut, not without pangs as when a Kaiser dies !

Least of all cities can Lyons escape. Lyons, which we saw in dread sunblaze, that Autumn night when the Powder-tower sprang aloft, was clearly verging towards a sad end. Inevitable : what could desperate valour and Précy do; Dubois-Crancé, deaf as Destiny, stern as Doom, capturing their 'redoubts of cotton-bags ;' hemming them in, ever closer, with his Artillery-lava ? Never would that *ci-devant* D'Autichamp arrive; never any help from Blankenberg. The Lyons Jacobins were hidden in cellars; the Girondin Municipality waxed pale, in famine, treason and red fire. Précy drew his sword, and some Fifteen Hundred with him ; sprang to saddle, to cut their way to Switzerland. They cut fiercely ; and were fiercely cut, and cut down; not hundreds, hardly units of them ever saw Switzerland.[3] Lyons, on the 9th of October, surrenders at discretion; it is become a devoted Town. Abbé

[3] *Deux Amis*, xi. 145.

Lamourette, now Bishop Lamourette, whilom Legislator, he of the old *Baiser-l'Amourette* or Delilah-Kiss, is seized here; is sent to Paris to be guillotined : ' he made the sign of the cross,' they say, when Tinville intimated his death-sentence to him; and died as an eloquent Constitutional Bishop. But wo now to all Bishops, Priests, Aristocrats and Federalists that are in Lyons ! The *manes* of Chalier are to be appeased; the Republic, maddened to the Sibylline pitch, has bared her right arm. Behold ! Representative Fouché, it is Fouché of Nantes, a name to become well known; he with a Patriot company goes duly, in wondrous Procession, to raise the corpse of Chalier. An Ass housed in Priest's cloak, with a mitre on his head, and trailing the Mass-Books, some say the very Bible, at its tail, paces through Lyons streets : escorted by multitudinous Patriotism, by clangour as of the Pit; towards the grave of Martyr Chalier. The body is dug up, and burnt : the ashes are collected in an Urn; to be worshipped of Paris Patriotism. The Holy Books were part of the funeral pile; their ashes are scattered to the wind. Amid cries of "Vengeance ! Vengeance !" —which, writes Fouché, shall be satisfied.[4]

Lyons in fact is a Town to be abolished; not Lyons henceforth, but ' *Commune Affranchie*, Township Freed :' the very name of it shall perish. It is to be razed, this once great City, if Jacobinism prophesy right; and a Pillar to be erected on the ruins, with this Inscription, *Lyons rebelled against the Republic; Lyons is no more.* Fouché, Couthon, Collot, Convention Representatives succeed one another : there is work for the hangman; work for the hammerman, *not* in building. The very Houses of Aristocrats, we say, are doomed. Paralytic Couthon, borne in a chair, taps on the wall, with emblematic mallet, saying, " *La Loi te frappe*, The Law strikes thee; " masons, with wedge and crowbar, begin demolition. Crash of downfal, dim ruin and dust-clouds fly in the winter wind. Had Lyons been of soft stuff, it had all vanished in those weeks, and the Jacobin prophecy had been fulfilled. But Towns are not built of soap-froth; Lyons Town is built of stone. Lyons, though it rebelled against the Republic, *is* to this day.

Neither have the Lyons Girondins all one neck, that you could despatch it at one swoop. Revolutionary Tribunal here, and Military Commission, guillotining, fusillading, do what they can : the kennels of the Place des Terreaux run red; mangled corpses roll down the Rhone. Collot d'Herbois, they say, was once hissed

[4] *Moniteur* (du 17 Novembre 1793), &c.

on the Lyons stage: but with what sibilation, of world-catcall or
hoarse Tartarean Trumpet, will ye hiss him now, in this his new
character of Convention Representative,—not to be repeated!
Two-hundred and nine men are marched forth over the River, to
be shot in mass, by musket and cannon, in the Promenade of the
Brotteaux. It is the second of such scenes; the first was of some
Seventy. The corpses of the first were flung into the Rhone, but
the Rhone stranded some; so these now, of the second lot, are to
be buried on land. Their one long grave is dug; they stand
ranked, by the loose mould-ridge; the younger of them singing
the Marseillaise. Jacobin National Guards give fire; but have
again to give fire, and again; and to take the bayonet and the
spade, for though the doomed all fall, they do not all die;—and it
becomes a butchery too horrible for speech. So that the very
Nationals, as they fire, turn away their faces. Collot, snatching
the musket from one such National, and levelling it with unmoved
countenance, says, "It is thus a Republican ought to fire."

This is the second Fusillade, and happily the last: it is found
too hideous; even inconvenient. There were Two-hundred and
nine marched out; one escaped at the end of the Bridge: yet
behold, when you count the corpses, they are Two-hundred and *ten*.
Rede us this riddle, O Collot? After long guessing, it is called to
mind that two individuals, here in the Brotteaux ground, did
attempt to leave the rank, protesting with agony that they were
not condemned men, that they were Police Commissaries: which
two we repulsed, and disbelieved, and shot with the rest![5] Such
is the vengeance of an enraged Republic. Surely this, according
to Barrère's phrase, is Justice "under rough forms, *sous des formes
acerbes.*" But the Republic, as Fouché says, must "march to
Liberty over corpses." Or again, as Barrère has it: "None but
the dead do not come back, *Il n'y a que les morts qui ne reviennent
pas.*" Terror hovers far and wide: 'the Guillotine goes not ill.'

, But before quitting those Southern regions, over which History
can cast only glances from aloft, she will alight for a moment, and
look fixedly at one point: the Siege of Toulon. Much battering
and bombarding, heating of balls in furnaces or farm-houses,
serving of artillery well and ill, attacking of Ollioules Passes, Forts
Malbosquet, there has been: as yet to small purpose. We have
had General Cartaux here, a whilom Painter elevated in the
troubles of Marseilles; General Doppet, a whilom Medical man

---

[5] *Deux Amis*, xii. 251-62.

elevated in the troubles of Piemont, who, under Crancé, took Lyons, but cannot take Toulon. Finally we have General Dugommier, a pupil of Washington. Convention *Représentans* also we have had; Barrasses, Salicettis, Robespierres the Younger: —also an Artillery *Chef de brigade*, of extreme diligence, who often takes his nap of sleep among the guns; a short, taciturn, olive-complexioned young man, not unknown to us, by name Buonaparte; one of the best Artillery-officers yet met with. And still Toulon is not taken. It is the fourth month now; December, in slave-style; *Frostarious* or *Frimaire*, in new-style: and still their cursed Red-Blue Fag flies there. They are provisioned from the Sea; they have seized all heights, felling wood, and fortifying themselves; like the cony, they have built their nest in the rocks.

Meanwhile *Frostarious* is not yet become *Snowous* or *Nivose*, when a Council of War is called; Instructions have just arrived from Government and *Salut Public*. Carnot, in *Salut Public*, has sent us a plan of siege: on which plan General Dugommier has this criticism to make, Commissioner Salicetti has that; and criticisms and plans are very various; when that young Artillery-Officer ventures to speak; the same whom we saw snatching sleep among the guns, who has emerged several times in this History,— the name of him Napoleon Buonaparte. It is his humble opinion, for he has been gliding about with spy-glasses, with thoughts, That a certain Fort l'Eguillette can be clutched, as with lion-spring, on the sudden; wherefrom, were it once ours, the very heart of Toulon might be battered; the English Lines were, so to speak, turned inside out, and Hood and our Natural Enemies must next day either put to sea, or be burnt to ashes. Commissioners arch their eyebrows, with negatory sniff: who is this young gentleman with more wit than we all? Brave veteran Dugommier, however, thinks the idea worth a word; questions the young gentleman; becomes convinced; and there is for issue, Try it.

On the taciturn bronze-countenance therefore, things being now all ready, there sits a grimmer gravity than ever, compressing a hotter central-fire than ever. Yonder, thou seest, is Fort l'Eguillette; a desperate lion-spring, yet a possible one; this day to be tried!—Tried it is; and found *good*. By stratagem and valour, stealing through ravines, plunging fiery through the fire-tempest, Fort l'Eguillette is clutched at, is carried; the smoke having cleared, we see the Tricolor fly on it; the bronze-complexioned young man was right. Next morning, Hood, finding the interior of his lines

exposed, his defences turned inside out, makes for his shipping.
Taking such Royalists as wished it on board with him, he weighs
anchor; on this 19th of December 1793, Toulon is once more the
Republic's!

Cannonading has ceased at Toulon; and now the guillotining
and fusillading may begin. Civil horrors, truly: but at least
that infamy of an English domination is purged away. Let there
be Civic Feast universally over France: so reports Barrère, or
Painter David; and the Convention assist in a body.[6] Nay, it is
said, these infamous English (with an attention rather to their
own interests than to ours) set fire to our store-houses, arsenals,
war-ships in Toulon Harbour, before weighing; some score of
brave war-ships, the only ones we now had! However, it did not
prosper, though the flame spread far and high; some two ships
were burned, not more; the very galley-slaves ran with buckets
to quench. These same proud Ships, Ship *l'Orient* and the rest,
have to carry this same young Man to Egypt first: not yet can
they be changed to ashes, or to Sea-Nymphs; not yet to sky-
rockets, O ship *l'Orient;* nor become the prey of England,—before
their time!

And so, over France universally, there is Civic Feast and high-
tide: and Toulon sees fusillading, grapeshotting in mass, as Lyons
saw; and 'death is poured out in great floods, *vomie à grands
flots ;*' and Twelve-thousand Masons are requisitioned from the
neighbouring country, to raze Toulon from the face of the Earth.
For it is to be razed, so reports Barrère; all but the National
Shipping Establishments; and to be called henceforth not Toulon,
but *Port of the Mountain.* There in black death-cloud we must
leave it;—hoping only that Toulon too is built of stone; that
perhaps even Twelve-thousand Masons cannot pull it down, till
the fit pass.

One begins to be sick of 'death vomited in great floods.'
Nevertheless, hearest thou not, O Reader (for the sound reaches
through centuries), in the dead December and January nights,
over Nantes Town,—confused noises, as of musketry and tumult,
as of rage and lamentation; mingling with the everlasting moan
of the Loire waters there? Nantes Town is sunk in sleep; but
Représentant Carrier is not sleeping, the wool-capped Company of
Marat is not sleeping. Why unmoors that flatbottomed craft, that
galarre; about eleven at night; with Ninety Priests under

[6] *Moniteur*, 1793, Nos. 101 (31 Décembre), 95, 96, 98, &c.

hatches? They are going to Belle Isle? In the middle of the Loire stream, on signal given, the gabarre is scuttled; she sinks with all her cargo. 'Sentence of Deportation,' writes Carrier, 'was executed *vertically*.' The Ninety Priests, with their gabarre-coffin, lie deep! It is the first of the *Noyades*, what we may call *Drownages*, of Carrier; which have become famous forever.

Guillotining there was at Nantes, till the Headsman sank worn out: then fusillading 'in the Plain of Saint-Mauve;' little children fusilladed, and women with children at the breast; children and women, by the hundred and twenty; and by the five hundred, so hot is La Vendée: till the very Jacobins grew sick, and all but the Company of Marat cried, Hold! Wherefore now we have got Noyading; and on the 24th night of *Frostarious* year 2, which is 14th of December 1793, we have a second Noyade; consisting of 'a Hundred and Thirty-eight persons.' [7]

Or why waste a gabarre, sinking it with them? Fling them out; fling them out, with their hands tied: pour a continual hail of lead over all the space, till the last struggler of them be sunk! Unsound sleepers of Nantes, and the Sea-Villages thereabouts, hear the musketry amid the night-winds; wonder what the meaning of it is. And women were in that gabarre; whom the Red Nightcaps were stripping naked; who begged, in their agony, that their smocks might not be stript from them. And young children were thrown in, their mothers vainly pleading: "Wolflings," answered the Company of Marat, "who would grow to be wolves."

By degrees, daylight itself witnesses Noyades: women and men are tied together, feet and feet, hands and hands; and flung in: this they call *Mariage Républicain*, Republican Marriage. Cruel is the panther of the woods, the she-bear bereaved of her whelps: but there is in man a hatred crueler than that. Dumb, out of suffering now, as pale swoln corpses, the victims tumble confusedly seaward along the Loire stream; the tide rolling them back: clouds of ravens darken the River; wolves prowl on the shoal-places: Carrier writes, '*Quel torrent révolutionnaire*, What a torrent of Revolution!' For the man is rabid; and the Time is rabid. These are the Noyades of Carrier; twenty-five by the tale, for what is done in darkness comes to be investigated in sunlight:[8] not to be forgotten for centuries.—We will turn to another

---

[7] *Deux Amis*, xii. 266-72; *Moniteur*, du 2 Janvier 1794.
[8] *Procès de Carrier* (4 tomes, Paris, 1795).

aspect of the Consummation of Sansculottism; leaving this as the blackest.

But indeed men are all rabid; as the Time is. Representative Lebon, at Arras, dashes his sword into the blood flowing from the Guillotine; exclaims, "How I like it!" Mothers, they say, by his orders, have to stand by while the Guillotine devours their children: a band of music is stationed near; and, at the fall of every head, strikes up its *Ça-ira*.[9] In the Burgh of Bedouin, in the Orange region, the Liberty-tree has been cut down overnight. Representative Maignet, at Orange, hears of it; burns Bedouin Burgh to the last dog-hutch; guillotines the inhabitants, or drives them into the caves and hills.[10] Republic One and Indivisible! She is the newest Birth of Nature's waste inorganic Deep, which men name Orcus, Chaos, primeval Night; and knows one law, that of self-preservation. *Tigresse Nationale:* meddle not with a whisker of her! Swift-rending is her stroke; look what a paw she spreads;—pity has not entered into her heart.

Prudhomme, the dull-blustering Printer and Able Editor, as yet a Jacobin Editor, will become a renegade one, and publish large volumes, on these matters, *Crimes of the Revolution;* adding innumerable lies withal, as if the truth were not sufficient. We, for our part, find it more edifying to know, one good time, that this Republic and National Tigress *is* a New-Birth; a Fact of Nature among Formulas, in an Age of Formulas; and to look, oftenest in silence, how the so genuine Nature-Fact will demean itself among these. For the Formulas are partly genuine, partly delusive, supposititious: we call them, in the language of metaphor, regulated modelled *shapes;* some of which have bodies and life still in them; most of which, according to a German Writer, have only emptiness, 'glass-eyes glaring on you with a ghastly affecta-'tion of life, and in their interior unclean accumulation of beetles 'and spiders!' But the Fact, let all men observe, is a genuine and sincere one; the sincerest of Facts; terrible in its sincerity, as very Death. Whatsoever is equally sincere may front it, and beard it; but whatsoever is *not?*—

9 *Les Horreurs des Prisons d'Arras* (Paris, 1823).
10 Montgaillard, iv. 200.

CHAPTER IV.

CARMAGNOLE COMPLETE.

SIMULTANEOUSLY with this Tophet-black aspect, there unfolds itself another aspect, which one may call a Tophet-red aspect, the Destruction of the Catholic Religion; and indeed, for the time being, of Religion itself. We saw Romme's New Calendar establish its *Tenth* Day of Rest; and asked, what would become of the Christian Sabbath? The Calendar is hardly a month old, till all this is set at rest. Very singular, as Mercier observes: last *Corpus-Christi* Day 1792, the whole world, and Sovereign Authority itself, walked in religious gala, with a quite devout air;—Butcher Legendre, supposed to be irreverent, was like to be massacred in his Gig, as the thing went by. A Gallican Hierarchy, and Church, and Church Formulas seemed to flourish, a little brown-leaved or so, but not browner than of late years or decades; to flourish far and wide, in the sympathies of an unsophisticated People; defying Philosophism, Legislature and the Encyclopédie. Far and wide, alas, like a brown-leaved Vallombrosa: which waits but one whirl-blast of the November wind, and in an hour stands bare! Since that *Corpus-Christi* Day, Brunswick has come, and the Emigrants, and La Vendée, and eighteen months of Time: to all flourishing, especially to brown-leaved flourishing, there comes, were it never so slowly, an end.

On the 7th of November, a certain Citoyen Parens, Curate of Boissise-le-Bertrand, writes to the Convention that he has all his life been preaching a lie, and is grown weary of doing it; wherefore he will now lay down his Curacy and stipend, and begs that an august Convention would give him something else to live upon. '*Mention honorable*,' shall we give him? Or 'reference to Committee of Finances'? Hardly is this got decided, when goose Gobel, Constitutional Bishop of Paris, with his Chapter, with Municipal and Departmental escort in red nightcaps, makes his appearance, to do as Parens has done. Goose Gobel will now acknowledge 'no Religion but Liberty;' therefore he doffs his Priest-gear, and

receives the Fraternal embrace. To the joy of Departmental
Momoro, of Municipal Chaumettes and Héberts, of Vincent and
the Revolutionary Army! Chaumette asks, Ought there not, in
these circumstances, to be among our intercalary Days Sans-
breeches, a Feast of Reason?[1] Proper surely! Let Atheist
Maréchal, Lalande, and little Atheist Naigeon rejoice; let Clootz,
Speaker of Mankind, present to the Convention his *Evidences of
the Mahometan Religion,* 'a work evincing the nullity of all
Religions,'—with thanks. There shall be Universal Republic now,
thinks Clootz; and 'one God only, *Le Peuple.*'

The French nation is of gregarious imitative nature; it needed
but a fugle-motion in this matter; and goose Gobel, driven by
Municipality and force of circumstances, has given one. What
Curé will be behind him of Boissise; what Bishop behind him of
Paris? Bishop Grégoire, indeed, courageously declines; to the
sound of " We force no one; let Grégoire consult his conscience;"
but Protestant and Romish by the hundred volunteer and assent.
From far and near, all through November into December, till the
work is accomplished, come Letters of renegation, come Curates
who 'are learning to be Carpenters,' Curates with their new-
wedded Nuns: has not the day of Reason dawned, very swiftly,
and become noon? From sequestered Townships come Addresses,
stating plainly, though in Patois dialect, That 'they will have no
more to do with the black animal called Curay, *animal noir appelé
Curay.*'[2]

Above all things, there come Patriotic Gifts, of Church-furniture.
The remnant of bells, except for tocsin, descend from their belfries,
into the National meltingpot to make cannon. Censers and all
sacred vessels are beaten broad; of silver, they are fit for the
poverty-stricken Mint; of pewter, let them become bullets, to
shoot the 'enemies *du genre humain.*' Dalmatics of plush make
breeches for him who had none; linen albs will clip into shirts
for the Defenders of the Country: old-clothesmen, Jew or Heathen,
drive the briskest trade. Chalier's Ass-Procession, at Lyons, was
but a type of what went on, in those same days, in all Towns.
In all Towns and Townships as quick as the guillotine may go,
so quick goes the axe and the wrench: sacristies, lutrins, altar-
rails are pulled down; the Mass-Books torn into cartridge-papers:
men dance the Carmagnole all night about the bonfire. All

---

[1] *Moniteur*, Séance du 17 Brumaire (7th November), 1793.
[2] *Analyse du Moniteur* (Paris, 1801), ii. 280.

highways jingle with metallic Priest-tackle, beaten broad; sent
to the Convention, to the poverty-stricken Mint. Good Sainte-
Geneviève's *Chasse* is let down: alas, to be burst open, this time,
and burnt on the Place de Grève. Saint Louis's Shirt is burnt;—
might not a Defender of the Country have had it? At Saint-
Denis Town, no longer Saint-Denis but *Franciade*, Patriotism has
been down among the Tombs, rummaging; the Revolutionary
Army has taken spoil. This, accordingly, is what the streets of
Paris saw:

   'Most of these persons were still drunk, with the brandy they
'had swallowed out of chalices;—eating mackerel on the patenas!
'Mounted on Asses, which were housed with Priests' cloaks, they
'reined them with Priests' stoles; they held clutched with the
'same hand communion-cup and sacred wafer. They stopped at
'the doors of Dramshops; held out ciboriums: and the landlord,
'stoup in hand, had to fill them thrice. Next came Mules
'high-laden with crosses, chandeliers, censers, holy-water vessels,
'hyssops;—recalling to mind the Priests of Cybele, whose panniers,
'filled with the instruments of their worship, served at once as
'storehouse, sacristy and temple. In such equipage did these
'profaners advance towards the Convention. They enter there,
'in an immense train, ranged in two rows; all masked like
'mummers in fantastic sacerdotal vestments; bearing on hand-
'barrows their heaped plunder,—cirboriums, suns, candelabras,
'plates of gold and silver.'[3]

   The Address we do not give; for indeed it was in strophes, sung
vivâ voce, with all the parts;—Danton glooming considerably,
in his place; and demanding that there be prose and decency
in future.[4] Nevertheless the captors of such *spolia opima* crave,
not untouched with liquor, permission to dance the Carmagnole
also on the spot: whereto an exhilarated Convention cannot but
accede. Nay 'several Members,' continues the exaggerative
Mercier, who was not there to witness, being in Limbo now,
as one of Duperret's *Seventy-three*, 'several Members, quitting
'their curule chairs, took the hand of girls flaunting in Priests'
'vestures, and danced the Carmagnole along with them.'
Such Old-Hallowtide have they, in this year, once named of
Grace 1793.

     [3] Mercier, iv. 134. See *Moniteur*, Séance du 10 Novembre.
     [4] See also *Moniteur*, Séance du 26 Novembre.

Out of which strange fall of Formulas, tumbling there in confused welter, betrampled by the Patriotic dance, is it not passing strange to see a *new* Formula arise ? For the human tongue is not adequate to speak what 'triviality run distracted' there is in human nature. Black Mumbo-Jumbo of the woods, and most Indian Wau-waus, one can understand: but this of Procureur *Anaxagoras*, whilom John-Peter, Chaumette? We will say only : Man is a born idol-worshipper, *sight*-worshipper, so sensuous-imaginative is he; and also partakes much of the nature of the ape.

For the same day, while this brave Carmagnole-dance has hardly jigged itself out, there arrive Procureur Chaumette and Municipals and Departmentals, and with them the strangest freightage : a New Religion ! Demoiselle Candeille, of the Opera ; a woman fair to look upon, when well rouged ; she, borne on palanquin shoulderhigh ; with red woollen nightcap ; in azure mantle ; garlanded with oak ; holding in her hand the Pike of the Jupiter-*Peuple*, sails in : heralded by white young women girt in tricolor. Let the world consider it ! This, O National Convention wonder of the universe, is our New Divinity ; *Goddess of Reason*, worthy, and alone worthy of revering. Her henceforth we adore. Nay were it too much to ask of an august National Representation that it also went with us to the *ci-devant* Cathedral called of Notre-Dame, and executed a few strophes in worship of her ?

President and Secretaries give Goddess Candeille, borne at due height round their platform, successively the Fraternal kiss ; whereupon she, by decree, sails to the right-hand of the President and there alights. And now, after due pause and flourishes of oratory, the Convention, gathering its limbs, does get under way in the required procession towards Notre-Dame ;—Reason, again in her litter, sitting in the van of them, borne, as one judges, by men in the Roman costume ; escorted by wind-music, red nightcaps, and the madness of the world. And so, straightway, Reason taking seat on the high-altar of Notre-Dame, the requisite worship or quasi-worship is, say the Newspapers, *executed ;* National Convention chanting ' the *Hymn to Liberty*, words by Chénier, music by Gossec.' It is the first of the *Feasts of Reason ;* first communion-service of the New Religion of Chaumette.

' The corresponding Festival in the Church of Saint-Eustache,' says Mercier, ' offered the spectacle of a great tavern. The interior ' of the choir represented a landscape decorated with cottages and

'boskets of trees. Round the choir stood tables overloaded with
'bottles, with sausages, pork-puddings, pastries and other meats.
'The guests flowed in and out through all doors : whosoever pre-
'sented himself took part of the good things : children of eight,
'girls as well as boys, put hand to plate, in sign of Liberty; they
'drank also of the bottles, and their prompt intoxication created
'laughter. Reason sat in azure mantle aloft, in a serene manner;
'Cannoneers, pipe in mouth, serving her as acolytes. And out of
'doors,' continues the exaggerative man, 'were mad multitudes
'dancing round the bonfire of Chapel-balustrades, of Priests' and
'Canons' stalls; and the dancers,—I exaggerate nothing,—the
'dancers nigh bare of breeches, neck and breast naked, stockings
'down, went whirling and spinning, like those Dust-vortexes, fore-
'runners of Tempest and Destruction.' [5] At Saint-Gervais Church,
again, there was a terrible 'smell of herrings;' Section or Municipality having provided no food, no condiment, but left it to chance.
Other mysteries, seemingly of a Cabiric or even Paphian character,
we leave under the Veil, which appropriately stretches itself 'along
the pillars of the aisles,'—not to be lifted aside by the hand of
History.

But there is one thing we should like almost better to understand than any other : what Reason herself thought of it, all the
while. What articulate words poor Mrs. Momoro, for example,
uttered; when she had become ungoddessed again, and the
Bibliopolist and she sat quiet at home, at supper? For he was an
earnest man, Bookseller Momoro; and had notions of Agrarian
Law. Mrs. Momoro, it is admitted, made one of the best Goddesses
of Reason; though her teeth were a little defective.—And now if
the Reader will represent to himself that such visible Adoration of
Reason went on 'all over the Republic,' through these November
and December weeks, till the Church woodwork was burnt out,
and the business otherwise completed, he will perhaps feel sufficiently what an adoring Republic it was, and without reluctance quit
this part of the subject.

Such gifts of Church-spoil are chiefly the work of the *Armée
Révolutionnaire ;* raised, as we said, some time ago. It is an army
with portable guillotine : commanded by Playwright Ronsin in
terrible mustachioes; and even by some uncertain shadow of Usher
Maillard, the old Bastille Hero, Leader of the Menads, September

[5] Mercier, iv. 127-146.

Man in Gray! Clerk Vincent of the War-Office, one of Pache's old Clerks, 'with a head heated by the ancient orators,' had a main hand in the appointments, at least in the staff-appointments.

But of the marchings and retreatings of these Six-thousand no Xenophon exists. Nothing, but an inarticulate hum, of cursing and sooty frenzy, surviving dubious in the memory of ages! They scour the country round Paris; seeking Prisoners; raising Requisitions; seeing that Edicts are executed, that the Farmers have thrashed sufficiently; lowering Church-bells or metallic Virgins. Detachments shoot forth dim, towards remote parts of France; nay new Provincial Revolutionary Armies rise dim, here and there, as Carrier's Company of Marat, as Tallien's Bourdeaux Troop; like sympathetic clouds in an atmosphere all electric. Ronsin, they say, admitted, in candid moments, that his troops were the elixir of the Rascality of the Earth. One sees them drawn up in market-places; travel-splashed, rough-bearded, in *carmagnole complète:* the first exploit is to prostrate what Royal or Ecclesiastical monument, crucifix or the like, there may be: to plant a cannon at the steeple; fetch down the bell without climbing for it, bell and belfry together. This, however, it is said, depends somewhat on the size of the town: if the town contains much population, and these perhaps of a dubious choleric aspect, the Revolutionary Army will do its work gently, by ladder and wrench; nay perhaps will take its billet without work at all; and, refreshing itself with a little liquor and sleep, pass on to the next stage.[6] Pipe in cheek, sabre on thigh; in Carmagnole complete!

Such things have been; and may again be. Charles Second sent out his Highland Host over the Western Scotch Whigs: Jamaica Planters got Dogs from the Spanish Main to hunt their Maroons with: France too is bescoured with a Devil's Pack, the baying of which, at this distance of half a century, still sounds in the mind's ear.

---

[6] *Deux Amis,* xii. 62-5.

CHAPTER V.

LIKE A THUNDER-CLOUD.

BUT the grand and indeed substantially primary and generic aspect of the Consummation of Terror remains still to be looked at; nay blinkard History has for most part all but *over*looked this aspect, the soul of the whole; that which makes it terrible to the Enemies of France. Let Despotism and Cimmerian Coalitions consider. All French men and French things are in a State of Requisition; Fourteen Armies are got on foot; Patriotism, with all that it has of faculty in heart or in head, in soul or body or breeches-pocket, is rushing to the Frontiers, to prevail or die! Busy sits Carnot, in *Salut Public;* busy, for his share, in 'organising victory.' Not swifter pulses that Guillotine, in dread systole-diastole in the Place de la Révolution, than smites the Sword of Patriotism, smiting Cimmeria back to its own borders, from the sacred soil.

In fact, the Government is what we can call Revolutionary; and some men are '*à la hauteur,*' on a level with the circumstances; and others are not *à la hauteur,*—so much the worse for them. But the Anarchy, we may say, has *organised* itself: Society is literally overset; its old forces working with mad activity, but in the inverse order; destructive and self-destructive.

Curious to see how all still refers itself to some head and fountain; not even an Anarchy but must have a centre to revolve round. It is now some six months since the Committee of *Salut Public* came into existence; some three months since Danton proposed that all power should be given it, and 'a sum of fifty millions,' and the 'Government be declared Revolutionary.' He himself, since that day, would take no hand in it, though again and again solicited; but sits private in his place on the Mountain. Since that day, the Nine, or if they should even rise to Twelve, have become permanent, always reëlected when their term runs out; *Salut Public, Sûreté Générale* have assumed their ulterior form and mode of operating.

Committee of Public Salvation, as supreme; of General Surety, as subaltern: these, like a Lesser and Greater Council, most harmonious hitherto, have become the centre of all things. They ride this Whirlwind; they, raised by force of circumstances, insensibly, very strangely, thither to that dread height;—and guide it, and seem to guide it. Stranger set of Cloud-Compellers the Earth never saw. A Robespierre, a Billaud, a Collot, Couthon, Saint-Just; not to mention still meaner Amars, Vadiers, in *Sûreté Générale:* these are your Cloud-Compellers. Small intellectual talent is necessary: indeed where among them, except in the head of Carnot, busied organising victory, would you find any? The talent is one of instinct rather. It is that of divining aright what this great dumb Whirlwind wishes and wills; that of willing, with more frenzy than any one, what all the world wills. To stand at no obstacles; to heed no considerations, human or divine; to know well that, of divine or human, there is one thing needful Triumph of the Republic, Destruction of the Enemies of the Republic! With this one spiritual endowment, and so few others, it is strange to see how a dumb inarticulately storming Whirlwind of things puts, as it were, its reins into your hand, and invites and compels you to be leader of it.

Hard by sits a Municipality of Paris; all in red nightcaps since the fourth of November last: a set of men fully ' on a level with circumstances,' or even beyond it. Sleek Mayor Pache, studious to be safe in the middle; Chaumettes, Héberts, Varlets, and Henriot their great Commandant; not to speak of Vincent the War-clerk, of Momoros, Dobsents and suchlike: all intent to have Churches plundered, to have Reason adored, Suspects cut down, and the Revolution triumph. Perhaps carrying the matter *too* far? Danton was heard to grumble at the civic strophes; and to recommend prose and decency. Robespierre also grumbles that, in overturning Superstition, we did not mean to make a religion of Atheism. In fact, your Chaumette and Company constitute a kind of Hyper-Jacobinism, or rabid ' Faction *des Enragés;* ' which has given orthodox Patriotism some umbrage, of late months. To 'know a Suspect on the streets;' what is this but bringing the *Law of the Suspect* itself into ill odour? Men half-frantic, men zealous over-much,—they toil there, in their red nightcaps, rest-lessly, rapidly, accomplishing what of Life is allotted them.

And the Forty-four Thousand other Townships, each with Revolutionary Committee, based on Jacobin Daughter Society;

enlightened by the spirit of Jacobinism; quickened by the Forty
Sous a-day!—The French Constitution spurned always at anything
like Two Chambers; and yet, behold, has it not verily got Two
Chambers? National Convention, elected, for one; Mother of
Patriotism, self-elected, for another! Mother of Patriotism has
her Debates reported in the *Moniteur*, as important state-pro-
cedures; which indisputably they are. A Second Chamber of
Legislature we call this Mother Society;—if perhaps it were not
rather comparable to that old Scotch Body named *Lords of the
Articles*, without whose origination, and signal given, the so-called
Parliament could introduce no bill, could do no work? Robespierre
himself, whose words are a law, opens his incorruptible lips copiously in the Jacobins Hall. Smaller Council of *Salut Public*,
Greater Council of *Sûreté Générale*, all active Parties, come here
to plead; to shape beforehand what decision they must arrive at,
what destiny they have to expect. Now if a question arose,
Which of those Two Chambers, Convention, or Lords of the
Articles, was the *stronger?* Happily they as yet go hand in hand.

As for the National Convention, truly it has become a most
composed Body. Quenched now the old effervescence; the
Seventy-three locked in ward; once noisy Friends of the Girondins
sunk all into silent men of the Plain, called even 'Frogs of the
Marsh,' *Crapauds du Marais!* Addresses come, Revolutionary
Church-plunder comes; Deputations, with prose or strophes: these
the Convention receives. But beyond this, the Convention has
one thing mainly to do: to listen what *Salut Public* proposes,
and say, Yea.

Bazire followed by Chabot, with some impetuosity, declared,
one morning, that this was not the way of a Free Assembly.
"There ought to be an Opposition side, a *Côté Droit*," cried
Chabot: "if none else will form it, I will. People say to me,
You will all get guillotined in your turn, first you and Bazire,
then Danton, then Robespierre himself."[1] So spake the Dis-
frocked, with a loud voice: next week, Bazire and he lie in the
Abbaye; wending, one may fear, towards Tinville and the Axe;
and 'people say to me'—what seems to be proving true! Bazire's
blood was all inflamed with Revolution Fever; with coffee and
spasmodic dreams.[2] Chabot, again, how happy with his rich Jew-
Austrian wife, late Fräulein Frey! But he lies in Prison; and

---

[1] *Débats*, du 10 Novembre 1793.
[2] *Dictionnaire des Hommes Marquans*, i. 115.

his two Jew-Austrian Brothers-in-Law, the Bankers Frey, lie with
him; waiting the urn of doom.   Let a National Convention,
therefore, take warning, and know its function.   Let the Convention, all as one man, set its shoulder to the work; not with
bursts of Parliamentary eloquence, but in quite other and service-
abler ways!

Convention Commissioners, what we ought to call Representatives, '*Représentans* on mission,' fly, like the Herald Mercury, to
all points of the Territory; carrying your behests far and wide.
In their 'round hat, plumed with tricolor feathers, girt with
'flowing tricolor taffeta; in close frock, tricolor sash, sword and
'jack-boots,' these men are powerfuler than King or Kaiser.
They say to whomso they meet, Do; and he must do it: all men's
goods are at their disposal; for France is as one huge City in
Siege.   They smite with Requisitions and Forced-loan; they have
the power of life and death.   Saint-Just and Lebas order the rich
classes of Strasburg to 'strip-off their shoes,' and send them to
the Armies, where as many as 'ten-thousand pairs' are needed.
Also, that within four-and-twenty hours, 'a thousand beds' be
got ready;[3] wrapt in matting, and sent under way.   For the
time presses!—Like swift bolts, issuing from the fuliginous
Olympus of *Salut Public*, rush these men, oftenest in pairs;
scatter your thunder-orders over France; make France one
enormous Revolutionary thunder-cloud.

[3] *Moniteur*, du 27 Novembre 1793.

CHAPTER VI.

DO THY DUTY.

ACCORDINGLY, alongside of these bonfires of Church-balustrades, and sounds of fusillading and noyading, there rise quite another sort of fires and sounds: Smithy-fires and Proof-volleys for the manufacture of arms.

Cut off from Sweden and the world, the Republic must learn to make steel for itself; and, by aid of Chemists, she has learnt it. Towns that knew only iron, now know steel: from their new dungeons at Chantilly, Aristocrats may hear the rustle of our new steel furnace there. Do not bells transmute themselves into cannon; iron stancheons into the white-weapon (*arme blanche*), by sword-cutlery? The wheels of Langres scream, amid their sputtering fire-halo; grinding mere swords. The stithies of Charleville ring with gun-making. What say we, Charleville? Two-hundred and fifty-eight Forges stand in the open spaces of Paris itself; a hundred and forty of them in the Esplanade of the Invalides, fifty-four in the Luxembourg Garden: so many Forges stand; grim Smiths beating and forging at lock and barrel there. The Clock-makers have come, requisitioned, to do the touch-holes, the hard-solder and file-work. Five great Barges swing at anchor on the Seine Stream, loud with boring; the great press-drills grating harsh thunder to the general ear and heart. And deft Stock-makers do gouge and rasp; and all men bestir themselves, according to their cunning :—in the language of hope, it is reckoned that 'a thousand finished muskets can be delivered daily.'[1] Chemists of the Republic have taught us miracles of swift tanning:[2] the cordwainer bores and stitches ;—*not* of 'wood and pasteboard,' or he shall answer it to Tinville! The women sew tents and coats, the children scrape surgeon's-lint, the old men sit in the market-places; able men are on march; all men in requisition: from Town to Town flutters, on the Heaven's winds, this Banner, THE FRENCH PEOPLE RISEN AGAINST TYRANTS.

[1] *Choix des Rapports*, xiii. 189.   [2] Ibid. xv. 360.

All which is well. But now arises the question: What is to be done for saltpetre? Interrupted Commerce and the English Navy shut us out from saltpetre; and without saltpetre there is no gunpowder. Republican Science again sits meditative; discovers that saltpetre exists here and there, though in attenuated quantity; that old plaster of walls holds a sprinkling of it;—that the earth of the Paris Cellars holds a sprinkling of it, diffused through the common rubbish; that were these dug up and washed, saltpetre might be had. Whereupon, swiftly, see! the Citoyens, with up-shoved *bonnet rouge*, or with doffed bonnet, and hair toil-wetted; digging fiercely, each in his own cellar, for saltpetre. The Earth-heap rises at every door; the Citoyennes with hod and bucket carrying it up; the Citoyens, pith in every muscle, shovelling and digging: for life and saltpetre. Dig, my *braves;* and right well speed ye! What of saltpetre is essential the Republic shall not want.

Consummation of Sansculottism has many aspects and tints: but the brightest tint, really of a solar or stellar brightness, is this which the Armies give it. That same fervour of Jacobinism, which internally fills France with hatreds, suspicions, scaffolds and Reason-worship, does, on the Frontiers, show itself as a glorious *Pro patria mori*. Ever since Dumouriez's defection, three Convention Representatives attend every General. Committee of *Salut* has sent them; often with this Laconic order only: "Do thy duty, *Fais ton devoir.*" It is strange, under what impediments the fire of Jacobinism, like other such fires, will burn. These Soldiers have shoes of wood and pasteboard, or go booted in hay-ropes, in dead of winter; they skewer a bast mat round their shoulders, and are destitute of most things. What then? It is for Rights of Frenchhood, of Manhood, that they fight: the unquenchable spirit, here as elsewhere, works miracles. "With steel and bread," says the Convention Representative, "one may get to China." The Generals go fast to the guillotine; justly and unjustly. From which what inference? This, among others: That ill-success is death; that in victory alone is life! To conquer or die is no theatrical palabra, in these circumstances, but a practical truth and necessity. All Girondism, Halfness, Compromise is swept away. Forward, ye Soldiers of the Republic, captain and man! Dash, with your Gaelic impetuosity, on Austria, England, Prussia, Spain, Sardinia; Pitt, Cobourg, York, and the Devil and the World! Behind us is but the Guillotine; before us is Victory, Apotheosis and Millennium without end!

See, accordingly, on all Frontiers, how the Sons of Night, astonished after short triumph, do recoil;—the Sons of the Republic flying at them, with wild *Ça-ira* or Marseillese *Aux armes*, with the temper of cat-o'-mountain, or demon incarnate; which no Son of Night can stand! Spain, which came bursting through the Pyrenees, rustling with Bourbon banners, and went conquering here and there for a season, falters at such cat-o'-mountain welcome; draws itself in again; too happy now were the Pyrenees impassable. Not only does Dugommier, conqueror of Toulon, drive Spain back; he invades Spain. General Dugommier invades it by the Eastern Pyrenees; General Müller shall invade it by the Western. *Shall,* that is the word: Committee of *Salut Public* has said it; Representative Cavaignac, on mission there, must see it done. Impossible! cries Müller.—Infallible! answers Cavaignac. Difficulty, impossibility, is to no purpose. "The Committee is deaf on that side of its head," answers Cavaignac, "*n'entend pas de cette oreille là.* How many wantest thou of men, of horses, cannons? Thou shalt have them. Conquerors, conquered or hanged, forward we must." [3] Which things also, even as the Representatives spake them, were *done*. The Spring of the new Year sees Spain invaded: and redoubts are carried, and Passes and Heights of the most scarped description; Spanish Field-officerism struck mute at such cat-o'-mountain spirit, the cannon forgetting to fire. [4] Swept are the Pyrenees; Town after Town flies open, burst by terror or the petard. In the course of another year, Spain will crave Peace; acknowledge its sins and the Republic; nay, in Madrid, there will be joy as for a victory, that even Peace is got.

Few things, we repeat, can be notabler than these Convention Representatives, with their power more than kingly. Nay at bottom are they not Kings, *Able-men*, of a sort; chosen from the Seven-hundred and Forty-nine French Kings; with this order, Do thy duty? Representative Levasseur, of small stature, by trade a mere pacific Surgeon-Accoucheur, has mutinies to quell; mad hosts (mad at the Doom of Custine) bellowing far and wide; he alone amid

---

[3] There is, in *Prudhomme*, an atrocity *à la* Captain-Kirk reported of this Cavaignac; which has been copied into Dictionaries of *Hommes Marquans*, of *Biographie Universelle*, &c.; which not only has no truth in it, but, much more singular, is still capable of being proved to have none.

[4] *Deux Amis*, xiii. 205-30; Toulongeon, &c.

them, the one small Representative,—small, but as hard as flint, which also carries *fire* in it! So too, at Hondschooten, far in the afternoon, he declares that the Battle is not lost; that it must be gained; and fights, himself, with his own obstetric hand;—horse shot under him, or say on foot, ' up to the haunches in tide-water;' cutting stoccado and passado there, in defiance of Water, Earth, Air and Fire, the choleric little Representative that he was! Whereby, as natural, Royal Highness of York had to withdraw,— occasionally at full gallop; like to be swallowed by the tide: and his Siege of Dunkirk became a dream, realising only much loss of beautiful siege-artillery and of brave lives.[5]

General Houchard, it would appear, stood behind a hedge on this Hondschooten occasion; wherefore they have since guillotined him. A new General Jourdan, late Sergeant Jourdan, commands in his stead: he, in long-winded Battles of Watigny, 'murderous artillery-fire mingling itself with sound of Revolutionary battle-hymns,' forces Austria behind the Sambre again; has hopes of purging the soil of Liberty. With hard wrestling, with artillerying and *ça-ira*-ing, it shall be done. In the course of a new Summer, Valenciennes will see itself beleaguered; Condé beleaguered; whatsoever is yet in the hands of Austria beleaguered and bombarded: nay, by Convention Decree, we even summon them *all* 'either to surrender in twenty-four hours, or else be put to the sword;'—a high saying, which, though it remains unfulfilled, may show what spirit one is of.

Representative Drouet, as an Old-dragoon, could fight by a kind of second nature: but he was unlucky. Him, in a night-foray at Maubeuge, the Austrians took alive, in October last. They stript him almost naked, he says; making a show of him, as King-taker of Varennes. They flung him into carts; sent him far into the interior of Cimmeria, to 'a Fortress called Spitzberg' on the Danube River; and left him there, at an elevation of perhaps a hundred and fifty feet, to his own bitter reflections. Reflections; and also devices! For the indomitable Old-dragoon constructs wing-machinery, of Paperkite; saws window-bars; determines to fly down. He will seize a boat, will follow the River's course; land somewhere in Crim Tartary, in the Black-Sea or Constantinople region: *à la* Sindbad! Authentic History, accordingly, looking far into Cimmeria, discerns dimly a phenomenon. In the dead night-watches, the Spitzberg sentry is near fainting with terror:— Is it a huge vague Portent descending through the night-air? It

[5] Levasseur, *Mémoires*, ii. c. 2-7.

is a huge National Representative Old-dragoon, descending by Paper-kite; too rapidly, alas! For Drouet had taken with him 'a small provision-store, twenty pounds weight or thereby;' which proved accelerative: so he fell, fracturing his leg; and lay there, moaning, till day dawned, till you could discern clearly that he was not a Portent but a Representative.[6]

Or see Saint-Just, in the Lines of Weissembourg, though physically of a timid apprehensive nature, how he charges with his 'Alsatian Peasants armed hastily' for the nonce; the solemn face of him blazing into flame; his black hair and tricolor hat-taffeta flowing in the breeze! These our Lines of Weissembourg were indeed forced, and Prussia and the Emigrants rolled through: but we *re*-force the Lines of Weissembourg; and Prussia and the Emigrants roll back again still faster,—hurled with bayonet-charges and fiery *ça-ira*-ing.

Ci-devant Sergeant Pichegru, *ci-devant* Sergeant Hoche, risen now to be Generals, have done wonders here. Tall Pichegru was meant for the Church; was Teacher of Mathematics once, in Brienne School,—his remarkablest Pupil there was the Boy Napoleon Buonaparte. He then, not in the sweetest humour, enlisted, exchanging ferula for musket; and had got the length of the halberd, beyond which nothing could be hoped; when the Bastille barriers falling made passage for him, and he is here. Hoche bore a hand at the literal overturn of the Bastille; he was, as we saw, a Sergeant of the *Gardes Françaises*, spending his pay in rushlights and cheap editions of books. How the Mountains are burst, and many an Enceladus is disimprisoned; and Captains founding on Four parchments of Nobility are blown with their parchments across the Rhine, into Lunar Limbo!

What high feats of arms, therefore, were done in these Fourteen Armies; and how, for love of Liberty and hope of Promotion, lowborn valour cut its desperate way to Generalship; and, from the central Carnot in *Salut Public* to the outmost drummer on the Frontiers, men strove for their Republic, let Readers fancy. The snows of Winter, the flowers of Summer continue to be stained with warlike blood. Gaelic impetuosity mounts ever higher with victory; spirit of Jacobinism weds itself to national vanity: the Soldiers of the Republic are becoming, as we prophesied, very Sons of Fire. Barefooted, barebacked: but with bread and iron you can get to China! It is one Nation against the whole world; but

[6] His Narrative (in *Deux Amis*, xiv. 177-86).

the Nation has that within her which the whole world will not conquer. Cimmeria, astonished, recoils faster or slower; all round the Republic there rises fiery, as it were, a magic ring of musket-volleying and *ça-ira*-ing. Majesty of Prussia, as Majesty of Spain, will by and by acknowledge his sins and the Republic; and make a Peace of Bâle.

Foreign Commerce, Colonies, Factories in the East and in the West, are fallen or falling into the hands of sea-ruling Pitt, enemy of human nature. Nevertheless what sound is this that we hear, on the first of June 1794; sound as of war-thunder borne from the Ocean too, of tone most piercing? War-thunder from off the Brest waters: Villaret-Joyeuse and English Howe, after long manœuvering, have ranked themselves there; and are belching fire. The enemies of human nature are on their own element; cannot be conquered; cannot be kept from conquering. Twelve hours of raging cannonade; sun now sinking westward through the battle-smoke: six French Ships taken, the Battle lost; what Ship soever can still sail, making off! But how is it, then, with that *Vengeur* Ship, she neither strikes nor makes off? She is lamed, she cannot make off; strike she will not. Fire rakes her fore and aft from victorious enemies; the *Vengeur* is sinking. Strong are ye, Tyrants of the sea; yet we also, are we weak? Lo! all flags, streamers, jacks, every rag of tricolor that will yet run on rope, fly rustling aloft: the whole crew crowds to the upper deck; and with universal soul-maddening yell, shouts *Vive la République*, —sinking, sinking. She staggers, she lurches, her last drunk whirl; Ocean yawns abysmal: down rushes the *Vengeur*, carrying *Vive la République* along with her, unconquerable, into Eternity.[7] Let foreign Despots think of that. There is an Unconquerable in man, when he stands on his Rights of Man: let Despots and Slaves and all people know this, and only them that stand on the Wrongs of Man tremble to know it.—So has History written, nothing doubting, of the sunk *Vengeur*.

—— Reader! Mendez Pinto, Münchausen, Cagliostro, Psalma-nazar have been great; but they are not the greatest. O Barrère, Barrère, Anacreon of the Guillotine! must inquisitive pictorial History, in a new edition, ask again, 'How *is* it with the *Vengeur*,' in this its glorious suicidal sinking; and, with resentful brush, dash a bend-sinister of contumelious lampblack through thee and it? Alas, alas! The *Vengeur*, after fighting bravely, did sink altogether

---

[7] Compare Barrère (*Choix des Rapports*, xvi. 416-21); Lord Howe (*Annual Register* of 1794, p. 86), &c.

as other ships do, her captain and above two-hundred of her crew escaping gladly in British boats; and this same enormous inspiring Feat, and rumour 'of sound most piercing,' turns out to be an enormous inspiring Non-entity, extant nowhere save, as falsehood, in the brain of Barrère! Actually so.[8] Founded, like the World itself, on *Nothing;* proved by Convention Report, by solemn Convention Decree and Decrees, and wooden '*Model of the Vengeur;*' believed, bewept, besung by the whole French People to this hour, it may be regarded as Barrère's masterpiece; the largest, most inspiring piece of *blague* manufactured, for some centuries, by any man or nation. As such, and not otherwise, be it henceforth memorable.

CHAPTER VII.

FLAME-PICTURE.

IN this manner, mad-blazing with flame of all imaginable tints, from the red of Tophet to the stellar-bright, blazes off this Consummation of Sansculottism.

But the hundredth part of the things that were done, and the thousandth part of the things that were projected and decreed to be done, would tire the tongue of History. Statue of the *Peuple Souverain,* high as Strasburg Steeple; which shall fling its shadow from the Pont Neuf over Jardin National and Convention Hall;— enormous, in Painter David's Head! With other the like enormous Statues not a few: realised in paper Decree. For, indeed, the Statue of Liberty herself is still but Plaster, in the Place de la Révolution. Then Equalisation of Weights and Measures, with decimal division; Institutions, of Music and of much else; Institute in general; School of Arts, School of Mars, *Elèves de la Patrie,* Normal Schools: amid such Gun-boring, Altar-burning, Saltpetre-digging, and miraculous improvements in Tannery!

What, for example, is this that Engineer Chappe is doing, in the Park of Vincennes? In the Park of Vincennes; and onwards, they say, in the Park of Lepelletier Saint-Fargeau the assassinated Deputy; and still onwards to the Heights of Ecouen and farther, he has scaffolding set up, has posts driven in; wooden arms with

[8] Carlyle's *Miscellanies,* § Sinking of the Vengeur.

elbow-joints are jerking and fugling in the air, in the most rapid mysterious manner ! Citoyens ran up, suspicious. Yes, O Citoyens, we are signalling: it is a device this, worthy of the Republic; a thing for what we will call *Far-writing* without the aid of post-bags; in Greek it shall be named Telegraph.—*Télégraphe sacré!* answers Citoyenism: For writing to Traitors, to Austria?—and tears it down. Chappe had to escape, and get a new Legislative Decree. Nevertheless he has accomplished it, the indefatigable Chappe: this his *Far-writer*, with its wooden arms and elbow-joints, can intelligibly signal; and lines of them are set up, to the North Frontiers and elsewhither. On an Autumn evening of the Year Two, Far-writer having just written that Condé Town has surrendered to us, we send from the Tuileries Convention-Hall this response in the shape of Decree: 'The name of Condé is 'changed to *Nord-Libre*, North-Free. The Army of the North 'ceases not to merit well of the country.'—To the admiration of men! For lo, in some half hour, while the Convention yet debates, there arrives this new answer: 'I inform thee, *je t'annonce*, 'Citizen President, that the Decree of Convention, ordering change 'of the name Condé into *North-Free;* and the other, declaring that 'the Army of the North ceases not to merit well of the country; 'are transmitted and acknowledged by Telegraph. I have in-'structed my Officer at Lille to forward them to North-Free by 'express. *Signed*, CHAPPE.' [1]

Or see, over Fleurus in the Netherlands, where General Jourdan, having now swept the soil of Liberty, and advanced thus far, is just about to fight, and sweep or be swept, hangs there not in the Heaven's Vault some Prodigy, seen by Austrian eyes and spy-glasses: in the similitude of an enormous Wind-bag, with netting and enormous Saucer depending from it ? A Jove's Balance, O ye Austrian spy-glasses ? One saucer-scale of a Jove's Balance ; *your* poor Austrian scale having kicked itself quite aloft, out of sight ? By Heaven, answer the spy-glasses, it is a Montgolfier, a Balloon, and they are making signals! Austrian cannon-battery barks at this Montgolfier; harmless as dog at the Moon: the Montgolfier makes its signals ; detects what Austrian ambuscade there may be, and descends at its ease.[2]—What will not these devils incarnate contrive ?

On the whole, is it not, O Reader, one of the strangest Flame-

[1] *Choix des Rapports*, xv. 378, 384.

[2] 26th June 1794 (see *Rapport de Guyton-Morveau sur les Aérostats*, in *Moniteur* du 6 Vendémiaire, An 2).

Pictures that ever painted itself; flaming off there, on its ground
of Guillotine-black? And the nightly Theatres are Twenty-three;
and the *Salons de danse* are Sixty; full of mere *Egalité, Fraternité*
and *Carmagnole*. And Section Committee-rooms are Forty-eight;
redolent of tobacco and brandy: vigorous with twenty-pence a-day,
coercing the Suspect. And the Houses of Arrest are Twelve, for
Paris alone; crowded and even crammed. And at all turns, you
need your 'Certificate of Civism;' be it for going out, or for
coming in; nay without it you cannot, for money, get your daily
ounces of bread. Dusky red-capped Bakers'-queues; wagging
themselves; not in silence! For we still live by Maximum, in all
things; waited on by these two, Scarcity and Confusion. The
faces of men are darkened with suspicion; with suspecting, or
being suspect. The streets lie unswept; the ways unmended.
Law has shut her Books; speaks little, save impromptu, through
the throat of Tinville. Crimes go unpunished; not crimes against
the Revolution.[3] 'The number of foundling children,' as some
compute, 'is doubled.'

How silent now sits Royalism; sits all Aristocratism; Respectability that kept its Gig! The honour now, and the safety, is to
Poverty, not to Wealth. Your Citizen, who would be fashionable, walks abroad, with his Wife on his arm, in red-wool nightcap,
black-shag spencer, and carmagnole complete. Aristocratism
crouches low, in what shelter is still left; submitting to all requisitions, vexations; too happy to escape with life. Ghastly
châteaus stare on you by the wayside; disroofed, diswindowed;
which the National Housebroker is peeling for the lead and ashlar.
The old tenants hover disconsolate, over the Rhine with Condé; a
spectacle to men. *Ci-devant* Seigneur, exquisite in palate, will
become an exquisite Restaurateur Cook in Hamburg; *Ci-devant*
Madame, exquisite in dress, a successful *Marchande des Modes* in
London. In Newgate-Street, you meet M. le Marquis, with a
rough deal on his shoulder, adze and jack-plane under arm; he
has taken to the joiner trade; it being necessary to live (*faut
vivre*).[4]—Higher than all Frenchmen the domestic Stock-jobber
flourishes,—in a day of Paper-money. The Farmer also flourishes:
'Farmers' houses,' says Mercier, 'have become like Pawnbrokers'
shops;' all manner of furniture, apparel, vessels of gold and silver
accumulate themselves there: bread is precious. The Farmer's

---

[3] Mercier, v. 25; *Deux Amis*, xii. 142-199.

[4] See *Deux Amis*, xv. 189-192; *Mémoires de Genlis*; *Founders of the French
Republic*, &c. &c.

rent is Paper-money, and he alone of men has bread : Farmer is
better than Landlord, and will himself become Landlord.

And daily, we say, like a black Spectre, silently through that
Life-tumult, passes the Revolution Cart; writing on the walls its
MENE, MENE, *Thou art weighed, and found wanting !* A Spectre
with which one has grown familiar. Men have adjusted themselves : complaint issues not from that Death-tumbril. Weak
women and *ci-devants,* their plumage and finery all tarnished, sit
there; with a silent gaze, as if looking into the Infinite Black.
The once light lip wears a curl of irony, uttering no word ; and the
Tumbril fares along. They may be guilty before Heaven, or not ;
they are guilty, we suppose, before the Revolution. Then, does
not the Republic 'coin money' of them, with its great axe ? Red
Nightcaps howl dire approval : the rest of Paris looks on ; if with
a sigh, that is much : Fellow-creatures whom sighing cannot help;
whom black Necessity and Tinville have clutched.

One other thing, or rather two other things, we will still mention;
and no more : The Blond Perukes; the Tannery at Meudon. Great
talk is of these *Perruques blondes :* O Reader, they are made from
the Heads of Guillotined women ! The locks of a Duchess, in this
way, may come to cover the scalp of a Cordwainer ; her blonde
German Frankism his black Gaelic poll, if it be bald. Or they
may be worn affectionately, as relics ; rendering one suspect ?[5]
Citizens use them, not without mockery; of a rather cannibal sort.

Still deeper into one's heart goes that Tannery at Meudon ; not
mentioned among the other miracles of tanning ! 'At Meudon,'
says Montgaillard with considerable calmness, 'there was a Tan-
'nery of Human Skins; such of the Guillotined as seemed worth
'flaying : of which perfectly good wash-leather was made;' for
breeches, and other uses. The skin of the men, he remarks, was
superior in toughness (*consistance*) and quality to shamoy ; that of
the women was good for almost nothing, being so soft in texture ![6]
—History looking back over Cannibalism, through *Purchas's
Pilgrims* and all early and late Records, will perhaps find no
terrestrial Cannibalism of a sort, on the whole, so detestable. It is
a manufactured, soft-feeling, quietly elegant sort ; a sort *perfide!*
Alas, then, is man's civilisation only a wrappage, through which
the savage nature of him can still burst, infernal as ever ? Nature
still makes him ; and has an Infernal in her as well as a Celestial.

---

[5] Mercier, ii. 134.   [6] Montgaillard, iv. 290.

BOOK SIXTH.

THERMIDOR.

CHAPTER I.

THE GODS ARE ATHIRST.

WHAT, then, is this Thing called *La Révolution*, which, like an Angel of Death, hangs over France, noyading, fusillading, fighting, gun-boring, tanning human skins? *La Révolution* is but so many Alphabetic Letters; a thing nowhere to be laid hands on, to be clapt under lock and key: where is it? what is it? It is the Madness that dwells in the hearts of men. In this man it is, and in that man; as a rage or as a terror, it is in all men. Invisible, impalpable; and yet no black Azrael, with wings spread over half a continent, with sword sweeping from sea to sea, could be a truer Reality.

To explain, what is called explaining, the march of this Revolutionary Government, be no task of ours. Man cannot explain it. A paralytic Couthon, asking in the Jacobins, 'What hast thou done to be hanged if Counter-Revolution should arrive?' a sombre Saint-Just, not yet six-and-twenty, declaring that 'for Revolutionists there is no rest but in the tomb;' a seagreen Robespierre converted into vinegar and gall; much more an Amar and Vadier, a Collot and Billaud: to inquire what thoughts, predetermination or prevision, might be in the head of these men! Record of their thought remains not; Death and Darkness have swept it out utterly. Nay, if we even had their thought, all that they could have articulately spoken to us, how insignificant a fraction were that of the Thing which realised itself, which decreed itself, on signal given by them! As has been said more than once,

this Revolutionary Government is not a self-conscious but a blind
fatal one.   Each man, enveloped in his ambient-atmosphere of
revolutionary fanatic Madness, rushes on, impelled and impelling;
and has become a blind brute Force; no rest for him but in the
grave !   Darkness and the mystery of horrid cruelty cover it for
us, in History; as they did in Nature.   The chaotic Thunder-
cloud, with its pitchy black, and its tumult of dazzling jagged fire,
in a world all electric: thou wilt not undertake to show how that
comported itself,—what the secrets of its dark womb were; from
what sources, with what specialties, the lightning it held did, in
confused brightness of terror, strike forth, destructive and self-
destructive, till it ended ?   Like a Blackness naturally of Erebus,
which by will of Providence had for once mounted itself into
dominion and the Azure : is not this properly the nature of Sansculottism consummating itself ?   Of which Erebus Blackness be
it enough to discern that this and the other dazzling fire-bolt,
dazzling fire-torrent, does by small Volition and great Necessity,
verily issue,—in such and such succession; destructive so and so,
self-destructive so and so : till it end.

Royalism is extinct; 'sunk,' as they say, 'in the mud of the
Loire ;' Republicanism dominates without and within : what,
therefore, on the 15th day of March 1794, is this ?   Arrestment,
sudden really as a bolt out of the Blue, has hit strange victims:
Hébert *Père Duchesne*, Bibliopolist Momoro, Clerk Vincent, General
Ronsin ; high Cordelier Patriots, red-capped Magistrates of Paris,
Worshippers of Reason, Commanders of Revolutionary Army !
Eight short days ago, their Cordelier Club was loud, and louder
than ever, with Patriot denunciations.   Hébert *Père Duchesne* had
"held his tongue and his heart these two months, at sight of
"Moderates, Crypto-Aristocrats, Camilles, *Scélérats* in the Con-
"vention itself : but could not do it any longer; would, if other
"remedy were not, invoke the sacred right of Insurrection."   So
spake Hébert in Cordelier Session ; with vivats, till the roofs rang
again.[1]   Eight short days ago; and now already !   They rub their
eyes : it is no dream; they find themselves in the Luxembourg.
Goose Gobel too; and they that burnt Churches !   Chaumette
himself, potent Procureur, *Agent National* as they now call it, who
could 'recognise the Suspect by the very face of them,' he lingers
but three days ; on the third day he too is hurled in.   Most chop-

___
[1] *Moniteur*, du 17 Ventose (7th March), 1704.

fallen, blue, enters the National Agent this Limbo whither he has sent so many. Prisoners crowd round, jibing and jeering; "Sublime "National Agent," says one, "in virtue of thy immortal Proclama-"tion, lo there! I am suspect, thou art suspect, he is suspect, we "are suspect, ye are suspect, they are suspect!"

The meaning of these things? Meaning! It is a Plot; Plot of the most extensive ramifications; which, however, Barrère holds the threads of. Such Church-burning and scandalous masquerades of Atheism, fit to make the Revolution odious: where indeed could they originate but in the gold of Pitt? Pitt indubitably, as Preter-natural Insight will teach one, did hire this Faction of *Enragés*, to play their fantastic tricks; to roar in their Cordeliers Club about Moderatism; to print their *Père Duchesne ;* worship skyblue Reason in red nightcap; rob Altars,—and bring the spoil to *us !*

Still more indubitable, visible to the mere bodily sight, is this: that the Cordeliers Club sits pale, with anger and terror; and has 'veiled the Rights of Man,'—without effect. Likewise that the Jacobins are in considerable confusion; busy 'purging themselves, *s'épurant,*' as in times of Plot and public Calamity they have repeatedly had to do. Not even Camille Desmoulins but has given offence: nay there have risen murmurs against Danton him-self; though he bellowed them down, and Robespierre finished the matter by 'embracing him in the Tribune.'

Whom shall the Republic and a jealous Mother Society trust? In these times of temptation, of Preternatural Insight! For there are Factions of the Stranger, '*de l'étranger,*' Factions of Moderates, of Enraged; all manner of Factions: we walk in a world of Plots; strings universally spread, of deadly gins and falltraps, baited by the gold of Pitt! Clootz, Speaker of Mankind so-called, with his *Evidences of Mahometan Religion*, and babble of Universal Republic, him an incorruptible Robespierre has purged away. Baron Clootz, and Paine rebellious Needleman lie, these two months, in the Luxembourg; limbs of the Faction *de l'étranger*. Representative Phélippeaux is purged out: he came back from La Vendée with an ill report in his mouth against rogue Rossignol, and our method of warfare there. Recant it, O Phélippeaux, we entreat thee! Phélippeaux will not recant; and is purged out. Representative Fabre d'Eglantine, famed Nomenclator of Romme's Calendar, is purged out; nay, is cast into the Luxembourg: accused of Legis-lative Swindling 'in regard to moneys of the India Company.' There with his Chabots, Bazires, guilty of the like, let Fabre wait

his destiny. And Westermann friend of Danton, he who led the
Marseillese on the Tenth of August, and fought well in La Vendée,
but spoke not well of rogue Rossignol, is purged out. Lucky, if
he too go not to the Luxembourg. And your Prolys, Guzmans, of
the Faction of the Stranger, they have gone; Pereyra, though he
fled, is gone, 'taken in the disguise of a Tavern Cook.' I am
suspect, thou art suspect, he is suspect!—

The great heart of Danton is weary of it. Danton is gone to
native Arcis, for a little breathing-time of peace: Away, black
Arachne-webs, thou world of Fury, Terror and Suspicion; welcome,
thou everlasting Mother, with thy spring greenness, thy kind
household loves and memories; true art thou, were all else untrue!
The great Titan walks silent, by the banks of the murmuring
Aube, in young native haunts that knew him when a boy; wonders
what the end of these things may be.

But strangest of all, Camille Desmoulins is purged out. Couthon
gave as a test in regard to Jacobin purgation the question, 'What
hast thou done to be hanged if Counter-Revolution should arrive?'
Yet Camille, who could so well answer this question, is purged
out! The truth is, Camille, early in December last, began publishing a new Journal, or Series of Pamphlets, entitled the *Vieux
Cordelier*, Old Cordelier. Camille, not afraid at one time to
'embrace Liberty on a heap of dead bodies,' begins to ask now,
Whether among so many arresting and punishing Committees,
there ought not to be a 'Committee of Mercy'? Saint-Just, he
observes, is an extremely solemn young Republican, who 'carries
his head as if it were a *Saint-Sacrement*,' adorable Hostie, or divine
Real-Presence! Sharply enough, this *old* Cordelier,—Danton and
he were of the earliest primary Cordeliers,—shoots his glittering
war-shafts into your *new* Cordeliers, your Héberts, Momoros, with
their brawling brutalities and despicabilities; say, as the Sun-god
(for poor Camille is a Poet) shot into that Python Serpent sprung
of mud.

Whereat, as was natural, the Hébertist Python did hiss and
writhe amazingly; and threaten 'sacred right of Insurrection;'—
and, as we saw, get cast into Prison. Nay, with all the old wit,
dexterity and light graceful poignancy, Camille, translating 'out
of *Tacitus*, from the Reign of Tiberius,' pricks into the *Law of the
Suspect* itself; making it odious! Twice, in the Decade, his wild
Leaves issue; full of wit, nay of humour, of harmonious ingenuity
and insight,—one of the strangest phenomena of that dark time;

and smite, in their wild-sparkling way, at various monstrosities, Saint-Sacrament heads, and Juggernaut idols, in a rather reckless manner. To the great joy of Josephine Beauharnais, and the other Five-thousand and odd Suspect, who fill the Twelve Houses of Arrest; on whom a ray of hope dawns! Robespierre, at first approbatory, knew not at last what to think; then thought, with his Jacobins, that Camille must be expelled. A man of true Revolutionary spirit, this Camille; but with the unwisest sallies; whom Aristocrats and Moderates have the art to corrupt! Jacobinism is in uttermost crisis and struggle; enmeshed wholly in plots, corruptibilities, neck-gins and baited falltraps of Pitt *ennemi du genre humain*. Camille's First Number begins with '*O Pitt!*' —his last is dated 15 Pluviose Year 2, 3d February 1794; and ends with these words of Montezuma's, '*Les dieux ont soif*, The gods are athirst.'

Be this as it may, the Hébertists lie in Prison only some nine days. On the 24th of March, therefore, the Revolution Tumbrils carry through that Life-tumult a new cargo: Hébert, Vincent, Momoro, Ronsin, Nineteen of them in all; with whom, curious enough, sits Clootz Speaker of Mankind. They have been massed swiftly into a lump, this miscellany of Nondescripts; and travel now their last road. No help. They too must 'look through the little window;' they too 'must sneeze into the sack,' *éternuer dans le sac;* as they have done to others, so is it done to them. *Sainte-Guillotine,* meseems, is worse than the old Saints of Superstition; a man-devouring Saint? Clootz, still with an air of polished sarcasm, endeavours to jest, to offer cheering 'arguments of Materialism;' he requested to be executed last, 'in order to establish certain principles,'—which hitherto, I think, Philosophy has got no good of. General Ronsin too, he still looks forth with some air of defiance, eye of command: the rest are sunk in the stony paleness of despair. Momoro, poor Bibliopolist, no Agrarian Law yet realised,—they might as well have hanged thee at Evreux, twenty months ago, when Girondin Buzot hindered them. Hébert *Père Duchesne* shall never in this world rise in sacred right of insurrection; he sits there low enough, head sunk on breast; Red Nightcaps shouting round him, in frightful parody of his Newspaper Articles, "Grand choler of the Père Duchesne!" Thus perish they; the sack receives all their heads. Through some section of History, Nineteen spectre-chimeras shall flit, squeaking and gibbering; till Oblivion swallow them.

In the course of a week, the Revolutionary Army itself is disbanded; the General having become spectral. This Faction of Rabids, therefore, is also purged from the Republican soil; here also the baited falltraps of that Pitt have been wrenched up harmless; and anew there is joy over a Plot Discovered. The Revolution, then, is verily devouring its own children? All Anarchy, by the nature of it, is not only destructive but self-destructive.

CHAPTER II.

DANTON, NO WEAKNESS.

DANTON meanwhile has been pressingly sent for from Arcis: he must return instantly, cried Camille, cried Phélippeaux and Friends, who scented danger in the wind. Danger enough! A Danton, a Robespierre, chief-products of a victorious Revolution, are now arrived in immediate front of one another; must ascertain how they will live together, rule together. One conceives easily the deep mutual incompatibility that divided these two: with what terror of feminine hatred the poor seagreen Formula looked at the monstrous colossal Reality, and grew greener to behold him;— the Reality, again, struggling to think no ill of a chief-product of the Revolution; yet feeling at bottom that such chief-product was little other than a chief windbag, blown large by Popular air; not a man, with the heart of a man, but a poor spasmodic incorruptible pedant, with a logic-formula instead of heart; of Jesuit or Methodist-Parson nature; full of sincere-cant, incorruptibility, of virulence, poltroonery; barren as the eastwind! Two such chief-products are too much for one Revolution.

Friends, trembling at the results of a quarrel on their part, brought them to meet. "It is right," said Danton, swallowing much indignation, "to repress the Royalists: but we should not strike except where it is useful to the Republic; we should not confound the innocent and the guilty."—"And who told you," replied Robespierre with a poisonous look, "that one innocent person had perished?"—"Quoi," said Danton, turning round to

Friend Pâris self-named Fabricius, Juryman in the Revolutionary Tribunal: "*Quoi*, not one innocent? What sayest thou of it, Fabricius?"[1]—Friends, Westermann, this Pâris and others urged him to show himself, to ascend the Tribune and act. The man Danton was not prone to show himself; to act, or uproar for his own safety. A man of careless, large, hoping nature; a large nature that could rest: he would sit whole hours, they say, hearing Camille talk, and liked nothing so well. Friends urged him to fly; his Wife urged him: "Whither fly?" answered he: "If freed France cast me out, there are only dungeons for me elsewhere. One carries not his country with him at the sole of his shoe!" The man Danton sat still. Not even the arrestment of Friend Hérault, a member of *Salut*, yet arrested by *Salut*, can rouse Danton.—On the night of the 30th of March Juryman Pâris came rushing in; haste looking through his eyes: A clerk of the *Salut* Committee had told him Danton's warrant was made out, he is to be arrested this very night! Entreaties there are and trepidation, of poor Wife, of Pâris and Friends: Danton sat silent for a while; then answered, "*Ils n'oseraient*, They dare not;" and would take no measures. Murmuring "They dare not," he goes to sleep as usual.

And yet, on the morrow morning, strange rumour spreads over Paris City: Danton, Camille, Phélippeaux, Lacroix have been arrested overnight! It is verily so: the corridors of the Luxembourg were all crowded, Prisoners crowding forth to see this giant of the Revolution enter among them. "Messieurs," said Danton politely, "I hoped soon to have got you all out of this: but here I am myself; and one sees not where it will end."—Rumour may spread over Paris: the Convention clusters itself into groups; wide-eyed, whispering "Danton arrested!" Who, then, is safe? Legendre, mounting the Tribune, utters, at his own peril, a feeble word for him; moving that he be heard at that Bar before indictment; but Robespierre frowns him down: "Did you hear Chabot or Bazire? Would you have two weights and measures?" Legendre cowers low: Danton, like the others, must take his doom.

Danton's Prison-thoughts were curious to have; but are not given in any quantity: indeed few such remarkable men have been left so obscure to us as this Titan of the Revolution. He was heard to ejaculate: "This time twelvemonth, I was moving the creation of that same Revolutionary Tribunal. I crave pardon

---

[1] *Biographie des Ministres*, § Danton.

for it of God and man. They are all Brothers Cain; Brissot
would have had me guillotined as Robespierre now will. I leave
the whole business in a frightful welter (*gâchis épouvantable*): not
one of them understands anything of government. Robespierre
will follow me; I drag down Robespierre. O, it were better to
be a poor fisherman than to meddle with governing of men."—
Camille's young beautiful Wife, who had made him rich not in
money alone, hovers round the Luxembourg, like a disembodied
spirit, day and night. Camille's stolen letters to her still exist;
stained with the mark of his tears.[2] "I carry my head like a
Saint-Sacrament?" so Saint-Just was heard to mutter: "perhaps
he will carry his like a Saint-Denis."

Unhappy Danton, thou still unhappier light Camille, once light
Procureur de la Lanterne, ye also have arrived, then, at the Bourne
of Creation, where, like Ulysses Polytlas at the limit and utmost
Gades of his voyage, gazing into that dim Waste beyond Creation,
a man does see *the Shade of his Mother*, pale, ineffectual;—and
days when his Mother nursed and wrapped him are all-too sternly
contrasted with this day! Danton, Camille, Hérault, Westermann,
and the others, very strangely massed up with Bazires, Swindler
Chabots, Fabre d'Eglantines, Banker Freys, a most motley Batch,
'*Fournée*' as such things will be called, stand ranked at the Bar of
Tinville. It is the 2d of April 1794. Danton has had but three
days to lie in Prison; for the time presses.

What is your name? place of abode? and the like, Fouquier
asks; according to formality. "My name is Danton," answers he;
"a name tolerably known in the Revolution: my abode will soon
be Annihilation (*dans le Néant*); but I shall live in the Pantheon
of History." A man will endeavour to say something forcible, be
it by nature or not! Hérault mentions epigrammatically that he
"sat in this Hall, and was detested of Parlementeers." Camille
makes answer, "My age is that of the *bon Sansculotte Jésus;* an
age fatal to Revolutionists." O Camille, Camille! And yet in
that Divine Transaction, let us say, there did lie, among other
things, the fatalest Reproof ever uttered here below to Worldly
Right-honourableness; 'the highest fact,' so devout Novalis calls
it, 'in the Rights of Man.' Camille's real age, it would seem, is
thirty-four. Danton is one year older.

---

[2] *Aperçus sur Camille Desmoulins* (in *Vieux Cordelier*, Paris, 1825),
pp. 1-29.

Some five months ago, the Trial of the Twenty-two Girondins was the greatest that Fouquier had then done. But here is a still greater to do; a thing which tasks the whole faculty of Fouquier; which makes the very heart of him waver. For it is the voice of Danton that reverberates now from these domes; in passionate words, piercing with their wild sincerity, winged with wrath. Your best Witnesses he shivers into ruin at one stroke. He demands that the Committee-men themselves come as Witnesses, as Accusers; he "will cover them with ignominy." He raises his huge stature, he shakes his huge black head, fire flashes from the eyes of him,—piercing to all Republican hearts: so that the very Galleries, though we filled them by ticket, murmur sympathy; and are like to burst down and raise the People, and deliver him! He complains loudly that he is classed with Chabots, with swindling Stockjobbers; that his Indictment is a list of platitudes and horrors. "Danton hidden on the 10th of August?" reverberates he, with the roar of a lion in the toils: "where are the men that had to press Danton to show himself, that day? Where are these high-gifted souls of whom he borrowed energy? Let them appear, these Accusers of mine: I have all the clearness of my self-possession when I demand them. I will unmask the three shallow scoundrels," *les trois plats coquins*, Saint-Just, Couthon, Lebas, "who fawn on Robespierre, and lead him towards his destruction. Let them produce themselves here; I will plunge them into Nothingness, out of which they ought never to have risen." The agitated President agitates his bell; enjoins calmness, in a vehement manner: "What is it to thee how I defend myself?" cries the other: "the right of *dooming* me is thine always. The voice of a man speaking for his honour and his life may well drown the jingling of thy bell?" Thus Danton, higher and higher; till the lion-voice of him 'dies away in his throat:' speech will not utter what is in that man. The Galleries murmur ominously; the first day's Session is over.

O Tinville, President Herman, what will ye do? They have two days more of it, by strictest Revolutionary Law. The Galleries already murmur. If this Danton were to burst your meshwork!—Very curious indeed to consider. It turns on a hair: and what a hoitytoity were *there*, Justice and Culprit changing places; and the whole History of France running changed! For in France there is this Danton only that could still try to govern France. He only, the wild amorphous Titan;—and perhaps that other

olive-complexioned individual, the Artillery-Officer at Toulon,
whom we left pushing his fortune in the South?

On the evening of the second day, matters looking not better
but worse and worse, Fouquier and Herman, distraction in their
aspect, rush over to *Salut Public*. What is to be done? *Salut
Public* rapidly concocts a new Decree; whereby if men 'insult
Justice,' they may be 'thrown out of the Debates.' For indeed,
withal, is there not 'a Plot in the Luxembourg Prison'? *Ci-devant*
General Dillon, and others of the Suspect, plotting with Camille's
Wife to distribute *assignats*; to force the Prisons, overset the
Republic? Citizen Laflotte, himself Suspect but desiring enfran-
chisement, has reported said Plot for us:—a report that may bear
fruit! Enough, on the morrow morning, an obedient Convention
passes this Decree. *Salut* rushes off with it to the aid of Tinville,
reduced now almost to extremities. And so, *Hors de Débats*, Out
of the Debates, ye insolents! Policemen, do your duty! In such
manner, with a dead-lift effort, *Salut*, Tinville, Herman, Leroi
Dix-Août, and all stanch jurymen setting heart and shoulder to
it, the Jury becomes 'sufficiently instructed;' Sentence is passed,
is sent by an Official, and torn and trampled on: *Death this day*.
It is the 5th of April 1794. Camille's poor Wife may cease
hovering about this Prison. Nay let her kiss her poor children;
and prepare to enter it, and to follow!—

Danton carried a high look in the Death-cart. Not so Camille:
it is but one week, and all is so topsyturvied; angel Wife left
weeping; love, riches, revolutionary fame, left all at the Prison-
gate; carnivorous Rabble now howling round. Palpable, and yet
incredible; like a madman's dream! Camille struggles and
writhes; his shoulders shuffle the loose coat off them, which hangs
knotted, the hands tied: "Calm, my friend," said Danton; "heed
not that vile canaille (*laissez là cette vile canaille*)." At the foot
of the Scaffold, Danton was heard to ejaculate: "O my Wife, my
well-beloved, I shall never see thee more, then!"—but, interrupt-
ing himself: "Danton, no weakness!" He said to Hérault-
Séchelles stepping forward to embrace him: "Our heads will meet
there," in the Headsman's sack. His last words were to Samson
the Headsman himself: "Thou wilt show my head to the people:
it is worth showing."

So passes, like a gigantic mass of valour, ostentation, fury,
affection and wild revolutionary force and manhood, this Danton,
to his unknown home. He was of Arcis-sur-Aube; born of 'good

farmer-people' there. He had many sins; but one worst sin he had not, that of Cant. No hollow Formalist, deceptive and self-deceptive, *ghastly* to the natural sense, was this; but a very Man: with all his dross he was a Man; fiery-real, from the great fire-bosom of Nature herself. He saved France from Brunswick; he walked straight his own wild road, whither it led him. He may live for some generations in the memory of men.

CHAPTER III.

THE TUMBRILS.

Next week, it is still but the 10th of April, there comes a new Nineteen; Chaumette, Gobel, Hébert's Widow, the Widow of Camille: these also roll their fated journey; black Death devours them. Mean Hébert's Widow was weeping, Camille's Widow tried to speak comfort to her. O ye kind Heavens, azure, beautiful, eternal behind your tempests and Time-clouds, is there not pity in store for all! Gobel, it seems, was repentant; he begged absolution of a Priest; died as a Gobel best could. For Anaxagoras Chaumette, the sleek head now stripped of its *bonnet rouge*, what hope is there? Unless Death *were* 'an eternal sleep'? Wretched Anaxagoras, God shall judge thee, not I.

Hébert, therefore, is gone, and the Hébertists; they that robbed Churches, and adored blue Reason in red nightcap. Great Danton, and the Dantonists; they also are gone. Down to the catacombs; they are become silent men! Let no Paris Municipality, no Sect or Party of this hue or that, resist the will of Robespierre and *Salut*. Mayor Pache, not prompt enough in denouncing these Pitt Plots, may congratulate about them now. Never so heartily; it skills not! His course likewise is to the Luxembourg. We appoint one Fleuriot-Lescot Interim-Mayor in his stead: an 'architect from Belgium,' they say, this Fleuriot; he is a man one can depend on. Our new Agent-National is Payan, lately Juryman; whose cynosure also is Robespierre.

Thus then, we perceive, this confusedly electric Erebus-cloud of Revolutionary Government has altered its shape somewhat.

Two masses, or wings, belonging to it; an over-electric mass of Cordelier Rabids, and an under-electric of Dantonist Moderates and Clemency-men,—these two masses, shooting bolts at one another, so to speak, have annihilated one another. For the Erebus-cloud, as we often remark, is of suicidal nature; and, in jagged irregularity, darts its lightning withal into itself. But now these two discrepant masses being mutually annihilated, it is as if the Erebus-cloud had got to internal composure; and did only pour its hellfire lightning on the World that lay under it. In plain words, Terror of the Guillotine was never terrible till now. Systole, diastole, swift and ever swifter goes the Axe of Samson. Indictments cease by degrees to have so much as plausibility: Fouquier chooses from the Twelve Houses of Arrest what he calls Batches, '*Fournées*,' a score or more at a time; his Jurymen are charged to make *feu de file*, file-firing till the ground be *clear*. Citizen Laflotte's report of Plot in the Luxembourg is verily bearing fruit! If no speakable charge exist against a man, or Batch of men, Fouquier has always this: a Plot in the Prison. Swift and ever swifter goes Samson; up, finally, to threescore and more at a Batch. It is the highday of Death: none but the Dead return not.

O dusky D'Espréménil, what a day is this the 22d of April, thy last day! The Palais Hall here is the same stone Hall, where thou, five years ago, stoodest perorating, amid endless pathos of rebellious Parlement, in the gray of the morning; bound to march with D'Agoust to the Isles of Hières. The stones are the same stones: but the rest, Men, Rebellion, Pathos, Peroration, see, it has all fled, like a gibbering troop of ghosts, like the phantasms of a dying brain. With D'Espréménil, in the same line of Tumbrils, goes the mornfulest medley. Chapelier goes, *ci-devant* popular President of the Constituent; whom the Menads and Maillard met in his carriage, on the Versailles Road. Thouret likewise, *ci-devant* President, father of Constitutional Law-acts; he whom we heard saying, long since, with a loud voice, "The Constituent Assembly has fulfilled its mission!" And the noble old Malesherbes, who defended Louis and could not speak, like a gray old rock dissolving into sudden water: he journeys here now, with his kindred, daughters, sons and grandsons, his Lamoignons, Châteaubriands; silent, towards Death.—One young Châteaubriand alone is wandering amid the Natchez, by the roar of Niagara Falls, the moan of endless forests: Welcome thou great Nature, savage, but not false, not unkind, unmotherly; no Formula thou, or rabid jangle of Hypothesis, Parliamentary Eloquence, Constitution-building and the Guillotine; speak thou to me, O Mother, and sing my sick heart thy mystic everlasting lullaby-song, and let all the rest be far!—

Another row of Tumbrils we must notice : that which holds Elizabeth, the Sister of Louis. Her Trial was like the rest; for Plots, for Plots. She was among the kindliest, most innocent of women. There sat with her, amid four-and-twenty others, a once timorous Marchioness de Crussol; courageous now; expressing towards her the liveliest loyalty. At the foot of the Scaffold, Elizabeth with tears in her eyes thanked this Marchioness; said she was grieved she could not reward her. "Ah, Madame, would your Royal Highness deign to embrace me, my wishes were complete!"—"Right willingly, Marquise de Crussol, and with my whole heart." [1] Thus they : at the foot of the Scaffold. The Royal Family is now reduced to two : a girl and a little boy. The boy, once named Dauphin, was taken from his Mother while she yet lived; and given to one Simon, by trade a Cordwainer, on service then about the Temple-Prison, to bring him up in principles of Sansculottism. Simon taught him to drink, to swear, to sing the *carmagnole*. Simon is now gone to the Municipality : and the poor boy, hidden in a tower of the Temple, from which in his fright and bewilderment and early decrepitude he wishes not to stir out, lies perishing, 'his shirt not changed for six months;' amid squalor and darkness, lamentably,[2]—so as none but poor Factory Children and the like are wont to perish, and *not* be lamented!

The Spring sends its green leaves and bright weather, bright May, brighter than ever : Death pauses not. Lavoisier, famed Chemist, shall die and not live : Chemist Lavoisier was Farmer-General Lavoisier too, and now 'all the Farmers-General are arrested;' all, and shall give an account of their moneys and incomings; and die for 'putting water in the tobacco' they sold.[3] Lavoisier begged a fortnight more of life, to finish some experiments : but "the Republic does not need such;" the axe must do its work. Cynic Chamfort, reading these inscriptions of *Brotherhood or Death*, says, "it is a Brotherhood of Cain:" arrested,

---

[1] Montgaillard, iv. 200.

[2] Duchesse d'Angoulême, *Captivité à la Tour du Temple*, pp. 37-71.

[3] *Tribunal Révolutionnaire* du 8 Mai 1794 (*Moniteur*, No. 231).

then liberated; then about to be arrested again, this Chamfort
cuts and slashes himself with frantic uncertain hand; gains, not
without difficulty, the refuge of death. Condorcet has lurked
deep, these many months; Argus-eyes watching and searching
for him. His concealment is become dangerous to others and
himself; he has to fly again, to skulk, round Paris, in thickets
and stone-quarries. And so at the Village of Clamars, one
bleared May morning, there enters a Figure, ragged, rough-
bearded, hunger-stricken; asks breakfast in the tavern there.
Suspect, by the look of him! "Servant out of place, sayest
thou?" Committee-President of Forty-Sous finds a Latin Horace
on him: "Art not thou one of those *Ci-devants* that were wont
to keep servants? *Suspect!*" He is haled forthwith, breakfast
unfinished, towards Bourg-la-Reine, on foot: he faints with
exhaustion; is set on a peasant's horse; is flung into his damp
prison-cell: on the morrow, recollecting him, you enter; Condorcet lies dead on the floor. They die fast, and disappear: the
Notabilities of France disappear, one after one, like lights in a
Theatre, which you are snuffing out.

Under which circumstances, is it not singular, and almost
touching, to see Paris City drawn out, in the meek May nights,
in civic ceremony, which they call ' *Souper Fraternel*,' Brotherly
Supper? Spontaneous, or partially spontaneous, in the twelfth,
thirteenth, fourteenth nights of this May month, it is seen. Along
the Rue Saint-Honoré, and main Streets and Spaces, each Citoyen
brings forth what of supper the stingy *Maximum* has yielded him,
to the open air; joins it to his neighbour's supper; and with
common table, cheerful light burning frequent, and what due
modicum of cut-glass and other garnish and relish is convenient,
they eat frugally together, under the kind stars.[4] See it, O Night!
With cheerfully pledged wine-cup, hobnobbing to the Reign of
Liberty, Equality, Brotherhood, with their wives in best ribands,
with their little ones romping round, the Citoyens, in frugal
Love-feast, sit there. Night in her wide empire sees nothing
similar. O my brothers, why is the reign of Brotherhood *not*
come! It is come, it shall have come, say the Citoyens frugally
hobnobbing.—Ah me! these everlasting stars, do they not look
down ' like glistening eyes, bright with immortal pity, over the lot
of man'!—

[4] *Tableaux de la Révolution,* § Soupers Fraternels; Mercier, ii. 150.

One lamentable thing, however, is, that individuals will attempt assassination—of Representatives of the People. Representative Collot, Member even of *Salut*, returning home, 'about one in the morning,' probably touched with liquor, as he is apt to be, meets on the stairs the cry "*Scélérat!*" and also the snap of a pistol: which latter flashes in the pan; disclosing to him, momentarily, a pair of truculent saucer-eyes, swart grim-clenched countenance; recognisable as that of our little fellow-lodger, Citoyen Amiral, formerly 'a clerk in the Lotteries.' Collot shouts *Murder*, with lungs fit to awaken all the *Rue Favart;* Amiral snaps a second time; a second time flashes in the pan; then darts up into his apartment; and, after there firing, still with inadequate effect, one musket at himself and another at his captor, is clutched and locked in Prison.[5] An indignant little man this Amiral, of Southern temper and complexion, of 'considerable muscular force.' He denies not that he meant to "purge France of a Tyrant;" nay avows that he had an eye to the Incorruptible himself, but took Collot as more convenient!

Rumour enough hereupon; heaven-high congratulation of Collot, fraternal embracing, at the Jacobins and elsewhere. And yet, it would seem, the assassin mood proves catching. Two days more, it is still but the 23d of May, and towards nine in the evening, Cécile Rénault, Paper-dealer's daughter, a young woman of soft blooming look, presents herself at the Cabinet-maker's in the Rue Saint-Honoré; desires to see Robespierre. Robespierre cannot be seen; she grumbles irreverently. They lay hold of her. She has left a basket in a shop hard by: in the basket are female change of raiment and two knives! Poor Cécile, examined by Committee, declares she "wanted to see what a tyrant was like:" the change of raiment was "for my own use in the place I am surely going to."—"What place?"—"Prison; and then the Guillotine," answered she.—Such things come of Charlotte Corday; in a people prone to imitation, and monomania! Swart choleric men try Charlotte's feat, and their pistols miss fire; soft blooming young women try it, and, only half-resolute, leave their knives in a shop.

O Pitt, and ye Faction of the Stranger, shall the Republic never have rest; but be torn continually by baited springes, by wires of explosive spring-guns? Swart Amiral, fair young Cécile, and all that knew them, and many that did not know them, lie locked, waiting the scrutiny of Tinville.

[5] Riouffe, p. 73; *Deux Amis*, xii. 298-302.

CHAPTER IV.

MUMBO-JUMBO.

But on the day they call *Décadi*, New-Sabbath, 20 *Prairial*,
8th June by old style, what thing is this going forward in the
Jardin National, whilom Tuileries Garden?

All the world is there, in holiday clothes:[1] foul linen went
out with the Hébertists; nay Robespierre, for one, would never
once countenance that; but went always elegant and frizzled,
not without vanity even,—and had his room hung round with
seagreen Portraits and Busts. In holiday clothes, we say, are
the innumerable Citoyens and Citoyennes: the weather is of the
brightest; cheerful expectation lights all countenances. Juryman
Vilate gives breakfast to many a Deputy, in his official Apartment,
in the Pavillon *ci-devant* of Flora; rejoices in the bright-looking
multitudes, in the brightness of leafy June, in the auspicious
Décadi, or New-Sabbath. This day, if it please Heaven, we are
to have, on improved Anti-Chaumette principles: a New Religion.

Catholicism being burned out, and Reason-worship guillotined,
was there not need of one? Incorruptible Robespierre, not unlike
the Ancients, as Legislator of a free people, will now also be Priest
and Prophet. He has donned his sky-blue coat, made for the
occasion; white silk waistcoat broidered with silver, black silk
breeches, white stockings, shoe-buckles of gold. He is President
of the Convention; he has made the Convention *decree*, so they
name it, *décréter* the 'Existence of the Supreme Being,' and likewise '*ce principe consolateur* of the Immortality of the Soul.'
These consolatory principles, the basis of rational Republican
Religion, are getting decreed; and here, on this blessed *Décadi*,
by help of Heaven and Painter David, is to be our first act of
worship.

See, accordingly, how after Decree passed, and what has been
called 'the scraggiest Prophetic Discourse ever uttered by man,'—
Mahomet Robespierre, in sky-blue coat and black breeches, frizzled

---

[1] Vilate, *Causes Secrètes de la Révolution du 9 Thermidor.*

and powdered to perfection, bearing in his hand a bouquet of flowers and wheat-ears, issues proudly from the Convention Hall; Convention following him, yet, as is remarked, with an interval. Amphitheatre has been raised, or at least *Monticule* or Elevation; hideous Statues of Atheism, Anarchy and suchlike, thanks to Heaven and Painter David, strike abhorrence into the heart. Unluckily, however, our Monticule is too small. On the top of it not half of us can stand; wherefore there arises indecent shoving, nay treasonous irreverent growling. Peace, thou Bourdon de l'Oise; peace, or it may be worse for thee!

The seagreen Pontiff takes a torch, Painter David handing it; mouths some other froth-rant of vocables, which happily one cannot hear; strides resolutely forward, in sight of expectant France; sets his torch to Atheism and Company, which are but made of pasteboard steeped in turpentine. They burn up rapidly; and, from within, there rises 'by machinery,' an incombustible Statue of Wisdom, which, by ill hap, gets besmoked a little; but does stand there visible in as serene attitude as it can.

And then? Why, then, there is other Processioning, scraggy Discoursing, and—this *is* our Feast of the *Être Suprême;* our new Religion, better or worse, is come!—Look at it one moment, O Reader, not two. The shabbiest page of Human Annals: or is there, that thou wottest of, one shabbier? Mumbo-Jumbo of the African woods to me seems venerable beside this new Deity of Robespierre; for this is a *conscious* Mumbo-Jumbo, and *knows* that he is machinery. O seagreen Prophet, unhappiest of windbags blown nigh to bursting, what distracted Chimera among realities art thou growing to! This then, this common pitch-link for artificial fireworks of turpentine and pasteboard; *this* is the miraculous Aaron's Rod thou wilt stretch over a hag-ridden hell-ridden France, and bid her plagues cease? Vanish, thou and it!— "*Avec ton Être Suprême*," said Billaud, "*tu commences m'embêter:* With thy *Être Suprême* thou beginnest to be a bore to me." [2]

Catherine Théot, on the other hand, 'an ancient serving-maid seventy-nine years of age,' inured to Prophecy and the Bastille from of old, sits in an upper room in the Rue de Contrescarpe, poring over the Book of Revelations, with an eye to Robespierre; finds that this astonishing thrice-potent Maximilien really is the Man

[2] See Vilate, *Causes Secrètes.* (Vilate's Narrative is very curious; but is not to be taken as true, without sifting; being, at bottom, in spite of its title, not a Narrative but a Pleading.)

spoken of by Prophets, who is to make the Earth young again.
With her sit devout old Marchionesses, *ci-devant* honourable
women; among whom Old-Constituent Dom Gerle, with his addle
head, cannot be wanting. They sit there, in the Rue de Contrescarpe; in mysterious adoration: Mumbo is Mumbo, and Robespierre is his Prophet. A conspicuous man this Robespierre.
He has his volunteer Bodyguard of *Tappedurs*, let us say *Strike-
sharps*, fierce Patriots with feruled sticks; and Jacobins kissing
the hem of his garment. He enjoys the admiration of many, the
worship of some; and is well worth the wonder of one and all.

The grand question and hope, however, is: Will not this
Feast of the Tuileries Mumbo-Jumbo be a sign perhaps that the
Guillotine is to abate? Far enough from that! Precisely on the
second day after it, Couthon, one of the 'three shallow scoundrels,'
gets himself lifted into the Tribune; produces a bundle of papers.
Couthon proposes that, as Plots still abound, the *Law of the Suspect*
shall have extension, and Arrestment new vigour and facility.
Farther, that as in such case business is like to be heavy, our
Revolutionary Tribunal too shall have extension; be divided, say,
into Four Tribunals, each with its President, each with its
Fouquier or Substitute of Fouquier, all labouring at once, and
any remnant of shackle or dilatory formality be struck off: in
this way it may perhaps still overtake the work. Such is Couthon's
Decree of the Twenty-second Prairial, famed in those times. At
hearing of which Decree, the very Mountain gasped, awestruck;
and one Ruamps ventured to say that if it passed without adjourn-
ment and discussion, he, as one Representative, "would blow his
brains out." Vain saying! The Incorruptible knit his brows;
spoke a prophetic fateful word or two: the *Law of Prairial* is
Law; Ruamps glad to leave his rash brains where they are.
Death then, and always Death! Even so. Fouquier is enlarging
his borders; making room for Batches of a Hundred and fifty at
once;—getting a Guillotine set up of improved velocity, and to
work under cover, in the apartment close by. So that *Salut* itself
has to intervene, and forbid him: "Wilt thou *demoralise* the
Guillotine," asks Collot, reproachfully, "*démoraliser le supplice!*"

There is indeed danger of that; were not the Republican faith
great, it were already done. See, for example, on the 17th of June,
what a *Batch*, Fifty-four at once! Swart Amiral is here, he of the
pistol that missed fire; young Cécile Rénault, with her father,
family, entire kith and kin; the Widow of D'Espréménil; old M.

de Sombreuil of the Invalides, with his Son,—poor old Sombreuil, seventy-three years old, his Daughter saved him in September, and it was but for *this*. Faction of the Stranger, fifty-four of them! In red shirts and smocks, as Assassins and Faction of the Stranger, they flit along there; red baleful Phantasmagory, towards the land of Phantoms.

Meanwhile will not the people of the Place de la Révolution, the inhabitants along the Rue Saint-Honoré, as these continual Tumbrils pass, begin to look gloomy? Republicans too have bowels. The Guillotine is shifted, then again shifted; finally set up at the remote extremity of the South-east:[3] Suburbs Saint-Antoine and Saint-Marceau, it is to be hoped, if they have bowels, have very tough ones.

CHAPTER V.

THE PRISONS.

IT is time now, however, to cast a glance into the Prisons. When Desmoulins moved for his Committee of Mercy, these Twelve Houses of Arrest held five-thousand persons. Continually arriving since then, there have now accumulated twelve-thousand. They are Ci-devants, Royalists; in far greater part, they are Republicans, of various Girondin, Fayettish, Un-Jacobin colour. Perhaps no human Habitation or Prison ever equalled in squalor, in noisome horror, these Twelve Houses of Arrest. There exist records of personal experience in them, *Mémoires sur les Prisons;* one of the strangest Chapters in the Biography of Man.

Very singular to look into it: how a kind of order rises up in all conditions of human existence; and wherever two or three are gathered together, there are formed modes of existing together, habitudes, observances, nay gracefulness, joys! Citoyen Coittant will explain fully how our lean dinner, of herbs and carrion, was consumed not without politeness and *place-aux-dames:* how Seigneur and Shoeblack, Duchess and Doll-Tearsheet, flung pell-mell into a heap, ranked themselves according to method: at what hour 'the Citoyennes took to their needlework;' and we, yielding

[3] Montgaillard, iv. 237.

the chairs to them, endeavoured to talk gallantly in a standing posture, or even to sing and harp more or less. Jealousies, enmities, are not wanting; nor flirtations, of an effective character.

Alas, by degrees, even needlework must cease: Plot in the Prison rises, by Citoyen Laflotte and Preternatural Suspicion. Suspicious Municipality snatches from us all implements; all money and possession, of means or metal, is ruthlessly searched for, in pocket, in pillow and paillasse, and snatched away: red-capped Commissaries entering every cell. Indignation, temporary desperation, at robbery of its very thimble, fills the gentle heart. Old Nuns shriek shrill discord; demand to be killed forthwith. No help from shrieking! Better was that of the two shifty male Citizens, who, eager to preserve an implement or two, were it but a pipe-picker, or needle to darn hose with, determined to defend themselves: by tobacco. Swift then, as your fell Red Caps are heard in the Corridor rummaging and slamming, the two Citoyens light their pipes, and begin smoking. Thick darkness envelops them. The Red Nightcaps, opening the cell, breathe but one mouthful; burst forth into chorus of barking and coughing. "*Quoi, Messieurs,*" cry the two Citoyens, "you don't smoke? Is the pipe disagreeable? *Est-ce que vous ne fumez pas?*" But the Red Nightcaps have fled, with slight search: "*Vous n'aimez pas la pipe?*" cry the Citoyens, as their door slams-to again.[1] My poor brother Citoyens, O surely, in a reign of Brotherhood, you are not the two I would guillotine!

Rigour grows, stiffens into horrid tyranny; Plot in the Prison getting ever rifer. This Plot in the Prison, as we said, is now the stereotype formula of Tinville: against whomsoever he knows no crime, this is a ready-made crime. His Judgment-bar has become unspeakable; a recognised mockery; known only as the wicket one passes through, towards Death. His Indictments are drawn out in blank; you insert the Names after. He has his *moutons,* detestable traitor jackals, who report and bear witness; that they themselves may be allowed to live,—for a time. His *Fournées,* says the reproachful Collot, 'shall in no case exceed threescore;' that is his *maximum.* Nightly come his Tumbrils to the Luxembourg, with the fatal Roll-call; list of the *Fournée* of tomorrow. Men rush towards the Grate; listen, if their name be in it? One deep-drawn breath, when the name is not in; we live still one day!

[1] *Maison d'Arrêt de Port-Libre,* par Coittant, &c. (*Mémoires sur les Prisons,* ii.)

And yet some score or scores of names were in. Quick these, they clasp their loved ones to their heart, one last time; with brief adieu, wet-eyed or dry-eyed, they mount, and are away. This night to the Conciergerie; through the Palais misnamed *of Justice*, to the Guillotine tomorrow.

Recklessness, defiant levity, the Stoicism if not of strength yet of weakness, has possessed all hearts. Weak women and *Ci-devants*, their locks not yet made into blond perukes, their skins not yet tanned into breeches, are accustomed to 'act the Guillotine' by way of pastime. In fantastic mummery, with towel-turbans, blanket-ermine, a mock Sanhedrim of Judges sits, a mock Tinville pleads; a culprit is doomed, is guillotined by the oversetting of two chairs. Sometimes we carry it farther: Tinville himself, in his turn, is doomed, and not to the Guillotine alone. With blackened face, hirsute, horned, a shaggy Satan snatches him not unshrieking; shows him, with outstretched arm and voice, the fire that is not quenched, the worm that dies not; the monotony of Hell-pain, and the *What hour?* answered by, *It is Eternity.*[2]

And still the Prisons fill fuller, and still the Guillotine goes faster. On all high roads march flights of Prisoners, wending towards Paris. Not *Ci-devants* now; they, the noisy of them, are mown down; it is Republicans now. Chained two and two they march; in exasperated moments singing their *Marseillaise*. A hundred and thirty-two men of Nantes, for instance, march towards Paris, in these same days: Republicans, or say even Jacobins to the marrow of the bone; but Jacobins who had not approved Noyading.[3] *Vive la République* rises from them in all streets of towns: they rest by night in unutterable noisome dens, crowded to choking; one or two dead on the morrow. They are wayworn, weary of heart; can only shout: *Live the Republic;* we, as under horrid enchantment, dying in this way for it!

Some Four-hundred Priests, of whom also there is record, ride at anchor 'in the roads of the Isle of Aix,' long months; looking out on misery, vacuity, waste Sands of Oleron and the ever-moaning brine. Ragged, sordid, hungry; wasted to shadows: eating their unclean ration on deck, circularly, in parties of a dozen, with finger and thumb; beating their scandalous clothes between two stones; choked in horrible miasmata, closed under hatches, seventy of them in a berth, through night; so that the

[2] Montgaillard, iv. 218; Riouffe, p. 273.
[3] *Voyage de Cent Trente-deux Nantais (Prisons, ii. 288-325).*

' aged Priest is found lying dead in the morning, in the attitude of
prayer ! ' [4]—How long, O Lord !

Not forever; no. All Anarchy, all Evil, Injustice, is, by the
nature of it, *dragon's-teeth ;* suicidal, and cannot endure.

CHAPTER VI.

TO FINISH THE TERROR.

IT is very remarkable, indeed, that since the *Être-Suprême* Feast,
and the sublime continued harangues on it, which Billaud feared
would become a bore to him, Robespierre has gone little to Committee; but held himself apart, as if in a kind of pet. Nay they
have made a Report on that old Catherine Théot, and her
Regenerative Man spoken of by the Prophets; not in the best
spirit. This Théot mystery they affect to regard as a Plot; but
have evidently introduced a vein of satire, of irreverent banter, not
against the Spinster alone, but obliquely against her Regenerative
Man ! Barrère's light pen was perhaps at the bottom of it : read
through the solemn snuffling organs of old Vadier of the *Sûreté
Générale*, the Théot Report had its effect; wrinkling the general
Republican visage into an iron grin. Ought these things to be ?

We note farther, that among the Prisoners in the Twelve Houses
of Arrest, there is one whom we have seen before. Senhora Fontenai, *born* Cabarus, the fair Proserpine whom Representative
Tallien Pluto-like did gather at Bourdeaux, not without effect on
himself ! Tallien is home, by recall, long since, from Bourdeaux;
and in the most alarming position. Vain that he sounded, louder
even than ever, the note of Jacobinism, to hide past shortcomings :
the Jacobins purged him out; two times has Robespierre growled
at him words of omen from the Convention Tribune. And now
his fair Cabarus, hit by denunciation, lies Arrested, Suspect, in
spite of all he could do !—Shut in horrid pinfold of death, the
Senhora smuggles out to her red-gloomy Tallien the most pressing
entreaties and conjurings : Save me; save thyself. Seest thou

---

[4] *Relation de ce qu'ont souffert pour la Religion les Prêtres déportés en* 1794,
dans la rade de l'île d'Aix (*Prisons*, ii. 387-485).

not that thy own head is doomed; thou with a too fiery audacity; a Dantonist withal; against whom lie grudges? Are ye not all doomed, as in the Polyphemus Cavern: the fawningest slave of you will be but eaten last!—Tallien feels with a shudder that it is true. Tallien has had words of omen, Bourdon has had words, Fréron is hated and Barras: each man 'feels his head if it yet stick on his shoulders.'

Meanwhile Robespierre, we still observe, goes little to Convention, not at all to Committee; speaks nothing except to his Jacobin House of Lords, amid his bodyguard of *Tappe-durs*. These 'forty-days,' for we are now far in July, he has not showed face in Committee; could only work there by his three shallow scoundrels, and the terror there was of him. The Incorruptible himself sits apart; or is seen stalking in solitary places in the fields, with an intensely meditative air; some say, 'with eyes red-spotted,' [1] fruit of extreme bile: the lamentablest seagreen Chimera that walks the Earth that July! O hapless Chimera,—for thou too hadst a life, and heart of flesh,—what is this that the stern gods, seeming to smile all the way, have led and let thee to! Art not thou he, who, few years ago, was a young Advocate of promise; and gave up the Arras Judgeship rather than sentence one man to die?—

What his thoughts might be? His plans for finishing the Terror? One knows not. Dim vestiges there flit of Agrarian Law; a victorious Sansculottism become Landed Proprietor; old Soldiers sitting in National Mansions, in Hospital Palaces of Chambord and Chantilly; peace bought by victory; breaches healed by Feast of *Être Suprême*;—and so, through seas of blood, to Equality, Frugality, worksome Blessedness, Fraternity, and Republic of the virtues. Blessed shore, of such a sea of Aristocrat blood: but how to land on it? Through one last wave: blood of corrupt Sansculottists; traitorous or semi-traitorous Conventionals, rebellious Talliens, Billauds, to whom with my *Être Suprême* I have become a bore; with my Apocalyptic Old Woman a laughing-stock!—So stalks he, this poor Robespierre, like a seagreen ghost, through the blooming July. Vestiges of schemes flit dim. But *what* his schemes or his thoughts were will never be known to man.

New Catacombs, some say, are digging for a huge simultaneous butchery. Convention to be butchered, down to the right pitch, by General Henriot and Company: Jacobin House of Lords made

---

[1] *Deux Amis*, xii. 347-73.

dominant; and Robespierre Dictator.[2]   There is actually, or else
there is not actually, a List made out; which the Hairdresser has
got eye on, as he frizzled the Incorruptible locks. Each man asks
himself, Is it I ?

Nay, as Tradition and rumour of Anecdote still convey it, there
was a remarkable bachelor's dinner, one hot day, at Barrère's. For
doubt not, O Reader, this Barrère and others of them gave
dinners; had 'country-house at Clichy,' with elegant enough
sumptuosities, and pleasures high-rouged.[3]   But at this dinner we
speak of, the day being so hot, it is said, the guests all stript their
coats, and left them in the drawing-room: from the dinner-table
Carnot glided out, driven by a necessity, needing of all things
paper; groped in Robespierre's pocket; found a list of Forty, his
own name among them;—and tarried not at the wine-cup that
day !—Ye must bestir yourselves, O Friends; ye dull Frogs of the
Marsh, mute ever since Girondism sank under, even you now must
croak or die ! Councils are held, with word and beck; nocturnal,
mysterious as death. Does not a feline Maximilien stalk there;
voiceless as yet; his green eyes red-spotted; back bent, and hair
up ? Rash Tallien, with his rash temper and audacity of tongue;
he shall *bell the cat.* Fix a day; and be it soon, lest never !

Lo, before the fixed day, on the day which they call Eighth of
Thermidor, 26th July 1794, Robespierre himself reappears in
Convention; mounts to the Tribune ! The biliary face seems
clouded with new gloom: judge whether your Talliens, Bourdons,
listened with interest. It is a voice bodeful of death or of life.
Longwinded, unmelodious as the screech-owl's, sounds that prophetic voice: Degenerate condition of Republican spirit; corrupt
Moderatism; *Sûreté, Salut* Committees themselves infected; backsliding on this hand and on that; I, Maximilien, alone left incorruptible, ready to die at a moment's warning. For all which
what remedy is there ? The Guillotine; new vigour to the all-
healing Guillotine; death to traitors of every hue ! So sings the
prophetic voice; into its Convention sounding-board. The old
song this: but today, O Heavens, has the sounding-board ceased
to act ? There is not resonance in this Convention; there is, so
to speak, a gasp of silence; nay a certain grating of one knows not
what !—Lecointre, our old Draper of Versailles, in these questionable circumstances, sees nothing he can do so safe as rise, 'insidiously' or not insidiously, and move, according to established wont,

       [2] *Deux Amis*, xii. 350-8.   [3] See Vilate.

that the Robespierre Speech be 'printed and sent to the Departments.' Hark: gratings, even of dissonance! Honourable Members hint dissonance; Committee-Members, inculpated in the Speech, utter dissonance, demand 'delay in printing.' Ever higher rises the note of dissonance; inquiry is even made by Editor Fréron: "What has become of the Liberty of Opinions in this Convention?" The Order to print and transmit, which had got passed, is rescinded. Robespierre, greener than ever before, has to retire, foiled; discerning that it is mutiny, that evil is nigh!

Mutiny is a thing of the fatalest nature in all enterprises whatsoever; a thing so incalculable, swift-frightful: not to be dealt with in *fright*. But mutiny in a Robespierre Convention, above all,—it is like fire seen sputtering in the ship's powder-room! One death-defiant plunge at it, this moment, and you may still tread it out: hesitate till next moment,—ship and ship's captain, crew and cargo are shivered far; the ship's voyage has suddenly ended between sea and sky. If Robespierre can, tonight, produce his Henriot and Company, and get his work done by them, he and Sansculottism may still subsist some time; if not, probably not. Oliver Cromwell, when that Agitator Sergeant stept forth from the ranks, with plea of grievances, and began gesticulating and demonstrating, as the mouthpiece of Thousands expectant there,—discerned, with those truculent eyes of his, how the matter lay; plucked a pistol from his holsters; blew Agitator and Agitation instantly out. Noll was a man fit for such things.

Robespierre, for his part, glides over at evening to his Jacobin House of Lords; unfolds there, instead of some adequate resolution, his woes, his uncommon virtues, incorruptibilities; then, secondly, his rejected screech-owl Oration;—reads this latter over again; and declares that he is ready to die at a moment's warning. Thou shalt not die! shouts Jacobinism from its thousand throats. "Robespierre, I will drink the hemlock with thee," cries Painter David, " *Je boirai la cigue avec toi;* "—a thing not essential to *do*, but which, in the fire of the moment, can be said.

Our Jacobin sounding-board, therefore, does act! Applauses heaven-high cover the rejected Oration; fire-eyed fury lights all Jacobin features: Insurrection a sacred duty; the Convention to be purged; Sovereign People under Henriot and Municipality; we will make a new June-Second of it: To your tents, O Israel! In this key pipes Jacobinism; in sheer tumult of revolt. Let Tallien

and all Opposition men make off.   Collot d'Herbois, though of the
supreme *Salut*, and so lately near shot, is elbowed, bullied; is glad
to escape alive.   Entering Committee-room of *Salut*, all dishevelled,
he finds sleek sombre Saint-Just there, among the rest; who in his
sleek way asks, "What is passing at the Jacobins?"—"What is
passing?" repeats Collot, in the unhistoric Cambyses vein: "What
is passing?   Nothing but revolt and horrors are passing.   Ye want
our lives; ye shall not have them."   Saint-Just stutters at such
Cambyses oratory; takes his hat to withdraw.   That *Report* he
had been speaking of, Report on Republican Things in General
we may say, which is to be read in Convention on the morrow, he
cannot show it them, at this moment: a friend has it; he, Saint-
Just, will get it, and send it, were he once home.   Once home, he
sends not it, but an answer that he will not send it; that they will
hear it from the Tribune tomorrow.

Let every man, therefore, according to a well-known good-advice,
'pray to Heaven, and keep his powder dry'!   Paris, on the morrow,
will see a thing.   Swift scouts fly dim or invisible, all night, from
Sûreté and *Salut*; from conclave to conclave; from Mother Society
to Townhall.   Sleep, can it fall on the eyes of Talliens, Frérons,
Collots?   Puissant Henriot, Mayor Fleuriot, Judge Coffinhal, Procureur Payan, Robespierre and all the Jacobins are getting ready.

CHAPTER VII

GO DOWN TO.

TALLIEN'S eyes beamed bright, on the morrow, Ninth of
Thermidor, 'about nine o'clock,' to see that the Convention had
actually met.   Paris is in rumour: but at least we are met, in
Legal Convention here; we have not been snatched seriatim;
treated with a *Pride's Purge* at the door.   "*Allons*, brave men of
the Plain," late Frogs of the Marsh!   cried Tallien with a squeeze
of the hand, as he passed in; Saint-Just's sonorous voice being
now audible from the Tribune, and the game of games begun.

Saint-Just is verily reading that Report of his; green Vengeance,
in the shape of Robespierre, watching nigh.   Behold, however,

Saint-Just has read but few sentences, when interruption rises, rapid *crescendo;* when Tallien starts to his feet, and Billaud, and this man starts and that,—and Tallien, a second time, with his: "Citoyens, at the Jacobins last night, I trembled for the Republic. I said to myself, if the Convention dare not strike the Tyrant, then I myself dare ; and with this I will do it, if need be," said he, whisking out a clear-gleaming Dagger, and brandishing it there ; the Steel of Brutus, as we call it. Whereat we all bellow, and brandish, impetuous acclaim. "Tyranny! Dictatorship! Triumvirate!" And the *Salut* Committee-men accuse, and all men accuse, and uproar, and impetuously acclaim. And Saint-Just is standing motionless, pale of face ; Couthon ejaculating, "Triumvir?" with a look at his paralytic legs. And Robespierre is struggling to speak, but President Thuriot is jingling the bell against him, but the Hall is sounding against him like an Æolus-Hall : and Robespierre is mounting the Tribune-steps and descending again ; going and coming, like to choke with rage, terror, desperation :— and mutiny is the order of the day ![1]

O President Thuriot, thou that wert Elector Thuriot, and from the Bastille battlements sawest Saint-Antoine rising like the Ocean-tide, and hast seen much since, sawest thou ever the like of this ? Jingle of bell, which thou jinglest against Robespierre, is hardly audible amid the Bedlam storm ; and men rage for life. "President of Assassins," shrieks Robespierre, " I demand speech of thee for the last time!" It cannot be had. "To you, O virtuous men of the Plain," cries he, finding audience one moment, "I appeal to you!" The virtuous men of the Plain sit silent as stones. And Thuriot's bell jingles, and the Hall sounds like Æolus's Hall. Robespierre's frothing lips are grown 'blue;' his tongue dry, cleaving to the roof of his mouth. "The blood of Danton chokes him," cry they. "Accusation! Decree of Accusation!" Thuriot swiftly puts that question. Accusation passes; the incorruptible Maximilien is decreed Accused.

"I demand to share my Brother's fate, as I have striven to share his virtues," cries Augustin, the Younger Robespierre : Augustin also is decreed. And Couthon, and Saint-Just, and Lebas, they are all decreed ; and packed forth,—not without difficulty, the Ushers almost trembling to obey. Triumvirate and Company are packed forth, into *Salut* Committee-room ; their tongue cleaving to the roof of their mouth. You have but to

[1] *Moniteur*, Nos. 311, 312 ; *Débats*, iv. 421-42 ; *Deux Amis*, xii. 390-411.

summon the Municipality; to cashier Commandant Henriot, and
launch Arrest at him; to regulate formalities; hand Tinville his
victims. It is noon: the Æolus-Hall has delivered itself; blows
now victorious, harmonious, as one irresistible wind.

And so the work is finished? One thinks so: and yet it is not
so. Alas, there is yet but the first-act finished; three or four
other acts still to come; and an uncertain catastrophe! A huge
City holds in it so many confusions: seven hundred thousand
human heads; not one of which knows what its neighbour is
doing, nay not what itself is doing.—See, accordingly, about three
in the afternoon, Commandant Henriot, how instead of sitting
cashiered, arrested, he gallops along the Quais, followed by Municipal Gendarmes, 'trampling down several persons!' For the
Townhall sits deliberating, openly insurgent: Barriers to be shut;
no Gaoler to admit any Prisoner this day;—and Henriot is
galloping towards the Tuileries, to deliver Robespierre. On the
Quai de la Ferraillerie, a young Citoyen, walking with his wife,
says aloud: "Gendarmes, that man is not your Commandant; he
is under arrest." The Gendarmes strike down the young Citoyen
with the flat of their swords.[2]

Representatives themselves (as Merlin the Thionviller), who
accost him, this puissant Henriot flings into guard-houses. He
bursts towards the Tuileries Committee-room, "to speak with
Robespierre:" with difficulty, the Ushers and Tuileries Gendarmes,
earnestly pleading and drawing sabre, seize this Henriot; get the
Henriot Gendarmes persuaded not to fight; get Robespierre and
Company packed into hackney-coaches, sent off under escort, to
the Luxembourg and other Prisons. This, then, is the end? May
not an exhausted Convention adjourn now, for a little repose and
sustenance, 'at five o'clock'?

An exhausted Convention did it; and repented it. The end
was not come; only the end of the *second-act*. Hark, while exhausted Representatives sit at victuals,—tocsin bursting from all
steeples, drums rolling, in the summer evening: Judge Coffinhal is
galloping with new Gendarmes, to deliver Henriot from Tuileries
Committee-room; and does deliver him! Puissant Henriot vaults
on horseback; sets to haranguing the Tuileries Gendarmes; cor-
rupts the Tuileries Gendarmes too; trots off with them to Townhall. Alas, and Robespierre is not in Prison: the Gaoler showed

[2] *Précis des Evénemens du Neuf Thermidor*, par C. A. Méda, ancient
Gendarme (Paris, 1825).

his Municipal order, durst not, on pain of his life, admit any Prisoner; the Robespierre Hackney-coaches, in this confused jangle and whirl of uncertain Gendarmes, have floated safe—into the Townhall! There sit Robespierre and Company, embraced by Municipals and Jacobins in sacred right of Insurrection; redacting Proclamations; sounding tocsins; corresponding with Sections and Mother Society. Is not here a pretty enough third-act of a *natural* Greek Drama; catastrophe more uncertain than ever?

The hasty Convention rushes together again, in the ominous nightfall: President Collot, for the chair is his, enters with long strides, paleness on his face; claps-on his hat; says with solemn tone: "Citoyens, armed Villains have beset the Committee-rooms, and got possession of them. The hour is come, to die at our post!" "*Oui*," answer one and all: "We swear it!" It is no rodomontade, this time, but a sad fact and necessity; unless we *do* at our posts, we must verily die. Swift therefore, Robespierre, Henriot, the Municipality, are declared Rebels; put *Hors la Loi*, Out of Law. Better still, we appoint Barras Commandant of what Armed-force is to be had; send Missionary Representatives to all Sections and quarters, to preach, and raise force; will die at least with harness on our back.

What a distracted City; men riding and running, reporting and hearsaying; the Hour clearly in travail,—child not to be *named* till born! The poor Prisoners in the Luxembourg hear the rumour; tremble for a new September. They see men making signals to them, on skylights and roofs, apparently signals of hope; cannot in the least make out what it is.[3] We observe, however, in the eventide, as usual, the Death-tumbrils faring Southeastward, through Saint-Antoine, towards their Barrier du Trône. Saint-Antoine's tough bowels melt; Saint-Antoine surrounds the Tumbrils; says, It shall not be. O Heavens, why should it! Henriot and Gendarmes, scouring the streets that way, bellow, with waved sabres, that it must. Quit hope, ye poor Doomed! The Tumbrils move on.

But in this set of Tumbrils there are two other things notable: one notable person; and one want of a notable person. The notable person is Lieutenant-General Loiserolles, a nobleman by birth and by nature; laying down his life here for his son. In the Prison of Saint-Lazare, the night before last, hurrying to the Grate to hear the Death-list read, he caught the name of his son. The

[3] *Mémoires sur les Prisons,* ii. 277.

son was asleep at the moment. " I am Loiserolles," cried the old man : at Tinville's bar, an error in the Christian name is little ; small objection was made.—The want of the notable person, again, is that of Deputy Paine ! Paine has sat in the Luxembourg since January ; and seemed forgotten ; but Fouquier had pricked him at last. The Turnkey, List in hand, is marking with chalk the outer doors of tomorrow's *Fournée*. Paine's outer door happened to be open, turned back on the wall ; the Turnkey marked it on the side next him, and hurried on : another Turnkey came, and shut it ; no chalk-mark now visible, the *Fournée* went without Paine. Paine's life lay not there.—

Our fifth-act, of this natural Greek Drama, with its natural unities, can only be painted in gross ; somewhat as that antique Painter, driven desperate, did the *foam*. For through this blessed July night, there is clangour, confusion very great, of marching troops ; of Sections going this way, Sections going that ; of Missionary Representatives reading Proclamations by torchlight ; Missionary Legendre, who has raised force somewhere, emptying out the Jacobins, and flinging their key on the Convention table : "I have locked their door ; it shall be Virtue that reopens it." Paris, we say, is set against itself, rushing confused, as Ocean-currents do ; a huge Mahlstrom, sounding there, under cloud of night. Convention sits permanent on this hand ; Municipality most permanent on that. The poor prisoners hear tocsin and rumour ; strive to bethink them of the signals apparently of hope. Meek continual Twilight streaming up, which will be Dawn and a Tomorrow, silvers the Northern hem of Night ; it wends and wends there, that meek brightness, like a silent prophecy, along the great ring-dial of the Heaven. So still, eternal ! and on Earth all is confused shadow and conflict ; dissidence, tumultuous gloom and glare ; and 'Destiny as yet sits wavering, and shakes her doubtful urn.'

About three in the morning the dissident Armed-forces have *met*. Henriot's Armed-force stood ranked in the Place de Grève ; and now Barras's, which he has recruited, arrives there ; and they front each other, cannon bristling against cannon. Citoyens ! cries the voice of Discretion loudly enough, Before coming to bloodshed, to endless civil-war, hear the Convention Decree read : 'Robespierre and all rebels Out of Law !'—Out of Law ? There is terror in the sound. Unarmed Citoyens disperse rapidly home. Municipal Cannoneers, in sudden whirl, anxiously unanimous, range themselves on the Convention side, with shouting. At which shout,

Henriot descends from his upper room, far gone in drink as some say; finds his Place de Grève empty; the cannons' mouth turned *towards* him; and on the whole,—that it is now the catastrophe!

Stumbling in again, the wretched drunk-sobered Henriot announces: "All is lost!" "*Misérable*, it is thou that hast lost it!" cry they; and fling him, or else he flings himself, out of window: far enough down; into masonwork and horror of cesspool; not into death but worse. Augustin Robespierre follows him; with the like fate. Saint-Just, they say, called on Lebas to kill him; who would not. Couthon crept under a table; attempting to kill himself; not doing it.—On entering that Sanhedrim of Insurrection, we find all as good as extinct; undone, ready for seizure. Robespierre was sitting on a chair, with pistol-shot blown through not his head but his under-jaw; the suicidal hand had failed.[4] With prompt zeal, not without trouble, we gather these wrecked Conspirators; fish up even Henriot and Augustin, bleeding and foul; pack them all, rudely enough, into carts; and shall, before sunrise, have them safe under lock and key. Amid shoutings and embracings.

Robespierre lay in an anteroom of the Convention Hall, while his Prison-escort was getting ready; the mangled jaw bound up rudely with bloody linen: a spectacle to men. He lies stretched on a table, a deal-box his pillow; the sheath of the pistol is still clenched convulsively in his hand. Men bully him, insult him: his eyes still indicate intelligence; he speaks no word. 'He had on the sky-blue coat he had got made for the Feast of the *Être Suprême*'—O Reader, can thy hard heart hold out against that? His trousers were nankeen; the stockings had fallen down over the ankles. He spake no word more in this world.

And so, at six in the morning, a victorious Convention adjourns. Report flies over Paris as on golden wings; penetrates the Prisons; irradiates the faces of those that were ready to perish: turnkeys and *moutons*, fallen from their high estate, look mute and blue. It is the 28th day of July, called 10th of Thermidor, year 1794.

Fouquier had but to identify; his Prisoners being already Out of Law. At four in the afternoon, never before were the streets of Paris seen so crowded. From the Palais de Justice to the Place de

---

[4] Méda, p. 384. (Méda asserts that it was he who, with infinite courage though in a lefthanded manner, shot Robespierre. Méda got promoted for his services of this night; and died General and Baron. Few credited Méda in what was otherwise incredible.)

la Révolution, for *thither* again go the Tumbrils this time, it is one dense stirring mass; all windows crammed; the very roofs and ridge-tiles budding forth human Curiosity, in strange gladness. The Death-tumbrils, with their motley Batch of Outlaws, some Twenty-three or so, from Maximilien to Mayor Fleuriot and Simon the Cordwainer, roll on. All eyes are on Robespierre's Tumbril, where he, his jaw bound in dirty linen, with his half-dead Brother and half-dead Henriot, lie shattered; their 'seventeen hours' of agony about to end. The Gendarmes point their swords at him, to show the people which is he. A woman springs on the Tumbril; clutching the side of it with one hand, waving the other Sibyl-like; and exclaims: " The death of thee gladdens my very heart, *m'enivre de joie ;*" Robespierre opened his eyes; "*Scélérat,* go down to Hell, with the curses of all wives and mothers ! "—At the foot of the scaffold, they stretched him on the ground till his turn came. Lifted aloft, his eyes again opened ; caught the bloody axe. Samson wrenched the coat off him ; wrenched the dirty linen from his jaw : the jaw fell powerless, there burst from him a cry;—hideous to hear and see. Samson, thou canst not be too quick !

Samson's work done, there bursts forth shout on shout of applause. Shout, which prolongs itself not only over Paris, but over France, but over Europe, and down to this generation. Deservedly, and also undeservedly. O unhappiest Advocate of Arras, wert thou worse than other Advocates ? Stricter man, according to his Formula, to his Credo and his Cant, of probities, benevolences, pleasures-of-virtue, and suchlike, lived not in that age. A man fitted, in some luckier settled age, to have become one of those incorruptible barren Pattern-Figures, and have had marble-tablets and funeral-sermons. His poor landlord, the Cabinet-maker in the Rue Saint-Honoré, loved him; his Brother died for him. May God be merciful to him and to us !

This is the end of the Reign of Terror ; new glorious *Revolution* named *of Thermidor;* of Thermidor 9th, year 2; which being interpreted into old slave-style means 27th of July 1794. Terror is ended; and death in the Place de la Révolution, were the 'Tail of Robespierre' once executed; which service Fouquier, in large Batches, is swiftly managing.

BOOK SEVENTH.

VENDÉMIAIRE.

CHAPTER I.

DECADENT.

How little did anyone suppose that here was the end not of Robespierre only, but of the Revolution System itself! Least of all did the mutinying Committee-men suppose it; who had mutinied with no view whatever except to continue the National Regeneration with their own heads on their shoulders. And yet so it verily was. The insignificant stone they had struck out, so insignificant anywhere else, proved to be the Keystone; the whole arch-work and edifice of Sansculottism began to loosen, to crack, to yawn; and tumbled piecemeal, with considerable rapidity, plunge after plunge; till the Abyss had swallowed it all, and in this upper world Sansculottism was no more.

For despicable as Robespierre himself might be, the death of Robespierre was a signal at which great multitudes of men, struck dumb with terror heretofore, rose out of their hiding-places; and, as it were, saw one another, how multitudinous they were; and began speaking and complaining. They are countable by the thousand and the million; who have suffered cruel wrong. Ever louder rises the plaint of such a multitude; into a universal sound, into a universal continuous peal, of what they call Public Opinion. Camille had demanded a 'Committee of Mercy,' and could not get it; but now the whole Nation resolves itself into a Committee of Mercy: the Nation has tried Sansculottism, and is weary of it. Force of Public Opinion! What King or Convention can withstand it? You in vain struggle: the thing that is rejected as 'calumnious' to day must pass as veracious with triumph another day: gods and men have declared that Sansculottism cannot be. Sansculottism, on that Ninth night of Thermidor suicidally 'fractured its under-jaw;' and lies writhing, never to rise more.

Through the next fifteen months, it is what we may call the death-agony of Sansculottism. Sansculottism, Anarchy of the Jean-Jacques Evangel, having now got deep enough, is to perish in a new singular system of Culottism and Arrangement. For Arrangement is indispensable to man; Arrangement, were it grounded only on that old primary Evangel of Force, with Sceptre in the shape of Hammer! Be there method, be there order, cry all men; were it that of the Drill-sergeant! More tolerable is the drilled Bayonet-rank, than that undrilled Guillotine, incalculable as the wind.—How Sansculottism, writhing in death-throes, strove some twice, or even three times, to get on its feet again; but fell always, and was flung resupine the next instant; and finally breathed out the life of it, and stirred no more: this we are now, from a due distance, with due brevity, to glance at; and then—O Reader!—Courage, I see land!

Two of the first acts of the Convention, very natural for it after this Thermidor, are to be specified here: the first is, renewal of the Governing Committees. Both *Sûreté Générale* and *Salut Public*, thinned by the Guillotine, need filling up: we naturally fill them up with Talliens, Frérons, victorious Thermidorian men. Still more to the purpose, we appoint that they shall, as Law directs, not in name only but in deed, be renewed and changed from period to period; a fourth part of them going out monthly. The Convention will no more lie under bondage of Committees, under terror of death; but be a free Convention; free to follow its own judgment, and the Force of Public Opinion. Not less natural is it to enact that Prisoners and Persons under Accusation shall have right to demand some 'Writ of Accusation,' and see clearly what they are accused of. Very natural acts: the har-bingers of hundreds not less so.

For now Fouquier's trade, shackled by Writ of Accusation, and legal proof, is as good as gone; effectual only against Robespierre's Tail. The Prisons give up their Suspect; emit them faster and faster. The Committees see themselves besieged with Prisoners' friends; complain that they are hindered in their work: it is as with men rushing out of a crowded place; and obstructing one

another. Turned are the tables: Prisoners pouring out in floods;
Jailors, *Moutons* and the Tail of Robespierre going now whither
they were wont to send!—The Hundred and thirty-two Nantese
Republicans, whom we saw marching in irons, have arrived;
shrunk to Ninety-four, the fifth man of them choked by the road.
They arrive: and suddenly find themselves not pleaders for life,
but denouncers to death. Their Trial is for acquittal, and more.
As the voice of a trumpet, their testimony sounds far and wide,
mere atrocities of a Reign of Terror. For a space of nineteen
days; with all solemnity and publicity. Representative Carrier,
Company of Marat; Noyadings, Loire Marriages, things done in
darkness, come forth into light: clear is the voice of these poor
resuscitated Nantese; and Journals, and Speech, and universal
Committee of Mercy reverberate it loud enough, into all ears and
hearts. Deputation arrives from Arras; denouncing the atrocities
of Representative Lebon. A tamed Convention loves its own life:
yet what help? Representative Lebon, Representative Carrier
must wend towards the Revolutionary Tribunal; struggle and
delay as we will, the cry of a Nation pursues them louder and
louder. Them also Tinville must abolish;—if indeed Tinville
himself be not abolished.

We must note, moreover, the decrepit condition into which a
once omnipotent Mother of Society has fallen. Legendre flung
her keys on the Convention table, that Thermidor night; her
President was guillotined with Robespierre. The once mighty
Mother came, some time after, with a subdued countenance,
begging back her keys: the keys were restored her; but the
strength could not be restored her; the strength had departed
forever. Alas, one's day is done. Vain that the Tribune in
mid-air sounds as of old: to the general ear it has become a
horror, and even a weariness. By and by, Affiliation is prohibited: the mighty Mother sees herself suddenly childless; mourns
as so hoarse a Rachel may.

The Revolutionary Committees, without Suspects to prey upon,
perish fast; as it were, of famine. In Paris the old Forty-eight of
them are reduced to Twelve; their *Forty sous* are abolished: yet
a little while, and Revolutionary Committees are no more. *Maximum* will be abolished; let Sansculottism find food where it can.[1]
Neither is there now any Municipality, any centre at the Townhall. Mayor Fleuriot and Company perished; whom we shall

[1] 24th December 1794 (*Moniteur*, No. 97).

not be in haste to replace. The Townhall remains in a broken submissive state; knows not well what it is growing to; knows only that it is grown weak, and must obey. What if we should split Paris into, say, a Dozen separate Municipalities; incapable of concert! The Sections were thus rendered safe to act with:—or indeed might not the Sections themselves be abolished? You had then merely your Twelve manageable pacific Townships, without centre or subdivision:[2] and sacred right of Insurrection fell into abeyance!

So much is getting abolished; fleeting swiftly into the Inane. For the Press speaks, and the human tongue; Journals, heavy and light, in Philippic and Burlesque: a renegade Fréron, a renegade Prudhomme, loud they as ever, only the contrary way. And *Cidevants* show themselves, almost parade themselves; resuscitated as from death-sleep; publish what death-pains they have had. The very Frogs of the Marsh croak with emphasis. Your protesting Seventy-three shall, with a struggle, be emitted out of Prison, back to their seats; your Louvets, Isnards, Lanjuinais, and wrecks of Girondism, recalled from their haylofts, and caves in Switzerland, will resume their place in the Convention:[3] natural foes of Terror!

Thermidorian Talliens, and mere foes of Terror, rule in this Convention, and out of it. The compressed Mountain shrinks silent more and more. Moderatism rises louder and louder: not as a tempest, with threatenings; say rather, as the rushing of a mighty organ-blast, and melodious deafening Force of Public Opinion, from the Twenty-five million windpipes of a Nation all in Committee of Mercy: which how shall any detached body of individuals withstand?

[2] October 1795 (Dulaure, viii. 454-6).   [3] *Deux Amis*, xiii. 3-39.

CHAPTER II.

LA CABARUS.

How, above all, shall a poor National Convention withstand it? In this poor National Convention, broken, bewildered by long terror, perturbations and guillotinement, there is no Pilot, there is not now even a Danton, who could undertake to steer you anywhither, in such press of weather. The utmost a bewildered Convention can do, is to veer, and trim, and try to keep itself steady; and rush, undrowned, before the wind. Needless to struggle; to fling helm a-lee, and make *'bout ship!* A bewildered Convention sails not in the teeth of the wind; but is rapidly blown round again. So strong is the wind, we say; and so changed; blowing fresher and fresher, as from the sweet Southwest; your devastating North-easters, and wild Tornado-gusts of Terror, blown utterly out! All Sanculottic things are passing away; all things are becoming Culottic.

Do but look at the cut of clothes; that light visible Result, significant of a thousand things which are not so visible. In winter 1793, men went in red nightcap; Municipals themselves in *sabots;* the very Citoyennes had to petition against such head-gear. But now in this winter 1794, where is the red nightcap? With the things beyond the Flood. Your moneyed Citoyen ponders in what most elegant style he shall dress himself; whether he shall not even dress himself as the Free Peoples of Antiquity. The more adventurous Citoyenne has already done it. Behold her, that beautiful adventurous Citoyenne: in costume of the Ancient Greeks, such Greek as Painter David could teach; her sweeping tresses snooded by glittering antique fillet; bright-dyed tunic of the Greek women; her little feet naked, as in Antique Statues, with mere sandals, and winding-strings of riband,—defying the frost!

There is such an effervescence of Luxury. For your Emigrant *Ci-devants* carried not their mansions and furnitures out of the country with them; but left them standing here: and in the swift

changes of property, what with money coined on the Place de
la Révolution, what with Army-furnishings, sales of Emigrant
Domains and Church Lands and King's Lands, and then with the
Aladdin's-lamp of Agio in a time of Paper-money, such mansions
have found new occupants.   Old wine, drawn from *Ci-devant*
bottles, descends new throats.   Paris has swept herself, relighted
herself; Salons, Soupers not Fraternal, beam once more with
suitable effulgence, very singular in colour.   The fair Cabarus is
come out of Prison; wedded to her red-gloomy Dis, whom they
say she treats too loftily: fair Cabarus gives the most brilliant
soirées.   Round her is gathered a new Republican Army, of
Citoyennes in sandals; *Ci-devants* or other: what remnants soever
of the old grace survive are rallied there.   At her right-hand, in
this cause, labours fair Josephine the Widow Beauharnais, though
in straitened circumstances: intent, both of them, to blandish-down
the grimness of Republican austerity, and recivilise mankind.

Recivilise, even as of old they were civilised: by witchery of
the Orphic fiddle-bow, and Euterpean rhythm; by the Graces,
by the Smiles!   Thermidorian Deputies are there in those soirées:
Editor Fiéron, *Orateur du Peuple*; Barras, who has known other
dances than the Carmagnole.   Grim Generals of the Republic are
there; in enormous horse-collar neckcloth, good against sabre-
cuts; the hair gathered all into one knot, 'flowing down behind,
fixed with a comb.'   Among which latter do we not recognise,
once more, that little bronze-complexioned Artillery-Officer of
Toulon, home from the Italian Wars!   Grim enough; of lean,
almost cruel aspect: for he has been in trouble, in ill health;
also in ill favour, as a man promoted, deservedly or not, by the
Terrorists and Robespierre Junior.   But does not Barras know
him?   Will not Barras speak a word for him?   Yes,—if at any
time it will serve Barras so to do.   Somewhat forlorn of fortune, for
the present, stands that Artillery-Officer; looks, with those deep
earnest eyes of his, into a future as waste as the most.   Taciturn;
yet with the strangest utterances in him, if you awaken him,
which smite home, like light or lightning;—on the whole, rather
dangerous?   A 'dissocial' man?   Dissocial enough; a natural
terror and horror to all Phantasms, being himself of the genus
Reality!   He stands here, without work or outlook, in this forsaken manner;—glances nevertheless, it would seem, at the kind
glance of Josephine Beauharnais; and, for the rest, with severe
countenance, with open eyes, and closed lips, waits what will
betide.

That the Balls, therefore, have a new figure this winter, we can see. Not Carmagnoles, rude 'whirlblasts of rags,' as Mercier called them, 'precursors of storm and destruction :' no, soft Ionic motions; fit for the light sandal and antique Grecian tunic! Efflorescence of Luxury has come out: for men have wealth; nay new-got wealth; and under the Terror you durst not dance, except in rags. Among the innumerable kinds of Balls, let the hasty reader mark only this single one: the kind they call Victim Balls, *Bals à Victime.* The dancers, in choice costume, have all crape round the left arm: to be admitted, it needs that you be a *Victime;* that you have lost a relative under the Terror. Peace to the Dead; let us *dance* to their memory! For in all ways one must dance.

It is very remarkable, according to Mercier, under what varieties of figure this great business of dancing goes on. 'The women,' says he, 'are Nymphs, Sultanas; sometimes Minervas, Junos, 'even Dianas. In lightly-unerring gyrations they swim there; 'with such earnestness of purpose; with perfect silence, so ab-'sorbed are they. What is singular,' continues he, 'the onlookers 'are as it were mingled with the dancers; form, as it were, a 'circumambient element round the different contre-dances, yet 'without deranging them. It is rare, in fact, that a Sultana in 'such circumstances experiences the smallest collision. Her 'pretty foot darts down, an inch from mine; she is off again; 'she is as a flash of light: but soon the measure recalls her to 'the point she set out from. Like a glittering comet she travels 'her ellipse; revolving on herself, as by a double effect of gravi-'tation and attraction.'[1] Looking forward a little way, into Time, the same Mercier discerns *Merveilleuses* in 'flesh-coloured drawers' with gold circlets; mere dancing Houris of an artificial Ma-homet's-Paradise: much too Mahometan. Montgaillard, with his splenetic eye, notes a no less strange thing; that every fashionable Citoyenne you meet is in an interesting situation. Good Heavens, *every?* Mere pillows and stuffing! adds the acrid man ;—such in a time of depopulation by war and guillotine, being the fashion.[2] No farther seek its merits to disclose.

Behold also, instead of the old grim *Tappe-durs* of Robespierre, what new street-groups are these? Young men habited not in black-shag Carmagnole spencer, but in superfine *habit carré,* or spencer with rectangular tail appended to it; 'square-tailed coat,'

[1] Mercier, *Nouveau Paris,* iii. 138, 153.   [2] Montgaillard, iv. 436-42.

with elegant anti-guillotinish specialty of collar; 'the hair plaited
at the temples,' and knotted back, long-flowing, in military wise :
young men of what they call the *Muscadin* or Dandy species!
Fréron, in his fondness, names them *Jeunesse Dorée,* Golden or
Gilt Youth. They have come out, these Gilt Youths, in a kind
of resuscitated state; they wear crape round the left arm, such of
them as were *Victims.* More, they carry clubs loaded with lead;
in an angry manner: any *Tappe-dur,* or remnant of Jacobinism
they may fall in with, shall fare the worse. They have suffered
much : their friends guillotined; their pleasures, frolics, superfine
collars ruthlessly repressed : 'ware now the base Red Nightcaps
who did it! Fair Cabarus and the Army of Greek sandals smile
approval. In the Théâtre Feydeau, young Valour in square-tailed
coat eyes Beauty in Greek sandals, and kindles by her glances :
Down with Jacobinism! No Jacobin hymn or demonstration,
only Thermidorian ones, shall be permitted here: we beat down
Jacobinism with clubs loaded with lead.

But let any one who has examined the Dandy nature, how
petulant it is, especially in the gregarious state, think what an
element, in sacred right of insurrection, this Gilt Youth was!
Broils and battery; war without truce or measure! Hateful is
Sansculottism, as Death and Night. For indeed is not the Dandy
culottic, habilatory, by law of existence; 'a cloth-animal; one
that lives, moves and has his being in cloth'?

So goes it, waltzing, bickering; fair Cabarus, by Orphic witchery,
struggling to recivilise mankind. Not unsuccessfully, we hear.
What utmost Republican grimness can resist Greek sandals, in
Ionic motion, the very toes covered with gold rings?[3] By degrees
the indisputablest new-politeness rises; grows, with vigour. And
yet, whether, even to this day, that inexpressible tone of society
known under the old Kings, when Sin had 'lost all its deformity'
(with or without advantage to us), and airy Nothing had obtained
such a local habitation and establishment as she never had,—be
recovered? Or even, whether it be not lost beyond recovery?[4]—
Either way, the world must contrive to struggle on.

[3] Montgaillard, Mercier (ubi suprà).
[4] De Staël, *Considérations,* iii. c. 10, &c.

CHAPTER III.

QUIBERON.

BUT, indeed, do not these long-flowing hair-queues of a *Jeunesse Dorée* in semi-military costume betoken, unconsciously, another still more important tendency? The Republic, abhorrent of her Guillotine, loves her Army.

And with cause. For, surely, if good fighting be a kind of honour, as it is in its season; and be with the vulgar of men, even the chief kind of honour; then here is good fighting, in good season, if there ever was. These Sons of the Republic, they rose, in mad wrath, to deliver her from Slavery and Cimmeria. And have they not done it? Through Maritime Alps, through gorges of Pyrenees, through Low Countries, Northward along the Rhine-valley, far is Cimmeria hurled back from the sacred Motherland. Fierce as fire, they have carried her Tricolor over the faces of all her enemies;—over scarped heights, over cannon-batteries, it has flown victorious, winged with rage. She has 'Eleven hundred-thousand fighters on foot,' this Republic: 'at one particular moment she had,' or supposed she had, 'Seventeen-hundred thousand.'[1] Like a ring of lightning, they, volleying and *ça-ira*-ing, begirdle her from shore to shore. Cimmerian Coalition of Despots recoils, smitten with astonishment and strange pangs.

Such a fire is in these Gaelic Republican men; high-blazing; which no Coalition can withstand! Not scutcheons, with four degrees of nobility; but *ci-devant* Sergeants, who have had to clutch Generalship out of the cannon's throat, a Pichegru, a Jourdan, a Hoche lead them on. They have bread, they have iron; 'with bread and iron you can get to China.'—See Pichegru's soldiers, this hard winter, in their looped and windowed destitution, in their 'straw-rope shoes and cloaks of bast-mat,' how they overrun Holland, like a demon-host, the ice having bridged all waters; and rush shouting from victory to victory! Ships in the

---

[1] Toulongeon, iii. c. 7; v. c. 10 (p. 194).

Texel are taken by hussars on horseback : fled is York; fled is the Stadtholder, glad to escape to England, and leave Holland to fraternise.[2] Such a Gaelic fire, we say, blazes in this People, like the conflagration of grass and dry-jungle; which no mortal can withstand,—for the moment.

And even so it will blaze and run, scorching all things; and, from Cadiz to Archangel, mad Sansculottism, drilled now into Soldier-ship, led on by some 'armed Soldier of Democracy' (say, that monosyllabic Artillery-Officer), will set its foot cruelly on the necks of its enemies ; and its shouting and their shrieking shall fill the world !—Rash Coalised Kings, such a fire have ye kindled; yourselves fireless, *your* fighters animated only by drill-sergeants, mess-room moralities and the drummer's cat !　However, it is begun, and will not end: not for a matter of twenty years.　So long, this Gaelic fire, through its successive changes of colour and character, will blaze over the face of Europe, and afflict and scorch all men :—till it provoke all men; till it kindle another kind of fire, the Teutonic kind, namely ; and be swallowed up, so to speak, in a day !　For there is a fire comparable to the burning of dry-jungle and grass ; most sudden, high-blazing: and another fire which we liken to the burning of coal, or even of anthracite coal; difficult to kindle, but then which no known thing will put out. The ready Gaelic fire, we can remark farther,—and remark not in Pichegrus only, but in innumerable Voltaires, Racines, Laplaces, no less ; for a man, whether he fight, or sing, or think, will remain the same unity of a man,—is admirable for roasting eggs, in every conceivable sense.　The Teutonic anthracite again, as we see in Luthers, Leibnitzes, Shakspeares, is preferable for smelting metals. How happy is our Europe that has both kinds !—

But be this as it may, the Republic is clearly triumphing.　In the spring of the year, Mentz Town again sees itself besieged ; will again change master : did not Merlin the Thionviller, 'with wild beard and look,' say it was not for the last time they saw him there ?　The Elector of Mentz circulates among his brother Potentates this pertinent query, Were it not advisable to treat of Peace ?　Yes ! answers many an Elector from the bottom of his heart.　But, on the other hand, Austria hesitates ; finally refuses, being subsidied by Pitt.　As to Pitt, whoever hesitate, he, suspend-ing his Habeas-corpus, suspending his Cash-payments, stands inflexible,—spite of foreign reverses ; spite of domestic obstacles,

[2] 19th January 1795 (Montgaillard, iv. 287-311).

of Scotch National Conventions and English Friends of the People, whom he is obliged to arraign, to hang, or even to see acquitted with jubilee : a lean inflexible man. The Majesty of Spain, as we predicted, makes Peace ; also the Majesty of Prussia: and there is a Treaty of Bâle.[3] Treaty with black Anarchists and Regicides! Alas, what help? You cannot hang this Anarchy; it is like to hang you : you must needs treat with it.

Likewise, General Hoche has even succeeded in pacificating La Vendée. Rogue Rossignol and his 'Infernal Columns' have vanished : by firmness and justice, by sagacity and industry, General Hoche has done it. Taking 'Movable Columns,' not infernal; girdling-in the Country; pardoning the submissive, cutting down the resistive, limb after limb of the Revolt is brought under. La Rochejacquelin, last of our Nobles, fell in battle; Stofflet himself makes terms ; Georges-Cadoudal is back to Brittany, among his Chouans: the frightful gangrene of La Vendée seems veritably extirpated. It has cost, as they reckon in round numbers, the lives of a Hundred-thousand fellow-mortals; with noyadings, conflagratings by infernal column, which defy arithmetic. This is the La Vendée War.[4]

Nay in few months, it does burst-up once more, but once only; —blown upon by Pitt, by our Ci-devant Puisaye of Calvados, and others. In the month of July 1795, English Ships will ride in Quiberon roads. There will be debarkation of chivalrous Ci-devants, of volunteer Prisoners-of-war—eager to desert; of fire-arms, Proclamations, clothes-chests, Royalists and specie. Where-upon also, on the Republican side, there will be rapid stand-to-arms ; with ambuscade marchings by Quiberon beach, at midnight; storming of Fort Penthièvre ; war-thunder mingling with the roar of the nightly main; and such a morning light as has seldom dawned : debarkation hurled back into its boats, or into the de-vouring billows, with wreck and wail ;—in one word, a Ci-devant Puisaye as totally ineffectual here as he was in Calvados, when he rode from Vernon Castle without boots.[5]

Again, therefore, it has cost the lives of many a brave man. Among whom the whole world laments the brave Son of Som-breuil. Ill-fated family ! The father and younger son went to the

---

[3] 5th April 1795 (Montgaillard, iv. 319).

[4] *Histoire de la Guerre de la Vendée*, par M. le Comte de Vauban ; *Mémoires de Madame de la Rochejacquelin*, &c.

[5] *Deux Amis*, xiv. 94-106 ; Puisaye, *Mémoires*, iii.-vii.

guillotine; the heroic daughter languishes, reduced to want, hides
her woes from History: the elder son perishes here; shot by
military tribunal as an Emigrant; Hoche himself cannot save him.
If all wars, civil and other, are misunderstandings, what a thing
must right-understanding be!

CHAPTER IV.

LION NOT DEAD.

THE Convention, borne on the tide of Fortune towards foreign
Victory, and driven by the strong wind of Public Opinion towards
Clemency and Luxury, is rushing fast; all skill of pilotage is
needed, and more than all, in such a velocity.

Curious to see, how we veer and whirl, yet must ever whirl
round again, and scud before the wind. If, on the one hand, we
re-admit the Protesting Seventy-three, we, on the other hand, agree
to consummate the Apotheosis of Marat; lift his body from the
Cordeliers Church, and transport it to the Pantheon of Great Men,
—flinging out Mirabeau to make room for him. To no purpose:
so strong blows Public Opinion! A Gilt Youthhood, in plaited
hair-tresses, tears down his Busts from the Théâtre Feydeau;
tramples them under foot; scatters them, with vociferation, into
the Cesspool of Montmartre.[1] Swept is his Chapel from the Place
du Carrousel; the Cesspool of Montmartre will receive his very
dust. Shorter godhood had no divine man. Some four months in
this Pantheon, Temple of All the Immortals; then to the Cesspool, grand *Cloaca* of Paris and the World! 'His Busts at one
time amounted to four thousand.' Between Temple of All the
Immortals and Cloaca of the World, how are poor human creatures
whirled!

Furthermore the question arises, When will the Constitution of
Ninety-three, of 1793, come into action? Considerate heads surmise, in all privacy, that the Constitution of Ninety-three will
never come into action. Let them busy themselves to get ready a
better.

---

[1] *Moniteur*, du 25 Septembre 1794, du 4 Février 1795.

Or, again, where now are the Jacobins? Childless, most decrepit, as we saw, sat the mighty Mother; gnashing not teeth, but empty gums, against a traitorous Thermidorian Convention and the current of things. Twice were Billaud, Collot and Company accused in Convention, by a Lecointre, by a Legendre; and the second time, it was not voted calumnious. Billaud from the Jacobin tribune says, "The lion is not dead; he is only sleeping." They ask him in Convention, What he means by the awakening of the lion? And bickerings, of an extensive sort, arose in the Palais-Egalité between *Tappe-durs* and the Gilt Youthhood; cries of "Down with the Jacobins, the *Jacoquins*," *coquin* meaning scoundrel! The Tribune in mid-air gave battle-sound; answered only by silence and uncertain gasps. Talk was, in Government Committees, of 'suspending' the Jacobin Sessions. Hark, there!—it is in All-hallow-time, or on the Hallow-eve itself, month *ci-devant* November, year once named of Grace 1794, sad eve for Jacobinism,— volley of stones dashing through our windows, with jingle and execration! The female Jacobins, famed *Tricoteuses* with knitting-needles, take flight; are met at the doors by a Gilt Youthhood and 'mob of four thousand persons;' are hooted, flouted, hustled; fustigated in a scandalous manner, *cotillons retroussés;*—and vanish in mere hysterics. Sally out, ye male Jacobins! The male Jacobins sally out; but only to battle, disaster and confusion. So that armed Authority has to intervene: and again on the morrow to intervene; and suspend the Jacobin Sessions forever and a day.[2]—Gone are the Jacobins; into invisibility; in a storm of laughter and howls. Their Place is made a Normal School, the first of the kind seen; it then vanishes into a 'Market of Thermidor Ninth;' into a Market of Saint-Honoré, where is now peaceable chaffering for poultry and greens. The solemn temples, the great globe itself; the baseless fabric! Are not we such stuff, we and this world of ours, as Dreams are made of?

Maximum being abrogated, Trade was to take its own free course. Alas, Trade, shackled, topsyturvied in the way we saw, and now suddenly let-go again, can for the present take no course at all; but only reel and stagger. There is, so to speak, no Trade what-ever for the time being. Assignats, long sinking, emitted in such quantities, sink now with an alacrity beyond parallel. " *Combien?* " said one, to a Hackney-coachman, "What fare?" "Six thousand livres," answered he: some three hundred pounds sterling, in

---

[2] *Moniteur*, Séances du 10-12 Novembre 1794; *Deux Amis*, xiii. 43-49.

Paper-money.[3] Pressure of Maximum withdrawn, the things it compressed likewise withdraw. 'Two ounces of bread per day' is the modicum allotted: wide-waving, doleful are the Bakers' Queues; Farmers' houses are become pawnbrokers' shops.

One can imagine, in these circumstances, with what humour Sansculottism growled in its throat "*La Cabarus;*" beheld Ci-devants return dancing, the Thermidor effulgence of recivilisation, and Balls in flesh-coloured drawers. Greek tunics and sandals; hosts of *Muscadins* parading, with their clubs loaded with lead;— and we here, cast out, abhorred, 'picking offals from the street;'[4] agitating in Baker's Queue for our two ounces of bread! Will the Jacobin lion, which they say is meeting secretly 'at the Ar-chevêché, in *bonnet rouge* with loaded pistols,' not awaken? Seem-ingly, not. Our Collot, our Billaud, Barrère, Vadier, in these last days of March 1795, are found worthy of *Déportation*, of Banish-ment beyond seas; and shall, for the present, be trundled off to the Castle of Ham. The lion is dead;—or writhing in death-throes!

Behold, accordingly, on the day they call Twelfth of Germinal (which is also called First of April, not a lucky day), how lively are these streets of Paris once more! Floods of hungry women, of squalid hungry men; ejaculating, "Bread, bread, and the Con-stitution of Ninety-three!" Paris has risen, once again, like the Ocean-tide; is flowing towards the Tuileries, for Bread and a Constitution. Tuileries Sentries do their best; but it serves not: the Ocean-tide sweeps them away; inundates the Convention Hall itself; howling, "Bread and the Constitution!"

Unhappy Senators, unhappy People, there is yet, after all toils and broils, no Bread, no Constitution. "*Du pain, pas tant de longs discours,* Bread, not bursts of Parliamentary eloquence!" so wailed the Menads of Maillard, five years ago and more; so wail ye to this hour. The Convention, with unalterable countenance, with what thought one knows not, keeps its seat in this waste howling chaos; rings its storm-bell from the Pavilion of Unity. Section Lepelletier, old *Filles Saint-Thomas,* who are of the money-changing species; these and Gilt Youthhood fly to the rescue: sweep chaos forth again, with levelled bayonets. Paris is declared 'in a state of

---

[3] Mercier, ii. 94. ('1st February 1796: at the Bourse of Paris, the gold louis,' of 20 francs in silver, 'costs 5,300 francs in assignats.' Montgaillard, iv. 419.)

[4] Fantin Desodoards, *Histoire de la Révolution,* vii. c. 4.

LION NOT DEAD.

siege.' Pichegru, Conqueror of Holland, who happens to be here, is named Commandant, till the disturbance end. He, in one day so to speak, ends it. He accomplishes the transfer of Billaud, Collot and Company; dissipating all opposition ' by two cannon-shots,' blank cannon-shots, and the terror of his name; and thereupon, announcing, with a Laconicism which should be imitated, "Representatives, your decrees are executed," [5] lays down his Commandantship.

This Revolt of Germinal, therefore, has passed, like a vain cry. The Prisoners rest safe in Ham, waiting for ships; some nine-hundred 'chief Terrorists of Paris' are disarmed. Sansculottism, swept forth with bayonets, has vanished, with its misery, to the bottom of Saint-Antoine and Saint-Marceau.—Time was when Usher Maillard with Menads could alter the course of Legislation; but that time is not. Legislation seems to have got bayonets; Section Lepelletier takes its firelock, not for us! We retire to our dark dens; our cry of hunger is called a Plot of Pitt; the Saloons glitter, the flesh-coloured Drawers gyrate as before. It was for " The Cabarus," then, and her Muscadins and Money-changers that we fought? It was for Balls in flesh-coloured drawers that we took Feudalism by the beard, and did and dared, shedding our blood like water? Expressive Silence, muse thou their praise!—

[5] Moniteur, Séance du 13 Germinal (2d April), 1795.

CHAPTER V.

LION SPRAWLING ITS LAST.

REPRESENTATIVE Carrier went to the Guillotine, in December
last; protesting that he acted by orders. The Revolutionary
Tribunal, after all it has devoured, has now only, as Anarchic
things do, to devour itself. In the early days of May, men see a
remarkable thing: Fouquier-Tinville pleading at the Bar once his
own. He and his chief Jurymen, Leroi *August-Tenth*, Juryman
Vilate, a Batch of Sixteen; pleading hard, protesting that they
acted by orders: but pleading in vain. Thus men break the axe
with which they have done hateful things; the axe itself having
grown hateful. For the rest, Fouquier died hard enough: "Where
are thy Batches?" howled the people.—"Hungry *canaille*," asked
Fouquier, "is thy Bread cheaper, wanting them?"

Remarkable Fouquier; once but as other Attorneys and Law-
beagles, which hunt ravenous on this Earth, a well-known phasis
of human nature; and now thou art and remainest the most
remarkable Attorney that ever lived and hunted in the Upper
Air! For, in this terrestrial Course of Time, there was to be an
Avatar of Attorneyism; the Heavens had said, Let there be an
Incarnation, not divine, of the venatory Attorney-spirit which
keeps its eye on the bond only;—and lo, this was it; and they
have attorneyed it in its turn. Vanish, then, thou rat-eyed Incarnation of Attorneyism; who at bottom wert but as other
Attorneys, and too hungry sons of Adam! Juryman Vilate had
striven hard for life, and published, from his Prison, an ingenious
Book, not unknown to us; but it would not stead: he also had to
vanish; and this his Book of the *Secret Causes of Thermidor*, full
of lies, with particles of truth in it undiscoverable otherwise, is all
that remains of him.

Revolutionary Tribunal has done; but vengeance has not done.
Representative Lebon, after long struggling, is handed over to the
ordinary Law Courts, and by them guillotined. Nay at Lyons and
elsewhere, resuscitated Moderatism, in its vengeance, will not wait

the slow process of Law; but bursts into the Prisons, sets fire to
the Prisons; burns some threescore imprisoned Jacobins to dire
death, or chokes them 'with the smoke of straw.' There go
vengeful truculent 'Companies of Jesus,' 'Companies of the Sun;'
slaying Jacobinism wherever they meet with it; flinging it into the
Rhone-stream; which once more bears seaward a horrid cargo.[1]
Whereupon, at Toulon, Jacobinism rises in revolt; and is like to
hang the National Representatives.—With such action and reaction,
is not a poor National Convention hard bested? It is like the
settlement of winds and waters, of seas long tornado-beaten; and
goes on with jumble and with jangle. Now flung aloft, now sunk
in trough of the sea, your Vessel of the Republic has need of all
pilotage and more.

What Parliament that ever sat under the Moon had such a
series of destinies as this National Convention of France? It
came together to make the Constitution; and instead of that, it
has had to make nothing but destruction and confusion : to burn-up
Catholicisms, Aristocratisms; to worship Reason and dig Saltpetre;
to fight Titanically with itself and with the whole world. A Convention decimated by the Guillotine; above the tenth man has
bowed his neck to the axe. Which has seen Carmagnoles danced
before it, and patriotic strophes sung amid Church-spoils; the
wounded of the Tenth of August defile in handbarrows; and, in
the Pandemonial Midnight, Egalité's dames in tricolor drink
lemonade, and spectrum of Sieyes mount, saying, *Death sans
phrase*. A Convention which has effervesced, and which has con-
gealed; which has been red with rage, and also pale with rage;
sitting with pistols in its pocket, drawing sword (in a moment of
effervescence): now storming to the four winds, through a Danton-
voice, Awake, O France, and smite the tyrants; now frozen mute
under its Robespierre, and answering his dirge-voice by a dubious
gasp. Assassinated, decimated; stabbed at, shot at, in baths, on
streets and staircases; which has been the nucleus of Chaos. Has
it not heard the chimes at midnight? It has deliberated, beset
by a Hundred-thousand armed men with artillery-furnaces and
provision-carts. It has been betocsined, bestormed; overflooded
by black deluges of Sansculottism; and has heard the shrill cry,
Bread and Soap. For, as we say, it was the nucleus of Chaos : it
sat as the centre of Sansculottism; and had spread its pavilion on
the waste Deep, where is neither path nor landmark, neither

[1] *Moniteur*, du 27 Juin, du 31 Août, 1795 ; *Deux Amis*, xiii. 121-9.

bottom nor shore. In intrinsic valour, ingenuity, fidelity, and general force and manhood, it has perhaps not far surpassed the average of Parliaments; but in frankness of purpose, in singularity of position, it seeks its fellow. One other Sanculottic submersion, or at most two, and this wearied vessel of a Convention reaches land.

Revolt of Germinal Twelfth ended as a vain cry; moribund Sansculottism was swept back into invisibility. There it has lain moaning, these six weeks : moaning, and also scheming. Jacobins disarmed, flung forth from their Tribune in mid-air, must needs try to help themselves, in secret conclave under ground. Lo therefore, on the First day of the month *Prairial*, 20th of May 1795, sound of the *générale* once more; beating sharp ran-tan, To arms, To arms !

Sansculottism has risen, yet again, from its death-lair; waste, wild-flowing, as the unfruitful Sea. Saint-Antoine is afoot: " Bread and the Constitution of Ninety-three," so sounds it; so stands it written with chalk on the hats of men. They have their pikes, their firelocks; Paper of Grievances ; standards ; printed Proclamation, drawn-up in quite official manner,—considering this, and also considering that, they, a much-enduring Sovereign People, are in Insurrection; will have Bread and the Constitution of Ninety-three. And so the Barriers are seized, and the *générale* beats, and tocsins discourse discord. Black deluges overflow the Tuileries ; spite of sentries, the Sanctuary itself is invaded: enter, to our Order of the Day, a torrent of dishevelled women, wailing, " Bread ! Bread ! " President may well cover himself; and have his own tocsin rung in 'the Pavilion of Unity ;' the ship of the State again labours and leaks; overwashed, near to swamping, with unfruitful brine.

What a day, once more ! Women are driven out : men storm irresistibly in ; choke all corridors, thunder at all gates. Deputies, putting forth head, obtest, conjure ; Saint-Antoine rages, " Bread and Constitution." Report has risen that the 'Convention is assassinating the women :' crushing and rushing, clangor and furor ! The oak doors have become as oak tambourines, sounding under the axe of Saint-Antoine ; plaster-work crackles, wood-work booms and jingles ; door starts up ;—bursts-in Saint-Antoine with frenzy and vociferation, with Rag-standards, printed Proclamation, drum-music: astonishment to eye and ear. Gendarmes, loyal Sectioners charge through the other door ; they are re-charged ;

musketry exploding: Saint-Antoine cannot be expelled. Obtesting
Deputies obtest vainly : Respect the President; approach not the
President ! Deputy Féraud, stretching out his hands, baring his
bosom scarred in the Spanish wars, obtests vainly; threatens and
resists vainly. Rebellious Deputy of the Sovereign, if thou have
fought, have not we too ? We have no Bread, no Constitution !
They wrench poor Féraud ; they tumble him, trample him, wrath
waxing to see itself work : they drag him into the corridor, dead
or near it; sever his head, and fix it on a pike. Ah, did an
unexampled Convention want this variety of destiny, too, then ?
Féraud's bloody head goes on a pike. Such a game has begun ;
Paris and the Earth may wait how it will end.

And so it billows free through all Corridors ; within and without,
far as the eye reaches, nothing but Bedlam, and the great Deep
broken loose ! President Boissy d'Anglas sits like a rock : the
rest of the Convention is floated 'to the upper benches ;' Sectioners
and Gendarmes still ranking there to form a kind of wall for
them. And Insurrection rages; rolls its drums; will read its
Paper of Grievances, will have this decreed, will have that.
Covered sits President Boissy; unyielding; like a rock in the
beating of seas. They menace him, level muskets at him, he
yields not; they hold up Féraud's bloody head to him, with grave
stern air he bows to it, and yields not.

And the Paper of Grievances cannot get itself read for uproar :
and the drums roll, and the throats bawl; and Insurrection, like
sphere-music, is inaudible for very noise : Decree us this, Decree
us that. One man we discern bawling 'for the space of an hour
at all intervals,' " *Je demande l'arrestation des coquins et des lâches.*"
Really one of the most comprehensive Petitions ever put up;
which indeed, to this hour, includes all that you can reasonably
ask Constitution of the Year One, Rotten-Borough, Ballot-Box, or
other miraculous Political Ark of the Covenant to do for you to
the end of the world ! I also *demand arrestment of the Knaves and
Dastards,* and nothing more whatever.—National Representation,
deluged with black Sansculottism, glides out; for help elsewhere,
for safety elsewhere , here is no help.

About four in the afternoon, there remain hardly more than
some Sixty Members : mere friends, or even secret leaders; a
remnant of the Mountain-crest, held in silence by Thermidorian
thraldom. Now is the time for them; now or never let them
descend, and speak ! They descend, these Sixty, invited by

Sansculottism: Romme of the New Calendar, Ruhl of the Sacred Phial, Goujon, Duquesnoy, Soubrany, and the rest. Glad Sansculottism forms a ring for them; Romme takes the President's chair; they begin resolving and decreeing. Fast enough now comes Decree after Decree, in alternate brief strains, or strophe and antistrophe,—what will cheapen bread, what will awaken the dormant lion. And at every new decree, Sansculottism shouts "Decreed, decreed!" and rolls its drums.

Fast enough; the work of months in hours,—when see, a Figure enters, whom in the lamp-light we recognise to be Legendre; and utters words: fit to be hissed out! And then see, Section Lepelletier or other Muscadin Section enters, and Gilt Youth, with levelled bayonets, countenances screwed to the sticking-place! Tramp, tramp, with bayonets gleaming in the lamp-light: what can one do, worn down with long riot, grown heartless, dark, hungry, but roll back, but rush back, and escape who can? The very windows need to be thrown up, that Sansculottism may escape fast enough. Money-changer Sections and Gilt Youth sweep them forth, with steel besom, far into the depths of Saint-Antoine. Triumph once more! The Decrees of that Sixty are not so much as rescinded; they are declared null and non-extant. Romme, Ruhl, Goujon and the ringleaders, some thirteen in all, are decreed Accused. Permanent-session ends at three in the morning.[2] Sansculottism, once more flung resupine, lies sprawling; sprawling its *last*.

Such was the First of Prairial, 20th of May 1795. Second and Third of Prairial, during which Sansculottism still sprawled, and unexpectedly rang its tocsin, and assembled in arms, availed Sansculottism nothing. What though with our Rommes and Ruhls, accused but not yet arrested, we make a new 'True National Convention' of our own, over in the East; and put the others Out of Law? What though we rank in arms and march? Armed Force and Muscadin Sections, some thirty-thousand men, environ that old False Convention: we can but bully one another; bandying nicknames, "*Muscadins*," against "Blood-drinkers, *Buveurs de Sang*." Féraud's Assassin, taken with the red hand, and sentenced, and now near to Guillotine and Place de Grève, is retaken; is carried back into Saint-Antoine:—to no purpose. Convention Sectionaries and Gilt Youth come, according to Decree, to seek him; nay to disarm Saint-Antoine! And they do

[2] *Deux Amis*, xiii. 129-46.

disarm it: by rolling of cannon, by springing upon enemy's cannon; by military audacity, and terror of the Law. Saint-Antoine surrenders its arms; Santerre even advising it, anxious for life and brewhouse. Féraud's Assassin flings himself from a high roof: and all is lost.[3]

Discerning which things, old Ruhl shot a pistol through his old white head; dashed his life in pieces, as he had done the Sacred Phial of Rheims. Romme, Goujon and the others stand ranked before a swiftly-appointed, swift Military Tribunal. Hearing the sentence, Goujon drew a knife, struck it into his breast, passed it to his neighbour Romme; and fell dead. Romme did the like; and another all-but did it; Roman-death rushing on there, as in electric-chain, before your Bailiffs could intervene! The Guillotine had the rest.

They were the *Ultimi Romanorum*. Billaud, Collot and Company are now ordered to be tried for life; but are found to be already off, shipped for Sinamarri, and the hot mud of Surinam. There let Billaud surround himself with flocks of tame parrots; Collot take the yellow fever, and drinking a whole bottle of brandy, burn up his entrails.[4] Sansculottism sprawls no more. The dormant lion has become a dead one; and now, as we see, any hoof may smite him.

[3] Toulongeon, v. 297 ; *Moniteur*, Nos. 244, 5, 6.
[4] *Dictionnaire des Hommes Marquans*, §§ Billaud, Collot.

CHAPTER VI.

GRILLED HERRINGS.

So dies Sansculottism, the *body* of Sansculottism; or is changed.
Its ragged Pythian Carmagnole-dance has transformed itself into
a Pyrrhic, into a dance of Cabarus Balls. Sansculottism is dead;
extinguished by new *isms* of that kind, which were its own natural
progeny; and is buried, we may say, with such deafening jubilation
and disharmony of funeral-knell on their part, that only after
some half-century or so does one begin to learn clearly why it ever
was alive.

And yet a meaning lay in it: Sansculottism verily was alive,
a New-Birth of TIME; nay it still lives, and is not dead but
changed. The *soul* of it still lives; still works far and wide,
through one bodily shape into another less amorphous, as is the
way of cunning Time with his New-Births:—till, in some perfected
shape, it embrace the whole circuit of the world! For the wise
man may now everywhere discern that he must found on his
manhood, not on the garnitures of his manhood. He who, in these
Epochs of our Europe, founds on garnitures, formulas, culottisms
of what sort soever, is founding on old cloth and sheepskin, and
cannot endure. But as for the body of Sansculottism, that is
dead and buried,—and, one hopes, need not reappear, in primary
amorphous shape, for another thousand years.

It was the frightfulest thing ever born of Time? One of the
frightfulest. This Convention, now grown Anti-jacobin, did, with
an eye to justify and fortify itself, publish Lists of what the
Reign of Terror had perpetrated: Lists of Persons Guillotined.
The Lists, cries splenetic Abbé Montgaillard, were not complete.
They contain the names of, How many persons thinks the Reader?
—Two-thousand all but a few. There were above Four-thousand,
cries Montgaillard: so many were guillotined, fusilladed, noyaded,
done to dire death; of whom Nine-hundred were women. It is
a horrible sum of human lives, M. l'Abbé:—some ten times as

---

[1] Montgaillard, iv. 241.

many shot rightly on a field of battle, and one might have had
his Glorious-Victory with *Te-Deum*. It is not far from the two-
hundredth part of what perished in the entire Seven-Years War.
By which Seven-Years War, did not the great Fritz wrench
Silesia from the great Theresa; and a Pompadour, stung by
epigrams, satisfy herself that she could not be an Agnès Sorel?
The head of man is a strange vacant sounding-shell, M. l'Abbé;
and studies Cocker to small purpose.

But what if History somewhere on this Planet were to hear
of a Nation, the third soul of whom had not, for thirty weeks each
year, as many third-rate potatoes as would sustain him?[2] History,
in that case, feels bound to consider that starvation is starvation;
that starvation from age to age presupposes much; History
ventures to assert that the French Sansculotte of Ninety-three,
who, roused from long death-sleep, could rush at once to the
frontiers, and die fighting for an immortal Hope and Faith of
Deliverance for him and his, was but the *second*-miserablest of
men! The Irish Sans-potato, had he not senses, then, nay a soul?
In his frozen darkness, it was bitter for him to die famishing;
bitter to see his children famish. It was bitter for him to be a
beggar, a liar and a knave. Nay, if that dreary Greenland-wind
of benighted Want, perennial from sire to son, had frozen him
into a kind of torpor and numb callosity, so that he saw not, felt
not,—was this, for a creature with a soul in it, some assuagement;
or the cruelest wretchedness of all?

Such things were; such things are; and they go on in silence
peaceably:—and Sansculottisms follow them. History, looking
back over this France through long times, back to Turgot's time
for instance, when dumb Drudgery staggered up to its King's
Palace, and in wide expanse of sallow faces, squalor and winged
raggedness, presented hieroglyphically its Petition of Grievances;
and for answer got hanged on a 'new gallows forty feet high,'—
confesses mournfully that there is no period to be met with, in
which the general Twenty-five Millions of France suffered *less* than
in this period which they name Reign of Terror! But it was not
the Dumb Millions that suffered here; it was the Speaking
Thousands, and Hundreds, and Units; who shrieked and published,
and made the world ring with their wail, as they could and should:
that is the grand peculiarity. The frightfulest Births of Time are
never the loud-speaking ones, for these soon die; they are the

[2] *Report of the Irish Poor-Law Commission*, 1836.

silent ones, which can live from century to century! Anarchy,
hateful as Death, is abhorrent to the whole nature of man; and so
must itself soon die.

Wherefore let all men know what of depth and of height is still
revealed in man; and with fear and wonder, with just sympathy
and just antipathy, with clear eye and open heart, contemplate it
and appropriate it; and draw innumerable inferences from it.
This inference, for example, among the first: That 'if the gods of
'this lower world will sit on their glittering thrones, indolent as
'Epicurus' gods, with the living Chaos of Ignorance and Hunger
'weltering uncared-for at their feet, and smooth Parasites preach-
'ing, Peace, peace, when there is no peace,' then the dark Chaos,
it would seem, will rise;—has risen, and, O Heavens, has it not
tanned their skins into breeches for itself? That there be no
second Sansculottism in our Earth for a thousand years, let us
understand well what the first was; and let Rich and Poor of us
go and do *otherwise*.—But to our tale.

The Muscadin Sections greatly rejoice; Cabarus Balls gyrate:
the well-nigh insoluble problem, *Republic without Anarchy*, have
not we solved it?—Law of Fraternity or Death is gone: chimerical
Obtain-who-need has become practical *Hold-who-have*. To anarchic
Republic of the Poverties there has succeeded orderly Republic of
the Luxuries; which will continue as long as it can.

On the Pont au Change, on the Place de Grève, in long sheds,
Mercier, in these summer evenings, saw working men at their
repast. One's allotment of daily bread has sunk to an ounce and
a half. 'Plates containing each three grilled herrings, sprinkled
'with shorn onions, wetted with a little vinegar; to this add some
'morsel of boiled prunes, and lentils swimming in a clear sauce: at
'these frugal tables, the cook's gridiron hissing near by, and the
'pot simmering on a fire between two stones, I have seen them
'ranged by the hundred; consuming, without bread, their scant
'messes, far too moderate for the keenness of their appetite and
'the extent of their stomach.'[3] Seine water, rushing plenteous
by, will supply the deficiency.

O Man of Toil, thy struggling and thy daring, these six long
years of insurrection and tribulation, thou hast profited nothing by
it, then? Thou consumest thy herring and water, in the blessed
gold-red evening. O why was the Earth so beautiful, becrimsoned
with dawn and twilight, if man's dealings with man were to make

[3] *Nouveau Paris*, iv. 118.

it a vale of scarcity, of tears, not even soft tears? Destroying of
Bastilles, discomfiting of Brunswicks, fronting of Principalities and
Powers, of Earth and Tophet, all that thou hast dared and endured,
—it was for a Republic of the Cabarus Saloons? Patience; thou
must have patience : the end is not yet.

CHAPTER VII.

THE WHIFF OF GRAPESHOT.

In fact, what can be more natural, one may say inevitable, as a
Post-Sansculottic transitionary state, than even this? Confused
wreck of a Republic of the Poverties, which ended in Reign of
Terror, is arranging itself into such composure as it can. Evangel
of Jean-Jacques, and most other Evangels, becoming incredible,
what is there for it but return to the old Evangel of Mammon?
Contrat-Social is true or untrue, Brotherhood is Brotherhood or
Death ; but money always will buy money's worth : in the wreck
of human dubitations, this remains indubitable, that Pleasure is
pleasant. Aristocracy of Feudal Parchment has passed away with
a mighty rushing; and now, by a natural course, we arrive at
Aristocracy of the Moneybag. It is the course through which all
European Societies are, at this hour, travelling. Apparently a still
baser sort of Aristocracy? An infinitely baser; the basest yet
known.

In which, however, there is this advantage, that, like Anarchy
itself, it cannot continue. Hast thou considered how Thought is
stronger than Artillery-parks, and (were it fifty years after death
and martyrdom, or were it two thousand years) writes and unwrites
Acts of Parliament, removes mountains; models the World like
soft clay? Also how the beginning of all Thought, worth the
name, is Love; and the wise head never yet was, without first the
generous heart? The Heavens cease not their bounty; they send
us generous hearts into every generation. And now what generous
heart can pretend to itself, or be hoodwinked into believing, that
Loyalty to the Moneybag is a noble Loyalty? Mammon, cries the
generous heart out of all ages and countries, is the basest of known

Gods, even of known Devils. In him what glory is there, that ye should worship him? No glory discernible; not even terror: at best, detestability, ill-matched with despicability! — Generous hearts, discerning, on this hand, wide-spread Wretchedness, dark without and within, moistening its ounce-and-half of bread with tears; and, on that hand, mere Balls in flesh-coloured drawers, and inane or foul glitter of such sort,—cannot but ejaculate, cannot but announce: Too much, O divine Mammon; somewhat too much! —The voice of these, once announcing itself, carries *fiat* and *pereat* in it, for all things here below.

Meanwhile we will hate Anarchy as Death, which it is; and the things worse than Anarchy shall be hated *more*. Surely Peace alone is fruitful. Anarchy is destruction; a burning up, say, of Shams and Insupportabilities; but which leaves Vacancy behind. Know this also, that out of a world of Unwise nothing but an Unwisdom can be made. Arrange it, constitution-build it, sift it through ballot-boxes as thou wilt, it is and remains an Unwisdom, —the new prey of new quacks and unclean things, the latter end of it slightly better than the beginning. Who can bring a wise thing out of men unwise? Not one. And so Vacancy and general Abolition having come for this France, what can Anarchy do more? Let there be Order, were it under the Soldier's Sword; let there be Peace, that the bounty of the Heavens be not spilt; that what of Wisdom they do send us bring fruit in its season!— It remains to be seen how the quellers of Sansculottism were themselves quelled, and sacred right of Insurrection was blown away by gunpowder; wherewith this singular eventful History called *French Revolution* ends.

The Convention, driven such a course by wild wind, wild tide, and steerage and non-steerage, these three years, has become weary of its own existence, sees all men weary of it; and wishes heartily to finish. To the last it has to strive with contradictions: it is now getting fast ready with a Constitution, yet knows no peace. Sieyes, we say, is making the Constitution once more; has as good as made it. Warned by experience, the great Architect alters much, admits much. Distinction of Active and Passive Citizen, that is, Money-qualification for Electors: nay Two Chambers, 'Council of Ancients,' as well as 'Council of Five-hundred;' to that conclusion have we come! In a like spirit, eschewing that fatal self-denying ordinance of your Old Constituents, we enact not only that actual Convention Members are reëligible, but that Two-thirds of them must be reëlected. The Active Citizen Electors shall for this time have free choice of only One-third of their National Assembly. Such enactment, of Two-thirds to be reëlected, we append to our Constitution; we submit our Constitution to the Townships of France, and say, Accept *both,* or reject both. Unsavoury as this appendix may be, the Townships, by overwhelming majority, accept and ratify. With Directory of Five; with Two good Chambers, double-majority of them nominated by ourselves, one hopes this Constitution may prove final. *March* it will; for the legs of it, the reëlected Two-thirds, are already here, able to march. Sieyes looks at his paper-fabric with just pride.

But now see how the contumacious Sections, Lepelletier foremost, kick against the pricks. Is it not manifest infraction of one's Elective Franchise, Rights of Man, and Sovereignty of the People, this appendix of reëlecting *your* Two-thirds? Greedy tyrants, who would perpetuate yourselves!—For the truth is, victory over Saint-Antoine, and long right of Insurrection, has spoiled these men. Nay spoiled all men. Consider, too, how each man was free to hope what he liked; and now there is to be no hope, there is to be fruition, fruition of *this.*

In men spoiled by long right of Insurrection, what confused ferments will rise, tongues once begun wagging! Journalists declaim, your Lacretelles, Laharpes; Orators spout. There is Royalism traceable in it, and Jacobinism. On the West Frontier, in deep secrecy, Pichegru, durst he trust his Army, is treating with Condé: in these Sections, there spout wolves in sheep's clothing, masked Emigrants and Royalists.[1] All men, as we say, had hoped, each that the Election would do something for his own side: and now there is no Election, or only the third of one. Black is united with white against this clause of the Two-thirds; all the Unruly of France, who see their trade thereby near ending.

Section Lepelletier, after Addresses enough, finds that such clause is a manifest infraction; that it, Lepelletier for one, will simply not conform thereto; and invites all other free Sections to join it, 'in central Committee,' in resistance to oppression.[2] The Sections join it, nearly all; strong with their Forty-thousand fighting men. The Convention therefore may look to itself! Lepelletier, on this 12th day of Vendémiaire, 4th of October 1795,

---

[1] Napoleon, Las Cases (*Choix des Rapports,* xvii. 398-411).
[2] *Deux Amis,* xiii. 375-406.

is sitting in open contravention, in its Convent of Filles Saint-
Thomas, Rue Vivienne, with guns primed. The Convention has
some Five-thousand regular troops at hand; Generals in abundance; and a Fifteen-hundred of miscellaneous persecuted Ultra-
Jacobins, whom in this crisis it has hastily got together and
armed, under the title of *Patriots of Eighty-nine*. Strong in Law,
it sends its General Menou to disarm Lepelletier.

General Menou marches accordingly, with due summons and
demonstration; with no result. General Menou, about eight in
the evening, finds that he is standing ranked in the Rue Vivienne,
emitting vain summonses; with primed guns pointed out of every
window at him; and that he cannot disarm Lepelletier. He has
to return, with whole skin, but without success; and be thrown
into arrest, as 'a traitor.' Whereupon the whole Forty-thousand
join this Lepelletier which cannot be vanquished: to what hand
shall a quaking Convention now turn? Our poor Convention,
after such voyaging, just entering harbour, so to speak, has *struck
on the bar;*—and labours there frightfully, with breakers roaring
round it, Forty-thousand of them, like to wash it, and its Sieyes
Cargo and the whole future of France, into the deep! Yet one
last time, it struggles, ready to perish.

Some call for Barras to be made Commandant; he conquered
in Thermidor. Some, what is more to the purpose, bethink them
of the Citizen Buonaparte, unemployed Artillery-Officer, who took
Toulon. A man of head, a man of action: Barras is named
Commandant's-Cloak; this young Artillery-Officer is named
Commandant. He was in the Gallery at the moment, and heard
it; he withdrew, some half-hour, to consider with himself: after a
half-hour of grim compressed considering, to be or not to be, he
answers *Yea.*

And now, a man of head being at the centre of it, the whole
matter gets vital. Swift, to Camp of Sablons; to secure the
Artillery, there are not twenty men guarding it! A swift Adjutant,
Murat is the name of him, gallops; gets thither some minutes
within time, for Lepelletier was also on march that way: the
Cannon are ours. And now beset this post, and beset that; rapid
and firm: at Wicket of the Louvre, in Cul-de-sac Dauphin, in
Rue Saint-Honoré, from Pont-Neuf all along the north Quays,
southward to Pont *ci-devant* Royal,—rank round the Sanctuary of
the Tuileries, a ring of steel discipline; let every gunner have his
match burning, and all men stand to their arms!

Thus there is Permanent-session through the night; and thus at sunrise of the morrow, there is seen sacred Insurrection once again: vessel of State labouring on the bar; and tumultuous sea all round her, beating *générale*, arming and sounding,—not ringing tocsin, for we have left no tocsin but our own in the Pavilion of Unity. It is an imminence of shipwreck, for the whole world to gaze at. Frightfully she labours, that poor ship, within cable-length of port; huge peril for her. However, she has a man at the helm. Insurgent messages, received and not received; messenger admitted blindfolded; counsel and counter-counsel: the poor ship labours!—Vendémiaire 13th, year 4: curious enough, of all days, it is the 5th day of October, anniversary of that Menad-march, six years ago; by sacred right of Insurrection we are got thus far.

Lepelletier has seized the Church of Saint-Roch; has seized the Pont-Neuf, our piquet there retreating without fire. Stray shots fall from Lepelletier; rattle down on the very Tuileries Staircase. On the other hand, women advance dishevelled, shrieking, Peace; Lepelletier behind them waving his hat in sign that we shall fraternise. Steady! The Artillery-Officer is steady as bronze; can, if need were, be quick as lightning. He sends eight-hundred muskets with ball-cartridges to the Convention itself; honourable Members shall act with these in case of ex-tremity: whereat they look grave enough. Four of the after-noon is struck.[3] Lepelletier, making nothing by messengers, by fraternity or hat-waving, bursts out, along the Southern Quai Voltaire, along streets and passages, treble-quick, in huge veritable onslaught! Whereupon, thou bronze Artillery-Officer—? "Fire!" say the bronze lips. And roar and thunder, roar and again roar, continual, volcano-like, goes his great gun, in the Cul-de-sac Dauphin against the Church of Saint-Roch; go his great guns on the Pont-Royal; go all his great guns;—blow to air some two-hundred men, mainly about the Church of Saint-Roch! Lepelletier cannot stand such horse-play; no Sectioner can stand it; the Forty-thousand yield on all sides, scour towards covert. 'Some hundred or so of them gathered about the Théâtre de la 'République; but,' says he, 'a few shells dislodged them. It was 'all finished at six.'

The Ship is *over* the bar, then; free she bounds shoreward,— amid shouting and vivats! Citoyen Buonaparte is 'named General

[3] *Moniteur*, Séance du 5 Octobre 1795.

of the Interior, by acclamation;' quelled Sections have to disarm
in such humour as they may; sacred right of Insurrection is gone
forever! The Sieyes Constitution can disembark itself, and begin
marching. The miraculous Convention Ship has got to land;—
and is there, shall we figuratively say, changed, as Epic Ships are
wont, into a kind of *Sea Nymph*, never to sail more; to roam the
waste Azure, a Miracle in History!

'It is false,' says Napoleon, 'that we fired first with blank
charge; it had been a waste of life to do that.' Most false: the
firing was with sharp and sharpest shot: to all men it was plain
that here was no sport; the rabbets and plinths of Saint-Roch
Church show splintered by it to this hour.—Singular: in old
Broglie's time, six years ago, this Whiff of Grapeshot was promised;
but it could not be given then; could not have profited then. Now,
however, the time is come for it, and the man; and behold, you
have it; and the thing we specifically call *French Revolution* is
blown into space by it, and become a thing that was!—

CHAPTER VIII.

FINIS.

HOMER'S Epos, it is remarked, is like a Bas-Relief sculpture:
it does not conclude, but merely ceases. Such, indeed, is the
Epos of Universal History itself. Directorates, Consulates,
Emperorships, Restorations, Citizen-Kingships succeed this Business in due series, in due genesis one out of the other. Nevertheless the First-parent of all these may be said to have gone to
air in the way we see. A Babœuf Insurrection, next year, will
die in the birth; stifled by the Soldiery. A Senate, if tinged
with Royalism, can be purged by the Soldiery; and an Eighteenth
of Fructidor transacted by the mere show of bayonets.[1] Nay
Soldiers' bayonets can be used *à posteriori* on a Senate, and make
it leap out of window,—still bloodless; and produce an Eighteenth
of Brumaire.[2] Such changes must happen: but they are managed

---

[1] *Moniteur*, du 4 Septembre 1797.

[2] 9th November 1799 (*Choix des Rapports*, xvii. 1-96).

by intriguings, caballings, and then by orderly word of command; almost like mere changes of Ministry. Not in general by sacred right of Insurrection, but by milder methods growing ever milder, shall the events of French History be henceforth brought to pass.

It is admitted that this Directorate, which owned, at its starting, these three things, an 'old table, a sheet of paper, and an ink-bottle,' and no visible money or arrangement whatever,[3] did wonders: that France, since the Reign of Terror hushed itself, has been a new France, awakened like a giant out of torpor; and has gone on, in the Internal Life of it, with continual progress. As for the External form and forms of Life, what can we say, except that out of the Eater there comes Strength; out of the Unwise there comes *not* Wisdom!—Shams are burnt up; nay, what as yet is the peculiarity of France, the very Cant of them is burnt up. The new Realities are not yet come: ah no, only Phantasms, Paper models, tentative Prefigurements of such! In France there are now Four Million Landed Properties; that black portent of an Agrarian Law is, as it were, *realised*. What is still stranger, we understand all Frenchmen have 'the right of duel;' the Hackney-coachman with the Peer, if insult be given: such is the law of Public Opinion. Equality at least in death! The Form of Government is by Citizen King, frequently shot at, not yet shot.

On the whole, therefore, has it not been fulfilled what was prophesied, *ex postfacto* indeed, by the Arch-quack Cagliostro, or another? He, as he looked in rapt vision and amazement into these things, thus spake:[4] 'Ha! What is *this?* Angels, 'Uriel, Anachiel, and ye other Five; Pentagon of Rejuvenes-'cence; Power that destroyedst Original Sin; Earth, Heaven, 'and thou Outer Limbo, which men name Hell! Does the 'EMPIRE OF IMPOSTURE waver? Burst there, in starry sheen, 'updarting, Light-rays from out of *its* dark foundations; as it 'rocks and heaves, not in travail-throes but in death-throes? 'Yea, Light-rays, piercing, clear, that salute the Heavens,—lo, 'they *kindle* it; their starry clearness becomes as red Hellfire!

'IMPOSTURE is in flames, Imposture is burnt up: one red 'sea of Fire, wild-billowing, enwraps the World; with its fire-'tongue licks at the very Stars. Thrones are hurled into it,

---

[3] Bailleul, *Examen critique des Considérations de Mad. de Staël,* ii. 275.

[4] *Diamond Necklace* (Carlyle's *Miscellanies*).

'and Dubois Mitres, and Prebendal Stalls that drop fatness,
'and—ha! what see I?—all the *Gigs* of Creation: all, all! Wo is
'me! Never since Pharaoh's Chariots, in the Red Sea of water,
'was there wreck of Wheel-vehicles like this in the Sea of Fire.
'Desolate, as ashes, as gases, shall they wander in the wind.

 'Higher, higher yet flames the Fire-Sea; crackling with new
'dislocated timber; hissing with leather and prunella. The metal
'Images are molten; the marble Images become mortar-lime;
'the stone Mountains sulkily explode. RESPECTABILITY, with all
'her collected Gigs inflamed for funeral pyre, wailing, leaves the
'Earth: not to return save under new Avatar. Imposture how
'it burns, through generations: how it is burnt up; for a time.
'The World is black ashes;—which, ah, when will they grow
'green? The Images all run into amorphous Corinthian brass;
'all Dwellings of men destroyed; the very mountains peeled and
'riven, the valleys black and dead: it is an empty World! Wo
'to them that shall be born then!——A King, a Queen (ah me!)
'were hurled in; did rustle once; flew aloft, crackling, like paper-
'scroll. Iscariot Egalité was hurled in; thou grim De Launay,
'with thy grim Bastille; whole kindreds and peoples; five mil-
'lions of mutually destroying Men. For it is the End of the
'dominion of IMPOSTURE (which is Darkness and opaque Fire-
'damp); and the burning up, with unquenchable fire, of all the
'Gigs that are in the Earth.' This Prophecy, we say, has it not
been fulfilled, is it not fulfilling?

 And so here, O Reader, has the time come for us two to
part. Toilsome was our journeying together; not without offence;
but it is done. To me thou wert as a beloved shade, the disembodied or not yet embodied spirit of a Brother. To thee I
was but as a Voice. Yet was our relation a kind of sacred one;
doubt not that! For whatsoever once sacred things become
hollow jargons, yet while the Voice of Man speaks with Man,
hast thou not there the living fountain out of which all sacrednesses sprang, and will yet spring? Man, by the nature of
him, is definable as 'an incarnated Word.' Ill stands it with
me if I have spoken falsely: thine also it was to hear truly.
Farewell.

CHRONOLOGICAL SUMMARY

OF

THE FRENCH REVOLUTION.

[Drawn-up by "Philo," for Edition 1857.]

———◇———

THE BASTILLE.

(*May* 10*th*, 1774—*October* 5*th*, 1789.)

1774.

LOUIS XV. dies, at Versailles, *May* 10*th*, 1774; of small-pox, after a short illness: Great-grandson of Louis XIV.; age then 64; in the 59th year of his nominal 'reign.' Retrospect to 1774: sad decay of 'Realised Ideals,' secular and sacred. Scenes about Louis XV.'s deathbed. Scene of the Noblesse entering, 'with a noise like thunder,' to do homage to the New King and Queen. New King, Louis XVI., was his Predecessor's Grandson; age then near 20,—born *August* 23*d*, 1754. New Queen was Marie-Antoinette, Daughter (8th daughter, 12th child) of the great Empress Maria-Theresa and her Emperor Francis (originally 'Duke of Lorraine,' but with no territory there); her age at this time was under 19 (born *November* 2*d*, 1755). Louis and she were wedded four years ago (*May* 16*th*, 1770); but had as yet no children;—none till 1778, when their first was born; a Daughter known long afterwards as Duchess d'Angoulême. Two Sons followed, who were successively called "Dauphin;" but died both, the second in very miserable circumstances, while still in boyhood. Their fourth and last child, a Daughter (1786), lived only 11 months. These two were now King and Queen, piously reckoning themselves "too young to reign."

December 16*th*, 1773, Tea, a celebrated cargo of it, had been flung out in the harbour of Boston, Massachusetts: *June* 7*th*, 1775, Battle of Bunker's Hill, first of the American War, is fought in the same neighbourhood,—far over seas.

1774—1783.

Change of Administration. Maurepas, a man now 73 years old and of great levity, is appointed Prime-Minister; Vergennes favourably known for his correct habits, for his embassies in Turkey, in Sweden, gets the Department of Foreign Affairs.   Old Parlement is reinstated ; "Parlement Maupeou," which had been invented for getting edicts, particularly tax-edicts, 'registered,' and made available in law, is dismissed.   Turgot, made Controller-General of Finances ("Chancellor of the Exchequer" and something more), *August 24th*, 1774, gives rise to high hopes, being already known as a man of much intelligence speculative and practical, of noble patriotic intentions, and of a probity beyond question.

There are many changes ; but one steady fact, of supreme significance, continued Deficit of Revenue,—that is the only History of the Period. Noblesse and Clergy are exempt from direct imposts; no tax that can be devised, on such principle, will yield due ways and means.   Meanings of that fact ; little surmised by the then populations of France.   Turgot aiming at juster principles, cannot : 'Corn-trade' (domestic) 'made free,' and many improvements and high intentions ;—much discontent at Court in consequence ; famine-riots withal, and 'gallows forty feet high.'   Turgot will tax Noblesse and Clergy like the other ranks ; tempest of astonishment and indignation in consequence : Turgot dismissed, *May* 1776.   *Flat* snuff-boxes come out, this summer, under the name of *Turgotines*, as being "*platitudes*" (in the notion of a fashionable snuffing public), like the Plans of this Controller.   Necker, a Genevese become rich by Banking in Paris, and well seen by the Philosophe party, is appointed Controller in his stead (1776) ;—and there is continued Deficit of Revenue.

For the rest, Benevolence, Tolerance, Doctrine of universal Love and Charity to good and bad.   Scepticism, Philosophism, Sensualism : portentous 'Electuary,' of sweet taste, into which 'Good and Evil,' the distinctions of them lost, have been mashed up.   Jean-Jacques, *Contrat-Social :* universal Millennium, of Liberty, Brotherhood, and whatever is desirable, expected to be rapidly approaching on those terms.   Balloons, Horse-races, Anglomania. Continued Deficit of Revenue.   Necker's plans for 'filling up the Deficit' are not approved of, and are only partially gone into : Frugality is of slow operation ; curtailment of expenses occasions numerous dismissals, numerous discontents at Court : from Noblesse and Clergy, if their privilege of exemption be touched, what is to be hoped ?

American-English War (since *April* 1775) ; Franklin, and Agents of the Revolted Colonies, at Paris (1776 and afterwards), where their Cause is in high favour.   French Treaty with Revolted Colonies, *February 6th*, 1778 ; extensive Official smugglings of supplies to them (in which Beaumarchais is much concerned) for some time before.   Departure of French " volunteer " Auxiliaries, under Lafayette, 1778.   " Volunteers " these, not sanctioned, only countenanced and furthered, the public clamour being strong that way. War from England, in consequence ; Rochambeau to America, with public Auxiliaries, in 1780 :—War not notable, except by the Siege of Gibraltar, and by the general result arrived at shortly after.

Continued Deficit of Revenue : Necker's ulterior plans still less approved of ; by Noblesse and Clergy, least of all.   *January* 1781, he publishes a *Compte Rendu* ('Account Rendered,' of himself and them), 'Two hundred thousand copies of it sold ;'—and is dismissed in the *May* following.   Returns to Switzerland ; and there writes New Books, on the same interesting subject or pair of subjects.   Maurepas dies, *November* 21*st*, 1781 : the essential

" Prime-Minister " is henceforth the Controller-General, if any such could be found ; there being an ever-increasing Deficit of Revenue,—a Millennium thought to be just coming on, and evidently no money in its pocket.

Siege of Gibraltar (*September* 13*th*, to middle of *November*, 1782) : Siege futile on the part of France and Spain ; hopeless since that day (*September* 13*th*) of the red-hot balls. General result arrived at is important : American Independence recognised (*Peace of Versailles, January* 20*th*, 1783). Lafayette returns in illustrious condition : named *Scipio Americanus* by some able-editors of the time.

1783—1787.

Ever-increasing Deficit of Revenue. Worse, not better, since Necker's dismissal. After one or two transient Controllers, who can do nothing, Calonne, a memorable one, is nominated, *November* 1783. Who continues, with lavish expenditure raised by loans, contenting all the world by his liberality, 'quenching fire by oil thrown on it ; ' for three years and more. " All the world was holding out its hand, I held out my hat." Ominous scandalous Affair called of the *Diamond Necklace* (Cardinal de Rohan, Dame de Lamotte, Arch-Quack Cagliostro the principal actors), tragically compromising the Queen's name who had no vestige of concern with it, becomes public as Criminal-Trial, 1785 ; penal sentence on the above active parties and others, *May* 31*st*, 1786 : with immense rumour and conjecture from all mankind. Calonne, his borrowing resources being out, convokes the Notables (First Convocation of the Notables) *February* 22*d*, 1787, to sanction his new Plans of Taxing ; who will not hear of them or of him : so that he is dismissed, and 'exiled,' *April* 8*th*, 1787. First Convocation of Notables,—who treat not of this thing only, but of all manner of public things, and mention States-General among others,—sat from *February* 22*d* to *May* 25*th*, 1787.

1787.

Cardinal Loménie de Brienne, who had long been ambitious of the post, succeeds Calonne. A man now of sixty ; dissolute, worthless ;—devises Tax-Edicts, Stamptax (*Edit du Timbre, July* 6*th*, 1787) and others, with ' successive loans,' and the like ; which the Parlement, greatly to the joy of the Public, will not register. Ominous condition of the Public, all virtually in opposition ; Parlements, at Paris and elsewhere, have a cheap method of becoming glorious. Contests of Loménie and Parlement. Beds-of-Justice (first of them, *August* 6*th*, 1787) ; *Lettres-de-Cachet*, and the like methods ; general 'Exile' of Parlement (*August* 15*th*, 1787), who return upon conditions, *September* 20*th*. Increasing ferment of the Public. Loménie helps himself by temporary shifts till he can, privately, get ready for wrestling down the rebellious Parlement.

1788. *January—September.*

Spring of 1788, grand scheme of dismissing the Parlement altogether, and nominating instead a " Plenary Court (*Cour Plénière*)," which shall be obedient in 'registering' and in other points. Scheme detected before quite ripe : Parlement in permanent session thereupon ; haranguing all night (*May*

3d); applausive idle crowds inundating the Outer Courts; D'Espréménil and Goeslard de Monsabert seized by military in the gray of the morning (*May 4th*), and whirled off to distant places of imprisonment: Parlement itself dismissed to exile. Attempt to govern (that is, to raise supplies) by Royal Edict simply,—" Plenary Court " having expired in the birth. Rebellion of all the Provincial Parlements; idle Public more and more noisily approving and applauding. Destructive Hailstorm, *July 13th*, which was remembered next year. Royal Edict (*August 8th*), That States-General, often vaguely promised before, shall actually assemble in May next. Proclamation (*August 16th*), That 'Treasury Payments be henceforth three-fifths in cash, two-fifths in paper,'—in other words, that the Treasury is fallen insolvent. Loménie thereupon immediately dismissed: with immense explosion of popular rejoicing, more riotous than usual. Necker, favourite of all the world, is immediately (*August 24th*) recalled from Switzerland to succeed him, and be "Saviour of France."

1788.   *November—December.*

Second Convocation of the Notables (*November 6th—December 12th*), by Necker, for the purpose of settling *how*, in various essential particulars, the States-General shall be held. For instance, Are the Three Estates to meet as one Deliberative Body? Or as Three, or Two? Above all, what is to be the relative force, in deciding, of the Third Estate or Commonalty? Notables, as other less formal Assemblages had done and do, depart without settling any of the points in question; most points remain unsettled,—especially that of the Third Estate and its relative force. Elections begin everywhere, *January 1789*. Troubles of France seem now to be about becoming Revolution in France. Commencement of the "French Revolution,"—henceforth a phenomenon absorbing all others for mankind,—is commonly dated here.

1789.   *May—June.*

Assembling of States-General at Versailles; Procession to the Church of St. Louis there, *May 4th*. Third Estate has the Nation behind it; wishes to be a main element in the business. Hopes, and (led by Mirabeau and other able heads) decides, that it must be the main element of all,—and will continue 'inert,' and do nothing, till that come about: namely, till the other Two Estates, Noblesse and Clergy, be joined with it; in which conjunct state it can outvote them, and may become what it wishes. 'Inertia,' or the scheme of doing only harangues and adroit formalities, is adopted by it; adroitly persevered in, for seven weeks: much to the hope of France; to the alarm of Necker and the Court.

Court decides to intervene. Hall of Assembly is found shut (*Saturday June 20th*); Third-Estate Deputies take Oath, celebrated "Oath of the Tennis-Court," in that emergency. Emotion of French mankind. *Monday June 22d*, Court does intervene, but with reverse effect: *Séance Royale*, Royal Speech, giving open intimation of much significance, "If you Three Estates cannot agree, I the King will myself achieve the happiness of my People." Noblesse and Clergy leave the Hall along with King; Third Estate remains pondering this intimation. Enter Supreme-Usher de Brézé, to command departure;

Mirabeau's fulminant words to him : exit De Brézé, fruitless and worse, 'amid seas of angry people.' All France on the edge of blazing out : Court recoils ; Third Estate, other Two now joining it on order, triumphs, successful in every particular. The States-General are henceforth " National Assembly ;" called in Books distinctively " Constituent Assembly ;" that is, Assembly met "to make the Constitution,"—perfect Constitution, under which the French People might realise their Millennium.

1789. June—July.

Great hope, great excitement, great suspicion. Court terrors and plans : old Maréchal Broglio,—this is the Broglio who was young in the Seven-Years War ; son of a Marshal Broglio, and grandson of another, who much filled the Newspapers in their time. *Gardes Françaises* at Paris need to be confined to their quarters ; and cannot (*June 26th*). *Sunday July 12th*, News that Necker is dismissed, and gone homewards overnight : panic terror of Paris, kindling into hot frenzy ;—ends in besieging the Bastille ; and in taking it, chiefly by infinite noise, the *Gardes Françaises* at length mutely assisting in the rear. Bastille falls, 'like the City of Jericho, by sound,' *Tuesday July 14th*, 1789. Kind of 'fire-baptism' to the Revolution ; which continues insuppressible thenceforth, and beyond hope of suppression. All France, 'as National Guards, to suppress Brigands and enemies to the making of the Constitution,' takes arms.

1789. August—October.

Scipio Americanus, Mayor Bailly and 'Patrollotism versus Patriotism' (*August, September*). Hope, terror, suspicion, excitement, rising ever more, towards the transcendental pitch ;—continued scarcity of grain. Progress towards *Fifth of October*, called here 'Insurrection of Women.' Regiment de Flandre has come to Versailles (*September 23d*) ; Officers have had a dinner (*October 3d*), with much demonstration and gesticulative foolery, of an anti-constitutional and monarchic character. Paris, semi-delirious, hears of it (*Sunday October 4th*), with endless emotion ;—next day, some '10,000 women' (men being under awe of 'Patrollotism') march upon Versailles ; followed by endless miscellaneous multitudes, and finally by Lafayette and National Guards. Phenomena and procedure there. Result is, they bring the Royal Family and National Assembly home with them to Paris ; Paris thereafter Centre of the Revolution, and *October Five* a memorable day.

1789. October—December.

'First Emigration,' of certain higher Noblesse and Princes of the Blood ; which more or less continues through the ensuing years, and at length on an altoge her profuse scale. Much legal inquiring and procedure as to Philippe d'Orléans and his (imaginary) concern in this *Fifth of October* ; who retires to England for a while, and is ill seen by the polite classes there.

THE CONSTITUTION.

(*January* 1790—*August* 12*th*, 1792.)

1790.

Constitution-building, and its difficulties and accompaniments. Clubs, Journalisms ; advent of anarchic souls from every quarter of the world. *February* 4*th*, King's visit to Constituent Assembly ; emotion thereupon and National Oath, which flies over France. Progress of swearing it, detailed. General "Federation," or mutual Oath of all Frenchmen, otherwise called 'Feast of Pikes' (*July* 14*th*, Anniversary of Bastille-day), which also is a memorable Day. Its effects on the Military, in Lieutenant Napoleon Buonaparte's experience.

General disorganisation of the Army, and attempts to mend it. Affair of Nanci (catastrophe is *August* 31*st*) ; called "Massacre of Nanci :" irritation thereupon. Mutineer Swiss sent to the Galleys ; solemn Funeral-service for the Slain at Nanci (*September* 20*th*), and riotous menaces and mobs in consequence. Steady progress of disorganisation, of anarchy spiritual and practical. Mirabeau, desperate of Constitution-building under such accompaniments, has interviews with the Queen, and contemplates great things.

1791. *April—July.*

Death of Mirabeau (*April* 2*d*) : last chance of guiding or controlling this Revolution gone thereby. Royal Family, still hopeful to control it, means to get away from Paris as the first step. Suspected of such intention ; visit to St. Cloud violently prevented by the Populace (*April* 19*th*). Actual Flight to Varennes (*June* 20*th*) ; and misventures there : return captive to Paris, in a frightfully worsened position, the fifth evening after (*June* 25*th*). "Republic" mentioned in Placards, during King's Flight ; generally reprobated. Queen and Barnave. A Throne held up ; as if 'set on its vertex,' to be held there by hand. Should not this runaway King be deposed ? Immense assemblage, petitioning at Altar of Fatherland to that effect (*Sunday July* 17*th*), is dispersed by musketry, from Lafayette and Mayor Bailly, with extensive shrieks following, and leaving remembrances of a very bitter kind.

1791. *August.*

Foreign Governments, who had long looked with disapproval on the French Revolution, now set about preparing for actual interference. Convention of Pilnitz (*August* 25*th*-27*th*) : Emperor Leopold II., Friedrich Wilhelm II. King of Prussia, with certain less important Potentates, and Emigrant Princes of the Blood, assembling at this Pilnitz (Electoral Country-house near Dresden), express their sorrow and concern at the impossible posture of his now French Majesty, which they think calls upon regular Governments to interfere and mend it : they themselves, prepared at present to "resist French aggression" on their own territories, will coöperate with said Governments in "interfering by effectual methods." This Document, of date *August 27th*, 1791, rouses violent indignations in France; which blaze up higher and higher, and are not quenched for twenty-five years after. Constitution finished; accepted by the King (*September 14th*). Constituent Assembly proclaims 'in a sonorous voice' (*September 30th*), that its Sessions are all ended;—and goes its ways amid 'illuminations.'

1791. *October—December.*

Legislative Assembly, elected according to the Constitution, the first and also the last Assembly of that character, meets *October 1st*, 1791 : sat till *September 21st*, 1792 ; a Twelvemonth all but nine days. More republican than its predecessor ; inferior in talent ; destitute, like it, of parliamentary experience. Its debates, futilities, staggering parliamentary procedure (Book V. cc. 1-3). Court 'pretending to be dead,'—not 'aiding the Constitution to march.' *Sunday October 16th*, L'Escuyer, at Avignon, murdered in a Church ; Massacres in the Ice-Tower follow. Suspicions of their King, and of each other ; anxieties about foreign attack, and whether they are in a right condition to meet it ; painful questionings of Ministers, continual changes of Ministry, —occupy France and its Legislative with sad debates, growing ever more desperate and stormy in the coming months. Narbonne (Madame de Staël's friend) made War-Minister, *December 7th ;* continues for nearly half a year ; then Servan, who lasts three months ; then Dumouriez, who, in that capacity, lasts only five days (had, with Roland as Home-Minister, been otherwise in place for a year or more) ; mere 'Ghosts of Ministries.'

1792. *February—April.*

Terror of rural France (*February-March*) ; Camp of Jalès ; copious Emigration. *February 7th*, Emperor Leopold and the King of Prussia, mending their Pilnitz offer, make public Treaty, That they specially will endeavour to keep down disturbance, and if attacked will assist one another. Sardinia, Naples, Spain, and even Russia and the Pope, understood to be in the rear of these two. *April 20th*, French Assembly, after violent debates, decrees War against Emperor Leopold. This is the first Declaration of War ; which the others followed, *pro* and *contra*, all round, like pieces of a great Firework blazing out now here now there. The Prussian Declaration, which followed first, some months after, is the immediately important one.

1792. *June.*

In presence of these alarming phenomena, Government cannot act ; will not, say the People. Clubs, Journalists, Sections (organised population of Paris) growing ever more violent and desperate. Issue forth (*June 20th*) in vast Procession, the combined Sections and leaders, with banners, with demonstrations ; marching through the streets of Paris, "To quicken the Executive," and give it a fillip as to the time of day. Called "Procession of the Black Breeches" in this Book. Immense Procession, peaceable but dangerous ; finds the Tuileries gates closed, and no access to his Majesty ; squeezes, crushes, and is squeezed, crushed against the Tuileries gates and doors till they give way ;

and the admission to his Majesty, and the dialogue with him, and behaviour in his House, are of an utterly chaotic kind, dangerous and scandalous, though not otherwise than peaceable. Giving rise to much angry commentary in France and over Europe. *June Twenty* henceforth a memorable Day. General Lafayette suddenly appears in the Assembly ; without leave, as is splenetically observed : makes fruitless attempt to reinstate authority in Paris (*June* 28*th*) ; withdraws as an extinct popularity.

1792. *July.*

July 6*th*, Reconciliatory Scene in the Assembly, derisively called *Baiser L'amourette.* 'Third Federation,' *July* 14*th*, being at hand, could not the assembling 'Federates' be united into some Nucleus of Force near Paris ? Court answers, No ; not without reason of its own. Barbaroux writes to Marseilles for " 500 men that know how to die ; " who accordingly get under way, though like to be too late for the Federation. *Sunday July* 22*d*, Solemn Proclamation that the " Country is in Danger."

July 24*th*, Prussian Declaration of War ; and Duke of Brunswick's celebrated Manifesto, threatening France 'with military execution' if Royalty were meddled with : the latter bears date, *Coblentz, July* 27*th*, 1792, in the name of both Emperor and King of Prussia. Duke of Brunswick commands in chief : Nephew (sister's son) of Frederick the Great ; and Father of our unlucky 'Queen Caroline :' had served, very young, in the Seven-Years War, under his Father's Brother, Prince Ferdinand ; often in command of detachments bigger or smaller ; and had gained distinction by his swift marches, audacity and battle-spirit : never hitherto commanded any wide system of operations ; nor ever again, till 1806, when he suddenly encountered ruin and death at the very starting (Battle of Jena, *October* 14*th* of that year). This Proclamation, which awoke endless indignation in France and much criticism in the world elsewhere, is understood to have been prepared by other hands (French-Emigrant chiefly, who were along with him in force), and to have been signed by the Duke much against his will. '*Insigne vengeance*,' 'military execution,' and other terms of overbearing menace : Prussian Army, and Austrians from Netherlands, are advancing in that humour. Marseillese, 'who know how to die,' arrive in Paris (*July* 29*th*) ; dinner-scene in the *Champs Elysées.*

1792. *August.*

Indignation waxing desperate at Paris : France, boiling with ability and will, tied up from defending itself by "an inactive Government" (fatally unable to act). Secret conclaves, consultations of Municipality and Clubs ; Danton understood to be the presiding genius there. Legislative Assembly is itself plotting and participant ; no other course for it. *August* 10*th*, Universal Insurrection of the Armed Population of Paris ; Tuileries forced, Swiss Guards cut to pieces. King, when once violence was imminent, and before any act of violence, had with Queen and Dauphin sought shelter in the Legislative-Assembly Hall. They continue there till *August* 13*th* (*Friday-Monday*), listening to the debates, in a reporter's box. Are conducted thence to the Temple "as Hostages,"—do not get out again except to die. Legislative

Assembly has its Decree ready, That in terms of the Constitution in such alarming crisis a *National Convention* (Parliament with absolute powers) shall be elected ; Decree issued that same day, *August* 10*th*, 1792. After which the Legislative only waits in existence till it be fulfilled.

THE GUILLOTINE.

(*August* 10*th*, 1792—*October* 4*th*, 1795.)

1792. *August—September*.

Legislative continues its sittings till Election be completed. Enemy advancing, with armed Emigrants, enter France, Luxembourg region ; take Longwy, almost without resistance (*August* 23*d*) ; prepare to take Verdun. Austrians besieging Thionville ; cannot take it. Dumouriez seizes the Passes of Argonne, *August* 29*th*. Great agitation in Paris. *Sunday September* 2*d* and onwards till *Thursday* 6*th*, September Massacres : described Book I. cc. 4-6. Prussians have taken Verdun, *September* 2*d* (*Sunday*, while the Massacres are beginning): except on the score of provisions and of weather, little or no hindrance. Dumouriez waiting in the Passes of Argonne. Prussians detained three weeks forcing these. Famine, and torrents of rain. Battle or Cannonade of Valmy (*September* 20*th*) : French do not fly, as expected. Convention meets, *September* 22*d*, 1792 ; Legislative had sat till the day before, and now gives place to it : Republic decreed, same day. Austrians, renouncing Thionville, besiege Lille (*September* 28*th*—*October* 8*th*) ; cannot : 'fashionable shaving-dish,' the splinter of a Lille bombshell. Prussians, drenched deep in mud, in dysentery and famine, are obliged to retreat : Goethe's account of it. Total failure of that Brunswick Enterprise.

1792. *December*—1793. *January*.

Revolutionary activities in Paris and over France ; King shall be brought to "trial." Trial of the King (*Tuesday December* 11*th*—*Sunday* 16*th*). Three Votes (*January* 15*th*-17*th*, 1793) : Sentence, Death without respite. Executed, *Monday January* 21*st*, 1793, morning about 10 o'clock. English Ambassador quits Paris ; French Ambassador ordered to quit England (*January* 24*th*). War between the two countries imminent.

1793. *February*.

Dumouriez, in rear of the retreating Austrians, has seized the whole Austrian Netherlands, in a month or less (*November* 4*th*—2*d December* last) ; and now holds that territory. *February* 1*st*, France declares War against England and Holland ; England declares in return, *February* 11*th* : Dumouriez immediately invades Holland ; English, under Duke of York, go to the rescue : rather successful at first. Committee of *Salut Public* (instituted *January* 21*st*, day of the King's Execution) the supreme Administrative Body at Paris.

1793.   *March—July.*

Mutual quarrel of Parties once the King was struck down : Girondins or Limited " legal " Republicans *versus* Mountain or Unlimited : their strifes detailed, Book III. cc. 3, 7-9. War to Spain, *March 7th.* Three Epochs in the wrestle of Girondins and Mountain : first, *March 10th,* when the Girondins fancy they are to be "Septembered " by the anarchic population : anarchic population does demand "Arrestment of Twenty-two" by name, in return. Revolutionary Tribunal instituted, Danton's contrivance, that same day (*March 10th*). Battle of Neerwinden in Holland (*March 18th*) ; Dumouriez, quite beaten, obliged to withdraw homewards faster and faster. Second Girondin Epoch, *April 1st,* when they broke with Danton. General Dumouriez, a kind of Girondin in his way, goes over to the Enemy (*April 3d*). Famine, or scarcity in all kinds : *Law of Maximum* (fixing a price on commodities), *May 20th.* Third Girondin Epoch, "*illa suprema dies,*" Convention begirt by Armed Sections under Henriot (*Sunday June 2d*) ; Girondins, the Twenty-two and some more, put "under arrest in their own houses ;"— never got out again, but the reverse, as it proved.

1793.   *July.*

Revolt of the Departments in consequence, who are of Girondin temper ; their attempt at civil war. Comes to nothing ; ends in 'a mutual shriek' (at Vernon in Normandy, *July 15th*) : Charlotte Corday has assassinated Marat at Paris two days before (*Saturday July 13th*). Great Republican vengeances in consequence : Girondin Deputies, Barbaroux, Pétion, Louvet, Gaudet &c. wander ruined, disguised over France ; the Twenty-two, Brissot, Vergniaud &c. now imprisoned, await trial ; Lyons and other Girondin Cities to be signally punished. Valenciennes, besieged by Duke of York since May, surrenders *July 26th.*

1793.   *August—October.*

Mountain, victorious, resting on the 'Forty-four thousand Jacobin Clubs and Municipalities ;' its severe summary procedure rapidly developing itself into a "Reign of Terror." Law of the *Forty Sous* (Sectioners to be paid for attending meetings), Danton's Contrivance, *August 5th.* Austrians force the Lines of Weissembourg, penetrate into France on the East side : Dunkirk besieged by Duke of York (*August 22d*) : Lyons bombarded by Dubois-Crancé of the Mountain, Powder-Magazine explodes ; Barrère's Proclamation of Levy in Mass, "France risen against Tyrants" (*August 23d*). 'Revolutionary Army' (anarchic Police-force of the Mountain), *September 5th-11th.* Law of the Suspect, *September 17th.* Lyons, after frightful sufferings, surrenders to Dubois-Crancé (*October 9th*) : "To be razed from the Earth." Same day Gorsas at Paris, a Girondin Deputy, captured in a state of outlawry, is 'immediately guillotined' (*October 9th*) : first Deputy who died in that manner. Execution of the Queen Marie-Antoinette, *Wednesday October 16th.* Execution of the Twenty-two, after trial of some length, '*Marseillaise* sung in chorus' at the scaffold (*October 31st*).—General Jourdan has driven Cobourg and the Austrians over the Sambre again, *October* 16*th* (day of the Queen's death) ; Duke of York repulsed from Dunkirk, 'like to be swallowed by the tide,' a month before.

1793. *November—December.*

Reign of Terror, and Terror the Order of the Day. Execution of d'Orléans Egalité, *November* 6*th ;* of Madame Roland, *November* 8*th ;* of Mayor Bailly, *November* 10*th.* Goddess of Reason (first of them, at Paris) sails into the Convention, same day (*November* 10*th*): Plunder of Churches ; 'Carmagnole complete.' Convention "*Representatives* on Mission :" St. Just and Lebon, at Strasburg, "Strip off your shoes ; 10,000 pairs wanted ; likewise 1000 beds,— under way in 24 hours" (*November* 27*th*). Spanish War, neglected hitherto, and not successful ; may become important ? Toulon, dangerously Girondin in dangerous vicinity, Hood and the English and even "Louis XVIII." there ; is besieged, Napoleon serving in the Artillery ; is captured, *December* 19*th :* "To be razed from the Earth." Carrier at Nantes : *Noyadings* by night, second of them *December* 14*th ;* become "Marriages of the Loire," and other horrors. Lebon at Arras. Maignet at Orange. 'Death poured out in great floods (*vomie à grands flots*).' Lines of Weissembourg 'retaken by St. Just charging with Peasants' (*ends* the Year).

1794.

'Revolution eating its own children :' the Hébertists guillotined, Anacharsis Clootz among them, *March* 24*th ;* Danton himself and the Dantonists (*April* 3*d*), which is the acme of the process. Armies successful : Pichegru in the Netherlands ; defeat of Austrians at Moneron, *April* 29*th ;* of Austrian Emperor at Turcoing, *May* 18*th :* successes of Dugommier against Spain (*May* 23*d*), which continue in brilliant series, till the business ends, and he ends 'killed by a cannon-shot,' six months hence. *June* 1*st,* Howe's Sea-victory ; and Fable of the *Vengeur.* General Jourdan : Battle of Fleurus, sore stroke against the Austrian Netherlands (*June* 26*th*).

Conspiracy of Mountain against Robespierre : Tallien and others desirous not to be 'eaten.' Last scenes of Robespierre : *July* 28*th* (10 *Thermidor,* Year 2), guillotined with his Consorts ;—which, unexpectedly, ends the Reign of Terror. Victorious French Armies : enter Cologne, *October* 6*th ;* masters of Spanish bulwarks (Dugommier shot), *October* 17*th :* Duke of York and Dutch Stadtholder in a ruinous condition. Reaction against Robespierre : 'whole Nation a Committee of Mercy.' Jacobins Club assaulted by mob ; shut up, *November* 10*th-*12*th.* Law of Maximum abolished, *December* 24*th.* Duke of York gone home ; Pichegru and 70,000 overrun Holland ; frost so hard, 'hussars can take ships.'

1795.

Stadtholder quits Holland, *January* 19*th ;* glad to get across to England : Spanish Cities 'opening to the petard' (Rosas first, *January* 5*th,* and rapidly thereafter, till almost Madrid come in view). Continued downfall of Sans-culottism. Effervescence of luxury ; La Cabarus ; Greek Costumes ; *Jeunesse*

Dorée; balls in flesh-coloured drawers. Sansculottism rises twice in Insurrection; both times in vain. Insurrection of Germinal ('12 Germinal,' Year 3, *April 1st,* 1795); ends by 'two blank cannon-shot' from Pichegru.

1795. *April—October.*

Prussia makes Peace of Bâle (Basel), *April 5th;* Spain, Peace of Bâle a three months later. Armies everywhere successful: Catalogue of Victories and Conquests hung up in the Convention Hall. Famine of the lower classes. Fouquier Tinville guillotined (*May 8th*). Insurrection of Prairial, the Second attempt of Sansculottism to recover power ('1 Prairial,' *May 20th*); Deputy Féraud massacred:—issues in the Disarming and Finishing of Sansculottism. Emigrant Invasion, in English ships, lands at Quiberon, and is blown to pieces (*July 15th-20th*): La Vendée, which had before been three years in Revolt, is hereby kindled into a 'Second' less important 'Revolt of La Vendée,' which lasts some eight months. Reactionary "Companies of Jesus," "Companies of the Sun," assassinating Jacobins in the Rhone Countries (*July-August*). New Constitution: Directory and Consuls,—Two-thirds of the Convention to be reëlected. Objections to that clause. Section Lepelletier, and miscellaneous Discontented, revolt against it: Insurrection of Vendémiaire, Last of the Insurrections ('13 Vendémiaire, Year 4,' *October 5th,* 1795); quelled by Napoleon. On which "The Revolution," as defined here, ends,—Anarchic Government, if still anarchic, proceeding by softer methods than that of continued insurrection.

PAST AND PRESENT.

PAST AND PRESENT

BY

THOMAS CARLYLE

Ernſt iſt das Leben. SCHILLER

———————

LONDON: CHAPMAN AND HALL

LIMITED

1885

CONTENTS.

BOOK I.

BOOK II.

BOOK III.

THE MODERN-WORKER.

BOOK IV.

HOROSCOPE.

BOOK FIRST.

PROEM.

PAST AND PRESENT.

CHAPTER I.

MIDAS.

THE condition of England, on which many pamphlets are now in the course of publication, and many thoughts unpublished are going on in every reflective head, is justly regarded as one of the most ominous, and withal one of the strangest, ever seen in this world. England is full of wealth, of multifarious produce, supply for human want in every kind; yet England is dying of inanition. With unabated bounty the land of England blooms and grows; waving with yellow harvests; thick-studded with workshops, industrial implements, with fifteen millions of workers, understood to be the strongest, the cunningest and the willingest our Earth ever had; these men are here; the work they have done, the fruit they have realised is here, abundant, exuberant on every hand of us: and behold, some baleful fiat as of Enchantment has gone forth, saying, "Touch it not, ye workers, ye master-workers, ye master-idlers; none of you can touch it, no man of you shall be the better for it; this is enchanted fruit!" On the poor workers such fiat falls first, in its rudest shape; but on the rich master-workers too it falls; neither can the rich master-idlers, nor any richest or highest man escape, but all are like to be brought low with it, and made 'poor' enough, in the money sense or a far fataler one.

Of these successful skilful workers some two millions, it is now counted, sit in Workhouses, Poor-law Prisons; or have 'out-door relief' flung over the wall to them,—the workhouse Bastille being filled to bursting, and the strong Poor-law broken asunder by a stronger.[1] They sit there, these many months now; their hope of deliverance as yet small. In workhouses, pleasantly so-named, because work cannot be done in them. Twelve-hundred-thousand workers in England alone; their cunning right-hand lamed, lying idle in their sorrowful bosom; their hopes, outlooks, share of this fair world, shut-in by narrow walls. They sit there, pent up, as in a kind of horrid enchantment; glad to be imprisoned and enchanted, that they may not perish starved. The picturesque Tourist, in a sunny autumn day, through this bounteous realm of England, descries the Union Workhouse on his path. 'Passing by 'the Workhouse of St. Ives in Huntingdonshire, on a bright day 'last autumn,' says the picturesque Tourist, 'I saw sitting on 'wooden benches, in front of their Bastille and within their ring-'wall and its railings, some half-hundred or more of these men. 'Tall robust figures, young mostly or of middle age; of honest 'countenance, many of them thoughtful and even intelligent-'looking men. They sat there, near by one another; but in a 'kind of torpor, especially in a silence, which was very striking. 'In silence: for, alas, what word was to be said? An Earth all 'lying round, crying, Come and till me, come and reap me;—yet 'we here sit enchanted! In the eyes and brows of these men 'hung the gloomiest expression, not of anger, but of grief and 'shame and manifold inarticulate distress and weariness; they 'returned my glance with a glance that seemed to say, "Do not 'look at us. We sit enchanted here, we know not why. The 'Sun shines and the Earth calls; and, by the governing Powers 'and Impotences of this England, we are forbidden to obey. It is 'impossible, they tell us!" There was something that reminded me 'of Dante's Hell in the look of all this; and I rode swiftly away.'

So many hundred thousands sit in workhouses: and other hundred thousands have not yet got even workhouses; and in thrifty Scotland itself, in Glasgow or Edinburgh City, in their dark lanes, hidden from all but the eye of God, and of rare Benevolence the minister of God, there are scenes of woe and destitution and desolation, such as, one may hope, the Sun never saw before in the most barbarous regions where men dwelt. Competent witnesses, the brave and humane Dr. Alison, who speaks what he knows, whose noble Healing Art in his charitable hands becomes once more a truly sacred one, report these things for us:

---

[1] The Return of Paupers for England and Wales, at Ladyday 1842, is 'In-door 221,687, Out-door 1,207,402, Total 1,429,089.' *Official Report.*

these things are not of this year, or of last year, have no reference
to our present state of commercial stagnation, but only to the
common state. Not in sharp fever-fits, but in chronic gangrene
of this kind is Scotland suffering. A Poor-law, any and every
Poor-law, it may be observed, is but a temporary measure; an
anodyne, not a remedy: Rich and Poor, when once the naked
facts of their condition have come into collision, cannot long subsist
together on a mere Poor-law. True enough:—and yet, human
beings cannot be left to die! Scotland too, till something better
come, must have a Poor-law, if Scotland is not to be a byword
among the nations. O, what a waste is there; of noble and thrice-
noble national virtues; peasant Stoicisms, Heroisms; valiant
manful habits, soul of a Nation's worth,—which all the metal of
Potosi cannot purchase back; to which the metal of Potosi, and
all you can buy with *it*, is dross and dust!

Why dwell on this aspect of the matter? It is too indisputable,
not doubtful now to any one. Descend where you will into the
lower class, in Town or Country, by what avenue you will, by
Factory Inquiries, Agrictural Inquiries, by Revenue Returns, by
Mining-Labourer Committees, by opening your own eyes and
looking, the same sorrowful result discloses itself: you have to
admit that the working body of this rich English Nation has sunk
or is fast sinking into a state, to which, all sides of it considered,
there was literally never any parallel. At Stockport Assizes,—
and this too has no reference to the present state of trade, being
of date prior to that,—a Mother and a Father are arraigned and
found guilty of poisoning three of their children, to defraud a
'burial-society' of some 3*l*. 8*s*. due on the death of each child:
they are arraigned, found guilty; and the official authorities, it
is whispered, hint that perhaps the case is not solitary, that
perhaps you had better not probe farther into that department
of things. This is in the autumn of 1841; the crime itself is of
the previous year or season. "Brutal savages, degraded Irish,"
mutters the idle reader of Newspapers; hardly lingering on this
incident. Yet it is an incident worth lingering on; the depravity,
savagery and degraded Irishism being never so well admitted.
In the British land, a human Mother and Father, of white skin
and professing the Christian religion, had done this thing; they,
with their Irishism and necessity and savagery, had been driven
to do it. Such instances are like the highest mountain apex
emerged into view; under which lies a whole mountain region and

land, not yet emerged. A human Mother and Father had said to themselves, What shall we do to escape starvation? We are deep sunk here, in our dark cellar; and help is far.—Yes, in the Ugolino Hunger-tower stern things happen; best-loved little Gaddo fallen dead on his Father's knees!—The Stockport Mother and Father think and hint: Our poor little starveling Tom, who cries all day for victuals, who will see only evil and not good in this world: if he were out of misery at once; he well dead, and the rest of us perhaps kept alive? It is thought, and hinted; at last it is done. And now Tom being killed, and all spent and eaten, Is it poor little starveling Jack that must go, or poor little starveling Will?—What a committee of ways and means!

In starved sieged cities, in the uttermost doomed ruin of old Jerusalem fallen under the wrath of God, it was prophesied and said, 'The hands of the pitiful women have sodden their own children.' The stern Hebrew imagination could conceive no blacker gulf of wretchedness; that was the ultimatum of degraded god-punished man. And we here, in modern England, exuberant with supply of all kinds, besieged by nothing if it be not by invisible Enchantments, are we reaching that?——How come these things? Wherefore are they, wherefore should they be?

Nor are they of the St. Ives workhouses, of the Glasgow lanes, and Stockport cellars, the only unblessed among us. This successful industry of England, with its plethoric wealth, has as yet made nobody rich; it is an enchanted wealth, and belongs yet to nobody. We might ask, Which of us has it enriched? We can spend thousands where we once spent hundreds; but can purchase nothing good with them. In Poor and Rich, instead of noble thrift and plenty, there is idle luxury alternating with mean scarcity and inability. We have sumptuous garnitures for our Life, but have forgotten to *live* in the middle of them. It is an enchanted wealth; no man of us can yet touch it. The class of men who feel that they are truly better off by means of it, let them give us their name!

Many men eat finer cookery, drink dearer liquors,—with what advantage they can report, and their Doctors can: but in the heart of them, if we go out of the dyspeptic stomach, what increase of blessedness is there? Are they better, beautifuler, stronger, braver? Are they even what they call 'happier'? Do they look with satisfaction on more things and human faces

in this God's-Earth; do more things and human faces look
with satisfaction on them? Not so. Human faces gloom discordantly, disloyally on one another. Things, if it be not
mere cotton and iron things, are growing disobedient to man.
The Master Worker is enchanted, for the present, like his Workhouse Workman; clamours, in vain hitherto, for a very simple
sort of 'Liberty:' the liberty 'to buy where he finds it cheapest,
to sell where he finds it dearest.' With guineas jingling in every
pocket, he was no whit richer; but now, the very guineas threatening to vanish, he feels that he is poor indeed. Poor Master
Worker! And the Master Unworker, is not he in a still fataler
situation? Pausing amid his game-preserves, with awful eye,—as
he well may! Coercing fifty-pound tenants; coercing, bribing,
cajoling; 'doing what he likes with his own.' His mouth full of
loud futilities, and arguments to prove the excellence of his Corn-
law; and in his heart the blackest misgiving, a desperate half-
consciousness that his excellent Corn-law is *in*defensible, that his
loud arguments for it are of a kind to strike men too literally *dumb*.

To whom, then, is this wealth of England wealth? Who is it
that it blesses; makes happier, wiser, beautifuler, in any way
better? Who has got hold of it, to make it fetch and carry for
him, like a true servant, not like a false mock-servant; to do him
any real service whatsoever? As yet no one. We have more
riches than any Nation ever had before; we have less good
of them than any Nation ever had before. Our successful
industry is hitherto unsuccessful; a strange success, if we stop
here! In the midst of plethoric plenty, the people perish; with
gold walls, and full barns, no man feels himself safe or satisfied.
Workers, Master Workers, Unworkers, all men, come to a pause;
stand fixed, and cannot farther. Fatal paralysis spreading inwards,
from the extremities, in St. Ives workhouses, in Stockport cellars,
through all limbs, as if towards the heart itself. Have we actually
got enchanted, then; accursed by some god?—

Midas longed for gold, and insulted the Olympians. He got
gold, so that whatsoever he touched became gold,—and he, with
his long ears, was little the better for it. Midas had misjudged
the celestial music-tones; Midas had insulted Apollo and the gods:
the gods gave him his wish, and a pair of long ears, which also
were a good appendage to it. What a truth in these old Fables!

CHAPTER II.

THE SPHINX.

How true, for example, is that other old Fable of the Sphinx, who sat by the wayside, propounding her riddle to the passengers, which if they could not answer she destroyed them! Such a Sphinx is this Life of ours, to all men and societies of men. Nature, like the Sphinx, is of womanly celestial loveliness and tenderness; the face and bosom of a goddess, but ending in claws and the body of a lioness. There is in her a celestial beauty,—which means celestial order, pliancy to wisdom; but there is also a darkness, a ferocity, fatality, which are infernal. She is a goddess, but one not yet disimprisoned; one still half-imprisoned, —the articulate, lovely still encased in the inarticulate, chaotic. How true! And does she not propound her riddles to us? Of each man she asks daily, in mild voice, yet with a terrible significance, "Knowest thou the meaning of this Day? What thou canst do Today; wisely attempt to do?" Nature, Universe, Destiny, Existence, howsoever we name this grand unnamable Fact in the midst of which we live and struggle, is as a heavenly bride and conquest to the wise and brave, to them who can discern her behests and do them; a destroying fiend to them who cannot. Answer her riddle, it is well with thee. Answer it not, pass on regarding it not, it will answer itself; the solution for thee is a thing of teeth and claws; Nature is a dumb lioness, deaf to thy pleadings, fiercely devouring. Thou art not now her victorious bridegroom; thou art her mangled victim, scattered on the precipices, as a slave found treacherous, recreant, ought to be and must.

With Nations it is as with individuals: Can they rede the riddle of Destiny? This English Nation, will it get to know the meaning of *its* strange new Today? Is there sense enough extant, discoverable anywhere or anyhow, in our united twenty-seven million heads to discern the same; valour enough in our twenty-seven million hearts to dare and do the bidding thereof? It will be seen!—

The secret of gold Midas, which he with his long ears never could discover, was, That he had offended the Supreme Powers; —that he had parted company with the eternal inner Facts of this Universe, and followed the transient outer Appearances thereof; and so was arrived *here*. Properly it is the secret of all unhappy men and unhappy nations. Had they known Nature's right truth, Nature's right truth would have made them free. They have become enchanted; stagger spell-bound, reeling on the brink of huge peril, because they were not wise enough. They have forgotten the right Inner True, and taken up with the Outer Sham-true. They answer the Sphinx's question *wrong*. Foolish men cannot answer it aright! Foolish men mistake transitory semblance for eternal fact, and go astray more and more.

Foolish men imagine that because judgment for an evil thing is delayed, there is no justice, but an accidental one, here below. Judgment for an evil thing is many times delayed some day or two, some century or two, but it is sure as life, it is sure as death! In the centre of the world-whirlwind, verily now as in the oldest days, dwells and speaks a God. The great soul of the world is *just*. O brother, can it be needful now, at this late epoch of experience, after eighteen centuries of Christian preaching for one thing, to remind thee of such a fact; which all manner of Mahometans, old Pagan Romans, Jews, Scythians and heathen Greeks, and indeed more or less all men that God made, have managed at one time to see into; nay which thou thyself, till 'redtape' strangled the inner life of thee, hadst once some inkling of: That there *is* justice here below; and even, at bottom, that there is nothing else but justice! Forget that, thou hast forgotten all. Success will never more attend thee: how can it now? Thou hast the whole Universe against thee. No more success: mere sham-success, for a day and days; rising ever higher,—towards its Tarpeian Rock. Alas, how, in thy soft-hung Longacre vehicle, of polished leather to the bodily eye, of redtape philosophy, of expediencies, clubroom moralities, Parliamentary majorities to the mind's eye, thou beautifully rollest: but knowest thou whitherward? It is towards the *road's end*. Old use-and-wont; established methods, habitudes, *once* true and wise; man's noblest tendency, his perseverance, and man's ignoblest, his inertia ; whatsoever of noble and ignoble Conservatism there is in men and Nations, strongest always in the strongest men and Nations : all this is as a road to thee, paved smooth through the abyss,—till all this *end*. Till men's bitter necessities can endure thee no more. Till Nature's patience with thee is done ; and there is no road or footing any farther, and the abyss yawns sheer !—

Parliament and the Courts of Westminster are venerable to me ; how venerable ; gray with a thousand years of honourable age ! For a thousand years and more, Wisdom and faithful Valour, struggling amid much Folly and greedy Baseness, not without most sad distortions in the struggle, have built them up ; and they are as we see. For a thousand years, this English Nation has found them useful or supportable : they have served this English Nation's want ; *been* a road to it through the abyss of Time. They are venerable, they are great and strong. And yet it is good to remember always that they are not the venerablest, nor the greatest, nor the strongest ! Acts of Parliament are venerable ; but if they correspond not with the writing on the ' Adamant Tablet,' what are they ? Properly their one element of vener- ableness, of strength or greatness, is, that they at all times correspond therewith as near as by human possibility they can. They are cherishing destruction in their bosom every hour that they continue otherwise.

Alas, how many causes that can plead well for themselves in the Courts of Westminster ; and yet in the general Court of the Universe, and free Soul of Man, have no word to utter ! Honour- able Gentlemen may find this worth considering, in times like ours. And truly, the din of triumphant Law-logic, and all shaking of horse-hair wigs and learned-serjeant gowns having comfortably ended, we shall do well to ask ourselves withal, What says that high and highest Court to the verdict ? For it is the Court of Courts, that same ; where the universal soul of Fact and very Truth sits President ;—and thitherward, more and more swiftly, with a really terrible increase of swiftness, all causes do in these days crowd for revisal,—for confirmation, for modification, for reversal with costs. Dost thou know that Court ; hast thou had any Law- practice there ? What, didst thou never enter ; never file any petition of redress, reclaimer, disclaimer or demurrer, written as in thy heart's blood, for thy own behoof or another's ; and silently await the issue ? Thou knowest not such a Court ? Hast merely heard of it by faint tradition as a thing that was or had been? Of thee, I think, we shall get little benefit.

For the gowns of learned-serjeants are good: parchment records, fixed forms, and poor terrestrial Justice, with or without horse-hair, what sane man will not reverence these? And yet, behold, the man is not sane but insane, who considers these alone as venerable. Oceans of horse-hair, continents of parchment, and learned-serjeant eloquence, were it continued till the learned tongue wore itself small in the indefatigable learned mouth, cannot make unjust just. The grand question still remains, Was the judgment just? If unjust, it will not and cannot get harbour for itself, or continue to have footing in this Universe, which was made by other than One Unjust. Enforce it by never such statuting, three readings, royal assents; blow it to the four winds with all manner of quilted trumpeters and pursuivants, in the rear of them never so many gibbets and hangmen, it will not stand, it cannot stand. From all souls of men, from all ends of Nature, from the Throne of God above, there are voices bidding it: Away, away! Does it take no warning; does it stand, strong in its three readings, in its gibbets and artillery-parks? The more woe is to it, the frightfuler woe. It will continue standing for its day, for its year, for its century, doing evil all the while; but it has One enemy who is Almighty: dissolution, explosion, and the everlasting Laws of Nature incessantly advance towards it; and the deeper its rooting, more obstinate its continuing, the deeper also and huger will its ruin and overturn be.

In this God's-world, with its wild-whirling eddies and mad foam-oceans, where men and nations perish as if without law, and judgment for an unjust thing is sternly delayed, dost thou think that there is therefore no justice? It is what the fool hath said in his heart. It is what the wise, in all times, were wise because they denied, and knew forever not to be. I tell thee again, there is nothing else but justice. One strong thing I find here below: the just thing, the true thing. My friend, if thou hadst all the artillery of Woolwich trundling at thy back in support of an unjust thing; and infinite bonfires visibly waiting ahead of thee, to blaze centuries long for thy victory on behalf of it,—I would advise thee to call halt, to fling down thy baton, and say, "In God's name, No!" Thy 'success'? Poor devil, what will thy success amount to? If the thing is unjust, thou hast not succeeded; no, not though bonfires blazed from North to South, and bells rang, and editors wrote leading-articles, and the just thing lay trampled out of sight, to all mortal eyes an abolished and annihilated thing. Success? In few years thou wilt be dead and dark,—all cold, eyeless, deaf; no blaze of bonfires, ding-dong of bells or leading articles visible or audible to thee again at all forever: What kind of success is that!—

It is true, all goes by approximation in this world; with any not insupportable approximation we must be patient. There is a noble Conservatism as well as an ignoble. Would to Heaven, for the sake of Conservatism itself, the noble alone were left, and the ignoble, by some kind severe hand, were ruthlessly lopped away, forbidden evermore to show itself! For it is the right and noble alone that will have victory in this struggle; the rest is wholly an obstruction, a postponement and fearful imperilment of the victory. Towards an eternal centre of right and nobleness, and of that only, is all this confusion tending. We already know whither it is all tending; what will have victory, what will have none! The Heaviest will reach the centre. The Heaviest, sinking through complex fluctuating media and vortices, has its deflexions, its obstructions, nay at times its resiliences, its reboundings; where-upon some blockhead shall be heard jubilating, " See, your Heaviest ascends! "—but at all moments it is moving centreward, fast as is convenient for it; sinking, sinking; and, by laws older than the World, old as the Maker's first Plan of the World, it has to arrive there.

Await the issue. In all battles, if you await the issue, each fighter has prospered according to his right. His right and his might, at the close of the account, were one and the same. He has fought with all his might, and in exact proportion to all his right he has prevailed. His very death is no victory over him. He dies indeed; but his work lives, very truly lives. A heroic Wallace, quartered on the scaffold, cannot hinder that his Scotland become, one day, a part of England: but he does hinder that it become, on tyrannous unfair terms, a part of it; commands still, as with a god's voice, from his old Valhalla and Temple of the Brave, that there be a just real union as of brother and brother, not a false and merely semblant one as of slave and master. If the union with England be in fact one of Scotland's chief blessings, we thank Wallace withal that it was not the chief curse. Scotland is not Ireland: no, because brave men rose there, and said, " Behold, ye must not tread us down like slaves; and ye shall not,—and cannot!" Fight on, thou brave true heart, and falter not, through dark fortune and through bright. The cause thou fightest for, so far as it is true, no farther, yet precisely so far, is very sure of victory. The falsehood alone of it will be conquered, will be abolished, as it ought to be: but the truth of it is part of Nature's own Laws, coöperates with the World's eternal Tendencies, and cannot be conquered.

The *dust* of controversy, what is it but the *falsehood* flying off from all manner of conflicting true forces, and making such a loud dust-whirlwind,—that so the truths alone may remain, and embrace brother-like in some true resulting-force! It is ever so. Savage fighting Heptarchies: their fighting is an ascertainment, who has the right to rule over whom; that out of such waste-bickering Saxondom a peacefully coöperating England may arise. Seek through this Universe; if with other than owl's eyes, thou wilt find nothing nourished there, nothing kept in life, but what has right to nourishment and life. The rest, look at it with other than owl's eyes, is not living; is all dying, all as good as dead! Justice was ordained from the foundations of the world; and will last with the world and longer.

From which I infer that the inner sphere of Fact, in this present England as elsewhere, differs infinitely from the outer sphere and spheres of Semblance. That the Temporary, here as elsewhere, is too apt to carry it over the Eternal. That he who dwells in the temporary Semblances, and does not penetrate into the eternal Substance, will *not* answer the Sphinx-riddle of Today, or of any Day. For the substance alone is substantial; that *is* the law of Fact; if you discover not that, Fact, who already knows it, will let you also know it by and by!

What is Justice? that, on the whole, is the question of the Sphinx to us. The law of Fact is, that Justice must and will be done. The sooner the better; for the Time grows stringent, frightfully pressing! "What is Justice?" ask many, to whom cruel Fact alone will be able to prove responsive. It is like jesting Pilate asking, What is Truth? Jesting Pilate had not the smallest chance to ascertain what was Truth. He could not have known it, had a god shown it to him. Thick serene opacity, thicker than amaurosis, veiled those smiling eyes of his to Truth; the inner *retina* of them was gone paralytic, dead. He looked at Truth; and discerned her not, there where she stood. "What is Justice?" The clothed embodied Justice that sits in Westminster Hall, with penalties, parchments, tipstaves, is very visible. But the *un*embodied Justice, whereof that other is either an emblem, or else is a fearful indescribability, is not so visible! For the unembodied Justice is of Heaven; a Spirit, and Divinity of Heaven,—*in*visible to all but the noble and pure of soul. The impure ignoble gaze with eyes, and she is not there. They will prove it to you by logic, by endless Hansard Debatings, by bursts of Parliamentary eloquence. It is not consolatory to behold! For properly, as many men as there are in a Nation who *can* withal see Heaven's invisible Justice, and know it to be on Earth also omnipotent, so many men are there who stand between a Nation and perdition. So many, and no more. Heavy-laden England, how many hast thou in this hour? The Supreme Power sends new and ever new, all *born* at least with hearts of flesh and not of stone;—and heavy Misery itself, once heavy enough, will prove didactic!—

CHAPTER III.

MANCHESTER INSURRECTION.

BLUSTEROWSKI, Colacorde, and other Editorial prophets of the Continental-Democratic Movement, have in their leading-articles shown themselves disposed to vilipend the late Manchester Insurrection, as evincing in the rioters an extreme backwardness to battle; nay as betokening, in the English People itself, perhaps a want of the proper animal courage indispensable in these ages. A million hungry operative men started up, in utmost paroxysm of desperate protest against their lot; and, ask Colacorde and company, How many shots were fired? Very few in comparison! Certain hundreds of drilled soldiers sufficed to suppress this million-headed hydra, and tread it down, without the smallest appeasement or hope of such, into its subterranean settlements again, there to reconsider itself. Compared with our revolts in Lyons, in Warsaw and elsewhere, to say nothing of incomparable Paris City past or present, what a lamblike Insurrection!—

The present Editor is not here, with his readers, to vindicate the character of Insurrections; nor does it matter to us whether Blusterowski and the rest may think the English a courageous people or not courageous. In passing, however, let us mention that, to our view, this was not an unsuccessful Insurrection; that as Insurrections go, we have not heard lately of any that succeeded so well.

A million of hungry operative men, as Blusterowski says, rose all up, came all out into the streets, and—stood there. What other could they do? Their wrongs and griefs were bitter, insupportable, their rage against the same was just: but who are they that cause these wrongs, who that will honestly make effort to redress them? Our enemies are we know not who or what; our friends are we know not where! How shall we attack any one, shoot or be shot by any one? Oh, if the accursed invisible Nightmare, that is crushing out the life of us and ours, would take a shape; approach us like the Hyrcanian tiger, the Behemoth of Chaos, the Archfiend himself; in any shape that we could see, and fasten on!—A man can have himself shot with cheerfulness; but it needs first that he see clearly for what. Show him the divine face of Justice, then the diabolic monster which is eclipsing that: he will fly at the throat of such monster, never so monstrous, and need no bidding to do it. Woolwich grapeshot will sweep clear all streets, blast into invisibility so many thousand men: but if your Woolwich grapeshot be but eclipsing Divine Justice, and the God's-radiance itself gleam recognisable athwart such grapeshot,—then, yes then is the time come for fighting and attacking. All artillery-parks have become weak, and are about to dissipate: in the God's thunder, their poor thunder slackens, ceases; finding that it is, in all senses of the term, a *brute* one!—

That the Manchester Insurrection stood still, on the streets, with an indisposition to fire and bloodshed, was wisdom for it even as an Insurrection. Insurrection, never so necessary, is a most sad necessity; and governors who wait for that to instruct them, are surely getting into the fatalest courses,—proving themselves Sons of Nox and Chaos, of blind Cowardice, not of seeing Valour! How can there be any remedy in insurrection? It is a mere announcement of the disease,—visible now even to Sons of Night. Insurrection usually 'gains' little; usually wastes how much! One of its worst kinds of waste, to say nothing of the rest, is that of irritating and exasperating men against each other, by violence done; which is always sure to be injustice done, for violence does even justice unjustly.

Who shall compute the waste and loss, the obstruction of every sort, that was produced in the Manchester region by Peterloo alone! Some thirteen unarmed men and women cut down,—the number of the slain and maimed is very countable: but the treasury of rage, burning hidden or visible in all hearts ever since, more or less perverting the effort and aim of all hearts ever since, is of unknown extent. "How ye came among us, in your cruel armed blindness, ye unspeakable County Yeomanry, sabres flourishing, hoofs prancing, and slashed us down at your brute pleasure; deaf, blind to all *our* claims and woes and wrongs; of quick sight and sense to your own claims only! There lie poor sallow workworn weavers, and complain no more now; women themselves are slashed and sabred, howling terror fills the air; and ye ride prosperous, very victorious,—ye unspeakable: give *us* sabres too, and then come-on a little!" Such are Peterloos. In all hearts that witnessed Peterloo, stands written, as in fire-characters, or smoke-characters prompt to become fire again, a legible balance-account of grim vengeance; very unjustly balanced, much exaggerated, as is the way with such accounts: but payable readily at sight, in full with compound interest! Such things should be avoided as the very pestilence! For men's hearts ought not to be set against one another; but set *with* one another, and all against the Evil Thing only. Men's souls ought to be left to see clearly; not jaundiced, blinded, twisted all awry, by revenge, mutual abhorrence, and the like. An Insurrection that can announce the disease, and then retire with no such balance-account opened anywhere, has attained the highest success possible for it.

And this was what these poor Manchester operatives, with all the darkness that was in them and round them, did manage to perform. They put their huge inarticulate question, "What do you mean to do with us?" in a manner audible to every reflective soul in this kingdom; exciting deep pity in all good men, deep anxiety in all men whatever; and no conflagration or outburst of madness came to cloud that feeling anywhere, but everywhere it operates unclouded. All England heard the question: it is the first practical form of *our* Sphinx-riddle. England will answer it; or, on the whole, England will perish;—one does not yet expect the latter result!

For the rest, that the Manchester Insurrection could yet discern no radiance of Heaven on any side of its horizon ; but feared that all lights, of the O'Connor or other sorts, hitherto kindled, were but deceptive fish-oil transparencies, or bog will-o'-wisp lights, and no dayspring from on high : for this also we will honour the poor Manchester Insurrection, and augur well of it. A deep unspoken sense lies in these strong men,—inconsiderable, almost stupid, as all they can articulate of it is. Amid all violent stupidity of speech, a right noble instinct of what is doable and what is not doable never forsakes them : the strong inarticulate men and workers, whom *Fact* patronises ; of whom, in all difficulty and work whatsoever, there is good augury ! This work too is to be done : Governors and Governing Classes that *can* articulate and utter, in any measure, what the law of Fact and Justice is, may calculate that here is a Governed Class who will listen.

And truly this first practical form of the Sphinx-question, inarticulately and so audibly put there, is one of the most impressive ever asked in the world. " Behold us here, so many thousands, millions, and increasing at the rate of fifty every hour. We are right willing and able to work ; and on the Planet Earth is plenty of work and wages for a million times as many. We ask, If you mean to lead us towards work ; to try to lead us,—by ways new, never yet heard of till this new unheard-of Time ? Or if you declare that you cannot lead us ? And expect that we are to remain quietly unled, and in a composed manner perish of starvation ? What is it you expect of us ? What is it you mean to do with us ? " This question, I say, has been put in the hearing of all Britain ; and will be again put, and ever again, till some answer be given it.

Unhappy Workers, unhappy Idlers, unhappy men and women of this actual England. We are yet very far from an answer, and there will be no existence for us without finding one. " A fair day's-wages for a fair day's-work : " it is as just a demand as Governed men ever made of Governing. It is the everlasting right of man. Indisputable as Gospels, as arithmetical multiplication-tables : it must and will have itself fulfilled ;—and yet, in these times of ours, with what enormous difficulty, next-door to impossibility ! For the times are really strange ; of a complexity intricate with all the new width of the ever-widening world ; times here of half-frantic velocity of impetus, there of the deadest-looking stillness and paralysis ; times definable as showing two qualities, Dilettantism and Mammonism ;—most intricate obstructed times! Nay, if there were not a Heaven's radiance of Justice, prophetic, clearly of Heaven, discernible behind all these confused world-wide entanglements, of Landlord interests, Manufacturing interests, Tory-Whig interests, and who knows what other interests, expediencies, vested interests, established possessions, inveterate Dilettantisms, Midas-eared Mammonisms,—it would seem to every one a flat impossibility, which all wise men might as well at once abandon. If you do not know eternal Justice from momentary Expediency, and understand in your *heart of hearts how Justice, radiant, beneficent, as the all-victorious Light-element, is also in essence, if need be, an all-victorious *Fire*-element, and melts all manner of vested interests, and the hardest iron cannon, as if they were soft wax, and does ever in the long-run rule and reign, and allows nothing else to rule and reign,—you also would talk of impossibility! But it is only difficult, it is not impossible. Possible? It is, with whatever difficulty, very clearly inevitable.

Fair day's-wages for fair day's-work! exclaims a sarcastic man: Alas, in what corner of this Planet, since Adam first awoke on it, was that ever realised? The day's-wages of John Milton's day's-work, named *Paradise Lost* and *Milton's Works*, were Ten Pounds paid by instalments, and a rather close escape from death on the gallows. Consider that: it is no rhetorical flourish; it is an authentic, altogether quiet fact,—emblematic, quietly documentary of a whole world of such, ever since human history began. Oliver Cromwell quitted his farming; undertook a Hercules' Labour and lifelong wrestle with that Lernean Hydra-coil, wide as England, hissing heaven-high through its thousand crowned, coroneted, shovel-hatted quack-heads; and he did wrestle with it, the truest and terriblest wrestle I have heard of; and he wrestled it, and mowed and cut it down a good many stages, so that its hissing is ever since pitiful in comparison, and one can walk abroad in comparative peace from it;—and his wages, as I understand, were burial under the gallows-tree near Tyburn Turnpike, with his head on the gable of Westminster Hall, and two centuries now of mixed cursing and ridicule from all manner of men. His dust lies under the Edgware Road, near Tyburn Turnpike, at this hour; and his memory is—Nay what matters what his memory is? His memory, at bottom, is or yet shall be as that of a god: a terror and horror to all quacks and cowards and insincere persons; an everlasting encouragement, new memento, battleword, and pledge of victory to all the brave. It is the natural course and history of the Godlike, in every place, in every time. What god ever carried it with the Tenpound Franchisers; in Open Vestry, or with any Sanhedrim of considerable standing? When was a god found 'agreeable' to everybody? The regular way is to hang, kill, crucify your gods, and execrate and trample them under your stupid hoofs for a century or two; till you discover that they are gods,—and then take to braying over them, still in a very long-eared manner!—So speaks the sarcastic man; in his wild way, very mournful truths.

Day's-wages for day's-work? continues he: The Progress of Human Society consists even in this same, The better and better apportioning of wages to work. Give me this, you have given me all. Pay to every man accurately what he has worked for, what he has earned and done and deserved,—to this man broad lands and honours, to that man high gibbets and treadmills: what more have I to ask? Heaven's Kingdom, which we daily pray for, *has* come; God's will is done on Earth even as it is in Heaven! This *is* the radiance of celestial Justice; in the light or in the fire of which all impediments, vested interests, and iron cannon, are more and more melting like wax, and disappearing from the pathways of men. A thing ever struggling forward; irrepressible, advancing inevitable; perfecting itself, all days, more and more,—never to be *perfect* till that general Doomsday, the ultimate Consummation, and Last of earthly Days.

True, as to 'perfection' and so forth, answer we; true enough! And yet withal we have to remark, that imperfect Human Society holds itself together, and finds place under the Sun, in virtue simply of some *approximation* to perfection being actually made and put in practice. We remark farther, that there are supportable approximations, and then likewise insupportable. With some, almost with any, supportable approximation men are apt, perhaps too apt, to rest indolently patient, and say, It will do. Thus these poor Manchester manual workers mean only, by day's-wages for day's-work, certain coins of money adequate to keep them living; —in return for their work, such modicum of food, clothes and fuel as will enable them to continue their work itself! They as yet clamour for no more; the rest, still inarticulate, cannot yet shape itself into a demand at all, and only lies in them as a dumb wish; perhaps only, still more inarticulate, as a dumb, altogether unconscious want. *This* is the supportable approximation they would rest patient with, That by their work they might be kept alive to work more!—*This* once grown unattainable, I think your approximation may consider itself to have reached the *in*supportable stage; and may prepare, with whatever difficulty, reluctance and astonishment, for one of two things, for changing or perishing! With the millions no longer able to live, how can the units keep living? It is too clear the Nation itself is on the way to suicidal death.

Shall we say then, The world has retrograded in its talent of apportioning wages to work, in late days? The world had always a talent of that sort, better or worse. Time was when the mere *hand*worker needed not announce his claim to the world by Manchester Insurrections!—The world, with its Wealth of Nations, Supply-and-demand and suchlike, has of late days been terribly inattentive to that question of work and wages. We will not say, the poor world has retrograded even here: we will say rather, the world has been rushing on with such fiery animation to get work and ever more work done, it has had no time to think of dividing the wages; and has merely left them to be scrambled for by the Law of the Stronger, law of Supply-and-demand, law of Laissez-faire, and other idle Laws and Un-laws,—saying, in its dire haste to get the work done, That is well enough!

And now the world will have to pause a little, and take up that other side of the problem, and in right earnest strive for some solution of that. For it has become pressing. What is the use of your spun shirts? They hang there by the million unsaleable; and here, by the million, are diligent bare backs that can get no hold of them. Shirts are useful for covering human backs; useless otherwise, an unbearable mockery otherwise. You have fallen terribly behind with that side of the problem! Manchester Insurrections, French Revolutions, and thousandfold phenomena great and small, announce loudly that you must bring it forward a little again. Never till now, in the history of an Earth which to this hour nowhere refuses to grow corn if you will plough it, to yield shirts if you will spin and weave in it, did the mere manual two-handed worker (however it might fare with other workers) cry in vain for such 'wages' as *he* means by 'fair wages,' namely food and warmth! The Godlike could not and cannot be paid; but the Earthly always could. Gurth, a mere swineherd, born thrall of Cedric the Saxon, tended pigs in the wood, and did get some parings of the pork. Why, the four-footed worker

has already *got* all that this two-handed one is clamouring for!
How often must I remind you? There is not a horse in England,
able and willing to work, but *has* due food and lodging; and goes
about sleek-coated, satisfied in heart. And you say, It is
impossible. Brothers, I answer, if for you it be impossible, what
is to become of you? It is impossible for us to believe it to be
impossible. The human brain, looking at these sleek English
horses, refuses to believe in such impossibility for English men.
Do you depart quickly; clear the ways soon, lest worse befall.
We for our share do purpose, with full view of the enormous
difficulty, with total disbelief in the impossibility, to endeavour
while life is in us, and to die endeavouring, we and our sons, till
we attain it or have all died and ended.

Such a Platitude of a World, in which all working horses
could be well fed, and innumerable working men should die
starved, were it not best to end it: to have done with it, and
restore it once for all to the *Jötuns*, Mud-giants, Frost-giants, and
Chaotic Brute-gods of the Beginning? For the old Anarchic
Brute-gods it may be well enough; but it is a Platitude which
Men should be above countenancing by their presence in it. We
pray you, let the word *impossible* disappear from your vocabulary
in this matter. It is of awful omen; to all of us, and to yourselves
first of all.

CHAPTER IV.

MORRISON'S PILL.

WHAT is to be done, what would you have us do? asks many
a one, with a tone of impatience, almost of reproach; and then,
if you mention some one thing, some two things, twenty things
that might be done, turns round with a satirical tehee, and "These
are your remedies!" The state of mind indicated by such question,
and such rejoinder, is worth reflecting on.

It seems to be taken for granted, by these interrogative
philosophers, that there is some 'thing,' or handful of 'things,'
which could be done; some Act of Parliament, 'remedial measure'

or the like, which could be passed, whereby the social malady
were fairly fronted, conquered, put an end to; so that, with your
remedial measure in your pocket, you could then go on triumphant,
and be troubled no farther. "You tell us the evil," cry such
persons, as if justly aggrieved, "and do not tell us how it is to
be cured!"

How it is to be cured? Brothers, I am sorry I have got no
Morrison's Pill for curing the maladies of Society. It were
infinitely handier if we had a Morrison's Pill, Act of Parliament,
or remedial measure, which men could swallow, one good time,
and then go on in their old courses, cleared from all miseries and
mischiefs! Unluckily we have none such; unluckily the Heavens
themselves, in their rich pharmacopœia, contain none such.
There will no 'thing' be done that will cure you. There will
a radical universal alteration of your regimen and way of life take
place; there will a most agonising divorce between you and your
chimeras, luxuries and falsities, take place; a most toilsome, all-
but 'impossible' return to Nature, and her veracities and her
integrities, take place: that so the inner fountains of life may
again begin, like eternal Light-fountains, to irradiate and purify
your bloated, swollen, foul existence, drawing nigh, as at present,
to nameless death! Either death, or else all this will take
place. Judge if, with such diagnosis, any Morrison's Pill is like
to be discoverable!

But the Life-fountain within you once again set flowing, what
innumerable 'things,' whole sets and classes and continents of
'things,' year after year, and decade after decade, and century
after century, will then be doable and done! Not Emigration,
Education, Corn-Law Abrogation, Sanitary Regulation, Land
Property-Tax; not these alone, nor a thousand times as much as
these. Good·Heavens, there will then be light in the inner
heart of here and there a man, to discern what is just, what is
commanded by the Most High God, what *must* be done, were it
never so 'impossible.' Vain jargon in favour of the palpably
unjust will then abridge itself within limits. Vain jargon, on
Hustings, in Parliaments or wherever else, when here and there
a man has vision for the essential God's-Truth of the things
jargoned of, will become very vain indeed. The silence of here
and there such a man, how eloquent in answer to such jargon!
Such jargon, frightened at its own gaunt echo, will unspeakably
abate; nay, for a while, may almost in a manner disappear,—the

wise answering it in silence, and even the simple taking cue
from them to hoot it down wherever heard. It will be a blessed
time; and many 'things' will become doable,—and when the
brains are out, an absurdity will die! Not easily again shall
a Corn-Law argue ten years for itself; and still talk and argue,
when impartial persons have to say with a sigh that, for so long
back, they have heard no 'argument' advanced for it but such
as might make the angels and almost the very jackasses weep!—

Wholly a blessed time: when jargon might abate, and here
and there some genuine speech begin. When to the noble
opened heart, as to such heart they alone do, all noble things
began to grow visible; and the difference between just and unjust,
between true and false, between work and sham-work, between
speech and jargon, was once more, what to our happier Fathers
it used to be, *infinite*,—as between a Heavenly thing and an
Infernal: the one a thing which you were *not* to do, which you
were wise not to attempt doing; which it were better for you to
have a millstone tied round your neck, and be cast into the
sea, than concern yourself with doing!—Brothers, it will not be
a Morrison's Pill, or remedial measure, that will bring all this
about for us.

And yet, very literally, till, in some shape or other, it be
brought about, we remain cureless; till it begin to be brought
about, the cure does not begin. For Nature and Fact, not
Redtape and Semblance, are to this hour the basis of man's
life; and on those, through never such strata of these, man and
his life and all his interests do, sooner or later, infallibly come to
rest,—and to be supported or be swallowed according as they
agree with those. The question is asked of them, not, How do
you agree with Downing Street and accredited Semblance? but,
How do you agree with God's Universe and the actual Reality
of things? This Universe *has* its Laws. If we walk according
to the Law, the Law-Maker will befriend us; if not, not. Alas,
by no Reform Bill, Ballot-box, Five-point Charter, by no boxes or
bills or charters, can you perform this alchemy: 'Given a world
of Knaves, to produce an Honesty from their united action!' It
is a distillation, once for all, not possible. You pass it through
alembic after alembic, it comes out still a Dishonesty, with a new
dress on it, a new colour to it. 'While we ourselves continue
valets, how *can* any hero come to govern us?' We are governed,

very infallibly, by the 'sham-hero,'—whose name is Quack, whose work and governance is Plausibility, and also is Falsity and Fatuity; to which Nature says, and must say when it comes to *her* to speak, eternally No! Nations cease to be befriended of the Law-Maker, when they walk *not* according to the Law. The Sphinx-question remains unsolved by them, becomes ever more insoluble.

If thou ask again, therefore, on the Morrison's-Pill hypothesis, What is to be done? allow me to reply: By thee, for the present, almost nothing. Thou there, the thing for thee to do is, if possible, to cease to be a hollow sounding-shell of hearsays, egoisms, purblind dilettantisms; and become, were it on the infinitely small scale, a faithful discerning soul. Thou shalt descend into thy inner man, and see if there be any traces of a *soul* there; till then there can be nothing done! O brother, we must if possible resuscitate some soul and conscience in us, exchange our dilettantisms for sincerities, our dead hearts of stone for living hearts of flesh. Then shall we discern, not one thing, but, in clearer or dimmer sequence, a whole endless host of things that can be done. *Do* the first of these; do it; the second will already have become clearer, doabler; the second, third and three-thousandth will then have begun to be possible for us. Not any universal Morrison's Pill shall we then, either as swallowers or as venders, ask after at all; but a far different sort of remedies: Quacks shall no more have dominion over us, but true Heroes and Healers!

Will not that be a thing worthy of 'doing;' to deliver ourselves from quacks, sham-heroes; to deliver the whole world more and more from such? They are the one bane of the world. Once clear the world of them, it ceases to be a Devil's-world, in all fibres of it wretched, accursed; and begins to be a God's-world, blessed, and working hourly towards blessedness. Thou for one wilt not again vote for any quack, do honour to any edge-gilt vacuity in man's shape: cant shall be known to thee by the sound of it;— thou wilt fly from cant with a shudder never felt before; as from the opened litany of Sorcerers' Sabbaths, the true Devil-worship of this age, more horrible than any other blasphemy, profanity or genuine blackguardism elsewhere audible among men. It is alarming to witness,—in its present completed state! And Quack and Dupe, as we must ever keep in mind, are upper-side and under of the selfsame substance; convertible personages: turn up your dupe into the proper fostering element, and he himself can become a quack; there is in him the due prurient insincerity, open voracity for profit, and closed sense for truth, whereof quacks too, in all their kinds, are made.

Alas, it is not to the hero, it is to the sham-hero, that, of right and necessity, the valet-world belongs. 'What is to be done?' The reader sees whether it is like to be the seeking and swallowing of some 'remedial measure'!

CHAPTER V.

ARISTOCRACY OF TALENT.

WHEN an individual is miserable, what does it most of all behove him to do? To complain of this man or of that, of this thing or of that? To fill the world and the street with lamentation, objurgation? Not so at all; the reverse of so. All moralists advise him not to complain of any person or of any thing, but of himself only. He is to know of a truth that being miserable he has been unwise, he. Had he faithfully followed Nature and her Laws, Nature, ever true to her Laws, would have yielded fruit and increase and felicity to him: but he has followed other than Nature's Laws; and now Nature, her patience with him being ended, leaves him desolate; answers with very emphatic significance to him: No. Not by this road, my son; by another road shalt thou attain well-being: this, thou perceivest, is the road to ill-being; quit this!—So do all moralists advise: that the man penitently say to himself first of all, Behold I was not wise enough; I quitted the laws of Fact, which are also called the Laws of God, and mistook for them the Laws of Sham and Semblance, which are called the Devil's Laws; therefore am I here!

Neither with Nations that become miserable is it fundamentally otherwise. The ancient guides of Nations, Prophets, Priests, or whatever their name, were well aware of this; and, down to a late epoch, impressively taught and inculcated it. The modern guides of Nations, who also go under a great variety of names, Journalists, Political Economists, Politicians, Pamphleteers, have entirely forgotten this, and are ready to deny this. But it nevertheless remains eternally undeniable : nor is there any doubt but we shall all be taught it yet, and made again to confess it : we shall all be striped and scourged till we do learn it; and shall at last either get to know it, or be striped to death in the process. For it is undeniable ! When a Nation is unhappy, the old Prophet was right and not wrong in saying to it: Ye have forgotten God, ye have quitted the ways of God, or ye would not have been unhappy. It is not according to the laws of Fact that ye have lived and guided yourselves, but according to the laws of Delusion, Imposture, and wilful and unwilful *Mistake* of Fact; behold therefore the Unveracity is worn out; Nature's long-suffering with you is exhausted; and ye are here !

Surely there is nothing very inconceivable in this, even to the Journalist, to the Political Economist, Modern Pamphleteer, or any two-legged animal without feathers ! If a country finds itself wretched, sure enough that country has been *mis*guided : it is with the wretched Twenty-seven Millions, fallen wretched, as with the Unit fallen wretched: they, as he, have quitted the course prescribed by Nature and the Supreme Powers, and so are fallen into scarcity, disaster, infelicity; and pausing to consider themselves, have to lament and say: Alas, we were not wise enough ! We took transient superficial Semblance for everlasting central Substance; we have departed far away from the *Laws* of this Universe, and behold now lawless Chaos and inane Chimera is ready to devour us !—'Nature in late centuries,' says Sauerteig, 'was universally supposed to be dead; an old eight-day clock, 'made many thousand years ago, and still ticking, but dead as 'brass,—which the Maker, at most, sat looking at, in a distant, 'singular and indeed incredible manner : but now I am happy to 'observe, she is everywhere asserting herself to be not dead and 'brass at all, but alive and miraculous, celestial-infernal, with an 'emphasis that will again penetrate the thickest head of this Planet 'by and by !'——

Indisputable enough to all mortals now, the guidance of this country has not been sufficiently wise; men too foolish have been set to the guiding and governing of it, and have guided it *hither;* we must find wiser,—wiser, or else we perish ! To this length of insight all England has now advanced; but as yet no farther. All

England stands wringing its hands, asking itself, nigh desperate, What farther? Reform Bill proves to be a failure; Benthamee Radicalism, the gospel of 'Enlightened Selfishness,' dies out, or dwindles into Five-point Chartism, amid the tears and hootings of men : what next are we to hope or try? Five-point Charter, Free-trade, Church-extension, Sliding-scale; what, in Heaven's name, are we next to attempt, that we sink not in inane Chimera, and be devoured of Chaos ?—The case is pressing, and one of the most complicated in the world. ·A God's-message never came to thicker-skinned people; never had a God's-message to pierce through thicker integuments, into heavier ears. It is Fact, speaking once more, in miraculous thunder-voice, from out of the centre of the world;—how unknown its language to the deaf and foolish many; how distinct, undeniable, terrible and yet beneficent, to the hearing few : Behold, ye shall grow wiser, or ye shall die! Truer to Nature's Fact, or inane Chimera will swallow you; in whirlwinds of fire, you and your Mammonisms, Dilettantisms, your Midas-eared philosophies, double-barrelled Aristocracies, shall disappear !—Such is the God's-message to *us*, once more, in these modern days.

We must have more Wisdom to govern us, we must be governed by the Wisest, we must have an Aristocracy of Talent! cry many. True, most true; but how to get it? The following extract from our young friend of the *Houndsditch Indicator* is worth perusing : 'At this time,' says he, 'while there is a cry everywhere, articulate 'or inarticulate, for an "Aristocracy of Talent," a Governing Class 'namely which did govern, not merely which took the wages of 'governing, and could not with all our industry be kept from mis- 'governing,corn-lawing, and playing the very deuce with us,—it may 'not be altogether useless to remind some of the greener-headed sort 'what a dreadfully difficult affair the getting of such an Aristocracy 'is ! Do you expect, my friends, that your indispensable Aristocracy 'of Talent is to be enlisted straightway, by some sort of recruit- 'ment aforethought, out of the general population; arranged in 'supreme regimental order; and set to rule over us ? That it will 'be got sifted, like wheat out of chaff, from the Twenty-seven 'Million British subjects; that any Ballot-box, Reform Bill, or 'other Political Machine, with Force of Public Opinion never so 'active on it, is likely to perform said process of sifting ? Would 'to Heaven that we had a sieve; that we could so much as fancy 'any kind of sieve, wind-fanners, or ne-plus-ultra of machinery, 'devisable by man, that would do it !

'Done nevertheless, sure enough, it must be; it shall and will
'be. We are rushing swiftly on the road to destruction; every
'hour bringing us nearer, until it be, in some measure, done. The
'doing of it is not doubtful; only the method and the costs! Nay
'I will even mention to you an infallible sifting process whereby
'he that has ability will be sifted out to rule among us, and that
'same blessed Aristocracy of Talent be verily, in an approximate
'degree, vouchsafed us by and by: an infallible sifting-process; to
'which, however, no soul can help his neighbour, but each must,
'with devout prayer to Heaven, endeavour to help himself. It is,
'O friends, that all of us, that many of us, should acquire the true
'*eye* for talent, which is dreadfully wanting at present! The true
'eye for talent presupposes the true reverence for it,—O Heavens,
'presupposes so many things!

'For example, you Bobus Higgins, Sausage-maker on the great
'scale, who are raising such a clamour for this Aristocracy of
'Talent, what is it that you do, in that big heart of yours, chiefly
'in very fact pay reverence to? Is it to talent, intrinsic manly
'worth of any kind, you unfortunate Bobus? The manliest man
'that you saw going in a ragged coat, did you ever reverence him;
'did you so much as know that he was a manly man at all, till
'his coat grew better? Talent! I understand you to be able to
'worship the fame of talent, the power, cash, celebrity or other
'success of talent; but the talent itself is a thing you never saw
'with eyes. Nay what is it in yourself that you are proudest of,
'that you take most pleasure in surveying meditatively in thought-
'ful moments? Speak now, is it the bare Bobus stript of his very
'name and shirt, and turned loose upon society, that you admire
'and thank Heaven for; or Bobus with his cash-accounts and
'larders dropping fatness, with his respectabilities, warm garni-
'tures, and pony-chaise, admirable in some measure to certain
'of the flunky species? Your own degree of worth and talent, is
'it of *infinite* value to you; or only of finite,—measurable by the
'degree of currency, and conquest of praise or pudding, it has
'brought you to? Bobus, you are in a vicious circle, rounder than
'one of your own sausages; and will never vote for or promote any
'talent, except what talent or sham-talent has already *got* itself
'voted for!'—We here cut short the *Indicator;* all readers
perceiving whither he now tends.

'More Wisdom' indeed: but where to find more Wisdom? We

have already a Collective Wisdom, after its kind,—though 'class-legislation,' and another thing or two, affect it somewhat! On the whole, as they say, Like people like priest; so we may say, Like people like king. The man gets himself appointed and elected who is ablest—to be appointed and elected. What can the incorruptiblest *Bobuses* elect, if it be not some *Bobissimus*, should they find such?

Or again, perhaps there is not, in the whole Nation, Wisdom enough, 'collect' it as we may, to make an adequate Collective! That too is a case which may befall: a ruined man staggers down to ruin because there was not wisdom enough in him; so, clearly also, may Twenty-seven Million collective men!—But indeed one of the infalliblest fruits of Unwisdom in a Nation is that it cannot get the use of what Wisdom is actually in it: that it is not governed by the wisest it has, who alone have a divine right to govern in all Nations; but by the sham-wisest, or even by the openly not-so-wise, if they are handiest otherwise! This is the infalliblest result of Unwisdom; and also the balefulest, immeasurablest,—not so much what we can call a poison-*fruit*, as a universal death-disease, and poisoning of the whole tree. For hereby are fostered, fed into gigantic bulk, all manner of Unwisdoms, poison-fruits; till, as we say, the life-tree everywhere is made a upas-tree, deadly Unwisdom overshadowing all things; and there is done what lies in human skill to stifle all Wisdom everywhere in the birth, to smite our poor world barren of Wisdom,—and make your utmost Collective Wisdom, were it collected and elected by Rhadamanthus, Æacus and Minos, not to speak of drunken Ten-pound Franchisers with their ballot-boxes, an inadequate Collective! The Wisdom is not now there: how will you 'collect' it? As well wash Thames mud, by improved methods, to find more gold in it.

Truly, the first condition is indispensable, That Wisdom be there: but the second is like unto it, is properly one with it; these two conditions act and react through every fibre of them, and go inseparably together. If you have much Wisdom in your Nation, you will get it faithfully collected; for the wise love Wisdom, and will search for it as for life and salvation. If you have little Wisdom, you will get even that little ill-collected, trampled under foot, reduced as near as possible to annihilation; for fools do not love Wisdom; they are foolish, first of all, because they have never loved Wisdom,—but have loved their own appetites, ambitions, their coroneted coaches, tankards of heavy-wet. Thus is your candle lighted at both ends, and the progress towards consummation is swift. Thus is fulfilled that saying in the Gospel : To him that hath shall be given ; and from him that hath not shall be taken away even that which he hath. Very literally, in a very fatal manner, that saying is here fulfilled.

Our 'Aristocracy of Talent' seems at a considerable distance yet ; does it not, O Bobus ?

CHAPTER VI.

HERO-WORSHIP.

To the present Editor, not less than to Bobus, a Government of the Wisest, what Bobus calls an Aristocracy of Talent, seems the one healing remedy : but he is not so sanguine as Bobus with respect to the means of realising it. He thinks that we have at once missed realising it, and come to need it so pressingly, by departing far from the inner eternal Laws, and taking-up with the temporary outer semblances of Laws. He thinks that 'enlightened Egoism,' never so luminous, is not the rule by which man's life can be led. That 'Laissez-faire,' 'Supply-and-demand,' 'Cash-payment for the sole nexus,' and so forth, were not, are not and will never be, a practicable Law of Union for a Society of Men. The Poor and Rich, that Governed and Governing, cannot long live together on any such Law of Union. Alas, he thinks that man has a soul in him, *different* from the stomach in any sense of this word ; that if said soul be asphyxied, and lie quietly forgotten, the man and his affairs are in a bad way. He thinks that said soul will have to be resuscitated from its asphyxia ; that if it prove irresuscitable, the man is not long for this world. In brief, that Midas-eared Mammonism, double-barrelled Dilettantism, and their thousand adjuncts and corollaries, are *not* the Law by which God Almighty has appointed this his Universe to go. That, once for all, these are not the Law : and then farther that we shall have to return to what *is* the Law,—not by smooth flowery paths, it is like, and with 'tremendous cheers' in our throat ; but over steep untrodden places, through stormclad chasms, waste oceans, and the bosom of tornadoes; thank Heaven, if not through very Chaos and the Abyss! The resuscitating of a soul that has gone to asphyxia is no momentary or pleasant process, but a long and terrible one.

To the present Editor, 'Hero-worship,' as he has elsewhere named it, means much more than an elected Parliament, or stated Aristocracy, of the Wisest; for in his dialect it is the summary, ultimate essence, and supreme practical perfection of all manner of 'worship,' and true worthships and noblenesses whatsoever. Such blessed Parliament and, were it once in perfection, blessed Aristocracy of the Wisest, god-honoured and man-honoured, he does look for, more and more perfected,—as the topmost blessed practical apex of a whole world reformed from sham-worship, informed anew with worship, with truth and blessedness! He thinks that Hero-worship, done differently in every different epoch of the world, is the soul of all social business among men; that the doing of it well, or the doing of it ill, measures accurately what degree of well-being or of ill-being there is in the world's affairs. He thinks that we, on the whole, do our Hero-worship worse than any Nation in this world ever did it before: that the Burns an Exciseman, the Byron a Literary Lion, are intrinsically, all things considered, a baser and falser phenomenon than the Odin a God, the Mahomet a Prophet of God. It is this Editor's clear opinion, accordingly, that we must learn to do our Hero-worship better; that to do it better and better, means the awakening of the Nation's soul from its asphyxia, and the return of blessed life to us,—Heaven's blessed life, not Mammon's galvanic accursed one. To resuscitate the Asphyxied, apparently now moribund and in the last agony if not resuscitated: such and no other seems the consummation.

'Hero-worship,' if you will,—yes, friends; but, first of all, by being ourselves of heroic mind. A whole world of Heroes; a world not of Flunkies, where no Hero-King *can* reign: that is what we aim at! We, for our share, will put away all Flunkyism, Baseness, Unveracity from us; we shall then hope to have Noblenesses and Veracities set over us; never till then. Let Bobus and Company sneer, "That is your Reform!" Yes, Bobus, that is our Reform; and except in that, and what will follow out of that, we have no hope at all. Reform, like Charity, O Bobus, must begin at home. Once well at home, how will it radiate outwards, irrepressible, into all that we touch and handle, speak and work; kindling ever new light, by incalculable contagion, spreading in geometric ratio, far and wide,—doing good only, wheresoever it spreads, and not evil.

By Reform Bills, Anti-Corn-Law Bills, and thousand other bills and methods, we will demand of our Governors, with emphasis, and for the first time not without effect, that they cease to be quacks, or else depart; that they set no quackeries and block-headisms anywhere to rule over us, that they utter or act no cant to us,—it will be better if they do not. For we shall now know quacks when we see them; cant, when we hear it, shall be horrible to us! We will say, with the poor Frenchman at the Bar of the Convention, though in wiser style than he, and 'for the space' not 'of an hour' but of a lifetime: "*Je demande l'arrestation des coquins et des lâches.*" 'Arrestment of the knaves and dastards:' ah, we know what a work that is; how long it will be before *they* are all or mostly got 'arrested:'—but here is one; arrest him, in God's name; it is one fewer! We will, in all practicable ways, by word and silence, by act and refusal to act, energetically demand that arrestment,—"*je demande cette arrestation-là!*"—and by degrees infallibly attain it. Infallibly: for light spreads; all human souls, never so bedarkened, love light; light once kindled spreads, till all is luminous;—till the cry, "*Arrest* your knaves and dastards" rises imperative from millions of hearts, and rings and reigns from sea to sea. Nay how many of them may we not 'arrest' with our own hands, even now; we! Do not countenance them, thou there: turn away from their lacquered sumptuosities, their belauded sophistries, their serpent graciosities, their spoken and acted cant, with a sacred horror, with an *Apage Satanas.*— Bobus and Company, and all men will gradually join us. We demand arrestment of the knaves and dastards, and begin by arresting our own poor selves out of that fraternity. There is no other reform conceivable. Thou and I, my friend, can, in the most flunky world, make, each of us, *one* non-flunky, one hero, if we like: that will be two heroes to begin with:—Courage! even that is a whole world of heroes to end with, or what we poor Two can do in furtherance thereof!

Yes, friends: Hero-kings, and a whole world not unheroic,— there lies the port and happy haven, towards which, through all these stormtost seas, French Revolutions, Chartisms, Manchester

Insurrections, that make the heart sick in these bad days, the Supreme Powers are driving us. On the whole, blessed be the Supreme Powers, stern as they are! Towards that haven will we, O friends; let all true men, with what of faculty is in them, bend valiantly, incessantly, with thousandfold endeavour, thither, thither! There, or else in the Ocean-abysses, it is very clear to me, we shall arrive.

Well; here truly is no answer to the Sphinx-question; not the answer a disconsolate public, inquiring at the College of Health, was in hopes of! A total change of regimen, change of constitution and existence from the very centre of it; a new body to be got, with resuscitated soul,—not without convulsive travail-throes; as all birth and new-birth presupposes travail! This is sad news to a disconsolate discerning Public, hoping to have got off by some Morrison's Pill, some Saint-John's corrosive mixture and perhaps a little blistery friction on the back!—We were prepared to part with our Corn-Law, with various Laws and Unlaws: but this, what is this?

Nor has the Editor forgotten how it fares with your ill-boding Cassandras in Sieges of Troy. Imminent perdition is not usually driven away by words of warning. Didactic Destiny has other methods in store; or these would fail always. Such words should, nevertheless, be uttered, when they dwell truly in the soul of any man. Words are hard, are importunate; but how much harder the importunate events they foreshadow! Here and there a human soul may listen to the words,—who knows how many human souls?—whereby the importunate events, if not diverted and prevented, will be rendered *less* hard. The present Editor's purpose is to himself full of hope.

For though fierce travails, though wide seas and roaring gulfs lie before us, is it not something if a Loadstar, in the eternal sky, do once more disclose itself; an everlasting light, shining through all cloud-tempests and roaring billows, ever as we emerge from the trough of the sea: the blessed beacon, far off on the edge of far horizons, towards which we are to steer incessantly for life? Is it not something; O Heavens, is it not all? There lies the Heroic Promised Land; under that Heaven's-light, my brethren, bloom the Happy Isles,—there, O there! Thither will we;

'There dwells the great Achilles whom we knew.'[1]

---

[1] Tennyson's *Poems* (Ulysses).

There dwell all Heroes, and will dwell: thither, all ye heroic-minded!—The Heaven's Loadstar once clearly in our eye, how will each true man stand truly to *his* work in the ship; how, with undying hope, will all things be fronted, all be conquered. Nay, with the ship's prow once turned in that direction, is not all, as it were, already well? Sick wasting misery has become noble manful effort with a goal in our eye. 'The choking Nightmare 'chokes us no longer; for we *stir* under it; the Nightmare has 'already fled.'—

Certainly, could the present Editor instruct men how to know Wisdom, Heroism, when they see it, that they might do reverence to *it* only, and loyally make it ruler over them,—yes, he were the living epitome of all Editors, Teachers, Prophets, that now teach and prophesy; he were an *Apollo*-Morrison, a Trismegistus and *effective* Cassandra! Let no Able Editor hope such things. It is to be expected the present laws of copyright, rate of reward per sheet, and other considerations, will save him from that peril. Let no Editor hope such things: no;—and yet let all Editors aim towards such things, and even towards such alone! One knows not what the meaning of editing and writing is, if even this be not it.

Enough, to the present Editor it has seemed possible some glimmering of light, for here and there a human soul, might lie in these confused Paper-Masses now intrusted to him; wherefore he determines to edit the same. Out of old Books, new Writings, and much Meditation not of yesterday, he will endeavour to select a thing or two; and from the Past, in a circuitous way, illustrate the Present and the Future. The Past is a dim indubitable fact: the Future too is one, only dimmer; nay properly it is the *same* fact in new dress and development. For the Present holds it in both the whole Past and the whole Future;—as the LIFE-TREE IGDRASIL, wide-waving, many-toned, has its roots down deep in the Death-kingdoms, among the oldest dead dust of men, and with its boughs reaches always beyond the stars; and in all times and places is one and the same Life-tree!

BOOK SECOND.

THE ANCIENT MONK.

CHAPTER I.

JOCELIN OF BRAKELOND.

WE will, in this Second Portion of our Work, strive to penetrate a little, by means of certain confused Papers, printed and other, into a somewhat remote Century; and to look face to face on it, in hope of perhaps illustrating our own poor Century thereby. It seems a circuitous way; but it may prove a way nevertheless. For man has ever been a striving, struggling, and, in spite of wide-spread calumnies to the contrary, a veracious creature: the Centuries too are all lineal children of one another; and often, in the portrait of early grandfathers, this and the other enigmatic feature of the newest grandson shall disclose itself, to mutual elucidation. This Editor will venture on such a thing.

Besides, in Editors' Books, and indeed everywhere else in the world of Today, a certain latitude of movement grows more and more becoming for the practical man. Salvation lies not in tight lacing, in these times;—how far from that, in any province whatsoever! Readers and men generally are getting into strange habits of asking all persons and things, from poor Editors' Books up to Church Bishops and State Potentates, not, By what designation art thou called; in what wig and black triangle dost thou walk abroad? Heavens, I know thy designation and black triangle well enough! But, in God's name, what *art* thou? Not Nothing, sayest thou! Then, How much and what? This is the thing I would know; and even *must* soon know, such a pass am I come to!——What weather-symptoms,—not for the poor Editor of

Books alone! The Editor of Books may understand withal that if, as is said, 'many kinds are permissible,' there is one kind not permissible, 'the kind that has nothing in it, *le genre ennuyeux;*' and go on his way accordingly.

A certain Jocelinus de Brakelonda, a natural-born Englishman, has left us an extremely foreign Book,[1] which the labours of the Camden Society have brought to light in these days. Jocelin's Book, the 'Chronicle,' or private Boswellean Notebook, of Jocelin, a certain old St. Edmundsbury Monk and Boswell, now seven centuries old, how remote is it from us; exotic, extraneous; in all ways, coming from far abroad! The language of it is not foreign only but dead: Monk-Latin lies across not the British Channel, but the ninefold Stygian Marshes, Stream of Lethe, and one knows not where! Roman Latin itself, still alive for us in the Elysian Fields of Memory, is domestic in comparison. And then the ideas, life-furniture, whole workings and ways of this worthy Jocelin; covered deeper than Pompeii with the lava-ashes and inarticulate wreck of seven hundred years!

Jocelin of Brakelond cannot be called a conspicuous literary character; indeed few mortals that have left so visible a work, or footmark, behind them can be more obscure. One other of those vanished Existences, whose work has not yet vanished;—almost a pathetic phenomenon, were not the whole world full of such! The builders of Stonehenge, for example :—or, alas, what say we, Stonehenge and builders? The writers of the *Universal Review* and *Homer's Iliad;* the paviors of London streets;—sooner or later, the entire Posterity of Adam! It is a pathetic phenomenon; but an irremediable, nay, if well meditated, a consoling one.

By his dialect of Monk-Latin, and indeed by his name, this Jocelin seems to have been a Norman Englishman; the surname *de Brakelonda* indicates a native of St. Edmundsbury itself, *Brakelond* being the known old name of a street or quarter in that venerable Town. Then farther, sure enough, our Jocelin was a Monk of St. Edmundsbury Convent; held some '*obedientia,*' subaltern officiality there, or rather, in succession several; was, for one thing, 'chaplain to my Lord Abbot, living beside him night and day for the space of six years;'—which last, indeed, is the grand

---

[1] *Chronica* JOCELINI DE BRAKELONDA, *de rebus gestis Samsonis Abbatis Monasterii Sancti Edmundi: nunc primum typis mandata, curante Johanne Gage Rokewood.* (Camden Society, London, 1840.)

fact of Jocelin's existence, and properly the origin of this present
Book, and of the chief meaning it has for us now. He was, as we
have hinted, a kind of born *Boswell*, though an infinitesimally
small one; neither did he altogether want his *Johnson* even there
and then. Johnsons are rare; yet, as has been asserted, Boswells
perhaps still rarer,—the more is the pity on both sides! This
Jocelin, as we can discern well, was an ingenious and ingenuous, a
cheery-hearted, innocent, yet withal shrewd, noticing, quick-witted
man; and from under his monk's cowl has looked out on that
narrow section of the world in a really *human* manner; not in any
simial, canine, ovine, or otherwise *in*human manner,—afflictive to
all that have humanity! The man is of patient, peaceable, loving,
clear-smiling nature; open for this and that. A wise simplicity
is in him; much natural sense; a *veracity* that goes deeper than
words. Veracity: it is the basis of all; and, some say, means
genius itself; the prime essence of all genius whatsoever. Our
Jocelin, for the rest, has read his classical manuscripts, his Virgilius,
his Flaccus, Ovidius Naso; of course still more, his Homilies and
Breviaries, and if not the Bible, considerable extracts of the Bible.
Then also he has a pleasant wit; and loves a timely joke, though
in mild subdued manner: very amiable to see. A learned grown
man, yet with the heart as of a good child; whose whole life
indeed has been that of a child,—St. Edmundsbury Monastery a
larger kind of cradle for him, in which his whole prescribed duty
was to *sleep* kindly, and love his mother well! This is the Biography of Jocelin; 'a man of excellent religion,' says one of his
contemporary Brother Monks, '*eximiæ religionis, potens sermone
et opere.*'

For one thing, he had learned to write a kind of Monk or Dog-
Latin, still readable to mankind; and, by good luck for us, had
bethought him of noting down thereby what things seemed
notablest to him. Hence gradually resulted a *Chronica Jocelini;*
new Manuscript in the *Liber Albus* of St. Edmundsbury. Which
Chronicle, once written in its childlike transparency, in its innocent
good-humour, not without touches of ready pleasant wit and many
kinds of worth, other men liked naturally to read: whereby it
failed not to be copied, to be multiplied, to be inserted in the *Liber
Albus;* and so surviving Henry the Eighth, Putney Cromwell, the
Dissolution of Monasteries, and all accidents of malice and neglect
for six centuries or so, it got into the *Harleian Collection,*—and has
now therefrom, by Mr. Rokewood of the Camden Society, been

deciphered into clear print; and lies before us, a dainty thin quarto, to interest for a few minutes whomsoever it can.

Here too it will behove a just Historian gratefully to say that Mr. Rokewood, Jocelin's Editor, has done his editorial function well. Not only has he deciphered his crabbed Manuscript into clear print; but he has attended, what his fellow editors are not always in the habit of doing, to the important truth that the Manuscript so deciphered ought to have a meaning for the reader. Standing faithfully by his text, and printing its very errors in spelling, in grammar or otherwise, he has taken care by some note to indicate that they are errors, and what the correction of them ought to be. Jocelin's Monk-Latin is generally transparent, as shallow limpid water. But at any stop that may occur, of which there are a few, and only a very few, we have the comfortable assurance that a meaning does lie in the passage, and may by industry be got at; that a faithful editor's industry had already got at it before passing on. A compendious useful Glossary is given; nearly adequate to help the uninitiated through: sometimes one wishes it had been a trifle larger; but, with a Spelman and Ducange at your elbow, how easy to have made it far too large! Notes are added, generally brief; sufficiently explanatory of most points. Lastly, a copious correct Index; which no such Book should want, and which unluckily very few possess. And so, in a word, the *Chronicle of Jocelin* is, as it professes to be, unwrapped from its thick cerements, and fairly brought forth into the common daylight, so that he who runs, and has a smattering of grammar, may read.

We have heard so much of Monks; everywhere, in real and fictitious History, from Muratori Annals to Radcliffe Romances, these singular two-legged animals, with their rosaries and breviaries, with their shaven crowns, hair-cilices, and vows of poverty, masquerade so strangely through our fancy; and they are in fact so very strange an extinct species of the human family,—a veritable Monk of Bury St. Edmunds is worth attending to, if by chance made visible and audible. Here he is; and in his hand a magical speculum, much gone to rust indeed, yet in fragments still clear; wherein the marvellous image of his existence does still shadow itself, though fitfully, and as with an intermittent light! Will not the reader peep with us into this singular *camera lucida*, where an extinct species, though fitfully, can still be seen alive? Extinct

species, we say; for the live specimens which still go about under
that character are too evidently to be classed as spurious in Natural
History: the Gospel of Richard Arkwright once promulgated, no
Monk of the old sort is any longer possible in this world. But
fancy a deep-buried Mastodon, some fossil Megatherion, Ichthyo-
saurus, were to begin to *speak* from amid its rock-swathings, never
so indistinctly! The most extinct fossil species of Men or Monks
can do, and does, this miracle,—thanks to the Letters of the
Alphabet, good for so many things.

Jocelin, we said, was somewhat of a Boswell; but unfortunately,
by Nature, he is none of the largest, and distance has now dwarfed
him to an extreme degree. His light is most feeble, intermittent,
and requires the intensest kindest inspection; otherwise it will
disclose mere vacant haze. It must be owned, the good Jocelin,
spite of his beautiful child-like character, is but an altogether
imperfect 'mirror' of these old-world things! The good man, he
looks on us so clear and cheery, and in his neighbourly soft-smiling
eyes we see so well our *own* shadow,—we have a longing always to
cross-question him, to force from him an explanation of much.
But no; Jocelin, though he talks with such clear familiarity, like
a next-door neighbour, will not answer any question: that is the
peculiarity of him, dead these six hundred and fifty years, and
quite deaf to us, though still so audible! The good man, he
cannot help it, nor can we.

But truly it is a strange consideration this simple one, as we go
on with him, or indeed with any lucid simple-hearted soul like
him: Behold therefore, this England of the Year 1200 was no
chimerical vacuity or dreamland, peopled with mere vaporous
Fantasms, Rymer's Fœdera, and Doctrines of the Constitution;
but a green solid place, that grew corn and several other things.
The Sun shone on it; the vicissitude of seasons and human fortunes. Cloth was woven and worn; ditches were dug, furrow-
fields ploughed, and houses built. Day by day all men and cattle
rose to labour, and night by night returned home weary to their
several lairs. In wondrous Dualism, then as now, lived nations of
breathing men; alternating, in all ways, between Light and Dark;
between joy and sorrow, between rest and toil,—between hope,
hope reaching high as Heaven, and fear deep as very Hell. Not
vapour Fantasms, Rymer's Fœdera at all! Cœur-de-Lion was not
a theatrical popinjay with greaves and steel-cap on it, but a men
living upon victuals,—*not* imported by Peel's Tariff. Cœur-de-Lion

came palpably athwart this Jocelin at St. Edmundsbury; and had almost peeled the sacred gold '*Feretrum,*' or St. Edmund Shrine itself, to ransom him out of the Danube Jail.

These clear eyes of neighbour Jocelin looked on the bodily presence of King John; the very John *Sansterre,* or Lackland, who signed *Magna Charta* afterwards in Runnymead. Lackland, with a great retinue, boarded once, for the matter of a fortnight, in St. Edmundsbury Convent; daily in the very eyesight, palpable to the very fingers of our Jocelin: O Jocelin, what did he say, what did he do; how looked he, lived he;—at the very lowest, what coat or breeches had he on? Jocelin is obstinately silent. Jocelin marks down what interests *him;* entirely deaf to *us.* With Jocelin's eyes we discern almost nothing of John Lackland. As through a glass darkly, we with our own eyes and appliances, intensely looking, discern at most: A blustering, dissipated human figure, with a kind of blackguard quality air, in cramoisy velvet, or other uncertain texture, uncertain cut, with much plumage and fringing; amid numerous other human figures of the like; riding abroad with hawks; talking noisy nonsense;—tearing out the bowels of St. Edmundsbury Convent (its larders namely and cellars) in the most ruinous way, by living at rack and manger there. Jocelin notes only, with a slight subacidity of manner, that the King's Majesty, *Dominus Rex,* did leave, as gift for our St. Edmund Shrine, a handsome enough silk cloak,—or rather pretended to leave, for one of his retinue borrowed it of us, and *we* never got sight of it again; and, on the whole, that the *Dominus Rex,* at departing, gave us 'thirteen *sterlingii,*' one shilling and one penny, to say a mass for him; and so departed,—like a shabby Lackland as he was! 'Thirteen pence sterling,' this was what the Convent got from Lackland, for all the victuals he and his had made away with. We of course said our mass for him, having covenanted to do it,—but let impartial posterity judge with what degree of fervour!

And in this manner vanishes King Lackland; traverses swiftly our strange intermittent magic-mirror, jingling the shabby thirteen pence merely; and rides with his hawks into Egyptian night again. It is Jocelin's manner with all things; and it is men's manner and men's necessity. How intermittent is our good Jocelin; marking down, without eye to *us,* what *he* finds interesting! How much in Jocelin, as in all History, and indeed in all Nature, is at once inscrutable and certain; so dim, yet so indubitable; exciting us to endless considerations. For King Lackland *was* there, verily he; and did leave these *tredecim sterlingii*, if nothing more, and did live and look in one way or the other, and a whole world was living and looking along with him! There, we say, is the grand peculiarity; the immeasurable one; distinguishing, to a really infinite degree, the poorest historical Fact from all Fiction whatsoever. Fiction, 'Imagination,' 'Imaginative Poetry,' &c. &c., except as the vehicle for truth, or *fact* of some sort,—which surely a man should first try various other ways of vehiculating, and conveying safe,—what is it? Let the Minerva and other Presses respond!—

But it is time we were in St. Edmundsbury Monastery, and Seven good Centuries off. If indeed it be possible, by any aid of Jocelin, by any human art, to get thither, with a reader or two still following us?

CHAPTER II.

ST. EDMUNDSBURY.

THE *Burg*, Bury, or 'Berry' as they call it, of St. Edmund is still a prosperous brisk Town; beautifully diversifying, with its clear brick houses, ancient clean streets, and twenty or fifteen thousand busy souls, the general grassy face of Suffolk; looking out right pleasantly, from its hill-slope, towards the Rising Sun: and on the eastern edge of it, still runs, long, black and massive, a range of monastic ruins; into the wide internal spaces of which the stranger is admitted on payment of one shilling. Internal spaces laid out, at present, as a botanic garden. Here stranger or townsman, sauntering at his leisure amid these vast grim venerable ruins, may persuade himself that an Abbey of St. Edmundsbury did once exist; nay there is no doubt of it: see here the ancient massive Gateway, of architecture interesting to the eye of Dilettantism; and farther on, that other ancient Gateway, now about to tumble, unless Dilettantism, in these very months, can subscribe money to cramp it and prop it!

Here, sure enough, is an Abbey; beautiful in the eye of

Dilettantism. Giant Pedantry also will step in, with its huge *Dugdale* and other enormous *Monasticons* under its arm, and cheerfully apprise you, That this was a very great Abbey, owner and indeed creator of St. Edmund's Town itself, owner of wide lands and revenues; nay that its lands were once a county of themselves; that indeed King Canute or Knut was very kind to it, and gave St. Edmund his own gold crown off his head, on one occasion : for the rest, that the Monks were of such and such a genus, such and such a number; that they had so many carucates of land in this hundred, and so many in that; and then farther that the large Tower or Belfry was built by such a one, and the smaller Belfry was built by &c. &c.—Till human nature can stand no more of it ; till human nature desperately take refuge in forgetfulness, almost in flat disbelief of the whole business, Monks, Monastery, Belfries, Carucates and all! Alas, what mountains of dead ashes, wreck and burnt bones, does assiduous Pedantry dig up from the Past Time, and name it History, and Philosophy of History; till, as we say, the human soul sinks wearied and bewildered; till the Past Time seems all one infinite incredible gray void, without sun, stars, hearth-fires, or candle-light; dim offensive dust-whirlwinds filling universal Nature ; and over your Historical Library, it is as if all the Titans had written for themselves : DRY RUBBISH SHOT HERE !

And yet these grim old walls are not a dilettantism and dubiety; they are an earnest fact. It was a most real and serious purpose they were built for ! Yes, another world it was, when these black ruins, white in their new mortar and fresh chiselling, first saw the sun as walls, long ago. Gauge not, with thy dilettante compasses, with that placid dilettante simper, the Heaven's-Watchtower of our Fathers, the fallen God's-Houses, the Golgotha of true Souls departed !

Their architecture, belfries, land-carucates? Yes,—and that is but a small item of the matter. Does it never give thee pause, this other strange item of it, that men then had a *soul*,—not by hearsay alone, and as a figure of speech ; but as a truth that they *knew*, and practically went upon! Verily it was another world then. Their Missals have become incredible, a sheer platitude, sayest thou ? Yes, a most poor platitude ; and even, if thou wilt, an idolatry and blasphemy, should any one persuade *thee* to believe them, to pretend praying by them. But yet it is pity we had lost tidings of our souls :—actually we shall have to go in quest of them again, or worse in all ways will befall ! A certain degree of soul, as Ben Jonson reminds us, is indispensable to keep the very body from destruction of the frightfulest sort; to 'save us,' says he, 'the expense of *salt.*' Ben has known men who had soul enough to keep their body and five senses from becoming carrion, and save salt:—men, and also Nations. You may look in Manchester Hunger-mobs and Corn-law Commons Houses, and various other quarters, and say whether either soul or else salt is not somewhat wanted at present!—

Another world, truly: and this present poor distressed world might get some profit by looking wisely into it, instead of foolishly. But at lowest, O dilettante friend, let us know always that it *was* a world, and not a void infinite of gray haze with fantasms swimming in it. These old St. Edmundsbury walls, I say, were not peopled with fantasms; but with men of flesh and blood, made altogether as we are. Had thou and I then been, who knows but we ourselves had taken refuge from an evil Time, and fled to dwell here, and meditate on an Eternity, in such fashion as we could? Alas, how like an old osseous fragment, a broken blackened shin-bone of the old dead Ages, this black ruin looks out, not yet covered by the soil; still indicting what a once gigantic Life lies buried there! It is dead now, and dumb; but was alive once, and spake. For twenty generations, here was the earthly arena where painful living men worked out their life-wrestle,—looked at by Earth, by Heaven and Hell. Bells tolled to prayers; and men, of many humours, various thoughts, chanted vespers, matins;—and round the little islet of their life rolled forever (as round ours still rolls, though we are blind and deaf) the illimitable Ocean, tinting all things with *its* eternal hues and reflexes; making strange prophetic music! How silent now; all departed, clean gone. The World-Dramaturgist has written: *Exeunt.* The devouring Time-Demons have made away with it all: and in its stead, there is either nothing; or what is worse, offensive universal dust-clouds, and gray eclipse of Earth and Heaven, from 'dry rubbish shot here!'—

Truly it is no easy matter to get across the chasm of Seven Centuries, filled with such material. But here, of all helps, is not a Boswell the welcomest; even a small Boswell? Veracity, true simplicity of heart, how valuable are these always! He that speaks what *is* really in him, will find men to listen, though under never such impediments. Even gossip, springing free and cheery

from a human heart, this too is a kind of veracity and *speech ;*—
much preferable to pedantry and inane gray haze! Jocelin is
weak and garrulous, but he is human.　Through the thin watery
gossip of our Jocelin, we do get some glimpses of that deep-buried
Time; discern veritably, though in a fitful intermittent manner,
these antique figures and their life-method, face to face! Beautifully,
in our earnest loving glance, the old centuries melt from opaque to
partially translucent, transparent here and there; and the void
black Night, one finds, is but the summing-up of innumerable
peopled luminous *Days.*　Not parchment Chartularies, Doctrines
of the Constitution, O Dryasdust; not altogether, my erudite
friend!—

Readers who please to go along with us into this poor *Jocelini
Chronica* shall wander inconveniently enough, as in wintry twilight, through some poor stript hazel-grove, rustling with foolish
noises, and perpetually hindering the eyesight; but across which,
here and there, some real human figure is seen moving : very
strange ; whom we could hail if he would answer ;—and we look
into a pair of eyes deep as our own, *imaging* our own, but all
unconscious of us; to whom we, for the time, are become as spirits
and invisible!

CHAPTER III.

LANDLORD EDMUND.

SOME three centuries or so had elapsed since *Beodric's-worth* [1]
became St. Edmund's *Stow,* St. Edmund's *Town* and Monastery,

---

[1] Dryasdust puzzles and pokes for some biography of this Beodric ; and
repugns to consider him a mere East-Anglian Person of Condition, not in
need of a biography,—whose peopð, *weorth* or *worth,* that is to say, *Growth,*
Increase, or as we should now name it, *Estate,* that same Hamlet and wood
Mansion, now St. Edmund's Bury, originally was. For, adds our erudite
Friend, the Saxon peopðan, equivalent to the German *werden,* means to *grow,*
to *become;* traces of which old vocable are still found in the North-country
dialects; as, 'What is *word* of him?' meaning, 'What is *become* of him?' and
the like.　Nay we in modern English still say, 'Woe *worth* the hour' (Woe
befall the hour), and speak of the '*Weird* Sisters;' not to mention the

before Jocelin entered himself a Novice there.   'It was,' says
he, 'the year after the Flemings were defeated at Fornham St.
Genevieve.'

Much passes away into oblivion : this glorious victory over the
Flemings at Fornham has, at the present date, greatly dimmed
itself out of the minds of men. A victory and battle nevertheless
it was, in its time : some thrice-renowned Earl of Leicester, not of
the De Montfort breed (as may be read in Philosophical and other
Histories, could any human memory retain such things), had
quarrelled with his sovereign, Henry Second of the name; had
been worsted, it is like, and maltreated, and obliged to fly to
foreign parts ; but had rallied there into new vigour ; and so, in
the year 1173, returns across the German Sea with a vengeful army
of Flemings. Returns, to the coast of Suffolk ; to Framlingham
Castle, where he is welcomed; westward towards St. Edmundsbury and Fornham Church, where he is met by the constituted
authorities with *posse comitatus;* and swiftly cut in pieces, he and
his, or laid by the heels; on the right bank of the obscure river
Lark,—as traces still existing will verify.

For the river Lark, though not very discoverable, still runs or
stagnates in that country ; and the battle-ground is there ; serving
at present as a pleasure-ground to his Grace of Northumberland.
Copper pennies of Henry II. are still found there ;—rotted out
from the pouches of poor slain soldiers, who had not had *time* to
buy liquor with them. In the river Lark itself was fished up,
within man's memory, an antique gold ring; which fond Dilettantism can almost believe may have been the very ring Countess
Leicester threw away, in her flight, into that same Lark river or
ditch.[2] Nay, few years ago, in tearing out an enormous superannuated ash-tree, now grown quite corpulent, bursten, superfluous,
but long a fixture in the soil, and not to be dislodged without
revolution,—there was laid bare, under its roots, 'a circular mound
of skeletons wonderfully complete,' all radiating from a centre,
faces upwards, feet inwards; a 'radiation' not of Light, but of the
Nether Darkness rather; and evidently the fruit of battle ; for
'many of the heads were cleft, or had arrow-holes in them.' The

---

innumerable other names of places still ending in *weorth* or *worth*. And indeed,
our common noun *worth*, in the sense of *value*, does not this mean simply,
What a thing has *grown* to, What a man has *grown* to, How much he amounts
to,—by the Threadneedle-street standard or another !

    [2] Lyttelton's *History of Henry II.* (2d edition), v. 169, &c.

Battle of Fornham, therefore, is a fact, though a forgotten one;
no less obscure than undeniable,—like so many other facts.

Like the St. Edmund's Monastery itself! Who can doubt, after
what we have said, that there was a Monastery here at one time?
No doubt at all there was a Monastery here; no doubt, some three
centuries prior to this Fornham Battle, there dwelt a man in these
parts of the name of Edmund, King, Landlord, Duke or whatever
his title was, of the Eastern Counties;—and a very singular man
and landlord he must have been.

For his tenants, it would appear, did not in the least complain
of him; his labourers did not think of burning his wheat-stacks,
breaking into his game-preserves; very far the reverse of all that.
Clear evidence, satisfactory even to my friend Dryasdust, exists
that, on the contrary, they honoured, loved, admired this ancient
Landlord to a quite astonishing degree,—and indeed at last to an
immeasurable and inexpressible degree; for, finding no limits or
utterable words for their sense of his worth, they took to beatifying
and adoring him! 'Infinite admiration,' we are taught, 'means
worship.'

Very singular,—could we discover it! What Edmund's specific
duties were; above all, what his method of discharging them with
such results was, would surely be interesting to know; but are *not*
very discoverable now. His Life has become a poetic, nay a
religious *Mythus;* though, undeniably enough, it was once a prose
Fact, as our poor lives are; and even a very rugged unmanageable one. This landlord Edmund did go about in leather shoes,
with *femoralia* and bodycoat of some sort on him; and daily had
his breakfast to procure; and daily had contradictory speeches,
and most contradictory facts not a few, to reconcile with himself.
No man becomes a Saint in his sleep. Edmund, for instance,
instead of *reconciling* those same contradictory facts and speeches
to himself,—which means *subduing*, and in a manlike and godlike
manner conquering them to himself,—might have merely thrown
new contention into them, new unwisdom into them, and so been
conquered *by* them; much the commoner case! In that way he
had proved no 'Saint,' or Divine-looking Man, but a mere Sinner,
and unfortunate, blameable, more or less Diabolic-looking man!
No landlord Edmund becomes infinitely admirable in his sleep.

With what degree of wholesome rigour his rents were collected,
we hear not. Still less by what methods he preserved his game,

whether by 'bushing' or how,—and if the partridge-seasons were 'excellent,' or were indifferent. Neither do we ascertain what kind of Corn-bill he passed, or wisely-adjusted Sliding-scale:—but indeed there were few spinners in those days ; and the nuisance of spinning, and other dusty labour, was not yet so glaring a one.

How then, it may be asked, did this Edmund rise into favour; become to such astonishing extent a recognised Farmer's Friend ? Really, except it were by doing justly and loving mercy to an unprecedented extent, one does not know. The man, it would seem, 'had walked,' as they say, 'humbly with God ;' humbly and valiantly with God; struggling to make the Earth heavenly as he could : instead of walking sumptuously and pridefully with Mammon, leaving the Earth to grow hellish as it liked. Not sumptuously with Mammon ? How then could he 'encourage trade,'—cause Howel and James, and many wine-merchants, to bless him, and the tailor's heart (though in a very short-sighted manner) to sing for joy ? Much in this Edmund's Life is mysterious.

That he could, on occasion, do what he liked with his own, is meanwhile evident enough. Certain Heathen Physical-Force Ultra-Chartists, 'Danes' as they were then called, coming into his territory with their 'five points,' or rather with their five-and-twenty thousand *points* and edges too, of pikes namely and battle-axes; and proposing mere Heathenism, confiscation, spoliation, and fire and sword,—Edmund answered that he would oppose to the utmost such savagery. They took him prisoner; again required his sanction to said proposals. Edmund again refused. Cannot we kill you ? cried they.—Cannot I die ? answered he. My life, I think, is my own to do what I like with ! And he died, under barbarous tortures, refusing to the last breath; and the Ultra-Chartist Danes *lost* their propositions;—and went with their 'points' and other apparatus, as is supposed, to the Devil, the Father of them. Some say, indeed, these Danes were not Ultra-Chartists, but Ultra-Tories, demanding to reap where they had not sown, and live in this world without working, though all the world should starve for it; which likewise seems a possible hypothesis. Be what they might, they went, as we say, to the Devil; and Edmund doing what he liked with his own, the Earth was got cleared of them.

Another version is, that Edmund on this and the like occasions stood by his order; the oldest, and indeed only true order of

Nobility known under the stars, that of Just Men and Sons of
God, in opposition to Unjust and Sons of Belial,—which latter
indeed are *second*-oldest, but yet a very unvenerable order.
This, truly, seems the likeliest hypothesis of all. Names and
appearances alter so strangely, in some half-score centuries; and
all fluctuates chameleon-like, taking now this hue, now that.
Thus much is very plain, and does not change hue: Landlord
Edmund was seen and felt by all men to have done verily a man's
part in this life-pilgrimage of his; and benedictions, and out-
flowing love and admiration from the universal heart, were his
meed. Well-done! Well-done! cried the hearts of all men.
They raised his slain and martyred body; washed its wounds with
fast-flowing universal tears; tears of endless pity, and yet of a
sacred joy and triumph. The beautifulest kind of tears,—indeed
perhaps the beautifulest kind of thing: like a sky all flashing
diamonds and prismatic radiance; all weeping, yet shone on by the
everlasting Sun:—and *this* is not a sky, it is a Soul and living
Face! Nothing liker the *Temple of the Highest*, bright with some
real effulgence of the Highest, is seen in this world.

Oh, if all Yankee-land follow a small good 'Schnüspel the
distinguished Novelist' with blazing torches, dinner-invitations,
universal hep-hep-hurrah, feeling that he, though small, *is* something; how might all Angle-land once follow a hero-martyr and
great true Son of Heaven! It is the very joy of man's heart to
admire, where he can; nothing so lifts him from all his mean
imprisonments, were it but for moments, as true admiration. Thus
it has been said, 'all men, especially all women, are born worshippers;' and will worship, if it be but possible. Possible to
worship a Something, even a small one; not so possible a mere
loud-blaring Nothing! What sight is more pathetic than that of
poor multitudes of persons met to gaze at Kings' Progresses, Lord
Mayors' Shows, and other gilt-gingerbread phenomena of the
worshipful sort, in these times; each so eager to worship; each,
with a dim fatal sense of disappointment, finding that he cannot
rightly here! These be thy gods, O Israel? And thou art so
willing to worship,—poor Israel!

In this manner, however, did the men of the Eastern Counties
take up the slain body of their Edmund, where it lay cast forth
in the village of Hoxne; seek out the severed head, and reverently
reunite the same. They embalmed him with myrrh and sweet
spices, with love, pity, and all high and awful thoughts; conse-

crating him with a very storm of melodious adoring admiration, and sun-dyed showers of tears ;—joyfully, yet with awe (as all deep joy has something of the awful in it), commemorating his noble deeds and godlike walk and conversation while on Earth. Till, at length, the very Pope and Cardinals at Rome were forced to hear of it ; and they, summing up as correctly as they well could, with *Advocatus-Diaboli* pleadings and their other forms of process, the general verdict of mankind, declared : That he had, in very fact, led a hero's life in this world ; and being now *gone*, was gone, as they conceived, to God above, and reaping his reward *there*. Such, they said, was the best judgment they could form of the case ;—and truly not a bad judgment. Acquiesced in, zealously adopted, with full assent of ' private judgment,' by all mortals.

The rest of St. Edmund's history, for the reader sees he has now become a *Saint*, is easily conceivable. Pious munificence provided him a *loculus*, a *feretrum* or shrine ; built for him a wooden chapel, a stone temple, ever widening and growing by new pious gifts ;—such the overflowing heart feels it a blessedness to solace itself by giving. St. Edmund's Shrine glitters now with diamond flowerages, with a plating of wrought gold. The wooden chapel, as we say, has become a stone temple. Stately masonries, long-drawn arches, cloisters, sounding aisles buttress it, begirdle it far and wide. Regimented companies of men, of whom our Jocelin is one, devote themselves, in every generation, to meditate here on man's Nobleness and Awfulness, and celebrate and show forth the same, as they best can,—thinking they will do it better here, in presence of God the Maker, and of the so Awful and so Noble made by Him. In one word, St. Edmund's Body has raised a Monastery round it. To such length, in such manner, has the Spirit of the Time visibly taken body, and crystallised itself here. New gifts, houses, farms, *katalla* [3]—come ever in. King Knut, whom men call Canute, whom the Oceantide would not be forbidden to wet,—we heard already of this wise King, with his crown and gifts ; but of many others, Kings, Queens, wise men and noble loyal women, let Dryasdust and divine Silence be the record ! Beodric's-Worth has become St. Edmund's *Bury ;*—and lasts visible to this hour. All this that thou now seest, and namest Bury Town, is properly the Funeral Monument of Saint or

[3] Goods, properties ; what we now call *chattels*, and still more singularly *cattle*, says my erudite friend !

Landlord Edmund. The present respectable Mayor of Bury may be said, like a Fakeer (little as he thinks of it), to have his dwelling in the extensive, many-sculptured Tombstone of St. Edmund; in one of the brick niches thereof dwells the present respectable Mayor of Bury.

Certain Times do crystallise themselves in a magnificent manner; and others, perhaps, are like to do it in rather a shabby one!—But Richard Arkwright too will have his Monument, a thousand years hence: all Lancashire and Yorkshire, and how many other shires and countries, with their machineries and industries, for his monument! A true *pyr*amid or '*flame-mountain*,' flaming with steam fires and useful labour over wide continents, usefully towards the Stars, to a certain height;— how much grander than your foolish Cheops Pyramids or Sakhara clay ones! Let us withal be hopeful, be content or patient.

CHAPTER IV.

ABBOT HUGO.

IT is true all things have two faces, a light one and a dark. It is true, in three centuries much imperfection accumulates; many an Ideal, monastic or other, shooting forth into practice as it can, grows to a strange enough Reality; and we have to ask with amazement, Is this your Ideal! For, alas, the Ideal always has to grow in the Real, and to seek out its bed and board there, often in a very sorry way. No beautifulest Poet is a Bird-of-Paradise, living on perfumes; sleeping in the æther with outspread wings. The Heroic, *independent* of bed and board, is found in Drury-Lane Theatre only; to avoid disappointments, let us bear this in mind.

By the law of Nature, too, all manner of Ideals have their fatal limits and lot; their appointed periods, of youth, of maturity or perfection, of decline, degradation, and final death and disappearance. There is nothing born but has to die. Ideal monasteries,

once grown real, do seek bed and board in this world; do find it
more and more successfully; do get at length too intent on
finding it, exclusively intent on that.   They are then like diseased
corpulent bodies fallen idiotic, which merely eat and sleep; *ready*
for 'dissolution,' by a Henry the Eighth or some other.   Jocelin's
St. Edmundsbury is still far from this last dreadful state : but
here too the reader will prepare himself to see an Ideal not
sleeping in the æther like a bird-of-paradise, but roosting as the
common wood-fowl do, in an imperfect, uncomfortable, more or less
contemptible manner !—

Abbot Hugo, as Jocelin, breaking at once into the heart of the
business, apprises us, had in those days grown old, grown rather
blind, and his eyes were somewhat darkened, *aliquantulum caliga-*
verunt oculi ejus.   He dwelt apart very much, in his *Talamus* or
peculiar Chamber; got into the hands of flatterers, a set of mealy-
mouthed persons who strove to make the passing hour easy for
him,—for him easy, and for themselves profitable ; accumulating
in the distance mere mountains of confusion.   Old Dominus Hugo
sat inaccessible in this way, far in the interior, wrapt in his warm
flannels and delusions; inaccessible to all voice of Fact ; and bad
grew ever worse with us.   Not that our worthy old *Dominus Abbas*
was inattentive to the divine offices, or to the maintenance of a
devout spirit in us or in himself ; but the Account-Books of the
Convent fell into the frightfulest state, and Hugo's annual Budget
grew yearly emptier, or filled with futile expectations, fatal deficit,
wind and debts !

His one worldly care was to raise ready money; sufficient for
the day is the evil thereof.   And how he raised it : From usurious
insatiable Jews; every fresh Jew sticking on him like a fresh
horseleech, sucking his and our life out; crying continually, Give,
give ! Take one example instead of scores.   Our *Camera* having
fallen into ruin, William the Sacristan received charge to repair it ;
strict charge, but no money ; Abbot Hugo would, and indeed could,
give him no fraction of money.   The *Camera* in ruins, and Hugo
penniless and inaccessible, Willelmus Sacrista borrowed Forty
Marcs (some Seven-and-twenty Pounds) of Benedict the Jew, and
patched-up our Camera again.   But the means of repaying him ?
There were no means.   Hardly could *Sacrista, Cellerarius,* or any
public officer, get ends to meet, on the indispensablest scale, with
their shrunk allowances : ready money had vanished.

Benedict's Twenty-seven pounds grew rapidly at compound-interest; and at length, when it had amounted to a Hundred pounds, he, on a day of settlement, presents the account to Hugo himself. Hugo already owed him another Hundred of his own; and so here it has become Two Hundred! Hugo, in a fine frenzy, threatens to depose the Sacristan, to do this and do that; but, in the mean while, How to quiet your insatiable Jew? Hugo, for this couple of hundreds, grants the Jew his bond for Four hundred payable at the end of four years. At the end of four years there is, of course, still no money; and the Jew now gets a bond for Eight hundred and eighty pounds, to be paid by instalments, Fourscore pounds every year. Here was a way of doing business!

Neither yet is this insatiable Jew satisfied or settled with: he had papers against us of 'small debts fourteen years old;' his modest claim amounts finally to 'Twelve huudred pounds besides interest;'—and one hopes he never got satisfied in this world; one almost hopes he was one of those beleaguered Jews who hanged themselves in York Castle shortly afterwards, and had his usances and quittances and horseleech papers summarily set fire to! For approximate justice will strive to accomplish itself; if not in one way, then in another. Jews, and also Christians and Heathens, who accumulate in this manner, though furnished with never so many parchments, do, at times, 'get their grinder-teeth successively pulled out of their head, each day a new grinder,' till they consent to disgorge again. A sad fact,—worth reflecting on.

Jocelin, we see, is not without secularity: Our *Dominus Abbas* was intent enough on the divine offices; but then his Account-Books—?—One of the things that strike us most, throughout, in Jocelin's *Chronicle*, and indeed in Eadmer's *Anselm*, and other old monastic Books, written evidently by pious men, is this, That there is almost no mention whatever of 'personal religion' in them; that the whole gist of their thinking and speculation seems to be the 'privileges of our order,' 'strict exaction of our dues,' 'God's honour' (meaning the honour of our Saint), and so forth. Is not this singular? A body of men, set apart for perfecting and purifying their own souls, do not seem disturbed about that in any measure: the 'Ideal' says nothing about its idea; says much about finding bed and board for itself! How is this?

Why, for one thing, bed and board are a matter very apt to come to speech: it is much easier to *speak* of them than of ideas; and they are sometimes much more pressing with some! Nay, for another thing, may not this religious reticence, in these devout good souls, be perhaps a merit, and sign of health in them? Jocelin, Eadmer, and such religious men, have as yet nothing of ʻMethodism;' no Doubt or even root of Doubt. Religion is not a diseased self-introspection, an agonising inquiry: their duties are clear to them, the way of supreme good plain, indisputable, and they are travelling on it. Religion lies over them like an all-embracing heavenly canopy, like an atmosphere and life-element, which is not spoken of, which in all things is presupposed without speech. Is not serene or complete Religion the highest aspect of human nature; as serene Cant, or complete No-religion, is the lowest and miserablest? Between which two, all manner of earnest Methodisms, introspections, agonising inquiries, never so morbid, shall play their respective parts, not without approbation.

But let any reader fancy himself one of the Brethren in St. Edmundsbury Monastery under such circumstances! How can a Lord Abbot, all stuck-over with horseleeches of this nature, front the world? He is fast losing his life-blood, and the Convent will be as one of Pharaoh's lean kine. Old monks of experience draw their hoods deeper down; careful what they say: the monk's first duty is obedience. Our Lord the King, hearing of such work, sends down his Almoner to make investigations: but what boots it? Abbot Hugo assembles us in Chapter; asks, "If there is any complaint?" Not a soul of us dare answer, "Yes, thousands!" but we all stand silent, and the Prior even says that things are in a very comfortable condition. Whereupon old Abbot Hugo, turning to the royal messenger, says, "You see!"—and the business terminates in that way. I, as a brisk-eyed noticing youth and novice, could not help asking of the elders, asking of Magister Samson in particular: Why he, well-instructed and a knowing man, had not spoken out, and brought matters to a bearing? Magister Samson was Teacher of the Novices, appointed to breed us up to the rules, and I loved him well. "*Fili mi*," answered Samson, "the burnt child shuns the fire. Dost thou not know, our Lord the Abbot sent me once to Acre in Norfolk, to solitary confinement and bread-and-water, already? The Hinghams, Hugo and Robert, have just got home from banishment for speaking. This is the hour of darkness: the hour when flatterers rule and are believed. *Videat Dominus*, let the Lord see, and judge."

In very truth, what could poor old Abbot Hugo do? A frail old man, and the Philistines were upon him,—that is to say, the

Hebrews. He had nothing for it but to shrink away from them; get back into his warm flannels, into his warm delusions again. Happily, before it was quite too late, he bethought him of pilgriming to St. Thomas of Canterbury. He set out, with a fit train, in the autumn days of the year 1180; near Rochester City, his mule threw him, dislocated his poor kneepan, raised incurable inflammatory fever; and the poor old man got his dismissal from the whole coil at once. St. Thomas à Becket, though in a circuitous way, had *brought* deliverance! Neither Jew usurers, nor grumbling monks, nor other importunate despicability of men or mud-elements afflicted Abbot Hugo any more; but he dropt his rosaries, closed his account-books, closed his old eyes, and lay down into the long sleep. Heavy-laden hoary old Dominus Hugo, fare thee well.

One thing we cannot mention without a due thrill of horror: namely, that, in the empty exchequer of Dominus Hugo, there was not found one penny to distribute to the Poor that they might pray for his soul! By a kind of godsend, Fifty shillings did, in the very nick of time, fall due, or seem to fall due, from one of his Farmers (the *Firmarius* de Palegrava), and he paid it, and the Poor had it; though, alas, this too only *seemed* to fall due, and we had it to pay again afterwards. Dominus Hugo's apartments were plundered by his servants, to the last portable stool, in a few minutes after the breath was out of his body. Forlorn old Hugo, fare thee well forever.

CHAPTER V.

TWELFTH CENTURY.

OUR Abbot being dead, the *Dominus Rex*, Henry II., or Ranulf de Glanvill *Justiciarius* of England for him, set Inspectors or Custodiars over us;—not in any breathless haste to appoint a new Abbot, our revenues coming into his own *Scaccarium*, or royal Exchequer, in the mean while. They proceeded with some rigour, these Custodiars; took written inventories, clapt-on seals, exacted everywhere strict tale and measure: but wherefore should a living monk complain? The living monk has to do his devotional drill-exercise; consume his allotted *pitantia*, what we call *pittance*, or ration of victual; and possess his soul in patience.

Dim, as through a long vista of Seven Centuries, dim and very strange looks that monk-life to us; the ever-surprising circumstance this, That it is a *fact* and no dream, that we see it there, and gaze into the very eyes of it! Smoke rises daily from those culinary chimney-throats; there are living human beings there, who chant, loud-braying, their matins, nones, vespers; awakening *echoes*, not to the bodily ear alone. St. Edmund's Shrine, perpetually illuminated, glows ruddy through the Night, and through the Night of Centuries withal; St. Edmundsbury Town paying yearly Forty pounds for that express end. Bells clang out: on great occasions, all the bells. We have Processions, Preachings, Festivals, Christmas Plays, *Mysteries* shown in the Churchyard, at which latter the Townsfolk sometimes quarrel. Time was, Time is, as Friar Bacon's Brass Head remarked; and withal Time will be. There are three Tenses, *Tempora*, or Times; and there is one Eternity; and as for us,

'　We are such stuff as Dreams are made of !　'

Indisputable, though very dim to modern vision, rests on its hill-slope that same *Bury*, *Stow*, or Town of St. Edmund; already a considerable place, not without traffic, nay manufactures, would Jocelin only tell us what. Jocelin is totally careless of telling: but, through dim fitful apertures, we can see *Fullones*, 'Fullers,' see cloth-making; looms dimly going, dye-vats, and old women spinning yarn. We have Fairs too, *Nundinæ*, in due course; and the Londoners give us much trouble, pretending that they, as a metropolitan people, are exempt from toll. Besides there is Field-husbandry, with perplexed settlement of Convent rents: corn-ricks pile themselves within burgh, in their season : and cattle depart and enter; and even the poor weaver has his cow,—'dung-heaps' lying quiet at most doors (*ante foras*, says the incidental Jocelin), for the Town has yet no improved police. Watch and ward nevertheless we do keep, and have Gates,—as what Town must not; thieves so abounding; war, *werra*, such a frequent thing! Our thieves, at the Abbot's judgment-bar, deny; claim wager of battle; fight, are beaten, and *then* hanged. 'Ketel, the thief,' took this course; and it did nothing for him,—merely brought us, and indeed himself, new trouble !

Everyway a most foreign Time. What difficulty, for example, has our *Cellerarius* to collect the *repselver*, 'reaping silver,' or penny, which each householder is by law bound to pay for cutting down the Convent grain ! Richer people pretend that it is commuted, that it is this and the other; that, in short, they will not pay it. Our *Cellerarius* gives up calling on the rich. In the houses of the poor, our *Cellerarius* finding, in like manner, neither penny nor good promise, snatches, without ceremony, what *vadium* (pledge, *wad*) he can come at: a joint-stool, kettle, nay the very house-door, '*hostium;*' and old women, thus exposed to the un-feeling gaze of the public, rush out after him with their distaffs and the angriest shrieks: '*vetulæ exibant cum colis suis,*' says Jocelin, '*minantes et exprobrantes.*'

What a historical picture, glowing visible, as St. Edmund's Shrine by night, after Seven long Centuries or so! *Vetulæ cum colis:* My venerable ancient spinning grandmothers,—ah, and ye too have to shriek, and rush out with your distaffs; and become Female Chartists, and scold all evening with void doorway;—and in old Saxon, as we in modern, would fain demand some Five-point Charter, could it be fallen-in with, the Earth being too tyrannous! —Wise Lord Abbots, hearing of such phenomena, did in time abolish or commute the reap-penny, and one nuisance was abated. But the image of these justly offended old women, in their old wool costumes, with their angry features, and spindles brandished, lives forever in the historical memory. Thanks to thee, Jocelin Boswell. Jerusalem was taken by the Crusaders, and again lost by them; and Richard Cœur-de-Lion 'veiled his face' as he passed in sight of it: but how many other things went on, the while!

Thus, too, our trouble with the Lakenheath eels is very great. King Knut namely, or rather his Queen who also did herself honour by honouring St. Edmund, decreed by authentic deed yet extant on parchment, that the Holders of the Town Fields, once Beodric's, should, for one thing, go yearly and catch us four thousand eels in the marsh-pools of Lakenheath. Well, they went, they continued to go; but, in later times, got into the way of returning with a most short account of eels. Not the due six-score apiece; no, Here are two-score, Here are twenty, ten,—sometimes, Here are none at all; Heaven help us, we *could* catch no more, they were not there! What is a distressed *Cellerarius* to do? We agree that each Holder of so many acres shall pay one penny yearly, and let-go the eels as too slippery. But, alas, neither is this quite effectual: the Fields, in my time, have got divided among so many hands, there is no catching of *them* either; I have known our Cellarer get seven-and-twenty pence formerly, and now it is much if he get ten pence farthing (*vix decem denarios et obolum*). And then their sheep, which they are bound to fold nightly in our pens, for the manure's sake; and, I fear, do not always fold: and their *aver-pennies,* and their *avragiums,* and their *fodercorns,* and mill-and-market dues! Thus, in its undeniable but dim manner, does old St. Edmundsbury spin and till, and laboriously keep its pot boiling, and St. Edmund's Shrine lighted, under such conditions and averages as it can.

How much is still alive in England; how much has not yet come into life! A Feudal Aristocracy is still alive, in the prime of life; superintending the cultivation of the land, and less consciously the distribution of the produce of the land, the adjustment of the quarrels of the land; judging, soldiering, adjusting; everywhere governing the people,—so that even a Gurth, born thrall of Cedric, lacks not his due parings of the pigs he tends. Governing;—and, alas, also game-preserving; so that a Robert Hood, a William Scarlet and others have, in these days, put on Lincoln coats, and taking to living, in some universal-suffrage manner, under the greenwood-tree!

How silent, on the other hand, lie all Cotton-trades and suchlike; not a steeple-chimney yet got on end from sea to sea! North of the Humber, a stern Willelmus Conquæstor burnt the Country, finding it unruly, into very stern repose. Wild fowl scream in those ancient silences, wild cattle roam in those ancient solitudes; the scanty sulky Norse-bred population all coerced into silence,—feeling that, under these new Norman Governors, their history has probably as good as *ended.* Men and Northumbrian Norse populations know little what has ended, what is but beginning! The Ribble and the Aire roll down, as yet unpolluted by dyers' chemistry; tenanted by merry trouts and piscatory otters; the sunbeam and the vacant wind's-blast alone traversing those moors. Side by side sleep the coal-strata and the iron-strata for so many ages; no Steam-Demon has yet risen smoking into being. Saint Mungo rules in Glasgow; James Watt still slumbering in the deep of Time. *Mancunium,* Manceaster, what we now call Manchester, spins no cotton,—if it be not *wool* 'cottons,' clipped from the backs of mountain sheep. The Creek of the Mersey gurgles, twice in the four-and-twenty hours, with eddying brine, clangorous with sea-fowl; and is a *Lither*-Pool, a *lazy* or sullen Pool, no monstrous pitchy City, and Seahaven of the world! The Centuries are big; and the birth-hour is coming, not yet come. *Tempus ferax, tempus edax rerum.*

CHAPTER VI.

MONK SAMSON.

WITHIN doors, down at the hill-foot, in our Convent here, we are a peculiar people,—hardly conceivable in the Arkwright Corn-Law ages, of mere Spinning-Mills and Joe-Mantons! There is yet no Methodism among us, and we speak much of Secularities: no Methodism; our Religion is not yet a horrible restless Doubt, still less a far horribler composed Cant; but a great heaven-high Unquestionability, encompassing, interpenetrating the whole of Life. Imperfect as we may be, we are here, with our litanies, shaven crowns, vows of poverty, to testify incessantly and indisputably to every heart, That this Earthly Life and *its* riches and possessions, and good and evil hap, are not intrinsically a reality at all, but *are* a shadow of realities eternal, infinite; that this Time-world, as an air-image, fearfully *emblematic*, plays and flickers in the grand still mirror of Eternity; and man's little Life has Duties that are great, that are alone great, and go up to Heaven and down to Hell. This, with our poor litanies, we testify, and struggle to testify.

Which, testified or not, remembered by all men or forgotten by all men, does verily remain the fact, even in Arkwright Joe-Manton ages! But it is incalculable, when litanies have grown obsolete; when *fodercorns, avragiums,* and all human dues and reciprocities have been fully changed into one great due of *cash payment;* and man's duty to man reduces itself to handing him certain metal coins, or covenanted money-wages, and then shoving him out of doors; and man's duty to God becomes a cant, a doubt, a dim inanity, a 'pleasure of virtue' or suchlike; and the thing a man does infinitely fear (the real *Hell* of a man) is, 'that he do not make money and advance himself,'—I say, it is incalculable what a change has introduced itself everywhere into human affairs! How human affairs shall now circulate everywhere not healthy life-blood in them, but, as it were, a detestable copperas banker's ink; and all is grown acrid, divisive, threatening dissolution; and the huge tumultuous Life of Society is galvanic, devil-ridden, too truly possessed by a devil! For, in short, Mammon *is* not a god at all; but a devil, and even a very despicable devil. Follow the Devil faithfully, you are sure enough to *go* to the Devil: whither else can you go?—In such situations, men look back with a kind of mournful recognition even on poor limited Monk-figures, with their poor litanies; and reflect, with Ben Jonson, that soul is indispensable, some degree of soul, even to save you the expense of salt!—

For the rest, it must be owned, we Monks of St. Edmundsbury are but a limited class of creatures, and seem to have a somewhat dull life of it. Much given to idle gossip; having indeed no other work, when our chanting is over. Listless gossip, for most part, and a mitigated slander; the fruit of idleness, not of spleen. We are dull, insipid men, many of us; easy-minded; whom prayer and digestion of food will avail for a life. We have to receive all strangers in our Convent, and lodge them gratis; such and such sorts go by rule to the Lord Abbot and his special revenues; such and such to us and our poor Cellarer, however straitened. Jews themselves send their wives and little ones hither in war-time, into our *Pitanceria;* where they abide safe, with due *pittances,* —for a consideration. We have the fairest chances for collecting news. Some of us have a turn for reading Books; for meditation, silence; at times we even write Books. Some of us can preach, in English-Saxon, in Norman-French, and even in Monk-Latin; others cannot in any language or jargon, being stupid.

Failing all else, what gossip about one another! This is a perennial resource. How one hooded head applies itself to the ear of another, and whispers—*tacenda.* Willelmus Sacrista, for instance, what does he nightly, over in that Sacristy of his? Frequent bibations, '*frequentes bibationes et quædam tacenda,*'—eheu! We have '*tempora minutionis,*' stated seasons of blood-letting, when we are all let blood together; and then there is a general free-conference, a sanhedrim of clatter. Notwithstanding our vow of poverty, we can by rule amass to the extent of 'two shillings;' but it is to be given to our necessitous kindred, or in charity. Poor Monks! Thus too a certain Canterbury Monk was in the habit of 'slipping, *clanculo,* from his sleeve,' five shillings into the hand of his mother, when she came to see him, at the divine offices, every two months. Once, slipping the money clandestinely, just in the act of taking leave, he slipt it not into

her hand but on the floor, and another had it; whereupon the poor
Monk, coming to know it, looked mere despair for some days;
till Lanfranc the noble Archbishop, questioning his secret from
him, nobly made the sum *seven* shillings,[1] and said, Never mind !

One Monk, of a taciturn nature, distinguishes himself among
these babbling ones: the name of him Samson; he that answered
Jocelin, "*Fili mi*, a burnt child shuns the fire." They call him
'Norfolk *Barrator*,' or litigious person; for indeed, being of grave
taciturn ways, he is not universally a favourite; he has been
in trouble more than once. The reader is desired to mark this
Monk. A personable man of seven-and-forty; stout-made, stands
erect as a pillar; with bushy eyebrows, the eyes of him beaming
into you in a really strange way; the face massive, grave, with 'a
very eminent nose;' his head almost bald, its auburn remnants
of hair, and the copious ruddy beard, getting slightly streaked
with gray. This is Brother Samson; a man worth looking at.

He is from Norfolk, as the nickname indicates; from Tottington
in Norfolk, as we guess; the son of poor parents there. He has
told me Jocelin, for I loved him much, That once in his ninth year
he had an alarming dream;—as indeed we are all somewhat given
to dreaming here. Little Samson, lying uneasily in his crib at
Tottington, dreamed that he saw the Arch Enemy in person, just
alighted in front of some grand building, with outspread bat-wings,
and stretching forth detestable clawed hands to grip him, little
Samson, and fly-off with him: whereupon the little dreamer
shrieked desperate to St. Edmund for help, shrieked and again
shrieked; and St. Edmund, a reverend heavenly figure, did come,
—and indeed poor little Samson's mother, awakened by his
shrieking, did come; and the Devil and the Dream both fled away
fruitless. On the morrow, his mother, pondering such an awful
dream, thought it were good to take him over to St. Edmund's
own Shrine, and pray with him there. See, said little Samson at
sight of the Abbey-Gate; see, mother, this is the building I
dreamed of! His poor mother dedicated him to St. Edmund,—
left him there with prayers and tears: what better could she do?
The exposition of the dream, Brother Samson used to say, was
this: *Diabolus* with outspread bat-wings shadowed forth the
pleasures of this world, *voluptates hujus sœculi*, which were about
to snatch and fly away with me, had not St. Edmund flung his

[1] *Eadmeri Hist.* p. 8.

arms round me, that is to say, made me a monk of his. A monk,
accordingly, Brother Samson is; and here to this day where his
mother left him. A learned man, of devout grave nature; has
studied at Paris, has taught in the Town Schools here, and done
much else; can preach in three languages, and, like Dr. Caius,
'has had losses' in his time. A thoughtful, firm-standing man;
much loved by some, not loved by all; his clear eyes flashing into
you, in an almost inconvenient way!

Abbot Hugo, as we said, had his own difficulties with him;
Abbot Hugo had him in prison once, to teach him what authority
was, and how to dread the fire in future. For Brother Samson,
in the time of the Antipopes, had been sent to Rome on business;
and, returning successful, was too late,—the business had all mis-
gone in the interim! As tours to Rome are still frequent with us
English, perhaps the reader will not grudge to look at the method
of travelling thither in those remote ages. We happily have,
in small compass, a personal narrative of it. Through the clear
eyes and memory of Brother Samson one peeps direct into the
very bosom of that Twelfth Century, and finds it rather curious.
The actual *Papa*, Father, or universal President of Christendom,
as yet not grown chimerical, sat there; think of that only!
Brother Samson went to Rome as to the real Light-fountain of
this lower world; we now—!—But let us hear Brother Samson,
as to his mode of travelling:

'You know what trouble I had for that Church of Woolpit;
'how I was despatched to Rome in the time of the Schism between
'Pope Alexander and Octavian; and passed through Italy at
'that season, when all clergy carrying letters for our Lord Pope
'Alexander were laid hold of, and some were clapt in prison, some
'hanged; and some, with nose and lips cut off, were sent forward
'to our Lord the Pope, for the disgrace and confusion of him (*in*
'*dedecus et confusionem ejus*). I, however, pretended to be Scotch,
'and putting on the garb of a Scotchman, and taking the gesture
'of one, walked along; and when anybody mocked at me, I would
'brandish my staff in the manner of that weapon they call *gaveloc*,[2]
'uttering comminatory words after the way of the Scotch. To those
'that met and questioned me who I was, I made no answer but:
'*Ride, ride Rome; turne Cantwereberei.*[3] Thus did I, to conceal

---

[2] Javelin, missile pike. *Gaveloc* is still the Scotch name for *crowbar*.

[3] Does this mean, "Rome forever; Canterbury *not*" (which claims an
unjust Supremacy over us)! Mr. Rokewood is silent. Dryasdust would

'myself and my errand, and get safer to Rome under the guise of
'a Scotchman.

'Having at last obtained a Letter from our Lord the Pope
'according to my wishes, I turned homewards again. I had to
'pass through a certain strong town on my road; and lo, the
'soldiers thereof surrounded me, seizing me, and saying: "This
'vagabond (*iste solivagus*), who pretends to be Scotch, is either a
'spy, or has Letters from the false Pope Alexander." And whilst
'they examined every stitch and rag of me, my leggings (*caligas*),
'breeches, and even the old shoes that I carried over my shoulder
'in the way of the Scotch,—I put my hand into the leather scrip
'I wore, wherein our Lord the Pope's Letter lay, close by a little
'jug (*ciffus*) I had for drinking out of; and the Lord God so
'pleasing, and St. Edmund, I got out both the Letter and the jug
'together; in such a way that, extending my arm aloft, I held the
'Letter hidden between jug and hand: they saw the jug, but the
'Letter they saw not. And thus I escaped out of their hands in
'the name of the Lord. Whatever money I had, they took from
'me; wherefore I had to beg from door to door, without any pay-
'ment (*sine omni expensa*) till I came to England again. But
'hearing that the Woolpit Church was already given to Geoffry
'Ridell, my soul was struck with sorrow because I had laboured in
'vain. Coming home, therefore, I sat me down secretly under
'the Shrine of St. Edmund, fearing lest our Lord Abbot should
'seize and imprison me, though I had done no mischief; nor was
'there a monk who durst speak to me, nor a laic who durst bring
'me food except by stealth.'[4]

Such resting and welcoming found Brother Samson, with his
worn soles, and strong heart! He sits silent, revolving many
thoughts, at the foot of St. Edmund's Shrine. In the wide Earth,
if it be not Saint Edmund, what friend or refuge has he? Our
Lord Abbot, hearing of him, sent the proper officer to lead him
down to prison, and clap 'foot-gyves on him' there. Another poor
official furtively brought him a cup of wine; bade him "be comforted in the Lord." Samson utters no complaint; obeys in silence.
'Our Lord Abbot, taking counsel of it, banished me to Acre, and
there I had to stay long.'

Our Lord Abbot next tried Samson with promotions; made
perhaps explain it,—in the course of a week or two of talking; did one dare
to question him !

[4] *Jocelini Chronica*, p. 36.

him Subsacristan, made him Librarian, which he liked best of all, being passionately fond of Books: Samson, with many thoughts in him, again obeyed in silence; discharged his offices to perfection, but never thanked our Lord Abbot,—seemed rather as if looking into him, with those clear eyes of his. Whereupon Abbot Hugo said, *Se nunquam vidisse*, He had never seen such a man; whom no severity would break to complain, and no kindness soften into smiles or thanks:—a questionable kind of man !

In this way, not without troubles, but still in an erect clear-standing manner, has Brother Samson reached his forty-seventh year; and his ruddy beard is getting slightly grizzled. He is endeavouring, in these days, to have various broken things thatched in; nay perhaps to have the Choir itself completed, for he can bear nothing ruinous. He has gathered 'heaps of lime and sand;' has masons, slaters working, he and *Warinus monachus noster*, who are joint keepers of the Shrine; paying out the money duly, —furnished by charitable burghers of St. Edmundsbury, they say. Charitable burghers of St. Edmundsbury? To me Jocelin it seems rather, Samson, and Warinus whom he leads, have privily hoarded the oblations at the Shrine itself, in these late years of indolent dilapidation, while Abbot Hugo sat wrapt inaccessible; and are struggling, in this prudent way, to have the rain kept out![5]— Under what conditions, sometimes, has Wisdom to struggle with Folly; get Folly persuaded to so much as thatch out the rain from itself! For, indeed, if the Infant govern the Nurse, what dextrous practice on the Nurse's part will not be necessary !

It is a new regret to us that, in these circumstances, our Lord the King's Custodiars, interfering, prohibited all building or thatching from whatever source; and no Choir shall be completed, and Rain and Time, for the present, shall have their way. Willelmus Sacrista, he of 'the frequent bibations and some things not to be spoken of;' he, with his red nose, I am of opinion, had made complaint to the Custodiars : wishing to do Samson an ill turn :— Samson his *Sub*-sacristan, with those clear eyes, could not be a prime favourite of his! Samson again obeys in silence.

[5] *Jocelini Chronica*, p. 7.

CHAPTER VII.

THE CANVASSING.

Now, however, come great news to St. Edmundsbury: That
there is to be an Abbot elected; that our interlunar obscuration
is to cease; St. Edmund's Convent no more to be a doleful widow,
but joyous and once again a bride! Often in our widowed state
had we prayed to the Lord and St. Edmund, singing weekly a
matter of 'one-and-twenty penitential Psalms, on our knees in
the Choir,' that a fit Pastor might be vouchsafed us. And, says
Jocelin, had some known what Abbot we were to get, they had
not been so devout, I believe!—Bozzy Jocelin opens to mankind
the floodgates of authentic Convent gossip; we listen, as in a
Dionysius' Ear, to the inanest hubbub, like the voices at Virgil's
Horn-Gate of Dreams. Even gossip, seven centuries off, has
significance. List, list, how like men are to one another in all
centuries:

'*Dixit quidam de quodam*, A certain person said of a certain
'person, "He, that *Frater*, is a good monk, *probabilis persona*;
'knows much of the order and customs of the church; and, though
'not so perfect a philosopher as some others, would make a
'very good Abbot. Old Abbot Ording, still famed among us,
'knew little of letters. Besides, as we read in Fables, it is better
'to choose a log for king, than a serpent never so wise, that will
'venomously hiss and bite his subjects."—"Impossible!" answered
'the other: "How can such a man make a sermon in the Chapter,
'or to the people on festival-days, when he is without letters?
'How can he have the skill to bind and to loose, he who does not
'understand the Scriptures? How—?"'

And then 'another said of another, *alius de alio*, "That *Frater*
'is a *homo literatus*, eloquent, sagacious; vigorous in discipline;
'loves the Convent much, has suffered much for its sake." To
'which a third party answers, "From all your great clerks, good
'Lord deliver us! From Norfolk barrators and surly persons,
'That it would please thee to preserve us, We beseech thee to hear

'us, good Lord!" Then another *quidam* said of another *quodam*,
'"That *Frater* is a good manager (*husebondus*);" but was swiftly
'answered, "God forbid that a man who can neither read nor
'chant, nor celebrate the divine offices, an unjust person withal,
'and grinder of the faces of the poor, should ever be Abbot!"' One
man, it appears, is nice in his victuals. Another is indeed wise,
but apt to slight inferiors; hardly at the pains to answer, if they
argue with him too foolishly. And so each *aliquis* concerning his
aliquo,—through whole pages of electioneering babble. 'For,'
says Jocelin, 'So many men, as many minds.' Our Monks 'at
time of blood-letting, *tempore minutionis*,' holding their sanhedrim
of babble, would talk in this manner: Brother Samson, I remarked,
never said anything; sat silent, sometimes smiling; but he took
good note of what others said, and would bring it up, on occasion,
twenty years after. As for me Jocelin, I was of opinion that 'some
skill in Dialectics, to distinguish true from false,' would be good in
an Abbot. I spake, as a rash Novice in those days, some con-
scientious words of a certain benefactor of mine; 'and behold, one
of those sons of Belial' ran and reported them to him, so that
he never after looked at me with the same face again! Poor
Bozzy!—

Such is the buzz and frothy simmering ferment of the general
mind and no-mind; struggling to 'make itself up,' as the phrase
is, or ascertain what *it* does really want: no easy matter, in most
cases. St. Edmundsbury, in that Candlemas season of the year
1182, is a busily fermenting place. The very clothmakers sit
meditative at their looms; asking, Who shall be Abbot? The
sochemanni speak of it, driving their ox-teams afield; the old
women with their spindles: and none yet knows what the days
will bring forth.

The Prior, however, as our interim chief, must proceed to work;
get ready 'Twelve Monks,' and set off with them to his Majesty at
Waltham, there shall the election be made. An election, whether
managed directly by ballot-box on public hustings, or indirectly by
force of public opinion, or were it even by open alehouses, landlords'
coercion, popular club-law, or whatever electoral methods, is always
an interesting phenomenon. A mountain tumbling in great travail,
throwing up dustclouds and absurd noises, is visibly there; uncertain yetwhat mouse or monster it will give birth to.

Besides, it is a most important social act; nay, at bottom, the one important social act. Given the men a People choose, the People itself, in its exact worth and worthlessness, is given. A heroic people chooses heroes, and is happy; a valet or flunky people chooses sham-heroes, what are called quacks, thinking them heroes, and is not happy. The grand summary of a man's spiritual condition, what brings out all his herohood and insight, or all his flunkyhood and horn-eyed dimness, is this question put to him, What man dost thou honour? Which is thy ideal of a man; or nearest that? So too of a People: for a People too, every People, *speaks* its choice,—were it only by silently obeying, and not revolting,—in the course of a century or so. Nor are electoral methods, Reform Bills and suchlike, unimportant. A People's electoral methods are, in the long-run, the express image of its electoral *talent;* tending and gravitating perpetually, irresistibly, to a conformity with that: and are, at all stages, very significant of the People. Judicious readers, of these times, are not disinclined to see how Monks elect their Abbot in the Twelfth Century: how the St. Edmundsbury mountain manages its midwifery; and what mouse or man the outcome is.

CHAPTER VIII.

THE ELECTION.

Accordingly our Prior assembles us in Chapter; and we adjuring him before God to do justly, nominates, not by our selection, yet with our assent, Twelve Monks, moderately satisfactory. Of whom are Hugo Third-Prior, Brother Dennis a venerable man, Walter the *Medicus*, Samson *Subsacrista*, and other esteemed characters,—though Willelmus *Sacrista*, of the red nose, too is one. These shall proceed straightway to Waltham; and there elect the Abbot as they may and can. Monks are sworn to obedience; must not speak too loud, under penalty of foot-gyves, limbo, and bread-and-water: yet monks too would know what it is they are obeying. The St. Edmundsbury Community has no hustings, ballot-box, indeed no open voting: yet by various vague manipulations, pulse-feelings, we struggle to ascertain what its virtual aim is, and succeed better or worse.

This question, however, rises ; alas, a quite preliminary question : Will the *Dominus Rex* allow us to choose freely ? It is to be hoped ! Well, if so, we agree to choose one of our own Convent. If not, if the *Dominus Rex* will force a stranger on us, we decide on demurring, the Prior and his Twelve shall demur : we can appeal, plead, remonstrate ; appeal even to the Pope, but trust it will not be necessary. Then there is this other question, raised by Brother Samson : What if the Thirteen should not themselves be able to agree ? Brother Samson *Subsacrista,* one remarks, is ready oftenest with some question, some suggestion, that has wisdom in it. Though a servant of servants, and saying little, his words all tell, having sense in them ; it seems by his light mainly that we steer ourselves in this great dimness.

What if the Thirteen should not themselves be able to agree ? Speak, Samson, and advise.—Could not, hints Samson, Six of our venerablest elders be chosen by us, a kind of electoral committee, here and now : of these, ' with their hand on the Gospels, with their eye on the *Sacrosancta,*' we take oath that they will do faithfully ; let these, in secret and as before God, agree on Three whom they reckon fittest ; write their names in a Paper, and deliver the same sealed, forthwith, to the Thirteen : one of those Three the Thirteen shall fix on, if permitted. If not permitted, that is to say, if the *Dominus Rex* force us to demur,—the paper shall be brought back unopened, and publicly burned, that no man's secret bring him into trouble.

So Samson advises, so we act ; wisely, in this and in other crises of the business. Our electoral committee, its eye on the Sacrosancta, is soon named, soon sworn ; and we, striking-up the Fifth Psalm, ' *Verba mea,*

> ' Give ear unto my words, O Lord,
>   My meditation weigh,'

march out chanting, and leave the Six to their work in the Chapter here. Their work, before long, they announce as finished : they, with their eye on the Sacrosancta, imprecating the Lord to weigh and witness their meditation, have fixed on Three Names, and written them in this Sealed Paper. Let Samson Subsacrista, general servant of the party, take charge of it. On the morrow morning, our Prior and his Twelve will be ready to get under way.

This, then, is the ballot-box and electoral winnowing-machine they have at St. Edmundsbury : a mind fixed on the Thrice Holy, •

an appeal to God on high to witness their meditation : by far the best, and indeed the only good electoral winnowing-machine,—if men have souls in them. Totally worthless, it is true, and even hideous and poisonous, if men have no souls. But without soul, alas, what winnowing-machine in human elections can be of avail ? We cannot get along without soul; we stick fast, the mournfulest spectacle ; and salt itself will not save us !

On the morrow morning, accordingly, our Thirteen set forth ; or rather our Prior and Eleven ; for Samson, as general servant of the party, has to linger, settling many things. At length he too gets upon the road ; and, 'carrying the sealed Paper in a leather pouch hung round his neck ; and *froccum bajulans in ulnis*' (thanks to thee, Bozzy Jocelin), 'his frock-skirts looped over his elbow,' showing substantial stern-works, tramps stoutly along. Away across the Heath, not yet of Newmarket and horse-jockeying ; across your Fleam-dike and Devil's-dike, no longer useful as a Mercian East-Anglian boundary or bulwark : continually towards Waltham, and the Bishop of Winchester's House there, for his Majesty is in that. Brother Samson, as purse-bearer, has the reckoning always, when there is one, to pay ; ' delays are numerous,' progress none of the swiftest.

But, in the solitude of the Convent, Destiny thus big and in her birthtime, what gossiping, what babbling, what dreaming of dreams ! The secret of the Three our electoral elders alone know : some Abbot we shall have to govern us ; but which Abbot, oh, which ! One Monk discerns in a vision of the night-watches, that we shall get an Abbot of our own body, without needing to demur : a prophet appeared to him clad all in white, and said, "Ye shall have one of yours, and he will rage among you like a wolf, *sæviet ut lupus*." Verily !—then which of ours ? Another Monk now dreams : he has seen clearly which ; a certain Figure taller by head and shoulders than the other two, dressed in alb and *pallium*, and with the attitude of one about to fight ;—which tall Figure a wise Editor would rather not name at this stage of the business ! Enough that the vision is true : that Saint Edmund himself, pale and awful, seemed to rise from his Shrine, with naked feet, and say audibly, "He, *ille*, shall veil my feet;" which part of the vision also proves true. Such guessing, visioning, dim perscrutation of the momentous future : the very clothmakers, old women, all townsfolk speak of it, 'and more than once it is reported in St.

'Edmundsbury, This one is elected; and then, This one, and That
'other.' Who knows?

But now, sure enough, at Waltham 'on the second Sunday of
Quadragesima,' which Dryasdust declares to mean the 22d day of
February, year 1182, Thirteen St. Edmundsbury Monks are, at
last, seen processioning towards the Winchester Manorhouse; and,
in some high Presence-chamber and Hall of State, get access to
Henry II. in all his glory. What a Hall,—not imaginary in the
least, but entirely real and indisputable, though so extremely dim
to us; sunk in the deep distances of Night! The Winchester
Manorhouse has fled bodily, like a Dream of the old Night; not
Dryasdust himself can show a wreck of it. House and people,
royal and episcopal, lords and varlets, where are they? Why *there*,
I say, Seven Centuries off; sunk *so* far in the Night, there they
are; peep through the blankets of the old Night, and thou wilt
see! King Henry himself is visibly there; a vivid, noble-looking
man, with grizzled beard, in glittering uncertain costume; with
earls round him, and bishops, and dignitaries, in the like. The
Hall is large, and has for one thing an altar near it,—chapel and
altar adjoining it; but what gilt seats, carved tables, carpeting of
rush-cloth, what arras-hangings, and huge fire of logs:—alas, it
has Human Life in it; and is not that the grand miracle, in what
hangings or costume soever?—

The *Dominus Rex*, benignantly receiving our Thirteen with their
obeisance, and graciously declaring that he will strive to act for
God's honour and the Church's good, commands, 'by the Bishop of
Winchester and Geoffrey the Chancellor,'—*Galfridus Cancellarius*,
Henry's and the Fair Rosamond's authentic Son present here!—
commands, "That they, the said Thirteen, do now withdraw, and
fix upon Three from their own Monastery." A work soon done;
the Three hanging ready round Samson's neck, in that leather
pouch of his. Breaking the seal, we find the names,—what think
ye of it, ye higher dignitaries, thou indolent Prior, thou Willelmus
Sacrista with the red bottle-nose?—the names, in this order: of
Samson *Subsacrista*, of Roger the distressed Cellarer, of Hugo
Tertius-Prior.

The higher dignitaries, all omitted here, 'flush suddenly red in
the face;' but have nothing to say. One curious fact and question
certainly is, How Hugo Third-Prior, who was of the electoral
committee, came to nominate *himself* as one of the Three? A

Y 2

curious fact, which Hugo Third-Prior has never yet entirely explained, that I know of!—However, we return, and report to the
King our Three names ; merely altering the order ; putting Samson
last, as lowest of all. The King, at recitation of our Three, asks
us : "Who are they ? Were they born in my domain ? Totally
unknown to me ! You must nominate three others." Whereupon Willelmus Sacrista says, "Our Prior must be named, *quia
caput nostrum est*, being already our head." And the Prior re-
sponds, "Willelmus Sacrista is a fit man, *bonus vir est*,"—for all his
red nose. Tickle me, Toby, and I'll tickle thee ! Venerable
Dennis too is named ; none in his conscience can say nay. There
are now Six on our List. "Well," said the King, "they have
done it swiftly, they ! *Deus est cum eis.*" The Monks withdraw
again ; and Majesty revolves, for a little, with his *Pares* and
Episcopi, Lords or 'Law-wards' and Soul-Overseers, the thoughts
of the royal breast. The Monks wait silent in an outer room.

In short while, they are next ordered, To add yet another three ;
but not from their own Convent ; from other Convents, "for the
honour of my kingdom." Here,—what is to be done here ? We
will demur, if need be ! We do name three, however, for the
nonce : the Prior of St. Faith's, a good Monk of St. Neot's, a good
Monk of St. Alban's ; good men all ; all made abbots and dignitaries since, at this hour. There are now Nine upon our List.
What the thoughts of the Dominus Rex may be farther ? The
Dominus Rex, thanking graciously, sends out word that we shall
now strike off three. The three strangers are instantly struck off.
Willelmus Sacrista adds, that he will of his own accord decline,—
a touch of grace and respect for the *Sacrosancta*, even in Willelmus !
The King then orders us to strike off a couple more ; then yet one
more : Hugo Third-Prior goes, and Roger *Cellerarius*, and venerable
Monk Dennis ;—and now there remain on our List two only, Samson
Subsacrista and the Prior.

Which of these two ? It were hard to say,—by Monks who
may get themselves foot-gyved and thrown into limbo for speaking ! We humbly request that the Bishop of Winchester and
Geoffrey the Chancellor may again enter, and help us to decide.
"Which do you want ?" asks the Bishop. Venerable Dennis
made a speech, 'commending the persons of the Prior and
'Samson ; but always in the corner of his discourse, *in angulo*
'*sui sermonis*, brought Samson in.' "I see !" said the Bishop :
"We are to understand that your Prior is somewhat remiss ; that

you want to have him you call Samson for Abbot." "Either of
them is good," said venerable Dennis, almost trembling; "but we
would have the better, if it pleased God." "Which of the two *do*
you want?" inquires the Bishop pointedly. "Samson!" answered
Dennis; "Samson!" echoed all of the rest that durst speak or
echo anything: and Samson is reported to the King accordingly.
His Majesty, advising of it for a moment, orders that Samson be
brought in with the other Twelve.

The King's Majesty, looking at us somewhat sternly, then says:
"You present to me Samson; I do not know him: had it been
your Prior, whom I do know, I should have accepted him: how-
ever, I will now do as you wish. But have a care of yourselves.
By the true eyes of God, *per veros oculos Dei*, if you manage badly,
I will be upon you!" Samson, therefore, steps forward, kisses the
King's feet; but swiftly rises erect again, swiftly turns towards
the altar, uplifting with the other Twelve, in clear tenor-note, the
Fifty-first Psalm, ' *Miserere mei Deus,*

> ' After thy loving-kindness, Lord,
>   Have mercy upon *me* ; '

with firm voice, firm step and head, no change in his countenance
whatever. "By God's eyes," said the King, "that one, I think,
will govern the Abbey well." By the same oath (charged to your
Majesty's account), I too am precisely of that opinion! It is some
while since I fell in with a likelier man anywhere than this new
Abbot Samson. Long life to him, and may the Lord *have* mercy
on him as Abbot!

Thus, then, have the St. Edmundsbury Monks, without express
ballot-box or other good winnowing-machine, contrived to accomplish the most important social feat a body of men can do, to
winnow-out the man that is to govern them: and truly one sees
not that, by any winnowing-machine whatever, they could have
done it better. O ye kind Heavens, there is in every Nation
and Community a *fittest*, a wisest, bravest, best; whom could we
find and make King over us, all were in very truth well;—the best
that God and Nature had permitted *us* to make it! By what art
discover him? Will the Heavens in their pity teach us no art;
for our need of him is great!

Ballot-boxes, Reform Bills, winnowing-machines: all these are
good, or are not so good;—alas, brethren, how *can* these, I say,
be other than inadequate, be other than failures, melancholy to

behold? Dim all souls of men to the divine, the high and awful meaning of Human Worth and Truth, we shall never, by all the machinery in Birmingham, discover the True and Worthy. It is written, 'if we are ourselves valets, there shall exist no hero for us; 'we shall not know the hero when we see him;'—we shall take the quack for a hero; and cry, audibly through all ballot-boxes and machinery whatsoever, Thou art he; be thou King over us!

What boots it? Seek only deceitful Speciosity, money with gilt carriages, 'fame' with newspaper-paragraphs, whatever name it bear, you will find only deceitful Speciosity; godlike Reality will be forever far from you. The Quack shall be legitimate inevitable King of you; no earthly machinery able to exclude the Quack. Ye shall be born thralls of the Quack, and suffer under him, till your hearts are near broken, and no French Revolution or Manchester Insurrection, or partial or universal volcanic combustions and explosions, never so many, can do more than ' change the *figure* of your Quack;' the essence of him remaining, for a time and times.—"How long, O Prophet?" say some, with a rather melancholy sneer. Alas, ye *un*prophetic, ever till this come about: Till deep misery, if nothing softer will, have driven you out of your Speciosities *into* your Sincerities; and you find that there either is a Godlike in the world, or else ye are an unintelligible madness; that there is a God, as well as a Mammon and a Devil, and a Genius of Luxuries and canting Dilettantisms and Vain Shows! How long that will be, compute for yourselves. My unhappy brothers!—

CHAPTER IX.

ABBOT SAMSON.

So, then, the bells of St. Edmundsbury clang out one and all, and in church and chapel the organs go: Convent and Town, and all the west side of Suffolk, are in gala; knights, viscounts, weavers, spinners, the entire population, male and female, young and old, the very sockmen with their chubby infants,—out to have a holiday, and see the Lord Abbot arrive! And there is 'stripping barefoot' of the Lord Abbot at the Gate, and solemn leading of him in to the High Altar and Shrine; with sudden 'silence of all the bells and organs,' as we kneel in deep prayer there; and again with outburst of all the bells and organs, and loud *Te Deum* from the general human windpipe; and speeches by the leading viscount, and giving of the kiss of brotherhood; the whole wound-up with popular games, and dinner within doors of more than a thousand strong, *plus quam mille comedentibus in gaudio magno.*

In such manner is the selfsame Samson once again returning to us, welcomed on *this* occasion. He that went away with his frock-skirts looped over his arm, comes back riding high; suddenly made one of the dignitaries of this world. Reflective readers will admit that here was a trial for a man. Yesterday a poor mendicant, allowed to possess not above two shillings of money, and without authority to bid a dog run for him,—this man today finds himself a *Dominus Abbas*, mitred Peer of Parliament, Lord of manorhouses, farms, manors, and wide lands; a man with 'Fifty Knights under him,' and dependent, swiftly obedient multitudes of men. It is a change greater than Napoleon's; so sudden withal. As if one of the Chandos day-drudges had, on awakening some morning, found that *he* overnight was become Duke! Let Samson with his clear-beaming eyes see into that, and discern it if he can. We shall now get the measure of him by a new scale of inches, considerably more rigorous than the former was. For if a noble soul is rendered tenfold beautifuler by victory and prosperity, springing now radiant

as into his own due element and sun-throne; an ignoble one is
rendered tenfold and hundredfold uglier, pitifuler. Whatsoever
vices, whatsoever weaknesses were in the man, the parvenu will
show us them enlarged, as in the solar microscope, into frightful dis-
tortion. Nay, how many mere seminal principles of vice, hitherto
all wholesomely kept latent, may we now see unfolded, as in
the solar hothouse, into growth, into huge universally-conspicuous
luxuriance and development!

But is not this, at any rate, a singular aspect of what political
and social capabilities, nay, let us say, what depth and opulence of
true social vitality, lay in those old barbarous ages, That the fit
Governor could be met with under such disguises, could be recognised and laid hold of under such? Here he is discovered with a
maximum of two shillings in his pocket, and a leather scrip round
his neck; trudging along the highway, his frock-skirts looped over
his arm. They think this is he nevertheless, the true Governor;
and he proves to be so. Brethren, have we no need of discovering
true Governors, but will sham ones forever do for us? These were
absurd superstitious blockheads of Monks; and we are enlightened
Tenpound Franchisers, without taxes on knowledge! Where, I
say, are our superior, are our similar or at all comparable dis-
coveries? We also have eyes, or ought to have; we have hustings,
telescopes; we have lights, link-lights and rush-lights of an enlightened free Press, burning and dancing everywhere, as in a
universal torch-dance; singeing your whiskers as you traverse
the public thoroughfares in town and country. Great souls, true
Governors, go about under all manner of disguises now as then.
Such telescopes, such enlightenment,—and such discovery! How
comes it, I say; how comes it? Is it not lamentable; is it not
even, in some sense, amazing?

Alas, the defect, as we must often urge and again urge, is less
a defect of telescopes than of some eyesight. Those superstitious
blockheads of the Twelfth Century had no telescopes, but they
had still an eye; not ballot-boxes; only reverence for Worth,
abhorrence of Unworth. It is the way with all barbarians. Thus
Mr. Sale informs me, the old Arab Tribes would gather in liveliest
gaudeamus, and sing, and kindle bonfires, and wreathe crowns of
honour, and solemnly thank the gods that, in their Tribe too, a
Poet had shown himself. As indeed they well might; for what
usefuler, I say not nobler and heavenlier thing could the gods,

doing their very kindest, send to any Tribe or Nation, in any time or circumstances? I declare to thee, my afflicted quack-ridden brother, in spite of thy astonishment, it is very lamentable! We English find a Poet, as brave a man as has been made for a hundred years or so anywhere under the Sun; and do we kindle bonfires, or thank the gods? Not at all. We, taking due counsel of it, set the man to gauge ale-barrels in the Burgh of Dumfries; and pique ourselves on our 'patronage of genius.'

Genius, Poet: do we know what these words mean? An inspired Soul once more vouchsafed us, direct from Nature's own great fire-heart, to see the Truth, and speak it, and do it; Nature's own sacred voice heard once more athwart the dreary boundless element of hearsaying and canting, of twaddle and poltroonery, in which the bewildered Earth, nigh perishing, has *lost its way*. Hear once more, ye bewildered benighted mortals; listen once again to a voice from the inner Light-sea and Flame-sea, Nature's and Truth's own heart; know the Fact of your Existence what it is, put away the Cant of it which it is *not;* and knowing, do, and let it be well with you!—

George the Third is Defender of something we call 'the Faith' in those years; George the Third is head charioteer of the Destinies of England, to guide them through the gulf of French Revolutions, American Independences; and Robert Burns is Gauger of ale in Dumfries. It is an Iliad in a nutshell. The physiognomy of a world now verging towards dissolution, reduced now to spasms and death-throes, lies pictured in that one fact,— which astonishes nobody, except at me for being astonished at it. The fruit of long ages of confirmed Valethood, entirely confirmed as into a Law of Nature; cloth-worship and quack-worship: entirely *confirmed* Valethood,—which will have to *un*confirm itself again; God knows, with difficulty enough!—

Abbot Samson had found a Convent all in dilapidation; rain beating through it, material rain and metaphorical, from all quarters of the compass. Willelmus Sacrista sits drinking nightly, and doing mere *tacenda*. Our larders are reduced to leanness, Jew harpies and unclean creatures our purveyors; in our basket is no bread. Old women with their distaffs rush out on a distressed Cellarer in shrill Chartism. 'You cannot stir abroad but Jews and Christians pounce upon you with unsettled bonds;' debts boundless seemingly as the National Debt of England. For four years our new Lord Abbot never went abroad but Jew creditors and Christian, and all manner of creditors, were about him; driving him to very despair. Our Prior is remiss; our Cellarers, officials are remiss; our monks are remiss: what man is not remiss? Front this, Samson, thou alone art there to front it; it is thy task to front and fight this, and to die or kill it. May the Lord have mercy on thee!

To our antiquarian interest in poor Jocelin and his Convent, where the whole aspect of existence, the whole dialect, of thought, of speech, of activity, is so obsolete, strange, long-vanished, there now superadds itself a mild glow of human interest for Abbot Samson; a real pleasure, as at sight of man's work, especially of governing, which is man's highest work, done *well*. Abbot Samson had no experience in governing; had served no apprenticeship to the trade of governing,—alas, only the hardest apprenticeship to that of obeying. He had never in any court given *vadium* or *plegivm*, says Jocelin; hardly ever seen a court, when he was set to preside in one. But it is astonishing, continues Jocelin, how soon he learned the ways of business; and, in all sorts of affairs, became expert beyond others. Of the many persons offering him their service, 'he retained one Knight skilled in taking *vadia* and *plegia*;' and within the year was himself well skilled. Nay, by and by, the Pope appoints him Justiciary in certain causes; the King one of his new Circuit Judges: official Osbert is heard saying, "That Abbot is one of your shrewd ones, *disputator est*; if he go on as he begins, he will cut out every lawyer of us!"[1]

Why not? What is to hinder this Samson from governing? There is in him what far transcends all apprenticeships; in the man himself there exists a model of governing, something to govern by! There exists in him a heart-abhorrence of whatever is incoherent, pusillanimous, unveracious,—that is to say, chaotic, *un*governed; of the Devil, not of God. A man of this kind cannot help governing! He has the living ideal of a governor in him; and the incessant necessity of struggling to unfold the same out of him. Not the Devil or Chaos, for any wages, will he serve; no, this man is the born servant of Another than them. Alas, how little avail all apprenticeships, when there is in your governor himself what we may well call *nothing* to govern by: nothing;— a general gray twilight, looming with shapes of expediencies, parliamentary traditions, division-lists, election-funds, leading-articles; this, with what of vulpine alertness and adroitness soever, is not much!

But indeed what say we, apprenticeship? Had not this Samson served, in his way, a right good apprenticeship to governing; namely, the harshest slave-apprenticeship to obeying! Walk this world with no friend in it but God and St. Edmund, you will either fall into the ditch, or learn a good many things. To learn obeying is the fundamental art of governing. How much would many a Serene Highness have learned, had he travelled through the world with water-jug and empty wallet, *sine omni expensa;* and, at his victorious return, sat down not to newspaper-paragraphs and city-illuminations, but at the foot of St. Edmund's Shrine to shackles and bread-and-water! He that cannot be servant of many, will never be master, true guide and deliverer of many;— that is the meaning of true mastership. Had not the Monk-life extraordinary, 'political capabilities' in it; if not imitable by us, yet enviable? Heavens, had a Duke of Logwood, now rolling sumptuously to his place in the Collective Wisdom, but himself happened to plough daily, at one time, on seven-and-sixpence a week, with no out-door relief,—what a light, unquenchable by logic and statistic and arithmetic, would it have thrown on several things for him!

In all cases, therefore, we will agree with the judicious Mrs. Glass: 'First catch your hare!' First get your man; all is got: he can learn to do all things, from making boots, to decreeing judgments, governing communities; and will do them like a man. Catch your no-man,—alas, have you not caught the terriblest Tartar in the world! Perhaps all the terribler, the quieter and gentler he looks. For the mischief that one blockhead, that every blockhead does, in a world so feracious, teeming with endless results as ours, no ciphering will sum up. The quack bootmaker is considerable; as corn-cutters can testify, and desperate men reduced to buckskin and list-shoes. But the quack priest, quack high-priest, the quack king! Why do not all just citizens rush, half-frantic, to stop him, as they would a conflagration? Surely a just citizen *is* admonished by God and his own Soul, by all silent and articulate voices of this Universe, to do what in *him* lies towards relief of this poor blockhead-quack, and of a world that groans under him. Run swiftly; relieve him,—were it even by extinguishing him! For all things have grown so old, tinder-dry, combustible; and he is more ruinous than conflagration. Sweep him *down*, at least; keep him strictly within the hearth: he will then cease to be conflagration; he will then become useful, more or less, as culinary fire. Fire is the best of servants; but what a master! This poor blockhead too is born for uses: why, elevating him to mastership, will you make a conflagration, a parish-curse or world-curse of him?

CHAPTER X.

GOVERNMENT.

How Abbot Samson, giving his new subjects seriatim the kiss of fatherhood in the St. Edmundsbury chapterhouse, proceeded with cautious energy to set about reforming their disjointed distracted way of life; how he managed with his Fifty rough *Milites* (Feudal Knights), with his lazy Farmers, remiss refractory Monks, with Pope's Legates, Viscounts, Bishops, Kings; how on all sides he laid about him like a man, and putting consequence on premiss, and everywhere the saddle on the right horse, struggled incessantly to educe organic method out of lazily fermenting wreck,—the careful reader will discern, not without true interest, in these pages of Jocelin Boswell. In most antiquarian quaint costume, not of garments alone, but of thought, word, action, outlook and position, the substantial figure of a man with eminent nose, bushy brows and clear-flashing eyes, his russet beard growing daily grayer, is visible, engaged in true governing of men. It is beautiful how the chrysalis governing-soul, shaking off its dusty slough and prison, starts forth winged, a true royal soul! Our new Abbot has a right honest unconscious feeling, without insolence as without fear or flutter, of what he is and what others are. A courage to quell the proudest, an honest pity to encourage the humblest. Withal there is a noble reticence in this Lord Abbot: much vain unreason he hears; lays up without response. He is not there to expect reason and nobleness of others; he is there to give them of his own reason and nobleness. Is he not their servant, as we said, who can suffer from them, and for them; bear the burden their poor spindle-limbs totter and stagger under; and, in virtue

of *being* their servant, govern them, lead them out of weakness
into strength, out of defeat into victory!

One of the first Herculean Labours Abbot Samson undertook,
or the very first, was to institute a strenuous review and radical
reform of his economics. It is the first labour of every governing
man, from *Paterfamilias* to *Dominus Rex*. To get the rain thatched
out from you is the preliminary of whatever farther, in the way of
speculation or of action, you may mean to do. Old Abbot Hugo's
budget, as we saw, had become empty, filled with deficit and wind.
To see his account-books clear, be delivered from those ravening
flights of Jew and Christian creditors, pouncing on him like obscene harpies wherever he showed face, was a necessity for Abbot
Samson.

On the morrow after his instalment he brings in a load of
money-bonds, all duly stamped, sealed with this or the other
Convent Seal : frightful, unmanageable, a bottomless confusion of
Convent finance. There they are ;—but there at least they all
are ; all that shall be of them. Our Lord Abbot demands that all
the official seals in use among us be now produced and delivered
to him. Three-and-thirty seals turn up ; are straightway broken,
and shall seal no more : the Abbot only, and those duly authorised
by him shall seal any bond. There are but two ways of paying
debt : increase of industry in raising income, increase of thrift in
laying it out. With iron energy, in slow but steady undeviating
perseverance, Abbot Samson sets to work in both directions. His
troubles are manifold : cunning *milites*, unjust bailiffs, lazy sockmen, he an inexperienced Abbot ; relaxed lazy monks, not disinclined to mutiny in mass : but continued viligance, rigorous
method, what we call 'the eye of the master,' work wonders. The
clear-beaming eyesight of Abbot Samson, steadfast, severe, all-
penetrating,—it is like *Fiat lux* in that inorganic waste whirlpool ;
penetrates gradually to all nooks, and of the chaos makes a *kosmos*
or ordered world !

He arranges everywhere, struggles unweariedly to arrange, and
place on some intelligible footing, the 'affairs and dues, *res ac
redditus*,' of his dominion. The Lakenheath eels cease to breed
squabbles between human beings ; the penny of *reap-silver* to
explode into the streets the Female Chartism of St. Edmundsbury.
These and innumerable greater things. Wheresoever Disorder
may stand or lie, let it have a care ; here is the man that has
declared war with it, that never will make peace with it. Man is

the Missionary of Order; he is the servant not of the Devil and
Chaos, but of God and the Universe! Let all sluggards and
cowards, remiss, false-spoken, unjust, and otherwise diabolic persons
have a care: this is a dangerous man for them. He has a mild
grave face; a thoughtful sternness, a sorrowful pity: but there is
a terrible flash of anger in him too; lazy monks often have to
murmur, "*Sævit ut lupus,* He rages like a wolf; was not our Dream
true!" 'To repress and hold-in such sudden anger he was continually careful,' and succeeded well:—right, Samson; that it may
become in thee as noble central heat, fruitful, strong, beneficent;
not blaze out, or the seldomest possible blaze out, as wasteful
volcanoism to scorch and consume!

"We must first creep, and gradually learn to walk," had Abbot
Samson said of himself, at starting. In four years he had become
a great walker; striding prosperously along; driving much before
him. In less than four years, says Jocelin, the Convent Debts
were all liquidated: the harpy Jews not only settled with, but
banished, bag and baggage, out of the *Bannaleuca* (Liberties, *Ban-
lieue*) of St. Edmundsbury,—so has the King's Majesty been
persuaded to permit. Farewell to *you,* at any rate; let us, in no
extremity, apply again to you! Armed men march them over the
borders, dismiss them under stern penalties,—sentence of excommunication on all that shall again harbour them here: there were
many dry eyes at their departure.

New life enters everywhere, springs up beneficent, the Incubus
of Debt once rolled away. Samson hastes not; but neither does
he pause to rest. This of the Finance is a lifelong business with
him;—Jocelin's anecdotes are filled to weariness with it. As
indeed to Jocelin it was of very primary interest.

But we have to record also, with a lively satisfaction, that
spiritual rubbish is as little tolerated in Samson's Monastery as
material. With due rigour, Willelmus Sacrista, and his bibations
and *tacenda* are, at the earliest opportunity, softly yet irrevocably
put an end to. The bibations, namely, had to end; even the
building where they used to be carried on was razed from the soil
of St. Edmundsbury, and 'on its place grow rows of beans:'
Willelmus himself, deposed from the Sacristy and all offices, retires
into obscurity, into absolute taciturnity unbroken thenceforth to
this hour. Whether the poor Willelmus did not still, by secret
channels, occasionally get some slight wetting of vinous or alcoholic

liquor,—now grown, in a manner, indispensable to the poor man ? Jocelin hints not; one knows not how to hope, what to hope ! But if he did, it was in silence and darkness; with an ever-present feeling that teetotalism was his only true course.　Drunken dissolute Monks are a class of persons who had better keep out of Abbot Samson's way.　*Sævit ut lupus;* was not the Dream true ! murmured many a Monk.　Nay Ranulf de Glanvill, Justiciary in Chief, took umbrage at him, seeing these strict ways; and watched farther with suspicion: but discerned gradually that there was nothing wrong, that there was much the opposite of wrong.

CHAPTER XI.

THE ABBOT'S WAYS.

ABBOT SAMSON showed no extraordinary favour to the Monks who had been his familiars of old; did not promote them to offices, —*nisi essent idonei,* unless they chanced to be fit men !　Whence great discontent among certain of these, who had contributed to make him Abbot: reproaches, open and secret, of his being ' ungrateful, hard-tempered, unsocial, a Norfolk *barrator* and *paltenerius.*'

Indeed, except it were for *idonei,* ' fit men,' in all kinds, it was hard to say for whom Abbot Samson had much favour.　He loved his kindred well, and tenderly enough acknowledged the poor part of them; with the rich part, who in old days had never acknowledged him, he totally refused to have any business.　But even the former he did not promote into offices; finding none of them *idonei.* ' Some whom he thought suitable he put into situations ' in his own household, or made keepers of his country places: if ' they behaved ill, he dismissed them without hope of return.'　In his promotions, nay almost in his benefits, you would have said there was a certain impartiality.　' The official person who had, by ' Abbot Hugo's order, put the fetters on him at his return from ' Italy, was now supported with food and clothes to the end of his ' days at Abbot Samson's expense.'

Yet he did not forget benefits; far the reverse, when an opportunity

occurred of paying them at his own cost.　How pay them at
the public cost;—how, above all, by *setting fire* to the public, as we
said; clapping 'conflagrations' on the public, which the services
of blockheads, *non-idonei*, intrinsically are!　He was right willing
to remember friends, when it could be done.　Take these instances:
'A certain chaplain who had maintained him at the Schools of
'Paris by the sale of holy water, *quæstu aquæ benedictæ ;*—to this
'good chaplain he did give a vicarage, adequate to the comfortable
'sustenance of him.'　'The Son of Elias too, that is, of old Abbot
'Hugo's Cupbearer, coming to do homage for his Father's land,
'our Lord Abbot said to him in full Court: "I have, for these
'seven years, put off taking thy homage for the land which Abbot
'Hugo gave thy Father, because that gift was to the damage of
'Elmswell, and a questionable one: but now I must profess myself
'overcome; mindful of the kindness thy Father did me when I
'was in bonds; because he sent me a cup of the very wine his
'master had been drinking, and bade me be comforted in God."'

'To Magister Walter, son of Magister William de Dice, who
'wanted the vicarage of Chevington, he answered: "Thy Father
'was Master of the Schools; and when I was an indigent *clericus*,
'he granted me freely and in charity an entrance to his School,
'and opportunity of learning; wherefore I now, for the sake of
'God, grant to thee what thou askest."'　Or lastly, take this
good instance,—and a glimpse, along with it, into long-obsolete
times: 'Two *Milites* of Risby, Willelm and Norman, being ad-
'judged in Court to come under his mercy, *in misericordia ejus*,' for
a certain very considerable fine of twenty shillings, 'he thus
'addressed them publicly on the spot: "When I was a Cloister-
'monk, I was once sent to Durham on business of our Church;
'and coming home again, the dark night caught me at Risby, and
'I had to beg a lodging there.　I went to Dominus Norman's, and
'he gave me a flat refusal.　Going then to Dominus Willelm's,
'and begging hospitality, I was by him honourably received.　The
'twenty shillings therefore of *mercy*, I, without mercy, will exact
'from Dominus Norman; to Dominus Willelm, on the other hand,
'I, with thanks, will wholly remit the said sum."'　Men know not
always to whom they refuse lodgings; men have lodged Angels
unawares!—

It is clear Abbot Samson had a talent; he had learned to judge
better than Lawyers, to manage better than bred Bailiffs:—a
talent shining out indisputable, on whatever side you took him.

'An eloquent man he was,' says Jocelin, 'both in French and
'Latin; but intent more on the substance and method of what was
'to be said, than on the ornamental way of saying it. He could
'read English Manuscripts very elegantly, *elegantissime:* he was
'wont to preach to the people in the English tongue, though
'according to the dialect of Norfolk, where he had been brought
'up; wherefore indeed he had caused a Pulpit to be erected in our
'Church both for ornament of the same, and for the use of his
'audiences.' There preached he, according to the dialect of
Norfolk; a man worth going to hear.

That he was a just clear-hearted man, this, as the basis of all
true talent, is presupposed. How can a man, without clear vision
in his heart first of all, have any clear vision in the head? It is
impossible! Abbot Samson was one of the justest of judges;
insisted on understanding the case to the bottom, and then swiftly
decided without feud or favour. For which reason, indeed, the
Dominus Rex, searching for such men, as for hidden treasure and
healing to his distressed realm, had made him one of the new
Itinerant Judges,—such as continue to this day. "My curse on
that Abbot's court," a suitor was heard imprecating, "*Maledicta sit
curia istius Abbatis,* where neither gold nor silver can help me to
confound my enemy!" And old friendships and all connexions
forgotten, when you go to seek an office from him! "A kinless
loon," as the Scotch said of Cromwell's new judges,—intent on
mere indifferent fair-play!

Eloquence in three languages is good; but it is not the best.
To us, as already hinted, the Lord Abbot's eloquence is less
admirable than his *ineloquence,* his great invaluable 'talent of
silence'! '"*Deus, Deus,*" said the Lord Abbot to me once, when
'he heard the Convent were murmuring at some act of his, "I
'have much need to remember that Dream they had of me, that I
'was to rage among them like a wolf. Above all earthly things I
'dread their driving me to do it. How much do I hold in, and
'wink at; raging and shuddering in my own secret mind, and not
'outwardly at all!" He would boast to me at other times:
'"This and that I have seen, this and that I have heard; yet
'patiently stood it." He had this way, too, which I have never
'seen in any other man, that he affectionately loved many persons
'to whom he never or hardly ever showed a countenance of love.
'Once on my venturing to expostulate with him on the subject, he
'reminded me of Solomon: "Many sons I have; it is not fit that

'I should smile on them." He would suffer faults, damage from
'his servants, and know what he suffered, and not speak of it;
'but I think the reason was, he waited a good time for speaking
'of it, and in a wise way amending it. He intimated, openly in
'chapter to us all, that he would have no eavesdropping : "Let
'none," said he, "come to me secretly accusing another, unless he
'will publicly stand to the same; if he come otherwise, I will
'openly proclaim the name of him. I wish, too, that every Monk
'of you have free access to me, to speak of your needs or grievances
'when you will."'

The kinds of people Abbot Samson liked worst were these three :
'Mendaces, ebriosi, verbosi, Liars, drunkards and wordy or windy
persons ;'—not good kinds, any of them ! He also much condemned 'persons given to murmur at their meat or drink, especially Monks of that disposition.' We remark, from the very first,
his strict anxious order to his servants to provide handsomely for
hospitality, to guard 'above all things that there be no shabbiness
'in the matter of meat and drink; no look of mean parsimony, in
'novitate meâ, at the beginning of my Abbotship;' and to the last
he maintains a due opulence of table and equipment for others;
but he is himself in the highest degree indifferent to all such
things.

'Sweet milk, honey and other naturally sweet kinds of food,
'were what he preferred to eat: but he had this virtue,' says
Jocelin, 'he never changed the dish (ferculum) you set before him,
'be what it might. Once when I, still a novice, happened to be
'waiting table in the refectory, it came into my head' (rogue that I
was !) 'to try if this were true; and I thought I would place
'before him a ferculum that would have displeased any other
'person, the very platter being black and broken. But he, seeing
'it, was as one that saw it not: and now some little delay taking
'place, my heart smote me that I had done this; and so, snatching
'up the platter (discus), I changed both it and its contents for a
'better, and put down that instead ; which emendation he was
'angry at, and rebuked me for,'—the stoical monastic man ! 'For
'the first seven years he had commonly four sorts of dishes on his
'table; afterwards only three, except it might be presents, or
'venison from his own parks, or fishes from his ponds. And if, at
'any time, he had guests living in his house at the request of some
'great person, or of some friend, or had public messengers, or had
'harpers (citharœdos), or any one of that sort, he took the first

'opportunity of shifting to another of his Manor-houses, and so got
'rid of such superfluous individuals,' [1]—very prudently, I think.

As to his parks, of these, in the general repair of buildings,
general improvement and adornment of the St. Edmund Domains,
'he had laid out several, and stocked them with animals, retaining
'a proper huntsman with hounds: and, if any guest of great
'quality were there, our Lord Abbot with his Monks would sit in
'some opening of the woods, and see the dogs run; but he himself
'never meddled with hunting, that I saw.' [2]

'In an opening of the woods;'—for the country was still dark
with wood in those days; and Scotland itself still rustled shaggy
and leafy, like a damp black American Forest, with cleared spots
and spaces here and there. Dryasdust advances several absurd
hypotheses as to the insensible but almost total disappearance of
these woods; the thick wreck of which now lies as *peat*, sometimes
with huge heart-of-oak timber-logs imbedded in it, on many a
height and hollow. The simplest reason doubtless is, that by
increase of husbandry, there was increase of cattle; increase of
hunger for green spring food; and so, more and more, the new
seedlings got yearly eaten out in April; and the old trees, having
only a certain length of life in them, died gradually, no man
heeding it, and disappeared into *peat*.

A sorrowful waste of noble wood and umbrage! Yes,—but a
very common one; the course of most things in this world. Monachism itself, so rich and fruitful once, is now all rotted into *peat*;
lies sleek and buried,—and a most feeble bog-grass of Dilettantism
all the crop we reap from it! That also was frightful waste;
perhaps among the saddest our England ever saw. Why will
men destroy noble Forests, even when in part a nuisance, in such
reckless manner; turning loose four-footed cattle and Henry-the-
Eighths into them! The fifth part of our English soil, Dryasdust
computes, lay consecrated to 'spiritual uses,' better or worse;
solemnly set apart to foster spiritual growth and culture of the
soul, by the methods then known: and now—it too, like the four-
fifths, fosters what? Gentle shepherd, tell me what!

[1] *Jocelini Chronica*, p. 31.   [2] Ibid. p. 21.

CHAPTER XII.

THE ABBOT'S TROUBLES.

THE troubles of Abbot Samson, as he went along in this abstemious, reticent, rigorous way, were more than tongue can tell. The Abbot's mitre once set on his head, he knew rest no more. Double, double toil and trouble; that is the life of all governors that really govern: not the spoil of victory, only the glorious toil of battle can be theirs. Abbot Samson found all men more or less headstrong, irrational, prone to disorder; continually threatening to prove *un*governable.

His lazy Monks gave him most trouble. 'My heart is tortured,' said he, 'till we get out of debt, *cor meum cruciatum est.*' Your heart, indeed;—but not altogether ours! By no devisable method, or none of three or four that he devised, could Abbot Samson get these Monks of his to keep their accounts straight; but always, do as he might, the Cellerarius at the end of the term is in a coil, in a flat deficit,—verging again towards debt and Jews. The Lord Abbot at last declares sternly he will keep our accounts too himself; will appoint an officer of his own to see our Cellerarius keep them. Murmurs thereupon among us: Was the like ever heard? Our Cellerarius a cipher; the very Townsfolk know it: *subsannatio et derisio sumus*, we have become a laughingstock to mankind. The Norfolk barrator and paltener!

And consider, if the Abbot found such difficulty in the mere economic department, how much in more complex ones, in spiritual ones perhaps! He wears a stern calm face; raging and gnashing teeth, *fremens* and *frendens*, many times, in the secret of his mind. Withal, however, there is a noble slow perseverance in him; a strength of 'subdued rage' calculated to subdue most things: always, in the long-run, he contrives to gain his point.

Murmurs from the Monks, meanwhile, cannot fail; ever deeper murmurs, new grudges accumulating. At one time, on slight cause, some drop making the cup run over, they burst into open mutiny: the Cellarer will not obey, prefers arrest on bread-and-

water to obeying; the Monks thereupon strike work; refuse to do
the regular chanting of the day, at least the younger part of them
with loud clamour and uproar refuse :—Abbot Samson has withdrawn to another residence, acting only by messengers : the awful
report circulates through St. Edmundsbury that the Abbot is in
danger of being murdered by the Monks with their knives! How
wilt thou appease this, Abbot Samson! Return; for the Monastery
seems near catching fire!

Abbot Samson returns; sits in his *Talamus,* or inner room,
hurls out a bolt or two of excommunication : lo, one disobedient
Monk sits in limbo, excommunicated, with foot-shackles on him,
all day; and three more our Abbot has gyved 'with the lesser
sentence, to strike fear into the others'! Let the others think
with whom they have to do. The others think; and fear enters
into them. 'On the morrow morning we decide on humbling
'ourselves before the Abbot, by word and gesture, in order to
'mitigate his mind. And so accordingly was done. He, on the
'other side, replying with much humility, yet always alleging his
'own justice and turning the blame on us, when he saw that we
'were conquered, became himself conquered. And bursting into
'tears, *perfusus lachrymis,* he swore that he had never grieved so
'much for anything in the world as for this, first on his own
'account, and then secondly and chiefly for the public scandal
'which had gone abroad, that St. Edmund's Monks were going
'to kill their Abbot. And when he had narrated how he went
'away on purpose till his anger should cool, repeating this word
'of the philosopher, "I would have taken vengeance on thee, had
'not I been angry," he arose weeping, and embraced each and all
'of us with the kiss of peace. He wept; we all wept :'[1]—what a
picture! Behave better, ye remiss Monks, and thank Heaven
for such an Abbot; or know at least that ye must and shall obey
him.

Worn down in this manner, with incessant toil and tribulation,
Abbot Samson had a sore time of it; his grizzled hair and beard
grew daily grayer. Those Jews, in the first four years, had 'visibly
emaciated him:' Time, Jews, and the task of Governing, will
make a man's beard very gray! 'In twelve years,' says Jocelin,
'our Lord Abbot had grown wholly white as snow, *totus efficitur*
'*albus sicut nix.*' White atop, like the granite mountains :—

[1] *Jocelini Chronica,* p. 85.

but his clear-beaming eyes still look out, in their stern clearness, in their sorrow and pity; the heart within him remains unconquered.

Nay sometimes there are gleams of hilarity too; little snatches of encouragement granted even to a Governor. 'Once my Lord 'Abbot and I, coming down from London through the Forest, 'I inquired of an old woman whom we came up to, Whose wood 'this was, and of what manor; who the master, who the keeper?' —All this I knew very well beforehand, and my Lord Abbot too, Bozzy that I was! But 'the old woman answered, The wood 'belonged to the new Abbot of St. Edmund's, was of the manor 'of Harlow, and the keeper of it was one Arnald. How did he 'behave to the people of the manor? I asked farther. She 'answered that he used to be a devil incarnate, *dæmon vivus*, an 'enemy of God, and flayer of the peasants' skins,'—skinning them like live eels, as the manner of some is: 'but that now he dreads 'the new Abbot, knowing him to be a wise and sharp man, and 'so treats the people reasonably, *tractat homines pacifice.*' Whereat the Lord Abbot *factus est hilaris,*—could not but take a triumphant laugh for himself; and determines to leave that Harlow manor yet unmeddled with, for a while.[2]

A brave man, strenuously fighting, fails not of a little triumph now and then, to keep him in heart. Everywhere we try at least to give the adversary as good as he brings; and, with swift force or slow watchful manœuvre, extinguish this and the other solecism, leave one solecism less in God's Creation; and so *proceed* with our battle, not slacken or surrender in it! The Fifty feudal Knights, for example, were of unjust greedy temper, and cheated us, in the Installation-day, of ten knights'-fees;—but they know now whether that has profited them aught, and I Jocelin know. Our Lord Abbot for the moment had to endure it, and say nothing; but he watched his time.

Look also how my Lord of Clare, coming to claim his *undue* 'debt' in the Court of Witham, with barons and apparatus, gets a Roland for his Oliver! Jocelin shall report: 'The Earl, crowded 'round (*constipatus*) with many barons and men-at-arms, Earl 'Alberic and others standing by him, said, "That his bailiffs had 'given him to understand they were wont annually to receive for 'his behoof, from the Hundred of Risebridge and the bailiffs 'thereof, a sum of five shillings, which sum was now unjustly held 'back;" and he alleged farther that his predecessors had been

[2] *Jocelini Chronica,* p. 24.

'infeft, at the Conquest, in the lands of Alfric son of Wisgar, who
'was Lord of that Hundred, as may be read in Doomsday Book by
'all persons.—The Abbot, reflecting for a moment, without stirring
'from his place, made answer : "A wonderful deficit, my Lord Earl,
'this that thou mentionest ! King Edward gave to St. Edmund
'that entire Hundred, and confirmed the same with his Charter ;
'nor is there any mention there of those five shillings. It will
'behove thee to say, for what service, or on what ground, thou
'exactest those five shillings." Whereupon the Earl, consulting
'with his followers, replied, That he had to carry the Banner of
'St. Edmund in war-time, and for this duty the five shillings were
'his. To which the Abbot : "Certainly, it seems inglorious, if so
'great a man, Earl of Clare no less, receive so small a gift for
'such a service. To the Abbot of St. Edmund's it is no unbear-
'able burden to give five shillings. But Roger Earl Bigot holds
'himself duly seised, and asserts that he by such seisin has the
'office of carrying St. Edmund's Banner ; and he did carry it when
'the Earl of Leicester and his Flemings were beaten at Fornham.
'Then again Thomas de Mendham says that the right is his.
'When you have made out with one another, that this right is
'thine, come then and claim the five shillings, and I will promptly
'pay them !" Whereupon the Earl said, He would speak with
'Earl Roger his relative; and so the matter *cepit dilationem*,' and
lies undecided to the end of the world. Abbot Samson answers
by word or act, in this or the like pregnant manner, having justice
on his side, innumerable persons : Pope's Legates, King's Viscounts,
Canterbury Archbishops, Cellarers, *Sochemanni;*—and leaves
many a solecism extinguished.

On the whole, however, it is and remains sore work. 'One
'time, during my chaplaincy, I ventured to say to him : "*Domine*,
'I heard thee, this night after matins, wakeful, and sighing deeply,
'*valde suspirantem*, contrary to thy usual wont." He answered :
'" No wonder. Thou, son Jocelin, sharest in my good things, in
'food and drink, in riding and suchlike ; but thou little thinkest
'concerning the management of House and Family, the various and
'arduous businesses of the Pastoral Care, which harass me, and
'make my soul to sigh and be anxious." Whereto I, lifting up my
'hands to Heaven : "From such anxiety, Omnipotent merciful
'Lord deliver me !"—I have heard the Abbot say, If he had been
'as he was before he became a Monk, and could have anywhere
'got five or six marcs of income,' some three-pound ten of yearly

'revenue, whereby to support himself in the schools, he would
'never have been Monk nor Abbot. Another time he said with
'an oath, If he had known what a business it was to govern the
'Abbey, he would rather have been Almoner, how much rather
'Keeper of the Books, than Abbot and Lord. That latter office
'he said he had always longed for, beyond any other. *Quis*
'*talia crederet?*' concludes Jocelin, 'Who can believe such things?'

Three-pound ten, and a life of Literature, especially of quiet
Literature, without copyright, or world-celebrity of literary-
gazettes,—yes, thou brave Abbot Samson, for thyself it had been
better, easier, perhaps also nobler! But then, for thy disobedient
Monks, unjust Viscounts; for a Domain of St. Edmund overgrown
with Solecisms, human and other, it had not been so well. Nay
neither could *thy* Literature, never so quiet, have been easy.
Literature, when noble, is not easy; but only when ignoble.
Literature too is a quarrel, and internecine duel, with the whole
World of Darkness that lies without one and within one;—rather
a hard fight at times, even with the three-pound ten secure. Thou,
there where thou art, wrestle and duel along, cheerfully to the end;
and make no remarks!

CHAPTER XIII.

IN PARLIAMENT.

OF Abbot Samson's public business we say little, though that
also was great. He had to judge the people as Justice Errant,
to decide in weighty arbitrations and public controversies; to
equip his *milites*, send them duly in war-time to the King;—
strive every way that the Commonweal, in his quarter of it, take
no damage.

Once, in the confused days of Lackland's usurpation, while
Cœur-de-Lion was away, our brave Abbot took helmet himself,
having first excommunicated all that should favour Lackland;
and led his men in person to the siege of *Windleshora*, what we
now call Windsor; where Lackland had entrenched himself, the
centre of infinite confusions; some Reform Bill, then as now, being

greatly needed. There did Abbot Samson 'fight the battle of reform,'—with other ammunition, one hopes, than 'tremendous cheering' and suchlike! For these things he was called 'the magnanimous Abbot.'

He also attended duly in his place in Parliament *de arduis regni;* attended especially, as in *arduissimo,* when 'the news 'reached London that King Richard was a captive in Germany.' Here 'while all the barons sat to consult,' and many of them looked blank enough, 'the Abbot started forth, *prosiliit coram* '*omnibus,* in his place in Parliament, and said, That *he* was ready 'to go and seek his Lord the King, either clandestinely by sub- 'terfuge (*in tapinagio*), or by any other method; and search till 'he found him, and got certain notice of him; he for one! By 'which word,' says Jocelin, 'he acquired great praise for himself,' —unfeigned commendation from the Able Editors of that age.

By which word;—and also by which *deed:* for the Abbot actually went 'with rich gifts to the King in Germany;'[1] Usurper Lackland being first rooted out from Windsor, and the King's peace somewhat settled.

As to these 'rich gifts,' however, we have to note one thing: In all England, as appeared to the Collective Wisdom, there was not like to be treasure enough for ransoming King Richard; in which extremity certain Lords of the Treasury, *Justiciarii ad Scaccarium,* suggested that St. Edmund's Shrine, covered with thick gold, was still untouched. Could not it, in this extremity, be peeled off, at least in part; under condition, of course, of its being replaced when times mended? The Abbot, starting plumb up, *se erigens,* answered: "Know ye for certain, that I will in nowise do this thing; nor is there any man who could force me to consent thereto. But I will open the doors of the Church: Let him that likes enter; let him that dares come forward!" Emphatic words, which created a sensation round the woolsack. For the Justiciaries of the *Scaccarium* answered, 'with oaths, each for himself: "I won't come 'forward, for my share; nor will I, nor I! The distant and 'absent who offended him, Saint Edmund has been known to 'punish fearfully; much more will he those close by, who lay 'violent hands on his coat, and would strip it off!" These things 'being said, the Shrine was not meddled with, nor any ransom 'levied for it.'

[1] *Jocelini Chronica*, pp. 39, 40.   [2] Ibid. p. 71.

For Lords of the Treasury have in all times their impassable limits, be it by 'force of public opinion' or otherwise; and in those days a heavenly Awe overshadowed and encompassed, as it still ought and must, all earthly Business whatsoever.

CHAPTER XIV.

HENRY OF ESSEX.

Of St. Edmund's fearful avengements have they not the remarkablest instance still before their eyes? He that will go to Reading Monastery may find there, now tonsured into a mournful penitent Monk, the once proud Henry Earl of Essex; and discern how St. Edmund punishes terribly, yet with mercy! This Narrative is too significant to be omitted as a document of the Time. Our Lord Abbot, once on a visit at Reading, heard the particulars from Henry's own mouth; and thereupon charged one of his monks to write it down;—as accordingly the Monk has done, in ambitious rhetorical Latin; inserting the same, as episode, among Jocelin's garrulous leaves. Read it here; with ancient yet with modern eyes.

Henry Earl of Essex, standard-bearer of England, had high places and emoluments; had a haughty high soul, yet with various flaws, or rather with one many-branched flaw and crack, running through the texture of it. For example, did he not treat Gilbert de Cereville in the most shocking manner? He cast Gilbert into prison; and, with chains and slow torments, wore the life out of him there. And Gilbert's crime was understood to be only that of innocent Joseph: the Lady Essex was a Potiphar's Wife, and had accused poor Gilbert! Other cracks, and branches of that widespread flaw in the Standard-bearer's soul we could point out: but indeed the main stem and trunk of all is too visible in this, That he had no right reverence for the Heavenly in Man,—that far from showing due reverence to St. Edmund, he did not even show him common justice. While others in the Eastern Counties were adorning and enlarging with rich gifts St. Edmund's resting-place,

which had become a city of refuge for many things, this Earl of
Essex flatly defrauded him, by violence or quirk of law, of five
shillings yearly, and converted said sum to his own poor uses! Nay,
in another case of litigation, the unjust Standard-bearer, for his
own profit, asserting that the cause belonged not to St. Edmund's
Court, but to *his* in Lailand Hundred, 'involved us in travellings
'and innumerable expenses, vexing the servants of St. Edmund for
'a long tract of time.' In short, he is without reverence for the
Heavenly, this Standard-bearer; reveres only the Earthly, Gold-
coined; and has a most morbid lamentable flaw in the texture of
him. It cannot come to good.

Accordingly, the same flaw, or St.-Vitus' *tic*, manifests itself ere
long in another way. In the year 1157, he went with his Standard
to attend King Henry, our blessed Sovereign (whom *we* saw afterwards at Waltham), in his War with the Welsh. A somewhat
disastrous War; in which while King Henry and his force were
struggling to retreat Parthian-like, endless clouds of exasperated
Welshmen hemming them in, and now we had come to the 'difficult
pass of Coleshill,' and as it were to the nick of destruction,—Henry
Earl of Essex shrieks out on a sudden (blinded doubtless by his
inner flaw, or 'evil genius' as some name it), That King Henry is
killed, That all is lost,—and flings down his Standard to shift for
itself there! And, certainly enough, all *had* been lost, had all men
been as he;—had not brave men, without such miserable jerking
tic-douloureux in the souls of them, come dashing up, with blazing
swords and looks, and asserted, That nothing was lost yet, that all
must be regained yet. In this manner King Henry and his force
got safely retreated, Parthian-like, from the pass of Coleshill and
the Welsh War.[1] But, once home again, Earl Robert de Montfort,
a kinsman of this Standard-bearer's, rises up in the King's Assembly
to declare openly that such a man is unfit for bearing English
Standards, being in fact either a special traitor, or something almost
worse, a coward namely, or universal traitor. Wager of Battle in
consequence; solemn Duel, by the King's appointment, 'in a certain
'Island of the Thames-stream at Reading, *apud Radingas*, short
'way from the Abbey there.' King, Peers, and an immense
multitude of people, on such scaffoldings and heights as they can
come at, are gathered round, to see what issue the business will
take. The business takes this bad issue, in our Monk's own words
faithfully rendered:

[1] See Lyttelton's *Henry II.* ii. 384.

'And it came to pass, while Robert de Montfort thundered on
'him manfully (*viriliter intonásset*) with hard and frequent strokes,
'and a valiant beginning promised the fruit of victory, Henry of
'Essex, rather giving way, glanced round on all sides; and lo, at
'the rim of the horizon, on the confines of the River and land, he
'discerned the glorious King and Martyr Edmund, in shining
'armour, and as if hovering in the air; looking towards him with
'severe countenance, nodding his head with a mien and motion of
'austere anger. At St. Edmund's hand there stood also another
'Knight, Gilbert de Cereville, whose armour was not so splendid,
'whose stature was less gigantic; casting vengeful looks at him.
'This he seeing with his eyes, remembered that old crime brings
'new shame. And now wholly desperate, and changing reason
'into violence, he took the part of one blindly attacking, not
'skilfully defending. Who while he struck fiercely was more
'fiercely struck; and so, in short, fell down vanquished, and it was
'thought slain. As he lay there for dead, his kinsmen, Magnates
'of England, besought the King, that the Monks of Reading might
'have leave to bury him. However, he proved not to be dead, but
'got well again among them; and now, with recovered health,
'assuming the Regular Habit, he strove to wipe out the stain of
'his former life, to cleanse the long week of his dissolute history
'by at least a purifying sabbath, and cultivate the studies of Virtue
'into fruits of eternal Felicity.' [2]

Thus does the Conscience of man project itself athwart whatsoever of knowledge or surmise, of imagination, understanding,
faculty, acquirement, or natural disposition, he has in him; and,
like light through coloured glass, paint strange pictures 'on the
rim of the horizon' and elsewhere! Truly, this same 'sense of the
Infinite nature of Duty' is the central part of all with us; a ray
as of Eternity and Immortality, immured in dusky many-coloured
Time, and its deaths and births. Your 'coloured glass' varies so
much from century to century;—and, in certain money-making,
game-preserving centuries, it gets so terribly opaque! Not a
Heaven with cherubim surrounds you then, but a kind of vacant
leaden-coloured Hell. One day it will again cease to be *opaque*,
this 'coloured glass.' Nay, may it not become at once translucent and *uncoloured*? Painting no Pictures more for us, but
only the everlasting Azure itself? That will be a right glorious
consummation!—

[2] *Jocelini Chronica*, p. 52.

Saint Edmund from the horizon's edge, in shining armour, threatening the misdoer in his hour of extreme need: it is beautiful, it is great and true. So old, yet so modern, actual; true yet for every one of us, as for Henry the Earl and Monk! A glimpse as of the Deepest in Man's Destiny, which is the same for all times and ages. Yes, Henry my brother, there in thy extreme need, thy soul is *lamed;* and behold thou canst not so much as fight! For Justice and Reverence *are* the everlasting central Law of this Universe; and to forget them, and have all the Universe against one, God and one's own Self for enemies, and only the Devil and the Dragons for friends, is not that a 'lameness' like few? That some shining armed St. Edmund hang minatory on thy horizon, that infinite sulphur-lakes hang minatory, or do not now hang,— this alters no whit the eternal fact of the thing. I say, thy soul is lamed, and the God and all Godlike in it marred: lamed, paralytic, tending towards baleful eternal death, whether thou know it or not;—nay hadst thou never known it, that surely had been worst of all!—

Thus, at any rate, by the heavenly Awe that overshadows earthly Business, does Samson, readily in those days, save St. Edmund's Shrine, and innumerable still more precious things.

CHAPTER XV.

PRACTICAL-DEVOTIONAL.

HERE indeed, by rule of antagonisms, may be the place to mention that, after King Richard's return, there was a liberty of tourneying given to the fighting-men of England: that a Tournament was proclaimed in the Abbot's domain, 'between Thetford and St. Edmundsbury,'—perhaps in the Euston region, on Fakenham Heights, midway between these two localities: that it was publicly prohibited by our Lord Abbot; and nevertheless was held in spite of him,—and by the parties, as would seem, considered 'a gentle and free passage of arms.'

Nay, next year, there came to the same spot four-and-twenty young men, sons of Nobles, for another passage of arms; who

having completed the same, all rode into St. Edmundsbury to
lodge for the night. Here is modesty! Our Lord Abbot, being
instructed of it, ordered the Gates to be closed; the whole party
shut in. The morrow was the Vigil of the Apostles Peter and
Paul; no outgate on the morrow. Giving their promise not to
depart without permission, those four-and-twenty young bloods
dieted all that day (*manducaverunt*) with the Lord Abbot, waiting
for trial on the morrow. ' But after dinner,'—mark it, posterity!—
'the Lord Abbot retiring into his *Talamus*, they all started up,
' and began carolling and singing (*carolare et cantare*); sending into
' the Town for wine; drinking, and afterwards howling (*ululantes*);
' —totally depriving the Abbot and Convent of their afternoon's
' nap; doing all this in derision of the Lord Abbot, and spending
' in such fashion the whole day till evening, nor would they desist
' at the Lord Abbot's order! Night coming on, they broke the
' bolts of the Town-Gates, and went off by violence!' [1] Was the
like ever heard of? The roysterous young dogs; carolling, howling,
breaking the Lord Abbot's sleep,—after that sinful chivalry cock-
fight of theirs! They too are a feature of distant centuries, as of
near ones. St. Edmund on the edge of your horizon, or whatever
else there, young scamps, in the dandy state, whether cased in iron
or in whalebone, begin to caper and carol on the green Earth! Our
Lord Abbot excommunicated most of them; and they gradually
came in for repentance.

Excommunication is a great recipe with our Lord Abbot; the
prevailing purifier in those ages. Thus when the Townsfolk and
Monks' menials quarrelled once at the Christmas Mysteries in St.
Edmund's Churchyard, and ' from words it came to cuffs, and from
cuffs to cutting and the effusion of blood,'—our Lord Abbot
excommunicates sixty of the rioters, with bell, book and candle
(*accensis candelis*), at one stroke.[2] Whereupon they all come suppliant, indeed nearly naked, ' nothing on but their breeches, *omnino*
' *nudi præter femoralia*, and prostrate themselves at the Church-
' door.' Figure that!

In fact, by excommunication or persuasion, by impetuosity of
driving or adroitness in leading, this Abbot, it is now becoming
plain everywhere, is a man that generally remains master at last.
He tempers his medicine to the malady, now hot, now cool;
prudent though fiery, an eminently practical man. Nay sometimes
in his adroit practice there are swift turns almost of a surprising

---

[1] *Jocelini Chronica*, p. 40.   [2] Ibid. p. 68.

nature! Once, for example, it chanced that Geoffrey Riddell Bishop of Ely, a Prelate rather troublesome to our Abbot, made a request of him for timber from his woods towards certain edifices going on at Glemsford. The Abbot, a great builder himself, disliked the request; could not, however, give it a negative. While he lay, therefore, at his Manorhouse of Melford not long after, there comes to him one of the Lord Bishop's men or monks, with a message from his Lordship, "That he now begged permission to cut down the requisite trees in Elmswell Wood,"— so said the monk: Elms*well*, where there are no trees but scrubs and shrubs, instead of Elm*set*, our true *nemus* and high-towering oak-wood, here on Melford Manor! Elmswell? The Lord Abbot, in surprise, inquires privily of Richard his Forester; Richard answers that my Lord of Ely has already had his *carpentarii* in Elm*set*, and marked out for his own use all the best trees in the compass of it. Abbot Samson thereupon answers the monk: "Elmswell? Yes surely, be it as my Lord Bishop wishes." The successful monk, on the morrow morning, hastens home to Ely; but, on the morrow morning, 'directly after mass,' Abbot Samson too was busy! The successful monk, arriving at Ely, is rated for a goose and an owl; is ordered back to say that Elmset was the place meant. Alas, on arriving at Elmset, he finds the Bishop's trees, they 'and a hundred more,' all felled and piled, and the stamp of St. Edmund's Monastery burnt into them,—for roofing of the great tower we are building there! Your importunate Bishop must seek wood for Glemsford edifices in some other *nemus* than this. A practical Abbot!

We said withal there was a terrible flash of anger in him: witness his address to old Herbert the Dean, who in a too thrifty manner has erected a windmill for himself on his glebe-lands at Haberdon. On the morrow, after mass, our Lord Abbot orders the Cellerarius to send off his carpenters to demolish the said structure *brevi manu*, and lay up the wood in safe keeping. Old Dean Herbert, hearing what was toward, comes tottering along hither, to plead humbly for himself and his mill. The Abbot answers: "I am obliged to thee as if thou hadst cut off both my feet! By God's face, *per os Dei*, I will not eat bread till that fabric be torn in pieces. Thou art an old man, and shouldst have known that neither the King nor his Justiciary dare change aught within the Liberties without consent of Abbot and Convent: and thou hast presumed on such a thing? I tell thee, it will *not* be without damage to my mills; for the Townsfolk will go to thy mill, and grind their corn (*bladum suum*) at their own good pleasure; nor can I hinder them, since they are free men. I will allow no new mills on such principle. Away, away; before thou gettest home again, thou shalt see what thy mill has grown to!"[3]—The very reverend the old Dean totters home again, in all haste; tears the mill in pieces by his own *carpentarii*, to save at least the timber; and Abbot Samson's workmen, coming up, find the ground already clear of it.

Easy to bully-down poor old rural Deans, and blow their wind-mills away: but who is the man that dare abide King Richard's anger; cross the Lion in his path, and take him by the whiskers! Abbot Samson too; he is that man, with justice on his side. The case was this. Adam de Cokefield, one of the chief feudatories of St. Edmund, and a principal man in the Eastern Counties, died, leaving large possessions, and for heiress a daughter of three months; who by clear law, as all men know, became thus Abbot Samson's ward; whom accordingly he proceeded to dispose of to such person as seemed fittest. But now King Richard has another person in view, to whom the little ward and her great possessions were a suitable thing. He, by letter, requests that Abbot Samson will have the goodness to give her to this person. Abbot Samson, with deep humility, replies that she is already given. New letters from Richard, of severer tenor; answered with new deep humilities, with gifts and entreaties, with no promise of obedience. King Richard's ire is kindled; messengers arrive at St. Edmundsbury, with emphatic message to obey or tremble! Abbot Samson, wisely silent as to the King's threats, makes answer: "The King can send if he will, and seize the ward: force and power he has to do his pleasure, and abolish the whole Abbey. But I, for my part, never can be bent to wish this that he seeks, nor shall it by me be ever done. For there is danger lest such things be made a precedent of, to the prejudice of my successors. *Videat Altissimus,* Let the Most High look on it. Whatsoever thing shall befall I will patiently endure."

Such was Abbot Samson's deliberate decision. Why not? Cœur-de-Lion is very dreadful, but not the dreadfulest. *Videat Altissimus.* I reverence Cœur-de-Lion to the marrow of my bones, and will in all right things be *homo suus;* but it is not, properly

---

[3] *Jocelini Chronica,* p. 43.

speaking, with terror, with any fear at all. On the whole, have I not looked on the face of 'Satan with outspread wings;' steadily into Hell-fire these seven-and-forty years;—and was not melted into terror even at that, such the Lord's goodness to me? Cœur-de-Lion!

Richard swore tornado oaths, worse than our armies in Flanders, To be revenged on that proud Priest. But in the end he discovered that the Priest was right; and forgave him, and even loved him. 'King Richard wrote, soon after, to Abbot Samson, That he 'wanted one or two of the St. Edmundsbury dogs, which he 'heard were good.' Abbot Samson sent him dogs of the best; Richard replied by the present of a ring, which Pope Innocent the Third had given him. Thou brave Richard, thou brave Samson! Richard too, I suppose, 'loved a man,' and knew one when he saw him.

No one will accuse our Lord Abbot of wanting worldly wisdom, due interest in worldly things. A skilful man; full of cunning insight, lively interests; always discerning the road to his object, be it circuit, be it short-cut, and victoriously travelling forward thereon. Nay rather it might seem, from Jocelin's Narrative, as if he had his eye all but exclusively directed on terrestrial matters, and was much too secular for a devout man. But this too, if we examine it, was right. For it is *in* the world that a man, devout or other, has his life to lead, his work waiting to be done. The basis of Abbot Samson's, we shall discover, was truly religion, after all. Returning from his dusty pilgrimage, with such welcome as we saw, 'he sat down at the foot of St. Edmund's Shrine.' Not a talking theory, that; no, a silent practice: Thou, St. Edmund, with what lies in thee, thou now must help me, or none will!

This also is a significant fact: the zealous interest our Abbot took in the Crusades. To all noble Christian hearts of that era, what earthly enterprise so noble? 'When Henry II., having 'taken the cross, came to St. Edmund's, to pay his devotions 'before setting out, the Abbot secretly made for himself a cross 'of linen cloth: and, holding this in one hand and a threaded 'needle in the other, asked leave of the King to assume it.' The King could not spare Samson out of England;—the King himself indeed never went. But the Abbot's eye was set on the Holy Sepulchre, as on the spot of this Earth where the true cause of Heaven was deciding itself. 'At the retaking of Jerusalem by the

A A

'Pagans, Abbot Samson put on a cilice and hair-shirt, and wore
'under-garments of hair-cloth ever after; he abstained also from
'flesh and flesh-meats (*carne et carneis*) thenceforth to the end of
'his life.' Like a dark cloud eclipsing the hopes of Christendom,
those tidings cast their shadow over St. Edmundsbury too : Shall
Samson Abbas take pleasure while Christ's Tomb is in the hands
of the Infidel ? Samson, in pain of body, shall daily be reminded
of it, daily be admonished to grieve for it.

The great antique heart: how like a child's in its simplicity,
like a man's in its earnest solemnity and depth ! Heaven lies over
him wheresoever he goes or stands on the Earth; making all the
Earth a mystic Temple to him, the Earth's business all a kind of
worship. Glimpses of bright creatures flash in the common sunlight; angels yet hover doing God's messages among men: that
rainbow was set in the clouds by the hand of God! Wonder,
miracle encompass the man; he lives in an element of miracle;
Heaven's splendour over his head, Hell's darkness under his feet.
A great Law of Duty, high as these two Infinitudes, dwarfing all
else, annihilating all else, — making royal Richard as small as
peasant Samson, smaller if need be !—The 'imaginative faculties ?'
'Rude poetic ages ?' The 'primeval poetic element ?' Oh, for
God's sake, good reader, talk no more of all that ! It was not a
Dilettantism this of Abbot Samson. It was a Reality, and it is
one. The garment only of it is dead; the essence of it lives
through all Time and all Eternity !—

And truly, as we said above, is not this comparative silence of
Abbot Samson as to his religion precisely the healthiest sign of
him and of it ? 'The Unconscious is the alone Complete.' Abbot
Samson all along a busy working man, as all men are bound to be,
his religion, his worship was like his daily bread to him;—which
he did not take the trouble to talk much about; which he merely
ate at stated intervals, and lived and did his work upon ! This is
Abbot Samson's Catholicism of the Twelfth Century;—something
like the *Ism* of all true men in all true centuries, I fancy ! Alas,
compared with any of the *Isms* current in these poor days, what
a thing ! Compared with the respectablest, morbid, struggling
Methodism, never so earnest; with the respectablest, ghastly,
dead or galvanised Dilettantism, never so spasmodic !

Methodism with its eye forever turned on its own navel; asking
itself with torturing anxiety of Hope and Fear, "Am I right ? am

I wrong? Shall I be saved? shall I not be damned?"—what is this, at bottom, but a new phasis of *Egoism,* stretched out into the Infinite; not always the heavenlier for its infinitude! Brother, so soon as possible, endeavour to rise above all that. "Thou *art* wrong; thou art like to be damned:" consider that as the fact, reconcile thyself even to that, if thou be a man;—then first is the devouring Universe subdued under thee, and from the black murk of midnight and noise of greedy Acheron, dawn as of an everlasting morning, how far above all Hope and all Fear, springs for thee, enlightening thy steep path, awakening in thy heart celestial Memnon's music!

But of our Dilettantisms, and galvanised Dilettantisms; of Puseyism—O Heavens, what shall we say of Puseyism, in comparison to Twelfth-Century Catholicism? Little or nothing; for indeed it is a matter to strike one dumb.

> The Builder of this Universe was wise,
> He plann'd all souls, all systems, planets, particles:
> The Plan He shap'd all Worlds and Æons by,
> Was—Heavens!—Was thy small Nine-and-thirty Articles?

That certain human souls, living on this practical Earth, should think to save themselves and a ruined world by noisy theoretic demonstrations and laudations of *the* Church, instead of some unnoisy, unconscious, but *practical,* total, heart-and-soul demonstration of *a* Church: this, in the circle of revolving ages, this also was a thing we were to see. A kind of penultimate thing, precursor of very strange consummations; last thing but one? If there is no atmosphere, what will it serve a man to demonstrate the excellence of lungs? How much profitabler, when you can, like Abbot Samson, breathe; and go along your way!

CHAPTER XVI.

ST. EDMUND.

ABBOT SAMSON built many useful, many pious edifices; human dwellings, churches, church-steeples, barns;—all fallen now and vanished, but useful while they stood. He built and endowed 'the Hospital of Babwell;' built 'fit houses for the St. Edmundsbury Schools.' Many are the roofs once 'thatched with reeds' which he 'caused to be covered with tiles;' or if they were churches, probably 'with lead.' For all ruinous incomplete things, buildings or other, were an eye-sorrow to the man. We saw his 'great tower of St. Edmund's;' or at least the roof-timbers of it, lying cut and stamped in Elmset Wood. To change combustible decaying reed-thatch into tile or lead; and material, still more, moral wreck into rain-tight order, what a comfort to Samson!

One of the things he could not in any wise but rebuild was the great Altar, aloft on which stood the Shrine itself; the great Altar, which had been damaged by fire, by the careless rubbish and careless candle of two somnolent Monks, one night,—the Shrine escaping almost as if by miracle! Abbot Samson read his Monks a severe lecture: "A Dream one of us had, that he saw St. Edmund naked and in lamentable plight. Know ye the interpretation of that Dream? St. Edmund proclaims himself naked, because ye defraud the naked Poor of your old clothes, and give with reluctance what ye are bound to give them of meat and drink: the idleness moreover and negligence of the Sacristan and his people is too evident from the late misfortune by fire. Well might our Holy Martyr seem to lie cast out from his Shrine, and say with groans that he was stript of his garments, and wasted with hunger and thirst!"

This is Abbot Samson's interpretation of the Dream;—diametrically the reverse of that given by the Monks themselves, who scruple not to say privily, "It is *we* that are the naked and famished limbs of the Martyr; we whom the Abbot curtails of all

our privileges, setting his own official to control our very Cellarer!"
Abbot Samson adds, that this judgment by fire has fallen upon
them for murmuring about their meat and drink.

Clearly enough, meanwhile, the Altar, whatever the burning of
it mean or foreshadow, must needs be reëdified. Abbot Samson
reëdifies it, all of polished marble; with the highest stretch of
art and sumptuosity, reëmbellishes the Shrine for which it is to
serve as pediment. Nay farther, as had ever been among his
prayers, he enjoys, he sinner, a glimpse of the glorious Martyr's
very Body in the process; having solemnly opened the *Loculus*,
Chest or sacred Coffin, for that purpose. It is the culminating
moment of Abbot Samson's life. Bozzy Jocelin himself rises into
a kind of Psalmist solemnity on this occasion; the laziest monk
'weeps' warm tears, as *Te Deum* is sung.

Very strange;—how far vanished from us in these unworshipping ages of ours! The Patriot Hampden, best beatified man we
have, had lain in like manner some two centuries in his narrow
home, when certain dignitaries of us, 'and twelve grave-diggers
with pulleys,' raised him also up, under cloud of night, cut off his
arm with penknives, pulled the scalp off his head,—and otherwise
worshipped our Hero Saint in the most amazing manner! [1] Let
the modern eye look earnestly on that old midnight hour in St.
Edmundsbury Church, shining yet on us, ruddy-bright, through
the depths of seven hundred years; and consider mournfully what
our Hero-worship once was, and what it now is! We translate
with all the fidelity we can:

'The Festival of St. Edmund now approaching, the marble
'blocks are polished, and all things are in readiness for lifting of
'the Shrine to its new place. A fast of three days was held by
'all the people, the cause and meaning thereof being publicly set
'forth to them. The Abbot announces to the Convent that all
'must prepare themselves for transferring of the Shrine, and
'appoints time and way for the work. Coming therefore that
'night to matins, we found the great Shrine (*feretrum magnum*)
'raised upon the Altar, but empty; covered all over with white
'doeskin leather, fixed to the wood with silver nails; but one
'pannel of the Shrine was left down below, and resting thereon,
'beside its old column of the Church, the Loculus with the Sacred
'Body yet lay where it was wont. Praises being sung, we all

---

[1] *Annual Register* (year 1828, Chronicle, p. 93), *Gentleman's Magazine*,
&c. &c.

'proceeded to commence our disciplines (*ad disciplinas suscipiendas*).
'These finished, the Abbot and certain with him are clothed in
'their albs; and, approaching reverently, set about uncovering the
'Loculus.   There was an outer cloth of linen, enwrapping the
'Loculus and all; this we found tied on the upper side with
'strings of its own: within this was a cloth of silk, and then
'another linen cloth, and then a third; and so at last the Loculus
'was uncovered, and seen resting on a little tray of wood, that the
'bottom of it might not be injured by the stone.   Over the breast
'of the Martyr, there lay, fixed to the surface of the Loculus, a
'Golden Angel about the length of a human foot; holding in one
'hand a golden sword, and in the other a banner: under this there
'was a hole in the lid of the Loculus, on which the ancient
'servants of the Martyr had been wont to lay their hands for
'touching the Sacred Body.   And over the figure of the Angel was
'this verse inscribed :

'*Martiris ecce zoma servat Michaelis agalma.*[2]

'At the head and foot of the Loculus were iron rings whereby it
'could be lifted.

   'Lifting the Loculus and Body, therefore, they carried it to the
'Altar; and I put-to my sinful hand to help in carrying, though
'the Abbot had commanded that none should approach except
'called.   And the Loculus was placed in the Shrine; and the
'pannel it had stood on was put in its place, and the Shrine for
'the present closed.   We all thought that the Abbot would show
'the Loculus to the people ; and bring out the Sacred Body again,
'at a certain period of the Festival.   But in this we were wofully
'mistaken, as the sequel shows.

   'For in the fourth holiday of the Festival, while the Convent
'were all singing *Completorium*, our Lord Abbot spoke privily with
'the Sacristan and Walter the Medicus ; and order was taken that
'twelve of the Brethren should be appointed against midnight,
'who were strong for carrying the pannel-planks of the Shrine,
'and skilful in unfixing them, and putting them together again.
'The Abbot then said that it was among his prayers to look once
'upon the Body of his Patron ; and that he wished the Sacristan
'and Walter the Medicus to be with him.   The Twelve appointed
'Brethren were these : The Abbot's two Chaplains, the two Keepers
'of the Shrine, the two Masters of the Vestry ; and six more,

   [2] 'This is the Martyr's Garment, which Michael's Image guards.'

' namely, the Sacristan Hugo, Walter the Medicus, Augustin,
' William of Dice, Robert and Richard. I, alas, was not of the
' number.

　' The Convent therefore being all asleep, these Twelve, clothed
' in their albs, with the Abbot, assembled at the Altar; and
' opening a pannel of the Shrine, they took out the Loculus; laid
' it on a table, near where the Shrine used to be; and made ready
' for unfastening the lid, which was joined and fixed to the Loculus
' with sixteen very long nails. Which when, with difficulty, they
' had done, all except the two forenamed associates are ordered to
' draw back. The Abbot and they two were alone privileged to look
' in. The Loculus was so filled with the Sacred Body that you could
' scarcely put a needle between the head and the wood, or between
' the feet and the wood: the head lay united to the body, a little
' raised with a small pillow. But the Abbot, looking close, found
' now a silk cloth veiling the whole Body, and then a linen cloth
' of wondrous whiteness; and upon the head was spread a small
' linen cloth, and then another small and most fine silk cloth, as if
' it were the veil of a nun. These coverings being lifted off, they
' found now the Sacred Body all wrapt in linen; and so at length
' the lineaments of the same appeared. But here the Abbot
' stopped; saying he durst not proceed farther, or look at the
' sacred flesh naked. Taking the head between his hands, he thus
' spake, groaning: "Glorious Martyr, holy Edmund, blessed be the
' hour when thou wert born. Glorious Martyr, turn it not to my
' perdition that I have so dared to touch thee, I miserable and
' sinful; thou knowest my devout love, and the intention of my
' mind." And proceeding, he touched the eyes; and the nose,
' which was very massive and prominent (*valde grossum et valde
' eminentem*); and then he touched the breast and arms; and
' raising the left arm he touched the fingers, and placed his own
' fingers between the sacred fingers. And proceeding he found the
' feet standing stiff up, like the feet of a man dead yesterday; and
' he touched the toes and counted them (*tangendo numeravit*).

　' And now it was agreed that the other Brethren should be
' called forward to see the miracles; and accordingly those ten now
' advanced, and along with them six others who had stolen in
' without the Abbot's assent, namely, Walter of St. Alban's, Hugh
' the Infirmirarius, Gilbert brother of the Prior, Richard of
' Henham, Jocellus our Cellarer, and Turstan the Little; and all
' these saw the Sacred Body, but Turstan alone of them put forth

'his hand, and touched the Saint's knees and feet. And that there
'might be abundance of witnesses, one of our Brethren, John of
'Dice, sitting on the roof of the Church, with the servants of the
'Vestry, and looking through, clearly saw all these things.'

What a scene; shining luminous effulgent, as the lamps of St.
Edmund do, through the dark Night; John of Dice, with vestry-
men, clambering on the roof to look through; the Convent all
asleep, and the Earth all asleep,—and since then, Seven Centuries
of Time mostly gone to sleep! Yes, there, sure enough, is the
martyred Body of Edmund, landlord of the Eastern Counties, who,
nobly doing what he liked with his own, was slain three hundred
years ago: and a noble awe surrounds the memory of him, symbol
and promoter of many other right noble things.

But have not we now advanced to strange new stages of Hero-
worship, now in the little Church of Hampden, with our penknives out, and twelve grave-diggers with pulleys? The manner
of men's Hero-worship, verily it is the innermost fact of their
existence, and determines all the rest,—at public hustings, in
private drawing-rooms, in church, in market, and wherever else.
Have true reverence, and what indeed is inseparable therefrom,
reverence the right man, all is well; have sham-reverence, and
what also follows, greet with it the wrong man, then all is ill, and
there is nothing well. Alas, if Hero-worship becomes Dilettantism,
and all except Mammonism be a vain grimace, how much, in this
most earnest Earth, has gone and is evermore going to fatal
destruction, and lies wasting in quiet lazy ruin, no man regarding
it! Till at length no heavenly *Ism* any longer coming down upon
us, *Isms* from the other quarter have to mount up. For the
Earth, I say, is an earnest place; Life is no grimace, but a most
serious fact. And so, under universal Dilettantism much having
been stript bare, not the souls of men only, but their very bodies
and bread-cupboards having been stript bare, and life now no longer
possible,—all is reduced to desperation, to the iron law of Necessity
and very Fact again; and to temper Dilettantism, and astonish it,
and burn it up with infernal fire, arises Chartism, *Bare-back-ism*,
Sansculottism so-called! May the gods, and what of unworshipped heroes still remain among us, avert the omen!—

But however this may be, St. Edmund's Loculus, we find, has
the veils of silk and linen reverently replaced, the lid fastened

down again with its sixteen ancient nails; is wrapt in a new costly covering of silk, the gift of Hubert Archbishop of Canterbury: and through the sky-window John of Dice sees it lifted to its place in the Shrine, the pannels of this latter duly refixed, fit parchment documents being introduced withal;—and now John and his vestry-men can slide down from the roof, for all is over, and the Convent wholly awakens to matins. 'When we assembled to sing matins,' says Jocelin, 'and understood what had been done, grief took hold 'of all that had not seen these things, each saying to himself, '"Alas, I was deceived." Matins over, the Abbot called the Con-'vent to the great Altar; and briefly recounting the matter, alleged 'that it had not been in his power, nor was it permissible or fit, 'to invite us all to the sight of such things. At hearing of which, 'we all wept, and with tears sang *Te Deum laudamus;* and 'hastened to toll the bells in the Choir.'

Stupid blockheads, to reverence their St. Edmund's dead Body in this manner? Yes, brother;—and yet, on the whole, who knows how to reverence the Body of a Man? It is the most reverend phenomenon under this Sun. For the Highest God dwells visible in that mystic unfathomable Visibility, which calls itself "I" on the Earth. 'Bending before men,' says Novalis, 'is 'a reverence done to this Revelation in the Flesh. We touch 'Heaven when we lay our hand on a human Body.' And the Body of one Dead;—a temple where the Hero-soul once was and now is not: Oh, all mystery, all pity, all mute *awe* and wonder; *Super-*naturalism brought home to the very dullest; Eternity laid open, and the nether Darkness and the upper Light-Kingdoms, do con-join there, or exist nowhere! Sauerteig used to say to me, in his peculiar way: "A Chancery Lawsuit; justice, nay justice in mere money, denied a man, for all his pleading, till twenty, till forty years of his Life are gone seeking it: and a Cockney Funeral, Death reverenced by hatchments, horse-hair, brass-lacquer, and unconcerned bipeds carrying long poles and bags of black silk :— are not these two reverences, this reverence for Death and that reverence for Life, a notable pair of reverences among you English ?"

Abbot Samson, at this culminating point of his existence, may, and indeed must, be left to vanish with his Life-scenery from the eyes of modern men. He had to run into France, to settle with King Richard for the military service there of his St. Edmunds-bury Knights; and with great labour got it done. He had to decide on the dilapidated Coventry Monks; and with great labour, and much pleading and journeying, got them reinstated; dined with them all, and with the 'Masters of the Schools of Oxneford,' —the veritable Oxford *Caput* sitting there at dinner, in a dim but undeniable manner, in the City of Peeping Tom! He had, not without labour, to controvert the intrusive Bishop of Ely, the intrusive Abbot of Cluny. Magnanimous Samson, his life is but a labour and a journey; a bustling and a justling, till the still Night come. He is sent for again, over sea, to advise King Richard touching certain Peers of England, who had taken the Cross, but never followed it to Palestine; whom the Pope is inquiring after. The magnanimous Abbot makes preparation for departure; departs, and——And Jocelin's Boswellean Narrative, suddenly shorn-through by the scissors of Destiny, *ends*. There are no words more; but a black line, and leaves of blank paper. Irremediable: the miraculous hand, that held all this theatric-machinery, suddenly quits hold; impenetrable Time-Curtains rush down; in the mind's eye all is again dark, void; with loud dinning in the mind's ear, our real-phantasmagory of St. Edmundsbury plunges into the bosom of the Twelfth Century again, and all is over. Monks, Abbot, Hero-worship, Government, Obedience, Cœur-de-Lion and St. Edmund's Shrine, vanish like Mirza's Vision; and there is nothing left but a mutilated black Ruin amid green botanic expanses, and oxen, sheep and dilettanti pasturing in their places.

CHAPTER XVII.

THE BEGINNINGS.

WHAT a singular shape of a Man, shape of a Time, have we in this Abbot Samson and his history; how strangely do modes, creeds, formularies, and the date and place of a man's birth, modify the figure of the man!

Formulas too, as we call them, have a *reality* in Human Life. They are real as the very *skin* and *muscular tissue* of a Man's Life; and a most blessed indispensable thing, so long as they have *vitality* withal, and are a *living* skin and tissue to him! No man, or man's life, can go abroad and do business in the world without skin and tissues. No; first of all these have to fashion themselves,—as indeed they spontaneously and inevitably do. Foam itself, and this is worth thinking of, can harden into oyster-shell; all living objects do by necessity form to themselves a skin.

And yet, again, when a man's Formulas become *dead;* as all Formulas, in the progress of living growth, are very sure to do! When the poor man's integuments, no longer nourished from within, become dead skin, mere adscititious leather and callosity, wearing thicker and thicker, uglier and uglier; till no *heart* any longer can be felt beating through them, so thick, callous, calcified are they; and all over it has now grown mere calcified oyster-shell, or were it polished mother-of-pearl, inwards almost to the very heart of the poor man:—yes then, you may say, his usefulness once more is quite obstructed; once more, he cannot go abroad and do business in the world; it is time that *he* take to bed, and prepare for departure, which cannot now be distant!

Ubi homines sunt modi sunt. Habit is the deepest law of human nature. It is our supreme strength; if also, in certain circumstances, our miserablest weakness.—From Stoke to Stowe is as yet a field, all pathless, untrodden: from Stoke where I live, to Stowe where I have to make my merchandises, perform my businesses, consult my heavenly oracles, there is as yet no path or human footprint; and I, impelled by such necessities, must nevertheless undertake the journey. Let me go once, scanning my way with any earnestness of outlook, and successfully arriving, my footprints are an invitation to me a second time to go by the same way. It is easier than any other way: the industry of 'scanning' lies already invested in it for me; I can go this time with less of scanning, or without scanning at all. Nay the very sight of my footprints, what a comfort for me; and in a degree, for all my brethren of mankind! The footprints are trodden and retrodden; the path wears ever broader, smoother, into a broad highway, where even wheels can run; and many travel it;—till—till the Town of Stowe disappear from that locality (as towns have been known to do), or no merchandising, heavenly oracle, or real business any longer exist for one there: then why should anybody travel the way?—Habit is our primal, fundamental law; Habit and Imitation, there is nothing more perennial in us than these two. They are the source of all Working and all Apprenticeship, of all Practice and all Learning, in this world.

Yes, the wise man too speaks, and acts, in Formulas; all men do so. And in general, the more completely cased with Formulas a man may be, the safer, happier is it for him. Thou who, in an All of rotten Formulas, seemest to stand nigh bare, having indignantly shaken off the superannuated rags and unsound callosities of Formulas,—consider how thou too art still clothed! This English Nationality, whatsoever from uncounted ages is genuine and a fact among thy native People, in their words and ways: all this, has it not made for thee a skin or second-skin, adhesive actually as thy natural skin? This thou hast not stript off, this thou wilt never strip off: the humour that thy mother gave thee has to show itself through this. A common, or it may be an uncommon Englishman thou art: but, good Heavens, what sort of Arab, Chinaman, Jew-Clothesman, Turk, Hindoo, African Mandingo, wouldst thou have been, *thou* with those mother-qualities of thine!

It strikes me dumb to look over the long series of faces, such as any full Church, Courthouse, London-Tavern Meeting, or miscellany of men will show them. Some score or two of years ago, all these were little red-coloured pulpy infants; each of them capable of being kneaded, baked into any social form you chose: yet see now how they are fixed and hardened,—into artisans, artists, clergy, gentry, learned serjeants, unlearned dandies, and can and shall now be nothing else henceforth!

Mark on that nose the colour left by too copious port and viands;

to which the profuse cravat with exorbitant breast-pin, and the fixed, forward, and as it were menacing glance of the eyes correspond. That is a 'Man of Business;' prosperous manufacturer, house-contractor, engineer, law-manager; his eye, nose, cravat have, in such work and fortune, got such a character: deny him not thy praise, thy pity. Pity him too, the Hard-handed, with bony brow, rudely-combed hair, eyes looking out as in labour, in difficulty and uncertainty; rude mouth, the lips coarse, loose, as in hard toil and lifelong fatigue they have got the habit of hanging: —hast thou seen aught more touching than the rude intelligence, so cramped, yet energetic, unsubduable, true, which looks out of that marred visage? Alas, and his poor wife, with her own hands, washed that cotton neckcloth for him, buttoned that coarse shirt, sent him forth creditably trimmed as she could. In such imprisonment lives he, for his part; man cannot now deliver him : the red pulpy infant has been baked and fashioned *so.*.

Or what kind of baking was it that this other brother mortal got, which has baked him into the genus Dandy? Elegant Vacuum; serenely looking down upon all Plenums and Entities as low and poor to his serene Chimeraship and *Non*entity laboriously attained! Heroic Vacuum; inexpugnable, while purse and present condition of society hold out; curable by no hellebore. The doom of Fate was, Be thou a Dandy! Have thy eye-glasses, opera-glasses, thy Long-Acre cabs with white-breeched tiger, thy yawning impassivities, pococurantisms; *fix* thyself in Dandyhood, undeliverable; it is thy doom.

And all these, we say, were red-coloured infants; of the same pulp and stuff, few years ago; now irretrievably shaped and kneaded as we see! Formulas? There is no mortal extant, out of the depths of Bedlam, but lives all skinned, thatched, covered over with Formulas; and is, as it were, held in from delirium and the Inane by his Formulas! They are withal the most beneficent, indispensable of human equipments: blessed he who has a skin and tissues, so it be a living one, and the heart-pulse everywhere discernible through it. Monachism, Feudalism, with a real King Plantagenet, with real Abbots Samson, and their other living realities, how blessed!—

Not without a mournful interest have we surveyed that authentic image of a Time now wholly swallowed. Mournful reflections crowd on us;—and yet consolatory. How many brave men have lived before Agamemnon! Here is a brave governor Samson, a man fearing God, and fearing nothing else; of whom as First Lord of the Treasury, as King, Chief Editor, High Priest, we could be so glad and proud; of whom nevertheless Fame has altogether forgotten to make mention! The faint image of him, revived in this hour, is found in the gossip of one poor Monk, and in Nature nowhere else. Oblivion had so nigh swallowed him altogether, even to the echo of his ever having existed. What regiments and hosts and generations of such has Oblivion already swallowed! Their crumbled dust makes up the soil our life-fruit grows on. Said I not, as my old Norse Fathers taught me, The Life-tree Igdrasil, which waves round thee in this hour, whereof thou in this hour art portion, has its roots down deep in the oldest Death-Kingdoms; and grows; the Three Nornas, or *Times*, Past, Present, Future, watering it from the Sacred Well!

For example, who taught thee to *speak*? From the day when two hairy-naked or fig-leaved Human Figures began, as uncomfortable dummies, anxious no longer to be dumb, but to impart themselves to one another; and endeavoured, with gaspings, gesturings, with unsyllabled cries, with painful pantomime and interjections, in a very unsuccessful manner,—up to the writing of this present copyright Book, which also is not very successful! Between that day and this, I say, there has been a pretty space of time; a pretty spell of work, which *somebody* has done! Thinkest thou there were no poets till Dan Chaucer? No heart burning with a thought, which it could not hold, and had no word for; and needed to shape and coin a word for,—what thou callest a metaphor, trope, or the like? For every word we have, there was such a man and poet. The coldest word was once a glowing new metaphor, and bold questionable originality. ' Thy very ATTENTION, does it not mean an *attentio*, a STRETCHING-TO?' Fancy that act of the mind, which all were conscious of, which none had yet named,—when this new ' poet' first felt bound and driven to name it! His questionable originality, and new glowing metaphor, was found adoptable, intelligible; and remains our name for it to this day.

Literature :—and look at Paul's Cathedral, and the Masonries and Worships and Quasi-Worships that are there; not to speak of Westminster Hall and its wigs! Men had not a hammer to begin with, not a syllabled articulation: they had it all to make ;—and they have made it. What thousand thousand articulate, semi-articulate, earnest-stammering *Prayers* ascending up to Heaven,

from hut and cell, in many lands, in many centuries, from the
fervent kindled souls of innumerable men, each struggling to pour
itself forth incompletely, as it might, before the incompletest
Liturgy could be compiled! The Liturgy, or adoptable and generally adopted Set of Prayers and Prayer-Method, was what we can
call the Select Adoptabilities, 'Select Beauties' well edited (by
Œcumenic Councils and other Useful-Knowledge Societies) from
that wide waste imbroglio of Prayers already extant and accumulated, good and bad. The good were found adoptable by men; were
gradually got together, well-edited, accredited: the bad, found
inappropriate, unadoptable, were gradually forgotten, disused and
burnt. It is the way with human things. The first man who,
looking with opened soul on this august Heaven and Earth, this
Beautiful and Awful, which we name Nature, Universe and suchlike, the essence of which remains for ever UNNAMEABLE; he who
first, gazing into this, fell on his knees awestruck, in silence as is
likeliest,—he, driven by inner necessity, the 'audacious original'
that he was, had done a thing, too, which all thoughtful hearts saw
straightway to be an expressive, altogether adoptable thing! To
bow the knee was ever since the attitude of supplication. Earlier
than any spoken Prayers, *Litanias*, or *Leitourgias;* the beginning
of all Worship,—which needed but a beginning, so rational was it.
What a poet he! Yes, this bold original was a successful one
withal. The wellhead this one, hidden in the primeval dusks and
distances, from whom as from a Nile-source all *Forms of Worship*
flow :—such a Nile-river (somewhat muddy and malarious now!)
of Forms of Worship sprang there, and flowed, and flows, down to
Puseyism, Rotatory Calabash, Archbishop Laud at St. Catherine
Creed's, and perhaps lower!

Things rise, I say, in that way. The *Iliad* Poem, and indeed
most other poetic, especially epic things, have risen as the Liturgy
did. The great *Iliad* in Greece, and the small *Robin Hood's
Garland* in England, are each, as I understand, the well-edited
'Select Beauties' of an immeasurable waste imbroglio of Heroic
Ballads in their respective centuries and countries. Think what
strumming of the seven-stringed heroic lyre, torturing of the less
heroic fiddle-catgut, in Hellenic Kings' Courts, and English
wayside Public Houses; and beating of the studious Poetic brain,
and gasping here too in the semi-articulate windpipe of Poetic
men, before the Wrath of a Divine Achilles, the Prowess of a Will
Scarlet or Wakefield Pindar, could be adequately sung! Honour

to you, ye nameless great and greatest ones, ye long-forgotten brave !

Nor was the Statute *De Tallagio non concedendo,* nor any Statute, Law-method, Lawyer's-wig, much less were the Statute-Book and Four Courts, with Coke upon Lyttelton and Three Estates of Parliament in the rear of them, got together without human labour,—mostly forgotten now ! From the time of Cain's slaying Abel by swift head-breakage, to this time of killing your man in Chancery by inches, and slow heart-break for forty years,—there too is an interval ! Venerable Justice herself began by Wild-Justice; all Law is as a tamed furrowfield, slowly worked out, and rendered arable, from the waste jungle of Club-Law. Valiant Wisdom tilling and draining; escorted by owl-eyed Pedantry, by owlish and vulturish and many other forms of Folly;—the valiant husbandman assiduously tilling; the blind greedy enemy *too* assiduously sowing tares ! It is because there is yet in venerable wigged Justice some wisdom, amid such mountains of wiggeries and folly, that men have not cast her into the River; that she still sits there, like Dryden's Head in the *Battle of the Books,*—a huge helmet, a huge mountain of greased parchment, of unclean horse-hair, first striking the eye; and then in the innermost corner, visible at last, in size as a hazelnut, a real fraction of God's Justice, perhaps not yet unattainable to some, surely still indispensable to all;—and men know not what to do with her ! Lawyers were not all pedants, voluminous voracious persons; Lawyers too were poets, were heroes,—or their Law had been past the Nore long before this time. Their Owlisms, Vulturisms, to an incredible extent, will disappear by and by, their Heroisms only remaining, and the helmet be reduced to something like the size of the head, we hope !—

It is all work and forgotten work, this peopled, clothed, articulate-speaking, high-towered, wide-acred World. The hands of forgotten brave men have made it a World for us;—they,—honour to them; they, in *spite* of the idle and the dastard. This English Land, here and now, is the summary of what was found of wise, and noble, and accordant with God's Truth, in all the generations of English Men. Our English Speech is speakable because there were Hero-Poets of our blood and lineage; speakable in proportion to the number of these. This Land of England has its conquerors, possessors, which change from epoch to epoch, from day to day; but its real conquerors, creators, and eternal proprietors are these following, and their representatives if you can find them : All the Heroic Souls that ever were in England, each in their degree; all the men that ever cut a thistle, drained a puddle out of England, contrived a wise scheme in England, did or said a true and valiant thing in England. I tell thee, they had not a hammer to begin with; and yet Wren built St. Paul's: not an articulated syllable; and yet there have come English Literatures, Elizabethan Literatures, Satanic-School, Cockney-School, and other Literatures;— once more, as in the old time of the *Leitourgia*, a most waste imbroglio, and world-wide jungle and jumble; waiting terribly to be 'well-edited' and 'well-burnt'! Arachne started with forefinger and thumb, and had not even a distaff; yet thou seest Manchester, and Cotton Cloth, which will shelter naked backs, at twopence an ell.

Work ? The quantity of done and forgotten work that lies silent under my feet in this world, and escorts and attends me, and supports and keeps me alive, wheresoever I walk or stand, whatsoever I think or do, gives rise to reflections! Is it not enough, at any rate, to strike the thing called 'Fame' into total silence for a wise man ? For fools and unreflective persons, she is and will be very noisy, this 'Fame,' and talks of her 'immortals' and so forth : but if you will consider it, what is she ? Abbot Samson was not nothing because nobody *said* anything of him. Or thinkest thou, the Right Honourable Sir Jabez Windbag can be made something by Parliamentary Majorities and Leading Articles ? Her 'immortals'! Scarcely two hundred years back can Fame recollect articulately at all; and there she but maunders and mumbles. She manages to recollect a Shakspeare or so; and prates, considerably like a goose, about him;—and in the rear of that, onwards to the birth of Theuth, to Hengst's Invasion, and the bosom of Eternity, it was all blank; and the respectable Teutonic Languages, Teutonic Practices, Existences, all came of their own accord, as the grass springs, as the trees grow; no Poet, no work from the inspired heart of a Man needed there; and Fame has not an articulate word to say about it! Or ask her, What, with all conceivable appliances and mnemonics, including apotheosis and human sacrifices among the number, she carries in her head with regard to a Wodan, even a Moses, or other such ? She begins to be uncertain as to what they were, whether spirits or men of mould,—gods, charlatans; begins sometimes to have a misgiving that they were mere symbols, ideas of the mind; perhaps nonentities and Letters of the Alphabet! She is the noisiest, inarticulately babbling, hissing, screaming, foolishest, unmusicalest of fowls that fly; and needs no 'trumpet,' I think, but her own enormous goose-throat,—measuring several degrees of celestial latitude, so to speak. Her 'wings,' in these days, have grown far swifter than ever; but her goose-throat hitherto seems only larger, louder and foolisher than ever. *She* is transitory, futile, a goose-goddess:—if she were not transitory, what would become of us! It is a chief comfort that she forgets us all; all, even to the very Wodans; and grows to consider us, at last, as probably nonentities and Letters of the Alphabet.

Yes, a noble Abbot Samson resigns himself to Oblivion too; feels *it* no hardship, but a comfort; counts it as a still resting-place, from much sick fret and fever and stupidity, which in the night-watches often made his strong heart sigh. Your most sweet voices, making one enormous goose-voice, O Bobus and Company, how can they be a guidance for any Son of Adam? In *silence* of you and the like of you, the 'small still voices' will speak to him better; in which does lie guidance.

My friend, all speech and rumour is short-lived, foolish, untrue. Genuine WORK alone, what thou workest faithfully, that is eternal, as the Almighty Founder and World-Builder himself. Stand thou by that; and let 'Fame' and the rest of it go prating.

> ' Heard are the Voices,
> Heard are the Sages,
> The Worlds and the Ages :
> "Choose well ; your choice is
> Brief and yet endless.
>
> Here eyes do regard you,
> In Eternity's stillness ;
> Here is all fulness,
> Ye brave, to reward you ;
> Work, and despair not."'
>   *Goethe.*

BOOK THIRD.

THE MODERN WORKER.

CHAPTER I.

PHENOMENA.

But, it is said, our religion is gone: we no longer believe in St. Edmund, no longer see the figure of him 'on the rim of the sky,' minatory or confirmatory! God's absolute Laws, sanctioned by an eternal Heaven and an eternal Hell, have become Moral Philosophies, sanctioned by able computations of Profit and Loss, by weak considerations of Pleasures of Virtue and the Moral Sublime.

It is even so. To speak in the ancient dialect, we 'have forgotten God;'—in the most modern dialect and very truth of the matter, we have taken up the Fact of this Universe as it *is not*. We have quietly closed our eyes to the eternal Substance of things, and opened them only to the Shows and Shams of things. We quietly believe this Universe to be intrinsically a great unintelligible PERHAPS; extrinsically, clear enough, it is a great, most extensive Cattlefold and Workhouse, with most extensive Kitchen-ranges, Dining-tables,—whereat he is wise who can find a place! All the Truth of this Universe is uncertain; only the profit and loss of it, the pudding and praise of it, are and remain very visible to the practical man.

There is no longer any God for us! God's Laws are become a Greatest-Happiness Principle, a Parliamentary Expediency: the Heavens overarch us only as an Astronomical Time-keeper; a butt for Herschel-telescopes to shoot science at, to shoot sentimentalities at:—in our and old Jonson's dialect, man has lost the *soul* out of

him; and now, after the due period,—begins to find the want of
it! This is verily the plague-spot; centre of the universal Social
Gangrene, threatening all modern things with frightful death. To
him that will consider it, here is the stem, with its roots and
taproot, with its world-wide upas-boughs and accursed poison-
exudations, under which the world lies writhing in atrophy and
agony. You touch the focal-centre of all our disease, of our
frightful nosology of diseases, when you lay your hand on this.
There is no religion; there is no God; man has lost his soul, and
vainly seeks antiseptic salt. Vainly: in killing Kings, in passing
Reform Bills, in French Revolutions, Manchester Insurrections, is
found no remedy. The foul elephantine leprosy, alleviated for an
hour, reappears in new force and desperateness next hour.

For actually this is *not* the real fact of the world; the world
is not made so, but otherwise!—Truly, any Society setting out
from this No-God hypothesis will arrive at a result or two. The
*Un*veracities, escorted, each Unveracity of them by its corresponding Misery and Penalty; the Phantasms, and Fatuities, and
ten-years Corn-Law Debatings, that shall walk the Earth at noon-
day,—must needs be numerous! The Universe *being* intrinsically
a Perhaps, being too probably an 'infinite Humbug,' why should
any minor Humbug astonish us? It is all according to the order
of Nature; and Phantasms riding with huge clatter along the
streets, from end to end of our existence, astonish nobody. Enchanted St. Ives' Workhouses and Joe-Manton Aristocracies;
giant Working Mammonism near strangled in the partridge-
nets of giant-looking Idle Dilettantism,—this, in all its branches,
in its thousand-thousand modes and figures, is a sight familiar
to us.

The Popish Religion, we are told, flourishes extremely in these
years; and is the most vivacious-looking religion to be met with
at present. "*Elle a trois cents ans dans le ventre,*" counts Mr
Jouffroy; "*c'est pourquoi je la respecte!*"—The old Pope of Rome,
finding it laborious to kneel so long while they cart him through
the streets to bless the people on *Corpus-Christi* Day, complains
of rheumatism; whereupon his Cardinals consult;—construct him,
after some study, a stuffed cloaked figure, of iron and wood, with
wool or baked hair; and place it in a kneeling posture. Stuffed
figure, or rump of a figure; to this stuffed rump he, sitting at his
ease on a lower level, joins, by the aid of cloaks and drapery, his

living head and outspread hands : the rump with its cloaks kneels, the Pope looks, and holds his hands spread ; and so the two in concert bless the Roman population on *Corpus-Christi* Day, as well as they can.

I have considered this amphibious Pope, with the wool-and-iron back, with the flesh head and hands ; and endeavoured to calculate his horoscope. I reckon him the remarkablest Pontiff that has darkened God's daylight, or painted himself in the human retina, for these several thousand years. Nay, since Chaos first shivered, and ' sneezed,' as the Arabs say, with the first shaft of sunlight shot through it, what stranger product was there of Nature and Art working together ? Here is a Supreme Priest who believes God to be—What, in the name of God, *does* he believe God to be ? —and discerns that all worship of God is a scenic phantasmagory of wax-candles, organ-blasts, Gregorian chants, mass-brayings, purple monsignori, wool-and-iron rumps, artistically spread out,— to save the ignorant from worse.

O reader, I say not who are Belial's elect. This poor amphibious Pope too gives loaves to the Poor ; has in him more good latent than he is himself aware of. His poor Jesuits, in the late Italian Cholera, were, with a few German Doctors, the only creatures whom dastard terror had not driven mad : they descended fearless into all gulfs and bedlams ; watched over the pillow of the dying, with help, with counsel and hope ; shone as luminous fixed stars, when all else had gone out in chaotic night : honour to them ! This poor Pope,—who knows what good is in him ? In a Time otherwise too prone to forget, he keeps up the mournfulest ghastly memorial of the Highest, Blessedest, which once was ; which, in new fit forms, will again partly have to be. Is he not as a per- petual death's-head and cross-bones, with their *Resurgam*, on the grave of a Universal Heroism,—grave of a Christianity ? Such Noblenesses, purchased by the world's best heart's-blood, must not be lost ; we cannot afford to lose them, in what confusions soever. To all of us the day will come, to a few of us it has already come, when no mortal, with his heart yearning for a ' Divine Humility,' or other ' Highest form of Valour,' will need to look for it in death's-heads, but will see it round him in here and there a beautiful living head.

Besides, there is in this poor Pope, and his practice of the Scenic Theory of Worship, a frankness which I rather honour. Not half and half, but with undivided heart does *he* set about

worshipping by stage-machinery; as if there were now, and could
again be, in Nature no other. He will ask you, What other?
Under this my Gregorian Chant, and beautiful waxlight Phantasmagory, kindly hidden from you is an Abyss, of Black Doubt,
Scepticism, nay Sansculottic Jacobinism; an Orcus that has no
bottom. Think of that. ' Groby Pool *is* thatched with pancakes,'
—as Jeannie Deans's Innkeeper defied it to be! The Bottomless
of Scepticism, Atheism, Jacobinism, behold, it is thatched over,
hidden from your despair, by stage-properties judiciously arranged
This stuffed rump of mine saves not me only from rheumatism,
but you also from what other *isms!* In this your Life-pilgrimage
Nowhither, a fine Squallacci marching-music, and Gregorian
Chant, accompanies you, and the hollow Night of Orcus is well
hid !

Yes truly, few men that worship by the rotatory Calabash of
the Calmucks do it in half so great, frank or effectual a way.
Drury-Lane, it is said, and that is saying much, might learn
from him in the dressing of parts, in the arrangement of lights and
shadows. He is the greatest Play-actor that at present draws
salary in this world. Poor Pope; and I am told he is fast growing
bankrupt too; and will, in a measurable term of years (a great
way *within* the 'three hundred'), not have a penny to make his
pot boil! His old rheumatic back will then get to rest; and
himself and his stage-properties sleep well in Chaos forevermore.

Or, alas, why go to Rome for Phantasms walking the streets?
Phantasms, ghosts, in this midnight hour, hold jubilee, and screech
and jabber; and the question rather were, What high Reality
anywhere is yet awake? Aristocracy has become Phantasm-
Aristocracy, no longer able to *do* its work, not in the least conscious
that it has any work longer to do. Unable, totally careless to *do*
its work; careful only to clamour for the *wages* of doing its work,
—nay for higher, and *palpably* undue wages, and Corn-Laws and
increase of rents; the old rate of wages not being adequate now!
In hydra-wrestle, giant ' *Millo*cracy' so-called, a real giant, though
as yet a blind one and but half-awake, wrestles and wrings in
choking nightmare, 'like to be strangled in the partridge-nets of
Phantasm-Aristocracy,' as we said, which fancies itself still to be a
giant. Wrestles, as under nightmare, till it do awaken; and gasps
and struggles thousandfold, we may say, in a truly painful manner,
through all fibres of our English Existence, in these hours and

years! Is our poor English Existence wholly becoming a Nightmare; full of mere Phantasms?—

The Champion of England, cased in iron or tin, rides into Westminster Hall, 'being lifted into his saddle with little assistance,' and there asks, If in the four quarters of the world, under the cope of Heaven, is any man or demon that dare question the right of this King? Under the cope of Heaven no man makes intelligible answer,—as several men ought already to have done. Does not this Champion too know the world; that it is a huge Imposture, and bottomless Inanity, thatched over with bright cloth and other ingenious tissues? Him let us leave there, questioning all men and demons.

Him we have left to his destiny; but whom else have we found? From this the highest apex of things, downwards through all strata and breadths, how many fully awakened Realities have we fallen in with:—alas, on the contrary, what troops and populations of Phantasms, not God-Veracities but Devil-Falsities, down to the very lowest stratum,—which now, by such superincumbent weight of Unveracities, lies enchanted in St. Ives' Workhouses, broad enough, helpless enough! You will walk in no public thoroughfare or remotest byway of English Existence but you will meet a man, an interest of men, that has given up hope in the Everlasting, True, and placed its hope in the Temporary, half or wholly False. The Honourable Member complains unmusically that there is 'devil's-dust' in Yorkshire cloth. Yorkshire cloth,—why, the very Paper I now write on is made, it seems, partly of plaster-lime well smoothed, and obstructs my writing! You are lucky if you can find now any good Paper,—any work really *done;* search where you will, from highest Phantasm apex to lowest Enchanted basis.

Consider, for example, that great Hat seven-feet high, which now perambulates London Streets; which my Friend Sauerteig regarded justly as one of our English notabilities; "the topmost point as yet," said he, "would it were your culminating and returning point, to which English Puffery has been observed to reach!"—The Hatter in the Strand of London, instead of making better felt-hats than another, mounts a huge lath-and-plaster Hat, seven-feet high, upon wheels; sends a man to drive it through the streets; hoping to be saved *thereby.* He has not attempted to make better hats, as he was appointed by the Universe to do, and as with this ingenuity of his he could very probably have done;

but his whole industry is turned to *persuade* us that he has made such! He too knows that the Quack has become God. Laugh not at him, O reader; or do not laugh only. He has ceased to be comic; he is fast becoming tragic. Te me this all-deafening blast of Puffery, of poor Falsehood grown necessitous, of poor Heart-Atheism fallen now into Enchanted Workhouses, sounds too surely like a Doom's-blast! I have to say to myself in old dialect: "God's blessing is not written on all this; His curse is written on all this!" Unless perhaps the Universe *be* a chimera;—some old totally deranged eightday clock, dead as brass; which the Maker, if there ever was any Maker, has long ceased to meddle with?— To my Friend Sauerteig this poor seven-feet Hat-manufacturer, as the topstone of English Puffery, was very notable.

Alas, that we natives note him little, that we view him as a thing of course, is the very burden of the misery. We take it for granted, the most rigorous of us, that all men who have made anything are expected and entitled to make the loudest possible proclamation of it, and call on a discerning public to reward them for it. Every man his own trumpeter; that is, to a really alarming extent, the accepted rule. Make loudest possible proclamation of your Hat: true proclamation if that will do; if that will not do, then false proclamation,—to such extent of falsity as will serve your purpose; as will not seem too false to be credible!—I answer, once for all, that the fact is not so. Nature requires no man to make proclamation of his doings and hat-makings; Nature forbids all men to make such. There is not a man or hat-maker born into the world but feels, or has felt, that he is degrading himself if he speak of his excellencies and prowesses, and supremacy in his craft: his inmost heart says to him, "Leave thy friends to speak of these; if possible, thy enemies to speak of these; but at all events, thy friends!" He feels that he is already a poor braggart; fast hastening to be a falsity and speaker of the Untruth.

Nature's Laws, I must repeat, are eternal: her small still voice, speaking from the inmost heart of us, shall not, under terrible penalties, be disregarded. No one man can depart from the truth without damage to himself; no one million of men; no Twenty-seven Millions of men. Show me a Nation fallen every-where into this course, so that each expects it, permits it to others and himself, I will show you a Nation travelling with one assent on the broad way. The broad way, however many Banks of

England, Cotton-Mills and Duke's Palaces it may have. Not at happy Elysian fields, and everlasting crowns of victory, earned by silent Valour, will this Nation arrive; but at precipices, devouring gulfs, if it pause not. Nature has appointed happy fields, victorious laurel-crowns; but only to the brave and true: *Un*nature, what we call Chaos, holds nothing in it but vacuities, devouring gulfs. What are Twenty-seven Millions, and their unanimity? Believe them not: the Worlds and the Ages, God and Nature and All Men say otherwise.

'Rhetoric all this?' No, my brother, very singular to say, it is Fact all this. Cocker's Arithmetic is not truer. Forgotten in these days, it is old as the foundations of the Universe, and will endure till the Universe cease. It is forgotten now; and the first mention of it puckers thy sweet countenance into a sneer: but it will be brought to mind again,—unless indeed the Law of Gravitation chance to cease, and men find that they *can* walk on vacancy. Unanimity of the Twenty-seven Millions will do nothing; walk not thou with them; fly from them as for thy life. Twenty-seven Millions travelling on such courses, with gold jingling in every pocket, with vivats heaven-high, are incessantly advancing, let me again remind thee, towards the *firm-land's end*, —towards the end and extinction of what Faithfulness, Veracity, real Worth, was in their way of life. Their noble ancestors have fashioned for them a 'life-road;'—in how many thousand senses, this! There is not an old wise Proverb on their tongue, an honest Principle articulated in their hearts into utterance, a wise true method of doing and despatching any work or commerce of men, but helps yet to carry them forward. Life is still possible to them, because all is not yet Puffery, Falsity, Mammon-worship and Unnature; because somewhat is yet Faithfulness, Veracity and Valour. With a certain very considerable finite quantity of Unveracity and Phantasm, social life is still possible; not with an infinite quantity! Exceed your certain quantity, the seven-feet Hat, and all things upwards to the very Champion cased in tin, begin to reel and flounder,—in Manchester Insurrections, Chartisms, Sliding-scales; the Law of Gravitation not forgetting to act. You advance incessantly towards the land's end; you are, literally enough, 'consuming the way.' Step after step, Twenty-seven Million unconscious men;—till you are *at* the land's end; till there is not Faithfulness enough among you any more: and the next step now is lifted *not* over land, but into air, over ocean-deeps and roaring abysses:—unless perhaps the Law of Gravitation have forgotten to act?

Oh, it is frightful when a whole Nation, as our Fathers used to say, has 'forgotten God;' has remembered only Mammon, and what Mammon leads to! When your self-trumpeting Hatmaker is the emblem of almost all makers, and workers, and men, that make anything,—from soul-overseerships, body-overseerships, epic poems, acts of parliament, to hats and shoe-blacking! Not one false man but does uncountable mischief: how much, in a generation or two, will Twenty-seven Millions, mostly false, manage to accumulate? The sum of it, visible in every street, market-place, senate-house, circulating-library, cathedral, cotton-mill, and union-workhouse, fills one *not* with a comic feeling!

CHAPTER II.

GOSPEL OF MAMMONISM.

READER, even Christian Reader as thy title goes, hast thou any notion of Heaven and Hell? I rather apprehend, not. Often as the words are on our tongue, they have got a fabulous or semi-fabulous character for most of us, and pass on like a kind of transient similitude, like a sound signifying little.

Yet it is well worth while for us to know, once and always, that they are not a similitude, nor a fable nor semi-fable; that they are an everlasting highest fact! "No Lake of Sicilian or other sulphur burns now anywhere in these ages," sayest thou? Well, and if there did not! Believe that there does not; believe it if thou wilt, nay hold by it as a real increase, a rise to higher stages, to wider horizons and empires. All this has vanished, or has not vanished; believe as thou wilt as to all this. But that an Infinite of Practical Importance, speaking with strict arithmetical exactness, an *Infinite*, has vanished or can vanish from the Life of any Man: this thou shalt not believe! O brother, the Infinite of Terror, of Hope, of Pity, did it not at any moment disclose itself to thee, indubitable, unnameable? Came it never, like the gleam of *preter*natural eternal Oceans, like the voice of old Eternities, far-sounding through thy heart of hearts? Never? Alas, it was not thy Liberalism, then; it was thy Animalism! The Infinite is more sure than any other fact. But only men can discern it; mere building beavers, spinning arachnes, much more the predatory vulturous and vulpine species, do not discern it well!—

'The word Hell,' says Sauerteig, 'is still frequently in use 'among the English people: but I could not without difficulty 'ascertain what they meant by it. Hell generally signifies the 'Infinite Terror, the thing a man *is* infinitely afraid of, and 'shudders and shrinks from, struggling with his whole soul to 'escape from it. There is a Hell therefore, if you will consider, 'which accompanies man, in all stages of his history, and religious 'or other development: but the Hells of men and Peoples differ 'notably. With Christians it is the infinite terror of being found 'guilty before the Just Judge. With old Romans, I conjecture, it 'was the terror not of Pluto, for whom probably they cared little, 'but of doing unworthily, doing unvirtuously, which was their 'word for un*man*fully. And now what is it, if you pierce through 'his Cants, his oft-repeated Hearsays, what he calls his Worships 'and so forth,—what is it that the modern English soul does, in 'very truth, dread infinitely, and contemplate with entire despair? 'What *is* his Hell, after all these reputable, oft-repeated Hearsays, 'what is it? With hesitation, with astonishment, I pronounce it 'to be: The terror of "Not succeeding;" of not making money, 'fame, or some other figure in the world,—chiefly of not making 'money! Is not that a somewhat singular Hell?'

Yes, O Sauerteig, it is very singular. If we do not 'succeed,' where is the use of us? We had better never have been born. "Tremble intensely," as our friend the Emperor of China says: *there* is the black Bottomless of Terror; what Sauerteig calls the 'Hell of the English'!—But indeed this Hell belongs naturally to the Gospel of Mammonism, which also has its corresponding Heaven. For there *is* one Reality among so many Phantasms; about one thing we are entirely in earnest: The making of money. Working Mammonism does divide the world with idle game-preserving Dilettantism:—thank Heaven that there is even a Mammonism, *any*thing we are in earnest about! Idleness is worst, Idleness alone is without hope: work earnestly at anything, you will by degrees learn to work at almost all things. There is endless hope in work, were it even work at making money.

True, it must be owned, we for the present, with our Mammon-Gospel, have come to strange conclusions. We call it a Society; and go about professing openly the totalest separation, isolation. Our life is not a mutual helpfulness; but rather, cloaked under due laws-of-war, named 'fair competition' and so forth, it is a mutual hostility. We have profoundly forgotten everywhere that *Cash-payment* is not the sole relation of human beings; we think, nothing doubting, that *it* absolves and liquidates all engagements of man. "My starving workers?" answers the rich mill-owner: "Did not I hire them fairly in the market? Did I not pay them, to the last sixpence, the sum covenanted for? What have I to do with them more?" — Verily Mammon-worship is a melancholy creed. When Cain, for his own behoof, had killed Abel, and was questioned, "Where is thy brother?" he too made answer, "Am I my brother's keeper?" Did I not pay my brother *his* wages, the thing he had merited from me?

O sumptuous Merchant-Prince, illustrious game-preserving Duke, is there no way of 'killing' thy brother but Cain's rude way! 'A good man by the very look of him, by his very presence 'with us as a fellow wayfarer in this Life-pilgrimage, *promises* so 'much :' woe to him if he forget all such promises, if he never know that they were given! To a deadened soul, seared with the brute Idolatry of Sense, to whom going to Hell is equivalent to not making money, all 'promises' and moral duties, that cannot be pleaded for in Courts of Requests, address themselves in vain. Money he can be ordered to pay, but nothing more. I have not heard in all Past History, and expect not to hear in all Future History, of any Society anywhere under God's Heaven supporting itself on such Philosophy. The Universe is not made so; it is made otherwise than so. The man or nation of men that thinks it is made so, marches forward nothing doubting, step after step; but marches—whither we know! In these last two centuries of Atheistic Government (near two centuries now, since the blessed restoration of his Sacred Majesty, and Defender of the Faith, Charles Second), I reckon that we have pretty well exhausted what of 'firm earth' there was for us to march on;—and are now, very ominously, shuddering, reeling, and let us hope trying to recoil, on the cliff's edge!—

For out of this that we call Atheism come so many other *isms* and falsities, each falsity with its misery at its heels!—A SOUL is not like wind (*spiritus*, or breath) contained within a capsule; the

ALMIGHTY MAKER is not like a Clockmaker that once, in old immemorial ages, having *made* his Horologe of a Universe, sits ever since and sees it go! Not at all. Hence comes Atheism; come, as we say, many other *isms;* and as the sum of all, comes Valetism, the *reverse* of Heroism; sad root of all woes whatsoever. For indeed, as no man ever saw the above-said wind-element enclosed within its capsule, and finds it at bottom more deniable than conceivable; so too he finds, in spite of Bridgwater Bequests, your Clockmaker Almighty an entirely questionable affair, a deniable affair;—and accordingly denies it, and along with it so much else. Alas, one knows not what and how much else! For the faith in an Invisible, Unnameable, Godlike, present everywhere in all that we see and work and suffer, is the essence of all faith whatsoever; and that once denied, or still worse, asserted with lips only, and out of bound prayerbooks only, what other thing remains believable? That Cant well-ordered is marketable Cant; that Heroism means gas-lighted Histrionism; that seen with 'clear eyes' (as they call Valet-eyes), no man is a Hero, or ever was a Hero, but all men are Valets and Varlets. The accursed practical quintessence of all sorts of Unbelief! For if there be now no Hero, and the Histrio himself begin to be seen into, what hope is there for the seed of Adam here below? We are the doomed everlasting prey of the Quack; who, now in this guise, now in that, is to filch us, to pluck and eat us, by such modes as are convenient for him. For the modes and guises I care little. The Quack once inevitable, let him come swiftly, let him pluck and eat me;—swiftly, that I may at least have done with him; for in his Quack-world I can have no wish to linger. Though he slay me, yet will I *not* trust in him. Though he conquer nations, and have all the Flunkies of the Universe shouting at his heels, yet will I know well that *he* is an Inanity; that for him and his there is no continuance appointed, save only in Gehenna and the Pool. Alas, the Atheist world, from its utmost summits of Heaven and Westminster-Hall, downwards through poor seven-feet Hats and 'Unveracities fallen hungry,' down to the lowest cellars and neglected hunger-dens of it, is very wretched.

One of Dr. Alison's Scotch facts struck us much.[1] A poor Irish Widow, her husband having died in one of the Lanes of Edinburgh, went forth with her three children, bare of all resource, to solicit

---

[1] *Observations on the Management of the Poor in Scotland:* by William Pulteney Alison, M.D. (Edinburgh, 1840.)

help from the Charitable Establishments of that City. At this Charitable Establishment and then at that she was refused; referred from one to the other, helped by none;—till she had exhausted them all; till her strength and heart failed her: she sank down in typhus-fever; died, and infected her Lane with fever, so that 'seventeen other persons' died of fever there in consequence. The humane Physician asks thereupon, as with a heart too full for speaking, Would it not have been *economy* to help this poor Widow? She took typhus-fever, and killed seventeen of you!—Very curious. The forlorn Irish Widow applies to her fellow-creatures, as if saying, "Behold I am sinking, bare of help: ye must help me! I am your sister, bone of your bone; one God made us: ye must help me!" They answer, "No, impossible; thou art no sister of ours." But she proves her sisterhood; her typhus-fever kills *them*: they actually were her brothers, though denying it! Had human creature ever to go lower for a proof?

For, as indeed was very natural in such case, all government of the Poor by the Rich has long ago been given over to Supply-and-demand, Laissez-faire and suchlike, and universally declared to be 'impossible.' "You are no sister of ours; what shadow of proof is there? Here are our parchments, our padlocks, proving indisputably our money-safes to be *ours*, and you to have no business with them. Depart! It is impossible!"—Nay, what wouldst thou thyself have us do? cry indignant readers. Nothing, my friends, —till you have got a soul for yourselves again. Till then all things are 'impossible.' Till then I cannot even bid you buy, as the old Spartans would have done, two-pence worth of powder and lead, and compendiously shoot to death this poor Irish Widow: even that is 'impossible' for you. Nothing is left but that she prove her sisterhood by dying, and infecting you with typhus. Seventeen of you lying dead will not deny such proof that she *was* flesh of your flesh; and perhaps some of the living may lay it to heart.

'Impossible:' of a certain two-legged animal with feathers it is said, if you draw a distinct chalk-circle round him, he sits imprisoned, as if girt with the iron ring of Fate; and will die there, though within sight of victuals,—or sit in sick misery there, and be fatted to death. The name of this poor two-legged animal is— Goose; and they make of him, when well fattened, *Pâté de foie gras*, much prized by some!

CHAPTER III.

GOSPEL OF DILETTANTISM.

BUT after all, the Gospel of Dilettantism, producing a Governing Class who do not govern, nor understand in the least that they are bound or expected to govern, is still mournfuler than that of Mammonism. Mammonism, as we said, at least works; this goes idle. Mammonism has seized some portion of the message of Nature to man; and seizing that, and following it, will seize and appropriate more and more of Nature's message: but Dilettantism has missed it wholly. 'Make money:' that will mean withal, 'Do work in order to make money.' But, 'Go gracefully idle in Mayfair,' what does or can that mean? An idle, game-preserving and even corn-lawing Aristocracy, in such an England as ours : has the world, if we take thought of it, ever seen such a phenomenon till very lately? Can it long continue to see such?

Accordingly the impotent, insolent Donothingism in Practice and Saynothingism in Speech, which we have to witness on that side of our affairs, is altogether amazing. A Corn-Law demonstrating itself openly, for ten years or more, with 'arguments' to make the angels, and some other classes of creatures, weep! For men are not ashamed to rise in Parliament and elsewhere, and speak the things they do *not* think. 'Expediency,' 'Necessities of Party,' &c. &c.! It is not known that the Tongue of Man is a sacred organ; that Man himself is definable in Philosophy as an 'Incarnate *Word;*' the Word not there, you have no Man there either, but a Phantasm instead! In this way it is that Absurdities may live long enough,—still walking, and talking for themselves, years and decades after the brains are quite out! How are 'the knaves and dastards' ever to be got 'arrested' at that rate?—

"No man in this fashionable London of yours," friend Sauerteig would say, "speaks a plain word to me. Every man feels bound to be something more than plain; to be pungent withal, witty, ornamental. His poor fraction of sense has to be perked into some epigrammatic shape, that it may prick into me;—perhaps

(this is the commonest) to be topsyturvied, left standing on its
head, that I may remember it the better! Such grinning inanity
is very sad to the soul of man. Human faces should not grin on
one like masks; they should look on one like faces! I love honest
laughter, as I do sunlight; but not dishonest: most kinds of
dancing too; but the St.-Vitus kind not at all! A fashionable
wit, *ach Himmel!* if you ask, Which, he or a Death's-head, will be
the cheerier company for me? pray send *not* him!"

Insincere Speech, truly, is the prime material of insincere
Action. Action hangs, as it were, *dissolved* in Speech, in Thought
whereof Speech is the Shadow; and precipitates itself therefrom.
The kind of Speech in a man betokens the kind of Action you will
get from him. Our Speech, in these modern days, has become
amazing. Johnson complained, "Nobody speaks in earnest, Sir;
there is no serious conversation." To us all serious speech of men,
as that of Seventeenth-Century Puritans, Twelfth-Century Catho-
lics, German Poets of this Century, has become jargon, more or
less insane. Cromwell was mad and a quack; Anselm, Becket,
Goethe, *ditto ditto.*

Perhaps few narratives in History or Mythology are more significant than that Moslem one, of Moses and the Dwellers by the
Dead Sea. A tribe of men dwelt on the shores of that same
Asphaltic Lake; and having forgotten, as we are all too prone to
do, the inner facts of Nature, and taken up with the falsities and
outer semblances of it, were fallen into sad conditions,—verging
indeed towards a certain far deeper Lake. Whereupon it pleased
kind Heaven to send them the Prophet Moses, with an instructive
word of warning, out of which might have sprung 'remedial
measures' not a few. But no: the men of the Dead Sea discovered, as the valet-species always does in heroes or prophets, no
comeliness in Moses; listened with real tedium to Moses, with
light grinning, or with splenetic sniffs and sneers, affecting even to
yawn; and signified, in short, that they found him a humbug, and
even a bore. Such was the candid theory these men of the
Asphalt Lake formed to themselves of Moses, That probably he
was a humbug, that certainly he was a bore.

Moses withdrew; but Nature and her rigorous veracities did not
withdraw. The men of the Dead Sea, when we next went to visit
them, were all 'changed into Apes;'[1] sitting on the trees there,
grinning now in the most *un*affected manner; gibbering and

[1] Sale's *Koran* (Introduction).

chattering very genuine nonsense; finding the whole Universe now a most indisputable Humbug! The Universe has *become* a Humbug to these Apes who thought it one. There they sit and chatter, to this hour: only, I believe, every Sabbath there returns to them a bewildered half-consciousness, half-reminiscence; and they sit, with their wizened smoke-dried visages, and such an air of supreme tragicality as Apes may; looking out through those blinking smoke-bleared eyes of theirs, into the wonderfulest universal smoky Twilight and undecipherable disordered Dusk of Things; wholly an Uncertainty, Unintelligibility, they and it; and for commentary thereon, here and there an unmusical chatter or mew:—truest, tragicalest Humbug conceivable by the mind of man or ape! They made no use of their souls; and so have lost them. Their worship on the Sabbath now is to roost there, with unmusical screeches, and half-remember that they had souls.

Didst thou never, O Traveller, fall-in with parties of this tribe? Meseems they are grown somewhat numerous in our day.

CHAPTER IV.

HAPPY.

ALL work, even cotton-spinning, is noble; work is alone noble : be that here said and asserted once more. And in like manner too, all dignity is painful; a life of ease is not for any man, nor for any god. The life of all gods figures itself to us as a Sublime Sadness,—earnestness of Infinite Battle against Infinite Labour. Our highest religion is named the 'Worship of Sorrow.' For the son of man there is no noble crown, well worn or even ill worn, but is a crown of thorns!—These things, in spoken words, or still better, in felt instincts alive in every heart, were once well known.

Does not the whole wretchedness, the whole *Atheism* as I call it, of man's ways, in these generations, shadow itself for us in that unspeakable Life-philosophy of his: The pretension to be what he calls 'happy'? Every pitifulest whipster that walks within a skin has his head filled with the notion that he is, shall be, or by all human and divine laws ought to be 'happy.' His wishes, the pitifulest whipster's, are to be fulfilled for him; his days, the pitifulest whipster's, are to flow on in ever-gentle current of enjoyment, impossible even for the gods. The prophets preach to us, Thou shalt be happy; thou shalt love pleasant things, and find them. The people clamour, Why have we not found pleasant things?

We construct our theory of Human Duties, not on any Greatest-Nobleness Principle, never so mistaken; no, but on a Greatest-Happiness Principle. 'The word *Soul* with us, as in some Slavonic dialects, seems to be synonymous with *Stomach*.' We plead and speak, in our Parliaments and elsewhere, not as from the Soul, but from the Stomach;—wherefore indeed our pleadings are so slow to profit. We plead not for God's Justice; we are not ashamed to stand clamouring and pleading for our own 'interests,' our own rents and trade-profits; we say, They are the 'interests' of so many; there is such an intense desire in us for them! We demand Free-Trade, with much just vociferation and benevolence, That the poorer classes, who are terribly ill-off at present, may have cheaper New-Orleans bacon. Men ask on Free-trade platforms, How can the indomitable spirit of Englishmen be kept up without plenty of bacon? We shall become a ruined Nation!—Surely, my friends, plenty of bacon is good and indispensable: but, I doubt, you will never get even bacon by aiming only at that. You are men, not animals of prey, well-used or ill-used! Your Greatest-Happiness Principle seems to me fast becoming a rather unhappy one.—What if we should cease babbling about 'happiness,' and leave *it* resting on its own basis, as it used to do!

A gifted Byron rises in his wrath; and feeling too surely that he for his part is not 'happy,' declares the same in very violent language, as a piece of news that may be interesting. It evidently has surprised him much. One dislikes to see a man and poet reduced to proclaim on the streets such tidings: but on the whole, as matters go, that is not the most dislikable. Byron speaks the *truth* in this matter. Byron's large audience indicates how true it is felt to be.

'Happy,' my brother? First of all, what difference is it whether thou art happy or not! Today becomes Yesterday so fast, all To-morrows become Yesterdays; and then there is no question whatever of the 'happiness,' but quite another question. Nay, thou hast such a sacred pity left at least for thyself, thy very pains, once gone over into Yesterday, become joys to thee. Besides, thou knowest not what heavenly blessedness and indispensable sanative virtue was in them; thou shalt only know it after many days, when thou art wiser!—A benevolent old Surgeon sat once in our company, with a Patient fallen sick by gourmandising, whom he had just, too briefly in the Patient's judgment, been examining. The foolish Patient still at intervals continued to break in on our discourse, which rather promised to take a philosophic turn: "But I have lost my appetite," said he, objurgatively, with a tone of irritated pathos; "I have no appetite; I can't eat!"—"My dear fellow," answered the Doctor in mildest tone, "it isn't of the slightest consequence;"—and continued his philosophical discoursings with us!

Or does the reader not know the history of that Scottish iron Misanthrope? The inmates of some town-mansion, in those Northern parts, were thrown into the fearfulest alarm by indubitable symptoms of a ghost inhabiting the next house, or perhaps even the partition-wall! Ever at a certain hour, with preternatural gnarring, growling and screeching, which attended as running bass, there began, in a horrid, semi-articulate, unearthly voice, this song: "Once I was hap-hap-happy, but now I'm *mees*erable! Clack-clack-clack, gnarr-r-r, whuz-z: Once I was hap-hap-happy, but now I'm *mees*erable!"—Rest, rest, perturbed spirit;—or indeed, as the good old Doctor said: My dear fellow, it isn't of the slightest consequence! But no; the perturbed spirit could not rest; and to the neighbours, fretted, affrighted, or at least insufferably bored by him, it *was* of such consequence that they had to go and examine in his haunted chamber. In his haunted chamber, they find that the perturbed spirit is an unfortunate—Imitator of Byron? No, is an unfortunate rusty Meat-jack, gnarring and creaking with rust and work; and this, in Scottish dialect, is *its* Byronian musical Life-philosophy, sung according to ability!

Truly, I think the man who goes about pothering and uproaring for his 'happiness,'—pothering, and were it ballot-boxing, poem-making, or in what way soever fussing and exerting himself,—he is not the man that will help us to 'get our knaves and dastards arrested'! No; he rather is on the way to increase the number,—by at least one unit and his tail! Observe, too, that this is all a modern affair; belongs not to the old heroic times, but to these dastard new times. 'Happiness our being's end and aim,' all that very paltry speculation is at bottom, if we will count well, not yet two centuries old in the world.

The only happiness a brave man ever troubled himself with asking much about was, happiness enough to get his work done. Not "I can't eat!" but "I can't work!" that was the burden of all wise complaining among men. It is, after all, the one unhappiness of a man, That he cannot work; that he cannot get his destiny as a man fulfilled. Behold, the day is passing swiftly over, our life is passing swiftly over; and the night cometh, wherein no man can work. The night once come, our happiness, our unhappiness,—it is all abolished; vanished, clean gone; a thing that has been: 'not of the slightest consequence' whether we were happy as eupeptic Curtis, as the fattest pig of Epicurus, or unhappy as Job with potsherds, as musical Byron with Giaours and sensibilities of the heart; as the unmusical Meat-jack with hard labour and rust! But our work,—behold that is not abolished, that has not vanished: our work, behold, it remains, or the want of it remains;—for endless Times and Eternities, remains; and that is now the sole question with us forevermore! Brief brawling Day, with its noisy phantasms, its poor paper-crowns tinsel-gilt, is gone; and divine everlasting Night, with her star-diadems, with her silences and her veracities, is come! What hast thou done, and how? Happiness, unhappiness: all that was but the *wages* thou hadst; thou hast spent all that, in sustaining thyself hitherward; not a coin of it remains with thee, it is all spent, eaten: and now thy work, where is thy work? Swift, out with it; let us see thy work!

Of a truth, if man were not a poor hungry dastard, and even much of a blockhead withal, he would cease criticising his victuals to such extent; and criticise himself rather, what he does with his victuals!

CHAPTER V.

THE ENGLISH.

AND yet, with all thy theoretic platitudes, what a depth of practical sense in thee, great England! A depth of sense, of justice, and courage; in which, under all emergencies and world-bewilderments, and under this most complex of emergencies we now live in, there is still hope, there is still assurance!

The English are a dumb people. They can do great acts, but not describe them. Like the old Romans, and some few others, *their* Epic Poem is written on the Earth's surface: England her Mark! It is complained that they have no artists: one Shakspeare indeed; but for Raphael only a Reynolds; for Mozart nothing but a Mr. Bishop: not a picture, not a song. And yet they did produce one Shakspeare: consider how the element of Shakspearean melody does lie imprisoned in their nature; reduced to unfold itself in mere Cotton-mills, Constitutional Governments, and suchlike;—all the more interesting when it does become visible, as even in such unexpected shapes it succeeds in doing! Goethe spoke of the Horse, how impressive, almost affecting it was that an animal of such qualities should stand obstructed so; its speech nothing but an inarticulate neighing, its handiness mere *hoof*iness, the fingers all constricted, tied together, the finger-nails coagulated into a mere hoof, shod with iron. The more significant, thinks he, are those eye-flashings of the generous noble quadruped; those prancings, curvings of the neck clothed with thunder.

A Dog of Knowledge has free utterance; but the War-horse is almost mute, very far from free! It is even so. Truly, your freest utterances are not by any means always the best: they are the worst rather; the feeblest, trivialest; their meaning prompt, but small, ephemeral. Commend me to the silent English, to the silent Romans. Nay the silent Russians, too, I believe to be worth something: are they not even now drilling, under much obloquy, an immense semi-barbarous half-world from Finland to Kamtschatka, into rule, subordination, civilisation,—really in an old

Roman fashion; speaking no word about it; quietly hearing all
manner of vituperative Able Editors speak! While your ever-
talking, ever-gesticulating French, for example, what are they at
this moment drilling?—Nay of all animals, the freest of utterance,
I should judge, is the genus *Simia:* go into the Indian woods,
say all Travellers, and look what a brisk, adroit, unresting Ape-
population it is!

The spoken Word, the written Poem, is said to be an epitome
of the man; how much more the done work. Whatsoever of
morality and of intelligence; what of patience, perseverance, faithfulness, of method, insight, ingenuity, energy; in a word, whatsoever of Strength the man had in him will lie written in the
Work he does. To work: why, it is to try himself against Nature,
and her everlasting unerring Laws; these will tell a true verdict
as to the man. So much of virtue and of faculty did *we* find in
him; so much and no more! He had such capacity of harmonising
himself with *me* and my unalterable ever-veracious Laws; of co-
operating and working as *I* bade him;—and has prospered, and
has not prospered, as you see!—Working as great Nature bade
him: does not that mean virtue of a kind; nay of all kinds?
Cotton can be spun and sold, Lancashire operatives can be got to
spin it, and at length one has the woven webs and sells them, by
following Nature's regulations in that matter: by not following
Nature's regulations, you have them not. You have them not;—
there is no Cotton-web to sell: Nature finds a bill against you;
your 'Strength' is not Strength, but Futility! Let faculty be
honoured, so far as it is faculty. A man that can succeed in
working is to me always a man.

How one loves to see the burly figure of him, this thick-skinned,
seemingly opaque, perhaps sulky, almost stupid Man of Practice,
pitted against some light adroit Man of Theory, all equipt with
clear logic, and able anywhere to give you Why for Wherefore!
The adroit Man of Theory, so light of movement, clear of utterance,
with his bow full-bent and quiver full of arrow-arguments,—surely
he will strike down the game, transfix everywhere the heart of the
matter; triumph everywhere, as he proves that he shall and must
do? To your astonishment, it turns out oftenest No. The cloudy-
browed, thick-soled, opaque Practicality, with no logic utterance,
in silence mainly, with here and there a low grunt or growl, has
in him what transcends all logic-utterance: a Congruity with the

Unuttered. The Speakable, which lies atop, as a superficial film, or outer skin, is his or is not his: but the Doable, which reaches down to the World's centre, you find him there!

The rugged Brindley has little to say for himself; the rugged Brindley, when difficulties accumulate on him, retires silent, 'generally to his bed;' retires 'sometimes for three days together 'to his bed, that he may be in perfect privacy there,' and ascertain in his rough head how the difficulties can be overcome. The ineloquent Brindley, behold he *has* chained seas together; his ships do visibly float over valleys, invisibly through the hearts of mountains; the Mersey and the Thames, the Humber and the Severn have shaken hands: Nature most audibly answers, Yea! The Man of Theory twangs his full-bent bow: Nature's Fact ought to fall stricken, but does not: his logic-arrow glances from it as from a scaly dragon, and the obstinate Fact keeps walking its way. How singular! At bottom, you will have to grapple closer with the dragon; take it home to you, by real faculty, not by seeming faculty; try whether you are stronger, or it is stronger. Close with it, wrestle it: sheer obstinate toughness of muscle; but much more, what we call toughness of heart, which will mean persistence hopeful and even desperate, unsubduable patience, composed candid openness, clearness of mind: all this shall be 'strength' in wrestling your dragon; the whole man's real strength is in this work, we shall get the measure of him here.

Of all the Nations in the world at present the English are the stupidest in speech, the wisest in action. As good as a 'dumb' Nation, I say, who cannot speak, and have never yet spoken,— spite of the Shakspeares and Miltons who show us what possibilities there are!—O Mr. Bull, I look in that surly face of thine with a mixture of pity and laughter, yet also with wonder and veneration. Thou complainest not, my illustrious friend; and yet I believe the heart of thee is full of sorrow, of unspoken sadness, seriousness,— profound melancholy (as some have said) the basis of thy being. Unconsciously, for thou speakest of nothing, this great Universe is great to thee. Not by levity of floating, but by stubborn force of swimming, shalt thou make thy way. The Fates sing of thee that thou shalt many times be thought an ass and a dull ox, and shalt with a godlike indifference believe it. My friend,—and it is all untrue, nothing ever falser in point of fact! Thou art of those great ones whose greatness the small passer-by does not discern. Thy very stupidity is wiser than their wisdom. A grand *vis inertiæ*

is in thee; how many grand qualities unknown to small men!
Nature alone knows thee, acknowledges the bulk and strength of
thee: thy Epic, unsung in words, is written in huge characters on
the face of this Planet,—sea-moles, cotton-trades, railways, fleets
and cities, Indian Empires, Americas, New Hollands; legible
throughout the Solar System!

But the dumb Russians too, as I said, they, drilling all wild
Asia and wild Europe into military rank and file, a terrible yet
hitherto a prospering enterprise, are still dumber. The old Romans
also could not *speak*, for many centuries:—not till the world was
theirs; and so many speaking Greekdoms, their logic-arrows all
spent, had been absorbed and abolished. The logic-arrows, how
they glanced futile from obdurate thick-skinned Facts; Facts to be
wrestled down only by the real vigour of Roman thews!—As for
me, I honour, in these loud-babbling days, all the Silent rather. A
grand Silence that of Romans;—nay the grandest of all, is it not
that of the gods! Even Triviality, Imbecility, that can sit silent,
how respectable is it in comparison! The 'talent of silence' is our
fundamental one. Great honour to him whose Epic is a melodious
hexameter Iliad; not a jingling Sham-Iliad, nothing true in it but
the hexameters and forms merely. But still greater honour, if his
Epic be a mighty Empire slowly built together, a mighty Series of
Heroic Deeds,—a mighty Conquest over Chaos; *which* Epic the
'Eternal Melodies' have, and must have, informed and dwelt in, as
it sung itself! There is no mistaking that latter Epic. Deeds are
greater than Words. Deeds have such a life, mute but undeniable,
and grow as living trees and fruit-trees do; they people the vacuity
of Time, and make it green and worthy. Why should the oak
prove logically that it ought to grow, and will grow? Plant it, try
it; what gifts of diligent judicious assimilation and secretion it
has, of progress and resistance, of *force* to grow, will then declare
themselves. My much-honoured, illustrious, extremely inarticulate
Mr. Bull!—

Ask Bull his spoken opinion of any matter,—oftentimes the
force of dulness can no farther go. You stand silent, incredulous,
as over a platitude that borders on the Infinite. The man's
Churchisms, Dissenterisms, Puseyisms, Benthamisms, College
Philosophies, Fashionable Literatures, are unexampled in this
world. Fate's prophecy is fulfilled; you call the man an ox and
an ass. But set him once to work,—respectable man! His spoken
sense is next to nothing, nine-tenths of it palpable *non*sense: but

his unspoken sense, his inner silent feeling of what is true, what does agree with fact, what is doable and what is not doable,—this seeks its fellow in the world. A terrible worker; irresistible against marshes, mountains, impediments, disorder, incivilisation; everywhere vanquishing disorder, leaving it behind him as method and order. He 'retires to his bed three days,' and considers!

Nay withal, stupid as he is, our dear John,—ever, after infinite tumblings, and spoken platitudes innumerable from barrel-heads and parliament-benches, he does settle down somewhere about the just conclusion; you are certain that his jumblings and tumblings will end, after years or centuries, in the stable equilibrium. Stable equilibrium, I say; centre-of-gravity lowest;—not the unstable, with centre-of-gravity highest, as I have known it done by quicker people! For indeed, do but jumble and tumble sufficiently, you avoid that worst fault, of settling with your centre-of-gravity highest; your centre-of-gravity is certain to come lowest, and to stay there. If slowness, what we in our impatience call 'stupidity,' be the price of stable equilibrium over unstable, shall we grudge a little slowness? Not the least admirable quality of Bull is, after all, that of remaining insensible to logic; holding out for consider- able periods, ten years or more, as in this of the Corn-Laws, after all arguments and shadow of arguments have faded away from him, till the very urchins on the street titter at the arguments he brings. Logic,—Λογικὴ, the 'Art of speech,'—does indeed speak so and so; clear enough: nevertheless Bull still shakes his head; will see whether nothing else *illogical*, not yet 'spoken,' not yet able to be 'spoken,' do not lie in the business, as there so often does!—My firm belief is, that, finding himself now enchanted, hand-shackled, foot-shackled, in Poor-Law Bastilles and elsewhere, he will retire three days to his bed, and *arrive* at a conclusion or two! His three-years 'total stagnation of trade,' alas, is not that a painful enough 'lying in bed to consider himself'? Poor Bull!

Bull is a born Conservative; for this too I inexpressibly honour him. All great Peoples are conservative; slow to believe in novelties; patient of much error in actualities; deeply and forever certain of the greatness that is in LAW, in Custom once solemnly established, and now long recognised as just and final.—True, O Radical Reformer, there is no Custom that can, properly speaking, be final; none. And yet thou seest *Customs* which, in all civilised countries, are accounted final; nay, under the Old-Roman name of *Mores*, are accounted *Morality*, Virtue, Laws of God Himself. Such,

I assure thee, not a few of them are; such almost all of them once were. And greatly do I respect the solid character,—a blockhead, thou wilt say; yes, but a well-conditioned blockhead, and the best-conditioned,—who esteems all 'Customs once solemnly acknowledged' to be ultimate, divine, and the rule for a man to walk by, nothing doubting, not inquiring farther. What a time of it had we, were all men's life and trade still, in all parts of it, a problem, a hypothetic seeking, to be settled by painful Logics and Baconian Inductions! The Clerk in Eastcheap cannot spend the day in verifying his Ready-Reckoner; he must take it as verified, true and indisputable; or his Book-keeping by Double Entry will stand still. "Where is your Posted Ledger?" asks the Master at night.—"Sir," answers the other, "I was verifying my Ready-Reckoner, and find some errors. The Ledger is—!"—Fancy such a thing!

True, all turns on your Ready-Reckoner being moderately correct, being *not* insupportably incorrect! A Ready-Reckoner which has led to distinct entries in your Ledger such as these: '*Creditor* an 'English People by fifteen hundred years of good Labour; and '*Debtor* to lodging in enchanted Poor-Law Bastilles: *Creditor* by 'conquering the largest Empire the Sun ever saw; and *Debtor* to 'Donothingism and "Impossible" written on all departments of 'the government thereof: *Creditor* by mountains of gold ingots 'earned; and *Debtor* to No Bread purchasable by them:'—*such* Ready-Reckoner, methinks, is beginning to be suspect; nay is ceasing, and has ceased, to be suspect! Such Ready-Reckoner is a Solecism in Eastcheap; and must, whatever be the press of business, and will and shall be rectified a little. Business can go on no longer with *it*. The most Conservative English People, thickest-skinned, most patient of Peoples, is driven alike by its Logic and its Unlogic, by things 'spoken,' and by things not yet spoken or very speakable, but only felt and very unendurable, to be wholly a Reforming People. Their Life, as it is, has ceased to be longer possible for them.

Urge not this noble silent People; rouse not the Berserkir rage that lies in them! Do you know their Cromwells, Hampdens, their Pyms and Bradshaws? Men very peaceable, but men that can be made very terrible! Men who, like their old Teutsch Fathers in Agrippa's days, 'have a soul that despises death;' to whom 'death,' compared with falsehood and injustices, is light;— 'in whom there is a rage unconquerable by the immortal gods!'

Before this, the English People have taken very preternatural-looking Spectres by the beard; saying virtually: "And if thou *wert* 'preternatural'? Thou with thy 'divine-rights' grown diabolic-wrongs? Thou,—not even 'natural;' decapitable; totally extinguishable!"——Yes, just so godlike as this People's patience was, even so godlike will and must its impatience be. Away, ye scandalous Practical Solecisms, children actually of the Prince of Darkness; ye have near broken our hearts; we can and will endure you no longer. Begone, we say; depart, while the play is good! By the Most High God, whose sons and born missionaries true men are, ye shall not continue here! You and we have become incompatible; can inhabit one house no longer. Either you must go, or we. Are ye ambitious to try *which* it shall be?

O my Conservative friends, who still specially name and struggle to approve yourselves 'Conservative,' would to Heaven I could persuade you of this world-old fact, than which Fate is not surer, That Truth and Justice alone are *capable* of being 'conserved' and preserved! The thing which is unjust, which is *not* according to God's Law, will you, in a God's Universe, try to conserve that? It is so old, say you? Yes, and the hotter haste ought *you*, of all others, to be in, to let it grow no older! If but the faintest whisper in your hearts intimate to you that it is not fair,—hasten, for the sake of Conservatism itself, to probe it rigorously, to cast it forth at once and forever if guilty. How will or can you preserve *it*, the thing that is not fair? 'Impossibility' a thousandfold is marked on that. And ye call yourselves Conservatives, Aristocracies:—ought not honour and nobleness of mind, if they had departed from all the Earth elsewhere, to find their last refuge with you? Ye unfortunate!

The bough that is dead shall be cut away, for the sake of the tree itself. Old? Yes, it is too old. Many a weary winter has it swung and creaked there, and gnawed and fretted, with its dead wood, the organic substance and still living fibre of this good tree; many a long summer has its ugly naked brown defaced the fair green umbrage; every day it has done mischief, and that only: off with it, for the tree's sake, if for nothing more; let the Conservatism that would preserve cut *it* away. Did no wood-forester apprise you that a dead bough with its dead root left sticking there is extraneous, poisonous; is as a dead iron spike, some horrid rusty ploughshare driven into the living substance;—nay is far worse; for in every wind-storm ('commercial crisis' or the like), it frets and creaks, jolts itself to and fro, and cannot lie quiet as your dead iron spike would.

If I were the Conservative Party of England (which is another bold figure of speech), I would not for a hundred thousand pounds an hour allow those Corn-Laws to continue! Potosi and Golconda put together would not purchase my assent to them. Do you count what treasuries of bitter indignation they are laying up for you in every just English heart? Do you know what questions, not as to Corn-prices and Sliding-scales alone, they are *forcing* every reflective Englishman to ask himself? Questions insoluble, or hitherto unsolved; deeper than any of our Logic-plummets hitherto will sound: questions deep enough,—which it were better that we did not name even in thought! You are forcing us to think of them, to begin uttering them. The utterance of them is begun; and where will it be ended, think you? When two millions of one's brother-men sit in Workhouses, and five millions, as is insolently said, 'rejoice in potatoes,' there are various things that must be begun, let them end where they can.

CHAPTER VI.

TWO CENTURIES.

THE Settlement effected by our 'Healing Parliament' in the Year of Grace 1660, though accomplished under universal acclamations from the four corners of the British Dominions, turns out to have been one of the mournfulest that ever took place in this land of ours. It called and thought itself a Settlement of brightest hope and fulfilment, bright as the blaze of universal tar-barrels and bonfires could make it: and we find it now, on looking back on it with the insight which trial has yielded, a Settlement as of despair. Considered well, it was a Settlement to govern henceforth without God, with only some decent Pretence of God.

Governing by the Christian Law of God had been found a thing of battle, convulsion, confusion, an infinitely difficult thing: wherefore let us now abandon it, and govern only by so much of

God's Christian Law as—as may prove quiet and convenient for us. What is the end of Government? To guide men in the way wherein they should go; towards their true good in this life, the portal of infinite good in a life to come? To guide men in such way, and ourselves in such way, as the Maker of men, whose eye is upon us, will sanction at the Great Day?—Or alas, perhaps at bottom *is* there no Great Day, no sure outlook of any life to come; but only this poor life, and what of taxes, felicities, Nell-Gwyns and entertainments we can manage to muster here? In that case, the end of Government will be, To suppress all noise and disturbance, whether of Puritan preaching, Cameronian psalm-singing, thieves'-riot, murder, arson, or what noise soever, and—be careful that supplies do not fail! A very notable conclusion, if we will think of it, and not without an abundance of fruits for us. Oliver Cromwell's body hung on the Tyburn gallows, as the type of Puritanism found futile, inexecutable, execrable,—yes, that gallows-tree has been a finger-post into very strange country indeed. Let earnest Puritanism die; let decent Formalism, what-soever cant it be or grow to, live! We have had a pleasant journey in that direction; and are—arriving at our inn?

To support the Four Pleas of the Crown, and keep Taxes coming in: in very sad seriousness, has not this been, ever since, even in the best times, almost the one admitted end and aim of Government? Religion, Christian Church, Moral Duty; the fact that man had a soul at all; that in man's life there was any eternal truth or justice at all,—has been as good as left quietly out of sight. Church indeed,—alas, the endless talk and struggle we have had of High-Church, Low-Church, Church-Extension, Church-in-Danger: we invite the Christian reader to think whether it has not been a too miserable screech-owl phantasm of talk and struggle, as for a 'Church,'—which one had rather not define at present!

But now in these godless two centuries, looking at England and her efforts and doings, if we ask, What of England's doings the Law of Nature had accepted, Nature's King had actually furthered and pronounced to have truth in them,—where is our answer? Neither the 'Church' of Hurd and Warburton, nor the Anti-Church of Hume and Paine; not in any shape the Spiritualism of England: all this is already seen, or beginning to be seen, for what it is; a thing that Nature does *not* own. On the one side is dreary Cant, with a *reminiscence* of things noble and divine; on the other is but acrid Candour, with a *prophecy* of things brutal, infernal.   Hurd and Warburton are sunk into the sere and yellow leaf; no considerable body of true-seeing men looks thitherward for healing : the Paine-and-Hume Atheistic theory, of 'things well let alone,' with Liberty, Equality and the like, is also in these days declaring itself nought, unable to keep the world from taking fire.

The theories and speculations of both these parties, and, we may say, of all intermediate parties and persons, prove to be things which the Eternal Veracity did not accept; things superficial, ephemeral, which already a near Posterity, finding them already dead and brown-leafed, is about to suppress and forget.   The Spiritualism of England, for those godless years, is, as it were, all forgettable.   Much has been written : but the perennial Scriptures of Mankind have had small accession : from all English Books, in rhyme or prose, in leather binding or in paper wrappage, how many verses have been added to these ?   Our most melodious Singers have sung as from the throat outwards : from the inner Heart of Man, from the great Heart of Nature, through no Pope or Philips, has there come any tone.   The Oracles have been dumb.   In brief, the Spoken Word of England has not been true. The Spoken Word of England turns out to have been trivial; of short endurance ; not valuable, not available as a Word, except for the passing day.   It has been accordant with transitory Semblance ; discordant with eternal Fact.   It has been unfortunately not a Word, but a Cant ; a helpless involuntary Cant, nay too often a cunning voluntary one : either way, a very mournful Cant; the Voice not of Nature and Fact, but of something other than these.

With all its miserable shortcomings, with its wars, controversies, with its trades-unions, famine-insurrections,—it is her Practical Material Work alone that England has to show for herself !   This, and hitherto almost nothing more ; yet actually this.   The grim inarticulate veracity of the English People, unable to speak its meaning in words, has turned itself silently on things ; and the dark powers of Material Nature have answered, " Yes, this at least is true, this is not false ! "   So answers Nature.   " Waste desert-shrubs of the Tropical swamps have become Cotton-trees ; and here, under my furtherance, are verily woven shirts,—hanging unsold, undistributed, but capable to be distributed, capable to cover the bare backs of my children of men.   Mountains, old as the Creation, I have permitted to be bored through ; bituminous fuel-

stores, the wreck of forests that were green a million years ago,—
I have opened them from my secret rock-chambers, and they are
yours, ye English. Your huge fleets, steamships, do sail the sea;
huge Indias do obey you; from huge *New* Englands and Antipodal
Australias comes profit and traffic to this Old England of mine!"
So answers Nature. The Practical Labour of England is *not* a
chimerical Triviality: it is a Fact, acknowledged by all the
Worlds; which no man and no demon will contradict. It is, very
audibly, though very inarticulately as yet, the one God's Voice we
have heard in these two atheistic centuries.

And now to observe with what bewildering obscurations and
impediments all this as yet stands entangled, and is yet intelligible
to no man! How, with our gross Atheism, we hear it not to be
the Voice of God to us, but regard it merely as a Voice of earthly
Profit-and-Loss. And have a Hell in England,—the Hell of not
making money. And coldly see the all-conquering valiant Sons
of Toil sit enchanted, by the million, in their Poor-Law Bastille,
as if this were Nature's Law;—mumbling to ourselves some vague
janglement of Laissez-faire, Supply-and-demand, Cash-payment the
one nexus of man to man: Free-trade, Competition, and Devil take
the hindmost, our latest Gospel yet preached!

As if, in truth, there were no God of Labour; as if godlike
Labour and brutal Mammonism were convertible terms. A serious,
most earnest Mammonism grown Midas-eared; an unserious
Dilettantism, earnest about nothing, grinning with inarticulate
incredulous incredible jargon about all things, as the *enchanted*
Dilettanti do by the Dead Sea! It is mournful enough, for the
present hour; were there not an endless hope in it withal. Giant
LABOUR, truest emblem there is of God the World-Worker, Demiurgus, and Eternal Maker; noble LABOUR, which is yet to be
the King of this Earth, and sit on the highest throne,—staggering
hitherto like a blind irrational giant, hardly allowed to have his
common place on the street-pavements; idle Dilettantism, Dead-
Sea Apism crying out, "Down with him; he is dangerous!"

Labour must become a seeing rational giant, with a *soul* in the
body of him, and take his place on the throne of things,—leaving
his Mammonism, and several other adjuncts, on the lower steps of
said throne.

CHAPTER VII.

OVER-PRODUCTION.

BUT what will reflective readers say of a Governing Class, such as ours, addressing its Workers with an indictment of 'Over-production'! Over-production: runs it not so? "Ye miscellaneous, ignoble manufacturing individuals, ye have produced too much! We accuse you of making above two-hundred thousand shirts for the bare backs of mankind. Your trousers too, which you have made, of fustian, of cassimere, of Scotch-plaid, of jane, nankeen and woollen broadcloth, are they not manifold? Of hats for the human head, of shoes for the human foot, of stools to sit on, spoons to eat with—Nay, what say we hats or shoes? You produce gold-watches, jewelries, silver-forks, and epergnes, commodes, chiffoniers, stuffed sofas—Heavens, the Commercial Bazaar and multitudinous Howel-and-Jameses cannot contain you. You have produced, produced;—he that seeks your indictment, let him look around. Millions of shirts, and empty pairs of breeches, hang there in judgment against you. We accuse you of over-producing: you are criminally guilty of producing shirts, breeches, hats, shoes and commodities, in a frightful over-abundance. And now there is a glut, and your operatives cannot be fed!"

Never surely, against an earnest Working Mammonism was there brought, by Game-preserving aristocratic Dilettantism, a stranger accusation, since this world began. My lords and gentlemen,—why, it was *you* that were appointed, by the fact and by the theory of your position on the Earth, to 'make and administer Laws,'—that is to say, in a world such as ours, to guard against 'gluts;' against honest operatives, who had done their work, remaining unfed! I say, *you* were appointed to preside over the Distribution and Apportionment of the Wages of Work done; and to see well that there went no labourer without his hire, were it of money-coins, were it of hemp gallows-ropes: that function was yours, and from immemorial time has been: yours, and as yet no other's. These poor shirt-spinners have forgotten much, which by the virtual unwritten law of their position they should have remembered : but by any written recognised law of their position, what have they forgotten ? They were set to make shirts. The Community with all its voices commanded them, saying, " Make shirts ; "—and there the shirts are ! Too many shirts ? Well, that is a novelty, in this intemperate Earth, with its nine-hundred millions of bare backs ! But the Community commanded you, saying, " See that the shirts are well apportioned, that our Human Laws be emblem of God's Laws ; "—and where is the apportionment ? Two million shirtless or ill-shirted workers sit enchanted in Workhouse Bastilles, five million more (according to some) in Ugolino Hunger-cellars ; and for remedy, you say,—what say you ? —" Raise *our* rents ! " I have not in my time heard any stranger speech, not even on the Shores of the Dead Sea. You continue addressing those poor shirt-spinners and over-producers in really a *too* triumphant manner !

" Will you bandy accusations, will you accuse *us* of over-production ? We take the Heavens and the Earth to witness that we have produced nothing at all. Not from us proceeds this frightful overplus of shirts. In the wide domains of created Nature circulates no shirt or thing of our producing. Certain fox-brushes nailed upon our stable-door, the fruit of fair audacity at Melton Mowbray ; these we have produced, and they are openly nailed up there. He that accuses us of producing, let him show himself, let him name what and when. We are innocent of producing ;—ye ungrateful, what mountains of things have we not, on the contrary, had to ' consume ' and make away with ! Mountains of those your heaped manufactures, wheresoever edible or wearable, have they not disappeared before us, as if we had the talent of ostriches, of cormorants, and a kind of divine faculty to eat ? Ye ungrateful ! —and did you not grow under the shadow of our wings ? Are not your filthy mills built on these fields of ours ; on this soil of England, which belongs to—whom think you ? And we shall not offer you our own wheat at the price that pleases us, but that partly pleases you ? A precious notion ! What would become of you, if we chose, at any time, to decide on growing no wheat more ? "

Yes, truly, *here* is the ultimate rock-basis of all Corn-Laws ; whereon, at the bottom of much arguing, they rest as securely as they can : What would become of you, if we decided, some day, on growing no more wheat at all ? If we chose to grow only

partridges henceforth, and a modicum of wheat for our own uses?
Cannot we do what we like with our own?—Yes, indeed! For my
share, if I could melt Gneiss Rock, and create Law of Gravitation;
if I could stride out to the Doggerbank, some morning, and
striking down my trident there into the mud-waves, say, "Be land,
be fields, meadows, mountains and fresh-rolling streams!" by
Heaven, I should incline to have the letting of *that* land in per-
petuity, and sell the wheat of it, or burn the wheat of it, according to my own good judgment! My Corn-Lawing friends, you
affright me.

To the 'Millo-cracy' so-called, to the Working Aristocracy,
steeped too deep in mere ignoble Mammonism, and as yet all
unconscious of its noble destinies, as yet but an irrational or semi-
rational giant, struggling to awake some soul in itself,—the world
will have much to say, reproachfully, reprovingly, admonishingly.
But to the Idle Aristocracy, what will the world have to say?
Things painful, and not pleasant!

To the man who *works*, who attempts, in never so ungracious
barbarous a way, to get forward with some work, you will hasten
out with furtherances, with encouragements, corrections; you will
say to him: "Welcome; thou art ours; our care shall be of thee."
To the Idler, again, never so gracefully going idle, coming forward
with never so many parchments, you will not hasten out; you will
sit still, and be disinclined to rise. You will say to him: "Not
welcome, O complex Anomaly; would thou hadst stayed out of
doors: for who of mortals knows what to do with thee? Thy
parchments: yes, they are old, of venerable yellowness; and we
too honour parchment, old-established settlements, and venerable
use-and-wont. Old parchments in very truth:—yet on the whole,
if thou wilt remark, they are young to the Granite Rocks, to the
Groundplan of God's Universe! We advise thee to put up thy
parchments; to go home to thy place, and make no needless noise
whatever. Our heart's wish is to save thee: yet there as thou art,
hapless Anomaly, with nothing but thy yellow parchments, noisy
futilities, and shotbelts and fox-brushes, who of gods or men can
avert dark Fate? Be counselled, ascertain if no work exist for
thee on God's Earth; if thou find no commanded-duty there but
that of going gracefully idle? Ask, inquire earnestly, with a half-
frantic earnestness; for the answer means Existence or Annihilation
to thee. We apprise thee of the world-old fact, becoming sternly
disclosed again in these days, That he who cannot work in this

Universe cannot get existed in it: had he parchments to thatch the face of the world, these, combustible fallible sheepskin, cannot avail him. Home, thou unfortunate; and let us have at least no noise from thee!"

Suppose the unfortunate Idle Aristocracy, as the unfortunate Working one has done, were to 'retire three days to *its* bed,' and consider itself there, what o'clock it had become ?—

How have we to regret not only that men have 'no religion,' but that they have next to no reflection ; and go about with heads full of mere extraneous noises, with eyes wide-open but visionless, —for most part in the somnambulist state !

CHAPTER VIII.

UNWORKING ARISTOCRACY.

It is well said, ' Land is the right basis of an Aristocracy ; ' whoever possesses the Land, he, more emphatically than any other, is the Governor, Viceking of the people on the Land. It is in these days as it was in those of Henry Plantagenet and Abbot Samson; as it will in all days be. The Land is *Mother* of us all; nourishes, shelters, gladdens, lovingly enriches us all ; in how many ways, from our first wakening to our last sleep on her blessed mother-bosom, does she, as with blessed mother-arms, enfold us all !

The Hill I first saw the Sun rise over, when the Sun and I and all things were yet in their auroral hour, who can divorce me from it ? Mystic, deep as the world's centre, are the roots I have struck into my Native Soil; no *tree* that grows is rooted so. From noblest Patriotism to humblest industrial Mechanism ; from highest dying for your country, to lowest quarrying and coal-boring for it, a Nation's Life depends upon its Land. Again and again we have to say, there can be no true Aristocracy but must possess the Land.

Men talk of 'selling' Land. Land, it is true, like Epic Poems and even higher things, in such a trading world, has to be presented in the market for what it will bring, and as we say be

'sold:' but the notion of 'selling,' for certain bits of metal, the
Iliad of Homer, how much more the *Land* of the World-Creator,
is a ridiculous impossibility! We buy what is saleable of it;
nothing more was ever buyable. Who can or could sell it to
us? Properly speaking, the Land belongs to these two: To the
Almighty God; and to all His Children of Men that have ever
worked well on it, or that shall ever work well on it. No
generation of men can or could, with never such solemnity and
effort, sell Land on any other principle: it is not the property of
any generation, we say, but that of all the past generations
that have worked on it, and of all the future ones that shall work
on it.

Again, we hear it said, The soil of England, or of any country,
is properly worth nothing, except 'the labour bestowed on it.'
This, speaking even in the language of Eastcheap, is not correct.
The rudest space of country equal in extent to England, could a
whole English Nation, with all their habitudes, arrangements,
skills, with whatsoever they do carry within the skins of them and
cannot be stript of, suddenly take wing and alight on it,—would
be worth a very considerable thing! Swiftly, within year and
day, this English Nation, with its multiplex talents of ploughing,
spinning, hammering, mining, road-making and trafficking, would
bring a handsome value out of such a space of country. On the
other hand, fancy what an English Nation, once 'on the wing,'
could have done with itself, had there been simply no soil, not
even an inarable one, to alight on? Vain all its talents for
ploughing, hammering, and whatever else; there is no Earth-room
for this Nation with its talents: this Nation will have to *keep*
hovering on the wing, dolefully shrieking to and fro; and perish
piecemeal; burying itself, down to the last soul of it, in the waste
unfirmamented seas. Ah yes, soil, with or without ploughing, is
the gift of God. The soil of all countries belongs evermore, in a
very considerable degree, to the Almighty Maker! The last stroke
of labour bestowed on it is not the making of its value, but only
the increasing thereof.

It is very strange, the degree to which these truisms are
forgotten in our days; how, in the ever-whirling chaos of Formulas,
we have quietly lost sight of Fact,—which it is so perilous not to
keep forever in sight. Fact, if we do not see it, will make us *feel*
it by and by!—From much loud controversy, and Corn-Law
debating there rises, loud though inarticulate, once more in these

years, this very question among others, Who made the Land of
England ?   Who made it, this respectable English Land, wheat-
growing, metalliferous, carboniferous, which will let readily hand
over head for seventy millions or upwards, as it here lies : who
did make it ?—" We ! " answer the much-*consuming* Aristocracy ;
" We ! " as they ride in, moist with the sweat of Melton Mowbray :
" It is we that made it ; or are the heirs, assigns and representatives
of those who did ! "—My brothers, YOU ?   Everlasting honour to
you, then ; and Corn-Laws as many as you will, till your own deep
stomachs cry Enough, or some voice of Human pity for our famine
bids you Hold !   Ye are as gods, that can create soil.   Soil-
creating gods there is no withstanding.   They have the might to
sell wheat at what price they list ; and the right, to all lengths,
and famine-lengths,—if they be pitiless infernal gods !   Celestial
gods, I think, would stop short of the famine-price ; but no infernal nor any kind of god can be bidden stop !——Infatuated
mortals, into what questions are you driving every thinking man
in England ?

I say, you did *not* make the Land of England ; and, by the
possession of it, you *are* bound to furnish guidance and governance to England !   That is the law of your position on this
God's-Earth ; an everlasting act of Heaven's Parliament, not
repealable in St. Stephen's or elsewhere !   True government
and guidance ; not no-government and Laissez-faire ; how much
less, *mis*-government and Corn-Law !   There is not an imprisoned Worker looking out from these Bastilles but appeals,
very audibly in Heaven's High Courts, against you, and me,
and every one who is not imprisoned, " Why am I here ? "   His
appeal is audible in Heaven ; and will become audible enough on
Earth too, if it remain unheeded here.   His appeal is against you,
foremost of all ; you stand in the front-rank of the accused ; you,
by the very place you hold, have first of all to answer him and
Heaven !

What looks maddest, miserablest in these mad and miserable
Corn-Laws is independent altogether of their ' effect on wages,'
their effect on ' increase of trade,' or any other such effect : it is
the continual maddening proof they protrude into the faces of all
men, that our Governing Class, called by God and Nature and the
inflexible law of Fact, either to do something towards governing,
or to die and be abolished,—have not yet learned even to sit still

and do no mischief! For no Anti-Corn-Law League yet asks more of them than this;—Nature and Fact, very imperatively, asking so much more of them. Anti-Corn-Law League asks not, Do something; but, Cease your destructive misdoing, Do ye nothing!

Nature's message will have itself obeyed: messages of mere Free-Trade, Anti-Corn-Law League and Laissez-faire, will then need small obeying!—Ye fools, in name of Heaven, work, work, at the Ark of Deliverance for yourselves and us, while hours are still granted you! No: instead of working at the Ark, they say, "We cannot get our hands kept rightly warm;" and *sit obstinately burning the planks*. No madder spectacle at present exhibits itself under this Sun.

The Working Aristocracy; Mill-owners, Manufacturers, Commanders of Working Men: alas, against them also much shall be brought in accusation; much,—and the freest Trade in Corn, total abolition of Tariffs, and uttermost 'Increase of Manufactures' and 'Prosperity of Commerce,' will permanently mend no jot of it. The Working Aristocracy must strike into a new path; must understand that money alone is *not* the representative either of man's success in the world, or of man's duties to man; and reform their own selves from top to bottom, if they wish England reformed. England will not be habitable long, unreformed.

The Working Aristocracy—Yes, but on the threshold of all this, it is again and again to be asked, What of the Idle Aristocracy? Again and again, What shall we say of the Idle Aristocracy, the Owners of the Soil of England; whose recognised function is that of handsomely consuming the rents of England, shooting the partridges of England, and as an agreeable amusement (if the purchase-money and other conveniences serve), dilettante-ing in Parliament and Quarter-Sessions for England? We will say mournfully, in the presence of Heaven and Earth,—that we stand speechless, stupent, and know not what to say! That a class of men entitled to live sumptuously on the marrow of the earth; permitted simply, nay entreated, and as yet entreated in vain, to do nothing at all in return, was never heretofore seen on the face of this Planet. That such a class is transitory, exceptional, and, unless Nature's Laws fall dead, cannot continue. That it has continued now a moderate while; has, for the last fifty years, been rapidly attaining its state of perfection. That it will have to find its duties and do them; or else that it must and will cease to be seen on the face of this Planet, which is a Working one, not an Idle one.

Alas, alas, the Working Aristocracy, admonished by Trades-unions, Chartist conflagrations, above all by their own shrewd sense kept in perpetual communion with the fact of things, will assuredly reform themselves, and a working world will still be possible :—but the fate of the Idle Aristocracy, as one reads its horoscope hitherto in Corn-Laws and suchlike, is an abyss that fills one with despair. Yes, my rosy fox-hunting brothers, a terrible *Hippocratic look* reveals itself (God knows, not to my joy) through those fresh buxom countenances of yours. Through your Corn-Law Majorities, Sliding-Scales, Protecting-Duties, Bribery-Elections, and triumphant Kentish-fire, a thinking eye discerns ghastly images of ruin, too ghastly for words; a handwriting as of MENE, MENE. Men and brothers, on your Sliding-scale you seem sliding, and to have slid,—you little know whither ! Good God ! did not a French Donothing Aristocracy, hardly above half a century ago, declare in like manner, and in its featherhead believe in like manner, " We cannot exist, and continue to dress and parade ourselves, on the just rent of the soil of France; but we must have farther payment than rent of the soil, we must be exempted from taxes too,"—we must have a Corn-Law to extend our rent ? This was in 1789 : in four years more—Did you look into the Tanneries of Meudon, and the long-naked making for themselves breeches of human skins ! May the merciful Heavens avert the omen; may we be wiser, that so we be less wretched.

A High Class without duties to do is like a tree planted on precipices; from the roots of which all the earth has been crumbling. Nature owns no man who is not a Martyr withal. Is there a man who pretends to live luxuriously housed up; screened from all work, from want, danger, hardship, the victory over which is what we name work ;—he himself to sit serene, amid down-bolsters and appliances, and have all his work and battling done by other men ? And such man calls himself a *noble*-man ? His fathers worked for him, he says; or successfully gambled for him : here *he* sits; professes, not in sorrow but in pride, that he and his have done no work, time out of mind. It is the law of the land, and is thought to be the law of the Universe, that he, alone of recorded men, shall have no task laid on him, except that of eating his cooked victuals, and not flinging himself out of window. Once more I will say, there was no stranger spectacle ever shown under this Sun. A veritable fact in our England of the Nineteenth Century. His victuals he does eat: but as for keeping in the inside of the window,—have not his friends, like me, enough to do? Truly, looking at his Corn-Laws, Game-Laws, Chandos-Clauses, Bribery-Elections and much else, you do shudder over the tumbling and plunging he makes, held back by the lapels and coat-skirts; only a thin fence of window-glass before him,—and in the street mere horrid iron spikes! My sick brother, as in hospital-maladies men do, thou dreamest of Paradises and Eldorados, which are far from thee. 'Cannot I do what I like with my own?' Gracious Heaven, my brother, this that thou seest with those sick eyes is no firm Eldorado, and Corn-Law Paradise of Donothings, but a dream of thy own fevered brain. It is a glass-window, I tell thee, so many stories from the street; where are iron spikes and the law of gravitation!

What is the meaning of nobleness, if this be 'noble'? In a valiant suffering for others, not in a slothful making others suffer for us, did nobleness ever lie. The chief of men is he who stands in the van of men; fronting the peril which frightens back all others; which, if it be not vanquished, will devour the others. Every noble crown is, and on Earth will forever be, a crown of thorns. The Pagan Hercules, why was he accounted a hero? Because he had slain Nemean Lions, cleansed Augean Stables, undergone Twelve Labours only not too heavy for a god. In modern, as in ancient and all societies, the Aristocracy, they that assume the functions of an Aristocracy, doing them or not, have taken the post of honour; which is the post of difficulty, the post of danger,—of death, if the difficulty be not overcome. *Il faut payer de sa vie.* Why was our life given us, if not that we should manfully give it? Descend, O Donothing Pomp; quit thy down-cushions; expose thyself to learn what wretches feel, and how to cure it! The Czar of Russia became a dusty toiling shipwright; worked with his axe in the Docks of Saardam; and his aim was small to thine. Descend thou: undertake this horrid 'living chaos of Ignorance and Hunger' weltering round thy feet; say, "I will heal it, or behold I will die foremost in it." Such is verily the law. Everywhere and everywhen a man has to '*pay* with his life;' to do his work, as a soldier does, at the expense of life. In no Piepowder earthly Court can you sue an Aristocracy to do its work, at this moment: but in the Higher Court, which even *it* calls 'Court of Honour,' and which is the Court of Necessity withal, and the eternal Court of the Universe, in which all Fact comes to plead, and every Human Soul is an apparitor,—the Aristocracy is answerable, and even now answering, *there*.

Parchments? Parchments are venerable: but they ought at all times to represent, as near as they by possibility can, the writing of the Adamant Tablets; otherwise they are not so venerable! Benedict the Jew in vain pleaded parchments; his usuries were too many. The King said, "Go to, for all thy parchments, thou shalt pay just debt; down with thy dust, or observe this tooth-forceps!" Nature, a far juster Sovereign, has far terribler forceps. Aristocracies, actual and imaginary, reach a time when parchment pleading does not avail them. "Go to, for all thy parchments, thou shalt pay due debt!" shouts the Universe to them, in an emphatic manner. They refuse to pay, confidently pleading parchment: their best grinder-tooth, with horrible agony, goes out of their jaw. Wilt thou pay now? A second grinder, again in horrible agony, goes: a second, and a third, and if need be, all the teeth and grinders, and the life itself with them;—and *then* there is free payment, and an anatomist-subject into the bargain!

Reform Bills, Corn-Law Abrogation Bills, and then Land-Tax Bill, Property-Tax Bill, and still dimmer list of *etceteras;* grinder after grinder:—my lords and gentlemen, it were better for you to arise and begin doing your work, than sit there and plead parchments!

We write no Chapter on the Corn-Laws, in this place; the Corn-Laws are too mad to have a Chapter. There is a certain immorality, when there is not a necessity, in speaking about things finished; in chopping into small pieces the already slashed and slain. When the brains are out, why does not a Solecism die? It is at its own peril if it refuse to die; it ought to make all conceivable haste to die, and get itself buried! The trade of Anti-Corn-Law Lecturer in these days, still an indispensable, is a highly tragic one.

The Corn-Laws will go, and even soon go: would we were all as sure of the Millennium as they are of going! They go swiftly in these present months; with an increase of velocity, an ever-deepening, ever-widening sweep of momentum, truly notable. It is at the Aristocracy's own damage and peril, still more than at any other's whatsoever, that the Aristocracy maintains them;—at a damage, say only, as above computed, of a 'hundred thousand pounds an hour'! The Corn-Laws keep all the air hot: fostered by their fever-warmth, much that is evil, but much also, how much that is good and indispensable, is rapidly coming to life among us!

CHAPTER IX.

WORKING ARISTOCRACY.

A POOR Working Mammonism getting itself 'strangled in the partridge-nets of an Unworking Dilettantism,' and bellowing dreadfully, and already black in the face, is surely a disastrous spectacle! But of a Midas-eared Mammonism, which indeed at bottom all pure Mammonisms are, what better can you expect? No better;—if not this, then something other equally disastrous, if not still more disastrous. Mammonisms, grown asinine, have to become human again, and rational; they have, on the whole, to cease to be Mammonisms, were it even on compulsion, and pressure of the hemp round their neck!—My friends of the Working Aristocracy, there are now a great many things which you also, in your extreme need, will have to consider.

The Continental people, it would seem, are 'exporting our 'machinery, beginning to spin cotton and manufacture for them-'selves, to cut us out of this market and then out of that!' Sad news indeed ; but irremediable ;—by no means the saddest news. The saddest news is, that we should find our National Existence, as I sometimes hear it said, depend on selling manufactured cotton at a farthing an ell cheaper than any other People. A most narrow stand for a great Nation to base itself on! A stand which, with all the Corn-Law Abrogations conceivable, I do not think will be capable of enduring.

My friends, suppose we quitted that stand; suppose we came

honestly down from it, and said : " This is our minimum of cotton-prices. We care not, for the present, to make cotton any cheaper. Do you, if it seem so blessed to you, make cotton cheaper. Fill your lungs with cotton-fuzz, your hearts with copperas-fumes, with rage and mutiny; become ye the general gnomes of Europe, slaves of the lamp ! "—I admire a Nation which fancies it will die if it do not undersell all other Nations, to the end of the world. Brothers, we will cease to *under*sell them; we will be content to *equal*-sell them; to be happy selling equally with them ! I do not see the use of underselling them. Cotton-cloth is already two-pence a yard or lower; and yet bare backs were never more numerous among us. Let inventive men cease to spend their existence incessantly contriving how cotton can be made cheaper; and try to invent, a little, how cotton at its present cheapness could be somewhat justlier divided among us. Let inventive men consider, Whether the Secret of this Universe, and of Man's Life there, does, after all, as we rashly fancy it, consist in making money ? There is One God, just, supreme, almighty: but is Mammon the name of him ?—With a Hell which means 'Failing to make money,' I do not think there is any Heaven possible that would suit one well ; nor so much as an Earth that can be habitable long ! In brief, all this Mammon-Gospel, of Supply-and-demand, Competition, Laissez-faire, and Devil take the hindmost, begins to be one of the shabbiest Gospels ever preached ; or altogether the shabbiest. Even with Dilettante partridge-nets, and at a horrible expenditure of pain, who shall regret to see the entirely transient, and at best somewhat despicable life strangled out of *it* ? At the best, as we say, a somewhat despicable, unvenerable thing, this same ' Laissez-faire ;' and now, at the *worst*, fast growing an altogether detestable one !

"But what is to be done with our manufacturing population, with our agricultural, with our ever-increasing population ? " cry many.—Ay, what ? Many things can be done with them, a hundred things, and a thousand things,—had we once got a soul, and begun to try. This one thing, of doing for them by ' under-selling all people,' and filling our own bursten pockets and appetites by the road ; and turning over all care for any ' popula-tion,' or human or divine consideration except cash only, to the winds, with a " Laissez-faire " and the rest of it: this is evidently not the thing. Farthing cheaper per yard ? No great Nation can stand on the apex of such a pyramid ; screwing itself higher and

higher; balancing itself on its great-toe! Can England not
subsist without being *above* all people in working? England never
deliberately purposed such a thing. If England work better than
all people, it shall be well. England, like an honest worker, will
work as well as she can; and hope the gods may allow her to live
on that basis. Laissez-faire and much else being once well dead,
how many 'impossibles' will become possible! They are impossible,
as cotton-cloth at two-pence an ell was—till men set about making
it. The inventive genius of great England will not forever sit
patient with mere wheels and pinions, bobbins, straps and billy-
rollers whirring in the head of it. The inventive genius of
England is not a Beaver's, or a Spinner's or Spider's genius: it is
a *Man's* genius, I hope, with a God over him!

Laissez-faire, Supply-and-demand,—one begins to be weary of
all that. Leave all to egoism, to ravenous greed of money, of
pleasure, of applause:—it is the Gospel of Despair! Man *is* a
Patent-Digester, then: only give him Free Trade, Free digesting-
room; and each of us digest what he can come at, leaving the rest
to Fate! My unhappy brethren of the Working Mammonism, my
unhappier brethren of the Idle Dilettantism, no world was ever
held together in that way for long. A world of mere Patent-
Digesters will soon have nothing to digest: such world ends, and
by Law of Nature must end, in 'over-population;' in howling
universal famine, 'impossibility,' and suicidal madness, as of endless
dog-kennels run rabid. Supply-and-demand shall do its full part,
and Free Trade shall be free as air;—thou of the shotbelts, see
thou forbid it not, with those paltry, *worse* than Mammonish
swindleries and Sliding-scales of thine, which are seen to be
swindleries for all thy canting, which in times like ours are very
scandalous to see! And Trade never so well freed, and all Tariffs
settled or abolished, and Supply-and-demand in full operation,—
let us all know that we have yet done nothing; that we have
merely cleared the ground for doing.

Yes, were the Corn-Laws ended tomorrow, there is nothing yet
ended; there is only room made for all manner of things beginning.
The Corn-Laws gone, and Trade made free, it is as good as certain
this paralysis of industry will pass away. We shall have another
period of commercial enterprise, of victory and prosperity; during
which, it is likely, much money will again be made, and all the
people may, by the extant methods, still for a space of years, be kept
alive and physically fed. The strangling band of Famine will be

loosened from our necks; we shall have room again to breathe; time to bethink ourselves, to repent and consider! A precious and thrice-precious space of years; wherein to struggle as for life in reforming our foul ways; in alleviating, instructing, regulating our people; seeking, as for life, that something like spiritual food be imparted them, some real governance and guidance be provided them! It will be a priceless time. For our new period or paroxysm of commercial prosperity will and can, on the old methods of 'Competition and Devil take the hindmost,' prove but a paroxysm: a new paroxysm,—likely enough, if we do not use it better, to be our *last*. In this, of itself, is no salvation. If our Trade in twenty years, 'flourishing' as never Trade flourished, could double itself; yet then also, by the old Laissez-faire method, our Population is doubled: we shall then be as we are, only twice as many of us, twice and ten times as unmanageable!

All this dire misery, therefore; all this of our poor Workhouse Workmen, of our Chartisms, Trades-strikes, Corn-Laws, Toryisms, and the general downbreak of Laissez-faire in these days,—may we not regard it as a voice from the dumb bosom of Nature, saying to us: "Behold! Supply-and-demand is not the one Law of Nature; Cash-payment is not the sole nexus of man with man,— how far from it! Deep, far deeper than Supply-and-demand, are Laws, Obligations sacred as Man's Life itself: these also, if you will continue to do work, you shall now learn and obey. He that will learn them, behold Nature is on his side, he shall yet work and prosper with noble rewards. He that will not learn them, Nature is against him, he shall not be able to do work in Nature's empire,—not in hers. Perpetual mutiny, contention, hatred, isolation, execration shall wait on his footsteps, till all men discern that the thing which he attains, however golden it look or be, is not success, but the want of success."

Supply-and-demand,—alas! For what noble work was there ever yet any audible 'demand' in that poor sense? The man of Macedonia, speaking in vision to an Apostle Paul, "Come over and help us," did not specify what rate of wages he would give! Or was the Christian Religion itself accomplished by Prize-Essays, Bridgwater Bequests, and a 'minimum of Four thousand five hundred a year'? No demand that I heard of was made then, audible in any Labour-market, Manchester Chamber of Commerce, or other the like emporium and hiring establishment; silent were

all these from any whisper of such demand ;—powerless were all
these to 'supply' it, had the demand been in thunder and earth-
quake, with gold Eldorados and Mahometan Paradises for the reward.
Ah me, into what waste latitudes, in this Time-Voyage, have we
wandered ; like adventurous Sindbads ;—where the men go about as
if by galvanism, with meaningless glaring eyes, and have no soul,
but only a beaver-faculty and stomach ! The haggard despair of
Cotton-factory, Coal-mine operatives, Chandos Farm-labourers, in
these days, is painful to behold ; but not so painful, hideous to the
inner sense, as that brutish godforgetting Profit-and-Loss Philosophy and Life-theory, which we hear jangled on all hands of us,
in senate-houses, spouting-clubs, leading-articles, pulpits and platforms, everywhere as the Ultimate Gospel and candid Plain-
English of Man's Life, from the throats and pens and though s of
all-but all men !—

Enlightened Philosophies, like Molière Doctors, will tell you :
" Enthusiasms, Self-sacrifice, Heaven, Hell and suchlike : yes, all
that was true enough for old stupid times ; all that used to be
true : but we have changed all that, *nous avons changé tout cela !*"
Well ; if the heart be got round now into the right side, and the
liver to the left ; if man have no heroism in him deeper than the
wish to eat, and in his soul there dwell now no Infinite of Hope and
Awe, and no divine Silence can become imperative because it is not
Sinai Thunder, and no tie will bind if it be not that of Tyburn
gallows-ropes,—then verily you have changed all that ; and for it,
and for you, and for me, behold the Abyss and nameless Annihilation is ready. So scandalous a beggarly Universe deserves indeed
nothing else ; I cannot say I would save it from Annihilation.
Vacuum, and the serene Blue, will be much handsomer ; easier too
for all of us. I, for one, decline living as a Patent-Digester :
Patent-Digester, Spinning-Mule, Mayfair Clothes-Horse : many
thanks, but your Chaosships will have the goodness to excuse me !

CHAPTER X.

PLUGSON OF UNDERSHOT.

ONE thing I do know: Never, on this Earth, was the relation of man to man long carried on by Cash-payment alone. If, at any time, a philosophy of Laissez-faire, Competition and Supply-and-demand, start up as the exponent of human relations, expect that it will soon end.

Such philosophies will arise: for man's philosophies are usually the 'supplement of his practice;' some ornamental Logic-varnish, some outer skin of Articulate Intelligence, with which he strives to render his dumb Instinctive Doings presentable when they are done. Such philosophies will arise; be preached as Mammon-Gospels, the ultimate Evangel of the World; be believed, with what is called belief, with much superficial bluster, and a kind of shallow satisfaction real in its way:—but they are ominous gospels! They are the sure, and even swift, forerunner of great changes. Expect that the old System of Society is done, is dying and fallen into dotage, when it begins to rave in that fashion. Most Systems that I have watched the death of, for the last three thousand years, have gone just so. The Ideal, the True and Noble that was in them having faded out, and nothing now remaining but naked Egoism, vulturous Greediness, they cannot live; they are bound and inexorably ordained by the oldest Destinies, Mothers of the Universe, to die. Curious enough: they thereupon, as I have pretty generally noticed, devise some light comfortable kind of 'wine-and-walnuts philosophy' for themselves, this of Supply-and-demand or another; and keep saying, during hours of mastication and rumination, which they call hours of meditation: "Soul, take thy ease; it is all *well* that thou art a vulture-soul;"—and pangs of dissolution come upon them, oftenest before they are aware!

Cash-payment never was, or could except for a few years be, the union-bond of man to man. Cash never yet paid one man fully his deserts to another; nor could it, nor can it, now or henceforth to the end of the world. I invite his Grace of Castle-Rackrent to reflect on this;—does he think that a Land Aristocracy when it becomes a Land Auctioneership can have long to live? Or that Sliding-scales will increase the vital stamina of it? The indomitable Plugson too, of the respected Firm of Plugson, Hunks and Company, in St. Dolly Undershot, is invited to reflect on this; for to him also it will be new, perhaps even newer. Book-keeping by double entry is admirable, and records several things in an exact manner. But the Mother-Destinies also keep their Tablets; in Heaven's Chancery also there goes on a recording; and things, as my Moslem friends say, are 'written on the iron leaf.'

Your Grace and Plugson, it is like, go to Church occasionally : did you never in vacant moments, with perhaps a dull parson droning to you, glance into your New Testament, and the cash-account stated four times over, by a kind of quadruple entry,—in the Four Gospels there? I consider that a cash-account, and balance-statement of work done and wages paid, worth attending to. Precisely *such*, though on a smaller scale, go on at all moments under this Sun; and the statement and balance of them in the Plugson Ledgers and on the Tablets of Heaven's Chancery are discrepant exceedingly ;—which ought really to teach, and to have long since taught, an indomitable common-sense Plugson of Undershot, much more an unattackable *un*common-sense Grace of Rackrent, a thing or two !—In brief, we shall have to dismiss the Cash-Gospel rigorously into its own place : we shall have to know, on the threshold, that either there is some infinitely deeper Gospel, subsidiary, explanatory and daily and hourly corrective, to the Cash one ; or else that the Cash one itself and all others are fast travelling !

For all human things do require to have an Ideal in them; to have some Soul in them, as we said, were it only to keep the Body unputrefied. And wonderful it is to see how the Ideal or Soul, place it in what ugliest Body you may, will irradiate said Body with its own nobleness; will gradually, incessantly, mould, modify, new-form or reform said ugliest Body, and make it at last beautiful, and to a certain degree divine !—Oh, if you could dethrone that Brute-god Mammon, and put a Spirit-god in his place ! One way or other, he must and will have to be dethroned.

Fighting, for example, as I often say to myself, Fighting with steel murder-tools is surely a much uglier operation than Working, take it how you will. Yet even of Fighting, in religious Abbot

Samson's days, see what a Feudalism there had grown,—a 'glorious Chivalry,' much besung down to the present day. Was not that one of the 'impossiblest' things? Under the sky is no uglier spectacle than two men with clenched teeth, and hell-fire eyes, hacking one another's flesh; converting precious living bodies, and priceless living souls, into nameless masses of putrescence, useful only for turnip-manure. How did a Chivalry ever come out of that; how anything that was not hideous, scandalous, infernal? It will be a question worth considering by and by.

I remark, for the present, only two things: first, that the Fighting itself was not, as we rashly suppose it, a Fighting without cause, but more or less with cause. Man is created to fight; he is perhaps best of all definable as a born soldier; his life 'a battle and a march,' under the right General. It is forever indispensable for a man to fight: now with Necessity, with Barrenness, Scarcity, with Puddles, Bogs, tangled Forests, unkempt Cotton;—now also with the hallucinations of his poor fellow Men. Hallucinatory visions rise in the head of my poor fellow man; make him claim over me rights which are not his. All fighting, as we noticed long ago, is the dusty conflict of strengths, each thinking itself the strongest, or, in other words, the justest;—of Mights which do in the long-run, and forever will in this just Universe in the long-run, mean Rights. In conflict the perishable part of them, beaten sufficiently, flies off into dust: this process ended, appears the imperishable, the true and exact.

And now let us remark a second thing: how, in these baleful operations, a noble devout-hearted Chevalier will comport himself, and an ignoble godless Bucanier and Chactaw Indian. Victory is the aim of each. But deep in the heart of the noble man it lies forever legible, that as an Invisible Just God made him, so will and must God's Justice and this only, were it never so invisible, ultimately prosper in all controversies and enterprises and battles whatsoever. What an Influence; ever-present,—like a Soul in the rudest Caliban of a body; like a ray of Heaven, and illuminative creative *Fiat-Lux*, in the wastest terrestrial Chaos! Blessed divine Influence, traceable even in the horror of Battlefields and garments rolled in blood: how it ennobles even the Battlefield; and, in place of a Chactaw Massacre, makes it a Field of Honour! A Battlefield too is great. Considered well, it is a kind of Quintessence of Labour; Labour distilled into its utmost concentration; the significance of years of it compressed into an hour. Here too thou shalt be strong, and not in muscle only, if thou wouldst prevail. Here too thou shalt be strong of heart, noble of soul; thou shalt dread no pain or death, thou shalt not love ease or life; in rage, thou shalt remember mercy, justice;—thou shalt be a Knight and not a Chactaw, if thou wouldst prevail! It is the rule of all battles, against hallucinating fellow Men, against unkempt Cotton, or whatsoever battles they may be, which a man in this world has to fight.

Howel Davies dyes the West-Indian Seas with blood, piles his decks with plunder; approves himself the expertest Seaman, the daringest Seafighter: but he gains no lasting victory, lasting victory is not possible for him. Not, had he fleets larger than the combined British Navy all united with him in bucaniering. He, once for all, cannot prosper in his duel. He strikes down his man: yes; but his man, or his man's representative, has no notion to lie struck down; neither, though slain ten times, will he keep so lying;—nor has the Universe any notion to keep him so lying! On the contrary, the Universe and he have, at all moments, all manner of motives to start up again, and desperately fight again. Your Napoleon is flung out, at last, to St. Helena; the latter end of him sternly compensating the beginning. The Bucanier strikes down a man, a hundred or a million men: but what profits it? He has one enemy never to be struck down; nay two enemies: Mankind and the Maker of Men. On the great scale or on the small, in fighting of men or fighting of difficulties, I will not embark my venture with Howel Davies: it is not the Bucanier, it is the Hero only that can gain victory, that can do more than *seem* to succeed. These things will deserve meditating; for they apply to all battle and soldiership, all struggle and effort whatsoever in this Fight of Life. It is a poor Gospel, Cash-Gospel or whatever name it have, that does not, with clear tone, uncontradictable, carrying conviction to all hearts, forever keep men in mind of these things.

Unhappily, my indomitable friend Plugson of Undershot has, in a great degree, forgotten them;—as, alas, all the world has; as, alas, our very Dukes and Soul-Overseers have, whose special trade it was to remember them! Hence these tears.—Plugson, who has indomitably spun Cotton merely to gain thousands of pounds, I have to call as yet a Bucanier and Chactaw; till there come something better, still more indomitable from him. His hundred Thousand-pound Notes, if there be nothing other, are to me but as the hundred Scalps in a Chactaw wigwam. The blind

Plugson : he was a Captain of Industry, born member of the Ultimate genuine Aristocracy of this Universe, could he have known it ! These thousand men that span and toiled round him, they were a regiment whom he had enlisted, man by man ; to make war on a very genuine enemy : Bareness of back, and disobedient Cotton-fibre, which will not, unless forced to it, consent to cover bare backs. Here is a most genuine enemy ; over whom all creatures will wish him victory. He enlisted his thousand men : said to them, " Come, brothers, let us have a dash at Cotton ! " They follow with cheerful shout ; they gain such a victory over Cotton as the Earth has to admire and clap hands at : but, alas, it is yet only of the Bucanier or Chactaw sort,—as good as no victory ! Foolish Plugson of St. Dolly Undershot : does he hope to become illustrious by hanging up the scalps in his wigwam, the hundred thousands at his banker's, and saying, Behold my scalps ? Why, Plugson, even thy own host is all in mutiny : Cotton is conquered ; but the ' bare backs '—are worse covered than ever ! Indomitable Plugson, thou must cease to be a Chactaw ; thou and others ; thou thyself, if no other !

Did William the Norman Bastard, or any of his Taillefers, *Ironcutters*, manage so ? Ironcutter, at the end of the campaign, did not turn-off his thousand fighters, but said to them : " Noble fighters, this is the land we have gained ; be I Lord in it,—what we will call *Law-ward*, maintainer and *keeper* of Heaven's *Laws* : be I *Law-ward*, or in brief orthoepy *Lord* in it, and be ye Loyal Men around me in it ; and we will stand by one another, as soldiers round a captain, for again we shall have need of one another ! " Plugson, bucanier-like, says to them : " Noble spinners, this is the Hundred Thousand we have gained, wherein I mean to dwell and plant vineyards ; the hundred thousand is mine, the three and sixpence daily was yours : adieu, noble spinners ; drink my health with this groat each, which I give you over and above ! " The entirely unjust Captain of Industry, say I ; not Chevalier, but Bucanier ! ' Commercial Law ' does indeed acquit him ; asks, with wide eyes, What else ? So too Howel Davies asks, Was it not according to the strictest Bucanier Custom ? Did I depart in any jot or tittle from the Laws of the Bucaniers ?

After all, money, as they say, is miraculous. Plugson wanted victory ; as Chevaliers and Bucaniers, and all men alike do. He found money recognised, by the whole world with one assent, as the true symbol, exact equivalent and synonym of victory ;—

and here we have him, a grimbrowed, indomitable Bucanier, coming home to us with a 'victory,' which the whole world is *ceasing* to clap hands at! The whole world, taught somewhat impressively, is beginning to recognise that such victory is but half a victory; and that now, if it please the Powers, we must— have the other half!

Money is miraculous. What miraculous facilities has it yielded, will it yield us; but also what never-imagined confusions, obscurations has it brought in; down almost to total extinction of the moral-sense in large masses of mankind! 'Protection of property,' of what is '*mine*,' means with most men protection of money,— the thing which, had I a thousand padlocks over it, is least of all *mine*; is, in a manner, scarcely worth calling mine! The symbol shall be held sacred, defended everywhere with tipstaves, ropes and gibbets; the thing signified shall be composedly cast to the dogs. A human being who has worked with human beings clears all scores with them, cuts himself with triumphant completeness forever loose from them, by paying down certain shillings and pounds. Was it not the wages I promised you? There they are, to the last sixpence,—according to the Laws of the Bucaniers!— Yes, indeed;—and, at such times, it becomes imperatively necessary to ask all persons, bucaniers and others, Whether these same respectable Laws of the Bucaniers are written on God's eternal Heavens at all, on the inner Heart of Man at all; or on the respectable Bucanier Logbook merely, for the convenience of bucaniering merely? What a question;—whereat Westminster Hall shudders to its driest parchment; and on the dead wigs each particular horsehair stands on end!

The Laws of Laissez-faire, O Westminster, the laws of industrial Captain and industrial Soldier, how much more of idle Captain and industrial Soldier, will need to be remodelled, and modified, and rectified in a hundred and a hundred ways,—and *not* in the Sliding-scale direction, but in the totally opposite one! With two million industrial Soldiers already sitting in Bastilles, and five million pining on potatoes, methinks Westminster cannot begin too soon!—A man has other obligations laid on him, in God's Universe, than the payment of cash: these also Westminster, if it will continue to exist and have board-wages, must contrive to take some charge of:—by Westminster or by another, they must and will be taken charge of; be, with whatever difficulty, got articulated, got enforced, and to a certain approximate extent put

in practice. And, as I say, it cannot be too soon! For Mammonism, left to itself, has become Midas-eared; and with all its
gold mountains, sits starving for want of bread: and Dilettantism
with its partridge-nets, in this extremely earnest Universe of ours,
is playing somewhat too high a game. 'A man by the very look
of him promises so much:' yes; and by the rent-roll of him does
he promise nothing?—

Alas, what a business will this be, which our Continental friends,
groping this long while somewhat absurdly about it and about it,
call 'Organisation of Labour;'—which must be taken out of the
hands of absurd windy persons, and put into the hands of wise,
laborious, modest and valiant men, to begin with it straightway;
to proceed with it, and succeed in it more and more, if Europe, at
any rate if England, is to continue habitable much longer. Looking
at the kind of most noble Corn-Law Dukes or Practical *Duces* we
have, and also of right reverend Soul-Overseers, Christian Spiritual
Duces 'on a minimum of four thousand five hundred,' one's hopes
are a little chilled. Courage, nevertheless; there are many brave
men in England! My indomitable Plugson,—nay is there not
even in thee some hope? Thou art hitherto a Bucanier, as it was
written and prescribed for thee by an evil world: but in that grim
brow, in that indomitable heart which *can* conquer Cotton, do
there not perhaps lie other ten-times nobler conquests?

CHAPTER XI.

LABOUR.

FOR there is a perennial nobleness, and even sacredness, in
Work. Were he never so benighted, forgetful of his high calling,
there is always hope in a man that actually and earnestly works:
in Idleness alone is there perpetual despair. Work, never so
Mammonish, mean, *is* in communication with Nature; the real
desire to get Work done will itself lead one more and more to
truth, to Nature's appointments and regulations, which are truth.
The latest Gospel in this world is, Know thy work and do it.

'Know thyself:' long enough has that poor 'self' of thine tormented thee; thou wilt never get to 'know' it, I believe! Think it not thy business, this of knowing thyself; thou art an unknowable individual: know what thou canst work at; and work at it, like a Hercules! That will be thy better plan.

It has been written, 'an endless significance lies in Work;' a man perfects himself by working. Foul jungles are cleared away, fair seedfields rise instead, and stately cities; and withal the man himself first ceases to be a jungle and foul unwholesome desert thereby. Consider how, even in the meanest sorts of Labour, the whole soul of a man is composed into a kind of real harmony, the instant he sets himself to work! Doubt, Desire, Sorrow, Remorse, Indignation, Despair itself, all these like helldogs lie beleaguering the soul of the poor dayworker, as of every man: but he bends himself with free valour against his task, and all these are stilled, all these shrink murmuring far off into their caves. The man is now a man. The blessed glow of Labour in him, is it not as purifying fire, wherein all poison is burnt up, and of sour smoke itself there is made bright blessed flame!

Destiny, on the whole, has no other way of cultivating us. A formless Chaos, once set it *revolving*, grows round and ever rounder; ranges itself, by mere force of gravity, into strata, spherical courses; is no longer a Chaos, but a round compacted World. What would become of the Earth, did she cease to revolve? In the poor old Earth, so long as she revolves, all inequalities, irregularities disperse themselves; all irregularities are incessantly becoming regular. Hast thou looked on the Potter's wheel,—one of the venerablest objects; old as the Prophet Ezechiel and far older? Rude lumps of clay, how they spin themselves up, by mere quick whirling, into beautiful circular dishes. And fancy the most assiduous Potter, but without his wheel; reduced to make dishes, or rather amorphous botches, by mere kneading and baking! Even such a Potter were Destiny, with a human soul that would rest and lie at ease, that would not work and spin! Of an idle unrevolving man the kindest Destiny, like the most assiduous Potter without wheel, can bake and knead nothing other than a botch; let her spend on him what expensive colouring, what gilding and enamelling she will, he is but a botch. Not a dish; no, a bulging, kneaded, crooked, shambling, squint-cornered, amorphous botch,—a mere enamelled vessel of dishonour! Let the idle think of this.

Blessed is he who has found his work; let him ask no other

blessedness.   He has a work, a life-purpose; he has found it, and
will follow it!   How, as a free-flowing channel, dug and torn by
noble force through the sour mud-swamp of one's existence, like
an ever-deepening river there, it runs and flows;—draining-off the
sour festering water, gradually from the root of the remotest grass-
blade;   making, instead of pestilential swamp, a green fruitful
meadow with its clear-flowing stream.   How blessed for the
meadow itself, let the stream and *its* value be great or small!
Labour is Life: from the inmost heart of the Worker rises his
god-given Force, the sacred celestial Life-essence breathed into
him by Almighty God; from his inmost heart awakens him to all
nobleness,—to all knowledge, 'self-knowledge' and much else, so
soon as Work fitly begins.   Knowledge?   The knowledge that will
hold good in working, cleave thou to that; for Nature herself
accredits that, says Yea to that.   Properly thou hast no other knowledge but what thou hast got by working: the rest is yet all a
hypothesis of knowledge; a thing to be argued of in schools, a
thing floating in the clouds, in endless logic-vortices, till we try it
and fix it.   'Doubt, of whatever kind, can be ended by Action alone.'

And again, hast thou valued Patience, Courage, Perseverance,
Openness to light; readiness to own thyself mistaken, to do better
next time?   All these, all virtues, in wrestling with the dim brute
Powers of Fact, in ordering of thy fellows in such wrestle, there
and elsewhere not at all, thou wilt continually learn.   Set down
a brave Sir Christopher in the middle of black ruined Stone-heaps,
of foolish unarchitectural Bishops, redtape Officials, idle Nell-Gwyn
Defenders of the Faith; and see whether he will ever raise a
Paul's Cathedral out of all that, yea or no!   Rough, rude, contradictory are all things and persons, from the mutinous masons and
Irish hodmen, up to the idle Nell-Gwyn Defenders, to blustering
redtape Officials, foolish unarchitectural Bishops.   All these things
and persons are there not for Christopher's sake and his Cathedral's;
they are there for their own sake mainly!   Christopher will have
to conquer and constrain all these,—if he be able.   All these are
against him.   Equitable Nature herself, who carries her mathematics and architectonics not on the face of her, but deep in the
hidden heart of her,—Nature herself is but partially for him; will
be wholly against him, if he constrain her not!   His very money,
where is it to come from?   The pious munificence of England lies
far-scattered, distant, unable to speak, and say, "I am here;"—

must be spoken to before it can speak. Pious munificence, and all help, is so silent, invisible like the gods; impediment, contradictions manifold are so loud and near! O brave Sir Christopher, trust thou in those notwithstanding, and front all these; understand all these; by valiant patience, noble effort, insight, by man's-strength, vanquish and compel all these,—and, on the whole, strike down victoriously the last topstone of that Paul's Edifice; thy monument for certain centuries, the stamp 'Great Man' impressed very legibly on Portland-stone there!—

Yes, all manner of help, and pious response from Men or Nature, is always what we call silent; cannot speak or come to light, till it be seen, till it be spoken to. Every noble work is at first 'impossible.' In very truth, for every noble work the possibilities will lie diffused through Immensity; inarticulate, undiscoverable except to faith. Like Gideon thou shalt spread out thy fleece at the door of thy tent; see whether under the wide arch of Heaven there be any bounteous moisture, or none. Thy heart and life-purpose shall be as a miraculous Gideon's fleece, spread out in silent appeal to Heaven: and from the kind Immensities, what from the poor unkind Localities and town and country Parishes there never could, blessed dew-moisture to suffice thee shall have fallen!

Work is of a religious nature:—work is of a *brave* nature; which it is the aim of all religion to be. All work of man is as the swimmer's: a waste ocean threatens to devour him; if he front it not bravely, it will keep its word. By incessant wise defiance of it, lusty rebuke and buffet of it, behold how it loyally supports him, bears him as its conqueror along. 'It is so,' says Goethe, 'with all things that man undertakes in this world.'

Brave Sea-captain, Norse Sea-king,—Columbus, my hero, royalest Sea-king of all! it is no friendly environment this of thine, in the waste deep waters; around thee mutinous discouraged souls, behind thee disgrace and ruin, before thee the unpenetrated veil of Night. Brother, these wild water-mountains, bounding from their deep bases (ten miles deep, I am told), are not entirely there on thy behalf! Meseems *they* have other work than floating thee forward: —and the huge Winds, that sweep from Ursa Major to the Tropics and Equators, dancing their giant-waltz through the kingdoms of Chaos and Immensity, they care little about filling rightly or filling wrongly the small shoulder-of-mutton sails in this cockle-skiff of thine! Thou art not among articulate-speaking friends, my brother; thou art among immeasurable dumb monsters, tumbling, howling

wide as the world here.   Secret, far off, invisible to all hearts but
thine, there lies a help in them : see how thou wilt get at that.
Patiently thou wilt wait till the mad Southwester spend itself,
saving thyself by dextrous science of defence, the while : valiantly,
with swift decision, wilt thou strike in, when the favouring East,
the Possible, springs up.   Mutiny of men thou wilt sternly repress ;
weakness, despondency, thou wilt cheerily encourage : thou wilt
swallow down complaint, unreason, weariness, weakness of others
and thyself ;—how much wilt thou swallow down !   There shall be
a depth of Silence in thee, deeper than this Sea, which is but ten
miles deep : a Silence unsoundable; known to God only.   Thou
shalt be a Great Man.   Yes, my World-Soldier, thou of the World
Marine-service,—thou wilt have to be *greater* than this tumultuous
unmeasured World here round thee is : thou, in thy strong soul, as
with wrestler's arms, shalt embrace it, harness it down ; and make
it bear thee on,—to new Americas, or whither God wills !

CHAPTER XII.

REWARD.

'RELIGION,' I said; for, properly speaking, all true Work is
Religion : and whatsoever Religion is not Work may go and dwell
among the Brahmins, Antinomians, Spinning Dervishes, or where
it will; with me it shall have no harbour.   Admirable was that of
the old Monks, '*Laborare est Orare*, Work is Worship.'

Older than all preached Gospels was this unpreached, inarticulate,
but ineradicable, forever-enduring Gospel : Work, and therein have
wellbeing.   Man, Son of Earth and of Heaven, lies there not, in
the innermost heart of thee, a Spirit of active Method, a Force for
Work ;—and burns like a painfully-smouldering fire, giving thee
no rest till thou unfold it, till thou write it down in beneficent
Facts around thee !   What is immethodic, waste, thou shalt make
methodic, regulated, arable; obedient and productive to thee.
Wheresoever thou findest Disorder, there is thy eternal enemy;
attack him swiftly, subdue him ; make Order of him, the subject
not of Chaos, but of Intelligence, Divinity and Thee !   The thistle
that grows in thy path, dig it out, that a blade of useful grass, a

drop of nourishing milk, may grow there instead. The waste cotton-shrub, gather its waste white down, spin it, weave it; that, in place of idle litter, there may be folded webs, and the naked skin of man be covered.

But above all, where thou findest Ignorance, Stupidity, Brute-mindedness,—yes, there, with or without Church-tithes and Shovel-hat, with or without Talfourd-Mahon Copyrights, or were it with mere dungeons and gibbets and crosses, attack it, I say; smite it wisely, unweariedly, and rest not while thou livest and it lives; but smite, smite, in the name of God! The Highest God, as I understand it, does audibly so command thee; still audibly, if thou have ears to hear. He, even He, with his *un*spoken voice, awfuler than any Sinai thunders or syllabled speech of Whirlwinds; for the SILENCE of deep Eternities, of Worlds from beyond the morning-stars, does it not speak to thee? The unborn Ages; the old Graves, with their long-mouldering dust, the very tears that wetted it now all dry,—do not these speak to thee, what ear hath not heard? The deep Death-kingdoms, the Stars in their never-resting courses, all Space and all Time, proclaim it to thee in continual silent admonition. Thou too, if ever man should, shalt work while it is called Today. For the Night cometh, wherein no man can work.

All true Work is sacred; in all true Work, were it but true hand-labour, there is something of divineness. Labour, wide as the Earth, has its summit in Heaven. Sweat of the brow; and up from that to sweat of the brain, sweat of the heart; which includes all Kepler calculations, Newton meditations, all Sciences, all spoken Epics, all acted Heroisms, Martyrdoms,—up to that 'Agony of bloody sweat,' which all men have called divine! O brother, if this is not 'worship,' then I say, the more pity for worship; for this is the noblest thing yet discovered under God's sky. Who art thou that complainest of thy life of toil? Complain not. Look up, my wearied brother; see thy fellow Workmen there, in God's Eternity; surviving there, they alone surviving: sacred Band of the Immortals, celestial Bodyguard of the Empire of Mankind. Even in the weak Human Memory they survive so long, as saints, as heroes, as gods; they alone surviving; peopling, they alone, the unmeasured solitudes of Time! To thee Heaven, though severe, is *not* unkind; Heaven is kind,—as a noble Mother; as that Spartan Mother, saying while she gave her son his shield, "With it, my son, or upon it!" Thou too shalt return *home* in honour; to thy far-distant Home, in honour; doubt it not,—if in the battle thou keep thy shield ! Thou, in the Eternities and deepest Death-kingdoms, art not an alien; thou everywhere art a denizen ! Complain not; the very Spartans did not *complain*.

And who art thou that braggest of thy life of Idleness; complacently showest thy bright gilt equipages ; sumptuous cushions; appliances for folding of the hands to mere sleep ? Looking up, looking down, around, behind or before, discernest thou, if it be not in Mayfair alone, any *idle* hero, saint, god, or even devil ? Not a vestige of one. In the Heavens, in the Earth, in the Waters under the Earth, is none like unto thee. Thou art an original figure in this Creation ; a denizen in Mayfair alone, in this extraordinary Century or Half-Century alone ! One monster there is in the world : the idle man. What is his ' Religion ' ? That Nature is a Phantasm, where cunning beggary or thievery may sometimes find good victual. That God is a lie; and that Man and his Life are a lie.—Alas, alas, who of us *is* there that can say, I have worked ? The faithfulest of us are unprofitable servants ; the faithfulest of us know that best. The faithfulest of us may say, with sad and true old Samuel, " Much of my life has been trifled away ! " But he that has, and except ' on public occasions ' professes to have, no function but that of going idle in a graceful or graceless manner; and of begetting sons to go idle ; and to address Chief Spinners and Diggers, who at least *are* spinning and digging, " Ye scandalous persons who produce too much "—My Corn-Law friends, on what imaginary still richer Eldorados, and true iron-spikes with law of gravitation, are ye rushing !

As to the Wages of Work there might innumerable things be said ; there will and must yet innumerable things be said and spoken, in St. Stephen's and out of St. Stephen's ; and gradually not a few things be ascertained and written, on Law-parchment, concerning this very matter :—' Fair day's-wages for a fair day's-work ' is the most unrefusable demand !· Money-wages ' to the extent of keeping your worker alive that he may work more ; ' these, unless you mean to dismiss him straightway out of this world, are indispensable alike to the noblest Worker and to the least noble !

One thing only I will say here, in special reference to the former class, the noble and noblest; but throwing light on all the other classes and their arrangements of this difficult matter : The ' wages ' of every noble Work do yet lie in Heaven or else Nowhere.

Not in Bank-of-England bills, in Owen's Labour-bank, or any the most improved establishment of banking and money-changing, needest thou, heroic soul, present thy account of earnings. Human banks and labour-banks know thee not; or know thee after generations and centuries have passed away, and thou art clean gone from 'rewarding,' — all manner of bank-drafts, shop-tills, and Downing-street Exchequers lying very invisible, so far from thee! Nay, at bottom, dost thou need any reward? Was it thy aim and life-purpose to be filled with good things for thy heroism; to have a life of pomp and ease, and be what men call 'happy,' in this world, or in any other world? I answer for thee deliberately, No! The whole spiritual secret of the new epoch lies in this, that thou canst answer for thyself, with thy whole clearness of head and heart, deliberately, No!

My brother, the brave man has to give his Life away. Give it, I advise thee;—thou dost not expect to *sell* thy Life in an adequate manner? What price, for example, would content thee? The just price of thy LIFE to thee,—why, God's entire Creation to thyself, the whole Universe of Space, the whole Eternity of Time, and what they hold: that is the price which would content thee; that, and if thou wilt be candid, nothing short of that! It is thy all; and for it thou wouldst have all. Thou art an unreasonable mortal;—or rather thou art a poor *infinite* mortal, who, in thy narrow clay-prison here, *seemest* so unreasonable! Thou wilt never sell thy Life, or any part of thy Life, in a satisfactory manner. Give it, like a royal heart; let the price be Nothing: thou *hast* then, in a certain sense, got All for it! The heroic man, —and is not every man, God be thanked, a potential hero?—has to do so, in all times and circumstances. In the most heroic age, as in the most unheroic, he will have to say, as Burns said proudly and humbly of his little Scottish Songs, little dewdrops of Celestial Melody in an age when so much was unmelodious: " By Heaven, they shall either be invaluable or of no value; I do not need your guineas for them!" It is an element which should, and must, enter deeply into all settlements of wages here below. They never will be ' satisfactory ' otherwise; they cannot, O Mammon Gospel, they never can! Money for my little piece of work 'to the extent that will allow me to keep working;' yes, this,—unless you mean that I shall go my ways *before* the work is all taken out of me: but as to 'wages'—!—

On the whole, we do entirely agree with those old Monks,

Laborare est Orare. In a thousand senses, from one end of it to the other, true Work *is* Worship. He that works, whatsoever be his work, he bodies forth the form of Things Unseen; a small Poet every Worker is. The idea, were it but of his poor Delf Platter, how much more of his Epic Poem, is as yet 'seen,' half-seen, only by himself; to all others it is a thing unseen, impossible; to Nature herself it is a thing unseen, a thing which never hitherto was;—very 'impossible,' for it is as yet a No-thing! The Unseen Powers had need to watch over such a man; he works in and for the Unseen. Alas, if he look to the Seen Powers only, he may as well quit the business; his No-thing will never rightly issue as a Thing, but as a Deceptivity, a Sham-thing,—which it had better not do!

Thy No-thing of an Intended Poem, O Poet who hast looked merely to reviewers, copyrights, booksellers, popularities, behold it has not yet become a Thing; for the truth is not in it! Though printed, hotpressed, reviewed, celebrated, sold to the twentieth edition: what is all that? The Thing, in philosophical uncommercial language, is still a No-thing, mostly semblance and deception of the sight;—benign Oblivion incessantly gnawing at it, impatient till Chaos, to which it belongs, do reabsorb it!—

He who takes not counsel of the Unseen and Silent, from him will never come real visibility and speech. Thou must descend to the *Mothers*, to the *Manes*, and Hercules-like long suffer and labour there, wouldst thou emerge with victory into the sunlight. As in battle and the shock of war,—for is not this a battle?—thou too shalt fear no pain or death, shalt love no ease or life; the voice of festive Lubberlands, the noise of greedy Acheron shall alike lie silent under thy victorious feet. Thy work, like Dante's, shall 'make thee lean for many years.' The world and its wages, its criticisms, counsels, helps, impediments, shall be as a waste ocean-flood; the chaos through which thou art to swim and sail. Not the waste waves and their weedy gulf-streams, shalt thou take for guidance: thy star alone,—'*Se tu segui tua stella!*' Thy star alone, now clear-beaming over Chaos, nay now by fits gone out disastrously eclipsed: this only shalt thou strive to follow. O, it is a business, as I fancy, that of weltering your way through Chaos and the murk of Hell! Green-eyed dragons watching you, three-headed Cerberuses,—not without sympathy of *their* sort! "*Eccovi l' uom ch' è stato all' Inferno.*" For in fine, as Poet Dryden says, you do walk hand in hand with sheer Madness, all the way,— who is by no means pleasant company! You look fixedly into

Madness, and *her* undiscovered, boundless, bottomless Night-empire; that you may extort new Wisdom out of it, as an Eurydice from Tartarus. The higher the Wisdom, the closer was its neighbourhood and kindred with mere Insanity; literally so;—and thou wilt, with a speechless feeling, observe how highest Wisdom, struggling up into this world, has oftentimes carried such tinctures and adhesions of Insanity still cleaving to it hither !

All Works, each in their degree, are a making of Madness sane ; —truly enough a religious operation ; which cannot be carried on without religion. You have not work otherwise ; you have eye-service, greedy grasping of wages, swift and ever swifter manufacture of semblances to get hold of wages. Instead of better felt-hats to cover your head, you have bigger lath-and-plaster hats set travelling the streets on wheels. Instead of heavenly and earthly Guidance for the souls of men, you have 'Black or White Surplice' Controversies, stuffed hair-and-leather Popes ;—terrestrial *Law-wards*, Lords and Law-bringers, 'organising Labour' in these years, by passing Corn-Laws. With all which, alas, this distracted Earth is now full, nigh to bursting. Semblances most smooth to the touch and eye; most accursed, nevertheless, to body and soul. Semblances, be they of Sham-woven Cloth or of Dilettante Legislation, which are *not* real wool or substance, but Devil's-dust, accursed of God and man ! No man has worked, or can work, except religiously; not even the poor day-labourer, the weaver of your coat, the sewer of your shoes. All men, if they work not as in a Great Taskmaster's eye, will work wrong, work unhappily for themselves and you.

Industrial work, still under bondage to Mammon, the rational soul of it not yet awakened, is a tragic spectacle. Men in the rapidest motion and self-motion ; restless, with convulsive energy, as if driven by Galvanism, as if possessed by a Devil ; tearing asunder mountains,—to no purpose, for Mammonism is always Midas-eared ! This is sad, on the face of it. Yet courage : the beneficent Destinies, kind in their sternness, are apprising us that this cannot continue. Labour is not a devil, even while encased in Mammonism ; Labour is ever an imprisoned god, writhing unconsciously or consciously to escape out of Mammonism ! Plugson of Undershot, like Taillefer of Normandy, wants victory ; how much happier will even Plugson be to have a Chivalrous victory than a Chactaw one ! The unredeemed ugliness is that of a slothful People. Show me a People energetically busy; heaving, struggling, all shoulders at the wheel; their heart pulsing, every muscle swelling, with man's energy and will;—I show you a People of whom great good is already predicable; to whom all manner of good is yet certain, if their energy endure. By very working, they will learn; they have, Antæus-like, their foot on Mother Fact: how can they but learn?

The vulgarest Plugson of a Master-Worker, who can command Workers, and get work out of them, is already a considerable man. Blessed and thrice-blessed symptoms I discern of Master-Workers who are not vulgar men; who are Nobles, and begin to feel that they must act as such: all speed to these, they are England's hope at present! But in this Plugson himself, conscious of almost no nobleness whatever, how much is there! Not without man's faculty, insight, courage, hard energy, is this rugged figure. His words none of the wisest; but his actings cannot be altogether foolish. Think, how were it, stoodst thou suddenly in his shoes! He has to command a thousand men. And not imaginary commanding; no, it is real, incessantly practical. The evil passions of so many men (with the Devil in them, as in all of us) he has to vanquish; by manifold force of speech and of silence, to repress or evade. What a force of silence, to say nothing of the others, is in Plugson! For these his thousand men he has to provide rawmaterial, machinery, arrangement, houseroom; and ever at the week's end, wages by due sale. No Civil-List, or Goulburn-Baring Budget has he to fall back upon, for paying of his regiment; he has to pick his supplies from the confused face of the whole Earth and Contemporaneous History, by his dexterity alone. There will be dry eyes if he fail to do it!—He exclaims, at present, 'black in the face,' near strangled with Dilettante Legislation: "Let me have elbow-room, throat-room, and I will not fail! No, I will spin yet, and conquer like a giant: what 'sinews of war' lie in me, untold resources towards the Conquest of this Planet, if instead of hanging me, you husband them, and help me!"—My indomitable friend, it is *true;* and thou shalt and must be helped.

This is not a man I would kill and strangle by Corn-Laws, even if I could! No, I would fling my Corn-Laws and Shot-belts to the Devil; and try to help this man. I would teach him, by noble precept and law-precept, by noble example most of all, that Mammonism was not the essence of his or of my station in God's Universe; but the adscititious excrescence of it; the gross, terrene, godless embodiment of it; which would have to become, more or

less, a godlike one.   By noble *real* legislation, by true *noble's*-work,
by unwearied, valiant, and were it wageless effort, in my Parliament and in my Parish, I would aid, constrain, encourage him to
effect more or less this blessed change.   I should know that it
would have to be effected; that unless it were in some measure
effected, he and I and all of us, I first and soonest of all, were
doomed to perdition!—Effected it will be; unless it were a Demon
that made this Universe; which I, for my own part, do at no
moment, under no form, in the least believe.

May it please your Serene Highnesses, your Majesties, Lordships
and Law-wardships, the proper Epic of this world is not now
'Arms and the Man;' how much less, 'Shirt-frills and the Man:'
no, it is now 'Tools and the Man:' that, henceforth to all time, is
now our Epic;—and you, first of all others, I think, were wise to
take note of that!

CHAPTER XIII.

DEMOCRACY.

IF the Serene Highnesses and Majesties do not take note of
that, then, as I perceive, *that* will take note of itself!   The time
for levity, insincerity, and idle babble and play-acting, in all kinds,
is gone by; it is a serious, grave time.   Old long-vexed questions,
not yet solved in logical words or parliamentary laws, are fast
solving themselves in facts, somewhat unblessed to behold!   This
largest of questions, this question of Work and Wages, which
ought, had we heeded Heaven's voice, to have begun two generations ago or more, cannot be delayed longer without hearing
Earth's voice.   'Labour' will verily need to be somewhat 'organised,' as they say,—God knows with what difficulty.   Man will
actually need to have his debts and earnings a little better paid
by man; which, let Parliaments speak of them or be silent of them,
are eternally his due from man, and cannot, without penalty and
at length not without death-penalty, be withheld.   How much
ought to cease among us straightway; how much ought to begin
straightway, while the hours yet are!

Truly they are strange results to which this of leaving all to
'Cash;' of quietly shutting-up the God's Temple, and gradually
opening wide-open the Mammon's Temple, with 'Lassez-faire, and
Every man for himself,'—have led us in these days! We have
Upper, speaking Classes, who indeed do 'speak' as never man
spake before; the withered flimsiness, the godless baseness and
barrenness of whose Speech might of itself indicate what kind
of Doing and practical Governing went on under it! For Speech
is the gaseous element out of which most kinds of Practice and
Performance, especially all kinds of moral Performance, condense
themselves, and take shape; as the one is, so will the other be.
Descending, accordingly, into the Dumb Class in its Stockport
Cellars and Poor-Law Bastilles, have we not to announce that they
also are hitherto unexampled in the History of Adam's Posterity ?

Life was never a May-game for men : in all times the lot of the
dumb millions born to toil was defaced with manifold sufferings,
injustices, heavy burdens, avoidable and unavoidable ; not play at
all, but hard work that made the sinews sore and the heart sore.
As bond-slaves, *villani, bordarii, sochemanni,* nay indeed as dukes,
earls and kings, men were oftentimes made weary of their life ;
and had to say, in the sweat of their brow and of their soul,
Behold, it is not sport, it is grim earnest, and our back can bear no
more ! Who knows not what massacrings and harryings there
have been; grinding, long-continuing, unbearable injustices,—till
the heart had to rise in madness, and some "*Eu Sachsen, nimith
euer sachses,* You Saxons, out with your gully-knives, then !" You
Saxons, some 'arrestment,' partial 'arrestment of the Knaves and
Dastards' has become indispensable !—The page of Dryasdust is
heavy with such details.

And yet I will venture to believe that in no time, since the
beginnings of Society, was the lot of those same dumb millions of
toilers so entirely unbearable as it is even in the days now passing
over us. It is not to die, or even to die of hunger, that makes a
man wretched; many men have died ; all men must die,—the last
exit of us all is in a Fire-Chariot of Pain. But it is to live
miserable we know not why; to work sore and yet gain nothing;
to be heart-worn, weary, yet isolated, unrelated, girt-in with a cold
universal Laissez-faire : it is to die slowly all our life long,
imprisoned in a deaf, dead, Infinite Injustice, as in the accursed
iron belly of a Phalaris' Bull! This is and remains forever
intolerable to all men whom God has made. Do we wonder at

French Revolutions, Chartisms, Revolts of Three Days? The times, if we will consider them, are really unexampled.

Never before did I hear of an Irish Widow reduced to 'prove 'her sisterhood by dying of typhus-fever and infecting seventeen 'persons,'—saying in such undeniable way, "You *see* I was your sister!" Sisterhood, brotherhood, was often forgotten; but not till the rise of these ultimate Mammon and Shotbelt Gospels did I ever see it so expressly denied. If no pious Lord or *Law-ward* would remember it, always some pious Lady ('*Hlaf-dig*,' Bene-factress, '*Loaf-giveress*,' they say she is,—blessings on her beautiful heart!) was there, with mild mother-voice and hand, to remember it; some pious thoughtful *Elder*, what we now call 'Prester,' *Presbyter* or 'Priest,' was there to put all men in mind of it, in the name of the God who had made all.

Not even in Black Dahomey was it ever, I think, forgotten to the typhus-fever length. Mungo Park, resourceless, had sunk down to die under the Negro Village-Tree, a horrible White object in the eyes of all. But in the poor Black Woman, and her daughter who stood aghast at him, whose earthly wealth and funded capital consisted of one small calabash of rice, there lived a heart richer than *Laissez-faire:* they, with a royal munificence, boiled their rice for him; they sang all night to him, spinning assiduous on their cotton distaffs, as he lay to sleep: "Let us pity the poor white man; no mother has he to fetch him milk, no sister to grind him corn!" Thou poor black Noble One,—thou *Lady* too: did not a God make thee too; was there not in thee too something of a God!—

Gurth, born thrall of Cedric the Saxon, has been greatly pitied by Dryasdust and others. Gurth, with the brass collar round his neck, tending Cedric's pigs in the glades of the wood, is not what I call an exemplar of human felicity: but Gurth, with the sky above him, with the free air and tinted boscage and umbrage round him, and in him at least the certainty of supper and social lodging when he came home; Gurth to me seems happy, in com-parison with many a Lancashire and Buckinghamshire man of these days, not born thrall of anybody! Gurth's brass collar did not gall him: Cedric *deserved* to be his master. The pigs were Cedric's, but Gurth too would get his parings of them. Gurth had the inexpressible satisfaction of feeling himself related indisso-lubly, though in a rude brass-collar way, to his fellow-mortals in this Earth. He had superiors, inferiors, equals.—Gurth is now 'emancipated' long since; has what we call 'Liberty.' Liberty, I am told, is a divine thing. Liberty when it becomes the 'Liberty to die by starvation' is not so divine!

Liberty? The true liberty of a man, you would say, consisted in his finding out, or being forced to find out the right path, and to walk thereon. To learn, or to be taught, what work he actually was able for; and then by permission, persuasion, and even compulsion, to set about doing of the same! That is his true blessedness, honour, 'liberty' and maximum of wellbeing: if liberty be not that, I for one have small care about liberty. You do not allow a palpable madman to leap over precipices; you violate his liberty, you that are wise; and keep him, were it in strait-waistcoats, away from the precipices! Every stupid, every cowardly and foolish man is but a less palpable madman: his true liberty were that a wiser man, that any and every wiser man, could, by brass collars, or in whatever milder or sharper way, lay hold of him when he was going wrong, and order and compel him to go a little righter. O, if thou really art my *Senior*, Seigneur, my *Elder*, Presbyter or Priest,—if thou art in very deed my *Wiser*, may a beneficent instinct lead and impel thee to 'conquer' me, to command me! If thou do know better than I what is good and right, I conjure thee in the name of God, force me to do it; were it by never such brass collars, whips and handcuffs, leave me not to walk over precipices! That I have been called, by all the Newspapers, a 'free man' will avail me little, if my pilgrimage have ended in death and wreck. O that the Newspapers had called me slave, coward, fool, or what it pleased their sweet voices to name me, and I had attained not death, but life!—Liberty requires new definitions.

A conscious abhorrence and intolerance of Folly, of Baseness, Stupidity, Poltroonery and all that brood of things, dwells deep in some men: still deeper in others an *un*conscious abhorrence and intolerance, clothed moreover by the beneficent Supreme Powers in what stout appetites, energies, egoisms so-called, are suitable to it;—these latter are your Conquerors, Romans, Normans, Russians, Indo-English; Founders of what we call Aristocracies. Which indeed have they not the most 'divine right' to found;—being themselves very truly Ἄριστοι, BRAVEST, BEST; and conquering generally a confused rabble of WORST, or at lowest, clearly enough, of WORSE? I think their divine right, tried, with affirmatory verdict, in the greatest Law-Court known to me, was good! A class of men who are dreadfully exclaimed against by Dryasdust; of whom nevertheless beneficent Nature has oftentimes had need; and may, alas, again have need.

When, across the hundredfold poor scepticisms, trivialisms and constitutional cobwebberies of Dryasdust, you catch any glimpse of a William the Conqueror, a Tancred of Hauteville or suchlike, —do you not discern veritably some rude outline of a true God-made King; whom not the Champion of England cased in tin, but all Nature and the Universe were calling to the throne? It is absolutely necessary that he get thither. Nature does not mean her poor Saxon children to perish, of obesity, stupor or other malady, as yet: a stern Ruler and Line of Rulers therefore is called in,—a stern but most beneficent *perpetual House-Surgeon* is by Nature herself called in, and even the appropriate *fees* are provided for him! Dryasdust talks lamentably about Hereward and the Fen Counties; fate of Earl Waltheof; Yorkshire and the North reduced to ashes: all which is undoubtedly lamentable. But even Dryasdust apprises me of one fact: 'A child, in this William's reign, might have carried a purse of gold from end to end of England.' My erudite friend, it is a fact which outweighs a thousand! Sweep away thy constitutional, sentimental and other cobwebberies; look eye to eye, if thou still have any eye, in the face of this big burly William Bastard: thou wilt see a fellow of most flashing discernment, of most strong lion-heart;— in whom, as it were, within a frame of oak and iron, the gods have planted the soul of 'a man of genius'! Dost thou call that nothing? I call it an immense thing!—Rage enough was in this Willelmus Conquæstor, rage enough for his occasions;—and yet the essential element of him, as of all such men, is not scorching *fire*, but shining illuminative *light*. Fire and light are strangely interchangeable; nay, at bottom, I have found them different forms of the same most godlike 'elementary substance' in our world: a thing worth stating in these days. The essential element of this Conquæstor is, first of all, the most sun-eyed perception of what *is* really what on this God's-Earth;—which, thou wilt find, does mean at bottom 'Justice,' and 'Virtues' not a few: *Conformity* to what the Maker has seen good to make; that, I suppose, will mean Justice and a Virtue or two?—

Dost thou think Willelmus Conquæstor would have tolerated ten years' jargon, one hour's jargon, on the propriety of killing

Cotton-manufactures by partridge Corn-Laws ? I fancy, this was not the man to knock out of his night's-rest with nothing but a noisy bedlamism in your mouth ! "Assist us still better to bush the partridges ; strangle Plugson who spins the shirts ? "—" *Par la Splendeur de Dieu !*"— —Dost thou think Willelmus Conquæstor, in this new time, with Steamengine Captains of Industry on one hand of him, and Joe-Manton Captains of Idleness on the other, would have doubted which *was* really the BEST ; which did deserve strangling, and which not ?

I have a certain indestructible regard for Willelmus Conquæstor. A resident House-Surgeon, provided by Nature for her beloved English People, and even furnished with the requisite fees, as I said ; for he by no means felt himself doing Nature's work, this Willelmus, but his own work exclusively ! And his own work withal it was ; informed '*par la Splendeur de Dieu.*'—I say, it is necessary to get the work out of such a man, however harsh that be ! When a world, not yet doomed for death, is rushing down to ever-deeper Baseness and Confusion, it is a dire necessity of Nature's to bring in her ARISTOCRACIES, her BEST, even by forcible methods. When their descendants or representatives cease entirely to *be* the Best, Nature's poor world will very soon rush down again to Baseness ; and it becomes a dire necessity of Nature's to cast them out. Hence French Revolutions, Five-point Charters, Democracies, and a mournful list of *Etceteras*, in these our afflicted times.

To what extent Democracy has now reached, how it advances irresistible with ominous, ever-increasing speed, he that will open his eyes on any province of human affairs may discern. Democracy is everywhere the inexorable demand of these ages, swiftly fulfilling itself. From the thunder of Napoleon battles, to the jabbering of Open-vestry in St. Mary Axe, all things announce Democracy. A distinguished man, whom some of my readers will hear again with pleasure, thus writes to me what in these days he notes from the Wahngasse of Weissnichtwo, where our London fashions seem to be in full vogue. Let us hear the Herr Teufelsdröckh again, were it but the smallest word !

' Democracy, which means despair of finding any Heroes to 'govern you, and contented putting-up with the want of them,— 'alas, thou too, *mein Lieber*, seest well how close it is of kin to '*Atheism,* and other sad *Isms:* he who discovers no God whatever, 'how shall he discover Heroes, the visible Temples of God ?—

'Strange enough meanwhile it is, to observe with what thought-
'lessness, here in our rigidly Conservative Country, men rush into
'Democracy with full cry. Beyond doubt, his Excellenz the Titular-
'Herr Ritter Kauderwälsch von Pferdefuss-Quacksalber, he our
'distinguished Conservative Premier himself, and all but the
'thicker-headed of his Party, discern Democracy to be inevitable
'as death, and are even desperate of delaying it much !

'You cannot walk the streets without beholding Democracy
'announce itself : the very Tailor has become, if not properly
'Sansculottic, which to him would be ruinous, yet a Tailor uncon-
'sciously symbolising, and prophesying with his scissors, the reign
'of Equality. What now is our fashionable coat ? A thing of
'superfinest texture, of deeply meditated cut; with Malines-lace
'cuffs; quilted with gold; so that a man can carry, without diffi-
'culty, an estate of land on his back ? *Keineswegs*, By no manner
'of means ! The Sumptuary Laws have fallen into such a state of
'desuetude as was never before seen. Our fashionable coat is an
'amphibium between barn-sack and drayman's doublet. The
'cloth of it is studiously coarse; the colour a speckled soot-black
'or rust-brown gray; the nearest approach to a Peasant's. And
'for shape,—thou shouldst see it ! The last consummation of the
'year now passing over us is definable as Three Bags ; a big bag
'for the body, two small bags for the arms, and by way of collar a
'hem ! The first Antique Cheruscan who, of felt-cloth or bear's-
'hide, with bone or metal needle, set about making himself a coat,
'before Tailors had yet awakened out of Nothing,—did not he
'make it even so ? A loose wide poke for body, with two holes to
'let out the arms; this was his original coat: to which holes it
'was soon visible that two small loose pokes, or sleeves, easily
'appended, would be an improvement.

'Thus has the Tailor-art, so to speak, overset itself, like most
'other things; changed its centre-of-gravity; whirled suddenly
'over from zenith to nadir. Your Stulz, with huge somerset,
'vaults from his high shopboard down to the depths of primal
'savagery,—carrying much along with him ! For I will invite
'thee to reflect that the Tailor, as topmost ultimate froth of
'Human Society, is indeed swift-passing, evanescent, slippery to
'decipher; yet significant of much, nay of all. Topmost evanes-
'cent froth, he is churned-up from the very lees, and from all
'intermediate regions of the liquor. The general outcome he,
'visible to the eye, of what men aimed to do, and were obliged

'and enabled to do, in this one public department of symbolising
'themselves to each other by covering of their skins. A smack of
'all Human Life lies in the Tailor: its wild struggles towards
'beauty, dignity, freedom, victory; and how, hemmed-in by Sedan
'and Huddersfield, by Nescience, Dulness, Prurience, and other
'sad necessities and laws of Nature, it has attained just to this:
'Gray savagery of Three Sacks with a hem!

'When the very Tailor verges towards Sansculottism, is it not
'ominous? The last Divinity of poor mankind dethroning him-
'self; sinking *his* taper too, flame downmost, like the Genius of
'Sleep or of Death; admonitory that Tailor time shall be no
'more!—For, little as one could advise Sumptuary Laws at the
'present epoch, yet nothing is clearer than that where ranks do
'actually exist, strict division of costumes will also be enforced;
'that if we ever have a new Hierarchy and Aristocracy, acknow-
'ledged veritably as such, for which I daily pray Heaven, the
'Tailor will reawaken; and be, by volunteering and appointment,
'consciously and unconsciously, a safeguard of that same.'—
Certain farther observations, from the same invaluable pen, on our
never-ending changes of mode, our 'perpetual nomadic and even
ape-like appetite for change and mere change' in all the equipments of our existence, and the 'fatal revolutionary character'
thereby manifested, we suppress for the present. It may be
admitted that Democracy, in all meanings of the word, is in full
career; irresistible by any Ritter Kauderwälsch or other Son of
Adam, as times go. 'Liberty' is a thing men are determined to have.

But truly, as I had to remark in the mean while, 'the liberty of
not being oppressed by your fellow man' is an indispensable, yet
one of the most insignificant fractional parts of Human Liberty.
No man oppresses thee, can bid thee fetch or carry, come or go,
without reason shown. True; from all men thou art emancipated:
but from Thyself and from the Devil—? No man, wiser, unwiser,
can make thee come or go: but thy own futilities, bewilderments,
thy false appetites for Money, Windsor Georges and suchlike? No
man oppresses thee, O free and independent Franchiser: but does
not this stupid Porter-pot oppress thee? No Son of Adam can
bid thee come or go; but this absurd Pot of Heavy-wet, this can
and does! Thou art the thrall not of Cedric the Saxon, but of thy
own brutal appetites and this scoured dish of liquor. And thou
pratest of thy 'liberty'? Thou entire blockhead!

Heavy-wet and gin: alas, these are not the only kinds of thraldom. Thou who walkest in a vain show, looking out with ornamental dilettante sniff and serene supremacy at all Life and all Death; and amblest jauntily; perking up thy poor talk into crotchets, thy poor conduct into fatuous somnambulisms;—and *art* as an 'enchanted Ape' under God's sky, where thou mightest have been a man, had proper Schoolmasters and Conquerors, and Constables with cat-o'-nine tails, been vouchsafed thee; dost thou call that 'liberty'? Or your unreposing Mammon-worshipper again, driven, as if by Galvanisms, by Devils and Fixed-Ideas, who rises early and sits late, chasing the impossible; straining every faculty to 'fill himself with the east wind,'—how merciful were it, could you, by mild persuasion, or by the severest tyranny so-called, check him in his mad path, and turn him into a wiser one! All painful tyranny, in that case again, were but mild 'surgery;' the pain of it cheap, as health and life, instead of galvanism and fixed-idea, are cheap at any price.

Sure enough, of all paths a man could strike into, there *is*, at any given moment, a *best path* for every man; a thing which, here and now, it were of all things *wisest* for him to do;—which could he be but led or driven to do, he were then doing 'like a man,' as we phrase it; all men and gods agreeing with him, the whole Universe virtually exclaiming Well-done to him! His success, in such case, were complete; his felicity a maximum. This path, to find this path and walk in it, is the one thing needful for him. Whatsoever forwards him in that, let it come to him even in the shape of blows and spurnings, is liberty: whatsoever hinders him, were it wardmotes, open-vestries, pollbooths, tremendous cheers, rivers of heavy-wet, is slavery.

The notion that a man's liberty consists in giving his vote at election-hustings, and saying, "Behold, now I too have my twenty-thousandth part of a Talker in our National Palaver; will not all the gods be good to me?"—is one of the pleasantest! Nature nevertheless is kind at present; and puts it into the heads of many, almost of all. The liberty especially which has to purchase itself by social isolation, and each man standing separate from the other, having 'no business with him' but a cash-account: this is such a liberty as the Earth seldom saw;—as the Earth will not long put up with, recommend it how you may. This liberty turns out, before it have long continued in action, with all men flinging up their caps round it, to be, for the Working Millions a liberty to die by want of food; for the Idle Thousands and Units, alas, a still more fatal liberty to live in want of work; to have no earnest duty to do in this God's-World any more. What becomes of a man in such predicament? Earth's Laws are silent; and Heaven's speak in a voice which is not heard. No work, and the ineradicable need of work, give rise to new very wondrous life-philosophies, new very wondrous life-practices! Dilettantism, Pococurantism, Beau-Brummelism, with perhaps an occasional, half-mad, protesting burst of Byronism, establish themselves: at the end of a certain period,—if you go back to 'the Dead Sea,' there is, say our Moslem friends, a very strange 'Sabbath-day' trans-acting itself there!—Brethren, we know but imperfectly yet, after ages of Constitutional Government, what Liberty and Slavery are.

Democracy, the chase of Liberty in that direction, shall go its full course; unrestrainable by him of Pferdefuss-Quacksalber, or any of *his* household. The Toiling Millions of Mankind, in most vital need and passionate instinctive desire of Guidance, shall cast away False-Guidance; and hope, for an hour, that No-Guidance will suffice them: but it can be for an hour only. The smallest item of human Slavery is the oppression of man by his Mock-Superiors; the palpablest, but I say at bottom the smallest. Let him shake-off such oppression, trample it indignantly under his feet; I blame him not, I pity and commend him. But oppression by your Mock-Superiors well shaken off, the grand problem yet remains to solve: That of finding government by your Real-Superiors! Alas, how shall we ever learn the solution of that, benighted, bewildered, sniffing, sneering, godforgetting unfortunates as we are? It is a work for centuries; to be taught us by tribulations, confusions, insurrections, obstructions; who knows if not by conflagration and despair! It is a lesson inclusive of all other lessons; the hardest of all lessons to learn.

One thing I do know: Those Apes, chattering on the branches by the Dead Sea, never got it learned; but chatter there to this day. To them no Moses need come a second time; a thousand Moseses would be but so many painted Phantasms, interesting Fellow-Apes of new strange aspect,—whom they would 'invite to dinner,' be glad to meet with in lion-soirées. To them the voice of Prophecy, of heavenly monition, is quite ended. They chatter there, all Heaven shut to them, to the end of the world. The unfortunates! Oh, what is dying of hunger, with honest tools in your hand, with a manful purpose in your heart, and much real labour lying round you done, in comparison? You honestly quit your tools; quit a most muddy confused coil of sore work, short rations, of sorrow, dispiritments and contradictions, having now honestly done with it all;—and await, not entirely in a distracted manner, what the Supreme Powers, and the Silences and the Eternities may have to say to you.

A second thing I know: This lesson will have to be learned,—under penalties! England will either learn it, or England also will cease to exist among Nations. England will either learn to reverence its Heroes, and discriminate them from its Sham-Heroes and Valets and gaslighted Histrios; and to prize them as the audible God's-voice, amid all inane jargons and temporary market-cries, and say to them with heart-loyalty, "Be ye King and Priest, and Gospel and Guidance for us:" or else England will continue to worship new and ever-new forms of Quackhood,—and so, with what resiliences and reboundings matters little, go down to the Father of Quacks! Can I dread such things of England? Wretched, thick-eyed, gross-hearted mortals, why will ye worship lies, and 'Stuffed Clothes-suits created by the ninth-parts of men'! It is not your purses that suffer; your farm-rents, your commerces, your mill-revenues, loud as ye lament over these; no, it is not these alone, but a far deeper than these: it is your souls that lie dead, crushed down under despicable Nightmares, Atheisms, Brain-fumes; and are not souls at all, but mere succedanea for *salt* to keep your bodies and their appetites from putrefying! Your cotton-spinning and thrice-miraculous mechanism, what is this too, by itself, but a larger kind of Animalism? Spiders can spin, Beavers can build and show contrivance; the Ant lays-up accumulation of capital, and has, for aught I know, a Bank of Antland. If there is no soul in man higher than all that, did it reach to sailing on the cloud-rack and spinning sea-sand; then I say, man is but an animal, a more cunning kind of brute: he has no soul, but only a succe-daneum for salt. Whereupon, seeing himself to be truly of the beasts that perish, he ought to admit it, I think;—and also straightway universally to kill himself; and so, in a manlike manner at least *end*, and wave these brute-worlds *his* dignified farewell!—

CHAPTER XIV.

SIR JABESH WINDBAG.

OLIVER CROMWELL, whose body they hung on their Tyburn gallows because he had found the Christian Religion inexecutable in this country, remains to me by far the remarkablest Governor we have had here for the last five centuries or so. For the last five centuries, there has been no Governor among us with anything like similar talent; and for the last two centuries, no Governor, we may say, with the possibility of similar talent,—with an idea in the heart of him capable of inspiring similar talent, capable of co-existing therewith. When you consider that Oliver believed in a God, the difference between Oliver's position and that of any subsequent Governor of this Country becomes, the more you reflect on it, the more immeasurable!

Oliver, no volunteer in Public Life, but plainly a balloted soldier strictly ordered thither, enters upon Public Life; comports himself there like a man who carried his own life in his hand; like a man whose Great Commander's eye was always on him. Not without results. Oliver, well-advanced in years, finds now, by Destiny and his own Deservings, or as he himself better phrased it, by wondrous successive 'Births of Providence,' the Government of England put into his hands. In senate-house and battle-field, in counsel and in action, in private and in public, this man has proved himself a man: England and the voice of God, through waste awful whirlwinds and environments, speaking to his great heart, summon him to assert formally, in the way of solemn Public Fact and as a new piece of English Law, what informally and by Nature's eternal Law needed no asserting, That he, Oliver, was the Ablest Man of England, the King of England; that he, Oliver, would undertake governing England. His way of making this same 'assertion,' the one way he had of making it, has given rise to immense criticism: but the assertion itself, in what way soever 'made,' is it not somewhat of a solemn one, somewhat of a tremendous one!

And now do but contrast this Oliver with my right honourable friend Sir Jabesh Windbag, Mr. Facing-both-ways, Viscount Mealy-mouth, Earl of Windlestraw, or what other Cagliostro, Cagliostrino, Cagliostraccio, the course of Fortune and Parliamentary Majorities has constitutionally guided to that dignity, any time during these last sorrowful hundred-and-fifty years! Windbag, weak in the faith of a God, which he believes only at Church on Sundays, if even then; strong only in the faith that Paragraphs and Plausibilities bring votes; that Force of Public Opinion, as he calls it, is the primal Necessity of Things, and highest God we have :—Windbag, if we will consider him, has a problem set before him which may be ranged in the impossible class. He is a Columbus minded to sail to the indistinct country of NOWHERE, to the indistinct country of WHITHERWARD, by the *friendship* of those same waste-tumbling Water-Alps and howling waltz of All the Winds; not by conquest of them and in spite of them, but by friendship of them, when once *they* have made-up their mind! He is the most original Columbus I ever saw. Nay, his problem is not an impossible one : he will infallibly *arrive* at that same country of NOWHERE; his indistinct Whitherward will be a *Thither*ward! In the Ocean Abysses and Locker of Davy Jones, there certainly enough do he and *his* ship's company, and all their cargo and navigatings, at last find lodgment.

Oliver knew that his America lay THERE, Westward Ho;—and it was not entirely by *friendship* of the Water-Alps, and yeasty insane Froth-Oceans, that he meant to get thither! He sailed accordingly; had compass-card, and Rules of Navigation,—older and greater than these Froth-Oceans, old as the Eternal God! Or again, do but think of this. Windbag in these his probable five years of office has to prosper and get Paragraphs: the Paragraphs of these five years must be his salvation, or he is a lost man; redemption nowhere in the Worlds or in the Times discoverable for him. Oliver too would like his Paragraphs; successes, popu-larities in these five years are not undesirable to him : but mark, I say, this enormous circumstance: *after* these five years are gone and done, comes an Eternity for Oliver! Oliver has to appear before the Most High Judge : the utmost flow of Paragraphs, the utmost ebb of them, is now, in strictest arithmetic, verily no matter at all; its exact value *zero ;* an account altogether erased! Enor-mous:—which a man, in these days, hardly fancies with an effort! Oliver's Paragraphs are all done, his battles, division-lists, successes all summed: and now in that awful unerring Court of Review, the

real question first rises, Whether he has succeeded at all; whether
he has not been defeated miserably forevermore? Let him come
with world-wide *Io-Pæans*, these avail him not. Let him come
covered over with the world's execrations, gashed with ignominious
death-wounds, the gallows-rope about his neck: what avails that?
The word is, Come thou brave and faithful; the word is, Depart
thou quack and accursed!

O Windbag, my right honourable friend, in very truth I pity
thee. I say, these Paragraphs, and low or loud votings of thy
poor fellow-blockheads of mankind, will never guide thee in any
enterprise at all. Govern a country on such guidance? Thou
canst not make a pair of shoes, sell a pennyworth of tape, on such.
No, thy shoes are vamped up falsely to meet the market; behold,
the leather only *seemed* to be tanned; thy shoes melt under me
to rubbishy pulp, and are not veritable mud-defying shoes, but
plausible vendible similitudes of shoes,—thou unfortunate, and I!
O my right honourable friend, when the Paragraphs flowed in,
who was like Sir Jabesh? On the swelling tide he mounted;
higher, higher, triumphant, heaven-high. But the Paragraphs
again ebbed out, as unwise Paragraphs needs must: Sir Jabesh
lies stranded, sunk and forever sinking in ignominious ooze; the
Mud-nymphs, and ever-deepening bottomless Oblivion, his portion
to eternal time. 'Posterity'? Thou appealest to Posterity,
thou? My right honourable friend, what will Posterity do for
thee! The voting of Posterity, were it continued through
centuries in thy favour, will be quite inaudible, extra-forensic,
without any effect whatever. Posterity can do simply nothing
for a man; nor even seem to do much if the man be not brainsick.
Besides, to tell the truth, the bets are a thousand to one, Posterity
will not hear of thee, my right honourable friend! Posterity, I
have found, has generally his own windbags sufficiently trumpeted
in all market-places, and no leisure to attend to ours. Posterity,
which has made of Norse Odin a similitude, and of Norman William
a brute monster, what will or can it make of English Jabesh? O
Heavens, 'Posterity!'—

"These poor persecuted Scotch Covenanters," said I to my
inquiring Frenchman, in such stinted French as stood at command,
"*ils s'en appelaient à*"—"*A la Postérité*," interrupted he, helping
me out.—"*Ah, Monsieur, non, mille fois non!* They appealed to
the Eternal God; not to Posterity at all! *C'était différent.*"

CHAPTER XV.

MORRISON AGAIN.

NEVERTHELESS, O Advanced-Liberal, one cannot promise thee
any ' New Religion,' for some time ; to say truth, I do not think we
have the smallest chance of any !   Will the candid reader, by way
of closing this Book Third, listen to a few transient remarks on
that subject ?

Candid readers have not lately met with any man who had
less notion to interfere with their Thirty-Nine or other Church-
Articles ; wherewith, very helplessly as is like, they may have
struggled to form for themselves some not inconceivable hypothesis
about this Universe, and their own Existence there.   Superstition,
my friend, is far from me ; Fanaticism, for any *Fanum* likely to
arise soon on this Earth, is far.   A man's Church-Articles are
surely articles of price to him ; and in these times one has to be
tolerant of many strange ' Articles,' and of many still stranger
' No-articles,' which go about placarding themselves in a very
distracted manner,—the numerous long placard-poles, and questionable infirm paste-pots, interfering with one's peaceable thoroughfare
sometimes !

Fancy a man, moreover, recommending his fellow men to
believe in God, that so Chartism might abate, and the Manchester
Operatives be got to spin peaceably !   The idea is more distracted
than any placard-pole seen hitherto in a public thoroughfare of
men !   My friend, if thou ever do come to believe in God, thou
wilt find all Chartism, Manchester riot, Parliamentary incompe-
tence, Ministries of Windbag, and the wildest Social Dissolutions,
and the burning-up of this entire Planet, a most small matter in
comparison.   Brother, this Planet, I find, is but an inconsiderable
sand-grain in the continents of Being : this Planet's poor temporary
interests, thy interests and my interests there, when I look fixedly
into that eternal Light-Sea and Flame-Sea with *its* eternal
interests, dwindle literally into Nothing ; my speech of it is—
silence for the while.   I will as soon think of making Galaxies

and Star-Systems to guide little herring-vessels by, as of preaching Religion that the Constable may continue possible. O my Advanced-Liberal friend, this new second progress, of proceeding 'to invent God,' is a very strange one! Jacobinism unfolded into Saint-Simonism bodes innumerable blessed things; but the thing itself might draw tears from a Stoic!—As for me, some twelve or thirteen New Religions, heavy Packets, most of them unfranked, having arrived here from various parts of the world, in a space of six calendar months, I have instructed my invaluable friend the Stamped Postman to introduce no more of them, if the charge exceed one penny.

Henry of Essex, duelling in that Thames Island, 'near to Reading Abbey,' had a religion. But was it in virtue of his seeing armed Phantasms of St. Edmund 'on the rim of the horizon,' looking minatory on him? Had that, intrinsically, anything to do with his religion at all? Henry of Essex's religion was the Inner Light or Moral Conscience of his own soul; such as is vouchsafed still to all souls of men;—which Inner Light shone here 'through such intellectual and other media' as there were; producing 'Phantasms,' Kircherean Visual-Spectra, according to circumstances! It is so with all men. The clearer my Inner Light may shine, through the *less* turbid media, the *fewer* Phantasms it may produce,—the gladder surely shall I be, and not the sorrier! Hast thou reflected, O serious reader, Advanced-Liberal or other, that the one end, essence, use of all religion past, present and to come, was this only : To keep that same Moral Conscience or Inner Light of ours alive and shining;—which certainly the 'Phantasms' and the 'turbid media' were not essential for! All religion was here to remind us, better or worse, of what we already know better or worse, of the quite *infinite* difference there is between a Good man and a Bad; to bid us love infinitely the one, abhor and avoid infinitely the other,—strive infinitely to *be* the one, and not to be the other. 'All religion issues in due Practical Hero-worship.' He that has a soul unasphyxied will never want a religion; he that has a soul asphyxied, reduced to a succedaneum for salt, will never find any religion, though you rose from the dead to preach him one.

But indeed, when men and reformers ask for 'a religion,' it is analogous to their asking, 'What would you have us to do?' and suchlike. They fancy that their religion too shall be a kind of Morrison's Pill, which they have only to swallow once, and all will be well. Resolutely once gulp-down your Religion, your Morrison's Pill, you have it all plain sailing now : you can follow your affairs, your no-affairs, go along money-hunting, pleasure-hunting, dilettanteing, dangling, and miming and chattering like a Dead-Sea Ape : your Morrison will do your business for you. Men's notions are very strange !—Brother, I say there is not, was not, nor will ever be, in the wide circle of Nature, any Pill or Religion of that character. Man cannot afford thee such ; for the very gods it is impossible. I advise thee to renounce Morrison ; once for all, quit hope of the Universal Pill. For body, for soul, for individual or society, there has not any such article been made. *Non extat.* In Created Nature it is not, was not, will not be. In the void imbroglios of Chaos only, and realms of Bedlam, does some shadow of it hover, to bewilder and bemock the poor inhabitants *there.*

Rituals, Liturgies, Creeds, Hierarchies ; all this is not religion ; all this, were it dead as Odinism, as Fetishism, does not kill religion at all ! It is Stupidity alone, with never so many rituals, that kills religion. Is not this still a World ? Spinning Cotton under Arkwright and Adam Smith ; founding Cities by the Fountain of Juturna, on the Janiculum Mount ; tilling Canaan under Prophet Samuel and Psalmist David, man is ever man ; the missionary of Unseen Powers ; and great and victorious, while he continues true to his mission ; mean, miserable, foiled, and at last annihilated and trodden out of sight and memory, when he proves untrue. Brother, thou art a Man, I think ; thou art not a mere building Beaver, or two-legged Cotton-Spider ; thou hast verily a Soul in thee, asphyxied or otherwise ! Sooty Manchester, —it too is built on the infinite Abysses ; overspanned by the skyey Firmaments ; and there is birth in it, and death in it ;—and it is every whit as wonderful, as fearful, unimaginable, as the oldest Salem or Prophetic City. Go or stand, in what time, in what place we will, are there not Immensities, Eternities over us, around us, in us :

> 'Solemn before us,
> Veiled, the dark Portal,
> Goal of all mortal :—
> Stars silent rest o'er us,
> Graves under us silent !'

Between *these* two great Silences, the hum of all our spinning cylinders, Trades-Unions, Anti-Corn-Law Leagues and Carlton

Clubs goes on. Stupidity itself ought to pause a little and consider that. I tell thee, through all thy Ledgers, Supply-and-demand Philosophies, and daily most modern melancholy Business and Cant, there does shine the presence of a Primeval Unspeakable; and thou wert wise to recognise, not with lips only, that same!

The Maker's Laws, whether they are promulgated in Sinai Thunder, to the ear or imagination, or quite otherwise promulgated, are the Laws of God; transcendent, everlasting, imperatively demanding obedience from all men. This, without any thunder, or with never so much thunder, thou, if there be any soul left in thee, canst know of a truth. The Universe, I say, is made by Law; the great Soul of the World is just and not unjust. Look thou, if thou have eyes or soul left, into this great shoreless Incomprehensible: in the heart of its tumultuous Appearances, Embroilments, and mad Time-vortexes, is there not, silent, eternal, an All-just, an All-beautiful; sole Reality and ultimate controlling Power of the whole? This is not a figure of speech; this is a fact. The fact of Gravitation known to all animals, is not surer than this inner Fact, which may be known to all men. He who knows this, it will sink, silent, awful, unspeakable, into his heart. He will say with Faust: "Who *dare* name HIM?" Most rituals or 'namings' he will fall in with at present, are like to be 'namings'—which shall be nameless! In silence, in the Eternal Temple, let him worship, if there be no fit word. Such knowledge, the crown of his whole spiritual being, the life of his life, let him keep and sacredly walk by. He has a religion. Hourly and daily, for himself and for the whole world, a faithful, unspoken, but not ineffectual prayer rises, "Thy will be done." His whole work on Earth is an emblematic spoken or acted prayer, Be the will of God done on Earth,—not the Devil's will, or any of the Devil's servants' wills! He has a religion, this man; an everlasting Load-star that beams the brighter in the Heavens, the darker here on Earth grows the night around him. Thou, if thou know not this, what are all rituals, liturgies, mythologies, mass-chantings, turnings of the rotatory calabash? They are as nothing; in a good many respects they are as *less*. Divorced from this, getting half-divorced from this, they are a thing to fill one with a kind of horror; with a sacred inexpressible pity and fear. The most tragical thing a human eye can look on. It was said to the Prophet, "Behold, I will show thee worse things than these: women weeping to Thammuz." That was the acme of the Prophet's vision,—then as now.

Rituals, Liturgies, Credos, Sinai Thunder: I know more or less the history of these; the rise, progress, decline and fall of these. Can thunder from all the thirty-two azimuths, repeated daily for centuries of years, make God's Laws more godlike to me? Brother, No. Perhaps I am grown to be a man now; and do not need the thunder and the terror any longer! Perhaps I am above being frightened; perhaps it is not Fear, but Reverence alone, that shall now lead me!—Revelations, Inspirations? Yes: and thy own god-created Soul; dost thou not call that a 'revelation'? Who made THEE? Where didst Thou come from? The Voice of Eternity, if thou be not a blasphemer and poor asphyxied mute, speaks with that tongue of thine! *Thou* art the latest Birth of Nature; it is 'the Inspiration of the Almighty' that giveth *thee* understanding! My brother, my brother!—

Under baleful Atheisms, Mammonisms, Joe-Manton Dilettantisms, with their appropriate Cants and Idolisms, and whatsoever scandalous rubbish obscures and all but extinguishes the soul of man,—religion now is; its Laws, written if not on stone tables, yet on the Azure of Infinitude, in the inner heart of God's Creation, certain as Life, certain as Death! I say the Laws are there, and thou shalt not disobey them. It were better for thee not. Better a hundred deaths than yes. Terrible 'penalties,' withal, if thou still need 'penalties,' are there for disobeying. Dost thou observe, O redtape Politician, that fiery infernal Phenomenon, which men name FRENCH REVOLUTION, sailing, unlooked-for, unbidden; through thy inane Protocol Dominion:—far-seen, with splendour not of Heaven? Ten centuries will see it. There were Tanneries at Meudon for human skins. And Hell, very truly Hell, had power over God's upper Earth for a season. The cruelest Portent that has risen into created Space these ten centuries: let us hail it, with awestruck repentant hearts, as the voice once more of a God, though of one in wrath. Blessed be the God's-voice; for *it* is true, and Falsehoods have to cease before it! But for that same preternatural quasi-infernal Portent, one could not know what to make of this wretched world, in these days, at all. The deplorablest quack-ridden, and now hunger-ridden, downtrodden Despicability and *Flebile Ludibrium*, of redtape Protocols, rotatory Calabashes, Poor-Law Bastilles: who is there that could think of *its* being fated to continue?—

Penalties enough, my brother! This penalty inclusive of all: Eternal Death to thy own hapless Self, if thou heed no other.

Eternal Death, I say,—with many meanings old and new, of which let this single one suffice us here: The eternal impossibility for thee to be aught but a Chimera, and swift-vanishing deceptive Phantasm, in God's Creation;—swift-vanishing, never to reappear: why should *it* reappear! Thou hadst one chance, thou wilt never have another. Everlasting ages will roll on, and no other be given thee. The foolishest articulate-speaking soul now extant, may not he say to himself: "A whole Eternity I waited to be born; and now I have a whole Eternity waiting to see what I will do when born!" This is not Theology, this is Arithmetic. And thou but half-discernest this; thou but half-believest it? Alas, on the shores of the Dead Sea, on Sabbath, there goes on a Tragedy!—

But we will leave this of 'Religion;' of which, to say truth, it is chiefly profitable in these unspeakable days to keep silence. Thou needest no 'New Religion;' nor art thou like to get any. Thou hast already more 'religion' than thou makest use of. This day thou knowest ten commanded duties, seest in thy mind ten things which should be done, for one that thou doest! *Do* one of them; this of itself will show thee ten others which can and shall be done. "But my future fate?" Yes, thy future fate, indeed! Thy future fate, while thou makest *it* the chief question, seems to me—extremely questionable! I do not think it can be good. Norse Odin, immemorial centuries ago, did not he, though a poor Heathen, in the dawn of Time, teach us that for the Dastard there was, and could be, no good fate; no harbour anywhere, save down with Hela, in the pool of Night! Dastards, Knaves, are they that lust for Pleasure, that tremble at Pain. For this world and for the next Dastards are a class of creatures made to be 'arrested;' they are good for nothing else, can look for nothing else. A greater than Odin has been here. A greater than Odin has taught us— not a greater Dastardism, I hope! My brother, thou must pray for a *soul;* struggle, as with life-and-death energy, to get back thy soul! Know that 'religion' is no Morrison's Pill from without but a reawakening of thy own Self from within:—and, above all, leave me alone of thy 'religions'. and 'new religions' here and elsewhere! I am weary of this sick croaking for a Morrison's-Pill religion; for any and for every such. I want none such; and discern all such to be impossible. The resuscitation of old liturgies fallen dead; much more, the manufacture of new liturgies that will never be alive: how hopeless! Stylitisms, eremite fanaticisms and fakeerisms; spasmodic agonistic posture-makings, and narrow, cramped, morbid, if forever noble wrestlings: all this is not a thing desirable to me. It is a thing the world *has* done once,—when its beard was not grown as now!

And yet there is, at worst, one Liturgy which does remain forever unexceptionable: that of *Praying* (as the old Monks did withal) *by Working.* And indeed the Prayer which accomplished itself in special chapels at stated hours, and went not with a man, rising up from all his Work and Action, at all moments sanctifying the same, —what was it ever good for? 'Work is Worship:' yes, in a highly considerable sense,—which, in the present state of all 'worship,' who is there that can unfold! He that understands it well, understands the Prophecy of the whole Future; the last Evangel, which has included all others. *Its* cathedral the Dome of Immensity,— hast thou seen it? coped with the star-galaxies; paved with the green mosaic of land and ocean; and for altar, verily, the Star-throne of the Eternal! Its litany and psalmody the noble acts, the heroic work and suffering, and true heart-utterance of all the Valiant of the Sons of Men. Its choir-music the ancient Winds and Oceans, and deep-toned, inarticulate, but most speaking voices of Destiny and History,—supernal ever as of old. Between two great Silences:

> 'Stars silent rest o'er us,
>   Graves under us silent!'

Between which two great Silences, do not, as we said, all human Noises, in the naturalest times, most *preter*naturally march and roll?—

I will insert this also, in a lower strain, from Sauerteig's *Æsthe-tische Springwurzeln.* 'Worship?' says he: 'Before that inane 'tumult of Hearsay filled men's heads, while the world lay yet 'silent, and the heart true and open, many things were Worship! 'To the primeval man whatsoever good came, descended on him '(as, in mere fact, it ever does) direct from God; whatsoever duty 'lay visible for him, this a Supreme God had prescribed. To the 'present hour I ask thee, Who else? For the primeval man, in 'whom dwelt Thought, this Universe was all a Temple; Life 'everywhere a Worship.

   'What Worship, for example, is there not in mere Washing! 'Perhaps one of the most moral things a man, in common cases, 'has it in his power to do. Strip thyself, go into the bath, or were

'it into the limpid pool and running brook, and there wash and be
'clean; thou wilt step out again a purer and a better man.   This
'consciousness of perfect outer pureness, that to thy skin there now
'adheres no foreign speck of imperfection, how it radiates in on
'thee, with cunning symbolic influences, to thy very soul!   Thou
'hast an increase of tendency towards all good things whatsoever.
'The oldest Eastern Sages, with joy and holy gratitude, had felt it
'so,—and that it was the Maker's gift and will.   Whose else *is* it?
'It remains a religious duty, from oldest times, in the East.—Nor
'could Herr Professor Strauss, when I put the question, deny that
'for us at present it is still such here in the West!   To that dingy
'fuliginous Operative, emerging from his soot-mill, what is the first
'duty I will prescribe, and offer help towards?   That he clean the
'skin of him.   *Can* he pray, by any ascertained method?   One
'knows not entirely:—but with soap and a sufficiency of water,
'he can wash.   Even the dull English feel something of this;
'they have a saying, "Cleanliness is near akin to Godliness:"
'—yet never, in any country, saw I operative men worse washed,
'and, in a climate drenched with the softest cloud-water, such a
'scarcity of baths!'—Alas, Sauerteig, our 'operative men' are at
present short even of potatoes: what 'duty' can you prescribe
to them?

Or let us give a glance at China.   Our new friend, the Emperor
there, is Pontiff of three hundred million men; who do all live and
work, these many centuries now; authentically patronised by
Heaven so far; and therefore must have some 'religion' of a kind.
This Emperor-Pontiff has, in fact, a religious belief of certain Laws
of Heaven; observes, with a religious rigour, his 'three thousand
punctualities,' given out by men of insight, some sixty generations
since, as a legible transcript of the same,—the Heavens do seem to
say, not totally an incorrect one.   He has not much of a ritual, this
Pontiff-Emperor; believes, it is likest, with the old Monks, that
'Labour is Worship.'   His most public Act of Worship, it appears,
is the drawing solemnly at a certain day, on the green bosom of
our Mother Earth, when the Heavens, after dead black winter, have
again with their vernal radiances awakened her, a distinct red
Furrow with the Plough,—signal that all the Ploughs of China are
to begin ploughing and worshipping!   It is notable enough.   He,
in sight of the Seen and Unseen Powers, draws his distinct red
Furrow there; saying, and praying, in mute symbolism, so many
most eloquent things!

If you ask this Pontiff, "Who made him ?   What is to become
of him and us ? " he maintains a dignified reserve ; waves his hand
and pontiff-eyes over the unfathomable deep of Heaven, the 'Tsien,'
the azure kingdoms of Infinitude ; as if asking, " Is it doubtful that
we are right *well* made ?   Can aught that is *wrong* become of us ? "
—He and his three hundred millions (it is their chief ' punctuality')
visit yearly the Tombs of their Fathers ; each man the Tomb of his
Father and his Mother: alone there, in silence, with what of
' worship' or of other thought there may be, pauses solemnly each
man ; the divine Skies all silent over him ; the divine Graves, and
this divinest Grave, all silent under him ; the pulsings of his own
soul, if he have any soul, alone audible.   Truly it may be a kind
of worship !   Truly, if a man cannot get some glimpse into the
Eternities, looking through this portal,—through what other need
he try it ?

Our friend the Pontiff-Emperor permits cheerfully, though with
contempt, all manner of Buddists, Bonzes, Talapoins and suchlike,
to build brick Temples, on the voluntary principle ; to worship
with what of chantings, paper-lanterns and tumultuous brayings,
pleases them ; and make night hideous, since they find some comfort
in so doing.   Cheerfully, though with contempt.   He is a wiser
Pontiff than many persons think !   He is as yet the one Chief
Potentate or Priest in this Earth who has made a distinct systematic
attempt at what we call the ultimate result of all religion, '*Practical
Hero-worship* :' he does incessantly, with true anxiety, in such way
as he can, search and sift (it would appear) his whole enormous
population for the Wisest born among them ; by which Wisest, as
by born Kings, these three hundred million men are governed.
The Heavens, to a certain extent, do appear to countenance him.
These three hundred millions actually make porcelain, souchong
tea, with innumerable other things ; and fight, under Heaven's flag,
against Necessity ;—and have fewer Seven-Years Wars, Thirty-
Years Wars, French-Revolution Wars, and infernal fightings with
each other, than certain millions elsewhere have !

Nay in our poor distracted Europe itself, in these newest times,
have there not religious voices risen,—with a religion new and yet
the oldest ; entirely indisputable to all hearts of men ?   Some I
do know, who did not call or think themselves 'Prophets,' far
enough from that ; but who were, in very truth, melodious Voices
from the eternal Heart of Nature once again ;   souls forever

venerable to all that have a soul. A French Revolution is one phenomenon; as complement and spiritual exponent thereof, a poet Goethe and German Literature is to me another. The old Secular or Practical World, so to speak, having gone up in fire, is not here the prophecy and dawn of a new Spiritual World, parent of far nobler, wider, new Practical Worlds? A Life of Antique devoutness, Antique veracity and heroism, has again become possible, is again *seen* actual there, for the most modern man. A phenomenon, as quiet as it is, comparable for greatness to no other! 'The great event for the world is, now as always, the arrival in it of a new Wise Man.' Touches there are, be the Heavens ever thanked, of new Sphere-melody; audible once more, in the infinite jargoning discords and poor scrannel-pipings of the thing called Literature;—priceless there, as the voice of new Heavenly Psalms! Literature, like the old Prayer-Collections of the first centuries, were it 'well selected from and burnt,' contains precious things. For Literature, with all its printing-presses, puffing-engines and shoreless deafening triviality, *is* yet 'the Thought of Thinking Souls.' A sacred 'religion,' if you like the name, does live in the heart of that strange froth-ocean, not wholly froth, which we call Literature; and will more and more disclose itself therefrom;—not now as scorching Fire: the red smoky scorching Fire has purified itself into white sunny Light. Is not Light grander than Fire? It is the same element in a state of purity.

My ingenuous readers, we will march out of this Third Book with a rhythmic word of Goethe's on our lips; a word which perhaps has already sung itself, in dark hours and in bright, through many a heart. To me, finding it devout yet wholly credible and veritable, full of piety yet free of cant; to me, joyfully finding much in it, and joyfully missing so much in it, this little snatch of music, by the greatest German Man, sounds like a stanza in the grand *Road-Song* and *Marching-Song* of our great Teutonic Kindred, wending, wending, valiant and victorious, through the undiscovered Deeps of Time! He calls it *Mason-Lodge*,—not Psalm or Hymn:

> The Mason's ways are
> A type of Existence,
> And his persistence
> Is as the days are
> Of men in this world.

The Future hides in it
Gladness and sorrow ;
We press still thorow,
Nought that abides in it
Daunting us,—onward.

And solemn before us,
Veiled, the dark Portal,
Goal of all mortal :—
Stars silent rest o'er us,
Graves under us silent !

While earnest thou gazest,
Comes boding of terror,
Comes phantasm and error,
Perplexes the bravest
With doubt and misgiving.

But heard are the Voices,—
Heard are the Sages,
The Worlds and the Ages :
" Choose well ; your choice is
Brief and yet endless :

Here eyes do regard you,
In Eternity's stillness ;
Here is all fulness,
Ye brave, to reward you ;
Work, and despair not."

BOOK FOURTH.

HOROSCOPE.

CHAPTER I.

ARISTOCRACIES.

To predict the Future, to manage the Present, would not be so impossible, had not the Past been so sacrilegiously mishandled; effaced, and what is worse, defaced! The Past cannot be seen; the Past, looked at through the medium of 'Philosophical History' in these times, cannot even be *not* seen: it is misseen; affirmed to have existed,—and to have been a godless Impossibility. Your Norman Conquerors, true royal souls, crowned kings as such, were vulturous irrational tyrants: your Becket was a noisy egoist and hypocrite; getting his brains spilt on the floor of Canterbury Cathedral, to secure the main chance,—somewhat uncertain how! 'Policy, Fanaticism;' or say 'Enthusiasm,' even 'honest Enthusiasm,'—ah yes, of course:

> 'The Dog, to gain his private ends,
> *Went* mad, and bit the Man!'—

For in truth, the eye sees in all things 'what it brought with it the means of seeing.' A godless century, looking back on centuries that were godly, produces portraitures more miraculous than any other. All was inane discord in the Past; brute Force bore rule everywhere; Stupidity, savage Unreason, fitter for Bedlam than for a human World! Whereby indeed it becomes sufficiently natural that the like qualities, in new sleeker habiliments, should continue in our time to rule. Millions enchanted in Bastille Workhouses; Irish Widows proving their relationship by typhus-fever: what would you have? It was ever so, or worse. Man's History, was it not always even this: The cookery and eating-up of imbecile Dupedom by successful Quackhood; the battle, with various weapons, of vulturous Quack and Tyrant against vulturous Tyrant and Quack? No God was in the Past Time; nothing but Mechanisms and Chaotic Brute-Gods:—how shall the poor 'Philosophic Historian,' to whom his own century is all godless, see any God in other centuries?

Men believe in Bibles, and disbelieve in them: but of all Bibles the frightfulest to disbelieve in is this 'Bible of Universal History.' This is the Eternal Bible and God's-Book, 'which every born man,' till once the soul and eyesight are extinguished in him, 'can and must, with his own eyes, see the God's-Finger writing!' To discredit this, is an *infidelity* like no other. Such infidelity you would punish, if not by fire and faggot, which are difficult to manage in our times, yet by the most peremptory order, To hold its peace till it got something wiser to say. Why should the blessed Silence be broken into noises, to communicate only the like of this? If the Past have no God's-Reason in it, nothing but Devil's-Unreason, let the Past be eternally forgotten: mention *it* no more;—we whose ancestors were all hanged, why should we talk of ropes!

It is, in brief, not true that men ever lived by Delirium, Hypocrisy, Injustice, or any form of Unreason, since they came to inhabit this Planet. It is not true that they ever did, or ever will, live except by the reverse of these. Men will again be taught this. Their acted History will then again be a Heroism; their written History, what it once was, an Epic. Nay, forever it is either such, or else it virtually is—Nothing. Were it written in a thousand volumes, the Unheroic of such volumes hastens incessantly to be forgotten; the net content of an Alexandrian Library of Unheroics is, and will ultimately show itself to be, *zero*. What man is interested to remember *it;* have not all men, at all times, the liveliest interest to forget it?—'Revelations,' if not celestial, then infernal, will teach us that God is; we shall then, if needful, discern without difficulty that He has always been! The Dryas-dust Philosophisms and enlightened Scepticisms of the Eighteenth Century, historical and other, will have to survive for a while with the Physiologists, as a memorable *Nightmare-Dream*. All this haggard epoch, with its ghastly doctrines, and death's-head Philosophies 'teaching by example' or otherwise, will one day have become, what to our Moslem friends their godless ages are, 'the Period of Ignorance.'

If the convulsive struggles of the last Half-Century have taught poor struggling convulsed Europe any truth, it may perhaps be this as the essence of innumerable others: That Europe requires a real Aristocracy, a real Priesthood, or it cannot continue to exist. Huge French Revolutions, Napoleonisms, then Bourbonisms with their corollary of Three Days, finishing in very unfinal Louis-Philippisms: all this ought to be didactic! All this may have taught us, That False Aristocracies are insupportable; that No-Aristocracies, Liberty-and-Equalities are impossible; that true Aristocracies are at once indispensable and not easily attained.

Aristocracy and Priesthood, a Governing Class and a Teaching Class: these two, sometimes separate, and endeavouring to harmonise themselves, sometimes conjoined as one, and the King a Pontiff King:—there did no Society exist without these two vital elements, there will none exist. It lies in the very nature of man: you will visit no remotest village in the most republican country of the world, where virtually or actually you do not find these two powers at work. Man, little as he may suppose it, is necessitated to obey superiors. He is a social being in virtue of this necessity; nay he could not be gregarious otherwise. He obeys those whom he esteems better than himself, wiser, braver; and will forever obey such; and even be ready and delighted to do it.

The Wiser, Braver: these, a Virtual Aristocracy everywhere and everywhen, do in all Societies that reach any articulate shape, develop themselves into a ruling class, an Actual Aristocracy, with settled modes of operating, what are called laws and even *private-laws* or privileges, and so forth; very notable to look upon in this world.—Aristocracy and Priesthood, we say, are sometimes united. For indeed the Wiser and the Braver are properly but one class; no wise man but needed first of all to be a brave man, or he never had been wise. The noble Priest was always a noble *Aristos* to begin with, and something more to end with. Your Luther, your Knox, your Anselm, Becket, Abbot Samson, Samuel Johnson, if they had not been brave enough, by what possibility could they ever have been wise?—If, from accident or forethought, this your Actual Aristocracy have got discriminated into Two Classes, there can be no doubt but the Priest Class is the more dignified;

supreme over the other, as governing head is over active hand.
And yet in practice again, it is likeliest the reverse will be found
arranged;—a sign that the arrangement is already vitiated; that
a split is introduced into it, which will widen and widen till the
whole be rent asunder.

In England, in Europe generally, we may say that these two
Virtualities have unfolded themselves into Actualities, in by far
the noblest and richest manner any region of the world ever saw.
A spiritual Guideship, a practical Governorship, fruit of the grand
conscious endeavours, say rather of the immeasurable unconscious
instincts and necessities of men, have established themselves;
very strange to behold.   Everywhere, while so much has been
forgotten, you find the King's Palace, and the Viceking's Castle,
Mansion, Manorhouse; till there is not an inch of ground from sea
to sea but has both its King and Viceking, long due series of Vicekings, its Squire, Earl, Duke or whatever the title of him,—to
whom you have given the land, that he may govern you in it.

More touching still, there is not a hamlet where poor peasants
congregate, but, by one means and another, a Church-Apparatus
has been got together,—roofed edifice, with revenues and belfries;
pulpit, reading-desk, with Books and Methods: possibility, in
short, and strict prescription, That a man stand there and speak
of spiritual things to men.   It is beautiful;—even in its great
obscuration and decadence, it is among the beautifulest, most
touching objects one sees on the Earth.   This Speaking Man has
indeed, in these times, wandered terribly from the point; has, alas,
as it were, totally lost sight of the point: yet, at bottom, whom
have we to compare with him?   Of all public functionaries
boarded and lodged on the Industry of Modern Europe, is there
one worthier of the board he has?   A man even professing, and
never so languidly making still some endeavour, to save the souls
of men: contrast him with a man professing to do little but shoot
the partridges of men!   I wish he could find the point again, this
Speaking One; and stick to it with tenacity, with deadly energy;
for there is need of him yet!   The Speaking Function, this of
Truth coming to us with a living voice, nay in a living shape,
and as a concrete practical exemplar: this, with all our Writing
and Printing Functions, has a perennial place.   Could he but
find the point again,—take the old spectacles off his nose, and
looking up discover, almost in contact with him, what the *real*
Satanas, and soul-devouring, world-devouring *Devil*, now is!

Original Sin and suchlike are bad enough, I doubt not: but distilled Gin, dark Ignorance, Stupidity, dark Corn-Law, Bastille and Company, what are they! *Will* he discover our new real Satan, whom he has to fight; or go on droning through his old nose-spectacles about old extinct Satans; and never see the real one, till he *feel* him at his own throat and ours? That is a question, for the world! Let us not intermeddle with it here.

Sorrowful, phantasmal as this same Double Aristocracy of Teachers and Governors now looks, it is worth all men's while to know that the purport of it is and remains noble and most real. Dryasdust, looking merely at the surface, is greatly in error as to those ancient Kings. William Conqueror, William Rufus or Redbeard, Stephen Curthose himself, much more Henry Beauclerc and our brave Plantagenet Henry: the life of these men was not a vulturous Fighting; it was a valorous Governing,—to which occasionally Fighting did, and alas must yet, though far seldomer now, superadd itself as an accident, a distressing impedimental adjunct. The fighting too was indispensable, for ascertaining who had the might over whom, the right over whom. By much hard fighting, as we once said, ' the unrealities, beaten into dust, flew gradually off; ' and left the plain reality and fact, " Thou stronger than I; thou wiser than I; thou king, and subject I," in a somewhat clearer condition.

Truly we cannot enough admire, in those Abbot-Samson and William-Conqueror times, the arrangement they had made of their Governing Classes. Highly interesting to observe how the sincere insight, on their part, into what did, of primary necessity, behove to be accomplished, had led them to the way of accomplishing it, and in the course of time to get it accomplished! No imaginary Aristocracy would serve their turn; and accordingly they attained a real one. The Bravest men, who, it is ever to be repeated and remembered, are also on the whole the Wisest, Strongest, every-way Best, had here, with a respectable degree of accuracy, been got selected; seated each on his piece of territory, which was lent him, then gradually given him, that he might govern it. These Vicekings, each on his portion of the common soil of England, with a Head King over all, were a ' Virtuality perfected into an Actuality ' really to an astonishing extent.

For those were rugged stalwart ages; full of earnestness, of a rude God's-truth:—nay, at any rate, their *quilting* was so unspeakably *thinner* than ours; Fact came swiftly on them, if at any time

they had yielded to Phantasm! 'The Knaves and Dastards' had
to be 'arrested' in some measure; or the world, almost within
year and day, found that it could not live. The Knaves and
Dastards accordingly were got arrested. Dastards upon the very
throne had to be got arrested, and taken off the throne,—by such
methods as there were; by the roughest method, if there chanced
to be no smoother one! Doubtless there was much harshness of
operation, much severity; as indeed government and surgery are
often somewhat severe. Gurth, born thrall of Cedric, it is like,
got cuffs as often as pork-parings, if he misdemeaned himself; but
Gurth did belong to Cedric: no human creature then went about
connected with nobody; left to go his way into Bastilles or worse,
under *Laissez-faire;* reduced to prove his relationship by dying of
typhus-fever!—Days come when there is no King in Israel, but
every man is his own king, doing that which is right in his own
eyes;—and tarbarrels are burnt to 'Liberty,' 'Ten-pound Franchise'
and the like, with considerable effect in various ways!—

The Feudal Aristocracy, I say, was no imaginary one. To a
respectable degree, its *Jarls*, what we now call Earls, were *Strong-
Ones* in fact as well as etymology; its Dukes *Leaders;* its Lords
Law-wards. They did all the Soldiering and Police of the country,
all the Judging, Law-making, even the Church-Extension; whatsoever in the way of Governing, of Guiding and Protecting could
be done. It was a Land Aristocracy; it managed the Governing
of this English People, and had the reaping of the Soil of England
in return. It is, in many senses, the Law of Nature, this same
Law of Feudalism;—no right Aristocracy but a Land one! The
curious are invited to meditate upon it in these days. Soldiering,
Police and Judging, Church-Extension, nay real Government and
Guidance, all this was actually *done* by the Holders of the Land in
return for their Land. How much of it is now done by them;
done by anybody? Good Heavens, "Laissez-faire, Do ye nothing,
eat your wages and sleep," is everywhere the passionate half-wise
cry of this time; and they will not so much as do nothing, but
must do mere Corn-Laws! We raise Fifty-two millions, from the
general mass of us, to get our Governing done—or, alas, to get ourselves persuaded that it is done: and the 'peculiar burden of the
Land' is to pay, not all this, but to pay, as I learn, one twenty-
fourth part of all this. Our first Chartist Parliament, or Oliver
Redivivus, you would say, will know where to lay the new taxes of
England!—Or, alas, taxes? If we made the Holders of the Land

pay every shilling still of the expense of Governing the Land, what were all that? The Land, by mere hired Governors, cannot be got governed. You cannot hire men to govern the Land: it is by a mission not contracted for in the Stock-Exchange, but felt in their own hearts as coming out of Heaven, that men can govern a Land. The mission of a Land Aristocracy is a *sacred* one, in both the senses of that old word. The footing it stands on, at present, might give rise to thoughts other than of Corn-Laws !—

But truly a 'Splendour of God,' as in William Conqueror's rough oath, did dwell in those old rude veracious ages; did inform, more and more, with a heavenly nobleness, all departments of their work and life. Phantasms could not yet walk abroad in mere Cloth Tailorage; they were at least Phantasms 'on the rim of the horizon,' pencilled there by an eternal Light-beam from within. A most 'practical' Hero-worship went on, unconsciously or half-consciously, everywhere. A Monk Samson, with a maximum of two shillings in his pocket, could, without ballot-box, be made a Viceking of, being seen to be worthy. The difference between a good man and a bad man was as yet felt to be, what it forever is, an immeasurable one. Who *durst* have elected a Pandarus Dog-draught, in those days, to any office, Carlton Club, Senatorship, or place whatsoever? It was felt that the arch Satanas and no other had a clear right of property in Pandarus; that it were better for you to have no hand in Pandarus, to keep out of Pandarus his neighbourhood! Which is, to this hour, the mere fact; though for the present, alas, the forgotten fact. I think they were comparatively blessed times those, in their way! 'Violence,' 'war,' 'disorder:' well, what is war, and death itself, to such a perpetual life-in-death, and 'peace, peace, where there is no peace'! Unless some Hero-worship, in its new appropriate form, can return, this world does not promise to be very habitable long.

Old Anselm, exiled Archbishop of Canterbury, one of the purest-minded 'men of genius,' was travelling to make his appeal to Rome against King Rufus,—a man of rough ways, in whom the 'inner Lightbeam' shone very fitfully. It is beautiful to read, in Monk Eadmer, how the Continental populations welcomed and venerated this Anselm, as no French population now venerates Jean-Jacques or giant-killing Voltaire; as not even an American population now venerates a Schnüspel the distinguished Novelist! They had, by phantasy and true insight, the intensest conviction that a God's-Blessing dwelt in this Anselm,—as is my conviction too. They crowded round, with bent knees and enkindled hearts, to receive his blessing, to hear his voice, to see the light of his face. My blessings on them and on him!—But the notablest was a certain necessitous or covetous Duke of Burgundy, in straitened circumstances we shall hope,—who reflected that in all likelihood this English Archbishop, going towards Rome to appeal, must have taken store of cash with him to bribe the Cardinals. Wherefore he of Burgundy, for his part, decided to lie in wait and rob him. 'In an open space of a wood,' some 'wood' then green and growing, eight centuries ago, in Burgundian Land,—this fierce Duke, with fierce steel followers, shaggy, savage, as the Russian bear, dashes out on the weak old Anselm; who is riding along there, on his small quiet-going pony; escorted only by Eadmer and another poor Monk on ponies; and, except small modicum of roadmoney, not a gold coin in his possession. The steelclad Russian bear emerges, glaring: the old white-bearded man starts not,—paces on unmoved, looking into him with those clear old earnest eyes, with that venerable sorrowful time-worn face; of whom no man or thing need be afraid, and who also is afraid of no created man or thing. The fire-eyes of his Burgundian Grace meet these clear eye-glances, convey them swift to his heart: he bethinks him that probably this feeble, fearless, hoary Figure has in it something of the Most High God; that probably he shall be damned if he meddle with it,—that, on the whole, he had better not. He plunges, the rough savage, from his war-horse, down to his knees; embraces the feet of old Anselm: he too begs his blessing; orders men to escort him, guard him from being robbed, and under dread penalties see him safe on his way. *Per os Dei*, as his Majesty was wont to ejaculate!

Neither is this quarrel of Rufus and Anselm, of Henry and Becket, uninstructive to us. It was, at bottom, a great quarrel. For, admitting that Anselm was full of divine blessing, he by no means included in him all forms of divine blessing:—there were far other forms withal, which he little dreamed of; and William Redbeard was unconsciously the representative and spokesman of these. In truth, could your divine Anselm, your divine Pope Gregory have had their way, the results had been very notable. Our Western World had all become a European Thibet, with one Grand Lama sitting at Rome; our one honourable business that of singing mass, all day and all night. Which would not in the least have suited us. The Supreme Powers willed it not so.

It was as if King Redbeard unconsciously, addressing Anselm,

Becket and the others, had said : "Right Reverend, your Theory of the Universe is indisputable by man or devil. To the core of our heart we feel that this divine thing, which you call Mother Church, does fill the whole world hitherto known, and is and shall be all our salvation and all our desire. And yet—and yet—Behold, though it is an unspoken secret, the world is *wider* than any of us think, Right Reverend! Behold, there are yet other immeasurable Sacrednesses in this that you call Heathenism, Secularity! On the whole, I, in an obscure but most rooted manner, feel that I cannot comply with you. Western Thibet and perpetual mass-chanting,— No. I am, so to speak, in the family-way ; with child, of I know not what,—certainly of something far different from this! I have —*Per os Dei*, I have Manchester Cotton-trades, Bromwicham Iron-trades, American Commonwealths, Indian Empires, Steam Mechanisms and Shakspeare Dramas, in my belly ; and cannot do it, Right Reverend!"—So accordingly it was decided: and Saxon Becket spilt his life in Canterbury Cathedral, as Scottish Wallace did on Tower-hill, and as generally a noble man and martyr has to do,— not for nothing ; no, but for a divine something other than *he* had altogether calculated. We will now quit this of the hard, organic, but limited Feudal Ages ; and glance timidly into the immense Industrial Ages, as yet all inorganic, and in a quite pulpy condition, requiring desperately to harden themselves into some organism!

Our Epic having now become *Tools and the Man*, it is more than usually impossible to prophesy the Future. The boundless Future does lie there, predestined, nay already extant though unseen ; hiding, in its Continents of Darkness, 'gladness and sorrow:' but the supremest intelligence of man cannot prefigure much of it :— the united intelligence and effort of All Men in all coming generations, this alone will gradually prefigure it, and figure and form it into a seen fact! Straining our eyes hitherto, the utmost effort of intelligence sheds but some most glimmering dawn, a little way into its dark enormous Deeps: only huge outlines loom uncertain on the sight ; and the ray of prophecy, at a short distance, expires. But may we not say, here as always, Sufficient for the day is the evil thereof! To shape the whole Future is not our problem: but only to shape faithfully a small part of it, according to rules already known. It is perhaps possible for each of us, who will with due earnestness inquire, to ascertain clearly what he, for his own part, ought to do: this let him, with true heart, do, and continue doing.

The general issue will, as it has always done, rest well with a Higher Intelligence than ours.

One grand 'outline,' or even two, many earnest readers may perhaps, at this stage of the business, be able to prefigure for themselves,—and draw some guidance from. One prediction, or even two, are already possible. For the Life-tree Igdrasil, in all its new developments, is the selfsame world-old Life-tree: having found an element or elements there, running from the very roots of it in Hela's Realms, in the Well of Mimer and of the Three Nornas or TIMES, up to this present hour of it in our own hearts, we conclude that such will have to continue. A man has, in his own soul, an Eternal; can read something of the Eternal there, if he will look! He already knows what will continue; what cannot, by any means or appliance whatsoever, be made to continue!

One wide and widest 'outline' ought really, in all ways, to be becoming clear to us; this namely: That a 'Splendour of God,' in one form or other, will have to unfold itself from the heart of these our Industrial Ages too; or they will never get themselves 'organised;' but continue chaotic, distressed, distracted evermore, and have to perish in frantic suicidal dissolution. A second 'outline' or prophecy, narrower, but also wide enough, seems not less certain: That there will again *be* a King in Israel; a system of Order and Government; and every man shall, in some measure, see himself constrained to do that which is right in the King's eyes. This too we may call a sure element of the Future; for this too is of the Eternal;—this too is of the Present, though hidden from most; and without it no fibre of the Past ever was. An actual new Sovereignty, Industrial Aristocracy, real not imaginary Aristocracy, is indispensable and indubitable for us.

But what an Aristocracy; on what new, far more complex and cunningly devised conditions than that old Feudal fighting one! For we are to bethink us that the Epic verily is not *Arms and the Man*, but *Tools and the Man*,—an infinitely wider kind of Epic. And again we are to bethink us that men cannot now be bound to men by *brass-collars*,—not at all: that this brass-collar method, in all figures of it, has vanished out of Europe forevermore! Huge Democracy, walking the streets everywhere in its Sack Coat, has asserted so much; irrevocably, brooking no reply! True enough, man *is* forever the 'born thrall' of certain men, born master of certain other men, born equal of certain others, let him acknowledge the fact or not. It is unblessed for him when he cannot acknowledge this fact; he is in the chaotic state, ready to perish, till he do get the fact acknowledged. But no man is, or can henceforth be, the brass-collar thrall of any man; you will have to bind him by other, far nobler and cunninger methods. Once for all, he is to be loose of the brass-collar, to have a scope *as* wide as his faculties now are :—will he not be all the usefuler to you in that new state? Let him go abroad as a trusted one, as a free one ; and return home to you with rich earnings at night! Gurth could only tend pigs; this one will build cities, conquer waste worlds.—How, in conjunction with inevitable Democracy, indispensable Sovereignty is to exist: certainly it is the hugest question ever heretofore propounded to Mankind! The solution of which is work for long years and centuries. Years and centuries, of one knows not what complexion ;—blessed or unblessed, according as they shall, with earnest valiant effort, make progress therein, or, in slothful unveracity and dilettantism, only talk of making progress. For either progress therein, or swift and ever swifter progress towards dissolution, is henceforth a necessity.

It is of importance that this grand reformation were begun; that Corn-Law Debatings and other jargon, little less than delirious in such a time, had fled far away, and left us room to begin! For the evil has grown practical, extremely conspicuous; if it be not seen and provided for, the blindest fool will have to feel it ere long. There is much that can wait; but there is something also that cannot wait. With millions of eager Working Men imprisoned in 'Impossibility' and Poor-Law Bastilles, it is time that some means of dealing with them were trying to become 'possible'! Of the Government of England, of all articulate-speaking functionaries, real and imaginary Aristocracies, of me and of thee, it is imperatively demanded, "How do you mean to manage these men? Where are they to find a supportable existence? What is to become of them,—and of you!"

CHAPTER II.

BRIBERY COMMITTEE.

In the case of the late Bribery Committee, it seemed to be the conclusion of the soundest practical minds that Bribery could not be put down; that Pure Election was a thing we had seen the last of, and must now go on without, as we best could. A conclusion not a little startling; to which it requires a practical mind of some seasoning to reconcile yourself at once! It seems, then, we are henceforth to get ourselves constituted Legislators not according to what merit we may have, or even what merit we may seem to have, but according to the length of our purse, and our frankness, impudence and dexterity in laying out the contents of the same. Our theory, written down in all books and law-books, spouted forth from all barrel-heads, is perfect purity of Tenpound Franchise, absolute sincerity of question put and answer given;— and our practice is irremediable bribery; irremediable, unpunishable, which you will do more harm than good by attempting to punish! Once more, a very startling conclusion indeed; which, whatever the soundest practical minds in Parliament may think of it, invites all British men to meditations of various kinds.

A Parliament, one would say, which proclaims itself elected and eligible by bribery, tells the Nation that is governed by it a piece of singular news. Bribery: have we reflected what bribery is? Bribery means not only length of purse, which is neither qualification nor the contrary for legislating well; but it means dishonesty, and even impudent dishonesty;—brazen insensibility to lying and to making others lie; total oblivion, and flinging overboard, for the nonce, of any real thing you can call veracity, morality; with dextrous putting-on the cast-clothes of that real thing, and strutting about in them! What Legislating can you get out of a man in that fatal situation? None that will profit much, one would think! A Legislator who has left his veracity lying on the door-threshold, he, why verily *he*—ought to be sent out to seek it again!

Heavens, what an improvement, were there once fairly in Downing-street an Election-Office opened, with a tariff of Boroughs! Such and such a population, amount of property-tax, ground-rental, extent of trade; returns two Members, returns one Member, for so much money down: Ipswich so many thousands, Nottingham so many,—as they happened, one by one, to fall into this new Downing-street Schedule A! An incalculable improvement, in comparison: for now at least you have it fairly by length of purse, and leave the dishonesty, the impudence, the unveracity all handsomely aside. Length of purse and desire to be a Legislator ought to get a man into Parliament, not *with*, but if possible *without* the unveracity, the impudence and the dishonesty! Length of purse and desire, these are, as intrinsic qualifications, correctly equal to zero; but they are not yet *less* than zero,—as the smallest addition of that latter sort will make them!

And is it come to this? And does our venerable Parliament announce itself elected and eligible in this manner? Surely such a Parliament promulgates strange horoscopes of itself. What is to become of a Parliament elected or eligible in this manner? Unless Belial and Beelzebub have got possession of the throne of this Universe, such Parliament is preparing itself for new Reform-bills. We shall have to try it by Chartism, or any conceivable *ism*, rather than put-up with this! There is already in England 'religion' enough to get six hundred and fifty-eight Consulting Men brought together who do *not* begin work with a lie in their mouth. Our poor old Parliament, thousands of years old, is still good for something, for several things;—though many are beginning to ask, with ominous anxiety, in these days: For what thing? But for whatever thing and things Parliament be good, indisputably it must start with other than a lie in its mouth! On the whole, a Parliament working with a lie in its mouth, will have to take itself away. To no Parliament or thing, that one has heard of, did this Universe ever long yield harbour on that footing. At all hours of the day and night, some Chartism is advancing, some armed Cromwell is advancing, to apprise such Parliament: "Ye are no Parliament. In the name of God,—go!"

In sad truth, once more, how is our whole existence, in these present days, built on Cant, Speciosity, Falsehood, Dilettantism; with this one serious Veracity in it: Mammonism! Dig down where you will, through the Parliament-floor or elsewhere, how

infallibly do you, at spade's depth below the service, come upon
this universal *Liars*-rock substratum! Much else is ornamental;
true on barrel-heads, in pulpits, hustings, Parliamentary benches;
but this is forever true and truest: "Money does bring money's
worth; Put money in your purse." Here, if nowhere else, is the
human soul still in thorough earnest; sincere with a prophet's
sincerity: and 'the Hell of the English,' as Sauerteig said, 'is the
infinite terror of Not getting on, especially of Not making money.'
With results!

To many persons the horoscope of Parliament is more interesting than to me: but surely all men with souls must admit
that sending members to Parliament by bribery is an infamous
solecism; an act entirely immoral, which no man can have to
do with more or less, but he will soil his fingers more or less.
No Carlton Clubs, Reform Clubs, nor any sort of clubs or
creatures, or of accredited opinions or practices, can make a Lie
Truth, can make Bribery a Propriety. The Parliament should
really either punish and put away Bribery, or legalise it by
some Office in Downing-street. As I read the Apocalypses, a
Parliament that can do neither of these things is not in a good
way.—And yet, alas, what of Parliaments and their Elections?
Parliamentary Elections are but the topmost ultimate outcome
of an electioneering which goes on at all hours, in all places, in
every meeting of two or more men. It is *we* that vote wrong,
and teach the poor ragged Freemen of Boroughs to vote wrong.
We pay respect to those worthy of no respect.

Is not Pandarus Dogdraught a member of select clubs, and
admitted into the drawing-rooms of men? Visibly to all persons
he is of the offal of Creation; but he carries money in his purse,
due lacquer on his dog-visage, and it is believed will not steal
spoons. The human species does not with one voice, like the
Hebrew Psalmist, 'shun to sit' with Dogdraught, refuse totally to
dine with Dogdraught; men called of honour are willing enough
to dine with him, his talk being lively, and his champagne
excellent. We say to ourselves, "The man is in good society,"
—others have already voted for him; why should not I? We
forget the indefeasible right of property that Satan has in Dogdraught,—we are not afraid to be near Dogdraught! It is we
that vote wrong; blindly, nay with falsity prepense! It is we that
no longer know the difference between Human Worth and Human

Unworth; or feel that the one is admirable and alone admirable, the other detestable, damnable ! How shall *we* find out a Hero and Viceking Samson with a maximum of two shillings in his pocket ? We have no chance to do such a thing. We have got out of the Ages of Heroism, deep into the Ages of Flunkyism,—and must return or die. What a noble set of mortals are we, who, because there is no Saint Edmund threatening us at the rim of the horizon, are not afraid to be whatever, for the day and hour, is smoothest for us !

And now, in good sooth, why should an indigent discerning Freeman give his vote without bribes ? Let us rather honour the poor man that he does discern clearly wherein lies, for him, the true kernel of the matter. What is it to the ragged grimy Freeman of a Tenpound-Franchise Borough, whether Aristides Rigmarole Esq. of the Destructive, or the Hon. Alcides Dolittle of the Conservative Party be sent to Parliament;—much more, whether the two-thousandth part of them be sent, for that is the amount of his faculty in it ? Destructive or Conservative, what will either of them destroy or conserve of vital moment to this Freeman ? Has he found either of them care, at bottom, a sixpence for him or his interests, or those of his class or of his cause, or of any class or cause that is of much value to God or to man ? Rigmarole and Dolittle have alike cared for themselves hitherto; and for their own clique, and self-conceited crotchets,—their greasy dishonest interests of pudding, or windy dishonest interests of praise; and not very perceptibly for any other interest whatever. Neither Rigmarole nor Dolittle will accomplish any good or any evil for this grimy Freeman, like giving him a five-pound note, or refusing to give it him. It will be smoothest to vote according to value received. That is the veritable fact; and he indigent, like others that are not indigent, acts conformably thereto.

Why, reader, truly, if they asked thee or me, Which way we meant to vote ?—were it not our likeliest answer: Neither way ! I, as a Tenpound Franchiser, will receive no bribe ; but also I will not vote for either of these men. Neither Rigmarole nor Dolittle shall, by furtherance of mine, go and make laws for this country. I will have no hand in such a mission. How dare I ! If other men cannot be got in England, a totally other sort of men, different as light is from dark, as star-fire is from street-mud, what is the use of votings, or of Parliaments in England ? England ought to resign herself; there is no hope or possibility for England.

If England cannot get her Knaves and Dastards 'arrested,' in some degree, but only get them 'elected,' what is to become of England?

I conclude, with all confidence, that England will verily have to put an end to briberies on her Election Hustings and elsewhere, at what cost soever;—and likewise that we, Electors and Eligibles, one and all of us, for our own behoof and hers, cannot too soon begin, at what cost soever, to put an end to *bribeabilities* in ourselves. The death-leprosy, attacking in this manner, by purifying lotions from without and by rallying of the vital energies and purities from within, will probably abate somewhat! It has otherwise no chance to abate.

CHAPTER III.

THE ONE INSTITUTION.

WHAT our Government can do in this grand Problem of the Working Classes of England? Yes, supposing the insane Corn-Laws totally abolished, all speech of them ended, and 'from ten to twenty years of new possibility to live and find wages' conceded us in consequence: What the English Government might be expected to accomplish or attempt towards rendering the existence of our Labouring Millions somewhat less anomalous, somewhat less impossible, in the years that are to follow those 'ten or twenty,' if either 'ten' or 'twenty' there be?

It is the most momentous question. For all this of the Corn-Law Abrogation, and what can follow therefrom, is but as the shadow on King Hezekiah's Dial: the shadow has gone back twenty years; but will again, in spite of Free-Trades and Abrogations, travel forward its old fated way. With our present system of individual Mammonism, and Government by Laissez-faire, this Nation cannot live. And if, in the priceless interim, some new life and healing be not found, there is no second respite to be counted on. The shadow on the Dial advances thenceforth without pausing. What Government can do? This that they call 'Organising of Labour' is, if well understood, the Problem of the whole Future, for all who will in future pretend to govern men. But our first preliminary stage of it, How to deal with the Actual Labouring Millions of England? this is the imperatively pressing Problem of the Present, pressing with a truly fearful intensity and imminence in these very years and days. No Government can longer neglect it: once more, what can our Government do in it?

Governments are of very various degrees of activity: some, altogether Lazy Governments, in 'free countries' as they are called, seem in these times almost to profess to do, if not nothing, one knows not at first what. To debate in Parliament, and gain majorities; and ascertain who shall be, with a toil hardly second to Ixion's, the Prime Speaker and Spoke-holder, and keep the Ixion's-Wheel going, if not forward, yet round? Not altogether so: —much, to the experienced eye, is not what it seems! Chancery and certain other Law-Courts seem nothing; yet in fact they are, the worst of them, something: chimneys for the devilry and contention of men to escape by;—a very considerable something! Parliament too has its tasks, if thou wilt look; fit to wear-out the lives of toughest men. The celebrated Kilkenny Cats, through their tumultuous congress, cleaving the ear of Night, could they be said to do nothing? Hadst thou been of them, thou hadst seen! The feline heart laboured, as with steam up—to the bursting point; and death-doing energy nerved every muscle: they had a work there; and did it! On the morrow, two tails were found left, and peaceable annihilation; a neighbourhood *delivered* from despair.

Again, are not Spinning-Dervishes an eloquent emblem, significant of much? Hast thou noticed him, that solemn-visaged Turk, the eyes shut; dingy wool mantle circularly hiding his figure;— bell-shaped; like a dingy bell set spinning on the *tongue* of it? By centrifugal force the dingy wool mantle heaves itself; spreads more and more, like upturned cup widening into upturned saucer: thus spins he, to the praise of Allah and advantage of mankind, fast and faster, till collapse ensue, and sometimes death!—

A Government such as ours, consisting of from seven to eight hundred Parliamentary Talkers, with their escort of Able Editors and Public Opinion; and for head, certain Lords and Servants of the Treasury, and Chief Secretaries and others, who find themselves at once Chiefs and No-Chiefs, and often commanded rather than commanding,—is doubtless a most complicate entity, and none of the alertest for getting on with business! Clearly enough, if the Chiefs be not self-motive and what we call men, but mere patient lay-figures without self-motive principle, the Government will not move anywhither; it will tumble disastrously, and jumble, round its own axis, as for many years past we have seen it do. —And yet a self-motive man who is not a lay-figure, place him in the heart of what entity you may, will make it move more or less! The absurdest in Nature he will make a little *less* absurd, he. The unwieldiest he will make to move;—that is the use of his existing there. He will at least have the manfulness to depart out of it, if not; to say: "I cannot move in thee, and be a man; like a wretched drift-log dressed in man's clothes and minister's clothes, doomed to a lot baser than belongs to man, I will not continue with thee, tumbling aimless on the Mother of Dead Dogs here:—Adieu!"

For, on the whole, it is the lot of Chiefs everywhere, this same. No Chief in the most despotic country but was a Servant withal; at once an absolute commanding General, and a poor Orderly-Sergeant, ordered by the very men in the ranks,—obliged to collect the vote of the ranks too, in some articulate or inarticulate shape, and weigh well the same. The proper name of all Kings is Minister, Servant. In no conceivable Government can a lay-figure get forward! *This* Worker, surely he above all others has to 'spread out his Gideon's Fleece,' and collect the monitions of Immensity; the poor Localities, as we said, and Parishes of Palace-yard or elsewhere, having no due monition in them. A Prime Minister, even here in England, who shall dare believe the heavenly omens, and address himself like a man and hero to the great dumb-struggling heart of England; and speak out for it, and act out for it, the God's-Justice it is writhing to get uttered and perishing for want of,—yes, he too will see awaken round him, in passionate burning all-defiant loyalty, the heart of England, and such a 'support' as no Division-List or Parliamentary Majority was ever yet known to yield a man! Here as there, now as then, he who can and dare trust the heavenly Immensities, all earthly Localities are subject to him. We will pray for such a Man and First-Lord;—yes, and far better, we will strive and incessantly make ready, each of us, to be worthy to serve and second such a First-Lord! We shall then be as good as sure of his arriving; sure of many things, let him arrive or not.

Who can despair of Governments that passes a Soldier's Guard-house, or meets a redcoated man on the streets! That a body of men could be got together to kill other men when you bade them : this, *a priori*, does it not seem one of the impossiblest things? Yet look, behold it : in the stolidest of Donothing Governments, that impossibility is a thing done. See it there, with buff belts, red coats on its back; walking sentry at guard-houses, brushing white breeches in barracks; an indisputable palpable fact. Out of gray Antiquity, amid all finance-difficulties, *scaccarium*-tallies, ship-moneys, coat-and-conduct moneys, and vicissitudes of Chance and Time, there, down to the present blessed hour, it is.

Often, in these painfully decadent and painfully nascent Times, with their distresses, inarticulate gaspings and 'impossibilities;' meeting a tall Lifeguardsman in his snow-white trousers, or seeing those two statuesque Lifeguardsmen in their frowning bearskins, pipe-clayed buckskins, on their coal-black sleek-fiery quadrupeds, riding sentry at the Horse-Guards,—it strikes one with a kind of mournful interest, how, in such universal down-rushing and wrecked impotence of almost all old institutions, this oldest Fighting Institution is still so young! Fresh-complexioned, firm-limbed, six feet by the standard, this fighting man has verily been got up, and can fight. While so much has not yet got into being; while so much has gone gradually out of it, and become an empty Semblance or Clothes-suit; and highest king's-cloaks, mere chimeras parading under them so long, are getting unsightly to the earnest eye, unsightly, almost offensive, like a costlier kind of scarecrow's-blanket,—here still is a reality!

The man in horsehair wig advances, promising that he will get me 'justice :' he takes me into Chancery Law-Courts, into decades, half-centuries of hubbub, of distracted jargon; and does *get* me —disappointed, almost desperation; and one refuge : that of dismissing him and his 'justice' altogether out of my head. For I have work to do; I cannot spend my decades in mere arguing with other men about the exact wages of my work : I will work cheerfully with no wages, sooner than with a ten-years gangrene or Chancery Lawsuit in my heart! He of the horsehair wig is a sort of failure; no substance, but a fond imagination of the mind. He of the shovel-hat, again, who comes forward professing that he will save my soul—O ye Eternities, of him in this place be absolute silence!—But he of the red coat, I say, is a success and no failure! He will veritably, if he get orders, draw out a long sword and kill me. No mistake there. He is a fact and not a shadow. Alive in this Year Forty-three, able and willing to do *his* work. In dim old centuries, with William Rufus, William of Ipres, or far earlier, he began; and has come down safe so far. Catapult has given place to cannon, pike has given place to musket, iron mail-shirt to coat of red cloth, saltpetre ropematch to percussion-cap; equipments, circumstances have all changed, and again changed: but the human battle-engine in the inside of any or each of these, ready still to do battle, stands there, six feet in standard size. There are Pay-Offices, Woolwich Arsenals, there is a Horse-Guards, War-Office, Captain-General; persuasive Sergeants, with tap of drum, recruit in market-towns and villages:—and, on the whole, I say, here is your actual drilled fighting-man; here are your actual Ninety-thousand of such, ready to go into any quarter of the world and fight!

Strange, interesting, and yet most mournful to reflect on. Was this, then, of all the things mankind had some talent for, the one thing important to learn well, and bring to perfection; this of successfully killing one another? Truly you have learned it well, and carried the business to a high perfection. It is incalculable what, by arranging, commanding and regimenting, you can make of men. These thousand straight-standing firmset individuals, who shoulder arms, who march, wheel, advance, retreat; and are, for your behoof, a magazine charged with fiery death, in the most perfect condition of potential activity: few months ago, till the persuasive sergeant came, what were they? Multiform ragged losels, runaway apprentices, starved weavers, thievish valets; an entirely broken population, fast tending towards the treadmill. But the persuasive sergeant came; by tap of drum enlisted, or formed lists of them, took heartily to drilling them;—and he and you have made them this! Most potent, effectual for all work whatsoever, is wise planning, firm combining and commanding among men. Let no man despair of Governments who looks on these two sentries at the Horse-Guards and our United-Service Clubs! I could conceive an Emigration Service, a Teaching Service, considerable varieties of United and Separate Services, of the due thousands strong, all effective as this Fighting Service is; all doing *their* work, like it;—which work, much more than fighting, is henceforth the necessity of these New Ages we are got into! Much lies among us, convulsively, nigh desperately *struggling to be born.*

But mean Governments, as mean-limited individuals do, have stood by the physically indispensable; have realised that and nothing more. The Soldier is perhaps one of the most difficult things to realise; but Governments, had they not realised him, could not have existed: accordingly he is here. O Heavens, if we saw an army ninety-thousand strong, maintained and fully equipt, in continual real action and battle against Human Starvation, against Chaos, Necessity, Stupidity, and our real 'natural enemies,' what a business were it! Fighting and molesting not 'the French,' who, poor men, have a hard enough battle of their own in the like kind, and need no additional molesting from us; but fighting and incessantly spearing down and destroying Falsehood, Nescience, Delusion, Disorder, and the Devil and his Angels! Thou thyself, cultivated reader, hast done something in that alone true warfare; but, alas, under what circumstances was it? Thee no beneficent drill-sergeant, with any effectiveness, would rank in line beside thy fellows; train, like a true didactic artist, by the wit of all past experience, to do thy soldiering; encourage thee when right, punish thee when wrong, and everywhere with wise word-of-command say, Forward on this hand, Forward on that! Ah, no: thou hadst to learn thy small-sword and platoon exercise where and how thou couldst; to all mortals but thyself it was indifferent whether thou shouldst ever learn it. And the rations, and shilling a day, were they provided thee,—reduced as I have known brave Jean-Pauls, learning their exercise, to live on 'water *without* the bread'? The rations; or any furtherance of promotion to corporalship, lance-corporalship, or due cat-o'-nine tails, with the slightest reference to thy deserts, were not provided. Forethought, even as of a pipe-clayed drill-sergeant, did not preside over thee. To corporalship, lance-corporalship, thou didst attain; alas, also to the halberts and cat: but thy rewarder and punisher seemed blind as the Deluge: neither lance-corporalship, nor even drummer's cat, because both appeared delirious, brought thee due profit.

It was well, all this, we know;—and yet it was not well! Forty soldiers, I am told, will disperse the largest Spitalfields mob: forty to ten-thousand, that is the proportion between drilled and undrilled. Much there is which cannot yet be organised in this world; but somewhat also which can, somewhat also which must. When one thinks, for example, what Books are become and becoming for us, what Operative Lancashires are become; what a

Fourth Estate, and innumerable Virtualities not yet got to be
Actualities are become and becoming,—one sees Organisms enough
in the dim huge Future; and 'United Services' quite other than
the redcoat one; and much, even in these years, struggling to be
born!

Of Time-Bill, Factory-Bill and other such Bills the present
Editor has no authority to speak. He knows not, it is for others
than he to know, in what specific ways it may be feasible to
interfere, with Legislation, between the Workers and the Master-
Workers;—knows only and sees, what all men are beginning to
see, that Legislative interference, and interferences not a few are
indispensable; that as a lawless anarchy of supply-and-demand, on
market-wages alone, this province of things cannot longer be left.
Nay interference has begun: there are already Factory Inspectors,
—who seem to have no *lack* of work. Perhaps there might be
Mine-Inspectors too:—might there not be Furrowfield Inspectors
withal, and ascertain for us how on seven and sixpence a week
a human family does live! Interference has begun; it must
continue, must extensively enlarge itself, deepen and sharpen
itself. Such things cannot longer be idly lapped in darkness, and
suffered to go on unseen: the Heavens do see them; the curse,
not the blessing of the Heavens is on an Earth that refuses to see
them.

Again, are not Sanitary Regulations possible for a Legislature?
The old Romans had their Ædiles; who would, I think, in direct
contravention to supply-and-demand, have rigorously seen rammed
up into total abolition many a foul cellar in our Southwarks,
Saint-Gileses, and dark poison-lanes; saying sternly, "Shall a
Roman man dwell there?" The Legislature, at whatever cost
of consequences, would have had to answer, "God forbid!"—The
Legislature, even as it now is, could order all dingy Manufacturing
Towns to cease from their soot and darkness; to let-in the blessed
sunlight, the blue of Heaven, and become clear and clean; to burn
their coal-smoke, namely, and make flame of it. Baths, free air,
a wholesome temperature, ceilings twenty feet high, might be
ordained, by Act of Parliament, in all establishments licensed as
Mills. There are such Mills already extant;—honour to the
builders of them! The Legislature can say to others: Go ye and
do likewise; better if you can.

Every toiling Manchester, its smoke and soot all burnt, ought
it not, among so many world-wide conquests, to have a hundred

acres or so of free greenfield, with trees on it, conquered, for its
little children to disport in; for its all-conquering workers to take
a breath of twilight air in? You would say so! A willing
Legislature could say so with effect. A willing Legislature could
say very many things! And to whatsoever 'vested interest,' or
suchlike, stood up, gainsaying merely, "I shall lose profits,"—the
willing Legislature would answer, "Yes, but my sons and daughters
will gain health, and life, and a soul."—"What is to become of
our Cotton-trade?" cried certain Spinners, when the Factory Bill
was proposed; "What is to become of our invaluable Cotton-
trade?" The Humanity of England answered steadfastly: "Deliver me these rickety perishing souls of infants, and let your
Cotton-trade take its chance. God Himself commands the one
thing; not God especially the other thing. We cannot have
prosperous Cotton-trades at the expense of keeping the Devil a
partner in them!"—

Bills enough, were the Corn-Law Abrogation Bill once passed,
and a Legislature willing! Nay this one Bill, which lies yet
unenacted, a right Education Bill, is not this of itself the sure
parent of innumerable wise Bills,—wise regulations, practical
methods and proposals, gradually ripening towards the state of
Bills? To irradiate with intelligence, that is to say, with order,
arrangement and all blessedness, the Chaotic, Unintelligent: how,
except by educating, *can* you accomplish this? That thought,
reflection, articulate utterance and understanding be awakened
in these individual million heads, which are the atoms of your
Chaos: there is no other way of illuminating any Chaos! The
sum-total of intelligence that is found in it, determines the extent
of order that is possible for your Chaos,—the feasibility and
rationality of what your Chaos will dimly demand from you, and
will gladly obey when proposed by you! It is an exact equation;
the one accurately measures the other.—If the whole English
People, during these 'twenty years of respite,' be not educated,
with at least schoolmaster's educating, a tremendous responsibility,
before God and men, will rest somewhere! How dare any man,
especially a man calling himself minister of God, stand up in any
Parliament or place, under any pretext or delusion, and for a day
or an hour forbid God's Light to come into the world, and bid the
Devil's Darkness continue in it one hour more! For all light
and science, under all shapes, in all degrees of perfection, is
of God; all darkness, nescience, is of the Enemy of God. 'The

schoolmaster's creed is somewhat awry?' Yes, I have found few
creeds entirely correct; few light-beams shining *white*, pure of ad-
mixture : but of all creeds and religions now or ever before known,
was not that of thoughtless thriftless Animalism, of Distilled Gin,
and Stupor and Despair, unspeakably the least orthodox? We
will exchange *it* even with Paganism, with Fetishism; and, on the
whole, must exchange it with something.

An effective 'Teaching Service' I do consider that there must
be; some Education Secretary, Captain-General of Teachers, who
will actually contrive to get us *taught*. Then again, why should
there not be an 'Emigration Service,' and Secretary, with adjuncts,
with funds, forces, idle Navy-ships, and ever-increasing apparatus;
in fine an *effective system* of Emigration; so that, at length, before
our twenty years of respite ended, every honest willing Workman
who found England too strait, and the 'Organisation of Labour'
not yet sufficiently advanced, might find likewise a bridge built to
carry him into new Western Lands, there to 'organise' with more
elbow-room some labour for himself? There to be a real blessing,
raising new corn for us, purchasing new webs and hatchets from
us; leaving us at least in peace;—instead of staying here to be
a Physical-Force Chartist, unblessed and no blessing! Is it not
scandalous to consider that a Prime Minister could raise within
the year, as I have seen it done, a Hundred and Twenty Millions
Sterling to shoot the French; and we are stopt short for want
of the hundredth part of that to keep the English living? The
bodies of the English living, and the souls of the English living:
—these two 'Services,' an Education Service and an Emigration
Service, these with others will actually have to be organised!

A free bridge for Emigrants: why, we should then be on a par
with America itself, the most favoured of all lands that have no
government; and we should have, besides, so many traditions
and mementos of priceless things which America has cast away.
We could proceed deliberately to 'organise Labour,' not doomed to
perish unless we effected it within year and day;—every willing
Worker that proved superfluous, finding a bridge ready for him.
This verily will have to be done; the Time is big with this. Our
little Isle is grown too narrow for us; but the world is wide
enough yet for another Six Thousand Years. England's sure
markets will be among new Colonies of Englishmen in all quarters
of the Globe. All men trade with all men, when mutually convenient; and are even bound to do it by the Maker of men.

Our friends of China, who guiltily refused to trade, in these circumstances,—had we not to argue with them, in cannon-shot at
last, and convince them that they ought to trade! 'Hostile
Tariffs' will arise, to shut us out; and then again will fall, to let
us in: but the Sons of England, speakers of the English language
were it nothing more, will in all times have the ineradicable pre-
disposition to trade with England. Mycale was the *Pan-Ionion*,
rendezvous of all the Tribes of Ion, for old Greece: why should
not London long continue the *All-Saxon-home*, rendezvous of all
the 'Children of the Harz-Rock,' arriving, in select samples, from
the Antipodes and elsewhere, by steam and otherwise, to the
'season' here!—What a Future; wide as the world if we have
the heart and heroism for it,—which, by Heaven's blessing, we
shall:

> ' Keep not standing fixed and rooted,
> Briskly venture, briskly roam;
> Head and hand, where'er thou foot it,
> And stout heart are still at home.
>
> In what land the sun does visit
> Brisk are we, whate'er betide:
> To give space for wandering is it
> That the world was made so wide.'[1]

Fourteen hundred years ago, it was by a considerable 'Emigration
Service,' never doubt it, by much enlistment, discussion and
apparatus, that we ourselves arrived in this remarkable Island,—
and got into our present difficulties among others!

It is true the English Legislature, like the English People, is
of slow temper; essentially conservative. In our wildest periods
of reform, in the Long Parliament itself, you notice always the
invincible instinct to hold fast by the Old; to admit the *minimum*
of New; to expand, if it be possible, some old habit or method,
already found fruitful, into new growth for the new need. It is an
instinct worthy of all honour; akin to all strength and all wisdom.
The Future hereby is not dissevered from the Past, but based con-
tinuously on it; grows with all the vitalities of the Past, and is
rooted down deep into the beginnings of us. The English Legislature is entirely repugnant to believe in 'new epochs.' The
English Legislature does not occupy itself with epochs; has,
indeed, other business to do than looking at the Time-Horologe
and hearing it tick! Nevertheless new epochs do actually come;

[1] Goethe, *Wilhelm Meister.*

and with them new imperious peremptory necessities; so that even
an English Legislature has to look up, and admit, though with
reluctance, that the hour has struck. The hour having struck, let
us not say 'impossible:'—it will have to be possible! 'Contrary
to the habits of Parliament, the habits of Government?' Yes:
but did any Parliament or Government ever sit in a Year Forty-
three before? One of the most original, unexampled years and
epochs; in several important respects totally unlike any other!
For Time, all-edacious and all-feracious, does run on: and the
Seven Sleepers, awakening hungry after a hundred years, find
that it is not their old nurses who can now give them suck!

For the rest, let not any Parliament, Aristocracy, Millocracy,
or Member of the Governing Class, condemn with much triumph
this small specimen of 'remedial measures;' or ask again, with the
least anger, of this Editor, What is to be done, How that alarming
problem of the Working Classes is to be managed? Editors are
not here, foremost of all, to say How. A certain Editor thanks
the gods that nobody pays him three hundred thousand pounds a
year, two hundred thousand, twenty thousand, or any similar sum
of cash for saying How;—that his wages are very different, his
work somewhat fitter for him. An Editor's stipulated work is to
apprise _thee_ that it must be done. The 'way to do it,'—is to try
it, knowing that thou shalt die if it be not done. There is the
bare back, there is the web of cloth; thou shalt cut me a coat to
cover the bare back, thou whose trade it is. 'Impossible?' Hapless Fraction, dost thou discern Fate there, half unveiling herself
in the gloom of the future, with her gibbet-cords, her steel-whips,
and very authentic Tailor's Hell; waiting to see whether it is
'possible'? Out with thy scissors, and cut that cloth or thy own
windpipe!

CHAPTER IV.

CAPTAINS OF INDUSTRY.

IF I believed that Mammonism with its adjuncts was to continue henceforth the one serious principle of our existence, I should reckon it idle to solicit remedial measures from any Government, the disease being insusceptible of remedy. Government can do much, but it can in no wise do all. Government, as the most conspicuous object in Society, is called upon to give signal of what shall be done; and, in many ways, to preside over, further, and command the doing of it. But the Government cannot do, by all its signaling and commanding, what the Society is radically indisposed to do. In the long-run every Government is the exact symbol of its People, with their wisdom and unwisdom; we have to say, Like People like Government.—The main substance of this immense Problem of Organising Labour, and first of all of Managing the Working Classes, will, it is very clear, have to be solved by those who stand practically in the middle of it; by those who themselves work and preside over work. Of all that can be enacted by any Parliament in regard to it, the germs must already lie potentially extant in those two Classes, who are to obey such enactment. A Human Chaos *in* which there is no light, you vainly attempt to irradiate by light shed *on* it: order never can arise there.

But it is my firm conviction that the 'Hell of England' will *cease* to be that of 'not making money;' that we shall get a nobler Hell and a nobler Heaven! I anticipate light *in* the Human Chaos, glimmering, shining more and more; under manifold true signals from without That light shall shine. Our deity no longer being Mammon,—O Heavens, each man will then say to himself: "Why such deadly haste to make money? I shall not go to Hell, even if I do not make money! There is another Hell, I am told!" Competition, at railway-speed, in all branches of commerce and work will then abate :—good felt-hats for the head, in every sense, instead of seven-feet lath-and-plaster hats on wheels, will then be discoverable! Bubble-periods, with their panics and commercial crises, will again become infrequent; steady modest industry will take the place of gambling speculation. To be a noble Master, among noble Workers, will again be the first ambition with some few; to be a rich Master only the second. How the Inventive Genius of England, with the whirr of its bobbins and billy-rollers shoved somewhat into the backgrounds of the brain, will contrive and devise, not cheaper produce exclusively, but fairer distribution of the produce at its present cheapness! By degrees, we shall again have a Society with something of Heroism in it, something of Heaven's Blessing on it; we shall again have, as my German friend asserts, 'instead of Mammon-Feudalism with 'unsold cotton-shirts and Preservation of the Game, noble just 'Industrialism and Government by the Wisest!'

It is with the hope of awakening here and there a British man to know himself for a man and divine soul, that a few words of parting admonition, to all persons to whom the Heavenly Powers have lent power of any kind in this land, may now be addressed. And first to those same Master-Workers, Leaders of Industry; who stand nearest and in fact powerfulest, though not most prominent, being as yet in too many senses a Virtuality rather than an Actuality.

The Leaders of Industry, if Industry is ever to be led, are virtually the Captains of the World, if there be no nobleness in them, there will never be an Aristocracy more. But let the Captains of Industry consider: once again, are they born of other clay than the old Captains of Slaughter; doomed forever to be no Chivalry, but a mere gold-plated *Doggery*,—what the French well name *Canaille*, 'Doggery' with more or less gold carrion at its disposal? Captains of Industry are the true Fighters, henceforth recognisable as the only true ones: Fighters against Chaos, Necessity and the Devils and Jötuns; and lead on Mankind in that great, and alone true, and universal warfare; the stars in their courses fighting for them, and all Heaven and all Earth saying audibly, Well done! Let the Captains of Industry retire into their own hearts, and ask solemnly, If there is nothing but vulturous hunger, for fine wines, valet reputation and gilt carriages, discoverable there? Of hearts made by the Almighty God I will not believe such a thing. Deep-hidden under wretchedest godforgetting Cants, Epicurisms, Dead-Sea Apisms; forgotten as under foulest fat Lethe mud and weeds, there is yet, in all hearts

born into this God's-World, a spark of the Godlike slumbering.
Awake, O nightmare sleepers; awake, arise, or be forever fallen!
This is not playhouse poetry; it is sober fact. Our England, our
world cannot live as it is. It will connect itself with a God again,
or go down with nameless throes and fire-consummation to the
Devils. Thou who feelest aught of such a Godlike stirring in thee,
any faintest intimation of it as through heavy-laden dreams, follow
it, I conjure thee. Arise, save thyself, be one of those that save
thy country.

Bucaniers, Chactaw Indians, whose supreme aim in fighting is
that they may get the scalps, the money, that they may amass
scalps and money: out of such came no Chivalry, and never
will! Out of such came only gore and wreck, infernal rage and
misery; desperation quenched in annihilation. Behold it, I bid
thee, behold there, and consider! What is it that thou have a
hundred thousand-pound bills laid-up in thy strong-room, a
hundred scalps hung-up in thy wigwam? I value not them or
thee. Thy scalps and thy thousand-pound bills are as yet nothing,
if no nobleness from within irradiate them; if no Chivalry, in
action, or in embryo ever struggling towards birth and action, be
there.

Love of men cannot be bought by cash-payment; and without
love men cannot endure to be together. You cannot lead a
Fighting World without having it regimented, chivalried: the
thing, in a day, becomes impossible; all men in it, the highest at
first, the very lowest at last, discern consciously, or by a noble
instinct, this necessity. And can you any more continue to lead a
Working World unregimented, anarchic? I answer, and the
Heavens and Earth are now answering, No! The thing becomes
not 'in a day' impossible; but in some two generations it does.
Yes, when fathers and mothers, in Stockport hunger-cellars, begin
to eat their children, and Irish widows have to prove their relationship by dying of typhus-fever; and amid Governing 'Corporations
of the Best and Bravest,' busy to preserve their game by 'bushing,'
dark millions of God's human creatures start up in mad Chartisms,
impracticable Sacred-Months, and Manchester Insurrections:—and
there is a virtual Industrial Aristocracy as yet only half-alive,
spell-bound amid money-bags and ledgers; and an actual Idle
Aristocracy seemingly near dead in somnolent delusions, in
trespasses and double-barrels; 'sliding,' as on inclined-planes,
which every new year they *soap* with new Hansard's-jargon under

God's sky, and so are 'sliding,' ever faster, towards a 'scale' and balance-scale whereon is written *Thou art found Wanting*:—in such days, after a generation or two, I say, it does become, even to the low and simple, very palpably impossible! No Working World, any more than a Fighting World, can be led on without a noble Chivalry of Work, and laws and fixed rules which follow out of that,—far nobler than any Chivalry of Fighting was. As an anarchic multitude on mere Supply-and-demand, it is becoming inevitable that we dwindle in horrid suicidal convulsion and self-abrasion, frightful to the imagination, into *Chactaw* Workers. With wigwams and scalps,—with palaces and thousand-pound bills; with savagery, depopulation, chaotic desolation! Good Heavens, will not one French Revolution and Reign of Terror suffice us, but must there be two? There will be two if needed; there will be twenty if needed; there will be precisely as many as are needed. The Laws of Nature will have themselves fulfilled. That is a thing certain to me.

Your gallant battle-hosts and work-hosts, as the others did, will need to be made loyally yours; they must and will be regulated, methodically secured in their just share of conquest under you;—joined with you in veritable brotherhood, sonhood, by quite other and deeper ties than those of temporary day's wages! How would mere red-coated regiments, to say nothing of chivalries, fight for you, if you could discharge them on the evening of the battle, on payment of the stipulated shillings,—and they discharge you on the morning of it! Chelsea Hospitals, pensions, promotions, rigorous lasting covenant on the one side and on the other, are indispensable even for a hired fighter. The Feudal Baron, much more,—how could he subsist with mere temporary mercenaries round him, at sixpence a day; ready to go over to the other side, if sevenpence were offered? He could not have subsisted;—and his noble instinct saved him from the necessity of even trying! The Feudal Baron had a Man's Soul in him; to which anarchy, mutiny, and the other fruits of temporary mercenaries, were intolerable: he had never been a Baron otherwise, but had continued a Chactaw and Bucanier. He felt it precious, and at last it became habitual, and his fruitful enlarged existence included it as a necessity, to have men round him who in heart loved him; whose life he watched over with rigour yet with love; who were prepared to give their life for him, if need came. It was beautiful; it was human! Man lives not otherwise, nor can live contented, anywhere or anywhen. Isolation is the sum-total of wretchedness to man. To be cut off, to be left solitary : to have a world alien, not your world ; all a hostile camp for you ; not a home at all, of hearts and faces who are yours, whose you are ! It is the frightfulest enchantment ; too truly a work of the Evil One. To have neither superior, nor inferior, nor equal, united manlike to you. Without father, without child, without brother. Man knows no sadder destiny. 'How is each of us,' exclaims Jean Paul, 'so lonely in the wide bosom of the All !' Encased each as in his transparent 'ice-palace ;' our brother visible in his, making signals and gesticulations to us ;—visible, but forever unattainable : on his bosom we shall never rest, nor he on ours. It was not a God that did this ; no !

Awake, ye noble Workers, warriors in the one true war : all this must be remedied. It is you who are already half-alive, whom I will welcome into life ; whom I will conjure, in God's name, to shake off your enchanted sleep, and live wholly ! Cease to count scalps, gold-purses ; not in these lies your or our salvation. Even these, if you count only these, will not long be left. Let bucaniering be put far from you ; alter, speedily abrogate all laws of the bucaniers, if you would gain any victory that shall endure. Let God's justice, let pity, nobleness and manly valour, with more goldpurses or with fewer, testify themselves in this your brief Lifetransit to all the Eternities, the Gods and Silences. It is to you I call ; for ye are not dead, ye are already half-alive : there is in you a sleepless dauntless energy, the prime-matter of all nobleness in man. Honour to you in your kind. It is to you I call : ye know at least this, That the mandate of God to His creature man is : Work ! The future Epic of the World rests not with those that are near dead, but with those that are alive, and those that are coming into life.

Look around you. Your world-hosts are all in mutiny, in confusion, destitution ; on the eve of fiery wreck and madness ! They will not march farther for you, on the sixpence a day and supply-and-demand principle : they will not ; nor ought they, nor can they. Ye shall reduce them to order, begin reducing them. To order, to just subordination ; noble loyalty in return for noble guidance. Their souls are driven nigh mad ; let yours be sane and ever saner. Not as a bewildered bewildering mob ; but as a firm regimented mass, with real captains over them, will these men march any more. All human interests, combined human endeavours, and social growths in this world, have, at a certain stage of their development, required organising: and Work, the grandest of human interests, does now require it.

God knows, the task will be hard: but no noble task was ever easy. This task will wear away your lives, and the lives of your sons and grandsons: but for what purpose, if not for tasks like this, were lives given to men? Ye shall cease to count your thousand-pound scalps, the noble of you shall cease! Nay the very scalps, as I say, will not long be left if you count only these. Ye shall cease wholly to be barbarous vulturous Chactaws, and become noble European Nineteenth-Century Men. Ye shall know that Mammon, in never such gigs and flunky 'respectabilities,' is not the alone God; that of himself he is but a Devil, and even a Brute-god.

Difficult? Yes, it will be difficult. The short-fibre cotton; that too was difficult. The waste cotton-shrub, long useless, disobedient, as the thistle by the wayside,—have ye not conquered it: made it into beautiful bandana webs; white woven shirts for men; bright-tinted air-garments wherein flit goddesses? Ye have shivered mountains asunder, made the hard iron pliant to you as soft putty: the Forest-giants, Marsh-jötuns bear sheaves of golden-grain; Ægir the Sea-demon himself stretches his back for a sleek highway to you, and on Firehorses and Windhorses ye career. Ye are most strong. Thor red-bearded, with his blue sun-eyes, with his cheery heart and strong thunder-hammer, he and you have prevailed. Ye are most strong, ye Sons of the icy North, of the far East,—far marching from your rugged Eastern Wildernesses, hitherward from the gray Dawn of Time! Ye are Sons of the *Jötun*-land; the land of Difficulties Conquered. Difficult? You must try this thing. Once try it with the understanding that it will and shall have to be done. Try it as ye try the paltrier thing, making of money! I will bet on you once more, against all Jötuns, Tailor-gods, Double-barrelled Law-wards, and Denizens of Chaos whatsoever!

CHAPTER V.

PERMANENCE.

STANDING on the threshold, nay as yet outside the threshold, of a ' Chivalry of Labour,' and an immeasurable Future which it is to fill with fruitfulness and verdant shade; where so much has not yet come even to the rudimental state, and all speech of positive enactments were hazardous in those who know this business only by the eye,—let us here hint at simply one widest universal principle, as the basis from which all organisation hitherto has grown up among men, and all henceforth will have to grow : The principle of Permanent Contract instead of Temporary.

Permanent not Temporary :—you do not hire the mere red-coated fighter by the day, but by the score of years ! Permanence, persistence is the first condition of all fruitfulness in the ways of men. The ' tendency to persevere,' to persist in spite of hindrances, discouragements and 'impossibilities :' it is this that in all things distinguishes the strong soul from the weak; the civilised burgher from the nomadic savage,—the Species Man from the Genus Ape ! The Nomad has his very house set on wheels; the Nomad, and in a still higher degree the Ape, are all for 'liberty;' the privilege to flit continually is indispensable for them. Alas, in how many ways, does our humour, in this swift-rolling, self-abrading Time, show itself nomadic, apelike; mournful enough to him that looks on it with eyes ! This humour will have to abate; it is the first element of all fertility in human things, that such 'liberty' of apes and nomads do by freewill or constraint abridge itself, give place to a better. The civilised man lives not in wheeled houses. He builds stone castles, plants lands, makes lifelong marriage-contracts;— has long-dated hundred-fold possessions, not to be valued in the money-market; has pedigrees, libraries, law-codes; has memories and hopes, even for this Earth, that reach over thousands of years. Lifelong marriage-contracts: how much preferable were year-long or month-long—to the nomad or ape !

Month-long contracts please me little, in any province where
there can by possibility be found virtue enough for more. Month-
long contracts do not answer well even with your house-servants;
the liberty on both sides to change every month is growing very
apelike, nomadic;—and I hear philosophers predict that it will
alter, or that strange results will follow: that wise men, pestered
with nomads, with unattached ever-shifting spies and enemies
rather than friends and servants, will gradually, weighing substance
against semblance, with indignation, dismiss such, down almost to
the very shoeblack, and say, "Begone; I will serve myself rather,
and have peace!" Gurth was hired for life to Cedric, and Cedric
to Gurth. O Anti-Slavery Convention, loud-sounding long-eared
Exeter-Hall—But in thee too is a kind of instinct towards justice,
and I will complain of nothing. Only black Quashee over the
seas being once sufficiently attended to, wilt thou not perhaps open
thy dull sodden eyes to the ' sixty-thousand valets in London itself
' who are yearly dismissed to the streets, to be what they can,
' when the season ends;'—or to the hunger-stricken, pallid, _yellow-_
coloured ' Free Labourers' in Lancashire, Yorkshire, Buckinghamshire, and all other shires! These Yellow-coloured, for the present,
absorb all my sympathies: if I had a Twenty Millions, with Model-
Farms and Niger Expeditions, it is to these that I would give it!
Quashee has already victuals, clothing; Quashee is not dying of
such despair as the yellow-coloured pale man's. Quashee, it must
be owned, is hitherto a kind of blockhead. The Haiti Duke of
Marmalade, educated now for almost half a century, seems to have
next to no sense in him. Why, in one of those Lancashire Weavers,
dying of hunger, there is more thought and heart, a greater
arithmetical amount of misery and desperation, than in whole
gangs of Quashees. It must be owned, thy eyes are of the sodden
sort; and with thy emancipations, and thy twenty-millionings and
long-eared clamourings, thou, like Robespierre with his pasteboard
Être Suprême, threatenest to become a bore to us: _Avec ton Être_
Suprême tu commences m'embêter!—

In a Printed Sheet of the assiduous, much-abused, and truly
useful Mr. Chadwick's, containing queries and responses from far
and near as to this great question, ' What is the effect of education
on working-men, in respect of their value as mere workers?' the
present Editor, reading with satisfaction a decisive unanimous
verdict as to Education, reads with inexpressible interest this

special remark, put in by way of marginal incidental note, from a practical manufacturing Quaker, whom, as he is anonymous, we will call Friend Prudence. Prudence keeps a thousand workmen; has striven in all ways to attach them to him; has provided conversational soirées; play-grounds, bands of music for the young ones; went even 'the length of buying them a drum:' all which has turned out to be an excellent investment. For a certain person, marked here by a black stroke, whom we shall name Blank, living over the way,—he also keeps somewhere about a thousand men; but has done none of these things for them, nor any other thing, except due payment of the wages by supply-and-demand. Blank's workers are perpetually getting into mutiny, into broils and coils: every six months, we suppose, Blank has a strike; every one month, every day and every hour, they are fretting and obstructing the shortsighted Blank; pilfering from him, wasting and idling for him, omitting and committing for him. "I would not," says Friend Prudence, "exchange my workers for his *with seven thousand pounds to boot.*" [1]

Right, O honourable Prudence; thou art wholly in the right: Seven thousand pounds even as a matter of profit for this world, nay for the mere cash-market of this world! And as a matter of profit not for this world only, but for the other world and all worlds, it outweighs the Bank of England!—Can the sagacious reader descry here, as it were the outmost inconsiderable rock-ledge of a universal rock-foundation, deep once more as the Centre of the World, emerging so, in the experience of this good Quaker, through the Stygian mud-vortexes and general Mother of Dead Dogs, whereon, for the present, all swags and insecurely hovers, as if ready to be swallowed?

Some Permanence of Contract is already almost possible; the principle of Permanence, year by year, better seen into and elaborated, may enlarge itself, expand gradually on every side into a system. This once secured, the basis of all good results were laid. Once permanent, you do not quarrel with the first difficulty on your path, and quit it in weak disgust; you reflect that it cannot be quitted, that it must be conquered, a wise arrangement fallen on with regard to it. Ye foolish Wedded Two, who have quarrelled, between whom the Evil Spirit has stirred-up transient strife and bitterness, so that 'incompatibility' seems almost nigh, ye are

[1] *Report on the Training of Pauper Children* (1841), p. 18.

nevertheless the Two who, by long habit, were it by nothing more,
do best of all others suit each other: it is expedient for your own
two foolish selves, to say nothing of the infants, pedigrees and
public in general, that ye agree again ; that ye put away the Evil
Spirit, and wisely on both hands struggle for the guidance of a
Good Spirit!

The very horse that is permanent, how much kindlier do his
rider and he work, than the temporary one, hired on any hack
principle yet known! I am for permanence in all things, at the
earliest possible moment, and to the latest possible. Blessed is he
that continueth where he is. Here let us rest, and lay-out seedfields; here let us learn to dwell. Here, even here, the orchards
that we plant will yield us fruit; the acorns will be wood and
pleasant umbrage, if we wait. How much grows everywhere, if
we do but wait! Through the swamps we will shape causeways,
force purifying drains; we will learn to thread the rocky inaccessi-
bilities; and beaten tracks, worn smooth by mere travelling of
human feet, will form themselves. Not a difficulty but can trans-
figure itself into a triumph; not even a deformity but, if our own
soul have imprinted worth on it, will grow dear to us. The sunny
plains and deep indigo transparent skies of Italy are all indifferent
to the great sick heart of a Sir Walter Scott: on the back of the
Apennines, in wild spring weather, the sight of bleak Scotch firs,
and snow-spotted heath and desolation, brings tears into his eyes.[2]

O unwise mortals that forever change and shift, and say, Yonder,
not Here! Wealth richer than both the Indies lies everywhere
for man, if he will endure. Not his oaks only and his fruit-trees,
his very heart roots itself wherever he will abide;—roots itself,
draws nourishment from the deep fountains of Universal Being!
Vagrant Sam-Slicks, who rove over the Earth doing 'strokes of
trade,' what wealth have they ? Horseloads, shiploads of white or
yellow metal: in very sooth, what *are* these ? Slick rests nowhere,
he is homeless. He can build stone or marble houses; but to
continue in them is denied him. The wealth of a man is the
number of things which he loves and blesses, which he is loved
and blessed by! The herdsman in his poor clay shealing, where
his very cow and dog are friends to him, and not a cataract but
carries memories for him, and not a mountain-top but nods old
recognition: his life, all encircled as in blessed mother's-arms, is it
poorer than Slick's with the ass-loads of yellow metal on his back ?

[2] Lockhart's *Life of Scott.*

Unhappy Slick! Alas, there has so much grown nomadic, apelike, with us: so much will have, with whatever pain, repugnance and 'impossibility,' to alter itself, to fix itself again,—in some wise way, in any not delirious way!

A question arises here: Whether, in some ulterior, perhaps some not far-distant stage of this 'Chivalry of Labour,' your Master-Worker may not find it possible, and needful, to grant his Workers permanent *interest* in his enterprise and theirs? So that it become, in practical result, what in essential fact and justice it ever is, a joint enterprise; all men, from the Chief Master down to the lowest Overseer and Operative, economically as well as loyally concerned for it?—Which question I do not answer. The answer, near or else far, is perhaps, Yes;—and yet one knows the difficulties. Despotism is essential in most enterprises; I am told, they do not tolerate 'freedom of debate' on board a Seventy-four! Republican senate and *plebiscita* would not answer well in Cotton-Mills. And yet observe there too: Freedom, not nomad's or ape's Freedom, but man's Freedom; this is indispensable. We must have it, and will have it! To reconcile Despotism with Freedom:—well, is that such a mystery? Do you not already know the way? It is to make your Despotism *just*. Rigorous as Destiny; but just too, as Destiny and its Laws. The Laws of God: all men obey these, and have no 'Freedom' at all but in obeying them. The way is already known, part of the way;—and courage and some qualities are needed for walking on it!

CHAPTER VI.

THE LANDED.

A MAN with fifty, with five hundred, with a thousand pounds a day, given him freely, without condition at all,—on condition, as it now runs, that he will sit with his hands in his pockets and do no mischief, pass no Corn-Laws or the like,—he too, you would say, is or might be a rather strong Worker! He is a Worker with such tools as no man in this world ever before had. But in practice, very astonishing, very ominous to look at, he proves not a strong Worker;—you are too happy if he will prove but a No-worker, do nothing, and not be a Wrong-worker.

You ask him, at the year's end: "Where is your three-hundred thousand pound; what have you realised to us with that?" He answers, in indignant surprise: "Done with it? Who are you that ask? I have eaten it; I and my flunkies, and parasites, and slaves two-footed and four-footed, in an ornamental manner; and I am here alive by it; *I* am realised by it to you!"—It is, as we have often said, such an answer as was never before given under this Sun. An answer that fills me with boding apprehension, with foreshadows of despair. O stolid Use-and-wont of an atheistic Half-century, O Ignavia, Tailor-godhood, soul-killing Cant, to what passes art thou bringing us!—Out of the loud-piping whirl-wind, audibly to him that has ears, the Highest God is again announcing in these days: "Idleness shall not be." God has said it, man cannot gainsay.

Ah, how happy were it, if he this Aristocrat Worker would, in like manner, see *his* work and do it! It is frightful seeking another to do it for him. Guillotines, Meudon Tanneries, and half-a-million men shot dead, have already been expended in that busi-ness; and it is yet far from done. This man too is something; nay he is a great thing. Look on him there: a man of manful aspect; something of the 'cheerfulness of pride' still lingering in him. A free air of graceful stoicism, of easy silent dignity sits well on him; in his heart, could we reach it, lie elements of

generosity, self-sacrificing justice, true human valour. Why should
he, with such appliances, stand an incumbrance in the Present;
perish disastrously out of the Future! From no section of the
Future would we lose these noble courtesies, impalpable yet all-
controlling; these dignified reticences, these kingly simplicities;—
lose aught of what the fruitful Past still gives us token of, memento
of, in this man. Can we not save him:—can he not help us to
save him! A brave man, he too; had not undivine Ignavia
Héarsay, Speech without meaning,—had not Cant, thousandfold
Cant within him and around him, enveloping him like choke-damp,
like thick Egyptian darkness, thrown his soul into asphyxia, as it
were extinguished his soul; so that he sees not, hears not, and
Moses and all the Prophets address him in vain.

Will he awaken, be alive again, and have a soul; or is this
death-fit very death? It is a question of questions, for himself
and for us all! Alas, is there no noble work for this man too?
Has not he thickheaded ignorant boors; lazy, enslaved farmers,
weedy lands? Lands! Has not he weary heavy-laden ploughers
of land; immortal souls of men, ploughing, ditching, day-drudging;
bare of back, empty of stomach, nigh desperate of heart; and none
peaceably to help them but he, under Heaven? Does he find,
with his three-hundred thousand pounds, no noble thing trodden
down in the thoroughfares, which it were godlike to help up? Can
he do nothing for his Burns but make a Gauger of him; lionise
him, bedinner him, for a foolish while; then whistle him down the
wind, to desperation and bitter death?—His work too is difficult,
in these modern, far-dislocated ages. But it may be done; it may
be tried;—it must be done.

A modern Duke of Weimar, not a god he either, but a human
duke, levied, as I reckon, in rents and taxes and all incomings
whatsoever, less than several of our English Dukes do in rent
alone. The Duke of Weimar, with these incomings, had to
govern, judge, defend, everyway administer *his* Dukedom. He
does all this as few others did: and he improves lands besides all
this, makes river-embankments, maintains not soldiers only but
Universities and Institutions;—and in his Court were these four
men: Wieland, Herder, Schiller, Goethe. Not as parasites, which
was impossible; not as table-wits and poetic Katerfeltoes; but
as noble Spiritual Men working under a noble Practical Man.
Shielded by him from many miseries; perhaps from many shortcomings, destructive aberrations. Heaven had sent, once more,

heavenly Light into the world; and this man's honour was that he gave it welcome. A new noble kind of Clergy, under an old but still noble kind of King! I reckon that this one Duke of Weimar did more for the Culture of his Nation than all the English Dukes and *Duces* now extant, or that were extant since Henry the Eighth gave them the Church Lands to eat, have done for theirs!—I am ashamed, I am alarmed for my English Dukes: what word have I to say?

If our Actual Aristocracy, appointed 'Best-and-Bravest,' will be wise, how inexpressibly happy for us! If not,—the voice of God from the whirlwind is very audible to me. Nay, I will thank the Great God, that He has said, in whatever fearful ways, and just wrath against us, "Idleness shall be no more!" Idleness? The awakened soul of man, all but the asphyxied soul of man, turns from it as from worse than death. It is the life-in-death of Poet Coleridge. That fable of the Dead-Sea Apes ceases to be a fable. The poor Worker starved to death is not the saddest of sights. He lies there, dead on his shield; fallen down into the bosom of his old Mother; with haggard pale face, sorrow-worn, but stilled now into divine peace, silently appeals to the Eternal God and all the Universe,—the most silent, the most eloquent of men.

Exceptions,—ah yes, thank Heaven, we know there are exceptions. Our case were too hard, were there not exceptions, and partial exceptions not a few, whom we know, and whom we do not know. Honour to the name of Ashley,—honour to this and the other valiant Abdiel, found faithful still; who would fain, by work and by word, admonish their Order not to rush upon destruction! These are they who will, if not save their Order, postpone the wreck of it;—by whom, under blessing of the Upper Powers, 'a 'quiet euthanasia spread over generations, instead of a swift 'torture-death concentred into years,' may be brought about for many things. All honour and success to these. The noble man can still strive nobly to save and serve his Order;—at lowest, he can remember the precept of the Prophet: "Come out of her, my people; come out of her!"

To sit idle aloft, like living statues, like absurd Epicurus'-gods, in pampered isolation, in exclusion from the glorious fateful battle-field of this God's-World: it is a poor life for a man, when all Upholsterers and French-Cooks have done their utmost for it!— Nay what a shallow delusion is this we have all got into, That any man should or can keep himself apart from men, have 'no business' with them, except a cash-account 'business'! It is the silliest tale a distressed generation of men ever took to telling one another. Men cannot live isolated: we *are* all bound together, for mutual good or else for mutual misery, as living nerves in the same body. No highest man can disunite himself from any lowest. Consider it. Your poor 'Werter blowing out his distracted existence because Charlotte will not have the keeping thereof:' this is no peculiar phasis; it is simply the highest expression of a phasis traceable wherever one human creature meets another! Let the meanest crookbacked Thersites teach the supremest Agamemnon that he actually does not reverence him, the supremest Agamemnon's eyes flash fire responsive; a real pain and partial insanity has seized Agamemnon. Strange enough: a many-counselled Ulysses is set in motion by a scoundrel-blockhead; plays tunes, like a barrel-organ, at the scoundrel-blockhead's touch, —has to snatch, namely, his sceptre-cudgel, and weal the crooked back with bumps and thumps! Let a chief of men reflect well on it. Not in having 'no business' with men, but in having no unjust business with them, and in *having* all manner of true and just business, can either his or their blessedness be found possible, and this waste world become, for both parties, a home and peopled garden.

Men do reverence men. Men do worship in that 'one temple of the world,' as Novalis calls it, the Presence of a Man! Hero-worship, true and blessed, or else mistaken, false and accursed, goes on everywhere and everywhen. In this world there is one godlike thing, the essence of all that was or ever will be of godlike in this world: the veneration done to Human Worth by the hearts of men. Hero-worship, in the souls of the heroic, of the clear and wise,—it is the perpetual presence of Heaven in our poor Earth: when it is not there, Heaven is veiled from us; and all is under Heaven's ban and interdict, and there is no worship, or worth-ship, or worth or blessedness in the Earth any more!—

Independence, 'lord of the lion-heart and eagle-eye,'—alas, yes, he is one we have got acquainted with in these late times: a very indispensable one, for spurning-off with due energy innumerable sham-superiors, Tailor-made: honour to him, entire success to him! Entire success is sure to him. But he must not stop there, at that small success, with his eagle-eye. He has now a second

far greater success to gain : to seek out his real superiors, whom
not the Tailor but the Almighty God has made superior to him,
and see a little what he will do with these ! Rebel against these
also ? Pass by with minatory eagle-glance, with calm-sniffing
mockery, or even without any mockery or sniff, when these present
themselves ? The lion-hearted will never dream of such a thing.
Forever far be it from him ! His minatory eagle-glance will veil
itself in softness of the dove : his lion-heart will become a lamb's ;
all its just indignation changed into just reverence, dissolved in
blessed floods of noble humble love, how much heavenlier than
any pride, nay, if you will, how much prouder ! I know him, this
lion-hearted, eagle-eyed one ; have met him, rushing on, 'with
bosom bare,' in a very distracted dishevelled manner, the times
being hard ;—and can say, and guarantee on my life, That in him
is no rebellion ; that in him is the reverse of rebellion, the needful
preparation for obedience. For if you do mean to obey God-made
superiors, your first step is to sweep out the Tailor-made ones ; order
them, under penalties, to vanish, to make ready for vanishing !

Nay, what is best of all, he cannot rebel, if he would. Superiors
whom God has made for us we cannot order to withdraw ! Not in
the least. No Grand-Turk himself, thickest-quilted tailor-made
Brother of the Sun and Moon can do it : but an Arab Man, in
cloak of his own clouting ; with black beaming eyes, with flaming
sovereign-heart direct from the centre of the Universe ; and also,
I am told, with terrible ' horse-shoe vein ' of swelling wrath in his
brow, and lightning (if you will not have it as light) tingling through
every vein of him,—he rises ; says authoritatively : " Thickest-quilted
Grand-Turk, tailor-made Brother of the Sun and Moon, No :—*I*
withdraw not ; thou shalt obey me or withdraw ! " And so accordingly it is : thickest-quilted Grand-Turks and all their progeny, to
this hour, obey that man in the remarkablest manner ; preferring
not to withdraw.

O brother, it is an endless consolation to me, in this disorganic,
as yet so quack-ridden, what you may well call hag-ridden and
hell-ridden world, to find that disobedience to the Heavens, when
they send any messenger whatever, is and remains impossible. It
cannot be done ; no Turk grand or small can do it. ' Show the
' dullest clodpole,' says my invaluable German friend, ' show the
' haughtiest feather-head, that a soul higher than himself is here ;
' were his knees stiffened into brass, he must down and worship.'

CHAPTER VII.

THE GIFTED.

YES, in what tumultuous huge anarchy soever a Noble human Principle may dwell and strive, such tumult is in the way of being calmed into a fruitful sovereignty. It is inevitable. No Chaos can continue chaotic with a soul in it. Besouled with earnest human Nobleness, did not slaughter, violence and fire-eyed fury, grow into a Chivalry; into a blessed Loyalty of Governor and Governed? And in Work, which is of itself noble, and the only true fighting, there shall be no such possibility? Believe it not; it is incredible; the whole Universe contradicts it. Here too the Chactaw Principle will be subordinated; the Man Principle will, by degrees, become superior, become supreme.

I know Mammon too; Banks-of-England, Credit-Systems, world-wide possibilities of work and traffic; and applaud and admire them. Mammon is like Fire; the usefulest of all servants, if the frightfulest of all masters! The Cliffords, Fitzadelms and Chivalry Fighters 'wished to gain victory,' never doubt it: but victory, unless gained in a certain spirit, was no victory; defeat, sustained in a certain spirit, was itself victory. I say again and again, had they counted the scalps alone, they had continued Chactaws, and no Chivalry or lasting victory had been. And in Industrial Fighters and Captains is there no nobleness discoverable? To them, alone of men, there shall forever be no blessedness but in swollen coffers? To see beauty, order, gratitude, loyal human hearts around them, shall be of no moment; to see fuliginous deformity, mutiny, hatred and despair, with the addition of half-a-million guineas, shall be better? Heaven's blessedness not there; Hell's cursedness, and your half-million bits of metal, a substitute for that! Is there no profit in diffusing Heaven's blessedness, but only in gaining gold?—If so, I apprise the Mill-owner and Millionaire, that he too must prepare for vanishing; that neither is *he* born to be of the sovereigns of this world; that he will have to be trampled and chained down in whatever terrible ways, and brass-collared safe, among the born thralls of this world! We cannot have *Canailles* and Doggeries that will not make some Chivalry of themselves: our noble Planet is impatient of such; in the end, totally intolerant of such!

For the Heavens, unwearying in their bounty, do send other souls into this world, to whom yet, as to their forerunners, in Old Roman, in Old Hebrew and all noble times, the omnipotent guinea is, on the whole, an impotent guinea. Has your half-dead avaricious Corn-Law Lord, your half-alive avaricious Cotton-Law Lord, never seen one such? Such are, not one, but several; are, and will be, unless the gods have doomed this world to swift dire ruin. These are they, the elect of the world; the born champions, strong men, and liberatory Samsons of this poor world: whom the poor Delilah-world will not always shear of their strength and eyesight, and set to grind in darkness at *its* poor gin-wheel! Such souls are, in these days, getting somewhat out of humour with the world. Your very Byron, in these days, is at least driven mad; flatly refuses fealty to the world. The world with its injustices, its golden brutalities, and dull yellow guineas, is a disgust to such souls: the ray of Heaven that is in them does at least predoom them to be very miserable here. Yes:—and yet all misery is faculty misdirected, strength that has not yet found its way. The black whirlwind is mother of the lightning. No *smoke*, in any sense, but can become flame and radiance! Such soul, once graduated in Heaven's stern University, steps out superior to your guinea.

Dost thou know, O sumptuous Corn-Lord, Cotton-Lord, O mutinous Trades-Unionist, gin-vanquished, undeliverable; O much-enslaved World,—this man is not a slave with thee! None of thy promotions is necessary for him. His place is with the stars of Heaven: to thee it may be momentous, to thee it may be life or death, to him it is indifferent, whether thou place him in the lowest hut, or forty feet higher at the top of thy stupendous high tower, while here on Earth. The joys of Earth that are precious, they depend not on thee and thy promotions. Food and raiment, and, round a social hearth, souls who love him, whom he loves: these are already his. He wants none of thy rewards; behold also, he fears none of thy penalties. Thou canst not answer even by killing him: the case of Anaxarchus thou canst kill; but the self of Anaxarchus, the word or act of Anaxarchus, in no wise whatever. To this man death is not a bugbear; to this man life is already as earnest and awful, and beautiful and terrible, as death.

Not a May-game is this man's life; but a battle and a march, a warfare with principalities and powers. No idle promenade through fragrant orange-groves and green flowery spaces, waited on by the choral Muses and the rosy Hours: it is a stern pilgrimage through burning sandy solitudes, through regions of thick-ribbed ice. He walks among men; loves men, with inexpressible soft pity,—as they *cannot* love him: but his soul dwells in solitude, in the uttermost parts of Creation. In green oases by the palm-tree wells, he rests a space; but anon he has to journey forward, escorted by the Terrors and the Splendours, the Archdemons and Archangels. All Heaven, all Pandemonium are his escort. The stars keen-glancing, from the Immensities, send tidings to him; the graves, silent with their dead, from the Eternities. Deep calls for him unto Deep.

Thou, O World, how wilt thou secure thyself against this man? Thou canst not hire him by thy guineas; nor by thy gibbets and law-penalties restrain him. He eludes thee like a Spirit. Thou canst not forward him, thou canst not hinder him. Thy penalties, thy poverties, neglects, contumelies: behold, all these are good for him. Come to him as an enemy; turn from him as an unfriend; only do not this one thing,—infect him not with thy own delusion: the benign Genius, were it by very death, shall guard him against this!—What wilt thou do with him? He is above thee, like a god. Thou, in thy stupendous three-inch pattens, art under him. He is thy born king, thy conqueror and supreme lawgiver: not all the guineas and cannons, and leather and prunella, under the sky can save thee from him. Hardest thick-skinned Mammon-world, ruggedest Caliban shall obey him, or become not Caliban but a cramp. Oh, if in this man, whose eyes can flash Heaven's lightning, and make all Calibans into a cramp, there dwelt not, as the essence of his very being, a God's justice, human Nobleness, Veracity and Mercy,—I should tremble for the world. But his strength, let us rejoice to understand, is even this: The quantity of Justice, of Valour and Pity that is in him. To hypocrites and tailored quacks in high places his eyes are lightning; but they melt in dewy pity softer than a mother's to the down-pressed, maltreated; in his heart, in his great thought, is a sanctuary for all the wretched. This world's improvement is forever sure.

'Man of Genius?' Thou hast small notion, meseems, O Mæcenas Twiddledee, of what a Man of Genius is. Read in thy New

Testament and elsewhere,—if, with floods of mealy-mouthed
inanity; with miserable froth-vortices of Cant now several
centuries old, thy New Testament is not all bedimmed for thee.
Canst thou read in thy New Testament at all? The Highest
Man of Genius, knowest thou him; Godlike and a God to this
hour? His crown a Crown of Thorns? Thou fool, with *thy*
empty Godhoods, Apotheoses *edgegilt;* the Crown of Thorns made
into a poor jewel-room crown, fit for the head of blockheads; the
bearing of the Cross changed to a riding in the Long-Acre
Gig! Pause in thy mass-chantings, in thy litanyings, and
Calmuck prayings by machinery; and pray, if noisily, at least in a
more human manner. How with thy rubrics and dalmatics, and
clothwebs and cobwebs, and with thy stupidities and grovelling
baseheartedness, hast thou hidden the Holiest into all but
invisibility!—

'Man of Genius:' O Mæcenas Twiddledee, hast thou any notion
what a Man of Genius is? Genius is 'the inspired gift of God.'
It is the clearer presence of God Most High in a man. Dim,
potential in all men; in this man it has become clear, actual.
So says John Milton, who ought to be a judge; so answer him
the Voices of all Ages and all Worlds. Wouldst thou commune
with such a one? *Be* his real peer, then: does that lie in thee?
Know thyself and thy real and thy apparent place, and know him
and his real and his apparent place, and act in some noble conformity with all that. What! The star-fire of the Empyrean
shall eclipse itself, and illuminate magic-lanterns to amuse grown
children? He, the god-inspired, is to twang harps for thee, and
blow through scrannel-pipes, to soothe thy sated soul with visions
of new, still wider Eldorados, Houri Paradises, richer Lands of
Cockaigne? Brother, this is not he; this is a counterfeit, this
twangling, jangling, vain, acrid, scrannel-piping man. Thou dost
well to say with sick Saul, "It is nought, such harping!"—and in
sudden rage, to grasp thy spear, and try if thou canst pin such a
one to the wall. King Saul was mistaken in his man, but thou
art right in thine. It is the due of such a one: nail him to
the wall, and leave him there. So ought copper shillings to be
nailed on counters; copper geniuses on walls, and left there for a
sign!—

I conclude that the Men of Letters too may become a 'Chivalry,'
an actual instead of a virtual Priesthood, with result immeasurable,
—so soon as there is nobleness in themselves for that. And, to a

certainty, not sooner! Of intrinsic Valetisms you cannot, with whole Parliaments to help you, make a Heroism. Doggeries never so gold-plated, Doggeries never so escutcheoned, Doggeries never so diplomaed, bepuffed, gas-lighted, continue Doggeries, and must take the fate of such.

CHAPTER VIII.

THE DIDACTIC.

CERTAINLY it were a fond imagination to expect that any preaching of mine could abate Mammonism; that Bobus of Houndsditch will love his guineas less, or his poor soul more, for any preaching of mine! But there is one Preacher who does preach with effect, and gradually persuade all persons: his name is Destiny, is Divine Providence, and his Sermon the inflexible Course of Things. Experience does take dreadfully high school-wages; but he teaches like no other!

I revert to Friend Prudence the good Quaker's refusal of 'seven thousand pounds to boot.' Friend Prudence's practical conclusion will, by degrees, become that of all rational practical men whatsoever. On the present scheme and principle, Work cannot continue. Trades' Strikes, Trades' Unions, Chartisms; mutiny, squalor, rage and desperate revolt, growing ever more desperate, will go on their way. As dark misery settles down on us, and our refuges of lies fall in pieces one after one, the hearts of men, now at last serious, will turn to refuges of truth. The eternal stars shine out again, so soon as it is dark *enough*.

Begirt with desperate Trades' Unionism and Anarchic Mutiny, many an Industrial *Law-ward*, by and by, who has neglected to make laws and keep them, will be heard saying to himself: "Why have I realised five hundred thousand pounds? I rose early and sat late, I toiled and moiled, and in the sweat of my brow and of my soul I strove to gain this money, that I might become conspicuous, and have some honour among my fellow-creatures. I wanted them to honour me, to love me. The money is here, earned with my best lifeblood: but the honour? I am encircled with squalor, with hunger, rage, and sooty desperation. Not honoured, hardly even envied; only fools and the flunky-species so much as envy me. I am conspicuous,—as a mark for curses and brickbats. What good is it? My five hundred scalps hang here in my wigwam: would to Heaven I had sought something else than the scalps; would to Heaven I had been a Christian Fighter, not a Chactaw one! To have ruled and fought not in a Mammonish but in a Godlike spirit; to have had the hearts of the people bless me, as a true ruler and captain of my people; to have felt my own heart bless me, and that God above instead of Mammon below was blessing me,—this had been something. Out of my sight, ye beggarly five hundred scalps of banker's-thousands: I will try for something other, or account my life a tragical futility!"

Friend Prudence's 'rock-ledge,' as we called it, will gradually disclose itself to many a man; to all men. Gradually, assaulted from beneath and from above, the Stygian mud-deluge of Laissez-faire, Supply-and-demand, Cash-payment the one Duty, will abate on all hands; and the everlasting mountain-tops, and secure rock-foundations that reach to the centre of the world, and rest on Nature's self, will again emerge, to found on, and to build on. When Mammon-worshippers here and there begin to be God-worshippers, and bipeds-of-prey become men, and there is a Soul felt once more in the huge-pulsing elephantine mechanic Animalism of this Earth, it will be again a blessed Earth.

"Men cease to regard money?" cries Bobus of Houndsditch: "What else do all men strive for? The very Bishop informs me that Christianity cannot get on without a minimum of Four thousand five hundred in its pocket. Cease to regard money? That will be at Doomsday in the afternoon!"—O Bobus, my opinion is somewhat different. My opinion is, that the Upper Powers have not yet determined on destroying this Lower World. A respectable, ever-increasing minority, who do strive for something higher than money, I with confidence anticipate; ever-increasing, till there be a sprinkling of them found in all quarters, as salt of the Earth once more. The Christianity that cannot get on without a minimum of Four thousand five hundred, will give place to something better that can. Thou wilt not join our small minority, thou? Not till Doomsday in the afternoon? Well; *then,* at least, thou wilt join it, thou and the majority in mass!

But truly it is beautiful to see the brutish empire of Mammon cracking everywhere; giving sure promise of dying, or of being changed. A strange, chill, almost ghastly dayspring strikes up in Yankeeland itself : my Transcendental friends announce there, in a distinct, though somewhat lankhaired, ungainly manner, that the Demiurgus Dollar is dethroned ; that new unheard-of Demiurgusships, Priesthoods, Aristocracies, Growths and Destructions, are already visible in the gray of coming Time. Chronos is dethroned by Jove ; Odin by St. Olaf : the Dollar cannot rule in Heaven forever. No ; I reckon, not. Socinian Preachers quit their pulpits in Yankeeland, saying, " Friends, this is all gone to coloured cobweb, we regret to say ! "—and retire into the fields to cultivate onion-beds, and live frugally on vegetables. It is very notable. Old godlike Calvinism declares that its old body is now fallen to tatters, and done ; and its mournful ghost, disembodied, seeking new embodiment, pipes again in the winds ;—a ghost and spirit as yet, but heralding new Spirit-worlds, and better Dynasties than the Dollar one.

Yes, here as there, light is coming into the world ; men love not darkness, they do love light. A deep feeling of the eternal nature of Justice looks out among us everywhere,—even through the dull eyes of Exeter Hall ; an unspeakable religiousness struggles, in the most helpless manner, to speak itself, in Puseyisms and the like. Of our Cant, all condemnable, how much is not condemnable without pity ; we had almost said, without respect ! The *in*articulate worth and truth that is in England goes down yet to the Foundations.

Some 'Chivalry of Labour,' some noble Humanity and practical Divineness of Labour, will yet be realised on this Earth. Or why *will ;* why do we pray to Heaven, without setting our own shoulder to the wheel ? The Present, if it will have the Future accomplish, shall itself commence. Thou who prophesiest, who believest, begin thou to fulfil. Here or nowhere, now equally as at any time ! That outcast help-needing thing or person, trampled down under vulgar feet or hoofs, no help 'possible' for it, no prize offered for the saving of it,—canst not thou save it, then, without prize ? Put forth thy hand, in God's name ; know that 'impossible,' where Truth and Mercy and the everlasting Voice of Nature order, has no place in the brave man's dictionary. That when all men have said "Impossible," and tumbled noisily elsewhither, and thou alone art left, then first thy time and possibility have come. It is for thee now; do thou that, and ask no man's counsel, but thy own only, and God's. Brother, thou hast possibility in thee for much: the possibility of writing on the eternal skies the record of a heroic life. That noble downfallen or yet unborn 'Impossibility,' thou canst lift it up, thou canst, by thy soul's travail, bring it into clear being. That loud inane Actuality, with millions in its pocket, too 'possible' that, which rolls along there, with quilted trumpeters blaring round it, and all the world escorting it as mute or vocal flunky,—escort it not thou; say to it, either nothing, or else deeply in thy heart: "Loud-blaring Nonentity, no force of trumpets, cash, Long-acre art, or universal flunkyhood of men, makes thee an Entity; thou art a *Non*entity, and deceptive Simulacrum, more accursed than thou seemest. Pass on in the Devil's name, unworshipped by at least one man, and leave the thoroughfare clear!"

Not on Ilion's or Latium's plains; on far other plains and places henceforth can noble deeds be now done. Not on Ilion's plains; how much less in Mayfair's drawingrooms! Not in victory over poor brother French or Phrygians; but in victory over Frost-jötuns, Marsh-giants, over demons of Discord, Idleness, Injustice, Unreason, and Chaos come again. None of the old Epics is longer possible. The Epic of French and Phrygians was comparatively a small Epic: but that of Flirts and Fribbles, what is that? A thing that vanishes at cock-crowing,—that already begins to scent the morning air! Game-preserving Aristocracies, let them 'bush' never so effectually, cannot escape the Subtle Fowler. Game seasons will be excellent, and again will be indifferent, and by and by they will not be at all. The Last Partridge of England, of an England where millions of men can get no corn to eat, will be shot and ended. Aristocracies with beards on their chins will find other work to do than amuse themselves with trundling-hoops.

But it is to you, ye Workers, who do already work, and are as grown men, noble and honourable in a sort, that the whole world calls for new work and nobleness. Subdue mutiny, discord, widespread despair, by manfulness, justice, mercy and wisdom. Chaos is dark, deep as Hell; let light be, and there is instead a green flowery World. Oh, it is great, and there is no other greatness. To make some nook of God's Creation a little fruitfuller, better, more worthy of God; to make some human hearts a little wiser,

manfuler, happier,—more blessed, less accursed! It is work for a
God. Sooty Hell of mutiny and savagery and despair can, by
man's energy, be made a kind of Heaven; cleared of its soot, of its
mutiny, of its need to mutiny; the everlasting arch of Heaven's
azure overspanning *it* too, and its cunning mechanisms and tall
chimney-steeples, as a birth of Heaven; God and all men looking
on it well pleased.

Unstained by wasteful deformities, by wasted tears or heart's-
blood of men, or any defacement of the Pit, noble fruitful Labour,
growing ever nobler, will come forth,—the grand sole miracle of
Man; whereby Man has risen from the low places of this Earth,
very literally, into divine Heavens. Ploughers, Spinners, Builders;
Prophets, Poets, Kings; Brindleys and Goethes, Odins and Ark-
wrights; all martyrs, and noble men, and gods are of one grand
Host; immeasurable; marching ever forward since the beginnings
of the World. The enormous, all-conquering, flame-crowned Host,
noble every soldier in it; sacred, and alone noble. Let him who
is not of it hide himself; let him tremble for himself. Stars
at every button cannot make him noble; sheaves of Bath-garters,
nor bushels of Georges; nor any other contrivance but manfully
enlisting in it, valiantly taking place and step in it. O Heavens,
will he not bethink himself; he too is so needed in the Host! It
were so blessed, thrice-blessed, for himself and for us all! In hope
of the Last Partridge, and some Duke of Weimar among our
English Dukes, we will be patient yet a while.

> 'The Future hides in it
> Gladness and sorrow;
> We press still thorow,
> Nought that abides in it
> Daunting us,—onward.'

SUMMARY.

BOOK I.—PROEM.

Chap. I. *Midas.*

The condition of England one of the most ominous ever seen in this world: Full of wealth in every kind, yet dying of inanition. Workhouses, in which no work can be done. Destitution in Scotland. Stockport Assizes. (p. 1.)— England's unprofitable success: Human faces glooming discordantly on one another. Midas longed for gold, and the gods gave it him. (4.)

Chap. II. *The Sphinx.*

The grand unnamable Sphinx-riddle, which each man is called upon to solve. Notions of the foolish concerning justice and judgment. Courts of Westminster, and the general High Court of the Universe. The one strong thing, the just thing, the true thing. (p. 6.)—A noble Conservatism, as well as an ignoble. In all battles of men each fighter, in the end, prospers according to his right: Wallace of Scotland. (10.)—Fact and Semblance. What is Justice? As many men as there are in a Nation who can *see* Heaven's Justice, so many are there who stand between it and perdition. (11.)

Chap. III. *Manchester Insurrection.*

Peterloo not an unsuccessful Insurrection. Governors who wait for Insurrection to instruct them, getting into the fatalest courses. Unspeakable County Yeomanry. Poor Manchester operatives, and their huge inarticulate question: Unhappy Workers, unhappier Idlers, of this actual England! (p. 12.)—Fair day's-wages for fair day's-work: Milton's 'wages;' Cromwell's. Pay to each man what he has earned and done and deserved; what more have we to ask?—Some not *in*supportable approximation indispensable and inevitable. (16.)

Chap. IV. *Morrison's Pill.*

A state of mind worth reflecting on. No Morrison's Pill for curing the maladies of Society: Universal alteration of regimen and way of life: Vain jargon giving place to some genuine Speech again. (p. 19.)—If we walk according to the Law of this Universe, the Law-Maker will befriend us ; if not, not. Quacks, sham heroes, the one bane of the world. Quack and Dupe, upper side and under of the selfsame substance. (21.)

Chap. V. *Aristocracy of Talent.*

All misery the fruit of unwisdom : Neither with individuals nor with Nations is it fundamentally otherwise. Nature in late centuries universally supposed to be dead ; but now everywhere asserting herself to be alive and miraculous. The guidance of this country not sufficiently wise. (p. 23.)— Aristocracy of talent, or government by the Wisest, a dreadfully difficult affair to get started. The true *eye* for talent ; and the flunky eye for respectabilities, warm garnitures and larders dropping fatness : Bobus and Bobissimus. (26.)

Chap. VI. *Hero-worship.*

Enlightened Egoism, never so luminous, not the rule by which man's life can be led : A *soul,* different from a stomach in any sense of the word. Hero-worship done differently in every different epoch of the world. Reform, like Charity, must begin at home. 'Arrestment of the knaves and dastards,' beginning by arresting our own poor selves out of that fraternity. (p. 28.)—The present Editor's purpose to himself full of hope. A Load-star in the eternal sky : A glimmering of light, for here and there a human soul. (30.)

BOOK II.—THE ANCIENT MONK.

Chap. I. *Jocelin of Brakelond.*

How the Centuries stand lineally related to each other. The one Book not permissible, the kind that has nothing in it. Jocelin's 'Chronicle,' a private Boswellean Notebook, now seven centuries old. How Jocelin, from under his monk's cowl, looked out on that narrow section of the world in a really *human* manner : A wise simplicity in him ; a *veracity* that goes deeper than words. Jocelin's Monk-Latin ; and Mr. Rokewood's editorial helpfulness and fidelity. (p. 33.)—A veritable Monk of old Bury St. Edmunds worth attending to. This England of ours, of the year 1200: Cœur-de-Lion : King Lackland, and his thirteenpenny mass. The poorest historical Fact, and the grandest imaginative Fiction. (36.)

Chap. II. *St. Edmundsbury.*

St. Edmund's Bury, a prosperous brisk Town : Extensive ruins of the Abbey still visible. Assiduous Pedantry, and its rubbish-heaps called ' History.' Another world it was, when those black ruins first saw the sun as walls. At lowest, O dilettante friend, let us know always that it *was* a world. No easy matter to get across the chasm of Seven Centuries : Of all helps, a Boswell, even a small Boswell, the welcomest. (p. 39.)

Chap. III. *Landlord Edmund.*

'Battle of Fornham,' a fact, though a forgotten one. Edmund, Landlord of the Eastern Counties : A very singular kind of 'landlord.' How he came to be 'sainted.' Seen and felt to have done verily a man's part in this life-pilgrimage of his. How they took up the slain body of their Edmund, and reverently embalmed it. (p. 42.)—Pious munificence, ever growing by new pious gifts. Certain Times do crystallise themselves in a magnificent manner; others in a rather shabby one. (47.)

Chap. IV. *Abbot Hugo.*

All things have two faces, a light one and a dark : The Ideal has to grow in the Real, and to seek its bed and board there, often in a very sorry manner. Abbot Hugo, grown old and feeble. Jew debts and Jew creditors. How approximate justice strives to accomplish itself. (p. 48.)—In the old monastic Books almost no mention whatever of 'personal religion.' A poor Lord Abbot, all stuck-over with horse-leeches : A 'royal commission of inquiry,' to no purpose. A monk's first duty, obedience. Magister Samson, Teacher of the Novices. The Abbot's providential death. (51.)

Chap. V. *Twelfth Century.*

Inspectors or Custodiars ; the King not in any breathless haste to appoint a new Abbot. Dim and very strange looks that monk-life to us. Our venerable ancient spinning grandmothers, shrieking, and rushing out with their distaffs. Lakenheath eels too slippery to be caught. (p. 52.)—How much is alive in England, in that Twelfth Century ; how much not yet come into life. Feudal Aristocracy ; Willelmus Conquæstor : Not a steeple-chimney yet got on end from sea to sea. (55.)

Chap. VI. *Monk Samson.*

Monk-Life and Monk-Religion : A great heaven-high Unquestionability, encompassing, interpenetrating all human Duties. Our modern Arkwright Joe-Manton ages : All human dues and reciprocities changed into one great due of 'cash-payment.' The old monks but a limited class of creatures, with a somewhat dull life of it. (p. 56.)—One Monk of a taciturn nature distinguishes himself among those babbling ones. A Son of poor Norfolk parents. Little Samson's awful dream : His poor Mother dedicates him to St. Edmund. He grows to be a learned man, of devout grave nature. Sent to Rome on business ; and returns *too* successful : Method of travelling thither in those days. His tribulations at home : Strange conditions under which Wisdom has sometimes to struggle with folly. (58.)

Chap. VII. *The Canvassing.*

A new Abbot to be elected. Even gossip, seven centuries off, has significance. The Prior with Twelve Monks, to wait on his Majesty at Waltham.

An ' election' the one important social act : Given the Man a People choose,
the worth and worthlessness of the People itself is given. (p. 62.)

Chap. VIII. *The Election.*

Electoral methods and manipulations.   Brother Samson ready oftenest with
some question, some suggestion that has wisdom in it.   The Thirteen off to
Waltham, to choose their Abbot : In the solitude of the Convent, Destiny
thus big and in her birthtime, what gossiping, babbling, dreaming of dreams !
(p. 64.)—King Henry II. in his high Presence-chamber.   Samson chosen
Abbot : the King's royal acceptation. (67.)—St. Edmundsbury Monks, without
express ballot-box or other winnowing machine.   In every Nation and Community there is at all times *a fittest*, wisest, bravest, best.   Human Worth and
human Worthlessness. (69.)

Chap. IX. *Abbot Samson.*

The Lord Abbot's arrival at St. Edmundsbury : The selfsame Samson
yesterday a poor mendicant, this day finds himself a *Dominus Abbas* and
mitred Peer of Parliament. (p. 71.)—Depth and opulence of true social vitality
in those old barbarous ages.   True Governors go about under all manner of
disguises now as then.   Genius, Poet ; what these words mean.   George the
Third, head charioteer of England ; and Robert Burns, gauger of ale in
Dumfries. (72.)—How Abbot Samson found a Convent all in dilapidation.
His life-long harsh apprenticeship to governing, namely obeying.   First get
your Man ; all is got.   Danger of blockheads. (73.)

Chap. X. *Government.*

Beautiful, how the chrysalis governing-soul, shaking off its dusty slough
and prison, starts forth winged, a true royal soul !   One first labour, to institute a strenuous review and radical reform of his economics.   Wheresoever
Disorder may stand or lie, let it have a care ; here is a man that has declared
war with it. (p. 76.)— In less than four years the Convent debts are all
liquidated, and the harpy Jews banished from St. Edmundsbury.   New
life springs beneficent everywhere : Spiritual rubbish as little tolerated as
material. (78.)

Chap. XI. *The Abbot's Ways.*

Reproaches, open and secret, of ingratitude, unsociability : Except for 'fit
men' in all kinds, hard to say for whom Abbot Samson had much favour.
Remembrance of benefits. (p. 79.)—An eloquent man, but intent more on
substance than on ornament.   A just clear heart the basis of all true talent.
One of the justest of judges : His invaluable 'talent of silence.'   Kind of
people he liked worst.   Hospitality and stoicism. (81.)—The country in
those days still dark with noble wood and umbrage : How the old trees
gradually died out, no man heeding it.   Monachism itself, so rich and fruitful
once, now all rotted into *peat*.   Devastations of four-footed cattle and Henry-
the-Eighths. (83.)

CHAP. XII. *The Abbot's Troubles.*

The troubles of Abbot Samson more than tongue can tell. Not the spoil of victory, only the glorious toil of battle, can be theirs who really govern. An insurrection of the Monks: Behave better, ye remiss Monks, and thank Heaven for such an Abbot. (p. 84.)—Worn down with incessant toil and tribulation: Gleams of hilarity too; little snatches of encouragement granted even to a Governor. How my Lord of Clare, coming to claim his *un*due 'debt,' gets a Roland for his Oliver. A Life of Literature, noble and ignoble. (85.)

CHAP. XIII. *In Parliament.*

Confused days of Lackland's usurpation, while Cœur-de-Lion was away: Our brave Abbot took helmet himself, excommunicating all who should favour Lackland. King Richard a captive in Germany. (p. 88.)—St. Edmund's Shrine not meddled with: A heavenly Awe overshadowed and encompassed, as it still ought and must, all earthly Business whatsoever. (89.)

CHAP. XIV. *Henry of Essex.*

How St. Edmund punished terribly, yet with mercy: A Narrative significant of the Time. Henry Earl of Essex, standard-bearer of England: No right reverence for the Heavenly in Man. A traitor or a coward. Solemn Duel, by the King's appointment. An evil Conscience doth make cowards of us all. (p. 90.)

CHAP. XV. *Practical-Devotional.*

A Tournament proclaimed and held in the Abbot's domain, in spite of him. Roystering young dogs brought to reason. The Abbot a man that generally remains master at last: The importunate Bishop of Ely outwitted. A man that dare abide King Richard's anger, with justice on his side. Thou brave Richard, thou brave Samson! (p. 93.)—The basis of Abbot Samson's life truly religion. His zealous interest in the Crusades. The great antique heart, like a child's in its simplicity, like a man's in its earnest solemnity and depth. His comparative silence as to his religion precisely the healthiest sign of him and it. Methodism, Dilettantism, Puseyism. (97.)

CHAP. XVI. *St. Edmund.*

Abbot Samson built many useful, many pious edifices: All ruinous, incomplete things an eye-sorrow to him. Rebuilding the great Altar: A glimpse of the glorious Martyr's very Body. What a scene; how far vanished from us, in these unworshipping ages of ours! The manner of men's Hero-worship, verily the innermost fact of their existence, determining all the rest. (p. 100.)—On the whole, who knows how to reverence the Body of Man? Abbot Samson, at the culminating point of his existence: Our real-phantasmagory of St. Edmundsbury plunges into the bosom of the Twelfth Century again, and all is over. (105.)

CHAP. XVII. *The Beginnings.*

Formulas the very skin and muscular tissue of a Man's Life: Living Formulas and dead. Habit the deepest law of human nature. A pathway
through the pathless. Nationalities. Pulpy infancy, kneaded, baked into
any form you choose: The Man of Business; the hard-handed Labourer;
the genus Dandy. No Mortal out of the depths of Bedlam but lives by Formulas. (p. 106.)—The hosts and generations of brave men Oblivion has
swallowed: Their crumbled dust, the soil our life-fruit grows on. Invention
of Speech; Forms of Worship; Methods of Justice. This English Land,
here and now, the summary of what was wise and noble, and accordant
with God's Truth, in all the generations of English Men. The thing called
'Fame.' (109.)

BOOK III.—THE MODERN WORKER.

CHAP. I. *Phenomena.*

How men have 'forgotten God;' taken the Fact of this Universe as it *is
not;* God's Laws become a Greatest-Happiness Principle, a Parliamentary
Expediency. Man has lost the *soul* out of him, and begins to find the want
of it. (p. 115.)—The old Pope of Rome, with his stuffed dummy to do the
kneeling for him. Few men that worship by the rotatory Calabash, do it
in half so great, frank or effectual a way. (116.)—Our Aristocracy no longer
able to *do* its work, and not in the least conscious that it has any work to do.
The Champion of England 'lifted into his saddle.' The Hatter in the Strand,
mounting a huge lath-and-plaster Hat. Our noble ancestors have fashioned
for us, in how many thousand senses, a 'life-road;' and we their sons are
madly, literally enough, 'consuming the way.' (118.)

CHAP. II. *Gospel of Mammonism.*

Heaven and Hell, often as the words are on our tongue, got to be fabulous
or semi-fabulous for most of us. The real 'Hell' of the English. Cash-payment, *not* the sole or even chief relation of human beings. Practical Atheism,
and its despicable fruits. (p. 122.)—One of Dr. Alison's melancholy facts: A
poor Irish Widow, in the Lanes of Edinburgh, *proving* her sisterhood. Until
we get a human *soul* within us, all things are *im*possible: Infatuated geese,
with feathers and without. (126.)

CHAP. III. *Gospel of Dilettantism.*

Mammonism at least works; but 'Go gracefully idle in Mayfair,' what
does or can that mean?—Impotent, insolent Donothingism in Practice and
Saynothingism in Speech. No man now speaks a plain word: Insincere
Speech the prime material of insincere Action. (p. 127.)—Moslem parable of
Moses and the Dwellers by the Dead Sea: The Universe *become* a Humbug
to the Apes that thought it one. (128.)

Chap. IV. *Happy.*

All work noble ; and every noble crown a crown of thorns. Man's pitiful pretension to be what he calls 'happy :' His Greatest-Happiness Principle fast becoming a rather unhappy one. Byron's large audience. A philosophical Doctor : A disconsolate Meat-jack, gnarring and creaking with rust and work. (p. 129.)—The only ' happiness ' a brave man ever troubled himself much about, the happiness to get his work done. (131.)

Chap. V. *The English.*

With all thy theoretic platitudes, what a depth of practical sense in thee, great England ! A dumb people, who can do great acts, but not describe them. The noble Warhorse, and the Dog of Knowledge : The freest utterances not by any means the best. (p. 133.)—The done Work, much more than the spoken Word, an epitome of the man. The Man of Practice, and the Man of Theory : Ineloquent Brindley. The English, of all Nations the stupidest in speech, the wisest in action : Sadness and seriousness : Unconsciously this great Universe is great to them. The silent Romans. John Bull's admirable insensibility to Logic. (134.)—All great Peoples conservative. Kind of Ready-Reckoner a Solecism in Eastcheap. Berserkir rage. Truth and Justice alone *capable* of being 'conserved.' Bitter indignation engendered by the Corn-Laws in every just English heart. (137.)

Chap. VI. *Two Centuries.*

The 'Settlement' of the year 1660 one of the mournfulest that ever took place in this land of ours. The true end of Government, to guide men in the way they should go : The true good of this life, the portal of infinite good in the life to come. Oliver Cromwell's body hung on the Tyburn gallows, the type of Puritanism found futile, inexecutable, execrable. The Spiritualism of England, for two godless centuries, utterly forgettable : Her practical material Work alone memorable. (p. 140.)—Bewildering obscurations and impediments : Valiant Sons of Toil enchanted, by the million, in their Poor-Law Bastille. Giant Labour yet to be King of this Earth. (142.)

Chap. VII. *Over-Production.*

An idle Governing Class addressing its Workers with an indictment of ' Over-production.' Duty of justly apportioning the Wages of Work done. A game-preserving Aristocracy, guiltless of producing or apportioning anything. Owning the soil of England. (p. 144.)—The Working Aristocracy steeped in ignoble Mammonism : The Idle Aristocracy, with its yellow parchments and pretentious futilities. (145.)

Chap. VIII. *Unworking Aristocracy.*

Our Land the *Mother* of us all : No true Aristocracy but must possess the Land. Men talk of 'selling' Land : Whom it belongs to. Our much-consuming Aristocracy : By the law of their position bound to furnish guidance and governance. Mad and miserable Corn-Laws. (p. 147.)—The Working Aristocracy, and its terrible New-Work : The Idle Aristocracy, and its horoscope of despair. (149.)—A High Class without duties to do, like a tree planted

L L 2

on precipices. In a valiant suffering for others, not in a slothful making
others suffer for us, did nobleness ever lie. The Pagan Hercules ; the Czar of
Russia. (151.)—Parchments, venerable and not venerable. Benedict the Jew,
and his usuries. No Chapter on the Corn-Laws : The Corn-Laws too mad to
have a Chapter. (152.)

Chap. IX. *Working Aristocracy.*

Many things for the Working Aristocracy, in their extreme need, to consider. A National Existence supposed to depend on 'selling cheaper' than
any other People. Let inventive men try to invent a little how cotton at
its present cheapness could be somewhat justlier divided. Many 'impossibles' will have to become possible. (p. 154.)—Supply-and-demand : For
what noble work was there ever yet any audible 'demand' in that poor
sense ? (157.)

Chap. X. *Plugson of Undershot.*

Man's philosophies usually the 'supplement of his practice :' Symptoms of
social death. Cash-Payment : The Plugson Ledger, and the Tablets of
Heaven's Chancery, discrepant exceedingly. (p. 159.)—All human things do
require to have an Ideal in them. How murderous fighting became a
'glorious Chivalry.' Noble devout-hearted Chevaliers. Ignoble Bucaniers
and Chactaw Indians : Howel Davies. Napoleon flung out, at last, to St.
Helena ; the latter end of him sternly compensating for the beginning. (160.)
The indomitable Plugson, as yet a Bucanier and Chactaw. William Conqueror
and his Norman followers. Organisation of Labour : Courage, there are yet
many brave men in England ! (162.)

Chap. XI. *Labour.*

A perennial nobleness and even sacredness in Work. Significance of the
Potter's Wheel. Blessed is he who has found his Work ; let him ask no other
blessedness. (p. 165.)—A brave Sir Christopher, and his Paul's Cathedral :
Every noble work at first 'impossible.' Columbus royalest Sea-king of all :
A depth of Silence, deeper than the Sea ; a Silence unsoundable ; known to
God only. (167.)

Chap. XII. *Reward.*

Work is Worship : Labour, wide as the Earth, has its summit in Heaven.
One monster there is in the world, the idle man. (p. 169.)—'Fair day's-wages
for a fair day's-work,' the most unrefusable demand. The 'wages' of every
noble Work in Heaven, or else Nowhere : The brave man has to *give* his Life
away. He that works bodies forth the form of Things Unseen. Strange
mystic affinity of Wisdom and Insanity : All Work, in its degree, a making
of Madness sane. (171.)—Labour not a devil, even when encased in
Mammonism : The unredeemed ugliness, a slothful People. The vulgarest
Plugson of a Master-Worker, not a man to strangle by Corn-Laws and Shot-
belts. (175.)

Chap. XIII. *Democracy.*

Man must actually have his debts and earnings a little better paid by man. At no time was the lot of the dumb millions of toilers so entirely unbearable as now. Sisterhood, brotherhood often forgotten, but never before so expressly denied. Mungo Park and his poor Black Benefactress. (p. 176.) —Gurth, born thrall of Cedric the Saxon : Liberty a divine thing ; but 'liberty to die by starvation' not so divine. Nature's Aristocracies. William Conqueror, a resident House-Surgeon provided by Nature for her beloved English People. (179.)—Democracy, the despair of finding Heroes to govern us, and contented putting-up with the want of them. The very Tailor unconsciously symbolising the reign of Equality. Wherever ranks do actually exist, strict division of costumes will also be enforced. (181.)—Freedom from oppression, an indispensable yet most significant portion of Human Liberty. A *best path* does exist for every man ; a thing which, here and now, it were of all things *wisest* for him to do. Mock Superiors and Real Superiors. (183.)

Chap. XIV. *Sir Jabesh Windbag.*

Oliver Cromwell, the remarkablest Governor we have had for the last five centuries or so : No volunteer in Public Life, but plainly a balloted soldier : The Government of England put into his hands. (p. 187.)—Windbag, weak in the faith of a God ; strong only in the faith that Paragraphs and Plausibilities bring votes. Five years of popularity or unpopularity ; and *after* those five years, an Eternity. Oliver has to appear before the Most High Judge : Windbag, appealing to 'Posterity.' (188.)

Chap. XV. *Morrison again.*

New Religions : This new stage of progress, proceeding 'to invent God,' a very strange one indeed. (p. 190.)—Religion, the Inner Light or Moral Conscience of a man's soul. Infinite difference between a Good man and a Bad. The great Soul of the World, just and not unjust : Faithful, unspoken, but not ineffectual 'prayer.' Penalties : The French Revolution ; cruelest Portent that has risen into created Space these ten centuries. Man needs no 'New Religion ;' nor is like to get it : Spiritual Dastardism, and sick folly. (191.)—One Liturgy which does remain forever unexceptionable, that of *Praying by Working.* Sauerteig on the symbolic influences of Washing. Chinese Pontiff-Emperor and his significant 'punctualities.' (196.)—Goethe and German Literature. The great event for the world, now as always, the arrival in it of a new Wise Man. Goethe's *Mason-Lodge.* (199.)

BOOK IV.—HOROSCOPE.

Chap. I. *Aristocracies.*

To predict the Future, to manage the Present, would not be so impossible, had not the Past been so sacrilegiously mishandled : a godless century, looking back to centuries that were godly. (p. 201.)—A new real Aristocracy and Priesthood. The noble Priest always a noble *Aristos* to begin with, and something more to end with. Modern Preachers, and the *real* Satanas that now is. Abbot-Samson and William-Conqueror times. The mission of a Land Aristocracy a *sacred* one, in both senses of that old word. Truly a 'Splendour of God' did dwell in those old rude veracious ages. Old Anselm travelling to Rome, to appeal against King Rufus. Their quarrel at bottom a great quarrel. (203.)—The boundless Future, predestined, nay already extant though unseen. Our Epic, not *Arms and the Man*, but *Tools and the Man;* an infinitely wider kind of Epic. Important that our grand Reformation were begun. (210.)

Chap. II. *Bribery Committee.*

Our theory, perfect purity of Tenpound Franchise ; our practice, irremediable bribery. Bribery, indicative not only of length of purse, but of brazen dishonesty : Proposed improvements. A Parliament, starting with a lie in its mouth, promulgates strange horoscopes of itself. (p. 212.)— Respect paid to those worthy of no respect : Pandarus Dogdraught. The indigent discerning Freeman ; and the kind of men he is called upon to vote for. (214.)

Chap. III. *The one Institution.*

The 'Organisation of Labour,' if well understood, the Problem of the whole Future. Governments of various degrees of utility. Kilkenny Cats ; Spinning-Dervishes ; Parliamentary Eloquence. A Prime-Minister who would dare believe the heavenly omens. (p. 216.)—Who can despair of Governments, that passes a Soldier's Guard-house ?—Incalculable what, by arranging, commanding and regimenting, can be made of men. Organisms enough in the dim huge Future ; and 'United Services' quite other than the red-coat one. (219.)—Legislative interference between Workers and Master-Workers increasingly indispensable. Sanitary Reform : People's Parks : A right Education Bill, and effective Teaching Service. Free bridge for Emigrants : England's sure markets among her Colonies. London the *All-Saxon-Home*, rendezvous of all the 'Children of the Harz-Rock.' (221.)— The English essentially conservative : Always the invincible instinct to hold fast by the Old, to admit the *minimum* of New. Yet new epochs do actually come ; and with them new peremptory necessities. A certain Editor's stipulated work. (225.)

Chap. IV. *Captains of Industry.*

Government can do much, but it can in nowise do all. Fall of Mammon: To be a noble Master among noble Workers, will again be the first ambition with some few. (p. 227.)—The Leaders of Industry, virtually the Captains of the World: Doggeries and Chivalries. Isolation, the sum-total of wretchedness to man. All social growths in this world have required organising; and Work, the grandest of human interests, does now require it. (228.)

Chap. V. *Permanence.*

The 'tendency to persevere,' to persist in spite of hindrances, discouragements and 'impossibilities,' that which distinguishes the Species Man from the Genus Ape. Month-long contracts, and Exeter-Hall purblindness. A practical manufacturing Quaker's care for his workmen. (p. 233.)—Blessing of Permanent Contract: Permanence in all things, at the earliest possible moment, and to the latest possible. Vagrant Sam-Slicks. The wealth of a man the number of things he loves and blesses, which he is loved and blessed by. (236.) The Worker's *interest* in the enterprise with which he is connected. How to reconcile Despotism with Freedom. (237.)

Chap. VI. *The Landed.*

A man with fifty, with five hundred, with a thousand pounds a day, given him freely, without condition at all, might be a rather strong Worker: The sad reality, very ominous to look at. Will he awaken, be alive again; or is this death-fit very death?—Goethe's Duke of Weimar. Doom of Idleness. (p. 238.)—To sit idle aloft, like absurd Epicurus'-gods, a poor life for a man. Independence, 'lord of the lion-heart and eagle-eye:' Rejection of sham Superiors, the needful preparation for obedience to *real* Superiors. (241.)

Chap. VII. *The Gifted.*

Tumultuous anarchy calmed by noble effort into fruitful sovereignty. Mammon, like Fire, the usefulest of servants, if the frightfulest of masters. Souls to whom the omnipotent guinea is, on the whole, an impotent guinea: Not a May-game is this man's life; but a battle and stern pilgrimage: God's justice, human Nobleness, Veracity and Mercy, the essence of his very being. (p. 243.)—What a man of Genius is. The Highest 'Man of Genius.' Genius, the clearer presence of God Most High in a man. Of intrinsic Valetisms you cannot, with whole Parliaments to help you, make a Heroism. (246.)

Chap. VIII. *The Didactic.*

One preacher who does preach with effect, and gradually persuade all persons. Repentant Captains of Industry: A Chactaw Fighter become a Christian Fighter. (p. 247.)—Doomsday in the afternoon. The 'Christianity' that cannot get on without a minimum of Four-thousand-five-hundred, will give place to something better that can. Beautiful to see the brutish empire of Mammon cracking everywhere : A strange, chill, almost ghastly dayspring in Yankeeland itself. Here as there, Light is coming into the world. Whoso believes, let him begin to fulfil : 'Impossible,' where Truth and Mercy and the everlasting Voice of Nature order, can have no place in the brave man's dictionary. (249.)—Not on Ilion's or Latium's plains ; on far other plains and places henceforth can noble deeds be done. The last Partridge of England shot and ended : Aristocracies with beards on their chins. O, it is great, and there is no other greatness : To make some nook of God's Creation a little fruitfuler ; to make some human hearts a little wiser, manfuler, happier : It is work for a God ! (250.)

INDEX.

THE FRENCH REVOLUTION.

Girondins, 49, 106 ; National Convention and, 129, 173 ; Popular Tribunals of, 158 ; Couthon's Question in, 185 ; purges members, 187 ; to become dominant, 208 ; locked out by Legendre, 214 ; begs back its keys, 219 ; decline of, 229 ; mobbed, suspended, 229 ; hunted down, 233.

Jacobinism, spirit of, ii. 176.

Jalès, Camp of, i. 258 ; Royalists at, 448 ; destroyed, 448.

Jaucourt, Chevalier, and Liberty, i. 423.

Jay, Dame le, bookseller, i. 270.

Jemappes, battle of, ii. 47.

Jesuitism and Dame Dubarry, i. 15.

Jokei, French, described, i. 43, 44.

Jones, Paul, equipped for America, i. 40 ; at Paris, account of, 266, 291 ; burial of, 482.

Jounneau, Deputy, in danger, in September, ii. 8.

Jourdan, General, repels Austria, ii. 178.

Jourdan, Coupe-tête, at Versailles, i. 225, 238 ; leader of Avignon Brigands, 238, 428 ; costume of, 428 ; supreme in Avignon, 430 ; massacre by, 431 ; flight of, 431 ; guillotined, ii. 158.

Jourgniac. See St. Méard.

Journals (see Paris) ; placard, i. 272, 338.

Julien, Sieur Jean, guillotined, i. 531.

June Twentieth, 1792, i. 471.

Justice, bed of, i. 71.

Kaunitz, Prince, denounces Jacobins, i. 455.

Kellermann, at Valmy, ii. 23.

Kings, primitive, i. 10 ; divine right of, 10.

Kingship, decline of, in France, i. 11.

Klopstock, naturalised, i. 517.

Knox, John, and the Virgin, i. 332.

Korff, Baroness de, in flight to Varennes, i. 382 ; is Dame de Tourzel, 385.

Lacroix, of Mountain, i. 423.

Lafarge, President of Jacobins, Madame Lavergne and, i. 523.

Lafayette, bust of, erected, i. 41, 171 ; against Calonne, 63 ; demands by, in Notables, 68 ; Cromwell - Grandison, 124 ; Bastille time, Vice-President of National Assembly, 157, 170 ; General of National Guard, 172 ; resigns and reaccepts, 178 ; Scipio - Americanus, 198 ; thanked, rewarded, 206 ; French Guards and, 219 ; to Versailles, 220 ; at Versailles, Fifth October, 233 ; swears the Guards, 242 ; Feuillans, 276 ; on abolition of Titles, 293 ; at Champ-de-Mars Federation, 301 ; at De Castries' riot, 347 ; character of, 349 ; in Day of Poniards, 358 ; difficult position of, 360 ; at King's going to St. Cloud,

375 ; resigns and reaccepts, 376 ; at flight from Tuileries, 383 ; after escape of King, 386 ; moves for amnesty, 417 ; resigns, 419 ; decline of, 453 ; doubtful against Jacobins, 463, 467, 477 ; fruitless journey to Paris, 473 ; to be accused ? 482 ; flies to Holland, 509.

Laflotte, prison-plot, informer, ii. 194, 204.

Laïs, Sieur, Jacobin, with Louis Philippe, i. 275.

Lally, death of, i. 74. See Tollendal.

Lamarche, guillotined, ii. 154.

Lamarck's, Mirabeau sick at, i. 366.

Lamballe, Princess de, to England, i. 390 ; intrigues for Royalists, 440, 457 ; at La Force, 526 ; massacred, 537.

Lambesc, Prince, attacks Bust-procession, July 1789, i. 150.

Lameth, in Constituent Assembly, one of a trio, i. 189 ; brothers, notice of, 253 ; Jacobins, 274 ; Charles, duel with Duke de Castries, 347 ; brothers become constitutional, 408 ; Theodore, in First Parliament, 423.

Lamoignon, Keeper of Seals, i. 65, 79, 84 ; dismissed, 96 ; effigy burned, and death of, 97.

Lamotte, Countess de, and Diamond Necklace, i. 50 ; in the Salpêtrière, 60, 81 ; 'Memoirs' burned, 450 ; in London, 535 ; M. de, in prison, 535.

Lamourette, Abbé, kiss of, i. 425 ; guillotined, ii. 159.

Lanjuinais, Girondin, clothes torn, ii. 113 ; arrested, 114 ; recalled, 220.

Lanterne, death by the, i. 176.

Lapérouse, voyage of, i. 41.

Laporte, Intendant, guillotined, i. 520.

Larivière, Justice, imprisoned, i. 475.

Larochejaquelin, in La Vendée, i. 522 ; death of, 227.

Lasource, accuses Danton, ii. 102 ; president, and Marat, 105 ; arrested, 114 ; condemned, his saying, 144.

Latour-Maubourg, notice of, i. 406.

Launay, Marquis de, Governor of Bastille, i. 158 ; besieged, 161 ; unassisted, 162 ; to blow up Bastille, 166 ; massacred, 167.

Lavergne, surrenders Longwi, i. 522, 523.

Lavoisier, Chemist, guillotined, ii. 197.

Law, Martial, in Paris, i. 263, 412 ; Book of the, 424.

Lawyers, their influence on the Revolution, i. 14 ; number of, in Tiers Etat, 123 ; in Parliament First, 421.

Lazare, Maison de St., plundered, i. 154.

Lebas at Strasburg, ii. 174 ; arrested, 211.

Lebon, Priest, in National Convention, ii. 16 ; at Arras, 164 ; guillotined, 232.

Lebrun, forger of Assignats, i. 444.

PAST AND PRESENT.

Richard Clay and Sons, London and Bungay.